SAGALASSOS VI

SAGALASSOS VI

GEO- AND BIO-ARCHAEOLOGY AT SAGALASSOS AND IN ITS TERRITORY

Edited by
P. Degryse & M. Waelkens

Leuven University Press

Uitgegeven met de steun van de Universitaire Stichting van België

FU/US

Previous volumes **Sagalassos I – V** are published as a subseries in
ACTA ARCHAEOLOGICA LOVANIENSIA - MONOGRAPHIAE

ISBN 978 90 5867 661 0

D/2008/1869/28
NUR: 682

Dedicated to the memory of Prof. dr. Willy Viaene (1940-2000)

CONTENTS

GEO- AND BIO-ARCHAEOLOGY AT SAGALASSOS AND IN ITS TERRITORY

Marc WAELKENS

The papers presented in this volume offer an insight in the basic geo-archaeological, archaeometrical and bio-archaeological research performed since the publication of volume V (Waelkens and Loots, 2000) within the framework of the excavations and surveys in and around the ancient city of Sagalassos (SW Turkey) and its 1.200 km² large territory carried out between 1996 and 2006. Sagalassos has been the focus of interdisciplinary, archaeological research coordinated by Marc Waelkens of the Katholieke Universiteit Leuven since 1990 (Waelkens, 1993; Waelkens and Poblome, 1993; 1995, 1997; Waelkens and Loots, 2000). Starting in 1985 – together with its southern neighbour Kremna – Sagalassos became the second 'stop' of the 'Pisidia Project' of the 'British Archaeological Institute at Ankara' initiated in 1982 under the direction of Stephen Mitchell (then Swansea College, now University of Exeter). After three years (1982-1984) of surveying at Pisidian Antioch (Mitchell and Waelkens, 1998), whereby M. Waelkens was responsible right from the beginning for carrying out the architectural survey of the Pisidian sites, the 'Pisidia Project', was split up into a twin city survey both directed by S. Mitchell, who in the field rather supervised the work at Kremna (Mitchell, 1995), whereas M. Waelkens acted as a kind of 'second director' working with the same team at Sagalassos (Mitchell and Waelkens, 1987, 1988; Mitchell et al., 1989). As still is the case with most surveys in Anatolia today, these surveys were basically 'restricted to city-oriented architectural studies, rather than regional explorations' (Alcock, 1994: 181) and also had a major focus on recording new inscriptions. After, in 1987, a Potters' Quarter had been discovered at Sagalassos by our 'temsilçi' (representative of the Antiquities Department), Sabri Aydal and it had become clear that the site had once been a major pottery producing centre, in 1989, still under the umbrella of the British Archaeological Institute at Ankara, besides the urban survey, a rescue excavation was carried out in the Potters' Quarter in collaboration and under the supervision of the Burdur Museum (dir. Selçuk Başer), which only confirmed the importance of this craft at Sagalassos (Waelkens et al., 1990). The year after, our activities resumed as a collaborative effort between the Katholieke Universiteit Leuven, directed by M. Waelkens

and the Burdur Museum represented by its director, Ali Harmankaya, pending the decision of the Council of Ministers and the President of the Turkish Republic to grant a full scale excavation permit to M. Waelkens, which was eventually issued on August the 24th (Waelkens et al., 1991). Henceforth, Sagalassos became a Belgian enterprise, albeit from the beginning it always involved the participation of half a dozen and currently even a dozen of nationalities, representing various disciplines. Whereas in 1989 our team was composed of six archaeologists from the K.U.Leuven and five local Turkish workmen, nowadays each year some 120 scientists and some 80 local workmen are active on the slopes carrying the urban site and in the mountains and valleys around it.

Chronologically, this interdisciplinary research can be divided into four periods, whereby each period represents an important step forward toward the 'holistic archaeology', which we apply and propagate today:

– **the years 1989-1992**: As we decided that only an interdisciplinary approach would provide us with as much as possible archaeological and historical evidence, including all kinds of environmental (geo-archaeological and geobiological) studies and all categories of finds (artefacts and ecofacts), in **1989,** a geologist – the late Willy Viaene, to whose memory this volume is dedicated – was already a member of our small fieldwork team. In **1990**, F. De Puydt started to map the Potters' Quarter, whereas physical anthropologist Chr. Charlier initiated her study of the skeletons excavated inside tombs, which in this quarter alternated with workshops and sometimes even were recycled as secondary dumps for misfired pottery. The nature of the excavated remains also necessitated the presence of an engineer-conservator (ir. K. Van Baelen). Both coins and inscriptions were subjected to a preliminary study by M. Waelkens at Sagalassos proper, whereas subsequently squeezes of the former and casts of the latter were studied in detail at the K.U.Leuven, respectively by the late epigraphist H. Devijver, whose task has now been taken over by W. Eck, and numismatist S. Scheers.

By **1991**, the scientific team already included 42 scientists from five European countries, and 25 local workmen. Besides the disciplines involved already in the 1990 season, a number of new scientists made their entry, such as geomorphologists (the late J. De Ploey and E. Paulissen), who started the study of erosion, hydrology and vegetation on the site, an archaeozoologist, W.Van Neer from the '*Royal Museum of Central Africa*' *(RMCA)*. Illustrators and conservators of small finds also joined the team. As for the 'traditional' archaeology, L. Vandeput initiated her doctoral research on the architectural decoration of the local buildings (Vandeput 1997), whereas J. Poblome and R. Degeest, responsible for establishing a typology and a chronology of the locally produced fine *Sagalassos red slip ware* (Poblome, 1999) and coarse wares (Degeest, 2000) respectively saw their research being matched archaeometrically by a carefully selected coring program of local and regional clays, whereby those of the fine ware could already be attributed to the detrital clay beds from a side valley of the Mamakovası or Çanaklı basin, ca. 8 km south of Sagalassos. At the same time, W. Viaene and his colleague R. Ottenburgs completed a first study of limestone used in the monumental architecture of Sagalassos. In **1992**, all disciplines continued but the number of participants grew: W. Van Neer was thus joined by B. De Cupere and A. Lentacker, who reconstructed bone working processes – the former also starting her doctoral research on the faunal remains (De Cupere, 2001), whereas two additional geomorphologists; J. Poesen and G. Govers, complemented the late J. De Ploey and E. Paulissen in their study of the physical environment of the site. Archaeometrical research on the locally produced pottery mainly focussed on the mineralogical and firing properties of the locally used clays. As for conservation activities of large scale monuments, until 1997, K. Van Balen was assisted by T. Patrício.

– **the years 1993-1998**: In 1994, P.M. Vermeersch excavated Neolithic remains – be it not *in situ* – at Düldül Izi (near Dereköy, some 3,5 km N of the village of Yazır, east of Sagalassos). After having excavated some disturbed caves in Sagalassos proper, in 1997, he exposed a partially preserved Epipalaeolithic camp site at Karain Cave, near Dereköy, some 15 km. east of Sagalassos, which had been occupied temporarily by hunter-gatherings originating from the coastal areas of Pamphylia, ventured during the summer months along the Aksu river into later Sagalassian territory in search of game and good silex. In 1993, palynologists from the University of Groningen (The Netherlands), S. Bottema and H. Woldring, carried out the first corings in the valley of Çanaklı, a very time consuming research that eventually would be continued by M. Vermoere from the K.U.Leuven (Vermoere, 2003).

All the above mentioned palynological corings were carried out together with geomorphologist E. Paulissen, who studied the sedimentation in the territory, whereas his colleagues J. Poesen and G. Govers rather studied erosion risks, among others caused by animal trampling on scree slopes, which proved to have buried large surfaces of the upper city. In 1995, the team (I. Librecht, G. Verstraeten) of E. Paulissen also studied the limestone platforms resulting from giant mass movements, e.g. in Sagalassos itself, where at least one such event could be dated to the Imperial period, as well as the implications of environmental changes on slope evolution near the city.

The geological work by the late W. Viaene was continued by other K.U.Leuven geologists (Ph. Muchez, P. Degryse), who started producing a geological map of the whole territory, Together with geologists W. Viaene, Ph. Muchez and P. Degryse and palynologist M. Vermoere, they also made a preliminary study of travertine deposits in the vicinity of Sagalassos, which are studied in detail in this volume. As for archaeometrical research, the late W. Viaene assisted by R. Ottenburgs and H. Kucha, established the firing temperature of the *Sagalassos red slip ware* (our two ceramologists simultaneously had established methods for dating the local wares), the geochemical distribution of trace elements in the fine ware and the mineralogy and geochemistry of Roman common wares. In 1996, J. Poblome, together with the Burdur Museum excavated an early Byzantine tile kiln at Taşkapı.

Besides the study of clay, a second material became part of archaeometrical research: iron slag, of which the mineralogy, the geochemistry and the phase equilibriums as tracers of the iron making technology, as well as the kind of charcoal used in this production were analyzed. P. Degryse still continues the research on iron and its production technology today. Moreover, together with K. Callebaut, a first archaeometrical study of mortars used at Sagalassos was carried out. The year after, the same group focussed their research on lime mortars at Sagalassos (currently continued by J. Elsen).

The archaeozoologists experimentally studied the implication of sieving on their interpretation of faunal data, worked on the study and import of fish at Sagalassos, for which they surveyed the fauna of the Aksu (ancient Kestros River) and some SW Anatolian lakes and their implications for the fish trade. At the same time, together with B. De Cupere, I. Beuls started her doctoral research (Beuls, 2005) by following, together with B. De Cupere, in the field and throughout the year modern sheep and goat herding practices near Sagalassos and their relevance for reconstructing pastoral practices in Imperial times. The above-mentioned study of bone working at Sagalassos was repeated experimentally by Z. Parras, which provided us with a better insight of the whole process.

A Dutch biologist (J. Schelvis), also carried out some tests, trying to isolate and identify ancient mites, which are good indicators for minor changes in climate and environment, but unfortunately the latter proved to have been preserved only in large enough quantities in the Gravgaz marshes.

During the period between 1993 and 1998, other environmental approaches were incorporated into our activities in both the city and its *chora*, involving bioengineers studying ancient and modern land use and irrigation (S. Deckers; B. Raes, K. Donners from the K.U.Leuven), while palaeobotanist L. Vanhecke (*National Botanical Gardens at Meise*, Belgium), made a complete inventory of the current vegetation in the territory of Sagalassos. This area appears to be one of the richest zones of the Mediterranean, as far as the quantity of different plants and trees is concerned. This results from the fact that the city's 'chora' encompasses the transition from the Mediterranean coastal area to the more arid vegetation types of the Taurus belt and towards the beginning of the '*Axylon*' (the treeless Anatolian Central plateau). Forest engineers (B. Muys in collaboration with the Forestry Department of the University of Isparta), started to develop a forest deforestation and regeneration model covering the historical period, which is currently still going on by studying modern growth rates and the behaviour of the most important trees composing the ancient arboriculture, which depends on the influence of soil, climate, altitude and human behaviour. A macrobotanist (Th. Van Thuyne, K.U.Leuven) completed the pollen picture by identifying macroscopically plant remains found inside stratified urban contexts.

Chr. Charlier (K.U.Leuven) and later on E. Smits (V.U.Amsterdam) respectively studied cremated bones from the potters' quarter cremation burials and initiated a new physico-anthropological study of the skeletons of 24 burial sites – some multiple burials – excavated in 1994-1997 along the western slope of the Lower Agora. At the time of their exposure, they were considered to be the tombs of a population, which had continued living in the ruined city after the catastrophic earthquake, which had levelled most of it at some point in Early Byzantine times and was tentatively dated to the years around 650 AD. In 1998-1999, however, some new burials, thought to predate the seismic catastrophe, turned up between the above mentioned graveyard and a Christian cemetery, which since 2006 is being excavated around the Christian basilica, which in the early 5th century had replaced the Temple of Apollo Klarios. All its skeletons were analyzed by F.X. Ricaut and R. Decorte and dated by

means of AMS ^{14}C between the 10th and 13th century AD. It now seems most likely that the whole necropolis previously excavated on the west slope of the Lower Agora is part of the graveyard surrounding the Christian basilica above this western slope. In the mean time, AMS dating of small ruminant and bird bones found inside uhu owl pellets puked out by these owls inside the layers of mortar coating of the Roman baths' vaults, which seems to have fallen down during or shortly after the major earthquake, but before the brick faced concrete vaults gradually collapsed themselves, provided with a 95% degree of probability a date for this seismic event between 540-620 AD.

In 1996-1997, aDNA analysis was also applied by E. Jehaes (under the supervision of J.-J. Cassiman and R. Decorte) to the first group of burials in order to study family relationships, especially in the case of multiple burials, and establish genetic characteristics and connections of the city's ancient population (E. Jehaes 1998). Since 2006, a new physico-morphological and genetic (aDNA) study is performed on the most recent material by F.X. Ricaut of the '*Centre for Archaeological Sciences*' (see below) and by R. Decorte.

During the years 1993-1998, the on-site conservation team was first reinforced by ir. S. Ercan and during the final year also by arch. E. Torun, who both are still active on the site, where the latter recently has been officially appointed as 'site manager' From 1997 onwards, part of the fine conservation on the site would be carried out by a team of the 'Meşlik Yüksek Okulu' from Ankara University, which conserved and restored the mosaics of the Neon Library, and since five years is involved again in the fine on-site conservation. As for registering the site, from 1993 onwards F. Depuydt and his team started mapping the whole site, a work that would go on until 2005.

The year 1993 was not only important because of the start of an intensive palynological coring programme, which proved to be very rewarding throughout the years (Vermoere, 2004; articles by D. Kaniewski), but especially because of the fact that from that year onwards, the Turkish Antiquities Department required all excavation directors to make the inventory of the cultural heritage in the region around their excavation sites, which in our case represented the 1.200 km² large territory of Sagalassos. From 1993 to 1997, all 52 villages, 2 ilçes (Ağlasun and Çeltikçi, which are the seats of a 'kaymakam', a kind of regional sub-governor) as well as the provincial capital of the province, Burdur, were thus systematically investigated based on topographical maps, all published travel and epigraphical records, descriptions of sites and interviews with elderly people, especially shepherds and farmers, who were asked to point out localities with remains of abandoned structures, concentrations of sherds, stones or other anomalies, which they had noticed in the vicinity of their villages. Although ca. 250 new 'sites', typologically ranging from isolated farmsteads, over villa sites on estates with sometimes large mausoleums, hamlets, village – some of them nearly 'agro towns' of proto-urban size – fortresses, refugee fortified hilltop sites and caves, covering a time span of 12.000 years from the Epipaleolithic to late Ottoman times, were 'discovered' this way (Vanhaverbeke and Waelkens, 2003), the statistical reliability of these sites was not very high. This was mainly due to our survey approach and to the fact that Sagalassos from the 2nd century BC at the latest to the early 8 century AD, being a pottery production centre, monopolized local and regional consumption of ceramic fine ware, for which a relative dating system based on seriation had to be developed first (Poblome, 1999). On the other hand, many if not most of the coarse or common wares (Degeest, 2000), and certainly storage vessels such as amphorae produced in the territory – be it only from the 4th century AD onwards – had a highly non-diagnostic character, which originally was also the case for most pottery types dating between the Early Bronze Age II and the Hellenistic period on the one hand, and the post 7th century AD pottery on the other.

– **the years 1999-2003**: a new boost to our research and our reconstruction of the ancient settlement patterns in the territory and of the urban fabric of Sagalassos proper was enhanced by the development of 'state-of-the-art' surveying approaches in both the city and its suburbia (2 hours of walking from the city centre), by F. Martens (Martens, 2004) and H. Vanhaverbeke respectively. Although both approaches are based on on-line-walking by two groups of archaeologists, they had to adapt their methodology to respectively the very steep slopes and the resulting erosion of an urban site that has never been subjected to any form of farming, whereby ploughs year after year bring up new material to the surface, and a more gently sloping suburban area, subject to modern ploughing, but because of logistic reasons, not accessible during the best seasons of the year, i.e. the early spring and fall. On the other hand, the new survey strategies in both city and the suburbia profited enormously from the incorporation of a team of geophysicists from the University of Ljubljana in the annual campaigns, producing stunning results in the urban area despite it being full of limestone boulders of various sizes. As a result of this new approach, the regular street pattern in the lower city, the more pragmatic street orientation adapted to the rather steeps slopes of the unexcavated parts of the eastern domestic area and the presence of large buildings beyond the northern track of the late Roman defence wall could be established. However, the most stunning results were obtained in the Potters' Quarter, which was not an area with a rather dispersed distribution of workshops and tombs, as previously assumed, but proved to be a densely occupied city quarter, with large public monuments near its western edge (e.g. a gymnasium) and a continuous succession of workshops along winding streets, containing at least 72 kilns or furnaces. One of these workshops, the so-called coroplast workshop, specialized in the production of lamps and figurines was excavated based on geophysical (geomagnetic) mapping, whereby the results of the excavations confirmed those of the geophysical research.

During the same years, other new approaches included the creation at the K.U.Leuven '*Centre for Surface Catalysis*' directed by Prof. P. Jacobs of a 'residue analysis unit', which at first developed a new methodology for identifying the lipid fraction in ancient ceramics, thus allowing identifying different kinds of animal fats and bees wax in cooking vessels (Kimpe, 2003). The geomorphologic team was also expanded by S. Six and V. De Laet, who studied the Holocene geomorphologic evolution of the territory (Six, 2004) and reconstructed its geo-archaeological landscape by integrating geomorphic, GIS and remote sensing methods (De Laet, 2007) respectively. A group of geologists composed of Ph. Muchez, M. Sintubin, D. Similox-Tohon, G. Verhaert and K. Vanneste (*Royal Observatory Brussels*) developed new approaches for identifying seismic activity in prehistoric and historic times. Several active faults were identified both along the northern edge of the plain of Çanaklı, ca. 6 km south of the city, and at Sagalassos proper, of which the latter most likely was responsible for an earthquake ca. 500 AD and almost certainly for the big one dated by AMS 14C of the above mentioned owl pellets ca. 540-620 AD. The archaeozoological team also produced cutting-edge research by extracting for the first time in archaeology aDNA from ancient fish remains (Arndt et al., 2003) proving a centuries long import of Nile fish at Sagalassos and developed tools to elucidate small ruminant herd management in the Roman-Byzantine period (0-650 AD) (Beuls, 2005).

– **the years 2004 until now**: as far as surveying strategies are concerned, our approach profited enormously from the successful introduction of ground penetrating radar by our geophysical team from Ljubljana, which allows identifying time slices below the surface and locate older buildings at a much lower level covered by current subsurface structures.

Another major breakthrough was realized in the field of identifying previously 'non-diagnostic' pottery. Only recently, by systematic restudying of previously collected, but still undated material, which for the Early Iron Age can now be confronted with stratified ceramic evidence from Ur-

4

Sagalassos, the predecessor of current Sagalassos located at ca. 1.8 km to the southwest of the latter, at Tepe Düzen and apparently largely abandoned during the 4th century BC in favour of current Sagalassos, this picture has improved considerably and will further profit from the excavations at Tepe Düzen, started in 2005. Simultaneously, at the other end of the chronological time span, our post 7th century AD material, especially that of the Byzantine Dark Ages (8th to 10/11th century AD) is now also well documented by stratified evidence originating from two hamlets of the 'kastron' type located within the ruins of the Imperial city. The first one is represented by an 8th to 9th century fortified hamlet occupying the natural plateau, previously occupied by the sanctuary of the official Pisidian Imperial cult. Test excavations have produced fine and coarse wares of that period The second one (8th/9th to 10th century), which is also being excavated since 2005, surrounds the ruins of a Christian basilica into which the Temple of Apollo Klarios had been transformed during the early 5th century. The settlement was succeeded by a graveyard, whose skeletons dated by AMS, point towards a burial site covering the 10th to 13th centuries. For the Mid-Byzantine period, a fortified settlement, possibly a fortress if not a fortified hamlet, has been identified on top of the Alexander Hill and dated to the 12-13th century AD. Its local or regional ceramic material could be placed into the right chronological context by the presence of imported fine wares (e.g. from Cyprus and/or the Cyclades). During the last two years, dating and studying the whole Byzantine ceramic sequence from these hamlets and the territorial surveys, has also profited enormously by the involvement of A. Vionis, a Byzantine ceramologist, who became a member of our team. As a result of all this new material, the proportion of non diagnostic sherds has been drastically reduced for both the Protohistoric to Post-Classical period and for the Byzantine Dark Ages and the Mid-Byzantine period.

Another major breakthrough in the field of both archaeological and geomorphological surveying was realized in the doctoral dissertation of V. De Laet, in which, based on the characteristics of settlements belonging to a specific period (topographical location, orientation, distance from springs, roads etc.), a predictive model to identify zones within the territory with a high probability of containing thus far unidentified sites belonging to the same period was developed (De Laet, 2007). In the mean time, K. Romanus also developed a methodology to distinguish between wine and oil in the residue of amphorae (Romanus, 2007).

Two other major steps that should improve our holistic approach in Archaeology, were the fact that in 2003 Sagalassos could profit from an 'impulse financing' by the K.U.Leuven, which allowed us to create the 'Centre for

Geo- and Bio-Archaeological Sciences and Archaeological Image Processing', which made it possible to appoint D. Kaniewski as our new palynologist and anthracologist after the departure of M. Vermoere and also included the VISICS group of ESAT at the K.U.Leuven, directed by L. Van Gool with its expertise in improving images and developing 3-D models of structures. In 2005 our team of archaeologists (now also including our colleagues H. Willems working in Egypt, K.Van Lerberghe working in Syria and prehistorian Ph.Van Peer working in a.o. Egypt, Sudan…) and scientists from the above mentioned geo- and bioarchaeological sciences was recognized as a 'centre of excellence' by the K.U.Leuven under the name of 'Centre for Archaeological Sciences'. It absorbed the previous centre (with D. Kaniewski) and allowed us to attract foreign researchers, such as F.X. Ricaut (physical anthropology), J. Schneider (isotopic analysis), E. Marinova (macrobotanist and anthracologist) and J. Bakker (palynologist). On the other hand, some of our own recently promoted scientists, such as V. Linseele (archaeozoologist) and V. De Laet (GIS expertise and remote sensing) were appointed as staff members of the same centre. This has allowed us to develop and promote a 'Holistic Archaeology' according to which all finds are analyzed and studied as far as the provenance of their raw materials and production technology is concerned, but without neglecting their functional or symbolic meaning.

REFERENCES USED IN THIS INTRODUCTORY CHAPTER

S. ALCOCK (1994) Breaking up the Hellenistic world: survey and society, in: I. MORRIS (ed.) *Classical Greece: Ancient Histories and Modern Archaeologies (New Directions in Archaeology)* Cambridge (U.K.), 171-190.

A. ARNDT, W. VAN NEER, B. HELLEMANS, J. ROBBEN, F. VOLCKAERT and M. WAELKENS (2003) Roman trade relationships at Sagalassos (Turkey) elucidated from mtDNA of ancient fish remains, *Journal of Archaeological Science* 30, 1095-1105.

I. BEULS (2005) *Design of Odontological Tools to Elucidate Small Ruminant Herd Management at Sagalassos (SW Turkey) in the Roman-Byzantine Period (0-650 AD)*, Leuven, unpublished Ph. D. dissertation.

B. DE CUPERE (2001) *Animals at Ancient Sagalassos. Evidence of the Faunal Remains (Studies in Eastern Mediterranean Archaeology 4)*, Brepols, Turnhout.

R. DEGEEST (2000) *The Common Wares of Sagalassos. Typology and Chronology (Studies in Eastern Mediterranean Archaeology 3)*, Brepols, Turnhout.

V. DE LAET (2007) *Evolution and Reconstruction of the Geoarchaeological Landscape in the Territory of Sagalassos*

(SW Turkey): Integration of Geomorphic, GIS and Remote Sensing Methods, Leuven, Ph D dissertation.

K. KIMPE (2003) *Chemical Analysis of the Lipid Fraction from Ancient Ceramics of Sagalassos (Dissertationes De Agricultura* 553) Leuven. Ph.D.

F. MARTENS (2005) The archaeological urban survey of Sagalassos (SW Turkey): The possibilities and limitations of surveying a "non-typical" classical site, *Oxford Journal of Archaeology* 24.3, 229-254.

S. MITCHELL (1995) *Cremna in Pisidia. An Ancient City in Peace and War*, London.

S. MITCHELL and M. WAELKENS (1987) Sagalassos and Cremna 1986, *Anatolian Studies* 37, 37-48.

S. MITCHELL and M. WAELKENS (1988) Cremna and Sagalassos 1987, *Anatolian Studies* 38, 53-65.

S. MITCHELL, E. OWENS and M. WAELKENS (1989) Ariassos and Sagalassos, *Anatolian Studies* 39, 63-77.

S. MITCHELL and M. WAELKENS (1998) *Pisidian Antioch. The Site and its Monuments*, Swansea.

J. POBLOME (1999) *Sagalassos Red Slip Ware. Typology and Chronology (Studies in Eastern Mediterranean Archaeology 2)*, Brepols, Turnhout.

K. ROMANUS (2008) *Chemical Analysis of Lipids and Polyphenols in Archaeological Pottery from Sagalassos, Turkey (Dissertationes De Agricultura)*, Leuven, Ph.D. dissertation.

J. SCHELVIS (1960) *Mites and Archaeozoology. General Methods; Application to Dutch Sites*, Rijksuniversiteit Groningen, PhD dissertation.

S. SIX (2004) *Holocene Geomorphological Evolution of the Territory of Sagalassos. Contribution to the Palaeo-Environmental Reconstruction of Southwest Turkey*, Leuven, unpublished Ph.D. dissertation.

M. VERMOERE (2004) *Holocene Vegetation History in the Territory of Sagalassos (Southwest Turkey). A Palynological Approach (Studies in Eastern Mediterranean Archaeology 6)*, Bepols, Turnhout.

M. WAELKENS, S. BAŞER and W. VIAENE (1990) Sagalassos 1989. The rescue excavation in the potters' quarter and the "Sagalassos ware", *Acta Archaeologica Lovaniensia* 28-29, 75-98.

M. WAELKENS, A. HARMANKAYA A. and W. VIAENE (1991) The excavations at Sagalassos 1990, *Anatolian Studies* 41, 197-213.

M. WAELKENS, E. OWENS, A. HASENDONCKX, and B. ARIKAN (1992) The excavations at Sagalassos 1991, *Anatolian Studies* 42, 79-98.

M. WAELKENS (1993) The 1992 excavation season. A preliminary report, in: WAELKENS, M. and POBLOME, J. (eds.) (1993) *Sagalassos II. Report on the Third Excavation Campaign of 1992 (Acta Archaeologica Lovaniensia Monographiae* 6), Leuven University Press, Leuven: 9-41.

M. WAELKENS and J. POBLOME (eds.) (1993) *Sagalassos II. Report on the Third Excavation Campaign of 1992 (Acta Archaeologica Lovaniensia Monographiae* 6) Leuven University Press, Leuven.

M. WAELKENS and J. POBLOME (eds.) (1995) *Sagalassos III. Report on the Fourth Excavation Campaign of 1993 (Acta Archaeologica Lovaniensia Monographiae* 7), Leuven University Press, Leuven.

M. WAELKENS and J. POBLOME (eds.) (1997) *Sagalassos IV. Report on the Survey and Excavation Campaigns of 1994 and 1995 (Acta Archaeologica Lovaniensia Monographiae* 9), Leuven University Press, Leuven.

M. WAELKENS and L. LOOTS (eds.) (2000) *Sagalassos V. Report on the Survey and Excavation Campaigns of 1996 and 1997 (Acta Archaeologica Lovaniensia Monographiae* 11), Leuven University Press, Leuven.

Most of the above mentioned research topics are discussed in the *Sagalassos* volumes listed above, whereas the current volume presents the contribution of the geo- and bio-archaeological sciences to the interdisciplinary study of the city and the territory of Sagalassos since, in 2000, the last *Sagalassos* volume *(V)* had presented research carried out ending with the campaign of 1997. As in recent years, we also started publishing more and more in journals or congress proceedings, which usually are not that well known for archaeologists, a complete list of such studies covering the environmental sciences that have appeared in journals, congress proceedings or books, besides the *Sagalassos Series* is added separately at the end of this introductory chapter.

The work described in this volume, provides a solid base for a 'holistic' approach of archaeology, as described above, geological and geomorphologic maps allow the identification and precise location of raw materials that were exploited in the past, but also were a requirement for geomorphologic, palynological and soil-engineering studies of the area, as geology, climate and geomorphology will influence the physical and biological processes at the surface. The soil formation and flora are directly related to the nature of the subsurface and its properties, whereas the rocks form the substrate on which geomorphologic processes act. The study of the various lithologies and their structural features further contribute to the study of all resources, both mineral and organic, in the territory of Sagalassos. The following paragraphs summarize the content of the various parts in which the volume has been divided.

1. THE GEOLOGICAL SETTING (PART I)

A geological map has been made of the territory of ancient Sagalassos. This territory is delimited by limestone formations just north of the site and limestone around the village of Çanaklı in the south, whereas the siliciclastics at Taşkapı and Yazır form the western and eastern boundary respectively. The map has been completed on a 1/10.000 scale.

This geological map serves as a database for identifying potential provenances of most of the raw materials used in the building and ceramic industries at Sagalassos. For this purpose, all lithologies present have been petrographically and geochemically characterized.

The region of Sagalassos in SW Turkey, centred on the cities of Burdur and Isparta, is situated in the first-degree seismic hazard zone. Based on archaeological evidence, it could be inferred that the ancient city has been struck by numerous earthquakes during its history. A first step in the search for the causative fault(s) of the Sagalassos earthquakes is a remote sensing analysis in order to identify all structures in the wider surroundings that may represent active faults. Near surface geophysics and remote sensing, using satellite images, aerial photographs and a digital elevation model (DEM) helped to identify previously unknown active faults within a radius of 20 km of the archaeological site.

2. THE GEOMORPHOLOGICAL SETTING (PART II)

The archaeological research at Sagalassos is a project covering not only scientific disciplines traditionally linked to archaeology, but also new technologies such as multi-method geophysical survey and very high resolution remote sensing with a sufficient radiometric and spatial resolution (<2.5 m). GIS-, pixel- and object-based techniques for automatic extraction of surveyed and excavated archaeological features of the ancient town of Sagalassos based on very high-resolution Quickbird-2 satellite imagery are discussed in this volume. The results of this analysis are compared to a visual interpretation of the data. Also, an evaluation has been made to what extent Quickbird-2 imagery is able to provide new evidence about some previously unknown archaeological features. Besides the automatic extraction of surveyed and excavated structures also unknown surface features, even after detailed field surveying and geophysical prospecting, can be identified on the Quickbird-2 image.

In terms of stratigraphy, the finding of the Santorini tephra in the Gravgaz basin in the territory is somewhat unique for Turkey. It is the first time that the tephra layer is not found in a lake environment, but in colluvial deposits on a gentle foot slope. The finding suggests that the territory of Sagalassos must have been covered by a thin ash layer that was later eroded and/or mixed with slope deposits, in most places within a short time span after the fallout of the eruption. This explains why the ash layer has never been observed during the intensive fieldwork which was also part of the extensive archaeological surveys on the territory of Sagalassos. The reworked glass sherds could be used in the future as a tracer for post-Santorini deposits. Because of the depth (· 8.74m) at which the tephra layer was found, it is suggested that most if not all Bronze Age sites in the territory, situated in a similar geomorphologic position, i.e. on gentle foot slopes, may be covered by large amounts of colluvial deposits and have not yet been identified. In fact, most settlements dated to the Late Bronze Age thus far belong to well-defended hilltop sites, which may not have been permanently occupied, but served as a refugee centre for people and their domestic animals in times of danger. The Thera tephra thus remains one of the main stratigraphical key horizons in the area.

In a complementary study, based on sediment description, accumulation rates and palynology, the filling of the Gravgaz basin in the territory of Sagalassos is described and interpreted. Several climatic events and environmental changes can be inferred in this way. Cultivation of the landscape and soil conservation measures to control the erosion can be shown and dated, together with the influence of natural changes in the environment. The emergence of larger proto-urban settlements during the Early Iron Age may have set a trigger for deforestation, whereas intensive cultivation of the area in Imperial times may also have had its influence on the landscape formation.

3. THE CLIMATIC SETTING (PART III)

The cool water travertine in the village of Başköy, near the archaeological site of Sagalassos, is investigated petrographically and geochemically. This travertine has been dated as deposited during the Holocene. U/Th dating of one section indicated an age of 9000 ± 600 yr BP. Other travertine deposits were dated after the 1st-2nd century A.D. based on ceramics found in their deposits. Three main types of travertine facies can be distinguished: phytoherm framestone, detrital travertine and finely laminated travertine. The latter is built up by bacteria, blue-green algae, microdetrital sediments and bio-mediated calcite precipitation around larvae. This type of travertine was deposited in an alternating fluvial-barrage and paludal system, providing an indication of past palaeoecological conditions. Remains of palaeochannels can still be found and are filled by siliciclastic and travertine pebbles. Today, the system no longer exists. It must have largely disappeared some 1350 yr ago, since by that time tombs were being cut into the travertine walls.

In a second study, the historical buildings of the ancient city of Sagalassos, mainly constructed with local limestone, have been investigated from a weathering point of view. The paper handles the dependence of this weathering on the burial conditions, the nature of the limestone, atmospheric circumstances and biological factors. To investigate the above mentioned relationships, it is necessary to gain insight into the different weathering mechanisms, the nature of the surface and of the weathering layers of the limestone, the stability of the various types of limestone under different conditions, in relation to prevailing climatic conditions.

4. THE EXPLOITATION OF LOCAL RESOURCES AND THE IMPORT OF SUBSISTENCE GOODS (PART IV)

For more than a decade, a major archaeometrical research programme has been investigating and reconstructing the technology of the potters at Sagalassos. One of the aims of the programme is the integration of our archaeometrical knowledge to study every single aspect of the pottery manufacturing process of Sagalassos in detail. Our research allowed the identification of most raw materials used in this industry and resulted in the reconstruction of the environmental and socio-economic factors influencing the potters' craft. In the mean time, all local table and common ware fabrics have been characterized. Also, the source of the clays used for the local fine wares and their slip has been identified. Mineralogical, petrographical and geochemical techniques were successfully applied in this respect.

Different types of building stones were also macroscopically and petrographically characterized at the ancient city of Sagalassos (SW Turkey). The natural building stones include limestone, conglomerate, breccia, marble, travertine, granite and sand- to siltstone of different qualities. The provenance of most of the building stones may be related to local lithological units, both in the immediate area of the city and on its territory. Also, some stone types were clearly imported from considerable distance. Throughout the occupation of the city, local beige and pink limestone of good quality remained the most important building stone. Both the high quality white limestone from just beyond the territory of the city and marble imported from a distance of 250 km (from Dokimeion), represent only a small fraction of the total amount of building stones present. The selection of building stone went hand in hand with the assessment of

their structural strength and suitability for carving complex architectural ornaments, together with the desire to create a polychrome architecture.

Although the nature of quarrying evidence at Sagalassos does not allow the reconstruction of an exact chronological sequence, a tentative chronology can be proposed. The first building stones of Sagalassos were quarried at the site proper. The quarrying of the local bedrock can be traced to the Mid-Hellenistic period. Limestone from the Lycian nappe near monumental Sagalassos continued to be extracted throughout the Julio-Claudian and Hadrianic to Severan period. The unique limestone of the Sarıkaya quarry seems to have been used only in Late Hellenistic buildings. This indicates that this quarry may have been one of the main suppliers of building stones during this period. The local pink limestone was only identified in the Ağlasun Dağları quarry immediately to the north of Sagalassos, be it on the other side of the mountain crest. Although the quarry cannot be dated with certainty, petrographic and geochemical data indicate that this quarry was at least contemporaneous with the Sarıkaya quarry, and was still supplying building stone to Sagalassos during the first and second centuries AD. Some of the beige and possibly pink limestone used at Sagalassos, along with a high quality white limestone, was likely imported from the Lycian nappes in the Yarışlı area, located just beyond the south-western territory of the town This import became a trend from the Trajanic period (98-117 AD) onwards. The pink variety was used together with the high quality semi-crystallized white variety, to obtain bichromy (e.g. the Temple of the Divine Hadrian and of Antoninus Pius) or polychromy (e.g. the Late Antonine Nymphaeum on the Upper Agora). The white variety which is easily wrongly identified as marble, certainly replaced this material, of which the high quality varieties from Aphrodisias and especially from Dokimeion were imported for normal and colossal statuary, whereas the latter quarry did provide the very popular purple veined '*pavonazetto*' used for columns and wall veneer that was also exported in bulky transports. This means that the use of white Docimian marble was never imported to Sagalassos as a building material because of the distance (250 km) or the difficulty of bulky transport from there, but because the much closer high quality white Yarışlı limestone, could hardly be distinguished from it by the naked eye and because of the expenses of much shorter overland transport formed a better alternative. In fact, a keyword for quarrying limestone in the city area seems to be proximity. In the immediate vicinity of constructions consuming large volumes of stone, there are quarries which fit in size the volumes in question (e.g. the stadium quarry). This view is also supported by the integration of potential exhausted quarries in buildings (e.g. the '*episkopeion*' or bishop's palace). Another interesting aspect of the quarries is the almost complete lack of well organized quarries with systematic trenching separating blocks from one another before they were cut off below by means of wedging, which was characteristic of Greek and Roman quarry practice. This relates to the stone quality, as the abundance of natural fractures in the limestone deposits forced the quarrymen to follow these natural features as best as they could. Sagalassos is an important case study concerning the use of predominantly local stone for large building activities in Antiquity. The obvious relation between quarrying and the nearby use of stone in a monumental city provides excellent opportunities for the promotion of the significance of this quarry landscape to the wider public. The importance of the quarries can easily be seen when presented as an integral part of the extended "townscape" of antique Sagalassos.

Regarding subsistence studies, an analytic method to study the lipid fraction inside the residue on used ceramics was developed. Two extraction methods were compared: soxtec extraction and ultrasonic extraction. Soxtec extraction proved to be more effective and more practical. In this way the total lipid profile and the distribution of the common fatty acids can be analyzed. The total lipid extract is analyzed with a high temperature gas chromatograph coupled to a mass spectrometer (GC-MS). With the GC-MS even 'biomarker' compounds such as sterols and waxes could be identified. To analyze the common fatty acids, a second lipid extract is transesterified. The ratios of the most important fatty acids provide more information on the origin of the lipids. Combining the obtained information provides a good basis for the identification of original contents of ancient ceramics (ruminant fat, fat from omnivores, bees wax etc.).

The surveys of the Anatolian fish fauna and the compilation of ichthyologic literature has allowed refining the existing data on the geographical distribution of species, despite the many anthropogenic changes that occurred the last few decennia as a result of introduction of species, damming and irrigation projects, pollution and overfishing. It appears that long distance trade of fishes at Sagalassos was not limited to marine species and even various Nilotic taxa, but that also Anatolian freshwater fish was commonly traded over long distances. The modern zoogeographical data available thus far allowed the provenancing of one type of fish, namely *Pseudophoxinus handlirschi* that is limited to Lake Eğirdir. For the other species, that have a wider distribution, multiple provenances are possible and, therefore, the water bodies have been determined that are in closest proximity to Sagalassos. However, since fish trade was also practised over long distances, the closest occurrence of a species does not necessarily indicate its

provenance. Further geochemical analysis and possibly also ancient DNA studies may help elucidating where the species were exactly imported from.

5. CONCLUSION

Sagalassos is not an isolated case – a similar approach gradually directs the policy of other excavations. It is hoped that in a near future real interdisciplinary collaboration will become a widespread characteristic feature of 'classical archaeology'. This volume is another step in this direction of what one could call 'holistic archaeology'.

6. ACKNOWLEDGEMENTS

The research presented in this volume is dedicated to the memory of Prof. Dr. Willy Viaene, who participated in the interdisciplinary study of Sagalassos and its the territory from the very start of the project.

The research was supported through the *QuarryScapes Project* (contract no. 015416 of EU FP6 STREP-INCO programme) and by the Belgian *Programme on Interuniversitary Poles of Attraction* (*IAP V/9* and *VI/22*). The text also presents the results of projects funded by the *Research Fund of the K.U.Leuven* (*BOF-GOA02/2* and *GOA07/2*), a *Culture 2000* project "*Stone-Relief-Inscriptions*" and by projects of the *Fund for Scientific Research-Flanders (Belgium)* (*FWO G.0421.06, G.2145.94, G.0245.02*). This book was published with support of the University Foundation of Belgium ("Uitgegeven met steun van de Universitaire Stichting van België"). Scientific responsibility for all contents is assumed by the authors.

7. REFERENCES TO OTHER GEO- AND BIO-ARCHAEOLOGICAL PUBLICATIONS OF THE SAGALASSOS PROJECT

Besides the *Sagalassos Series* of which this book represents the sixth volume dedicated to geo- and bio-archaeological research in the city and its territory, another series called *Studies in Eastern Mediterranean Archaeology* (or *SEMA*) presents the results of archaeological doctorates or doctorates concerning other disciplines dealing with archaeological evidence at Sagalassos. Since the last *Sagalassos* volume appeared in 2000, publishing material of the campaigns in 1996-1997, the following *SEMA Volumes* dealing with geo- and bio-archaeological subjects have been published:

B. De Cupere (2001) *Animals at Ancient Sagalassos. Evidence of the Faunal Remains* (*SEMA IV*) Brepols, Turhnout.

H. Vanhaverbeke and M. Waelkens (2003) *The Chora of Sagalassos. The Evolution of the Settlement Pattern from Prehistoric untilRecent Times* (*SEMA V*) Brepols, Turnhout.: contains an overview of the physical setting, the vegetation history and climatic change.

M. Vermoere (2005) *Holocene Vegetation History in the Territory of Sagalassos (Southwest Turkey). A Palynological Approach* (*SEMA VI*) Brepols, Turnhout.

A third category of publications deals with articles published either in journals, in congress proceedings or in books. According to their subject, they can be subdivided into the following groups:

7.1. On mineral resources and artefact production

Stones and stone quarrying

L. Loots (2001) *The Building Materials and Building Techniques at Sagalassos, Turkey,* Leuven, unpublished Ph.D.

M. Waelkens, Ph. Muchez, L. Loots, P. Degryse, L. Vandeput, S. Ercan, L. Moens and P. De Paepe (2002) Marble and the marble trade at Sagalassos (Turkey), in: J.J. Hermann Jr., N. Herz and R. Newman (eds.) *Asmosia V. Fifth International Conference. June 11-15, 1998. Boston. Museum of Fine Arts*, 370-380.

M. Waelkens, P. Degryse, L. Vandeput, Ph. Muchez and L. Loots (2003) Polychrome architecture at Sagalassos (Pisidia) during the Hellenistic and Imperial Period against the background of Greco-Roman coloured architecture, in: L. Lazzarini (ed.) *Asmosia. VIth International Conference. Venice, June 15-18, 2000*, 517-530.

P. Degryse, Ph. Muchez, L. Loots, L. Vandeput and M. Waelkens (2003) The building stones of Roman Sagalassos (SW Turkey): facies analysis and provenance, *Facies* 48, 9-22.

P. Degryse, P. Muchez and M. Waelkens (2007) Geology and archaeology of late Hellenistic limestone quarries at Sagalassos, *MARMORA, 2, 9-20.*

Mortars

J. Elsen, P. Degryse and M. Waelkens (2001) Mineralogical and petrographic study of ancient mortars from Sagalassos in view of their conservation, in: *Proceedings of the 8th Euroseminar on Microscopy Applied to Building Materials, September 4-7, 2001, Athens, Greece*: 331-337.

P. Degryse, J. Elsen and M. Waelkens (2002) Study of ancient mortars from Sagalassos (Turkey) in view of their conservation, *Cement and Concrete Research*, 32, 1457-1463.

Clay and Ceramic Production

J. Poblome, P. Degryse, M. Schlits, R. Degeest, W. Viaene, I. Librecht, E. Paulissen and M. Waelkens (2000) The ceramic production centre of Sagalassos, *Rei Cretariae Romanae Fautorum. Acta* 36, Abingdon, 39-42.

J. Poblome, O. Bounegru, P. Degryse, W. Viaene, M. Waelkens and S. Erdemgil (2001) The sigillata manufactories of Pergamon and Sagalassos, *Journal of Roman Archaeology* 14, 143-165.

J. Poblome, P. Degryse, W. Viaene, R. Ottenburgs, M. Waelkens, R. Degeest and J. Naud (2002) The concept of a pottery production centre. An archaeometrical contribution from ancient Sagalassos, *Journal of Archaeological Science* 29, 873-882.

P. Degryse, J. Poblome, K. Donners, J. Deckers and M. Waelkens (2003) Geoarchaeological investigations of the "Potters' Quarter" at Sagalassos, Southwest Turkey, *Geoarchaeology* 18-2, 255-281.

Glass raw materials and glass production technology

P. Degryse, J. Schneider, J. Poblome, M. Waelkens, U. Haack and Ph. Muchez (2005) A geochemical study of Roman to early Byzantine Glass from Sagalassos, South-west Turkey, *Journal of Archaeological Science* 32, 287-299.

V. Lauwers, P. Degryse, J. Poblome and M. Waelkens (2005) Le verre de Sagalassos: de nouvelles preuves, in: H. Cabart (ed.) *Éclats de verre. 19ième Rencontres de l'Association Française pour l'Archéologie du Verre: Gaillac en Montans (France), 14-16 octobre, Bulletin de l'association française pour l'archéologie du verre, Paris 2005*, 26-29.

P. Degryse, J. Schneider, U. Haack, V. Lauwers, J. Poblome, M. Waelkens and Ph. Muchez (2006) Evidence for glass recycling using Pb and Sr isotopic ratios and Sr-mixing lines: the case of early Byzantine Sagalassos, *Journal of Archaeological Science* 33, 494-501.

V. Lauwers, P. Degryse and M. Waelkens (2007) A ceramic tool for the glass blower, *Oxford Journal of Archaeology* 26 (2), 193-200.

V. Lauwers, P. Degryse and M. Waelkens (2007) Evidence for Anatolian Glassworking in Antiquity: The Case of Sagalassos (Southwestern Turkey), *Journal of Glass Studies* 49, 39-46.

Metal ores and iron production

P. Degryse, Ph. Muchez, S. Six and M. Waelkens (2003) Identification of ore extraction and metal working in ancient times: a case study of Sagalassos (SW Turkey), *Journal of Geochemical Exploration* 77, 65-80.

P. Degryse, Ph. Muchez, J. Naud and M. Waelkens (2003) Iron production at the Roman to Byzantine city of Sagalassos: an archaeometrical case study, in: *Archaeometry* in Europe, Proceedings Vol. 1, Milan, September 24-26, Milan, 133-142.

P. DEGRYSE, PH. MUCHEZ, J. NAUD and M. WAELKENS (2003) Geochemical prospection for iron-mineralization (SW Turkey) and their use during Roman-Byzantine times, *Proceedings of the 7th Biennial SGA Meeting, 24 to 28 August 2003, Athens, Greece*, 669-672.

N. KELLENS, P. DEGRYSE, F. MARTENS and M. WAELKENS (2003) Iron production activities and products at Roman to Early Byzantine Sagalassos (SW Turkey), in: *Archaeometallurgy in Europe, vol. 1, International Conference, 24-26 September 2003, Milan*, Milan, 545-554.

P. DEGRYSE, J. SCHNEIDER, M. BRAUNS, PH. MUCHEZ and M. WAELKENS (2006) Provenance and selective use of iron ores at Roman to Byzantine Sagalassos: lead, strontium and osmium isotopic evidence, in: *Proceedings of the 34th International Archaeometry Conference, Zaragoza, Spain, 3-7 May 2004*, 155-159.

P. DEGRYSE, J.C. SCHNEIDER, N. KELLENS, M. WAELKENS and P. MUCHEZ (2007) Tracing the resources of iron working at ancient Sagalassos (SW Turkey): a combined lead and strontium isotope study on iron artefacts and ores, *Archaeometry*, 49 (1), 75-86.

7.2. Palaeoseismology

M. SINTUBIN, PH. MUCHEZ, D. SIMILOX-TOHON, G. VERHAERT, E. PAULISSEN and M. WAELKENS (2003) Seismic catastrophes at the ancient city of Sagalassos (SW Turkey) and their implications for seismotectonics in the Burdur-Isparta area, *Geological Journal* 38, 359-374.

D. SIMILOX-TOHON, K. VANNESTE, M. SINTUBIN, PH. MUCHEZ and M. WAELKENS (2004) Two-dimensional resistivity imaging: a tool in archaeoseismology. An example from ancient Sagalassos (Southwest Turkey), *Archaeological Prospection* 11, 1-18.

D. SIMILOX-TOHON, M. SINTUBIN, PH. MUCHEZ, H. VANHAVERBEKE and M. WAELKENS (2004) A historical surface-rupturing event at ancient Sagalassos (SW Turkey): palaeoseismological evidence, in: A.A. Chatzipetros and S.B. Pavlides (eds.) *Proceedings of the 5th International Symposium on Eastern Mediterranean Geology, Thessaloniki (Greece), 14-20 April 2004*, 952-955.

D. SIMILOX-TOHON, M. SINTUBIN, PH. MUCHEZ, H. VANHAVERBEKE, G. VERHAERT and M. WAELKENS (2005) Identification of a historical morphogenic earthquake through trenching at ancient Sagalassos (SW Turkey), *Journal of Geodynamics* 40, 279-293.

D. SIMILLOX-TOHON (2006) *An Integrated Geological and Archaeoseismological Approach of the Historical Seismicity in the Territory of Sagalassos (SW Turkey). Towards an Assessment of the Seismic Hazard in the Burdur-Isparta Region*, Leuven, Ph.D. dissertation.

G. VERHAERT (2006) *Normal Fault Architecture and Related Fluid Flow in Carbonate Rocks (Burdur-Isparta Region, SW Turkey)*, Leuven, PhD dissertation.

D. SIMILOX-TOHON, M. SINTUBIN, PH. MUCHEZ, G. VERHAERT, K. VANNESTE, M. FERNANDEZ, S. VANDYCKE, H. VANHAVERBEKE and M. WAELKENS (2006) The identification of an active fault by a multidisciplinary study at the archaeological site of Sagalassos (SW Turkey), *Tectonophysics* 420, 371-387.

G. VERHAERT, D. SIMILOX-TOHON, S. VANDYCKE, M. SINTUBIN and P. MUCHEZ (2006) Different stress states in the Burdur-Isparta region (SW Turkey) since Late Miocene times: a reflection of a transient stress regime, *Journal of Structural Geology* 28, 1067-1083.

7.3. Geomorphology and Remote sensing

S. SIX (2004) *Holocene Geomorphological Evolution of the Territory of Sagalassos. Contribution to the Palaeo-Environmental Reconstruction of Southwest Turkey*, Leuven, unpublished Ph.D. dissertation.

V. DE LAET (2007) *Evolution and Reconstruction of the Geo-archaeological Landscape in the Territory of Sagalassos (SW Turkey): Integration of Geomorphic, GIS and Remote Sensing Methods*, Leuven, Ph.D. dissertation.

V. DE LAET, E. PAULISSEN, M. WAELKENS (2007) Methods for the extraction of archaeological features from very high resolution Ikonos-2 remote sensing imagery, Hisar (southwest Turkey), *Journal of Archaeological Science* 34 (5), 830-841.

D. KANIEWSKI, V. DE LAET, E. PAULISSEN and M. WAELKENS (2007) Long-term effects of human impact on mountainous ecosystems, western Taurus Mountains, Turkey, *Journal of Biogeography*, 1-23.

D. KANIEWSKI, E. PAULISSEN, V. DE LAET, K. DOSSCHE and M. WAELKENS (2007) A high resolution Late Holocene landscape ecological history inferred from an intramontane basin in the Western Taurus Mountains, Turkey, *Quaternary Science Reviews* 26, 2201-2218.

7.4. Palynological and botanical studies

M. VERMOERE, L. VANHECKE, M. WAELKENS and E. SMETS (2000) A comparison between modern pollen spectra of moss cushions and Cundill pollen traps. Implications for the interpretation of fossil pollen data from Southwest Turkey, *Grana* 39, 146-158.

M. VERMOERE, M. WAELKENS, H. VANHAVERBEKE, L. VANHECKE, I. LIBRECHT, E. PAULISSEN and E. SMETS (2000) Late Holocene environmental change and the record of human impact at Gravgaz near Sagalassos, Southwest Turkey, *Journal of Archaeological Science* 27, 571-595.

M. Vermoere, L. Vanhecke, M. Waelkens and E. Smets (2001) Modern pollen studies in the territory of Sagalassos (Southwest Turkey) and their use in the interpretation of a Late Holocene pollen diagram, *Review of Palaeobotany and Palynology* 114, 29-56.

M. Vermoere, S. Bottema, L. Vanhecke, M. Waelkens, E. Paulissen and E. Smets (2002) Palynological evidence for late Holocene human occupation recorded in two wetlands in Southwest Turkey, *The Holocene* 12.5, 569-584.

M. Vermoere, T. Van Thuyne, S. Six, L. Vanhecke, M. Waelkens, E. Paulissen and E. Smets (2002) Late Holocene local vegetation dynamics in the marsh of Gravgaz (SW Turkey), *Journal of Paleolimnology* 27, 429-451.

M. Vermoere, L. Vanhecke, M. Waelkens and E. Smets (2003) Modern and ancient olive stands near Sagalassos (southwest Turkey) and reconstruction of the ancient agricultural landscape in two valleys, *Global Ecology and Biogeography* 12, 217-235.

M. Vermoere, S. Six, J. Poblome, P. Degryse, E. Paulissen, M. Waelkens and E. Smets (2003) Pollen sequences from the city of Sagalassos (Pisidia, Southwest Turkey), *Anatolian Studies* 53, 2003, 161-173.

M. Fontaine, R. Aerts, K. Özkan, A. Mert, S. Gülsoy, H. Süel, M. Waelkens, and B. Muys (2007) Elevation and exposition rather than soil types determine communities and site suitability in Mediterranean mountain forests of southern Anatolia, Turkey, *Forest Ecology and Management* 247, 18-25.

D. Kaniewski, V. De Laet, E. Paulissen and M. Waelkens (2007) Long-term effects of human impact on mountainous ecosystems, western Taurus Mountains, Turkey, *Journal of Biogeography*, 1-23.

D. Kaniewski, E. Paulissen, V. De Laet, K. Dossche and M. Waelkens (2007) 3000 years BP high-resolution physical landscape history inferred from an intramontane basin in the Western Taurus Mountains, Turkey, *Quaternary Science Reviews* 26 (17-18), 2201-2218.

D. Kaniewski, E. Paulissen, V. De Laet and M. Waelkens (2008) Late Holocene fire impact and post-fire regeneration from the Bereket basin, Taurus Mountains, Southwest Turkey, *Quaternary Research* 70, 228-239.

7.5. Archaezoology or faunal studies

B. De Cupere, A. Lentacker, W. Van Neer, M. Waelkens and L. Verslype (2000) Osteological evidence for the draught exploitation of cattle: first applications of a new methodology, *International Journal of Osteoarchaeology* 10, 254-267.

I. Beuls, L. Vanhecke, B. De Cupere, M. Vermoere, W. Van Neer and M. Waelkens (2002) The predictive value of dental microwear in the assessment of caprine diet, in:

H. Buitenhuis, A.M. Choyke, M. Mashkour and A.H. Al-Shiyab (eds.) *Archaeozoology of the Near East. V. Proceedings of the fifth International Symposium on the Archaeozoology of Southwestern Asia and Adjacent Areas (Archaeological Research and Consultancy-Publication 62)* Groningen, 337-355.

B. De Cupere and M. Waelkens (2002) Draught cattle and its osteological indications: the example of Sagalassos, in: H. Buitenhuis, A.M. Choyke, M. Mashkour and A.H. Al-Shiyab (eds.) *Archaeozoology of the Near East. V. Proceedings of the fifth International Symposium on the Archaeozoology of Southwestern Asia and Adjacent Areas (Archaeological Research and Consultancy-Publication 62)* Groningen, 305-315.

A. Arndt, W. Van Neer, B. Hellemans, J. Robben, F. Volckaert and M. Waelkens (2003) Roman trade relationships at Sagalassos (Turkey) elucidated from mtDNA of ancient fish remains, *Journal of Archaeological Science* 30, 1095-1105.

P. Degryse, Ph. Muchez, W. Van Neer and M. Waelkens (2004) Statistical treatment of trace element data from modern and ancient animal bone: evaluation of Roman and Byzantine environmental pollution, *Analytical Letters* 37-13, 2819-2834.

W. Van Neer, O. Lernau, R. Friedman, G. Mumford, J. Poblome and M. Waelkens (2004) Fish remains from archaeological sites as indicators of former trade connections in the Eastern Mediterranean, *Paléorient* 30, 101-148.

I. Beuls (2005) *Design of Odontological Tools to Elucidate Small Ruminant Herd Management at Sagalassos (SW Turkey) in the Roman-Byzantine Period (0-650 AD)*, Leuven, unpublished Ph. D. dissertation.

B. De Cupere, W. van Neer, H. Monchot, E. Rijmenants, M. Udrescu and M. Waelkens (2005) Ancient breeds of domestic fowl (*Gallus gallus* f. domestica) distinguished on the basis of traditional observations combined with mixture analysis, *Journal of Archaeological Science* 32, 1587-1597.

J. Schelvis, T. Van Thuyne and M. Waelkens (2005) Late Holocene environmental changes indicated by fossil remains of mites (Arthropoda; Acari) in the marsh of Gravgaz, Southwest Turkey, *Archaeofauna* 14, 215-225.

E. Dufour, C. Holmden, W. Van Neer, A. Zazzo, W.P. Patterson, P. Degryse and E. Keppens (2007) Oxygen and strontium isotopes as provenance indicators of fish at archaeological sites: the case study of Sagalassos, SW Turkey, *Journal of Archaeological Science* 34, 1226-1239.

W. Van Neer and M. Waelkens (2007) Fish remains from Bronze Age to Byzantine levels, in: J.N. Postgate and D.C. Thomas (eds.) *Excavations at Kilise Tepe 1994-98*, Ankara: The British Institute of Archaeology/ Cambridge

Mc Donald Institute for Archaeological Research, 607-612. Discusses also briefly some of the Sagalassos fish imports.

B. De Cupere, S. Thys, W. Van Neer, A. Ervynck, M. Corremans and M. Waelkens (2008) Eagle owl (*Bubo bubo*) pellets from Roman Sagalassos (SW Turkey): Distinguishing the prey remains from nest and roost sites, *International Journal of Osteoarchaeology*. Published online in *Wiley InterScience* (www. interscience.wiley. com) DOI: 10.1002/oa965

II. Van Haverbeke, P. Degryse, B. De Cupere, Ph. Muchez, W. Van Neer and M. Waelkens (resubmitted after a first review to *Antiquity*)) Geochemical analysis of archaeological animal bones as an indication for urban-rural integration at ancient Sagalassos (SW Turkey).

7.6. Residue analysis

K. Kimpe, P.A. Jacobs and M. Waelkens (2001) Analysis of oil used in late Roman oil lamps with different mass spectrometric techniques revealed the presence of predominantly olive oil together with traces of animal fat, *Journal of Chromatography A*, 937, 87-95.

K. Kimpe, P.A. Jacobs and M. Waelkens (2002) Mass spectrometric method prove the use of beeswax and ruminant fat in Late roman cooking pots, *Journal of Chromatography A* 968, 151-160.

K. Kimpe (2003) *Chemical Analysis of the Lipid Fraction from Ancient Ceramics of Sagalassos* (*Dissertationes De Agricultura* 553) Leuven. Ph.D.

K. Kimpe, C. Drybooms, E. Schrevens, P.A. Jacobs, R. Degeest and M. Waelkens (2004) Assessing the relationship between form and use of different kinds of pottery from the archaeological site Sagalassos (southwest Turkey) with lipid analysis, *Journal of Archaeological Science* 31, 1503-1510.

K. Kimpe, P.A. Jacobs and M. Waelkens (2005) Identification of animal fats in Late Roman cooking pots of Sagalassos (southwestern Turkey), in: J. Mulville and A. Outram (eds.), *The Zooarchaeology of Milk and Fats*, Durham, 183-192.

K. Romanus, J. Poblome, K. Verbeke, A. Luypaerts, P. Jacobs, D. De Vos and M. Waelkens (2007) An evaluation of analytical and interpretative methodologies for the extraction and identification of lipids associated with pottery sherds from the site of Sagalassos, Turkey, *Archaeometry* 49 (4).

K. Romanus, M. Demarcke, J. Poblome, P. Degryse, P. Jacobs, D. De Vos and M. Waelkens (in press) Assessing the content of local/regional fabric 4 amphorae from Sagalassos, SW Turkey, in: J. Poblome, P. Monsieur, F. Vermeulen and M. Waelkens (eds) *From Amphorae to Modelling the Late Roman Economy (International ROCT Workshop, 5-6 December 2005, Ghent) (FACTA; A Journal of Roman Material Culture Studies. Supplement 1)* Pisa-Rome.

J. Poblome, M. Corremans, Ph. Bes, K. Romanus and P. Degryse (in press), It is never too late…The late Roman initiation of amphora production in the territory of Sagalassos, in: I. Delemen, S. Cokay-Kepçe and A. Özdibay (eds), *EUERGETES. Prof. Dr. Haluk Abbasoğlu'na 65. Yaş Armağan. Studies Presented to Prof. Dr. Haluk Abbasoğlu at the Occasion of his 65. Anniversary*, Istanbul.

K. Romanus (2008) *Chemical Analysis of Lipids and Polyphenols in Archaeological Pottery from Sagalassos, Turkey (Dissertationes De Agricultura)*, Leuven, Ph.D. dissertation.

7.7. Physical Anthropology and aDNA analysis

E. Jehaes (1998) *Optimisation of Methods and Procedures for the Analysis of mtDNA Sequences and Their Applications in Molecular Archaeological and Historical Finds* (*Acta Biomedica Lovaniensia* 188) Leuven University Press: is largely based on human remains from Sagalassos.

F.X. Ricaut and M. Waelkens (2008) Cranial discrete traits investigation from a Byzantine population and Eastern Mediterranean population movements, *Human Biology*.

F.X. Ricaut, R. Decorte and M. Waelkens (2008) Analyse de l'ADN mitochondrial d'une population Byzantine du sud-ouest de l'Anatolie (Sagalassos 7ième-11ième siècle), in: *Peuplement de la Méditerranée: Synthèse et questions d'Avenir*. Editions Errance.

7.8. Site management and conservation

T. Patrício (2004) *La conservation de ruines archéologiques. Dessin d'une méthodologie*, Leuven, unpublished Ph.D. dissertation.

M.Waelkens, S. Ercan and E. Torun (2006) Principles of archaeological management at Sagalassos, in: Z. Ahunbay and Ü. Izmirligil (eds.), *Management and Preservation of Archaeological Sites, 4th Bilateral Meeting of ICOMOS Turkey – ICOMOS Greece, 29 April-2 May 2002, SIDE* (Antalya, Turkey), Side Foundation for Education Culture and Art, 67-77.

PART I

THE GEOLOGICAL SETTING

THE GEOLOGY OF THE AREA AROUND THE ANCIENT CITY OF SAGALASSOS

**Patrick DEGRYSE, Philippe MUCHEZ, Manuel SINTUBIN, Anton CLIJSTERS, Willy VIAENE[†],
Micky DEDEREN, Pieter SCHROOTEN and Marc WAELKENS**

1. TECTONIC SETTING

The eastern Mediterranean is tectonically a very active and complex region (Figure 1). South of Cyprus and the Aegean Sea, active subduction[1] takes place of the African oceanic lithosphere[2] underneath the Eurasian continental lithosphere. These arcuate subduction zones form the current plate boundary between the African and Eurasian plates. The Aegean Sea area is characterized by a thinned continental lithosphere caused by the gravitational collapse of the Alpine orogen extending from the Balkans into Turkey. This domain currently undergoes active NE-SW oriented extension. For the major part, Turkey acts as one single continental block, the Anatolian plate. This continental block is extruded towards the west (Aegean Sea area) due to the impingement of the Arabian plate into the Eurasian plate. This tectonic escape occurs along the dextral North-Anatolian Fault. The Isparta-Antalya area occupies a particular tectonic setting. Not only is it situated in the area between the acruate Hellenic and Cyprus trenches, where the plate boundaries are not well defined, but is also situated at the interface between areas with contrasting tectonic regimes, i.e. the NE-SW extensional regime towards the west (Aegean Sea area) and the compressional regime towards the northeast, resulting in the uplift of the Anatolian Plateau (Glover and Robertson, 1998). The Isparta-Antalya area itself is currently dominated by NE-SW extension, which leads to the development of the Aksu Basin.

Prior to the Miocene, the Anatolian Plate did not act as one single continental block. Most of the Mesozoic-Tertiairy history of Turkey is a complex drift and amalgamation history of continental fragments. Currently 6 major terranes[3] are recognized. A major suture[4] runs across Turkey (the Izmir-Ankara-Erzincan Suture; Okay and Tuysuz, 1999), separating the northern Pontide terrane assemblage, characterized by a Laurussian affinity,[5] from the southern Anatolide-Tauride terrane assemblage, showing a Gondwanan affinity.[6] Carbonate platforms, seamounts, and small interjacent oceanic basins were all telescoped in a tectonic stack, resulting in the terrrane assemblage currently recognized in Turkey.

On a smaller scale, within the Anatolide-Tauride terrane assemblage, the different terrane components can also be clearly recognized. This is the case in the Isparta-Antalya area. The complex amalgamation history in this area resulted in a particular triangular-shaped configuration, the so-called Isparta Angle (Dilek and Rowland, 1993), where four terranes can be recognized (Figure 2). Rock types and associated structures within the Isparta Angle indicate a progressive evolution from continental rifting and passive margin development to ocean basin formation during Triassic to late Cretaceous time (Dilek and Rowland, 1993). Regional compression began in the latest Cretaceous (Maastrichtian) (~65Ma ago) and led to subduction-accretion.[7] The Antalya Nappes were emplaced towards the north onto the Bey Dağları carbonate platform during latest-Cretaceous-Paleocene time (~60Ma ago). In the late Eocene (~35Ma ago) the platform was overthrusted from the northeast by the Sultan Dağ-Beyşehir Nappe Complex. In the late Miocene (~7Ma ago), the Lycean Nappe complex was emplaced onto the Bey Dağları platform from the northwest. Both nappe complexes consist of allochthonous[8] carbonate platforms and seamounts, derived from other continental fragments, and ophiolitic[9] and flysch[10] complexes, originating from the interjacent oceanic basins. During the emplacement of the Lycean nappe complex a foreland basin developed on the autochthonous[11] platform, which evolved into the Aksu Basin. Crustal extension and strike-slip faulting exploited the Isparta Angle suture zone in the Plio-Quaternary (last 5Ma), with the development of the north-south oriented Kovada graben (Robertson, 1993).

The Sagalassos area, of which a geological map is presented, is situated in the frontal area of the Lycean Nappe Complex on the western limb of the Isparta Angle (Figure 2). This western limb is composed of Mesozoic platform carbonates of the Bey Dağları Massif, overlain by the Lycean Nappe Complex, composed of Mesozoic to early Tertiary marine

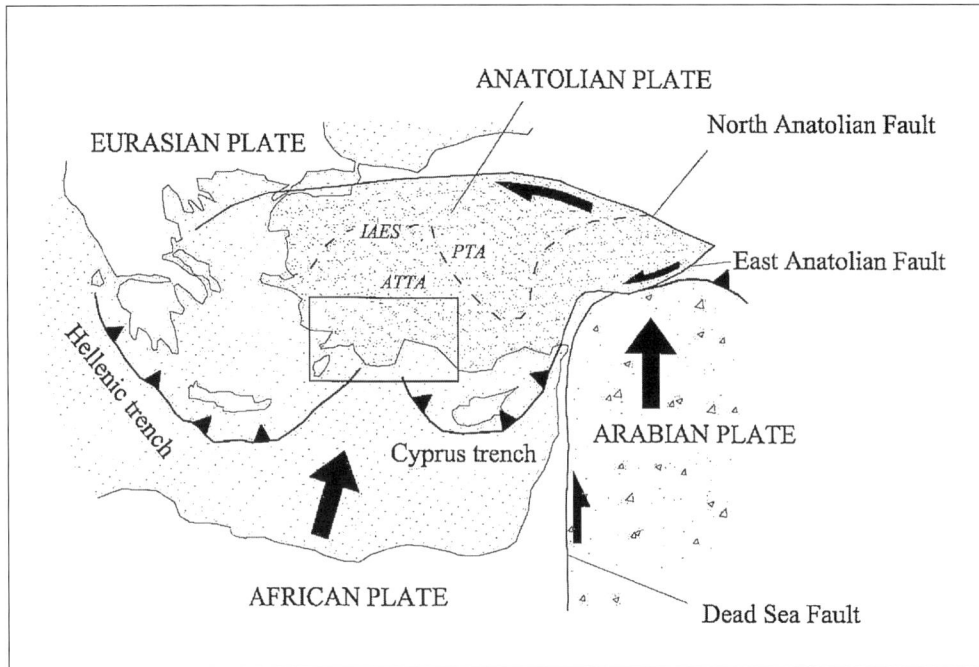

Figure 1: The current plate tectonic setting of the Eastern Mediterranean (after Jolivet and Patriat, 1999), with indication of the Izmir-Ankara-Erzincan Suture (IAES) separating the Pontide terrane assemblage (PTA) from the Anatolide-Tauride terrane assemblage (ATTA) (after Okay and Tüyüz, 1999).

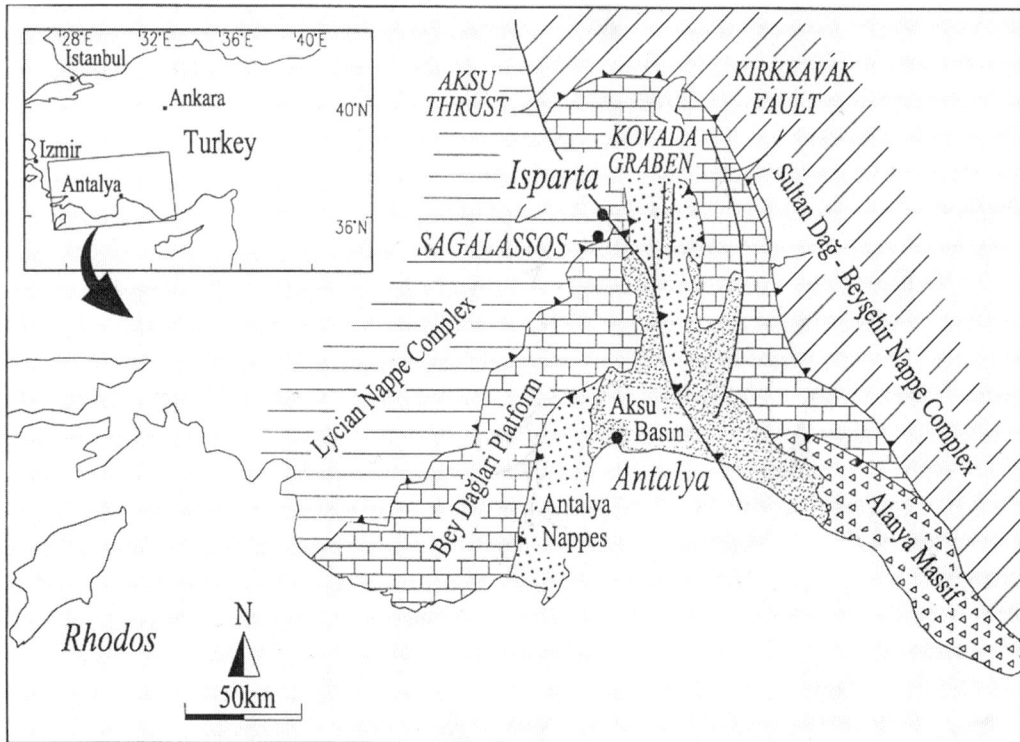

Figure 2: Simplified map of the Isparta Angle with indication of the main tectonic domains (after Brun *et al.*, 1970; Glover and Robertson, 1998; Marcoux *et al.*, 1989). The Aksu Thrust is post-Tortonian in age, and is related to the current convergence at the cyprus trench.

sediments and of peridotite and ophiolite sheets and by Cenozoic flysch and molasse[12] deposits.

The Bey Dağları Platform in the west consists of Triassic to lower Jurassic (Liassic) shallow-water limestone and dolomites up to 200 m thick, overlain by a sequence of neritic limestone (1.5 km thick) of Dogger to Cenomanian age (Poisson *et al.*, 1984). Pelagic limestone with ages between Turonian and late Palaeocene stratigraphically overlie the neritic limestone, indicating deep-water sedimentation during much of the late Cretaceous to early Tertiary time (Dilek and Rowland, 1993). The upper Palaeocene to lower Eocene olistostrome[13] deposits, containing ophiolitic material, rest on this pelagic limestone and are overlain by neritic Lutetian limestone (Poisson, 1977). Oligocene rocks are nearly absent from the Bey Dağları Platform, indicating a sedimentation stop and possibly a regional uplift until late Oligocene time (Dilek and Rowland, 1993). A sequence of neritic limestone of Aquitanian age, turbiditic flysch (Burdigalian) and deltaic conglomerates (Langhian) formed on top of the Eocene deposits (Poisson *et al.*, 1984).

The Mesozoic ophiolitic, sedimentary and volcanic rocks within the Isparta Angle are part of the Antalya, Beyşehir and Lycean nappe complexes, all of which tectonically rest on the platform carbonates (Dilek and Rowland, 1993). They present a large variety of units. Their protracted tectonic emplacement during late Cretaceous to early Palaeocene times explains the very different palaeogeographic origin of the units included in the imbricated stack of thrust sheets (Poisson *et al.*, 1984). The different units consist of shallow-water carbonates, radiolarites, limestone breccias, limestone with chert, detrital sediments with ophiolitic material and an ophiolitic mélange consisting of a chaotic sequence of ophiolitic material, radiolarites and pillow lavas. The ophiolitic material is characterized by serpentinite, harzburgite, dunite and multiple gabbro dykes. The nappes are strongly deformed, rendering the reconstruction of a detailed stratigraphy of these units difficult.

2. GEOLOGICAL MAP OF THE AREA AROUND SAGALASSOS

Geological mapping was carried out on a 1:10000 scale, using a Garmin™ GPS 40. Data obtained by the field study were plotted using the program Mapinfo ®. Also the existing geological maps of Poisson (1975) and Yalçinkaya (1983) were used.

2.1. Stratigraphy

The flysch consists of an alternation of sandstones and shales with some conglomerate levels. This sequence is very rich in lime. Sedimentary structures and the layering can easily be recognized, but the flysch is strongly deformed. Several folds with differently oriented fold hinge lines and multiple thrusts can be recognized over distances of a few meters. The recognized structures point to a synsedimentary deformation of the flysch (e.g. Hayward, 1984). The flysch is the result of the infill of a Miocene flexural foreland basin in front of the advancing Lycean Nappe Complex.

The red shale-limestone is characterized by the alternation of red limestone and red lime-rich shales. At some levels, blue nummulitic limestone is present. Large limestone and ophiolitic blocks in a shaly matrix form the olistostromes. The cherts in the grey-beige limestone have a black to blue-green colour. The grey micritic limestone comprises light to dark, pure mudstones. The grey limestone with dm-thick beige marl layers is coarse-grained and shows an internal layering. The grey micritic limestone and grey limestone with beige marl layers correspond to platform units of Cretaceous age (Robertson, 1993). These units are part of the Bey Dağları Platform. During Senonian times, a white limestone was deposited (Poisson, 1975). The latter corresponds to our grey-beige limestone with dark coloured cherts. After a disconformity[14] in the stratigraphy, the deposition of debris-flows occurred during the Palaeocene to early Eocene (Poisson, 1975; Robertson, 1993). The olistostrome unit belongs to this depositional system and stratigraphical interval. The red shale-limestones in the area around Sagalassos form part of the Eocene, pelagic marine shale and limestone (Poisson, 1975). A discontinuity is present between the olistostrome unit and the red shale-limestone. The flysch unconformably[15] overlies all these deposits.

The ophiolitic mélange contains a strongly weathered mélange of sedimentary and magmatic rocks. Only few consolidated rocks can be found. Some large fragments of basalt and radiolarite are present. The ophiolitic mélange of the Sagalassos area corresponds to the Kızıleadağ mélange, consisting of basalts, gabbros, red radiolarites and amphibolites (Poisson, 1975). Serpentine is often present. The beige limestone shows a large variety in appearances, with an uncertain stratigraphical relation: dark beige limestone, beige limestone with beige chert, homogeneous massive beige limestone, beige limestone with red chert, pink limestone, pinkish-beige limestone and red nodular clayey limestone. A detailed description of the petrography of this limestone, which was used in the building industry at Sagalassos, is given in Degryse *et al.* (this volume a). The limestone of the Lycean Allochthon (Robertson, 1993; Collins and Robertson,

1997) consists of a sequence of neritic limestone (Brunn *et al.*, 1976). According to Poisson (1975) the allochthonous limestone of the area of Sagalassos is part of the Domuz Dağ unit, of Permian to Palaeocene age. The homogeneous, massif beige limestone is part of this unit. This Domuz Dağ unit is interpreted by Collins and Robertson (1997) as part of the carbonate build-up of a volcanic seamount, which were detached during accretion of the seamount in a Lycean accretionary complex. The limestone with cherts is part of the Gülbahar unit of Triassic to Senonian age (Poisson, 1975).

West of the city of Sagalassos, a small outcrop of heterogeneous conglomerates, containing predominantly siliciclastic material, was recently discovered, lying unconformably on top of the ophiolitic mélange. Their stratigraphic position and origin is yet unknown. It is assumed that they form the remains of terraces of the paleo-Aksu river system (E. Paulissen, current research).

Alluvial, lacustrine and volcanic deposits form the upper part of the stratigraphy. The volcanic tuffs have a grey to red colour and are very porous. The alluvial and lake deposits are mainly composed of clays, but also of pebbles, gravel, travertine and volcanic tuffs. Some clay is rich in silt. Coarser fractions are generally found at the margins of the plains in which these deposits are located. The mineralogy and geochemistry of the Quaternary clay deposits, used in the ceramic industry at Sagalassos for the production of fine wares, common wares and building ceramics, has been discussed by Ottenburgs *et al.* (1993) and Degryse *et al.* (2000, this volume b). Schroyen *et al.* (2000) and Vermoere *et al.* (1999) studied the travertine deposits. The volcanic tuffs are of Miocene to Pliocene age and the alluvial and lake deposits of Quaternary age (Poisson, 1975; Robertson, 1993).

2.2. Structural observations

The southeastern quarter of the map (SE of Ağlasun), is composed of strata belonging to the western limb of the Bey Dağları platform. The overall orientation is NS24W. Based on the occurrence of the different lithologies on the map, a number of unconformities within this sequence can be deduced. The grey limestones are unconformably overlain by limestones with cherts, again unconformably overlain by the olistostrome unit, unconformably overlain by the red shale-limestone unit, and finally by the flysch.

The strongly deformed flysch has been overthrusted from the NW by the Lycean Allochthon. At the base of this complex a strongly deformed ophiolitic mélange is found. This water-rich ophiolitic sequence most probably acted as

a glide horizon on which the Domuz Dağı carbonate nappe was transported to the south. While in general the carbonate nappe is underlain by the ophiolitic sequence, in some areas the carbonate nappe directly lies upon the parautochthonous flysch. This is for e.g. the case on Alexander's Hill, at the southern outskirts of the city of Sagalassos. Also south of Başköy the carbonate nappe has overthrusted the flysch.

Taking into account the geometry of the trace of the nappes with respect to the topography, south-dipping, spoon-like, thrusts can be inferred. They seem to indicate a gravitational emplacement of the Lycean Allochthon within a foreland basin, in which the flysch was deposited. Moreover, the extent of the ophiolitic sequence is rather limited. Just south of the Gölçük volcanics, flysch crops out in a window[16] through the Domuz Dağı carbonate nappe, indicating the absence of the ophiolitic sequence in between. The undulous geometry of the thrusts in combination with the marked relief is responsible for the particular klippe-window-geometry west of Başköy. Also the presence of the ophiolitic mélange on the Başköy, Isparta and Akdağ passes indicates that the Domuz Dağı carbonate nappe is a south-dipping, relatively thin sliver on top of the ophiolitic mélange.

The isolated limestone massifs surrounded by ophiolitic material, also present in the direct vicinity of Sagalassos, raise some questions on their origin. Are these massifs klippes[17] and is their emplacement of Miocene age or are they blocks which resulted from mass movements on the topographic slope? Some of the contacts between the limestone and ophiolite show a few meters thick cataclastic zone with deeply red coloured silicified limestone. The red silicified limestone can be explained by dewatering of the ophiolite and subsequent water-rock interactions. These limestone massifs are definitively klippes some of which, located in the Imperial city of Sagalassos were selected as locations for monuments requiring a high visibility (e.g. Temple of Apollo Klarios) and are part of the Lycean carbonate nappe emplaced in Miocene times onto the water-rich ophiolitic sequence. The dewatering of the ophiolitic sequence occurred due to the vertical loading induced by the limestone nappes. This vertical loading caused the expulsion of the porewater and the transport of ions such as iron and silica in solution. The expulsed porewater interacted with the overlaying limestone resulting in the formation of a red coloured, often completely silicified limestone at the contact between the ophiolites and the limestone. This reaction zone forms a good indicator for the subaquatic, syntectonic emplacement of the limestone massifs. Other massifs do not show this red reaction zone. These massifs are caused by mass movements and can best be described as slumped limestone massifs (Verstraeten *et al.*, 2000). The true tectonic contact between the Domuz

Dağı limestone nappe and the ophiolitic mélange is therefore hard to trace, not only because of the presence of slumped limestone massifs, but also because of the important scree deposits obscuring the true contact.

The limestones of the Domuz Dağı limestone nappe are strongly fractured by different conjugate fracture sets. This intense fracturation may be related to the original nappe emplacement, but may also be partly or entirely caused by more recent brittle deformation. Numerous fractures are partly filled with miltiple calcite generations. Moreover, in all limestone units, subvertical limestone breccias with widths of a few centimeters to a few meters have been observed.

Finally, on Landsat satellite images it is apparent that the city of Sagalassos is situated on top of an N60E-trending lineament. This lineament is definitively not the expression of the surface geology. It is interpreted as a fault zone, cross-cutting all former structures of Miocene age. Related to this neotectonic feature, EW-trending extensional fissures filled with breccia are found. Earthquake-related damage, obvious in the city, is assumed to be related to nearby seismic activity (Waelkens *et al.*, 2000).

3. TECTONIC HISTORY OF THE SAGALASSOS AREA

In the Neotethys Ocean, several limestone platforms were present amid small oceans. One of these platforms, the Bey Dağları Platform, is cropping out in the southwestern part of the geological map (Figure 3, 4). After deposition of the shallow-marine limestone during Jurassic to late Cretaceous times (~200 to 65Ma ago), subsidence occurred with deposition of deep marine carbonates during the Maastrichtian (Robertson, 1993) (~65Ma ago). On top of these, the Paleocene (~65 to 55Ma ago) olistostrome deposits formed, containing limestone blocks and erosion material of oceanic crust. Oceanic crust and some limestone platforms were transported from the east to the west and were eroded during their obduction[18] onto the Bey Dağları Platform. The olistostromes are thus weathering products of the Antalya Allochthon (Figure 2).

To the northwest of the Bey Dağları Platform another oceanic domain was situated (Collins and Robertson, 1997), in which a northward intraoceanic subduction was active. Within this subduction zone an accretionary wedge (the future ophiolitic mélange) developed. In this accretionary wedge a seamount, capped with a neritic limestone platform (the Domuz Dağı limestone nappe) has been incorporated by tectonic erosion. Finally the accretionary wedge collided with

the Bey Dağları Platform, causing the final Miocene (~20 to 5Ma ago) nappe stacking. The tectonic loading related with this nappe stacking created a foreland basin, filled with the flysch deposits, which itself was incorporated in a final southeastward overthrusting phase during the Tortonian (~10Ma ago), coeval with hinterland extension.

Recent tectonics are expressed by the intense fracturation, brecciation and faulting. These faults crosscut the volcanics of Gölçük. Poisson (1975) places the first volcanic activity at the Miocene-Pliocene boundary Robertson (1993) restricts the volcanism to the Quaternary. This neotectonic activity may have extended into "historical" time, as inferred by the earthquake-related damage in the city of Sagalassos (Waelkens *et al.*, 2000).

Mass movements and other slope processes also dominate the recent landscaping. Alluvial and lake deposits formed in the valleys and plains through erosion of both autochthonous and allochthonous material. Robertson (1993) places these events in the light of a regional uplift of the area causing erosion. The conglomerates interpreted as remains of river terraces of the paleo-Aksu can also be framed in the overall uplift and erosion of the Sagalassos area.

4. ACKNOWLEDGEMENTS

The research was supported by the Belgian Programme on Interuniversitary Poles of Attraction (IAP V/9) and the Special Research Fund of the K.U.Leuven (BOF-GOA02/2).

5. REFERENCES

BRUNN, J.H., ARGYRIADIS, I., RICOU, L.E., POISSON, A., MARCOUX, J. and DE GRACIANSKY, P.C. (1976) Elements majeurs de liaisons entre Taurides et Hellénides, *Bulletin de la Société Géologique de France* 18: 481-497.

COLLINS, A.S. and ROBERTSON, A.H.F. (1997) Lycean melange, southwrestern Turkey: An emplaced Late Cretaceous accretionary complex, *Geology* 25(3): 255-258.

DEGRYSE, P., DEGEEST, R., OTTENBURGS, R., KUCHA, H., VIAENE, W., POBLOME, J. and WAELKENS, M. (2000) Mineralogy and geochemistry of Roman common wares produced at Sagalassos and its possible clay resources: determination of clay raw materials, in: M. WAELKENS and L. LOOTS (eds.) *Sagalassos V. Report on the Survey and Excavation Campaigns of 1996 and 1997* (Acta Archaeologica Monographiae Lovaniensia 10) Leuven University Press, Leuven: 703-716.

DEGRYSE, P., HELDAL, T., BLOXAM, E., STOREMYR, P., WAELKENS, M. and MUCHEZ, PH. (this volume a) The Sagalassos

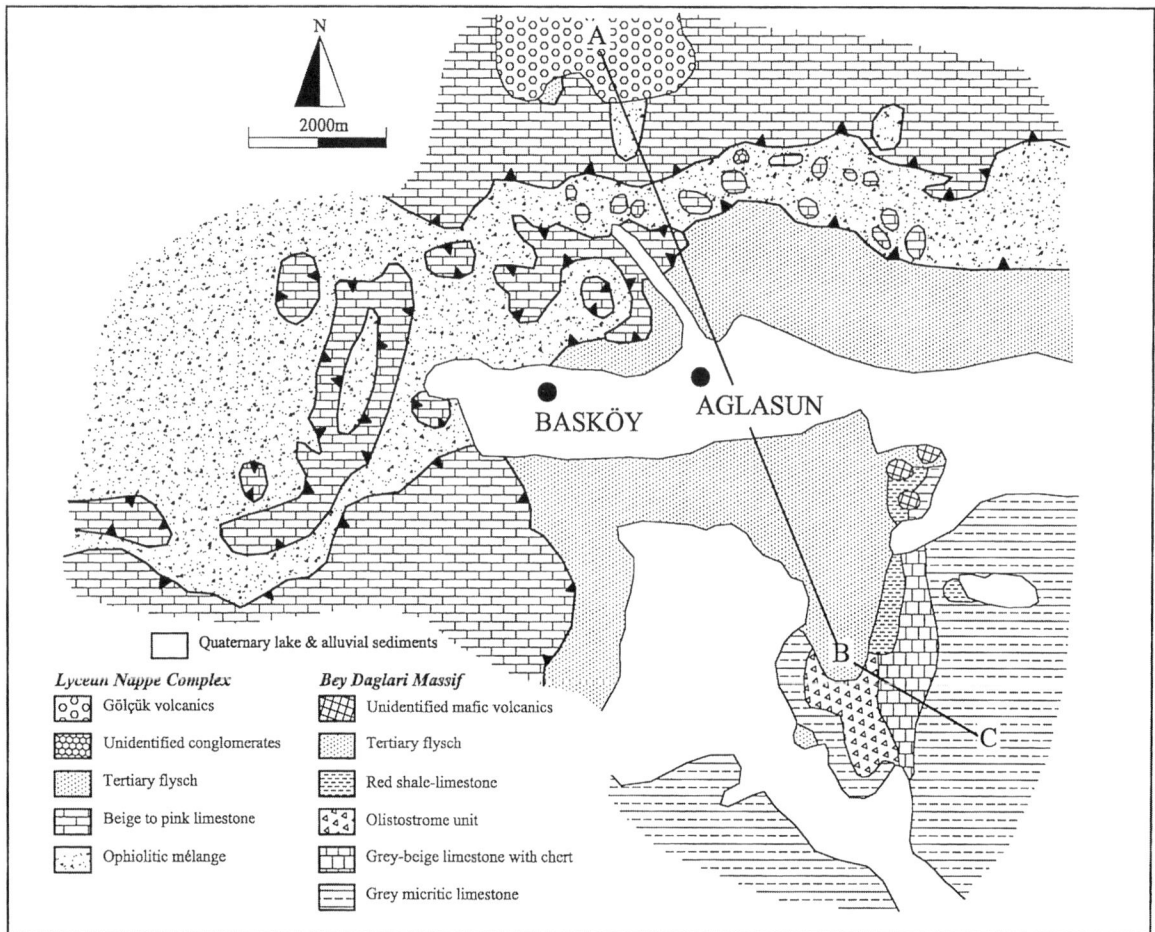

Figure 3: Geological map of the Sagalassos area.

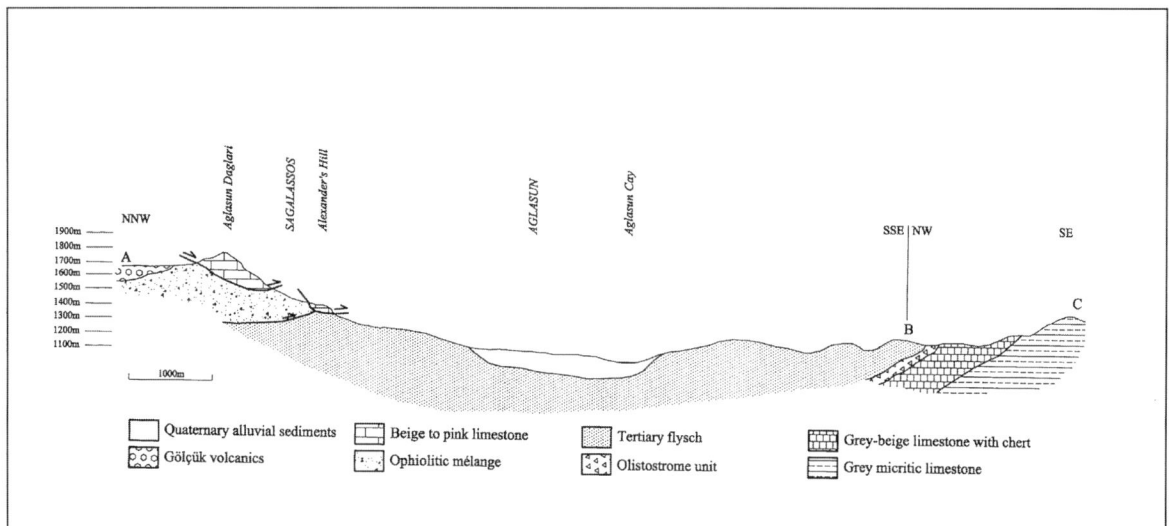

Figure 4: Geological cross-sections (section as shown on the geological map).

quarry landscape: bringing stone quarries in context, in: P. DEGRYSE and M. WAELKENS (eds.) *Sagalassos VI. Geo- and Bio-Archaeology at Sagalassos and in its Territory*, Leuven University Press, Leuven: 261-290.

DEGRYSE, P. and POBLOME, J. (this volume b) Clays for mass production of tablewares and coarse ceramics at Sagalassos, in: P. DEGRYSE and M. WAELKENS (eds.) *Sagalassos VI. Geo- and Bio-Archaeology at Sagalassos and in its Territory*, Leuven University Press, Leuven: 231-254.

DILEK, Y. and ROWLAND, J.C. (1993) Evolution of a conjugate passive margin pair in Mesozoic Southern Turkey, *Tectonics* 12: 954-970.

GLOVER, C.P. and ROBERTSON, A.H.F. (1998) Role of regional extension and uplift in the Plio-Pleistocene evolution of the Aksu Basin, SW Turkey, *Journal of the Geological Society, London* 155: 365-387.

HAYWARD, A.B. (1984) Miocene clastic sedimentation related to emplacement of the Lycean nappes and the Antalya Complex, SW Turkey, in: J.E. DIXON and A.H.F. ROBERTSON (eds.) *The Geological Evolution of the Eastern Mediterranean* (Geological Society of London, Special Publication, 17): 287-300.

JOLIVET, L. and PATRIAT, M. (1999) Ductile extension and the formation of the Aegean Sea, in: B. DURANT, L. JOLIVET, F. HORVÁTH and M. SÉRANNE (eds.) *The Mediterranean Basins: Tertiary Extension within the Alpine Orogen* (Special Publications. Geological Society, London): 427-456.

OKAY, A.I. and TÜYSÜZ, O. (1999) Tethyan sutures of northern Turkey, in: B. DURANT, L. JOLIVET, F. HORVÁTH and M. SÉRANNE (eds.) *The Mediterranean Basins: Tertiary Extension within the Alpine Orogen* (Special Publications. Geological Society, London): 475-515.

OTTENBURGS, R., JORISSEN, C. and VIAENE, W. (1993) Study of the clays, in: M. WAELKENS (ed.) *Sagalassos I* (*Acta Archaeologica Monographiae Lovaniensia 5*), Leuven University Press, Leuven: 163-169.

POISSON, A. (1975) *Geological Map of the Isparta Area*, Centre National de Recherche Scientifique, Paris.

POISSON, A. (1977) *Recherches géologiques dans les Taurides occidentales*, Thèse de Doctorat d'Etat, Orsay.

POISSON, A., AKAY, E., DUMONT, J.F. and UYSAL, S. (1984) The Isparta Angle : a Mesozoic paleorift in the Western Taurides, in: O. TEKELI and C. GONCÜOGLU (eds.) *Geology of the Taurus Belt* (*Proceedings of the International Symposium on the Geology of the Taurus Belt*), MTA, Ankara: 11-26.

ROBERTSON, A.H.F. (1993) Mesozoic-Tertiary sedimentary and tectonic evolution of Neotethyan carbonate platforms, margins and small ocean basins in the Antalya Complex, southwest Turkey, in: L.E. FROSTICK and R.J. STEEL (eds.) *Tectonic Controls and Signatures in Sedimentary Successions* (*Special Publication of the International Association of Sedimentologists 20*), Blackwell Scientific Publications, Oxford: 415-465.

SCHROYEN, K., VERMOERE, M., DEGRYSE, P., LIBRECHT, I., MUCHEZ, PH., VIAENE, W., SMETS, E., PAULISSEN, E., KEPPENS, E. and WAELKENS, M. (2000) Preliminary study of travertine deposits in the vicinity of Sagalassos: petrography, geochemistry, geomorphology and palynology, in: M. WAELKENS and L. LOOTS (eds.) *Sagalassos V. Report on the Survey and Excavation Campaigns of 1996 and 1997* (*Acta Archaeologica Monographiae Lovaniensia 10*) Leuven University Press, Leuven: 755-780.

VERMOERE, M., DEGRYSE, P., VANHECKE, L., MUCHEZ, PH., PAULISSEN, E., SMETS, E. and WAELKENS, M. (1999) Pollen analysis of two travertine sections in Başköy (southwestern Turkey): implications for environmental conditions during the early Holocene, *Review of Paleobotany and Palynology* 105: 93-110.

VERSTRAETEN, G., LIBRECHT, I., PAULISSEN, E. and WAELKENS, M. (2000) Limestone platforms around Sagalassos resulting from vast mass movements, in: M. WAELKENS and L. LOOTS (eds.) *Sagalassos V. Report on the Survey and Excavation Campaigns of 1996 and 1997* (*Acta Archaeologica Monographiae Lovaniensia 10*) Leuven University Press, Leuven: 783-798.

WAELKENS, M., SINTUBIN, M., MUCHEZ, P. and PAULISSEN, E. (2000) Archeological, geomorphological and geological evidence for a major earthquake at Sagalassos (SW Turkey) around the middle of the seventh century AD, in: W.J. McGUIRE, D.R. GRIFFITHS, P.L. HANCOCK and I. STEWART (eds.) *The Archaeology of Geological Catastrophes* (*Special Publications. Geological Society, London*): 373-383.

YALÇINKAYA, S. (1983) *Geological Map of the area of Isparta (M25-d1)*, MTA, Ankara.

6. GLOSSARY

[1] *Subduction*: the process taking place at a consuming plate margin, when oceanic lithosphere disappears underneath oceanic or continental lithosphere.

[2] *Lithosphere*: the outer part of the earth, consisting of the crust (oceanic or continental) and the upper part of the mantle.

[3] *Terrane*: a geological unit bounded by faults and characterized by a tectonometamorphic history, which differs from that of the neighbouring units or continent.

[4] *Suture*: A linear belt of highly deformed rocks, which is interpreted as the boundary between two collided continents or island arcs. This boundary may be diffuse rather than a narrow belt.

[5] *Laurussian affinity*: the paleontological record of the Palaeozoic rocks of these terranes indicates that it was

part of the Laurussian continent (North America, Northern Europe) during Palaeozoic times.

[6] *Gondwanan affinity*: the paleontological record of the Palaeozoic rocks of these terranes indicates that it was part of the Gondwanan supercontinent (Africa, South America, Antarctica, India, Australia) during Palaeozoic times.

[7] *Accretion*: Process by which an inorganic body grows in size by the addition of new particles. Here the addition of continental material to a pre-existing continent, usually at its edge.

[8] *Allochthon*: A body of rock that has been transported to its present position, usually over considerable distance.

[9] *Ophiolite*: typical ultramafic rock suite, which originated as a part of the oceanic crust.

[10] *Flysch*: a sequence of marine sediments, deposited in front of an advacing mountain front.

[11] *Autochthon*: A body of rock that was formed in its present position, no significant transport has occurred.

[12] *Molasse*: Shallow-marine and non-marine sediments produced from the erosion of a mountain belt after the final stage of uplift in an orogeny. It is now clear that much so-called molasse, however, are not post-tectonic but syntectonic, and some researchers therefore consider that the term should be abandoned.

[13] *Olistostrome*: A sedimentary deposit, which consists of a chaotic mass of rock with large clasts composed of material older than the enclosing sedimentary sequence.

[14] *Disconformity*: Unconformity so that the beds above and below the surface are parallel. This surface may be highly irregular.

[15] *Unconformity*: Surface of contact between two groups of unconformable strata, which represents a hiatus in the geologic record due to a combination of erosion and a cessation of sedimentation.

[16] *Window*: an isolated area where the parautochthonous material underneath a nappe can be seen because of erosional processes.

[17] *Klippe*: a part of an allochthonous unit which is completely isolated from the rest of the nappe because of erosional processes.

[18] *Obduction*: The lateral, sub-horizontal displacement of a lithospheric plate on to a continental margin at a destructive plate boundary. The opposite of subduction.

PETROGRAPHY, MINERALOGY AND GEOCHEMISTRY OF THE ROCKS IN THE AREA OF THE ARCHAEOLOGICAL SITE OF SAGALASSOS

Philippe MUCHEZ, Suzy LENS, Patrick DEGRYSE, Kristof CALLEBAUT, Micky DEDEREN, Jan HERTOGEN, Michael JOACHIMSKI, Eddy KEPPENS, Raoul OTTENBURGS, Kristof SCHROYEN and Marc WAELKENS

1. INTRODUCTION

Knowledge of the geology is essential to evaluate the potential occurrence of raw materials that could be exploited by man in Antiquity in a given area. It also forms the base for geomorphological and soil-engineering studies. The mineralogical and geochemical characterization of the immediate subsurface constitutes the background for environmental investigations such as the reconstruction of the palaeoclimate and to determine anthropogenic influences based on geochemistry. Since 1989, prof. Willy Viaene and his team carried out a systematic study of the geology in the area of the archaeological site of Sagalassos. The present work is a tribute to prof. Willy Viaene and summarizes the work performed by his group and colleagues to fully characterize and understand the rocks, exploited and used in ancient times.

2. GEOLOGICAL SETTING

Sagalassos is geologically located in the Isparta Angle. Rock types and associated structures within this area indicate a progressive evolution from continental rifting and passive margin development to ocean basin formation during the Triassic to the late Cretaceous (Dilek and Rowland, 1993). Regional compression began in the latest Cretaceous and led to subduction-accretion. The Antalya nappes were emplaced towards the north onto the Bey Dağları carbonate platform during the latest Cretaceous to Paleocene. In the late Eocene, this platform was overthrusted from the northeast by the Beyşehir-Hoyran-Hadım nappes. The Lycean nappes were emplaced onto the Bey Dağları platform from the northwest during the late Miocene. Sagalassos is situated in the frontal area of the Lycean nappes, on the western flank of the Isparta Angle.

The rocks studied can be subdivided into two main groups: the autochthonous and the allochthonous group. The autochthonous group consists of a Palaeozoic basement overlain by Mesozoic carbonates and siliciclastics, Cenozoic flysch and by Quaternary volcanic tuffs, lake and river sediments (Poisson, 1977). Especially the Bey Dağları sediments are well exposed to the south of Sagalassos (Degryse et al., this volume b). The autochthonous group was thrusted from the north over the allochthonous rocks. Sagalassos is underlain and flanked to the north by the Lycean nappes, consisting of an ophiolitic mélange and platform carbonates. The Beyşehir-Hoyran-Hadım nappes are not exposed in the study area, but are present to the northeast of it.

The autochthonous Bey Dağları massif is composed of Middle Jurassic to Cenomanian platform carbonates (Poisson et al., 1984; Robertson, 1993). During the late Cretaceous, deep-water pelagic carbonates were deposited, reflecting an increase in subsidence during this period (Dilek and Rowland, 1993). The Paleocene is characterized by olistostrome deposits (Poisson, 1975), related to the emplacement of the Antalya Complex, which thrusted from the east. These deposits are overlain by early Eocene pelagic shales and limestone (Poisson, 1975) and neritic limestone of Lutetian age (middle Eocene). The olistostrome, deep-sea and shallow water sediments are exposed to the southeast of the village of Ağlasun. No sediments were deposited during the Oligocene. Transgressive carbonates of Aquitanian age (earliest Miocene) formed due to flexural bending in the foreland basin of the Lycean nappes. During the main phase of this thrust emplacement, thick flysch sequences (Burdigalian) formed (Hayward, 1984). Deltaic conglomerates (Langhian), not present in the area investigated, overly the flysch (Poisson et al., 1984).

Volcanic tuffs of Tertiary (Poisson, 1975) and likely Quaternary age (Ota and Dincel, 1975), recognized in test trenches below the city, are well exposed to the north of the area under study. According to Savaşçin and Güleç (1990), two periods of volcanism can be distinguished in West-Anatolia: a calc-alcalic series, which developed during a compressional phase (up to the late Miocene), and an alcalic series. The latter formed during an extensional phase starting from the late Miocene. However, the transition from calc-alcalic to alcalic volcanism does not everywhere correspond to this change in tectonic regime. Both the calc-alcalic and alcalic series can result from fractionated crystallization of an alcalic-olivine-basaltic magma (Ota and Dincel, 1975). The volcanics of Gölçük, a lake to the northwest of Sagalassos, are alcalic Na- and K-rich and related to a post-orogenic extensional phase. The valleys of Ağlasun and Çanaklı are filled with Quaternary lake sediments. However, river sediments have also been identified, even up to a height of 1750m. Quaternary cool-water travertine deposits are well exposed in the valley of Başköy to the west of Sagalassos (Waelkens *et al.*, 1999; Vermoere *et al.*, 1999; Schroyen *et al.*, 2000; Degryse *et al.*, this volume a). U/Th dating of one section indicated an age of 9000 ± 600 yr (Degryse *et al.*, this volume a). Extensive cool-water tufa deposits (the traditional Antalya Travertine) developed to the southeast of Sagalassos, in the Aksu Basin (Glover and Robertson, 1998), i.e. the alluvial plains of the ancient Kestros river. They have a Pliocene to/or early Pleistocene age and are older than the travertines at Başköy.

The stratigraphy of the Lycean nappes (allochthonous group) is poorly constrained due to its intense disturbance, caused by the polyphase tectonic emplacement (Poisson *et al.*, 1984). In general two main units can be distinguished (Brunn *et al.*, 1976): an ophiolitic mélange and platform carbonates. The ophiolitic mélange in the area corresponds with the Kızıleadağ mélange (cfr. Poisson, 1975). In general, this unit is composed of a chaotic arrangement of ophiolitic, intrusive and extrusive rocks and radiolarites of Senomian age. The ophiolitic material is characterized by serpentinite, harzburgite, dunite and multiple gabbro dykes. Large shallow-water limestone is incorporated in this mélange (Collins and Robertson, 1997). According to Poisson (1975), the platform carbonates belong to the Domuz Dağ unit, with rocks of Permian to Paleocene age.

3. METHODOLOGY

Samples have been taken from the different rock types present in both the autochthonous and allochthonous units. Thin sections and polished sections were prepared for petrographic characterisation by transmitted and incident light microscopy respectively. Mineral identification was done by X-ray diffractometry on a Philips® PW3710 diffractometer. The operational parameters are graphite-monochromatized Cu K_α radiation, 45 kV, 30mA, automatic divergence slit and a receiving slit of 0.1°.

The geochemical composition of the individual minerals was semi-quantitatively investigated by a scanning electron microscope (JEOL JSM 6400) equipped with a Link energy dispersive X-ray analytical system (SEM/EDX). Major and trace element geochemistry was investigated using atomic emission spectrometry (DCP-AES), atomic absorption spectrometry (AAS), instrumental neutron activation analysis (INAA), X-ray fluorescence (XRF) and inductively coupled plasma – mass spectrometry (ICP-MS). The main elements SiO_2, Al_2O_3, Fe_2O_3, MnO, CaO, TiO_2 and P_2O_5 in magmatic rocks are analyzed with DCP-AES and K_2O and Na_2O with AAS. The dried samples are ground to a grain size less than 10μm. A representative part of each sample is dissolved in a lithium metaborate flux, which was subsequently dissolved in 30ml dilute HNO_3. INAA is applied to quantify the trace elements Sc, Cr, the lanthanides, Hf, Ta, Th and U in the rocks of the ophiolitic mélange. Rb, Sr, Y, Zr and Nb are analyzed with XRF. The Ba, Ce, Co, Cr, Cu, La, Nb, Ni, Pb, Rb, Sr, W, Y, Zn and Zr content of the volcanic tuff was determined by XRF analyses carried out by prof. J. Naud at the Université Catholique de Louvain-la-Neuve) and Ba, La and Sr by AES at the K.U.Leuven. Travertines have been analyzed for their Ca, Fe, Mg, Mn, Na, K, Zn, Sr, Cu, Ni, Pb content by AAS. The amount of insoluble residue (IR) was determined gravimetrically after HCl (12.5N) attack.

Stable isotope analyses were carried out both at the Free University of Brussels and at the University of Erlangen. The travertine carbonates were analyzed at Brussels. The samples were reacted in a vacuum with 100% H_3PO_4 which release CO_2 at 25°C. The gas was introduced into a Finnigan-MAT Delta-E mass spectrometer. Reproducibilities (2σ) were better than 0.05‰ for carbon and 0.1‰ for oxygen. Carbonate powders of limestone, dolomite, carbonate matrix of the flysch and of vein cements were reacted with 100% phosphoric acid at 75°C in an online carbonate preparation line (Carbo-Kiel – single acid bath) connected to a ThermoFinnigan 252 mass spectrometer at the University of Erlangen. All values are reported in per mil relative to VPDB by assigning a $\delta^{13}C$ value of +1.95‰ and a $\delta^{18}O$ value of –2.20‰ to NBS 19. Reproducibilty was checked by replicate analysis of laboratory standards and is better than 0.08‰ (1σ) for both $\delta^{13}C$ and $\delta^{18}O$.

4. PETROGRAPHY, MINERALOGY AND GEOCHEMISTRY

4.1. Magmatic rocks

4.1.1. Ophiolitic mélange

The ophiolitic mélange forms part of the Lycean nappes and is exposed to the north of the valley of Başköy. This mélange can be subdivided into three units: a serpentinite, a tectonic mélange and a volcanic-sedimentary unit.

4.1.1.1. Serpentinite unit

The serpentinite unit consits of serpentinite and gabbroid rocks. It is crosscut by tholleitic dykes of Cretaceous age (Juteau, 1980). Since the base of this unit is not exposed, the total thickness cannot be estimated, but is probably less than 200m. The dominant mineral in the serpentinite rocks is serpentine showing a mesh texture (Figure 1A) with subordinate chlorite. In addition to these secondary minerals, relics of the original rock, i.e. olivine, clinopyroxene, orthopyroxene and plagioclase can be recognized (Figure 1B). The latter is often altered to albite. Calcite veins and the opaque minerals ilmenite, chromite, magnetite, pyrite, chalcopyrite, pyrrhotite may be abundant (Figure 1C). The gabbroid rocks mainly consist of pyroxene (clino- and orthopyroxene) and plagioclase with minor olivine (Figure 1D). The plagioclase can be altered to albite. Secondary minerals also include chlorite and actinoliet (Figure 1E). Magnetite, ilmenite and chromite represent the opaque minerals (Figure 1F).

If the serpentinite is regarded solely as an alteration of ultramafic rocks by water, the geochemistry of the serpentinite mainly reflects the original composition of the ultramafic rocks. They are characterized by very low CaO, Al_2O_3 and TiO_2 and by elevated total Fe_2O_3 and MgO contents (Table 1, samples MD25, MD27, MD65, MD74 from the serpentinite unit and MD9 from the volcanic-sedimentary unit). The trace element content of the serpentinite are low except for Cr and Co, which are present in the relics of olivine and pyroxene (Table 2, MD9). The mineralogy and geochemistry indicates that these serpentinites were originally harzburgites. The magnetite results from this serpentinitisation. The gabbroid rocks show high Al_2O_3, CaO and MgO and low Fe_2O_3, TiO_2 and Na_2O contents (Table 1, samples MD70 and MD73) from the serpentinite unit, but MD48 from the volcanic-sedimentary unit, and MD53 and MD56 from the tectonic mélange unit). Their chemical composition varies little and they likely represent isolated gabbroid dykes, omnipresent in ophiolitic complexes in the Eastern Mediterranean region. The gabbroid rock (MD56

and MD73) has in general a low trace element content except for Cr and Co (Table 2), which are enriched in olivine, pyroxene and oxides.

4.1.1.2. Tectonic mélange

The tectonic mélange is well exposed to the north of Başköy and it occurs below the serpentinite unit. It is characterized by a chaotic texture with blocks of limestone and intrusive rocks present in a green-greyish matrix of extrusive rocks, serpentinite and deep-sea sediments. This unit is interpreted to have a late Cretaceous age. The extrusive rocks show a porphyritic or trachytic texture (Figure 2A). The phenocrysts in the porphyritic rocks are plagioclase (often albite), pyroxene and olivine (Figure 2B). Tiny plagioclase laths are recognized in the matrix. Opaque minerals include large chromite crystals and magnetite (Figure 2C). Secondary minerals are chlorite, quartz, calcite, pumpellyite and magnetite (Figure 2D). The intrusive rocks determined are gabbroid rocks and pyroxenites. The deep-sea sediments are characterized by radiolarites (Figure 2E).

The extrusive rocks may show a high TiO_2 (1.5%) and low K_2O (0.5%) content (Table 1, samples MD54, MD55, MD76, MD77). Most rocks have a high Na_2O content and those rich in olivine have high MgO and FeO concentrations. The high Na_2O content reflects the abundant occurrence of albite. The albite formed as a secondary mineral from hydrothermal alteration. Trace element analysis indicates a prominent enrichment in Ba (Table 2). This pattern is typical for subduction related rocks. During melting and subsequent crystallization, Ta and Nb are incorporated in oxides, which are stabilized by the hydration of the mantle and deeper crust above a subduction zone. Samples MD55 and MD76 show a rather flat REE pattern, characteristic for melts formed from a depleted mantle, with a negative Nb and Ta anomaly. These rocks are interpreted to have formed near an oceanic spreading centre in a subduction environment. According to geochemistry, the matrix of the tectonic mélange can be subdivided in two sets (Table 1, samples MD50, MD52, MD58, MD60). The first set (MD50, MD52) has higher SiO_2, Al_2O_3, FeO and MgO contents and represents a serpentinized matrix. The second set (MD58, MD60) is much richer in calcium carbonate and reflects the transition towards the overlying volcanic sedimentary unit.

4.1.1.3. Volcanic-sedimentary rocks

The volcanic-sedimentary unit partly underlies the city of Sagalassos, just below the massive carbonates of the Lycean nappes. The rocks are largely covered by talus slope of limestone. They are composed of sandstone, radiolarite,

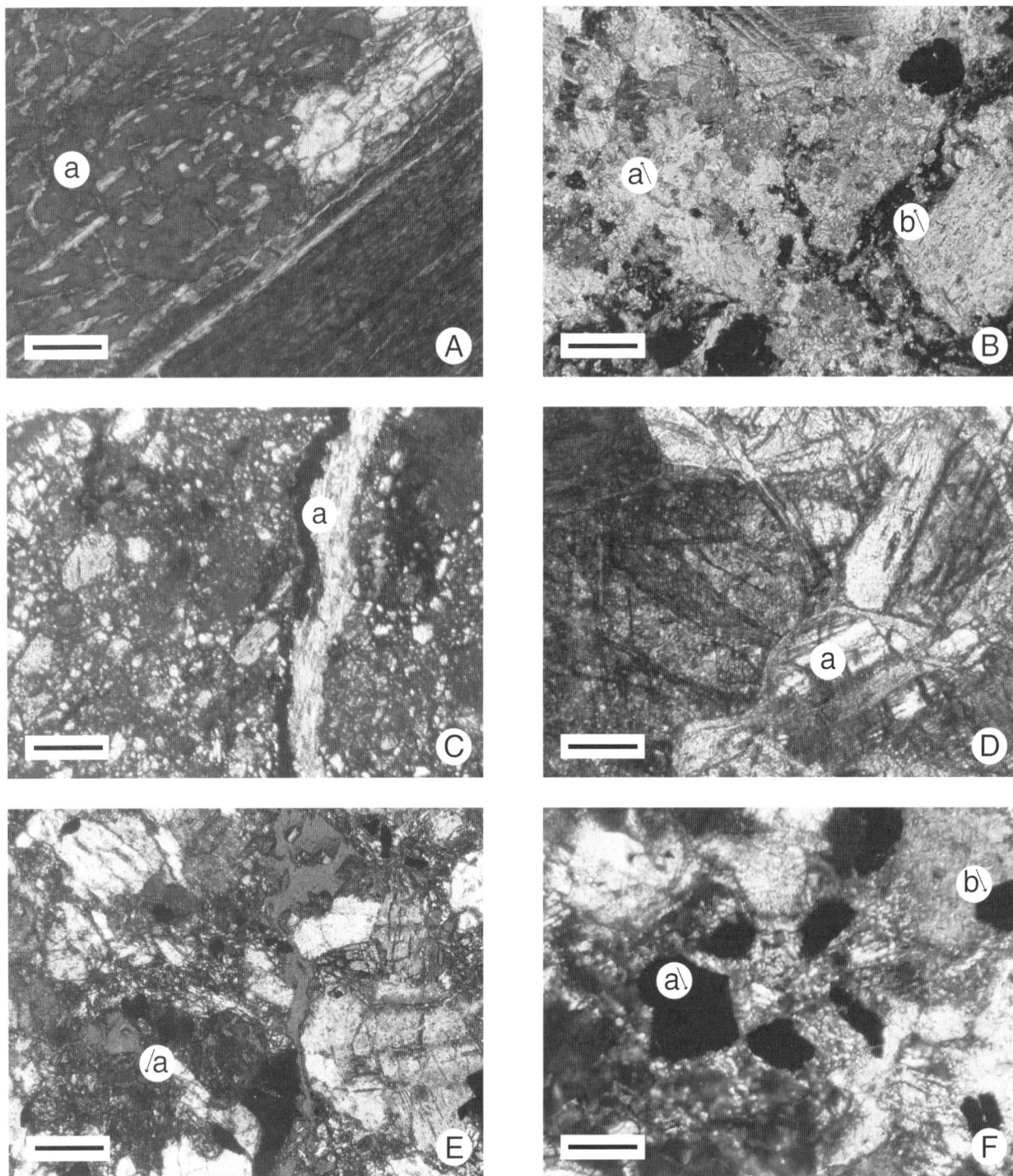

Figure 1: A. Serpentinite showing a mesh texture (a). The scale bar is 200 μm; B. Relics of olivine (a) and plagioclase (b) in serpentinized rock. The scale bar is 100 μm; C. Calcite veins (a) in serpentinite unit. The scale bar is 100 μm; D. Gabbroid rock with plagioclase (a). The scale bar is 100 μm; E. Chlorite and actinolite (a) occur as secondary minerals in the gabbroid rock. The scale bar is 100 μm; F. Magnetite (a) and ilmenite (b) occur as opaque minerals in the gabbroid rock. The scale bar is 50 μm.

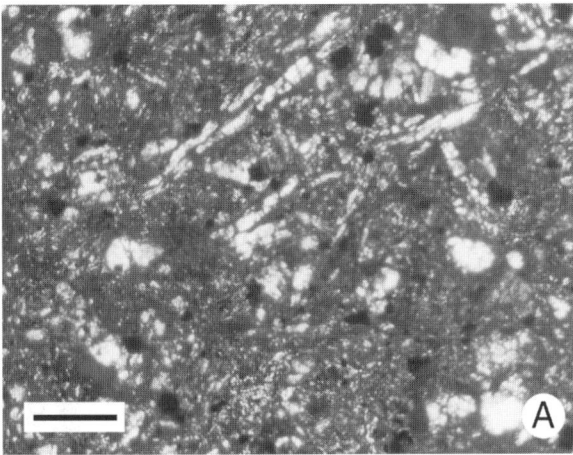

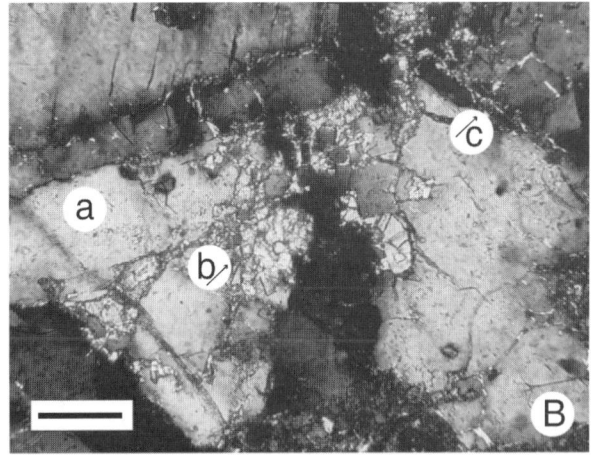

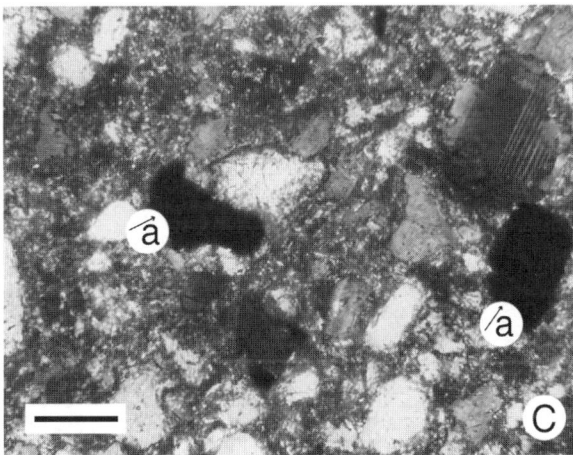

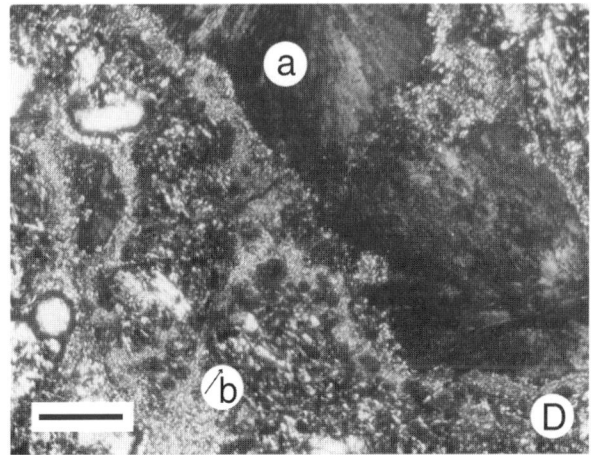

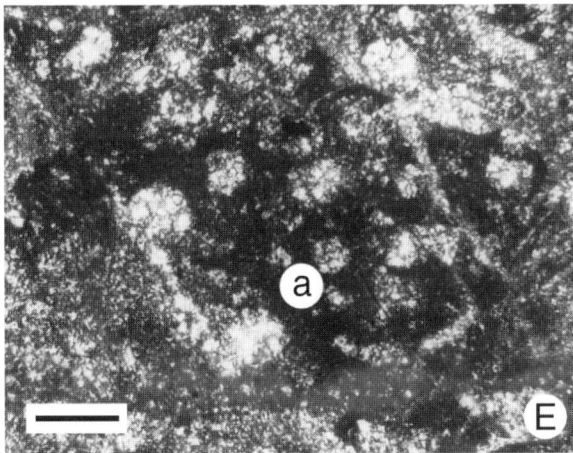

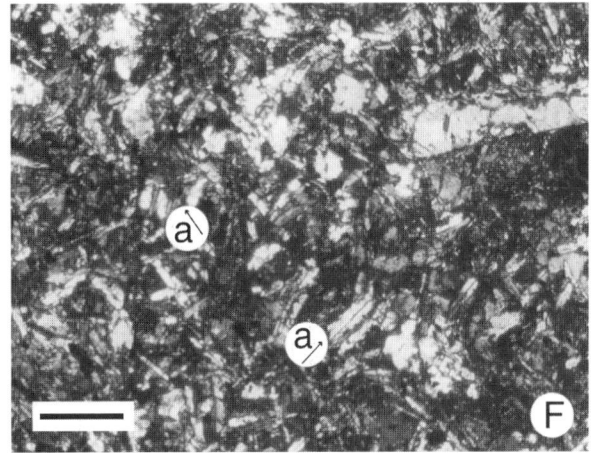

Figure 2: A. Extrusive rocks of the tectonic mélange showing a trachytic texture. The scale bar is 200 μm; B. Plagioclase (a), pyroxene (b) and olivine (c) occur as phenocrysts in porphyritic rocks of the tectonic mélange. The scale bar is 50 μm; C. Chromite and magnetite form the opaque minerals (a) in the extrusive rocks. The scale bar is 50 μm; D. Secondary minerals in the extrusive rocks are chlorite (a), quartz and calcite (b). The scale bar is 200 μm; E. Radiolarites (a) present in the tectonic mélange. The scale bar is 100 μm; F. Volcanics of the volcanic-sedimentary unit showing plagioclase laths (a). The scale bar is 200 μm.

	serpentinite				
	VSU	SU			
	MD 9	MD 25	MD 27	MD 65	MD 74
SiO_2	38.50	38.42	43.81	39.02	40.43
Al_2O_3	0.61	0.72	2.38	0.54	0.81
TotFe	8.09	10.07	6.34	11.75	9.14
FeO	6.19	7.70	4.85	8.99	6.99
Fe_2O_3	1.21	1.51	0.95	1.76	1.37
MnO	0.12	0.10	0.16	0.10	0.12
MgO	38.06	36.30	29.08	35.34	35.60
CaO	–	–	7.79	–	–
CaOmeas.	0.20	0.26	8.40	0.18	0.16
Na_2O	0.03	0.02	0.04	0.02	0.02
K_2O	0.05	0.04	0.04	0.05	0.05
TiO_2	0.02	0.02	0.06	0.02	0.05
P_2O_5	0.15	0.17	0.20	0.15	0.12
LOI	13.86	13.49	8.94	12.39	13.10
CO_2	–	–	0.48	–	–
TOT	99.69	99.61	99.45	99.56	99.60

	gabbroid rocks				
	VSU	TM		SU	
	MD 48	MD 53	MD 56	MD 70	MD 73
SiO_2	40.41	43.68	49.81	48.90	44.04
Al_2O_3	17.83	18.04	11.84	12.09	18.62
TotFe	4.20	3.56	3.27	6.42	2.97
FeO	3.21	2.72	2.50	4.91	2.27
Fe_2O_3	0.63	0.53	0.49	0.96	0.45
MnO	0.09	0.09	0.11	0.13	0.09
MgO	11.56	10.92	11.24	13.88	8.16
CaO	16.23	18.84	19.12	8.05	14.94
CaOmeas.	16.23	18.84	19.12	8.47	14.94

Table 1: Major element content (in wt%) of the magmatic rocks of the ophiolitic mélange forming part of the Lycean nappes. TotFe: total iron content expressed as Fe_2O_3; Ca: calcium content in all minerals, except in calciet; Ca_{meas}: total Ca content; SU: serpentinite unit; VSU: volcanic-sedimentary unit; TM: tectonic mélange unit; –: not given.

Na$_2$O	1.79	1.02	0.88	3.10	2.22
K$_2$O	0.03	0.03	0.03	0.32	0.03
TiO$_2$	0.15	0.11	0.11	0.07	0.08
P$_2$O$_5$	0.15	0.14	0.14	0.15	0.07
LOI	6.93	2.76	2.71	5.87	7.88
CO$_2$	<0.01	<0.01	<0.01	0.33	<0.01
TOT	99.37	99.19	99.26	99.40	99.10

	extrusive rocks				extrusive rocks			
	TM				VSU			
	MD 54	MD 55	MD 76	MD 77	MD 5	MD 10	MD 45	MD 63
SiO$_2$	71.30	59.87	48.02	62.26	59.96	51.78	52.64	42.43
Al$_2$O$_3$	12.30	12.47	13.77	18.45	12.58	15.97	13.01	16.45
TotFe	4.33	10.49	9.59	4.53	11.56	11.62	13.67	10.27
FeO	3.31	8.02	7.33	3.46	8.84	–	10.46	7.85
Fe$_2$O$_3$	0.65	1.57	1.44	0.68	1.73	–	2.05	1.54
MnO	0.04	0.15	0.24	0.06	0.12	0.14	0.10	0.14
MgO	1.00	3.17	8.68	0.87	3.79	5.24	4.16	6.27
CaO	2.88	3.74	6.18	6.00	3.02	4.20	5.17	10.33
CaOmeas.	2.88	3.74	7.02	6.33	3.02	4.20	5.45	14.21
Na$_2$O	5.98	4.74	4.60	2.96	4.65	6.18	4.98	3.59
K$_2$O	0.08	0.07	1.05	1.84	0.14	0.31	0.23	0.11
TiO$_2$	0.54	1.45	1.02	0.53	1.19	1.38	1.49	0.81
P$_2$O$_5$	0.13	0.05	0.14	0.20	0.18	0.14	0.16	0.18
LOI	0.64	3.36	5.44	1.16	2.39	2.29	3.67	5.10
CO$_2$	<0.01	<0.01	0.66	0.26	<0.01	<0.01	0.22	3.05
TOT	99.22	99.56	99.57	99.19	99.58	99.25	99.56	99.56

	matrix tectonic mélange				radiolarite	
	TM				VSU	
	MD 50	MD 52	MD 58	MD 60	MD 21	MD 22
SiO$_2$	35.89	48.10	19.71	12.51	91.74	71.29
Al$_2$O$_3$	11.09	1.66	0.70	2.55	1.86	0.96
TotFe	6.22	4.34	2.07	1.39	1.80	0.77
FeO	–	–	–	–	–	–

Table 1: (*cont.*)

Fe$_2$O$_3$	–	–	–	–	–	–
MnO	0.12	0.14	0.08	0.03	0.08	0.09
MgO	8.74	16.68	6.99	1.07	0.67	0.49
CaO	5.32	20.51	4.71	2.61	–	1.44
CaOmeas.	20.22	23.97	40.68	44.56	0.25	13.49
Na$_2$O	0.27	0.12	0.03	0.10	0.20	0.12
K$_2$O	0.20	0.03	0.04	0.48	0.35	0.19
TiO$_2$	0.18	0.09	0.07	0.19	0.10	0.04
P$_2$O$_5$	0.12	0.18	0.21	0.12	0.10	0.18
LOI	16.45	3.80	28.57	36.63	2.13	11.59
CO$_2$	11.71	2.72	28.26	32.96	–	9.47
TOT	99.50	99.11	99.15	99.63	99.28	99.21

Table 1: (*cont.*)

	Serpentinite	gabbroid rocks		extrusive rocks		
	VSU	TM	SU	TM		
	MD 9	MD 56	MD 73	MD 55	MD 76	MD 77
Na	<0.15	0.56	–	3.40	–	–
Sc	10.1	52.8	35.0	25.2	33.7	18.8
Cr	2825	1112	240	5	52	5
Fe	5.19	2.35	2.03	7.77	6.53	2.87
Co	108.0	25.6	20.7	22.0	33.8	4.9
Rb	<6	<8	<6	<7	17	50
Sr	–	–	178	–	408	460
Ba	<6	<1	<1	<1	260	800
La	<0.2	<0.4	<3.0	4.3	<4.0	28.0
Ce	<0.3	<0.5	<0.4	13.1	9.5	58.0
Nd	<0.4	<0.8	<0.5	12.7	9.8	28.3
Sm	<0.005	0.088	0.066	4.390	2.540	5.500
Eu	<0.03	<0.06	0.07	1.59	0.96	1.46
Tb	<0.04	0.05	<0.10	1.15	0.64	0.69
Yb	<0.1	0.21	0.16	5.00	2.69	2.15

Table 2: Trace element content (all elements in ppm, except Na and Fe in wt%) of magmatic rocks of the ophiolitic mélange forming part of the Lycean nappes. SU: serpentinite unit; VSU: volcanic-sedimentary unit; TM: tectonic mélange unit.

Lu	<0.02	<0.06	<0.03	0.74	0.38	0.31
Hf	<0.03	<0.10	<0.20	3.1	1.76	2.90
Ta	<0.08	<0.01	<0.01	0.14	0.08	0.22
Th	<0.03	<0.10	<0.05	0.27	0.30	5.90
U	<0.1	<0.3	<0.3	<0.3	<0.3	2.1

Table 2: (cont.)

serpentinite, gabbroid rocks and volcanics. The latter are fine-grained, often with plagioclase laths and tiny pyroxenes and olivine (Figure 2F). Actinolite, sericite and calcite represent the secondary minerals (Figure 3A). Opaque minerals identified are magnetite, ilmenite and hematite.

The geochemistry of the extrusive rocks present in the volcanic-sedimentary unit is comparable to that of the same rocks in the tectonic mélange unit (Table 1, samples MD5, MD10, MD45, MD63). The radiolarite (samples MD21, MD22) has a high SiO_2 content due to the silica originally present in the radiolaria.

4.1.2. Volcanic tuff

In the area around Gölçük, not only tuff deposits are present but also lava flows. The former became popular at Sagalassos as a building material in late Antiquity and early Byzantine times. Moreover, crushed volcanic tuff was added to locally produced cooking wares and mortars. K-Ar dating indicates a Pliocene age for these deposits (Lefèvre et al., 1983). The volcanic sequence consists of extrusive rocks, such as tefri-fonolite, trachy-andesites and andesites and pyroclastic series (Özgür et al., 1990). The volcanic rocks consist of mono- and polycrystalline inclusions in a matrix of submicroscopic crystals and a glass phase. Anorthite with typical plagioclase twins and K-feldspar with Carlsbad twins (Figure 3B) has been identified in the matrix. The texture is hypocrystalline or hypohyaline (Figure 3C). The inclusions can be subdivided into rock fragments and individual crystals. The rock fragments recognized are pumice, lava, sandstone and granodiorite. The size of the very porous pumice fragments varies between less than a mm up to a few centimeters. Biotite and augite occur in the pumice. The lava fragments are mainly andesites and form irregular inclusions of maximum a few centimeters. They are less porous than the pumice fragments. The texture is characterized by phenocrysts occurring in a fine-grained crystalline matrix (Figure 3D). The matrix consists of plagioclase and K-feldspar. The phenocrysts

are composed of the same feldspars, augite, biotite, magnetite and hornblende (Figure 3E). Sandstone fragments occur sporadically. They show a typical red-brown colour due to the presence of iron oxides and originate from the Miocene flysch. Also the granodiorite inclusions are rare. K-feldspar, quartz, hornblende and plagioclase have been identified in these inclusions (Figure 3F). The large individual crystals in the matrix are: euhedral to subsubhedral zoned plagioclase with polysynthetic twins, euhedral and anhedral K-feldspar with Carlsbad twins, zoned subhedral and euhedral augite, diopside, elongated biotite, hornblende and magnetite. SEM/EDX analysis of the augite indicates that the zonation is due to a decrease of the Mg and Ca content towards the rim and a simultaneous increase of the Fe and Na content. The zonation in the plagioclase results from a decrease of Ca and Al and an increase of K from core to rim. Three groups can be distinguished in chemical analyses of tuff and lava (Table 3): basaltic andesite (wt% SiO_2 between 53 and 57), andesite (wt% SiO_2 between 57 and 63) and dacite (wt% SiO_2 between 63 and 68). The basaltic andesite has a higher Fe, Mg and Ca content than the andesite and dacite. Higher K contens are present in the dacite. Most samples analyzed fall within the field of trachy-andesite with the exception of a few trachites, mugearites (contains oligoclase), benmorites and one basaltic trachite. The earlier classification, solely based on the SiO_2 content, has to be modified. Taking into account the high K_2O content of the volcanic rocks, they can also be subdivided into the shoshonitic class. Francalanci et al. (1990) described ultra K-rich rocks from the area of Isparta, associated with post-orogenic extension. The trace element content of the volcanics (Table 4) is characterized by a high Ba and Sr content. These values are much higher than could be expected from andesitic rocks (Jakes and White, 1972). The concentration of most trace elements largely varies. Only the elements with a low content such as Co and Cr, are more or less constant. The high Zr, Ce, Ba and Sr and low Ni and Cr content suggest an oceanic island basalt origin for these rocks.

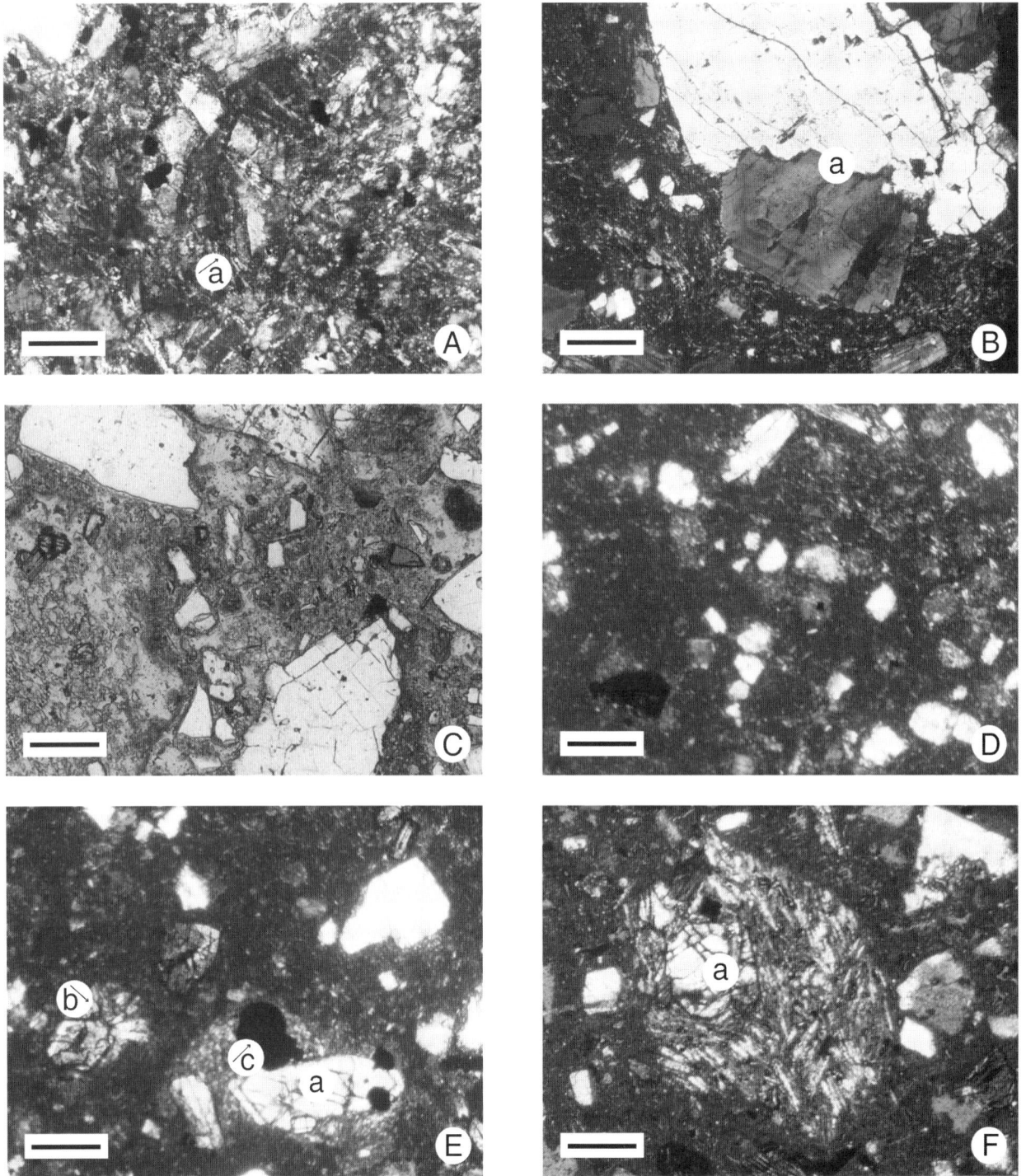

Figure 3: A. Actinolite (a) is present as a secondary mineral in the volcanics of the volcanic-sedimentary unit. The scale bar is 50 μm; B. K-feldspar (a) with Carlsbad twins in the volcanic tuff of Gölçük. The scale bar is 200 μm; C. Hypohaline texture of the volcanic tuff. The scale bar is 200 μm; D. Texture of a lava flow in the Gölçük area. The scale bar is 200 μm; E. Phenocrysts of K-feldspar (a), augite (b), biotite and magnetite (c) in the lava. The scale bar is 100 μm; F. Granodiorite inclusion (a) in the extrusive rocks showing K-feldspar, quartz, hornblende and plagioclase. The scale bar is 200 μm.

Basaltic andesite												
Sample/description	SiO₂	Al₂O₃	TotFe	MnO	MgO	CaO	Na₂O	K₂O	TiO₂	P₂O₅	LOI	TOT
SA95KC1 coarse porous tuff	56.54	16.23	4.57	0.13	2.42	5.46	3.15	4.91	0.59	0.27	5.09	99.36
SA95KC2 coarse porous tuff	56.85	16.15	4.37	0.12	2.33	5.78	3.09	5.08	0.57	0.27	4.78	99.39
SA95KC4 coarse porous tuff	56.53	16.41	4.56	0.13	2.07	5.57	2.79	5.02	0.58	0.28	5.41	99.35
SA95KC5 coarse porous tuff	56.52	16.29	4.65	0.12	2.20	5.76	2.72	4.98	0.59	0.30	5.18	99.31
SA95KC7 coarse porous tuff	56.66	16.42	4.72	0.14	2.29	5.65	3.01	4.90	0.58	0.31	4.65	99.33
SA95KC11 lava	53.77	16.93	6.67	0.12	2.95	7.11	3.95	5.16	0.79	0.48	1.57	99.50
SA95KC16 lava (white)	52.46	17.20	6.62	0.14	3.60	7.53	3.52	5.60	0.70	0.57	1.59	99.53
SA95KC16 lava (grey)	53.99	16.45	5.42	0.13	3.41	7.81	4.30	5.77	0.70	0.56	0.83	99.37
SA95KC26 coarse porous tuff	56.44	16.78	4.08	0.11	2.05	5.33	2.66	5.11	0.55	0.35	5.98	99.44
SA95KC29 coarse porous tuff	52.52	21.39	4.34	0.13	1.40	4.52	2.32	2.78	0.60	0.31	9.10	99.41
SA95KC37 coarse porous tuff	55.01	16.70	5.46	0.13	2.21	5.66	2.57	4.43	0.62	0.32	6.19	99.30
SA95KC44 coarse porous tuff	54.37	15.69	5.89	0.12	2.85	6.44	2.98	4.07	0.62	0.38	6.08	99.49
SA95KC48 coarse porous tuff	55.61	15.20	5.41	0.11	2.79	6.61	2.44	4.38	0.61	0.36	5.99	99.51
SA95KC25 coarse porous tuff	53.91	18.54	4.26	0.12	2.14	5.66	2.18	4.68	0.51	0.28	6.99	99.27
SA95KC32 coarse porous tuff	56.42	17.36	4.65	0.11	2.66	4.93	2.82	4.99	0.60	0.32	4.46	99.32
SA95KC33 coarse porous tuff	54.68	17.09	5.31	0.10	2.96	6.16	2.61	4.57	0.64	0.36	4.94	99.42

Andesite												
Sample/description	SiO₂	Al₂O₃	TotFe	MnO	MgO	CaO	Na₂O	K₂O	TiO₂	P₂O₅	LOI	TOT
SA95KC3 coarse porous tuff	57.42	16.31	4.51	0.11	2.14	5.08	3.97	4.94	0.58	0.26	3.97	99.29
SA95KC8b fine compact tuff	57.86	16.59	3.44	0.18	1.86	4.26	2.65	5.27	0.44	0.22	6.54	99.31

Table 3: Major element content of the volcanic rocks at Gölçük (in wt%). Por: porous; comp.: compact; incl.: inclusion; TFe: total iron content expressed as Fe₂O₃.

SA95KC12 lava	62.18	17.01	3.85	0.08	1.42	3.54	5.49	4.94	0.47	0.19	0.19	99.36
SA95KC24 fine compact tuff	60.53	17.46	2.49	0.08	1.09	3.09	4.24	5.4	0.34	0.16	4.27	99.15
SA95KC43 coarse porous tuff	57.15	18.05	4.82	0.16	1.94	4.44	3.84	5.34	0.53	0.28	2.77	99.32
SA95KC30 coarse porous tuff	57.19	17.40	4.78	0.12	2.67	4.77	3.45	5.04	0.57	0.27	2.95	99.21
SA95KC31 coarse porous tuff	57.31	17.49	4.71	0.11	2.63	4.64	3.48	4.98	0.59	0.29	3.02	99.25
SA95KC39A1 lava inclusions	59.32	18.03	4.67	0.13	1.81	4.30	4.78	5.27	0.57	0.35	0.17	99.40
SA95KC39A2 granodiorite inclusions	61.98	18.99	2.41	0.09	0.37	2.06	5.20	6.90	0.38	0.12	0.79	99.29

Dacite												
Sample/ description	SiO_2	Al_2O_3	TotFe	MnO	MgO	CaO	Na_2O	K_2O	TiO_2	P_2O_5	LOI	TOT
SA95KC42 lava	64.66	16.85	3.60	0.05	0.79	2.39	4.83	5.18	0.48	0.24	0.43	99.50

Table 3: (cont.)

Sample	Ba		Ce	Co	Cr	Cu	La	Nb		Ni
	XRF	AES	XRF	XRF	XRF	XRF	XRF	AES	XRF	XRF
KC1	3396	2813	458	20	18	255	281	133	46	52
KC2	3787	3033	475	19	25	326	282	135	41	45
KC3	3646	2873	413	17	15	244	294	134	47	73
KC4	5248	4023	481	20	19	377	302	136	45	50
KC5	3895	2990	463	19	20	262	320	132	41	43
KC7	3346	2907	488	19	18	228	298	135	44	35
KC8	13867	8228	424	14	12	613	355	151	52	49
KC11	3311	2909	563	17	19	195	498	215	56	56
KC12	2255	1909	163	14	14	126	157	79	34	48
KC16	3658	2853	431	19	27	218	312	142	36	38
KC24	2292	1802	330	13	19	146	233	109	35	33
KC29	4573	3677	785	18	10	218	389	176	78	44
KC30	4649	3432	568	20	29	227	363	87	37	48
KC42	1795	1500	259	13	17	85	162	139	35	46
KC48	3074	2361	499	20	27	189	304	161	34	41

Table 4: Trace element content of the volcanic rocks at Gölçük (in ppm). XRF: analyzed by X-ray fluorescence; AES: analyzed by atomic emission spectrometry.

Sample	Rb	Sr		W	Y	Zn	Zr	Pb	S
	XRF	XRF	AES	XRF	XRF	XRF	XRF	XRF	XRF
KC1	322	7498	6620	41	17	71	363	116	119
KC2	229	8208	6794	51	16	75	317	142	120
KC3	481	6525	5625	50	19	77	380	107	112
KC4	229	8279	7342	55	16	70	338	118	139
KC5	238	6990	6617	64	14	68	320	103	183
KC7	142	7105	6680	40	18	70	338	104	119
KC8	184	6084	6004	40	14	83	406	98	175
KC11	102	5464	5288	59	22	60	455	92	732
KC12	155	3679	3139	59	13	44	383	69	100
KC16	97	5580	5471	44	16	56	373	78	1493
KC24	176	3859	3522	61	11	78	362	125	81
KC29	69	4852	4487	36	32	80	596	115	133
KC30	172	4109	3999	34	17	95	355	123	236
KC42	147	2008	1829	88	16	43	376	78	96
KC48	168	4466	4399	48	17	94	333	102	103

Table 4: (*cont.*)

4.2. Carbonates

Limestone was the major building element at Sagalassos in Hellenistic and high Imperial times. It continued to be used into the third century AD as ashlars but was gradually replaced by mortared rubble alternating with brick layers or by brick-faced 'Roman' concrete.

4.2.1. Autochthonous carbonates

The autochthonous limestone studied was deposited on the Bey Dağları platform and is of Cretaceous age. It is character-ized by bioclastic, peloidal wacke- and packstone (Figure 4A) with intermediate grainstone textures (Figure 4B). The biota consists of foraminifers, crinoids, brachiopods, bivalves, calcispheres, algae, echinoid and brachiopod spines, ostra-cods, corals and gastropods. Allochems are presented by peloids, micritized grains and lithoclasts. The limestone texture and the biota present indicate that the limestone has mainly been deposited on an open marine shelf or ramp at or below wave base. Numerous, tiny non-ferroan calcite veins crosscut this limestone. Partial recrystallisation of the limestone and the formation of microsparite is sporadically

recognized (Figure 4C). Two vein generations occur. The first one contains calcite crystals with abundant twin planes. The second vein generation clearly crosscuts the first generation and calcite crystals do not show twinning. The allochems, the matrix (orthochems) and the first vein-filling calcites are non-luminescent. The second generation of vein-filling calcites is ochre to bright yellow luminescent and may be intensely zoned.

The main and trace element composition of the limestone is given in Table 5. The geochemistry varies little between the different samples analyzed and the trace element content is relatively low. The limestone is rather pure (low IR and Na and K content) and did not become enriched in Mn or Fe during subsequent diagenesis. Diagenetic processes did cause a decrease in the Sr and Mg contents. Compared with the limestone of the Lycean nappes, much higher uranium concentrations occur. The carbon and oxygen isotopic com-position varies between 1.0‰ and 3.9‰ and between –6.5 and –2.2‰ respectively (n = 14, Figure 5). The iron-poor vein calcites show a much wider range in the carbon (–5.2‰ to +4.0‰) and oxygen isotopic composition (–10.3‰ and +2.0‰, n = 4). The carbon isotopic values are within the

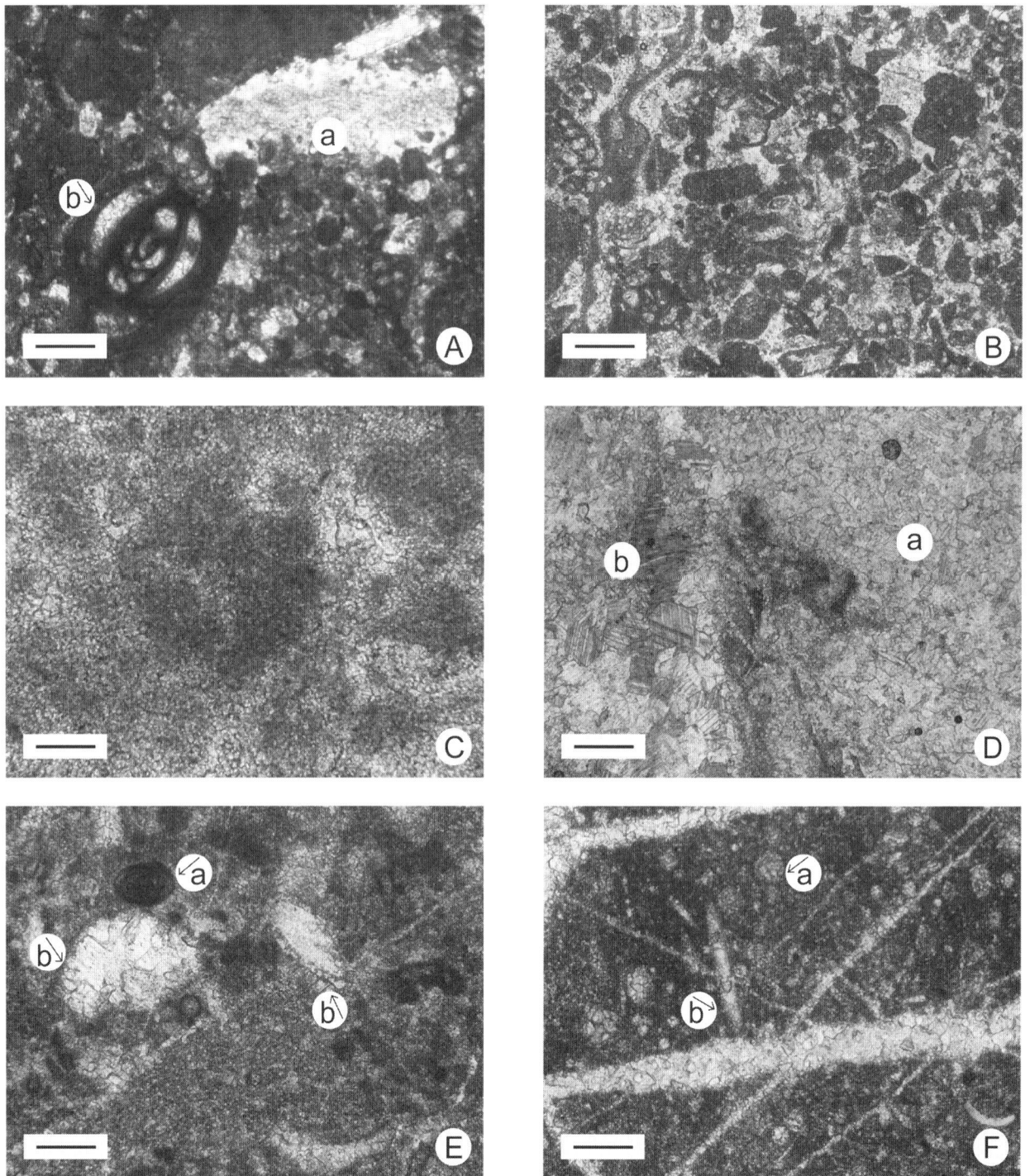

Figure 4: A. Bioclastic wackstone with crinoids (a) and foraminifers (b). The scale bar is 200 μm; B. Bioclastic, peloidal grainstone. The scale bar is 200 μm; C. Partial recrystallization of bioclastic peloidal packstone with the formation of microsparite. The scale bar is 200 μm; D. Intensely recrystallized (a) and veined (b) limestone of the allochthonous, Lycean nappes. The scale bar is 200 μm; E. Bioclastic wackestone with foraminifers (a) and bivalves (b). Massif beige limestone at the base of the allochthonous limestone (Lycean nappes) near Sagalassos. The scale bar is 200 μm; F. Bioclastic wacke-stone with radiolaria (a) and sponge spicules (b); beige limestone with white chert nodules of the allochthonous limestone. The scale bar is 200 μm.

Autochthonous limestone								
Sample	Ca	IR	Na	Mg	Fe	K	Mn	Sr
	%	%	ppm	ppm	ppm	ppm	ppm	ppm
PM53	37.2	2.7	60	2821	120	17	2	301
PM54	38.2	2.7	55	2794	120	18	3	202
PM55	37.3	2.8	80	3352	102	14	3	361
PM56	36.9	2.9	51	2900	102	9	3	200
PM57	36.8	2.0	58	2264	129	12	3	181
PM58	36.2	2.5	71	2450	102	11	7	181
PM59	38.8	2.2	49	2106	102	9	11	167
PM60	35.5	2.2	95	2397	94	17	3	200
PM61	37.1	2.9	132	2794	111	32	3	198
PM62	36.0	3.3	43	2053	111	12	5	155

Allochthonous limestone								
Sample	Ca	IR	Na	Mg	Fe	K	Mn	Sr
	%	%	ppm	ppm	ppm	ppm	ppm	ppm
PM8	37.7	0.4	16	1592	67	2	8	76
PM9	38.1	0.5	32	2070	57	5	8	75
PM10	38.0	0.4	14	1830	67	2	9	73
PM11	38.8	0.4	32	2160	57	3	7	156
PM12	37.6	0.2	25	9450	76	6	5	149
PM13	38.6	0.5	18	1794	67	6	257	144
PM14	24.7	0.5	96	11165	1323	5	23	41
PM15	37.7	1.1	36	3096	86	66	64	342
PM16	37.6	0.8	27	2515	200	36	98	314
PM17	37.4	1.4	32	3255	921	72	278	278
PM18	28.1	31.0	34	2018	247	54	49	184
PM19	26.3	33.0	30	1690	694	72	739	205
PM20	35.7	6.8	34	3276	1680	858	837	320
PM21	37.4	0.5	69	2713	323	13	577	254
PM22	35.6	5.9	60	3540	1614	812	691	581
PM23	29.6	22.0	39	2723	684	436	938	314

Table 5: Major and trace element content of autochtonous and allochthonous carbonates. Ca and IR in wt%, Na, Mg, Fe, K, Mn and Sr in ppm and Sc, Co, Ni, Cu, Zn, Se, Rb, Cd, Ba, Ce, Sm, Yb, Lu, Pb, Th and U in ppb.

PM24	36.4	1.4	11	2557	978	44	312	539
PM25	36.5	1.2	16	2863	1462	105	327	555
PM26	38.0	0.7	25	3458	304	53	31	306
PM27	38.8	0.6	29	1945	143	41	31	195
PM28	38.7	0.8	24	2874	323	52	40	101
PM29	37.1	0.6	15	3923	67	6	2	193
PM30	36.5	0.2	26	17370	86	16	2	92
PM31	26.0	0.9	112	90581	219	19	1	104
PM32	24.0	0.3	130	105630	314	50	2	102
PM33	24.9	0.3	159	103689	200	85	1	103
PM34	36.5	0.2	29	4204	143	19	2	128
PM35	36.1	0.6	33	10510	209	91	4	191
PM36	36.3	1.0	42	15510	333	157	3	479
PM37	36.4	0.8	20	19450	295	89	4	414
PM38	37.2	0.3	2	5504	171	9	18	102
PM39	37.0	0.9	17	2207	352	89	17	145
PM40	37.7	0.3	2	2039	57	4	6	120
PM41	37.4	0.4	13	2318	152	18	14	134
PM42	37.9	0.1	7	2202	95	8	7	116

Autochthonous limestone								
Sample	Sc	Co	Ni	Cu	Zn	Se	Rb	Cd
PM53	90	10	1550	<1	1100	2485	<1	<1
PM54	75	<1	1450	<1	1450	2735	<1	<1
PM55	95	<1	950	<1	1400	2685	<1	<1
PM56	50	<1	1850	<1	2600	2535	<1	<1
PM57	60	<1	1100	<1	1500	2535	<1	<1
PM58	65	<1	1000	<1	1500	2485	<1	<1
PM59	50	<1	1000	<1	1150	2435	<1	<1
PM60	40	5	850	<1	<1	2085	<1	<1
PM61	50	15	900	<1	1200	2385	<1	<1
PM62	75	30	800	<1	950	2235	<1	<1

Table 5: (*cont.*)

Sample	Ba	Ce	Sm	Yb	Lu	Pb	Th	U
PM53	<1	595	115	50	<1	<1	<1	910
PM54	<1	455	70	35	<1	<1	<1	1110
PM55	<1	845	170	70	<1	<1	<1	1010
PM56	<1	470	75	30	<1	<1	<1	1510
PM57	<1	495	90	40	<1	<1	<1	1810
PM58	<1	545	100	45	<1	<1	<1	1210
PM59	<1	330	45	35	15	<1	<1	1710
PM60	<1	175	<1	<1	<1	<1	<1	510
PM61	<1	200	30	<1	<1	<1	<1	610
PM62	<1	495	90	40	<1	<1	<1	1310

Allochthonous limestone								
Sample	Sc	Co	Ni	Cu	Zn	Se	Rb	Cd
PM8	84	416	1589	1345	3413	1875	111	310
PM9	52	463	1683	1340	3612	1546	109	348
PM10	79	604	1675	1231	2646	1850	241	436
PM11	64	637	1574	1348	2684	1889	276	444
PM12	37	479	1641	1091	2560	1641	43	180
PM13	53	447	1845	1384	4419	1887	22	448
PM14	16	478	1284	1306	5685	1017	1	222
PM15	238	605	1842	2204	2679	1880	581	140
PM16	656	569	2272	2471	2602	2546	591	359
PM17	385	650	3847	3439	10125	2169	549	446
PM18	197	357	1174	1758	2836	1183	238	111
PM19	197	370	1091	3097	4088	1238	389	49
PM20	901	1006	3508	5150	10765	2076	3413	131
PM21	122	572	1583	2053	12590	1639	49	102
PM22	1103	1149	3937	10140	20010	2129	3371	191
PM23	599	899	2345	2554	7145	1426	1823	176
PM24	244	536	1508	1151	7190	1775	322	178
PM25	275	526	1924	3042	6095	1942	627	7
PM26	256	736	1720	1919	5335	1687	284	250
PM27	175	503	1910	689	2072	1735	200	50

Table 5: (cont.)

PM28	519	591	1775	1495	2236	1731	308	153
PM29	17	280	1258	607	1	1722	1	27
PM30	20	333	1353	926	1295	1560	64	3
PM31	28	258	2374	1686	5050	631	81	188
PM32	23	287	2557	1476	5515	761	286	134
PM33	105	257	2726	2900	5870	732	393	178
PM34	52	244	2096	498	565	1335	196	113
PM35	86	191	2333	952	1275	1525	369	77
PM36	156	207	2406	1522	819	1476	644	93
PM37	120	235	2362	4308	957	1422	442	128
PM38	39	341	2014	409	259	1581	151	94
PM39	222	652	3486	1127	1532	1668	710	563
PM40	51	227	2012	270	1	1482	47	290
PM41	50	212	2436	3592	2329	1513	99	310
PM42	20	5280	2473	836	1151	1578	24	308

Sample	Ba	Ce	Sm	Yb	Lu	Pb	Th	U
PM8	2477	108	67	87	17	1037	27	157
PM9	1944	42	32	42	13	985	17	122
PM10	2195	79	71	87	26	1247	51	333
PM11	2050	97	71	74	27	879	50	323
PM12	1950	82	22	12	5	461	1	323
PM13	1414	67	129	126	12	1078	1	193
PM14	1452	280	51	16	3	1014	1	444
PM15	2902	829	589	300	30	722	34	1146
PM16	2754	2252	1740	773	80	1242	184	879
PM17	2441	2963	2236	912	62	1224	42	324
PM18	5490	716	634	296	20	545	1	505
PM19	3996	1857	1186	490	32	1086	1	1
PM20	5945	6381	3540	1128	67	1321	138	1
PM21	3156	521	273	151	15	211	1	520
PM22	10650	7636	4671	1209	77	1991	204	70
PM23	5170	3681	1850	614	44	1756	84	71
PM24	6130	2184	1128	516	36	847	12	47

Table 5: (cont.)

PM25	9580	2939	1534	616	40	554	17	1
PM26	1635	910	647	301	18	452	3	1480
PM27	1490	475	310	145	11	53	1	1002
PM28	1658	1258	801	348	24	284	19	790
PM29	957	25	3	1	1	1	1	2907
PM30	1284	88	16	5	1	1	1	3699
PM31	1191	281	13	1	5	274	47	2050
PM32	1036	155	11	3	11	36	37	4102
PM33	1299	288	37	26	26	266	51	7069
PM34	1487	195	28	20	25	248	37	1519
PM35	1663	270	17	2	5	1215	20	1627
PM36	2106	468	47	9	4	313	20	2263
PM37	2028	465	53	23	10	70	24	1219
PM38	1020	122	20	12	22	1	27	240
PM39	2352	527	217	186	100	218	91	704
PM40	1252	38	61	67	27	1	16	912
PM41	1181	122	43	44	11	1	5	241
PM42	1019	101	6	9	1	1	1	317

Table 5: (*cont.*)

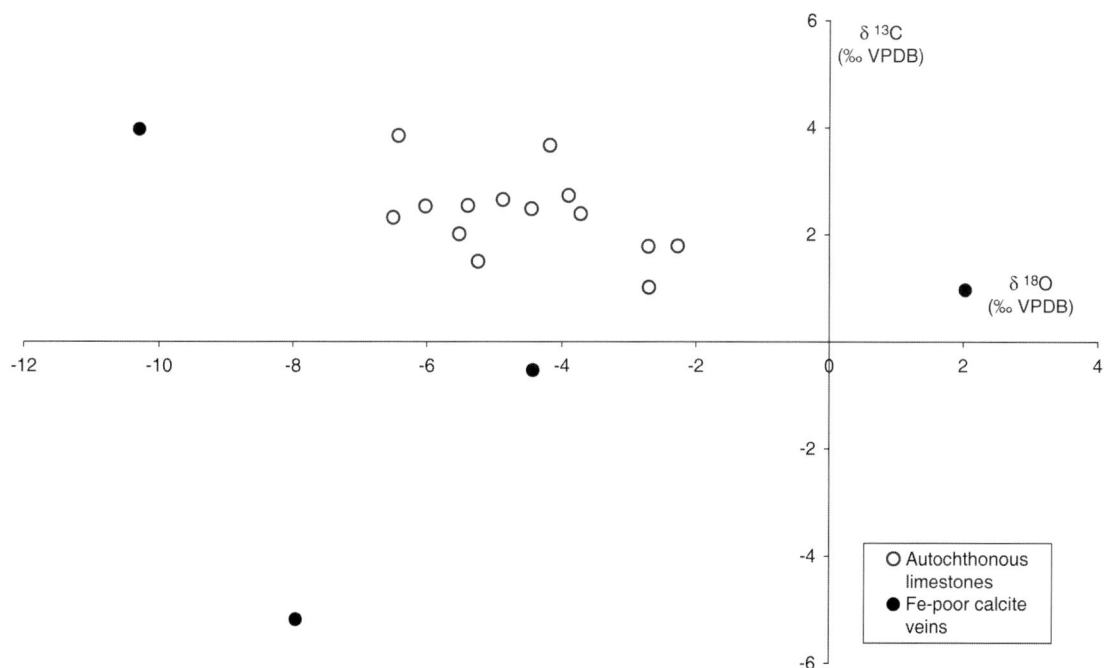

Figure 5: Carbon and oxygen isotopic composition of autochthonous limestone and non-ferroan calcite veins.

range generally measured on Cretaceous carbonates. The oxygen isotopic values are significantly lower (Lowenstam and Epstein, 1954), indicating an oxygen isotopic resetting during limestone diagenesis. The wide range in the isotopic composition of the vein-filling calcites is attributed to the fact that the two vein generations could not be sampled separately.

4.2.2. Allochthonous carbonates

The allochthonous carbonates are exposed to the north of the ancient city of Sagalassos and may be subdivided into six major lithological units: a massif beige limestone, a beige limestone with white chert nodules, a thin-bedded, red limestone with red chert layers and abundant veins, a massif beige limestone with white cherts, an intensely dolomitized unit and a massif beige to pink limestone. Most of these types of limestone are found in the Hellenistic to early Imperial architecture of Sagalassos (Degryse et al., this volume c). Very often the limestone is intensely veined and recrystallized (Figure 4D). The massif beige limestone is mainly characterized by bioclastic wackestone with crinoids, foraminifers, bivalves, calpionellids, ostracods, gastropods, sponge spicules, rudist fragments, pellets, micritized grains and clasts (Figure 4E). The fossils may be micritized. A clotted texture is locally observed. The limestone is mainly dark to non-luminescent under cathodoluminescence. Calcite cements may show a non-, bright yellow (very thin zone) and dull orange luminescent sequence. The beige limestone with white chert nodules is characterized by bioclastic wackestone with abundant radiolaria, sponge spicules, bivalves and rare gastropod shells (Figure 4F). The limestone (allochems and orthochems) shows a dull brown-orange luminescence. The thin-bedded, red limestone is composed of bioclastic wackestone with radiolaria, sponge spicules, bivalves and peloids. A thick, intercalated beige limestone bed is composed of an oolitic grainstone with crinoids, foraminifers, algae, bivalves, lithoclasts, coated and micritized grains (Figure 6A). The thin-bedded limestone and the oolitic grainstone mainly show an orange-ochre-brown luminescence. Parts of the limestone may still be non-luminescent, resulting in a patchy luminescence pattern. The massif beige limestone with white chert consists of bioclastic wackestone and peloidal packstone (Figure 6B). The allochems are pellets, radiolaria, sponge spicules, bivalves, foraminifers, crinoids and calpionellids. This limestone is often dark, brown-orange to non-luminescent. The overlying unit mainly consists of coarse-grained dolomites (Figure 6C), however, partly dolomitized limestone beds are present. The latter are peloidal pack- to grainstone. The dolomite and the limestone are non-luminescent. The thick unit forming the upper part of the limestone massif to the north of the site, is characterized by bioclastic mud-, wacke and packstone with pellets, micritized grains, clasts, bivalves, foraminifers, algae, crinoids, radiolaria and sponge spicules (Figure 6D). This limestone is mainly dark to non-luminescent. The veins in the whole allochthonous carbonate sequence can have different luminescence patterns. However, often the veins show the same luminescence as the host-rock. Veins may also have a zoned non- to yellow and a zoned bright yellow pattern (Figure 6E).

The IR and the Na, Fe, K, Mn and Sr contents of the massif beige limestone is low (Table 5). It represents pure limestone (low IR, Na and K), whose Mn and Fe contents did not increase during subsequent diagenesis. The low Sr and Mg content reflect their decrease during limestone diagenesis. The magnesium content of sample PM14 is high since this sample represents a dolomite. The latter shows a higher iron and a lower strontium concentration. The K, Mn, Sr, Mg, Fe, Sc, Cu, Rb, Ba, Ce, Sm, Yb, Lu, Th and U content are higher in the overlying beige limestone with white chert nodules. The content of most of these elements further increases in the thin-bedded, red limestone. This is mainly due to higher clay content. Also Mn, Co, Ni and Zn are more enriched in this more clayey limestone. The very high IR content (up to 33%) of several of the samples analyzed is due to the partly silicified nature of the limestone. In the massif beige limestone with white chert and the following units, the content of most elements decreases again. The lowest contents are present in the massif, beige and pink limestone forming the uppermost part of the nappe. The magnesium content is of course high in the coarse-grained dolomites and partly dolomitized limestone above the beige limestone with white chert (Table 5). The geochemical pattern of the allochthonous carbonates thus shows an increase in the trace element content with a maximum at the thin-bedded red limestone, followed by a decrease with minimum values at the top.

The thick limestone sequence shows a relatively narrow range in isotopic values. $\delta^{13}C$ values are between 1.5‰ and 3.6‰ and $\delta^{18}O$ values range from –4.1‰ to –0.2‰ (n = 34, Figure 7). Dolomite reflects a carbon and oxygen isotopic composition of +1.9‰ to 2.7‰ VPDB and –1.7‰ to –1.5‰ respectively (n = 3, Figure 7). Both the iron-poor (n = 5) and iron-rich calcite veins (n = 7) show values mostly between +2.1‰ and +3.4‰ for carbon and between –4.0‰ and –0.9‰ for oxygen (Figure 7).

4.3. Flysch deposits

The flysch deposits consist of conglomerate, sandstone and shale. The minerals determined are iron-rich calcite (44-71%)

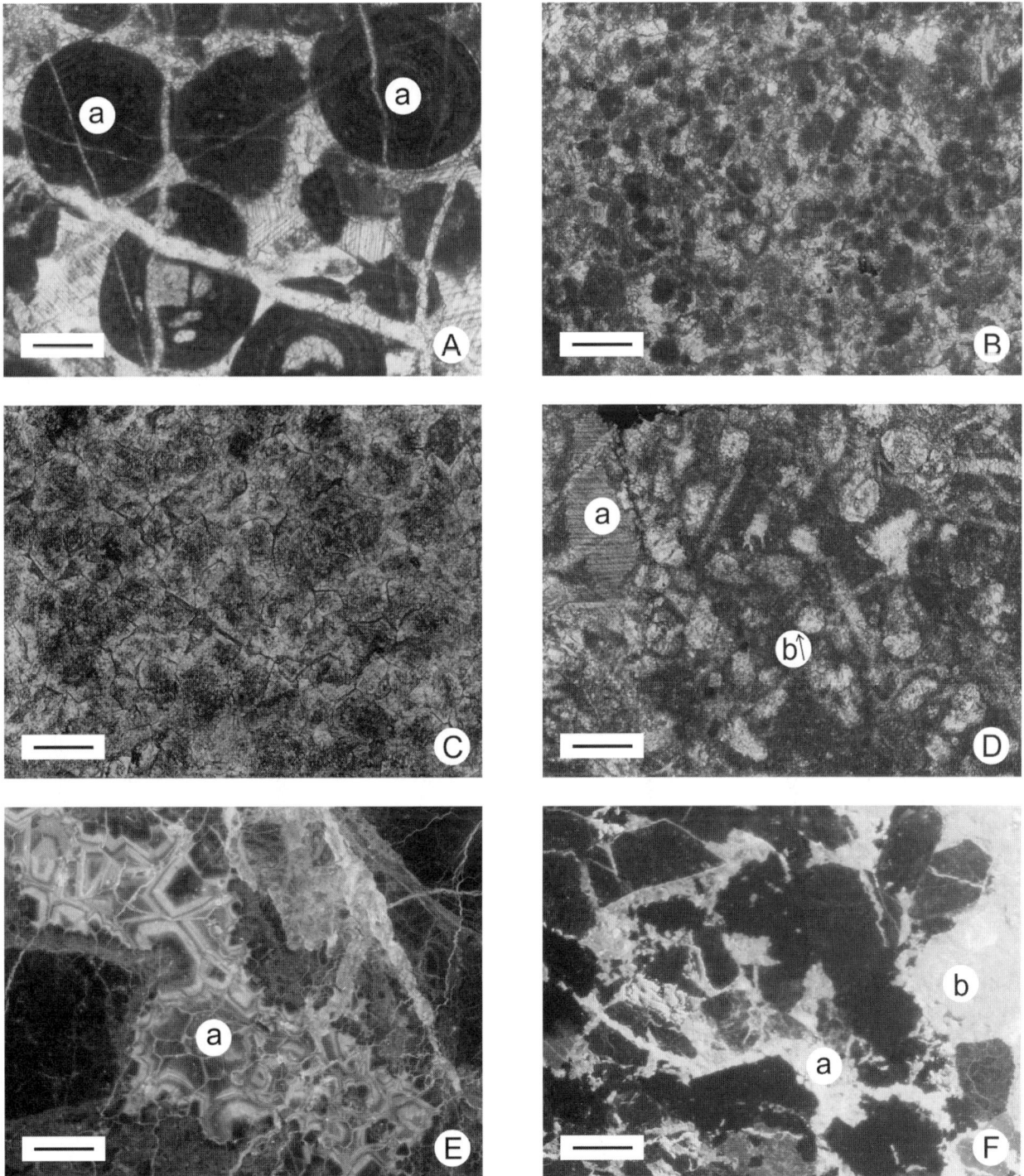

Figure 6: A. Thick oolitic (a) grainstone bed in a unit composed of thin-bedded red limestone of the Lycean nappes. The scale bar is 200 μm; B. Peloidal packstone. Massif limestone with white chert nodules of the allochthonous limestone. The scale bar is 200 μm; C. Dolomites of the Lycean nappes. The scale bar is 200 μm; D. Bioclastic wackestone with crinoids (a) and radiolaria (b). Beige to pink limestone at the top of the Lycean nappes. The scale bar is 200 μm; E. Luminescence pattern of calcite veins (a) in a recrystallized limestone. The scale bar is 100 μm.; F. Ochre luminescent iron-rich calcite forming the matrix (a) of the flysch and filling the fractures (b). The scale bar is 100 μm.

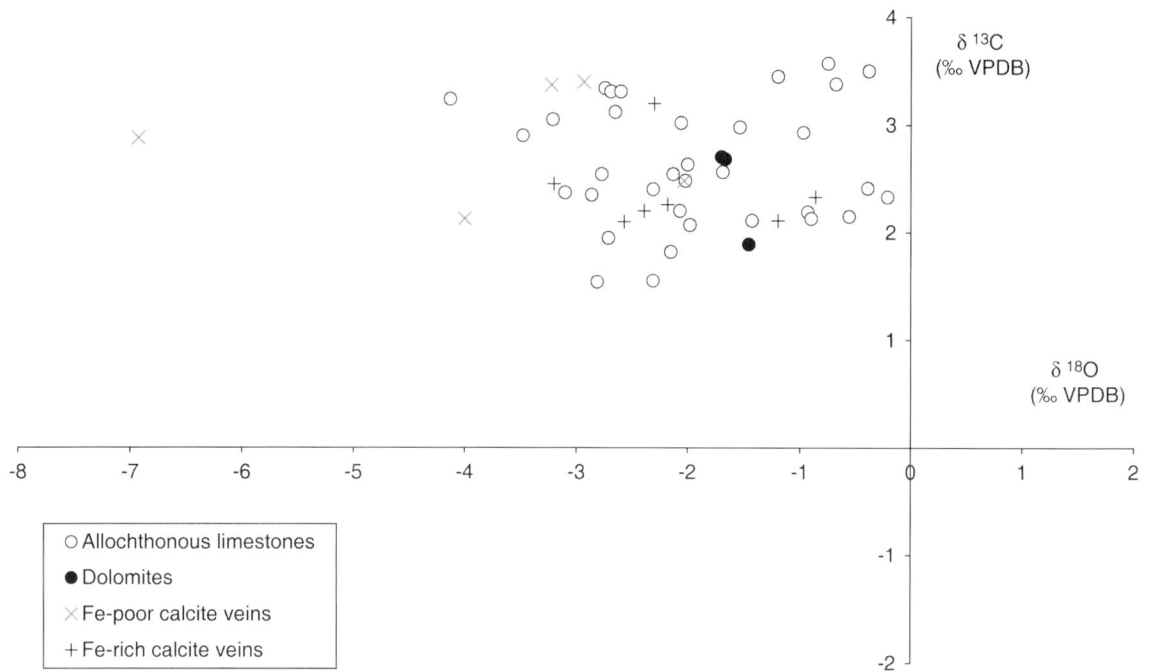

Figure 7: Carbon and oxygen isotopic composition of the allochthonous limestone and dolomite and calcite veins.

and quartz with minor amounts of dolomite, clay, feldspar, hematite and heavy minerals. The main components of the sandstone are small limestone fragments and quartz grains. The quartz grains are mono- or polycrystalline. Numerous, randomly oriented fractures filled with iron-rich calcite crosscut these siliciclastics. The iron-rich nature of the calcite has been identified by staining thin sections and polished slabs with potassium ferricyanide (Dickson, 1966). The calcite cement between the grains is similar to that filling the veins. This cement is iron-rich and shows the same ochre luminescence as the vein calcites (Figure 6F). The calcite grains may be non-, dark brown, ochre and even yellow luminescent. Mostly, veins with different orientations do not show crosscutting relationships, but the vein-filling calcites pass gradually from one vein into another. However, crosscutting relationships between veins is sometimes present and can be observed based on different intensities of purple during coloration and different hues of ochre present in the veins. In addition, veins with calcites showing twinning are crosscut by vein calcites without twin planes.

The geochemistry of the flysch clearly reflects the carbonate-rich nature of the rock (high Ca content and loss-of-ignition; Table 6). The relatively high content of most other elements, compared to pure sandstone, is due to the presence of clays (Al, Fe, Na, K), dolomite (Mg), hematite (Fe), heavy minerals (Ti) and the iron-rich nature of the calcites.

The oxygen and carbon isotopic composition of the total rock (limestone fragments, cement and tiny veins) vary respectively between –6.9‰ and –4.3‰ and –0.9‰ and 1.0‰ (n = 10, Figure 8). The stable isotopic composition of the Fe-rich calcite veins is similar for carbon (–0.8‰ to –0.1‰, n = 10) but systematically lower for oxygen (–7.3‰ to –6.5‰) when compared with the host-rock of the veins. These lower values are due to the incorporation of limestone fragments, with higher $\delta^{18}O$ values than the cement and veins in the bulk rock analyses.

4.4. Cool-water travertines

Travertine only scarcely appears as a building material in the architecture of Sagalassos. Three main types of cool-water travertine facies have been identified in the valley of Başköy: phytoherm framestone, detrital and finely laminated travertine. The latter is built up by bacteria, blue-green algae, microdetrital sediments and biomediated calcite precipitation around larvae (Degryse et al., this volume a). The facies analyses indicate that the travertines were deposited in an alternating fluvial-barrage and paludal system.

A first study by Schroyen et al. (2000) showed that the trace element content of the travertine correlates well with the insoluble residue, indicating that these elements are not significantly incorporated in the carbonate lattice. An X-ray

Sample/wt%	SiO$_2$	TiO$_2$	Al$_2$O$_3$	Fe$_2$O$_3$	MnO	MgO	CaO	Na$_2$O	K$_2$O	LOI
PM43	37.18	0.49	6.31	3.92	0.09	2.20	26.19	0.51	0.95	22.43
PM44	26.36	0.23	2.46	2.55	0.12	2.67	37.12	0.51	0.33	28.89
PM45	36.17	0.41	5.32	3.56	0.09	3.12	28.42	0.45	0.90	23.72
PM46	33.18	0.38	5.36	3.83	0.08	2.94	29.83	0.42	0.92	24.74
PM47	23.96	0.22	2.73	2.26	0.11	2.85	37.29	0.38	0.43	29.84
PM48	34.03	0.32	4.63	3.21	0.10	3.36	27.83	0.64	0.60	24.15
PM50	17.16	0.19	1.99	2.01	0.09	4.88	40.99	0.26	0.34	33.49
PM51	28.34	0.25	4.01	3.25	0.09	3.15	33.28	0.76	0.55	26.95
PM52	31.36	0.33	3.69	2.89	0.10	4.22	29.56	0.48	0.68	25.95

Table 6: Major and trace element content of the Miocene flysch deposits.

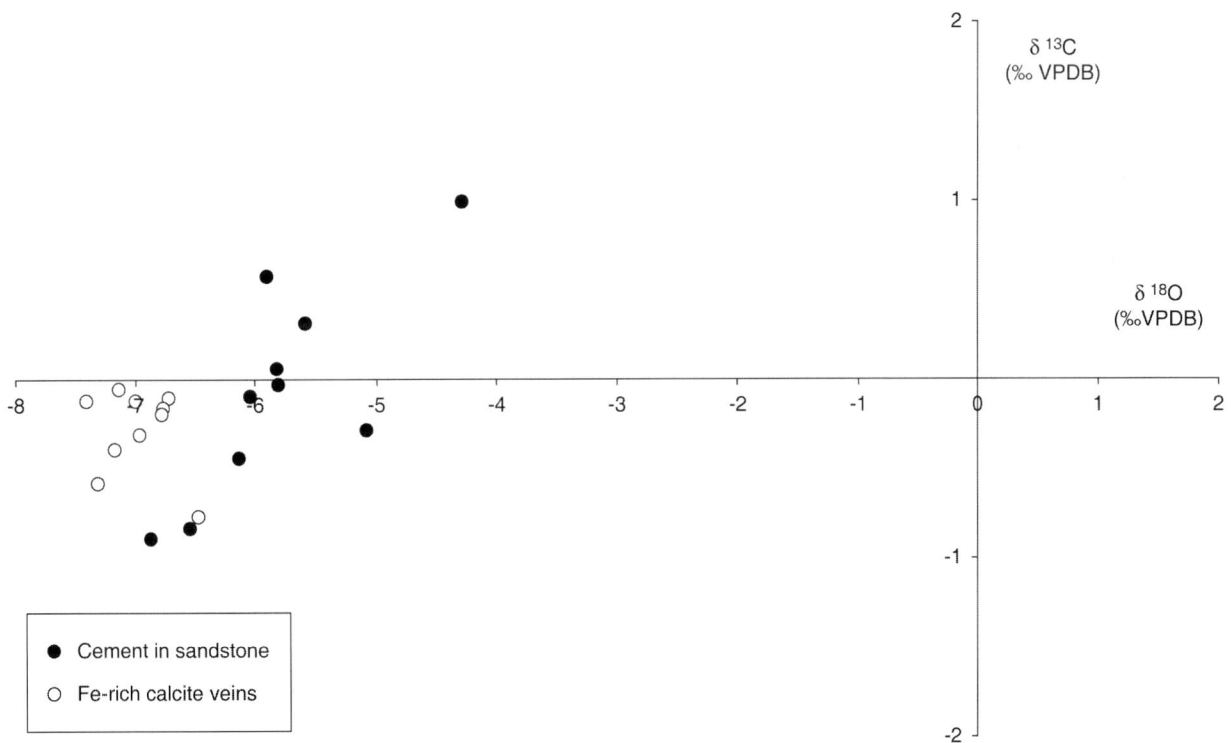

Figure 8: Carbon and oxygen isotopic composition of flysch and ferroan veins.

diffraction analysis of the insoluble residue shows the presence of illite, smectite, chlorite, kaolinite, quartz, hornblende, augite, diopside, magnetite, anorthite and Fe- and Mn-oxides and -hydroxides. Most elements analyzed are incorporated in phyllosilicates, diopside or augite or adsorbed on clay minerals or the oxides/hydroxides. The mineral assemblage is characteristic of the topographically higher situated ophiolitic mélange and their weathering products. The analyses of two new travertine sections are presented in Tables 7 and 8. The first profile (PD1A and PD1B) is characterized by a low IR and Fe and Mg content (Table 7). Higher values only occur in samples with higher K, Mn and Ni content. Macroscopically, these samples already show the presence of clay and/or Mn-oxides. The IR and Fe, Mn, Mn and K content is higher in the second profile (Table 8). Bivariant plots nicely show the correlation between Fe-Mg, Fe-Mn, Fe-K, Mn-K, Mg-Mn and Mg-K (Figure 9). X-ray analysis of the samples from the two profiles indicates the occurrence of illite, quartz, augite, diopside, anorthite, chlorite/illite (R = 1), hornblende, magnetite, hausmannite and possibly of kaolinite and limonite. Both the geochemistry and mineralogy confirm the earlier results of Schroyen et al. (2000), that the geochemistry of the cool-water travertine is mainly related to detrital minerals originating from the surrounding mountain slopes.

The carbon and oxygen stable isotopic composition of cool-water travertine has extensively been studied by Waelkens et al. (1999), Vermoere et al. (1999) and Schroyen et al. (2000). The results and interpretations will only be summarized. The carbon and oxygen isotopic composition of all travertines analyzed (n = 75) varies respectively between –0.4‰ and +4.6‰ VPDB and –9.6‰ and –7.3‰ VPDB (Figure 10). The positive $\delta^{13}C$ values could reflect a carbon isotopic equilibrium of the precipitating water with both the surrounding limestone aquifer and the atmosphere (Cerling, 1984; Schroyen et al., 2000). An organic origin of the carbon can, however, be excluded since calcites which incorporated a large amount of organic carbon, have much lower $\delta^{13}C$ values (Salomons et al., 1978). The $\delta^{18}O$ values are in agreement with the general values of meteoric carbonate precipitates (Wright and Tucker, 1990).

5. ACKNOWLEDGEMENTS

The research was supported by the Belgian Programme on Interuniversity Poles of Attraction (IAP V/9) and the Special Research Fund of the K.U.Leuven (BOF-GOA02/2). The authors are grateful to D. Coetermans for part of the geochemical analysis, H. Nijs for the preparation of the thin sections and D. Steeno for technical assistance.

6. REFERENCES

BRUNN, J.H., ARGYRIADIS, I., RICOU, L.E., POISSON, A., MARCOUX, J. and DE GRACIANSKY, P.C. (1976) Elements majeurs de liaisons entre Taurides et Héllenides, Bulletin de la Société Géologique de France 18: 481-497.

CERLING, T.E. (1984) The stable isotopic composition of modern soil carbonate and its relationship to climate, Earth and Planetary Science Letters 71: 229-240.

COLLINS, A.S. and ROBERTSON, A.H.F. (1997) Lycean melange, southwestern Turkey: An emplaced Late Cretaceous accretionary complex, Geology 25(3): 255-258.

DEGRYSE, P., MUCHEZ, PH., VIAENE, W., QUINIF, Y. and WAELKENS, M. (this volume a) Depositional environment and climatic implications of Holocene travertines in the valley of Başköy, in: P. DEGRYSE and M. WAELKENS (eds.) Sagalassos VI. Geo- and Bio-Archaeology at Sagalassos and in its Territory, Leuven University Press, Leuven: 211-214.

DEGRYSE, P., MUCHEZ, PH., SINTUBIN, M., CLIJSTERS, A., VIAENE, W., DEDEREN, M., SCHROOTEN, P. and WAELKENS, M. (this volume b) Geological mapping of the area around Sagalassos, in: P. DEGRYSE and M. WAELKENS (eds.) Sagalassos VI. Geo- and Bio-Archaeology at Sagalassos and in its Territory, Leuven University Press, Leuven: 17-24.

DEGRYSE, P., HELDAL, T., BLOXAM, E., STOREMYR, P., WAELKENS, M. and MUCHEZ, PH. (this volume c) The Sagalassos quarry landscape: bringing stone quarries in context, in: P. DEGRYSE and M. WAELKENS (eds.) Sagalassos VI. Geo- and Bio-Archaeology at Sagalassos and in its Territory, Leuven University Press, Leuven: 261-290.

DICKSON, J.A.D. (1966) Carbonate identification and genesis as revealed by staining, Journal of Sedimentary Petrology 36: 491-505.

DILEK, Y. and ROWLAND, J.C. (1993) Evolution of a conjugate passive margin pair in Mesozoic Southern Turkey, Tectonics 12: 954-970.

FRANCALANCI, L., CIVETTA, L., INNOCENTI, F. and MANETTI, P. (1990) Tertiary-Quaternary alkaline magmatism of the Aegean-Western Anatolian area: a petrological study in the light of new geochemical and isotopic data, in: M.Y. SAVAŞÇIN and A.H. ERONAT (eds.) IESCA 1990: 385-396.

GLOVER, C.P. and ROBERTSON, A.H.F. (1998) Role of regional extension and uplift in the Plio-Pleistocene evolution of the Aksu Basin, SW Turkey, Journal of the Geological Society, London 155: 365-387.

HAYWARD, A.B. (1984) Miocene clastic sedimentation related to emplacement of the Lycean nappes and the Antalya Complex, SW Turkey, in: J.E. DIXON and A.H.F. ROBERTSON (eds.) The Geological Evolution of the Eastern

Travertine section 1									
Sample	IR	Fe	Mg	Ca	Mn	Zn	Sr	Na	K
PD1A1	0.8	0.01	0.16	37.7	2	3	106	57	23
PD1A2	1.7	0.02	0.17	37.8	5	3	105	59	37
PD1A3	0.4	0.01	0.15	37.8	2	4	114	54	15
PD1A4	1.1	0.02	0.12	38.0	7	3	128	84	27
PD1A5	0.4	0.02	0.14	38.0	7	6	135	58	22
PD1A6	1.5	0.06	0.11	36.9	30	4	114	55	57
PD1A7	1.1	0.01	0.10	37.7	19	2	128	53	15
PD1A8	0.9	0.04	0.13	37.0	22	4	120	65	38
PD1A9	1.3	0.03	0.59	36.5	16	3	178	126	105
PD1A10	0.6	0.01	0.11	37.2	3	2	116	45	9
PD1A11a	0.3	0.01	0.11	36.7	7	2	106	52	12
PD1A11b	0.4	0.02	0.12	37.0	6	<2	101	61	11
PD1A12a	<0.1	0.04	0.11	37.2	40	2	104	66	35
PD1A12b	0.7	0.01	0.14	37.5	2	2	121	52	16
PD1A13	<0.1	0.01	0.13	36.8	2	2	117	51	10
PD1A14	0.5	0.01	0.12	37.3	2	<2	116	59	5
PD1A15	0.2	0.01	0.14	37.7	2	<2	109	46	7
PD1A16	<0.1	0.01	0.15	37.5	6	2	112	54	19
PD1A17	0.4	0.02	0.11	37.6	6	2	105	52	14
PD1A18	1.1	0.02	0.15	37.4	8	<2	115	55	26
PD1A19	0.7	0.02	0.12	37.7	6	<2	102	46	12
PD1A20	1.4	0.02	0.21	37.0	16	<2	126	81	37
PD1B1	2.9	0.02	0.17	36.1	170	5	114	58	276
PD1B2	0.9	0.01	0.10	37.2	2	<2	101	55	12
PD1B3	0.1	0.02	0.10	38.3	4	2	108	52	31
PD1B4	0.5	0.01	0.09	38.0	4	2	106	46	14
PD1B5	0.7	0.01	0.09	37.4	2	2	122	47	10
PD1B6	0.6	0.06	0.12	37.3	12	<2	127	50	54
PD1B7	0.1	0.03	0.11	36.6	6	<2	122	49	21
PD1B8	1.8	0.14	0.15	37.3	30	3	126	55	120
PD1B9	4.2	0.23	0.21	36.8	53	4	133	55	333
PD1B10	0.8	0.07	0.12	37.5	15	<2	116	55	94

Table 7: Major and trace element content of the travertine of profile 1 at Başköy. IR, Fe, Mg and Ca in wt% all other elements in ppm.

Travertine section 2									
Sample	IR	Fe	Mg	Ca	Mn	Zn	Sr	Na	K
MV67	3.3	0.16	0.16	38.2	60	6	192	54	121
MV68	4.1	0.17	0.18	37.8	65	8	180	64	119
MV69	1.5	0.09	0.12	38.3	40	7	195	45	70
MV70	2.7	0.13	0.14	38.6	49	7	203	48	97
MV71	2.7	0.15	0.16	38.1	50	5	195	49	118
MV72	5.7	0.14	0.14	38.3	47	8	197	52	115
MV73	3.1	0.12	0.13	38.2	48	6	200	50	111
MV74	4.9	0.06	0.10	38.8	45	5	217	43	60
MV75	3.0	0.06	0.11	38.8	29	4	208	44	59
MV76	2.9	0.10	0.13	38.5	50	5	198	44	89
MV77	3.4	0.12	0.13	38.2	45	4	202	50	92
MV78	1.9	0.11	0.12	36.8	43	3	213	46	80
MV79	1.5	0.10	0.13	39.1	49	4	225	49	73
MV80	2.6	0.15	0.16	37.5	54	5	171	67	109
MV81	2.4	0.14	0.16	37.9	54	5	175	101	106
MV82	1.8	0.12	0.15	37.4	49	4	184	57	94
MV83	1.9	0.13	0.15	37.5	55	5	195	61	107
MV84	1.5	0.08	0.11	36.7	36	4	205	50	68
MV85	1.2	0.10	0.13	37.6	44	5	193	53	82
MV86	1.3	0.06	0.10	36.5	29	5	199	51	61
MV87	1.5	0.08	0.12	36.7	38	4	204	53	63
MV88	2.1	0.15	0.15	36.5	50	6	210	48	134
MV90	2.0	0.11	0.13	36.6	40	4	212	47	88
MV91	1.4	0.10	0.12	35.7	42	4	217	61	89

Table 8: Major and trace element content of the travertine of profile 2 at Başköy. IR, Fe, Mg and Ca in wt% all other elements in ppm.

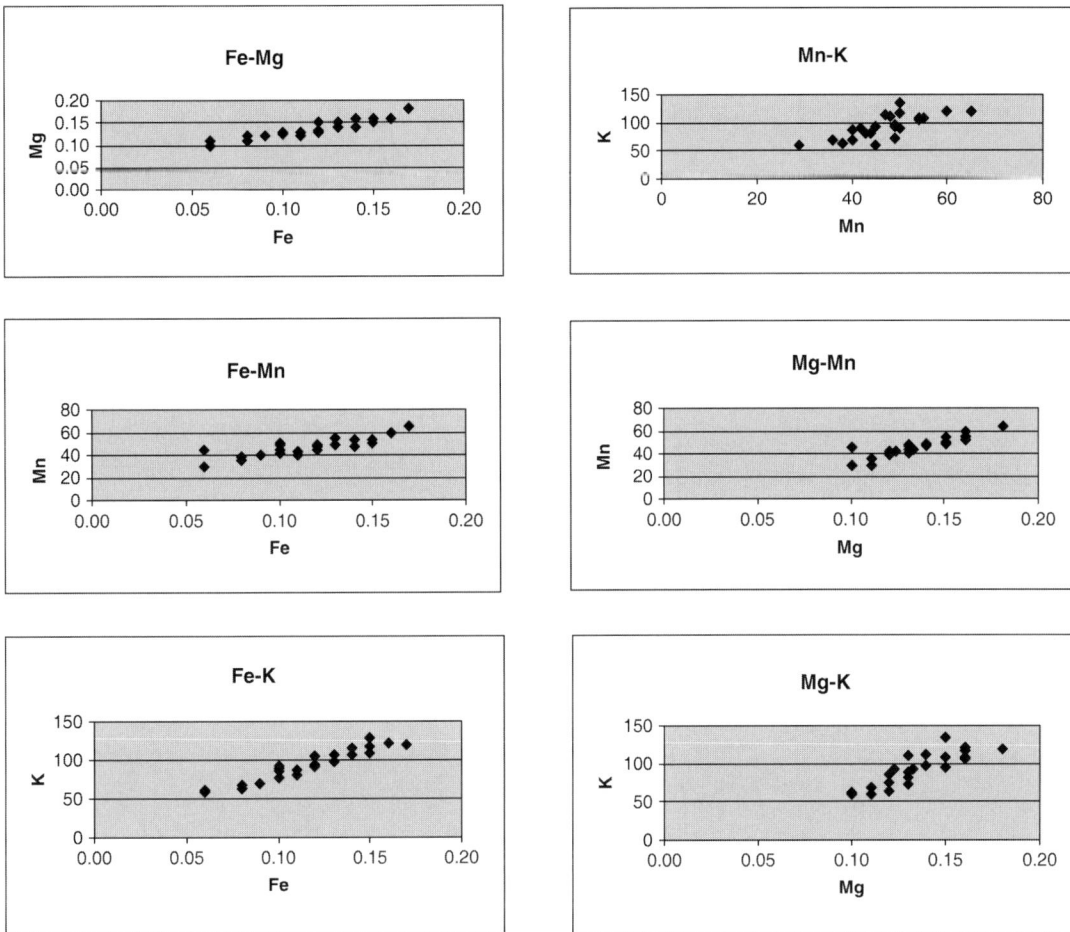

Figure 9: Bivariate plot of the element contents present in travertine profile 2.

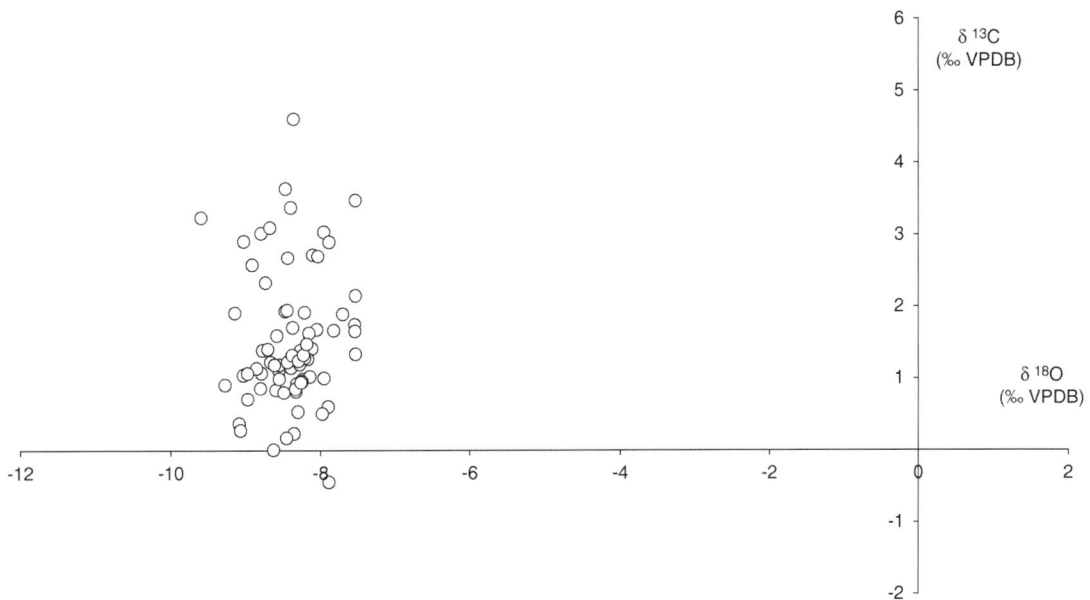

Figure 10: Carbon and oxygen isotopic composition of the travertine at Başköy.

Mediterranean (*Geological Society of London, Special Publication, 17*): 287-300.

Jakeš, P. and White, A.J.R. (1972) Major and trace element abundances in volcanic rocks of orogenic areas, *Geological Society of America Bulletin* 83: 29-40.

Juteau, T. (1980) Ophiolites of Turkey, *Ofioliti* 16: 199-236.

Lefèvre, C., Bellon, H. and Poisson, A. (1983) Présence de leucitites dans le volcanisme pliocène de la région d'Isparta (Taurides occidentales, Turquie), *Compte Rendu de l'Académie des Sciences de Paris* 297: 367-372.

Lowenstam, H.A. and Epstein, S. (1954) Paleotemperatures of the post-Aptian Cretaceous as determined by the oxygen isotope method, *Journal of Geology* 62: 207-248.

Ota, R. and Dincel, A. (1975) Volcanic rocks of Turkey, *Bulletin of the Geological Survey of Japan* 26: 393-419.

Özgür, N., Pekdeger, A. and Schneider, H.-J. (1990) Pliocene volcanism in the Gölçük area, Isparta/Western Taurides, in: M.Y. Savaşçin and A.H. Eronat (eds.) *IESCA 1990*: 411-419.

Poisson, A. (1975) *Geological Map of the Isparta Area*, Centre National de Recherche Scientifique, Paris.

Poisson, A. (1977) *Recherches géologiques dans les Taurides occidentales*, Thèse de Doctorat d'Etat, Orsay.

Poisson, A., Akay, E., Dumont, J.F. and Uysal, S. (1984) The Isparta Angle : a Mesozoic paleorift in the Western Taurides, in: O. Tekeli and C. Goncüoglu (eds.) *Geology of the Taurus Belt* (*Proceedings of the International Symposium on the Geology of the Taurus Belt*), MTA, Ankara: 11-26.

Robertson, A.H.F. (1993) Mesozoic-Tertiary sedimentary and tectonic evolution of Neotethyan carbonate platforms, margins and small ocean basins in the Antalya Complex, southwest Turkey, in: L.E. Frostick and R.J. Steel (eds.) *Tectonic Controls and Signatures in Sedimentary Successions* (*Special Publication of the International Association of Sedimentologists 20*), Blackwell Scientific Publications, Oxford: 415-465.

Salomons, W., Goudie, G. and Mook, W.G. (1978) Isotopic composition of calcrete deposits from Europe, *Earth Surface Processes* 3: 43-57.

Savaşçin, M.Y. and Güleç, N. (1990) Relationship between magmatic and tectonic activities in Western Turkey, in: M.Y. Savaşçin and A.H. Eronat (eds.) *IESCA 1990*: 300-313.

Schroyen, K., Vermoere, M., Degryse, P., Librecht, I., Muchez, Ph., Viaene, W., Smets, E., Paulissen, E., Keppens, E. and Waelkens, M. (2000) Preliminary study of travertine deposits in the vicinity of Sagalassos: petrography, geochemistry, geomorphology and palynology, in: M. Waelkens and L. Loots (eds.) *Sagalassos V. Report on the Survey and Excavation Campaigns of 1996 and 1997* (Acta Archaeologica Monographiae Lovaniensia 10) Leuven University Press, Leuven: 755-780.

Vermoere, M., Degryse, P., Vanhecke, L., Muchez, Ph., Paulissen, E., Smets, E. and Waelkens, M. (1999) Pollen analysis of two travertine sections in Başköy (southwestern Turkey): implications for environmental conditions during the early Holocene, *Review of Paleobotany and Palynology* 105: 93-110.

Waelkens, M., Paulissen, E., Vermoere, M., Degryse, P., Celis, D., Schroyen, K., De Cupere, B., Librecht, I., Nackaerts, K., Vanhaverbeke, H., Viaene, W., Muchez, P., Ottenburgs, R., Deckers, S., Van Neer, W., Smets, E., Govers, G., Verstraeten, G., Steegen, A. and Cauwenberghs, K. (1999) Man and environment in the territory of Sagalassos, a classical city in SW Turkey, *Quaternary Science Reviews* 18: 697-709.

Wright, V.P. and Tucker, M.E. (1990) Calcretes, *International Association of Sedimentologists, Reprint series 2*, Oxford: 1-22.

TESTING DIAGNOSTIC GEOMORPHOLOGICAL CRITERIA OF ACTIVE NORMAL FAULTS IN THE BURDUR-ISPARTA REGION (SW TURKEY)

Dominique SIMILOX-TOHON, Max FERNANDEZ-ALONSO, Marc WAELKENS, Philippe MUCHEZ and Manuel SINTUBIN

1. INTRODUCTION

The Lake Region in Southwest Turkey, centred on the cities of Burdur and Isparta, is situated in the first-degree seismic hazard zone (*Global Seismic Hazard Assessment Program* – www.seismo.ethz.ch/GSHAP/), inferring a relatively high risk for major earthquakes. The wider Burdur-Isparta region has indeed been struck by a number of large damaging earthquakes in the last century. Based on archaeological evidence (Waelkens *et al.*, 2000) at the archaeological site of Sagalassos, situated some 10 km SSW of Isparta and some 20 km ESE of Burdur, it could be inferred that the ancient city has been struck by a number of earthquake(s) during its history. The last during the late Roman and early Byzantine periods (6th to 7th century AD) turned out to have caused major damage. Based on archaeoseismological evidence (type of damage, extensive and widespread nature of damage) (Sintubin *et al.*, 2003), an intensity of at least VIII (MSK) is attributed to these earthquakes. Therefore, an epicentre in the direct proximity of the ancient city, i.e. within a radius of less than 20 km, should be considered (cf. Stiros, 1996). Within this radius around the archaeological site no active fault, however, is known to date (Figure 1).

A first step in the search for the causative fault(s) the Sagalassos earthquake(s) is a remote sensing analysis in order to identify all structures in the wider surroundings of Sagalassos that may be active faults. Remote sensing involves gathering data and information from the earth by detecting and measuring radiation, particles, and fields associated with objects located beyond the immediate vicinity of the sensor device(s). We want to gather information about active faults in the Burdur-Isparta area, particularly large ones capable of generating substantial earthquakes (≥ Ms 5.5), using satellite images, aerial photographs and a digital elevation model (DEM). The remote sensing analysis should help us to identify previously unknown active faults within a radius of 20 km of the archaeological site of Sagalassos. It is therefore not our goal to make a detailed cartography of all the faults in the target area but only to describe the major structures which may represent major active faults, relevant for the seismotectonics in the Burdur-Isparta area.

Assuming that a seismogenic fault has been active in the past over a time span of several tens of thousands of years, it is very likely that, depending on the style of faulting and rate of activity, comparable events repeatedly occurred in the past, and produced similar ground effects. Even if partially obliterated or masked by climatically driven or anthromorphic processes, the results of such past activity can be recognized in today's environment (Michetti and Hancock, 1997). In other words, it should always be possible to recognize a 'seismic landscape' (*sensu* Michetti and Hancock, 1997) that can be considered to be the result of one or more earthquakes that resulted in ground deformation, including surface faulting (Michetti *et al.*, 2005). A classic illustration of this concept is provided by a fault-generated mountain range front, regarded as the sum over time of the evolution of the free-face of a fault scarp (Stewart and Hancock, 1991; 1994). In many cases the high escarpments associated with active normal faults in the Aegean region dominate the landscape and are obvious features to recognize in a remote sensing analysis. Therefore, the geomorphology and drainage patterns of the known major active faults in the Burdur-Isparta area as seen on remote sensing images have been analyzed first. Then, the diagnostic criteria with respect to the geomorphology and drainage patterns of these active normal faults will be used as a guideline to further identify previously unknown active normal faults (Similox-Tohon *et al.*, this volume b).

We emphasize that we are concerned only with large active faults, defined as those with dimensions comparable to or greater than the thickness of the seismogenic upper crust. In the Aegean region these are normal fault segments that typically reach maximum lengths of 15 to 20 km, extend to depths of 10 to 15 km, and generate earthquakes of magnitude (Ms) 6.0 to 6.8 (Goldsworthy and Jackson,

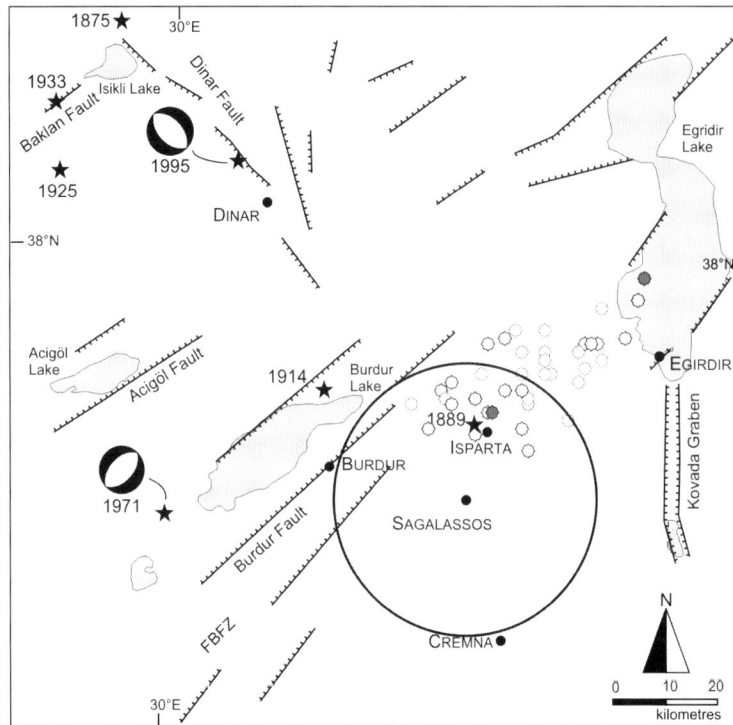

Figure 1: Simplified active fault map of the Lake Region centred on Burdur and Isparta at the northeastern extremity of the Fethiye-Burdur fault zone (FBFZ) (after Bozkurt, 2001; Eyidoğan and Barka, 1996; Senel, 1997), with indication of the epicentres of recent large earthquakes (stars), available focal mechanisms (after Eyidoğan and Barka, 1996; Taymaz and Price, 1992) and the microseismic activity in the Isparta-Eğirdir region (white circles are Md 3.0-3.9 events; gray circles are Md 4.0-4.9 events) (KOERI, 2002) (see also Similox-Tohon et al., this volume b). Also marked is the target area within a radius of 20 km around the archaeological site of Sagalassos.

2000). An important feature of normal faults on this scale is that they produce vertical motions in their footwalls and hanging walls, i.e. tilting, that die away from the surface rupture over distances of typically 10 to 15 km from the fault, i.e. measured normal to the fault strike (Goldsworthy and Jackson, 2000).

2. GEODYNAMIC SETTING

The Burdur-Isparta region is situated at the northeastern extremity of the **Fethiye-Burdur fault zone** (FBFZ). This NE-SW trending tectonic feature, running from Fethiye to Burdur, is commonly considered to be the northeastern on-land contin-uation of the left-lateral transform system of the Pliny-Strabo trench off the coast of Rhodes, linking it with the Hellenic arc (Barka et al., 1995; Bozkurt, 2001; ten Veen, 2004; ten Veen and Kleinspehn, 2002; 2003). Left-lateral motion of the FBFZ is corroborated with GPS measurements showing a movement of at least 15 mm/yr (Barka and Reilinger, 1997).

This has, however, not been demonstrated by fault plane solutions of recent earthquakes in the Burdur-Isparta region (Figure 1).

The current geodynamic setting of the Burdur-Isparta region started in Late Miocene to Early Pliocene times (ca. 5 Ma) (Bozkurt, 2001). The extensional regime is expressed by three NE-SW trending half-graben systems (Figures 1 and 5), bounded to the southeast by major NW dipping, slightly listric normal faults, the **Burdur**, **Acıgöl** and **Baklan faults** (Price and Scott, 1991; 1994). Quaternary basins developed within these graben depressions, occupying the central part of wider, fault-bounded Pliocene basins (Price and Scott, 1991). To the northeast, the graben system terminates against the NW-SE trending **Dinar fault** (Figures 1 and 8).

Although it is generally accepted that the **Burdur gra-ben system** is located at the diffuse eastern edge of the Aegean-Western Anatolian extensional province (Glover and Robertson, 1998), tectonic interpretations differ. Glover

54

and Robertson (1998) consider the Burdur area as part of the N-S trending right-lateral Isparta angle suture zone. Clockwise rotation of fault blocks within this right-lateral shear zone generated NE-SW trending left-lateral faults (Price and Scott, 1994). Barka *et al.* (1995) locate the Burdur graben system at the northeastern extremity of the left-lateral FBFZ. The Dinar fault is considered as a break-away fault in this graben system.

East of the city of Isparta, the neotectonic setting of the apex of the Isparta angle (Blumenthal, 1963) is dominated by the N-S trending **Kovada graben** and sub parallel lineaments (Glover and Robertson, 1998) (Figures 1 and 7). The Kovada graben is 25 km long and 2 to 3 km wide, running south from Lake Eğirdir, with the small Lake Kovada filling the southern end of the graben. Subordinate Quaternary N-S trending faults are mapped to the east of the Kovada graben over a distance of more than 20 km (Robertson, 1993), showing that extensional deformation is affecting a wider area. The graben itself is rather symmetrical, bounded by prominent faults on both sides, and developed in Mesozoic carbonates. There is, however, little evidence of active faulting (Glover and Robertson, 1998).

In recent history, seismic activity on a number of these faults has been recorded. The Burdur 1914 earthquake (Ms 7.0) and the Burdur 1971 earthquake (Ms 6.2) occurred on the Burdur fault (Ambraseys and Jackson, 1998; Eyidoğan and Barka, 1996) (Figure 1). A surface rupture of 23 km with a maximum offset of 150 cm (Ambraseys and Jackson, 1998) has been observed for the first event, while the second event ruptured the surface over 4 km with a maximum displacement of 30 cm (Ambraseys and Jackson, 1998). Fault-plane solution of the 1971 earthquake indicates pure normal faulting (Eyidoğan and Barka, 1996; Taymaz and Price, 1992). The Dinar 1933 earthquake (Ms 5.8) is considered to have occurred on the Baklan fault (Eyidoğan and Barka, 1996; Koral, 2000) (Figure 1). Eyidoğan and Barka (1996) also consider that the Dinar 1925 (Md 6.0) earthquake occurred on the Baklan fault, although its epicentre is located in the footwall of the Baklan fault. The Dinar 1995 earthquake (Ms 6.2) occurred on the Dinar fault (Ambraseys and Jackson, 1998) (Figure 1). The total length of surface rupture was 10 km with a maximum vertical offset of 50 cm (Altunel *et al.*, 1999) and a maximum lateral offset of 10 cm (Ambraseys and Jackson, 1998). Fault-plane solution indicates pure normal faulting (Eyidoğan and Barka, 1996; Taymaz and Price, 1992).

A medium magnitude earthquake has furthermore been reported in 1889 to have caused local damage concentrated at Isparta and the nearby village of Deregümü, a few km northwest of Isparta (Ambraseys, Waelkens, pers. comm., 2002). It is unknown which fault has caused this seismic event.

Finally, an inventory of the seismicity in the region in the last century (*Kandili Observatory and Earthquake Research Institute* earthquake catalogue 1900-2000) reveals three clusters of microseismic activity: (1) associated with the Burdur 1971 earhtquake; (2) associated with the Dinar 1995 earthquake and (3) a cluster in the region between Isparta and Eğirdir. This ENE-WSW trending elongated cluster extends over a region of 41 by 17 km (Figure 1). This microseismic activity may be related to the Isparta-Eğirdir fault zone (Similox-Tohon *et al.*, this volume b).

3. REMOTE SENSING ANALYSIS

3.1. Satellite images

A Landsat 5 Mulit-Spectral Scanner tape, a Landsat 7 Enhanced Thematic Mapper + tape, an Aster tape and an Ikonos tape were processed using ENVI (Figure 2).

The Landsat 5 tape dates from 26 August 1987 and has a resolution of 60 m for all visible and near-IR bands. The data were contrast-stretched and filtered. Various combinations of bands were used to try to pick out different features. A combination of bands 4, 2, 1 for red, green and blue respectively has most widely been used. The Landsat 5 images were analyzed for a first regional view (100 by 100 km) of the area, as it has one of the lowest resolution.

The Landsat 7 tape dates from 9 December 1999 and has a resolution of 30 m for the visible, near-IR and IR bands (1, 2, 3, 4, 5, and 7) and a resolution of 15 m for the panchromatic band (8). The data were contrast-stretched and filtered. Various combinations of bands were used to pick out different features. A combination of bands 4, 5, 7 for red, green and blue respectively was most widely used as this clearly showed the known major active faults. This image was analyzed for a more detailed, regional view (100 by 100 km) of the area than that from the Landsat 5 images. A fusion of bands 4, 5, 7 and 8 (panchromatic) was carried out for an even more detailed colour image. The resulting image has the colours of the bands 4, 5, 7 (30 m resolution) and the detail of band 8 (15 m resolution).

The Aster tape dates from 18 October 2001 and has a resolution of 90 m for the thermal bands (10, 11, 12, 13, and

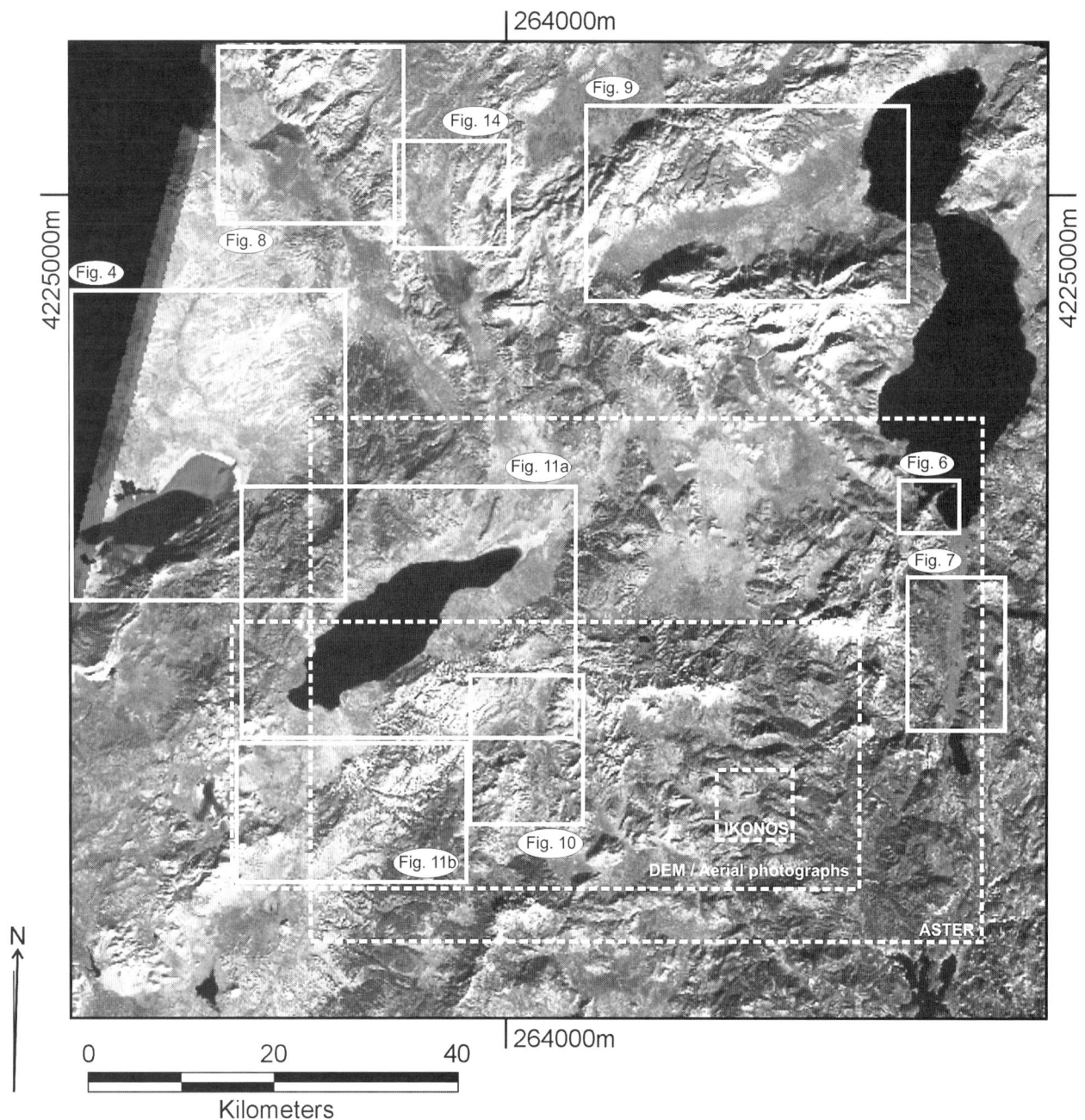

Figure 2: Landsat 7 Enhanced Thematic Mapper + image of the region of the lakes with a combination of bands 4, 5 and 7 for red, green and blue respectively. Projection is UTM Zone 36, Northern Hemisphere (WGS 84). Location of the used remote sensing imagery (boxes). Landsat 7 image used in figures 4, 7, 8, 9, 10, 11 and 14. Aster image used in figure 6. DEM used in figures 3, 10 and 11. Ikonos image used in Similox *et al.* (this volume c). Areas discussed in the paper: Acıgöl basin (Figure 4), Eğirdir (Figure 6), Kovada graben (Figure 7), Dinar fault (Figure 8), Hoyran basin (Figure 9), Kayaaltı fault (Figure 10), Burdur basin (Figure 11), Dinar system (Figure 14).

14), 30 m for the IR bands (4, 5, 6, 7, 8, and 9) and 15 m for the visible bands (1, 2, and 3). The data were contrast-stretched and filtered. Various combinations of bands were used to pick out different features. A combination of thermal bands 14, 12, 10, of IR bands 4, 7, 9 and of visible bands 1, 2, 3, each for red, green and blue respectively provided satisfactory images and were most widely used. The Aster images with the thermal bands were used in the same way as the Landsat 5 images, whereas the Aster images with the IR and visible bands were used in the same way as the Landsat 7 images. The visible area is however somewhat smaller (70 by 60 km) than the Landsat tapes (Figure 2). No fusions of bands with different resolution were carried out with the Aster data.

The Ikonos tape has a resolution of 4 m for the visible and near-IR bands and of 1 m for the panchromatic band. The data were contrast-stretched and filtered. Various combinations of bands were used to pick out different features. A combination of bands red, green and blue and a combination of bands near-IR, green and blue for red, green and blue respectively were most widely used. The Ikonos tape represents only a small area (8 by 7 km) W of the village of Çanaklı (Figure 2) and was used for a very detailed analysis of this area (Similox-Tohon *et al.*, this volume c). A fusion of bands near-IR, green, blue and the panchromatic band and also a fusion of bands red, green, blue and the panchromatic band was carried out for even more detailed colour images. The resulting images have the colours of the visible and near-IR bands (4 m resolution) and the detail of the panchromatic band (1 m resolution).

3.2. Digital Elevation Model (DEM)

A DEM was obtained by manually digitizing 1:25000-scale topographic maps (performed by the team of E. Paulissen, K.U.Leuven) of a 70 by 30 km large area (Figures 2 and 3). The accuracy resulting from digitizing is 10 m. Six shaded relief views were computed, using ENVI, with a sun angle of 60° and different values for sun azimuth (270°, 315°, 0°, 45° and 90°). A lineament analysis has been carried out on these images. The shaded relief view with a sun azimuth of 315° appeared to be one of the most useful images as this is subperpendicular to most lineament trends. Topographic profiles were made across some lineaments for a better geomorphological understanding of these lineaments. Moreover, the DEM was combined with the Landsat 7 fusion image to obtain a 3D view of the area.

3.3. Aerial photographs

Aerial photographs covering the same area as the DEM were analyzed at the *Akdeniz University* at Antalya, Turkey. The 1:40000-scale photographs date from February 1988 and were used to investigate more in detail some of the lineaments observed on the satellite images and DEM. Unfortunately, no copy of the photographs was allowed to be taken out of Turkey, so that the results of this study will be incorporated with the results from the satellite imagery.

4. DIAGNOSTIC CRITERIA FOR ACTIVE NORMAL FAULTS

Faults appear as linear features, called **lineaments**, on remote sensing images. These features may not be confused with other similar linear features, due to human activity (e.g. drainage works, etc.). All these linear features are traced on the images, i.e. a **lineament analysis**, and need afterwards to be inspected in the field. Active faults will appear as more distinct linear features since their 'recent' (neotectonic) activity may leave a clear imprint on both the geomorphology and drainage patterns of the faulted area, which are both evidenced on remote sensing images. Since the Burdur-Isparta area is characterized by an extensional neotectonic regime, expressed by major active normal faults, we will describe some of the major geomorphological features and drainage patterns associated with these faults. The descriptions are based on studies in the Basin and Range (western United States), Greece and SW Turkey (Goldsworthy and Jackson, 2000; 2001; Jackson and Leeder, 1994; Leeder and Alexander, 1987; Leeder and Gawthorpe, 1987; Leeder and Jackson, 1993; Leeder *et al.*, 1991; Paton, 1992; Roberts and Jackson, 1991). Afterwards, these criteria will be applied to the target area, i.e. within a radius of 20 km around the archaeological site of Sagalassos, to identify lineaments that may represent active faults (Similox-Tohon *et al.*, this volume b).

We will illustrate the variation in fault-related geomorphology and drainage patterns associated with different rock types in the footwall and hanging wall blocks of normal faults, distinguishing two main types: (1) Mesozoic limestone as resistant lithology; and (2) Neogene sediments, often lake or alluvial deposits, as less-resistant lithology. Moreover, attention will be paid to the predictable surface effects related to extensional half-graben/tilt-block systems that may provide supplementary criteria for the identification of active normal faults. The surface effects are predictable due to the primary control on depositional processes exerted by imposed tectonic slopes (Leeder and Gawthorpe, 1987).

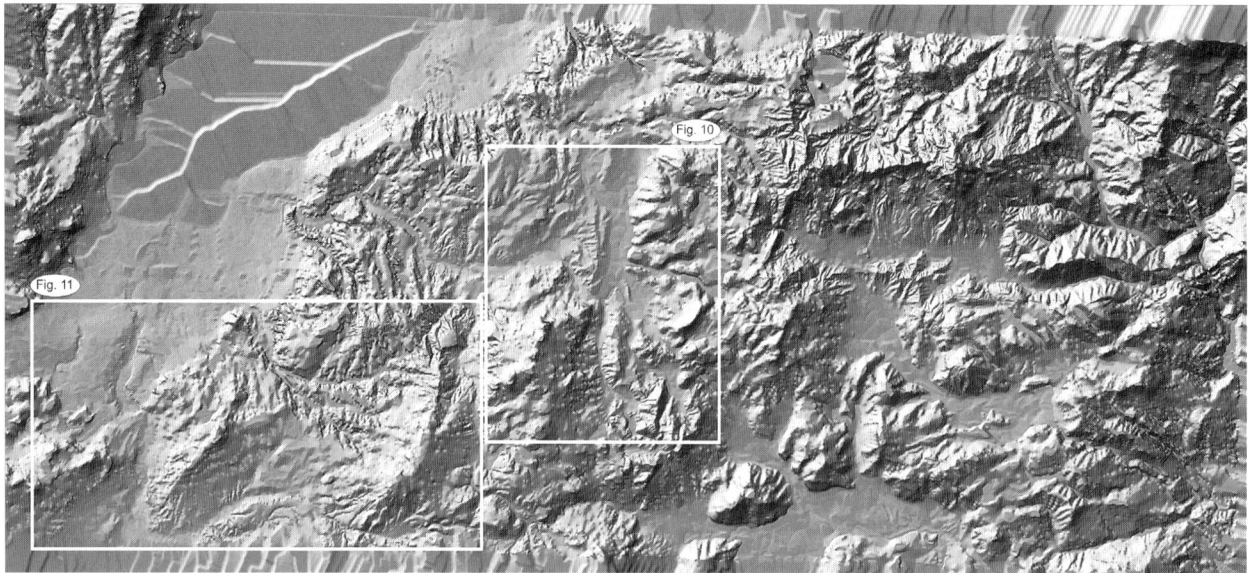

Figure 3: DEM image with shaded relief view of the territory of Sagalassos, illuminated from the NW. See figure 2 for location. Areas discussed in this paper: Kayaaltı (Figure 10), Burdur (Figure 11).

5. TESTING IN THE BURDUR-ISPARTA AREA

5.1. Normal faults in resistant lithology – Mesozoic limestones

The **Acıgöl fault** bounds the SE margin of Lake Acıgöl, located on the other side of the mountain ridge forming the western margin of Lake Burdur (Figures 1 and 4). The initiation of the Acıgöl fault cannot be dated precisely. Nevertheless it cuts the Lycian nappes, the last emplacement of which is dated early to middle Miocene (Temiz *et al.*, 1997). There have been no known historical or recent earthquakes linked to this fault. Despite the lack of historical and recent seismicity on the Acıgöl fault, a 15 m wide belt of incohesive breccia, underlain by a slip plane, is exposed along the steep limestone escarpment of the Acıgöl fault testifying its relatively recent activity (Taymaz and Price, 1992; Temiz *et al.*, 1997). The fault has been reactivated during Plio-Quaternary times as it cuts Pliocene lacustrine limestones (Temiz *et al.*, 1997). An erosional nick, i.e. an indentation in a surface, representing an old level of the lake, is also affected by a fault (probably post-Pliocene), which is parallel to the main fault (Temiz *et al.*, 1997). This erosional nick can not be seen on the satellite image. The Acıgöl fault is a 15 km long continuous fault segment and forms a steep escarpment, 1100 m high in limestone (Taymaz and Price, 1992). The surface trace of the fault is straight and trends NE-SW. The prominent footwall ridge, i.e. the fault scarp, is clear on the satellite image (Figure 4). Its northeastern continuation is poorly con-

strained since NE of Lake Acıgöl. Oligocene flysch in its footwall is rapidly eroding and there is no discernible fault trace (Taymaz and Price, 1992). On the satellite image, it appears that the Acıgöl fault steps to the SE in an at least 6 km long segment. This right-stepping segmentation is in accordance with the southwestern continuation of the Acıgöl fault, where the fault appears to step to the NW (Taymaz and Price, 1992). Comparable many other normal faults in limestone, drainage from the footwall enters the basin at topographic lows associated with the ends of fault segments or en-echelon steps between them. Two major catchments (Figure 4), S1 and S2, flow round the ends of the Acıgöl fault. Catchment S1 even flows through the gap between two right-stepping segments of the fault system. Catchment S1 forms a predominantly longitudinal drainage pattern in the footwall. Drainage of the steep fault face itself is minor, as the associated catchments are small. This pattern of drainage is typical for limestone footwall uplands (cf. Goldsworthy and Jackson, 2000). In such systems, fault segmentation is the dominant control on the position of fans in the main basin. However, alluvial fans sourced in the slope of the limestone footwall are poorly developed and of limited areal extent (generally less than 1 km²) (Taymaz and Price, 1992). By contrast, the hanging wall of the Acıgöl fault contains young lake deposits, formed in a fault-bounded basin. These sediments have now been tilted to the SE as a result of fault movement (Price and Scott, 1994). The result is a smooth slope with streams flowing down-dip over a length of ca. 15 km, which is the wavelength of the expected tilting (Figure 4).

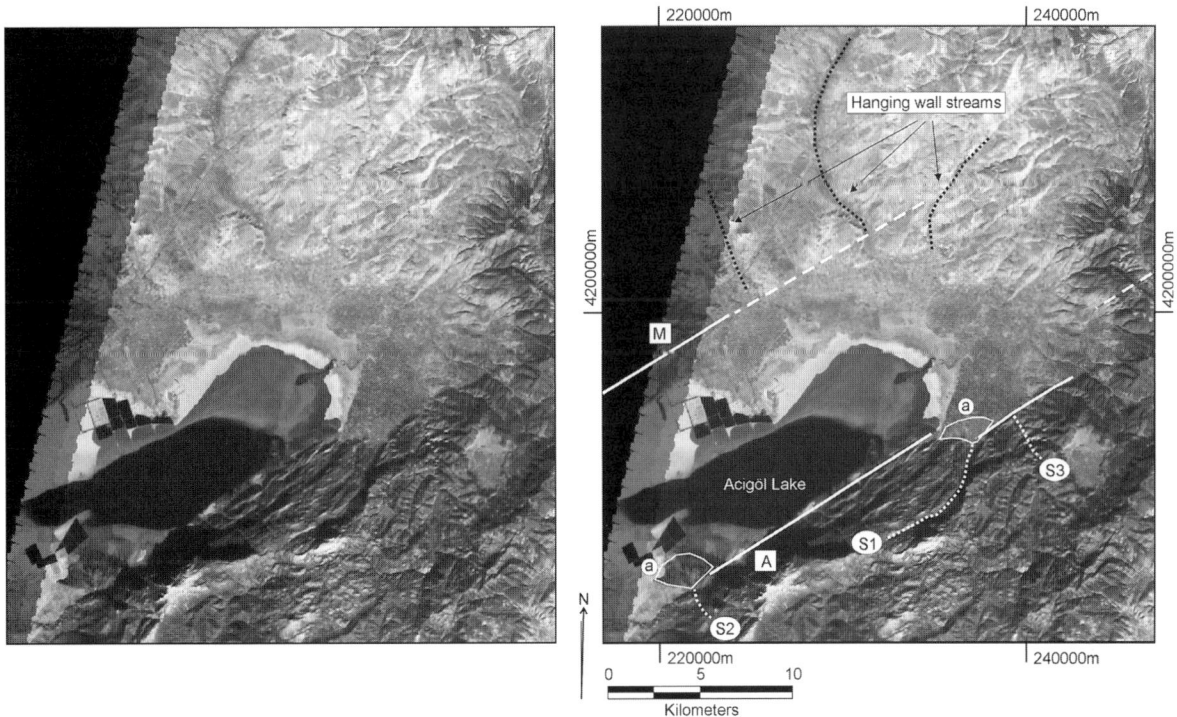

Figure 4: Landsat 7 Enhanced Thematic Mapper + image with a combination of bands 4, 5 and 7 for red, green and blue respectively, of the **Acıgöl basin**, showing the trace of the Acıgöl fault (A) and the Maymundağ fault (M), the major drainage systems (S1, S2, S3) and alluvial fans (a). Projection is UTM Zone 36, Northern Hemisphere (WGS 84). See figure 2 for location.

While the southeastern margin of the **Acıgöl basin** is controlled by the Acıgöl fault, the northwestern margin is controlled by the Maymundağ fault (Figure 4). The **Maymundağ fault** exposes Oligocene flysch in its footwall. The surface trace of the fault trends NE-SW. There is no well-developed slip plane or breccia associated with the Maymundağ fault (Taymaz and Price, 1992). It is assigned as a fault merely on the linearity of the basin margin and the relief of the Oligocene conglomerates in its footwall (Taymaz and Price, 1992). Quaternary deposits are banked unconformably against footwall strata on both margins of the Acıgöl basin (Taymaz and Price, 1992). Geomorphological evidence suggests the greatest rates of subsidence in the Acıgöl basin to be along its southeastern margin, adjacent to the scarp of the Acıgöl fault. The size of the footwall scarp associated with the Acıgöl fault (relief 1100 m) is much greater than that of the Maymundağ fault (relief 780 m) (Price and Scott, 1994). Also, the lake sits against the southeastern margin of the basin (Figure 4). Neogene fluvio-lacustrine deposits and Quaternary alluvium have also a general dip to the ESE further supporting a half-graben geometry with the major fault occurring on the southeastern side of the basin (Figure 5) (Price and Scott, 1994). The tilting of the Neogene deposits northeast of the footwall of

the Maymundağ fault resulted in streams flowing down-dip (Figure 4). The model of a continental half-graben basin with interior drainage (tectono-sedimentary facies model A of Leeder and Gawthorpe, 1987) closely approximates the present situation of the Acıgöl basin. On the satellite images, the playa fringes around the lake border can be seen (Figure 4).

As the limestone ridge erodes, the debris builds up along the base of the mountain as an apron of scree. These scree cones typically reach a similar height along the whole length of the fault ridge. This is clearly observed along an active normal fault scarp in the Lake Eğirdir area (Figures 1 and 6). The southern part of Lake Eğirdir is controlled by a NE-SW trending active normal fault, exposing limestone in its footwall (Glover and Robertson, 1998). The tectonic grabens hosting the lake were probably formed in Late Pliocene time (Nemec and Kazancı, 1999).

The N-S trending **Kovada graben** (Figure 1) and sub-parallel lineaments also clearly bear the geomorphological features diagnostic for normal faults in hard limestone (Goldsworthy and Jackson, 2000) The margins of the graben are clearly identified on the satellite imagery (Figure 7).

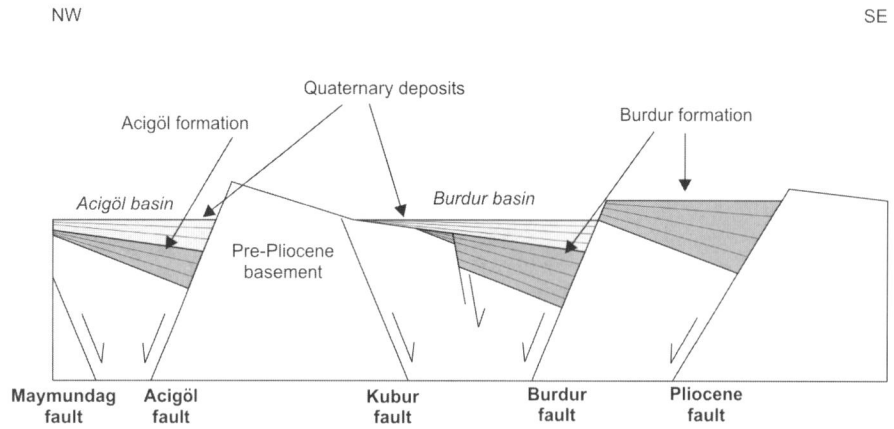

Figure 5: Simplified geological cross-section across the eastern part of the Burdur graben system (after Price and Scott, 1991, 1994). Quaternary deposits in light gray, Pliocene deposits in dark gray.

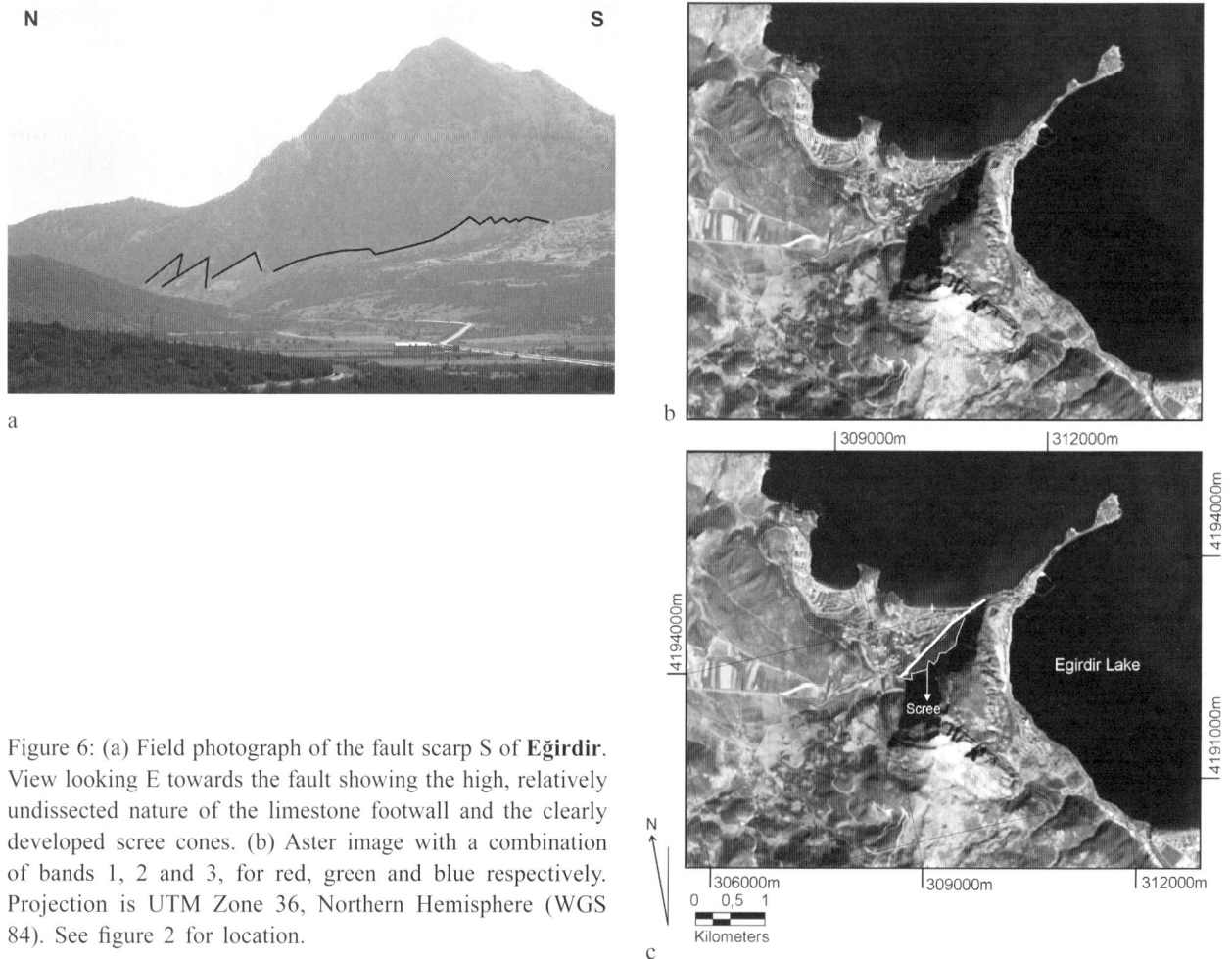

Figure 6: (a) Field photograph of the fault scarp S of **Eğirdir**. View looking E towards the fault showing the high, relatively undissected nature of the limestone footwall and the clearly developed scree cones. (b) Aster image with a combination of bands 1, 2 and 3, for red, green and blue respectively. Projection is UTM Zone 36, Northern Hemisphere (WGS 84). See figure 2 for location.

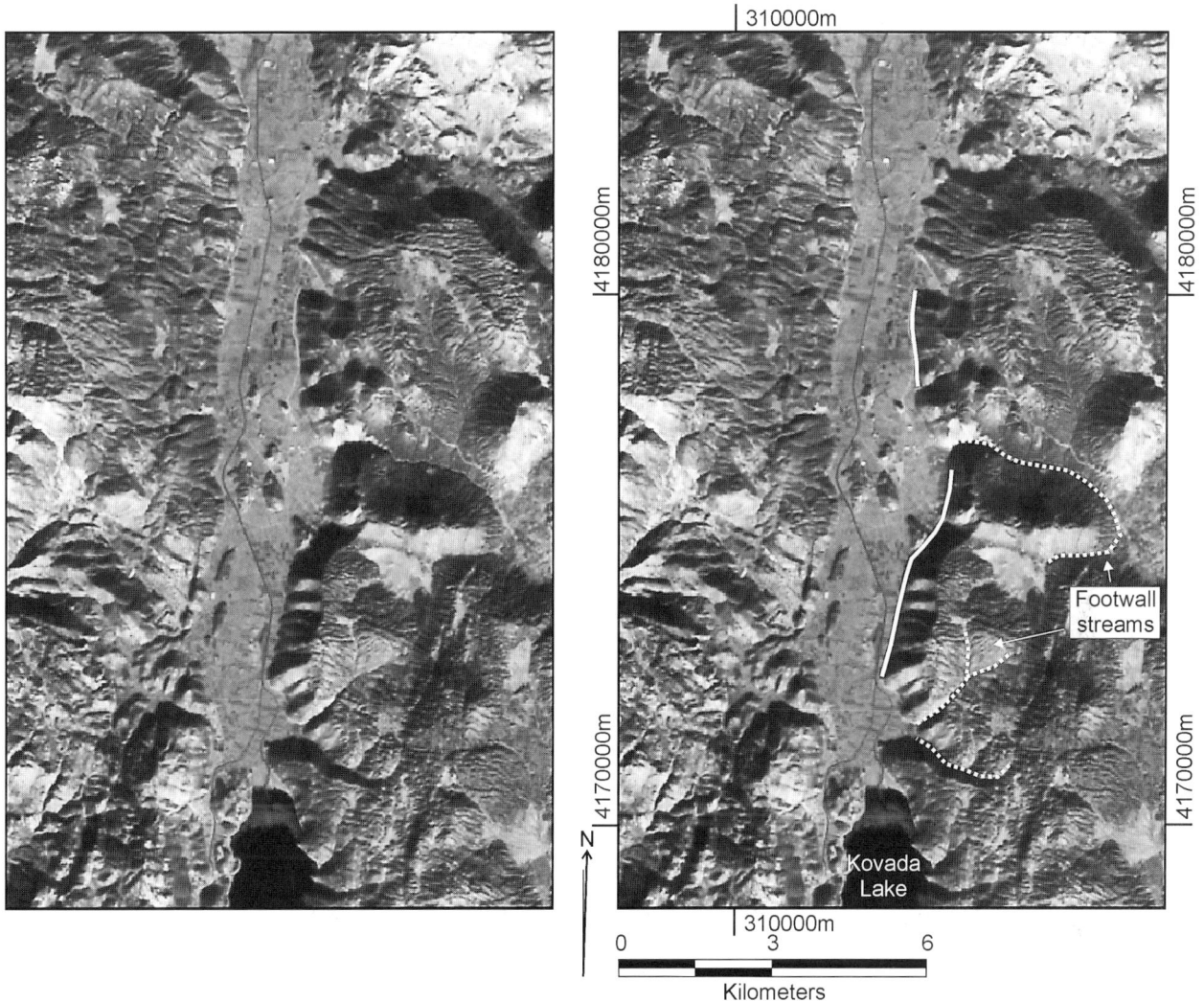

Figure 7: Landsat 7 Enhanced Thematic Mapper + image with a combination of bands 4, 5 and 7 for red, green and blue respectively, of the **Kovada graben**, showing the trace of some fault segments of the eastern graben margin and to some extent the control of major drainage systems by the fault segmentation. Projection is UTM Zone 36, Northern Hemisphere (WGS 84). See figure 2 for location.

However, most fault scarps are markedly eroded, with little evidence of active faulting (Glover and Robertson, 1998). This advanced degradation of fault planes in the Kovada graben is most likely the reason why the diagnostic features of active normal faulting are not observed. This means that the Kovada graben system is maybe no longer active. This conclusion is corroborated by an extensive paleostress study of the region (Verhaert et al., 2006) inferring the fading influence of the 'Kovada stress regime' (dominant E-W extension) at the expense of the 'Burdur stress regime' (dominant NW-SE extension).

The NW-SE trending, SW-dipping **Dinar fault** is about 75 km long, is formed by en-echelon segments, and is a predominantly normal fault separating Tertiary rocks in the NE from unconsolidated Quaternary deposits in the SW (Eyidoğan and Barka, 1996; Koral, 2000) (Figures 1 and 8). The 01.10.1995 Dinar earthquake (Ms 6.2) showed that this fault is still active. The major fault plane cuts through Mesozoic limestone (Temiz et al., 1997). It was initiated after the Aksu thrust, i.e. during Pliocene times, and has been reactivated several times (old slope breccia has been affected) (Temiz et al., 1997). Using the total displacement in trenches perpendicular to the 1995 rupture, a slip rate of about 1 mm/yr has been estimated for the Dinar fault (Altunel et al., 1999). Observations from these trenches suggest that the return period for large earthquakes in the Dinar area is about 1200-2000 yr.

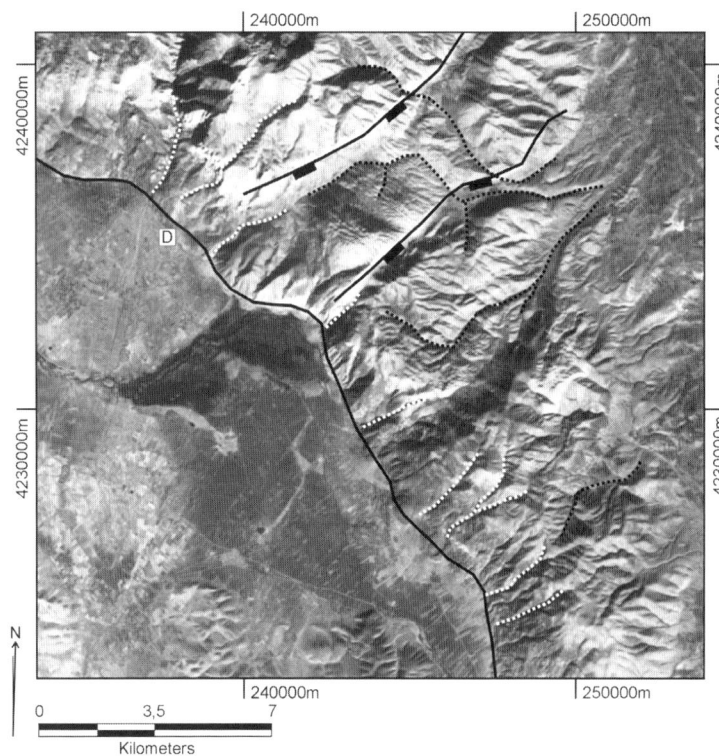

Figure 8: Landsat 7 Enhanced Thematic Mapper + image with a combination of bands 4, 5 and 7 for red, green and blue respectively, of the area NW of Dinar, showing the trace of part of the **Dinar fault** (D), two NE-SW trending faults (Temiz *et al.*, 1997), and the major drainage systems flowing towards (white) and away (black) of the Dinar fault scarp. The footwall in the southwestern part is more dissected since it is composed of Oligocene conglomerates (Temiz *et al.*, 1997). The NE-SW trending faults are older than the Dinar fault since they are truncated by the latter. Projection is UTM Zone 36, Northern Hemisphere (WGS 84). See figure 2 for location.

The NE-SW trending **Hoyran basin-bounding faults** control the position and shape of the northern part of Lake Eğirdir (Bozkurt, 2001) (Figures 1 and 9). The footwall of the northern basin-bounding faults is composed of Eocene flysch, while the footwall of the southern basin-bounding faults is composed of limestone (Yagmurlu et al., 1997). This difference of footwall lithology can be observed on the satellite image since the southern border fault is defined by undissected slopes, while the northern fault is much more dissected and resembles faults in Neogene sediments (Figure 9).

The NNE-SSW trending and ESE-dipping **Kayaaltı fault** (Price and Scott, 1994) is a normal fault separating basement limestone in the NW and Pliocene sediments in the SE (Figures 1 and 10). Price and Scott (1994) do not attribute any Quaternary activity to this fault but define it as a Pliocene fault. The Kayaaltı fault, south of Kayaaltı can according to the remote sensing imagery be followed northwards, separating Pliocene lake deposits in its footwall from Quaternary alluvium in the hanging wall. The footwall of the unnamed fault is made of Mesozoic limestone, ophiolitic mélange and olistostrome. The major drainage systems flow axially along these faults. The Ak Çayı flows from the hanging wall of the Kayaaltı fault towards its footwall, suggesting higher rates of subsidence in the area west of the fault, i.e. on the Burdur fault, than on the Kayaaltı fault itself. This supports that fault activity in Quaternary times was controlled by the Burdur fault and that possibly fault activity stopped in Quaternary times on the Kayaaltı fault.

5.2. Normal faults in less-resistant lithology – Neogene sediments

The segmented **Burdur fault** bounds the southeastern margin of the Lake Burdur, which formed the western boundary of Hellenistic to Imperial Sagalassos (Figures 1 and 11). The fault strikes NE-SW, dips NW, and has a footwall mainly composed of rapidly eroding Neogene sediments and to a lesser extend composed of Mesozoic limestone and Eo-Oligocene conglomerates (Taymaz and Price, 1992). In 1914 and 1971 earthquakes, respectively Ms 7.0 and Ms 6.2, occurred on the Burdur fault (Ambraseys, 2001). Waveform modeling of the main shock of the latter event by Taymaz and Price (1992) suggested that the slip vector of the fault at the hypocentre plunged at 35° ± 5° towards the NNW. The average slip plunge taken from striations measured on the most reliable slip plane at the surface is 66°. Taymaz and Price (1992) took these observations to indicate that the Burdur fault shallows at depth. The Burdur fault separates the Burdur basin from the high topography to the SE (Figure 11). The fault forms a sharp linear feature

bounding the edge of the plain and is clearly the dominant feature in the morphology. The city of Burdur is situated at the edge of a 20 km long fault scarp of Neogene and Oligocene sediments which trend NE-SW. The Burdur fault shows a curvilinear appearance at Burdur. No explanation has been postulated so far for this curvature. In contrast to the limestone footwall discussed earlier, sub-parallel streams flowing of the fault scarp in Neogene sediments incise into the footwall block giving the ridge a dissected appearance. Streams cross the fault at positions unrelated to its continuity or segmentation, but incision changes abruptly to deposition as the drainage crosses the line of the fault itself. It is this abrupt change along a linear escarpment that is the characteristic feature seen in the topography and satellite images (Figure 11). As streams dissect the range front, they leave narrow wine-glass canyons between truncated spurs with triangular facets, or flat irons (Figure 11d). The drainage divide in the footwall is up to 3 km from the fault itself due to stream-head erosion. Major sediment fans are produced that build out across the valley floor. Their position is not controlled by fault segmentation (Figure 11). In the southwestern continuation of the Burdur fault, the northwestern border of the Tefenni basin, separating Neogene sediments in the NW from Quaternary deposits in the SE, also seems to be fault-controlled as it displays similar characteristics as the Burdur fault (Figure 11b-c). It should be noted that since part of the Burdur fault exposes limestone in its footwall (darker/brown areas near the Tefenni basin in Figure 11b), as discussed previously, the drainage is to some extent controlled by this footwall lithology. The footwall drainage system SE of the Burdur fault segments, north of the Tefenni basin (e.g. Tozyurt D.) on figure 11b, flows around the Burdur fault segments exposing limestone.

On the northwestern side of Lake Burdur, an erosion surface is displaced by about 15 m along the **Kubur fault** (Figure 11), which exposes Eo-Oligocene conglomerates in its footwall (Taymaz and Price, 1992). The abrupt change of the drainage from incision to deposition along a linear scarp, SE and parallel to the Kubur fault, bounding the topography and separating Pliocene lake deposits in the footwall from Quaternary alluvium in the hanging wall, is clearly seen on satellite images (Figure 11a). In the southwestern continuation of the Kubur fault, another major NE-SW trending and SE-dipping normal fault, which exposes Eo-Oligocene conglomerates in its footwall (Senel, 1997a), displays a clear fault scarp (Figure 11a). Quaternary alluvium has a general dip to the ESE supporting a half-graben geometry with the major fault occurring on the southeastern side of the basin (Price and Scott, 1991) (Figure 5). Geomorphological evidence further suggests the greatest rates of subsidence in the Burdur basin to be located along its southeastern

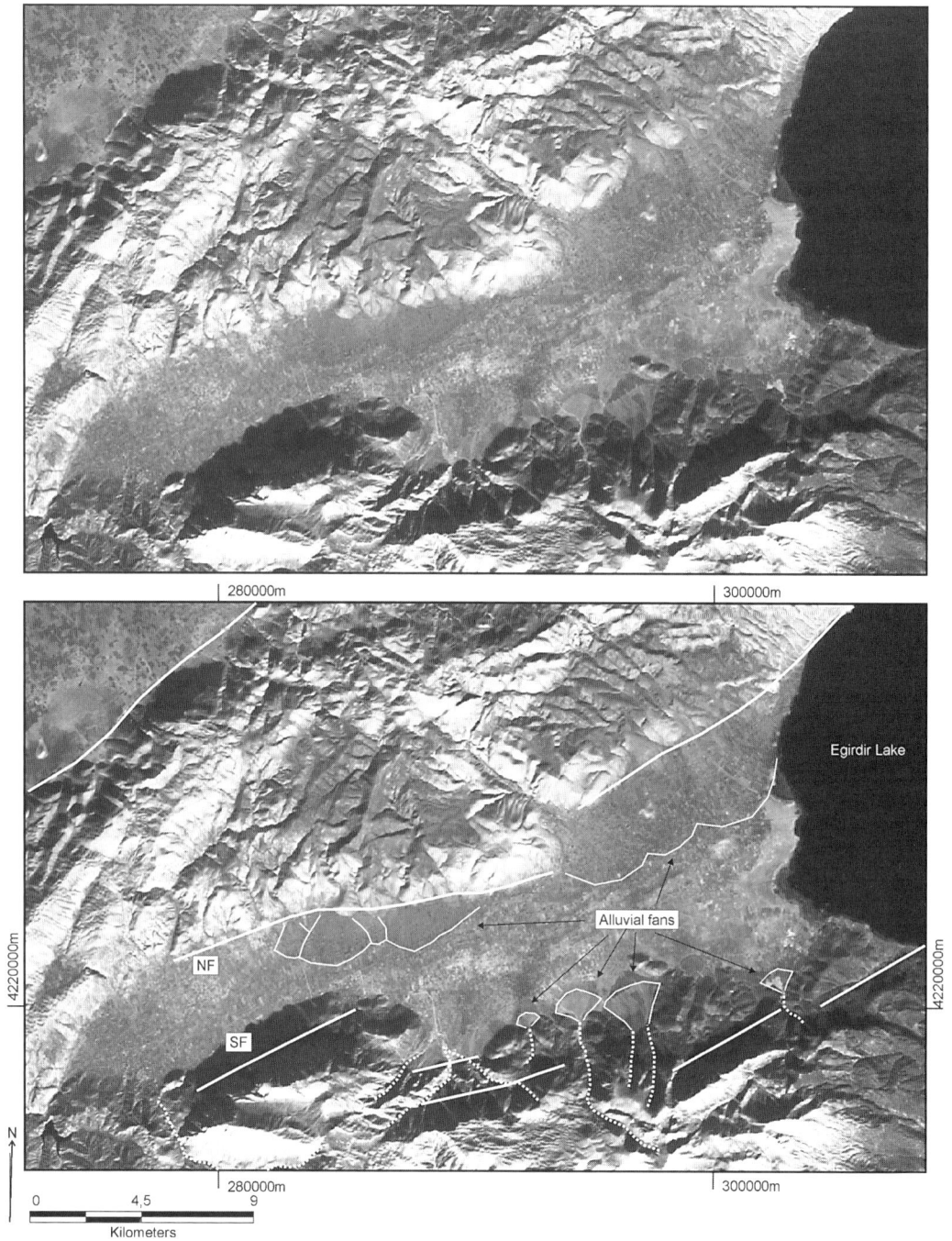

Figure 9: Landsat 7 Enhanced Thematic Mapper + image with a combination of bands 4, 5 and 7 for red, green and blue respectively, of the **Hoyran basin**, showing the trace of the northern basin-bounding fault (NF) and the southern basin-bounding fault (SF), the major drainage systems and alluvial fans. The footwall of the northern basin-bounding fault is composed of Eocene flysch and the drainage and alluvial fans are not related to the fault segmentation, while the footwall of the southern basin-bounding fault is composed of limestone and hence the drainage and alluvial fans is controlled by the fault segmentation. Projection is UTM Zone 36, Northern Hemisphere (WGS 84). See figure 2 for location.

64

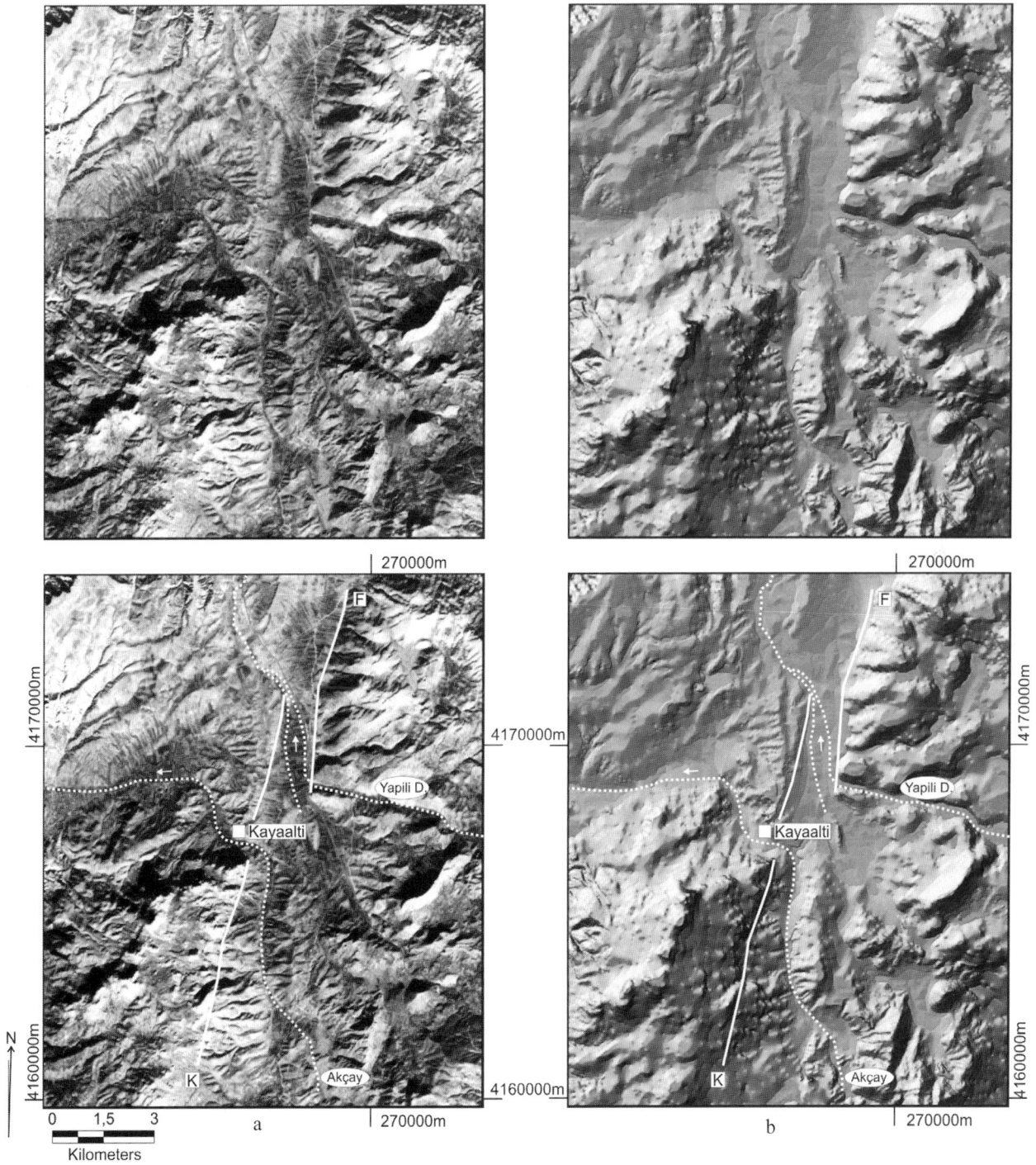

Figure 10: (a) Landsat 7 Enhanced Thematic Mapper + image with a combination of bands 4, 5 and 7 for red, green and blue respectively, of the area near the village of Kayaaltı, along the northern slopes of Mt. Beşparmak, showing the trace of the **Kayaaltı fault** (K) and an unnamed fault (F) (Price and Scott, 1994, Temiz *et al.*, 1997), and the major drainage systems. Projection is UTM Zone 36, Northern Hemisphere (WGS 84). (b) DEM image with shaded relief view of the same area, illuminated from the NW. See figures 2 and 3 for location.

Figure 11: (a) Landsat 7 Enhanced Thematic Mapper + image with a combination of bands 4, 5 and 7 for red, green and blue respectively, of the **Burdur basin**, showing the trace of the Acıgöl (A), Kubur (K) and Burdur (B) faults, the major drainage systems, alluvial fans (a) and drainage divide (dd). Projection is UTM Zone 36, Northern Hemisphere (WGS 84). (b) Landsat 7 Enhanced Thematic Mapper + image with a combination of bands 4, 5 and 7 for red, green and blue respectively, of the southern part of the Burdur basin, showing the trace of the Burdur (B) and Pliocene (Pl) faults and the major drainage systems. Projection is UTM Zone 36, Northern Hemisphere (WGS 84). (c) DEM image of the same area as in (b). (d) Perspective view of the enlarged Landsat TM image with a fusion of bands 4, 5, 7 and 8 of the Burdur fault (see box in a), showing the drainage divide (dd), the footwall uplands, the fault trace (ft) and the associated flat-irons. See figures 2 and 3 for location.

66

margin, adjacent to the scarp of the Burdur fault. The Eren river (Price and Scott, 1991), which flows axially through the basin, possibly displays a migration of active meander channels towards the Burdur fault (Figure 11b-c). The Eren river seems to occupy an asymmetrical meander belt with the abandoned part to the NW of the active channel. The channels of meandering rivers in half-grabens commonly move laterally towards the major basin-boundary fault (e.g. the area of maximum subsidence) (Leeder and Alexander, 1987; Leeder and Gawthorpe, 1987). In contrast to Lake Acıgöl, Lake Burdur occupies, axially, the central part of the Burdur graben and its shape is controlled by alluvial fans (Figure 11a). Major alluvial fans build out across the valley floor in front of the Burdur fault, tending to push the lake away from the fault towards the opposite side of the graben (Paton, 1992) (Figure 11a). Only, where the footwall of the Burdur fault is locally composed of ophiolitic mélange, olistostrome and limestone, Lake Burdur sits closely to the fault as no fans are produced. A combination of the model of a continental half-graben basin with interior drainage and the model of a continental half-graben basin with axial through-drainage (tectono-sedimentary facies model A and B of Leeder and Gawthorpe, 1987) closely approximates the present situation of the Burdur basin. The Quaternary Burdur basin formed towards the end of the Pliocene by dissecting an earlier Neogene basin (Taymaz and Price, 1992). Pliocene basin-bounding faults controlling a single older Pliocene basin became inactive and faulting moved to the NW, effectively dissecting the basin. As most of these faults became buried by the end of the Neogene, they are now poorly exposed and difficult to recognize (Price and Scott, 1994). Hence, these Pliocene faults do not display any clear morphological expression on remote sensing images (Figure 11). However, the location of the Pliocene faults can be inferred based on differences in lithology at both sides of the faults. These faults expose Pliocene fluvio-lacustrine sediments of the Burdur Formation in the hanging wall and basement serpentinite in the footwall (Price and Scott, 1994). The light areas on the satellite image correspond to Neogene strata, whereas the basement rocks are seen as darker areas (Figure 11). Moreover, the strong dissection of the Neogene strata, as a result from their uplift with the footwall block of the Burdur fault, can be depicted on the remote sensing images (Figure 11). Bedding dip profiles in the hanging wall of the Pliocene basin-bounding fault suggests a rotating planar fault geometry (Price and Scott, 1994). The Burdur Formation gently dips towards the SE at 10° to 15° into the NW-dipping basin-controlling fault system (Price and Scott, 1991) (Figure 5), suggesting a half-graben geometry. According to Temiz et al. (1997) the W- to NW-dipping fault NE of Kayaaltı (Figure 10) represents one of the old faults, which marked the border of the primitive Late Miocene-Early Pliocene lacustrine basin. This fault,

considered to be a normal fault, has been reactivated during the Quaternary and travertines of this age have been tilted about 15° towards the W (Temiz et al., 1997). The model of a continental basin with interior drainage (tectono-sedimentary facies model A of Leeder and Gawthorpe, 1987) closely approximates the situation at the time of deposition of the Burdur formation (Price and Scott, 1991).

Less than 1 km E from the village of Karaçal, the Eren river flows from the footwall of the seismogenic Burdur fault into the hanging wall of the Burdur basin (Figure 11b-c). At this site, two cross-sections, which crosscut the Burdur fault, were studied in detail in an excavated canal bedding, which was under construction on August, 6th, 2002 (Figure 12). A range of lithologies is present along the cross-sections. They comprise bedrock of Middle Triassic-Liassic limestone and the Upper Senonian ophiolitic mélange and olistostrome unit. The Pliocene lacustrine Burdur formation and Quaternary alluvium are deposited in the western part of the cross-sections. In the northern cross-section (Figure 12b), two faults crosscut the limestone (031/51 pitch 155; 190/75).[1] A single fault separates the limestone and the ophiolitic mélange (220/50). The Pliocene Burdur formation lies on top of the ophiolitic mélange and is intensely back-tilted at this fault. Both the Burdur formation and the ophiolitic mélange are characterized by an iron-rich red alteration zone at the contact with the fault plane. The ophiolitic mélange itself is intensely fractured and several fault planes could be detected (CI 065/73 pitch 102; CI 152/81 pitch 95; CN 242/80 pitch 45; CN 044/22 pitch 82; CN 161/40 pitch 67; CN 180/40 pitch 40; CN: certainly normal faulting; CI: certainly inverse faulting). To the west, two fault steps could be identified. The first fault step is a topographical step between the Burdur formation to the east and Quaternary alluvium to the west. The second fault step crosscuts the Quaternary alluvium and a height difference of several metres can be observed. In the Quaternary alluvium, synthetic and antithetic normal faults are present (230/70; 040/60). In the southern cross-section (Figure 12c), a dextral strike-slip fault displaces the ophiolitic mélange relative to the limestone (140/65 pitch 160). Another fault plane (180/85) displaces the back-tilted Pliocene Burdur formation relative to the ophiolitic mélange and olistostrome unit. Approximately 400 m south of the canal, both W- and E-dipping normal faults crosscut the back-tilted Pliocene lacustrine Burdur formation (Figure 12a).

---

[1]   Representation of orientation data of planar features uses the 'strike-dip' and 'azimuth' conventions; pitch is counted within the plane starting from strike direction.

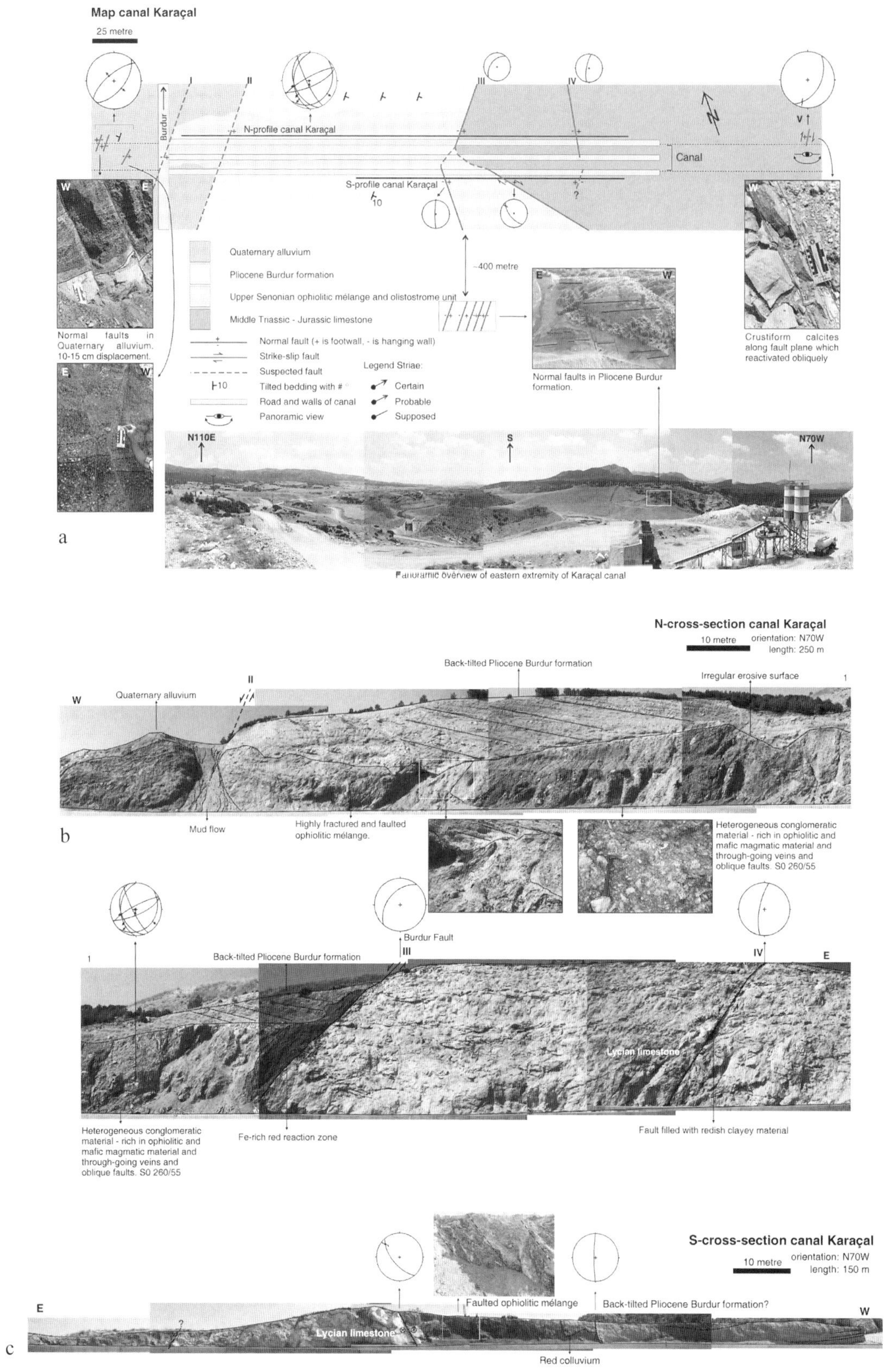

Map canal Karaçal

25 metre

Burdur

N-profile canal Karaçal

Canal

Normal faults in
Quaternary alluvium.
10-15 cm displacement.

S-profile canal Karaçal

~400 metre

Quaternary alluvium

Pliocene Burdur formation

Upper Senonian ophiolitic mélange and olistostrome unit

Middle Triassic - Jurassic limestone

Normal fault (+ is footwall, - is hanging wall)

Strike-slip fault

Suspected fault

Tilted bedding with #

Road and walls of canal

Panoramic view

Legend Striae:

Certain

Probable

Supposed

Normal faults in Pliocene Burdur
formation.

Crustiform   calcites
along fault plane which
reactivated obliquely

N110E   S   N70W

a

Panoramic overview of eastern extremity of Karaçal canal

N-cross-section canal Karaçal

10 metre   orientation: N70W
             length: 250 m

Back-tilted Pliocene Burdur formation

Irregular erosive surface

W

Quaternary alluvium

1

b

Mud flow

Highly fractured and faulted
ophiolitic mélange.

Heterogeneous conglomeratic
material - rich in ophiolitic and
mafic magmatic material and
through-going veins and
oblique faults. S0 260/55

Back-tilted Pliocene Burdur formation

Burdur Fault

1   III   IV   E

Lycian limestone

Heterogeneous conglomeratic
material - rich in ophiolitic and
mafic magmatic material and
through-going veins and
oblique faults. S0 260/55

Fe-rich red reaction zone

Fault filled with redish clayey material

S-cross-section canal Karaçal

10 metre   orientation: N70W
             length: 150 m

Faulted ophiolitic mélange   Back-tilted Pliocene Burdur formation?

E

Lycian limestone

W

c

Red colluvium

Figure 12: (a) Geological map of the Karaçal section (b) Northern Karaçal section. (c) Southern Karaçal section. Stereo-plots of fault data are lower-hemisphere equal-area projections.

68

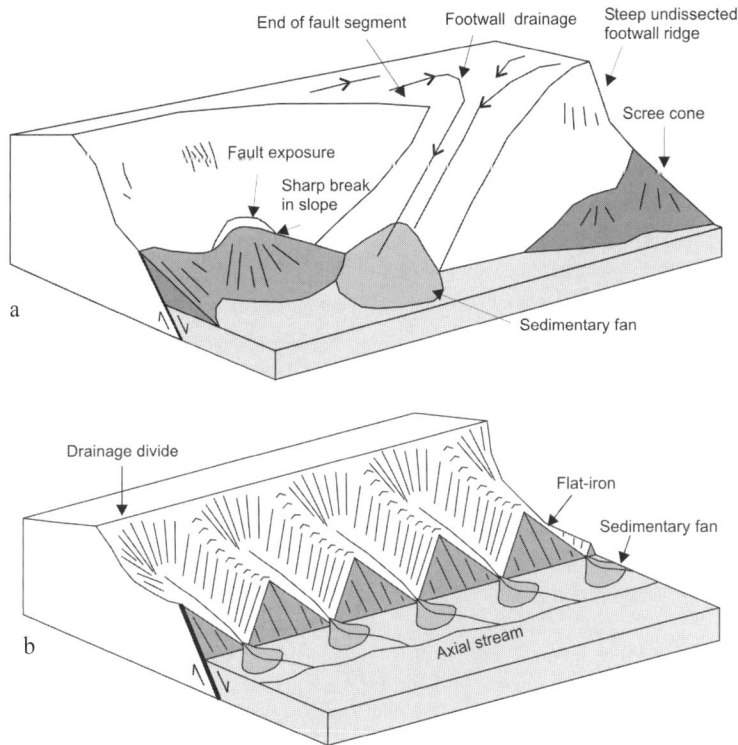

Figure 13: Schematic diagram (not to scale) summarizing the geomorphological features and drainage pattern generated by active normal faulting in (a) resistant lithology, i.e. Mesozoic limestone (after Goldsworthy and Jackson, 2000; Jackson and Leeder, 1994) and (b) less-resistant lithology, i.e. Neogene deposits (after Burbank and Anderson, 2001; Goldsworthy and Jackson, 2000).

A kinematic model is proposed for the different fault movements at Karaçal. The right-lateral oblique slip on the NW-SE trending fault, (140/65 pitch 160) displacing the ophiolitic mélange with respect to the limestone in the southern cross-section, is probably the oldest event, but motion can only be dated as post-Mesozoic. After deposition of the Pliocene Burdur formation, a NW-SE extension caused normal displacement and the back-tilting of this lacustrine formation. The fault plane at the southern cross-section has a slightly different orientation with respect to the overall NE-SW trend in the northern cross-section. This probably is the result of the preferential localisation of the fault plane at the contact between the ophiolitic mélange and the Burdur formation. In the Quaternary deposits, a NW-SE extension is responsible for the faults and probably for the two fault steps in the topography. It has to be stated that the dextral movement on the 140/65 oriented fault plane can also be explained by a NW-SE extension on the fault plane. At Karaçal, a ca. NW-SE general direction of extension characterized the kinematics during Pliocene and Quaternary times (Price and Scott, 1994; Temiz et al., 1997; Verhaert et al., 2006). This regime remains active at the present time as inferred from the focal mechanism of the 12.05.1971 earthquake

(Figure 1). Our observations, moreover, indicate that the Burdur fault is rather complex (cf. southern cross-section) but that nevertheless a good correlation exists between the surface geology and the geomorphological expression of the fault. However, neither a 1914 nor a 1971 surface rupture could be observed.

6. DISCUSSION AND CONCLUSIONS

In summary, the key features associated with normal faults in **resistant lithology**, such as the Mesozoic limestone, are a prominent relatively undissected footwall ridge, exposed fault surfaces along the top of the scree cones, and a footwall drainage controlled by the segmentation of the faults (Figure 13a) (Goldsworthy and Jackson, 2000). By contrast, hanging wall drainage in young sediments is controlled by tilting. The most useful characteristics of faults in **less-resistant lithology**, such as the Neogene sediments, and more in general relatively soft sediments, are the abrupt change of the drainage from incision to deposition along a linear scarp bounding the topography, and the generally roughly linear drainage divide set back by upstream incision hundreds of metres to a few km from the fault (Figure 13b) (Goldsworthy and Jackson, 2000). These stream systems are often more prominent on satellite images and topography than the fault scarp itself. These characteristic features can also be observed on a fault in the footwall of the Dinar fault, NE of Dinar (Figure 14). The most useful characteristic of **half-graben basins** are the relatively low-gradient hanging wall dip-slope with broad alluvial cones and the relatively high-gradient footwall scarp slope, which sources small alluvial fans whose depositional loci occur at the foot of the scarp on the lower hanging wall dip slope (Figure 15) (Leeder and Gawthorpe, 1987; Leeder and Jackson, 1993). Where basement lithology is invariant, footwall catchments are generally smaller, shorter and steeper than those of the hanging wall. As noted previously, large drainage systems frequently take advantage of areas between en-echelon fault terminations so that lager-than average cones may preferentially form in such locations. Basement geology may influence relative catchment size in the footwall block, e.g. larger catchments in more erosion-sensible portions of the footwall uplands. When local climatic conditions allow, permanent or playa lake bodies will form in the basin as close to the locus of maximum subsidence as the footwall-sourced fans allow. Axial rivers react to episodes of tectonic tilting, which influences river migration. Periodic abrupt channel movements, i.e. avulsions, cause the 'low-seeking' channel to persistently reoccupy the axis of maximum subsidence, leaving behind a abandoned meander belt.

As faults are weak zones, rivers tend to follow these lines. Hence, straight segments of a river can coincide with a fault line and the abrupt diversion of the course of a river can be caused by a fault. This is most likely the case along one of the Burdur fault segments where the NW-flowing Bügdüz Çayı, once a 150 m wide braided river forming the major connection between Sagalassos and its estates in the plain of Burdur (Waelkens *et al.*, 2000), makes a sharp 90° bend and flows for several kilometres SW before entering the Burdur basin again after a second 90° bend (Figure 11a).

We focused in this paper on the geomorphological expression of the known active normal faults and their associated basins in the Burdur-Isparta region. These faults display a set of diagnostic characteristics, enabling their identification on remote sensing images. The key features associated with normal faults in hard limestone turn out to be different than those associated with faults in relatively soft sediments. Moreover, the region is characterized by an extensional half-graben/tilt-block system. The predictable surface effects of such a system can provide supplementary criteria for the identification of active normal faults. All features discussed are well-known characteristics described in literature for active normal faults in the Basin and Range (western United Sates) and the Aegean region (Goldsworthy and Jackson, 2000; Leeder and Gawthorpe, 1987; Leeder and Jackson, 1993). These diagnostic criteria with respect to the geomorphology and drainage patterns of the known active normal faults will subsequently be used as a guideline in a remote sensing analysis of the direct surroundings of the ancient city of Sagalassos to identify previously unknown active normal faults (Similox-Tohon *et al.*, this volume b). The presence of such (a) fault(s) is indeed suggested by archaeoseismological studies (Sintubin *et al.*, 2003). These faults may potentially be hazardous and are possible candidates to be the causative fault(s) for the Sagalassos earthquake(s) in the 6th to 7th century AD (Waelkens *et al.*, 2000a).

7. ACKNOWLEDGMENTS

A version of this article in full colour is available from the authors. The research was supported by the Belgian Programme on Interuniversitary Poles of Attraction (IAP V/9) and the Research Fund of the K.U.Leuven (BOF-GOA02/2). The satellite images were provided by Prof. Dr. E. Paulissen (K.U.Leuven). Processing using ENVI was performed at the Royal Museum of Central Africa at Tervuren (Belgium). We thank the Akdeniz University of Antalya for the opportunity to study the aerial photographs. Manuel Sintubin is Research Professor of the Research Fund of the K.U.Leuven. Marc Waelkens, the excavation director of the archaeological site of Sagalassos, is acknowledged for enabling our research in and around the archaeological site. We are grateful to Patrick Degryse for taking this initiative and giving us the opportunity to publish results of our research in SW Turkey.

8. REFERENCES

Altunel, E., Barka, A.A. and Akyüz, S. (1999) Palaeoseismicity of the Dinar fault, SW Turkey, *Terra Nova* 11: 297-302.

Ambraseys, N.N. (2001) Reassessment of earthquakes, 1900-1999, in the Eastern Mediterranean and the Middle East, *Geophysical Journal International* 145: 471-485.

Ambraseys, N.N. and Jackson, J.A. (1998) Faulting associated with historical and recent earthquakes in the eastern Mediterranean region, *Geophysical Journal International* 133: 390-406.

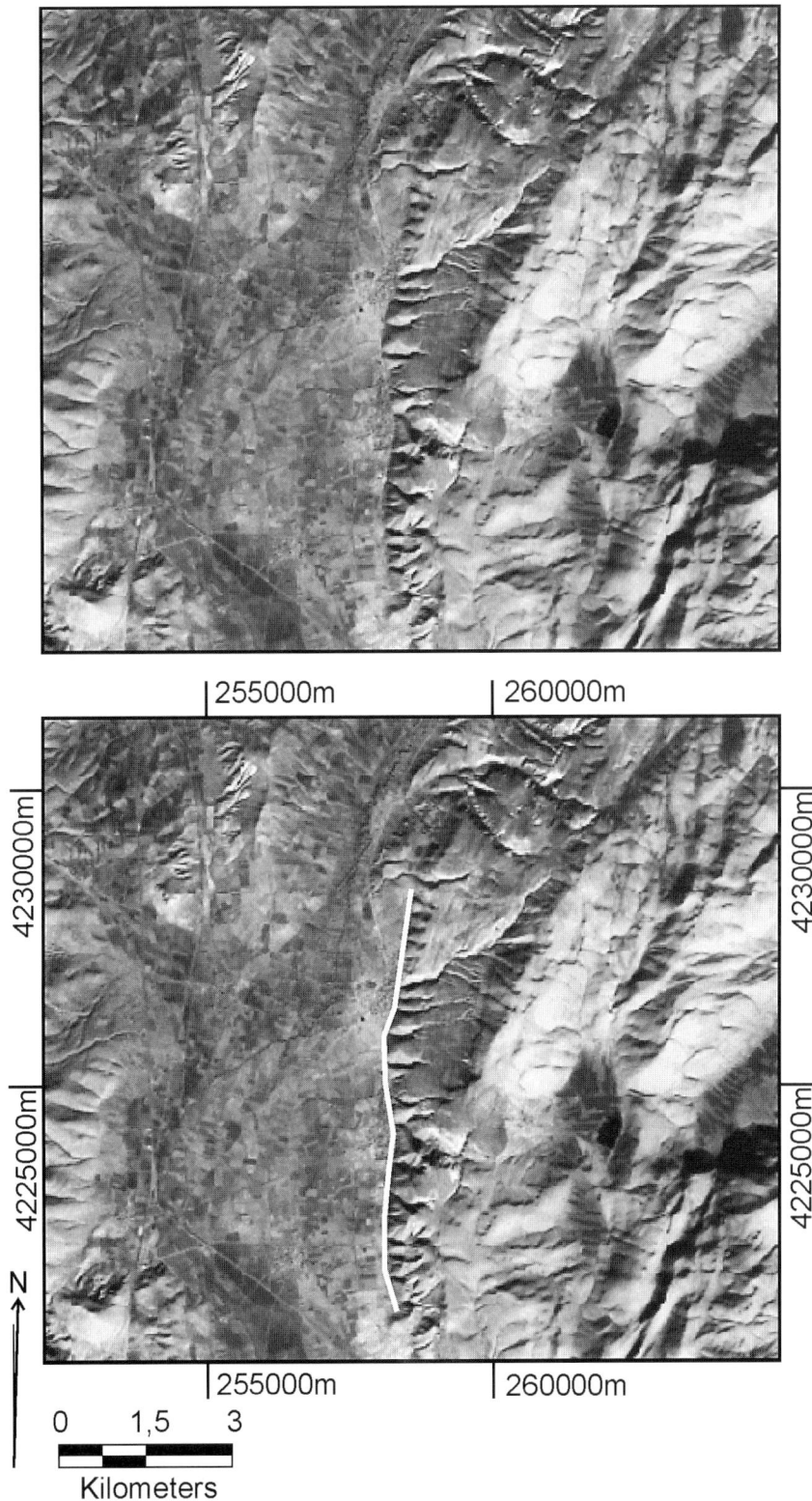

Figure 14: Landsat 7 Enhanced Thematic Mapper + image with a combination of bands 4, 5 and 7 for red, green and blue respectively, of the footwall area of the Dinar fault, NE of **Dinar**. It shows the abrupt change of the drainage from incision to deposition along a linear N-S trending scarp bounding a topography typical for active normal faults in a less-resistant lithology. Projection is UTM Zone 36, Northern Hemisphere (WGS 84). See figure 2 for location.

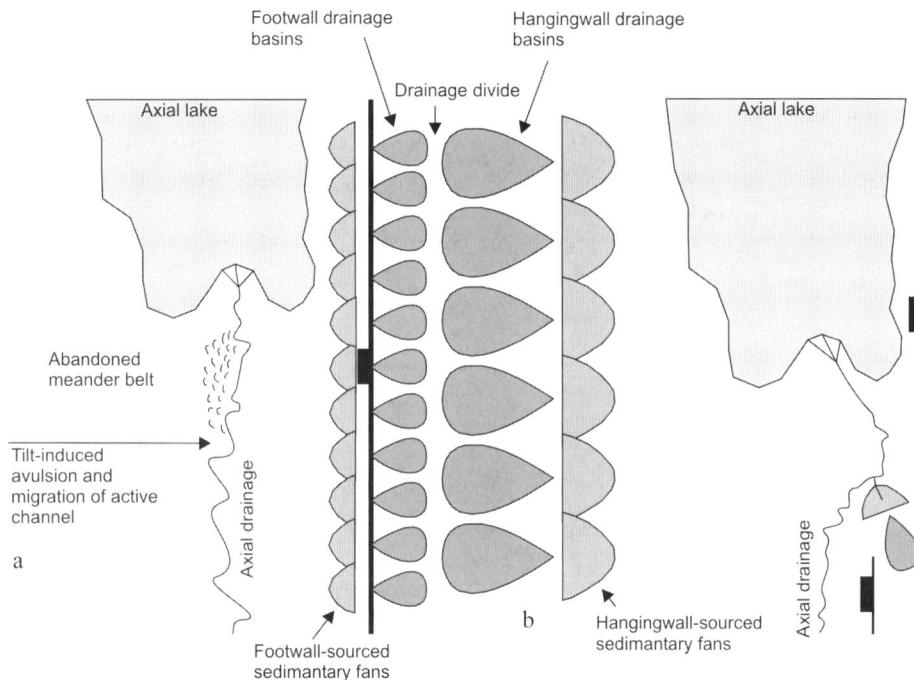

Figure 15: Idealized schematic diagram summarizing the characteristics related to extensional half-graben basins (modified after Leeder and Jackson, 1993). (a) Normal fault developing in resistant lithology. (b) Normal fault developing in less-resistant lithology.

BARKA, A.A. and REILINGER, R. (1997) Active tectonics of the eastern Mediterranean region: deduced from GPS, neotectonics and seismicity data, *Annali di Geofisica* 40: 587-610.

BARKA, A.A., REILINGER, R., SAROGLU, F. and SENGÖR, A.M.C. (1995) The Isparta Angle: Its importance in the neotectonics of the Eastern Mediterranean Region, *International Earth Sciences Colloqium on the Aegean Region* 1: 3-17.

BLUMENTHAL, M.M. (1963) Le système structural du Taurus sud Anatolien, *Mémoire de la Société Géologique de France* 1(2): 611-662.

BOZKURT, E. (2001) Neotectonics of Turkey – a synthesis, *Geodinamica Acta* 14: 3-30.

BURBANK, D.W. and ANDERSON, R.S. (2001) *Tectonic Geomorphology*, Blackwell Science, Malden, Massachusetts.

EYIDOĞAN, H. and BARKA, A.A. (1996) The 1 October 1995 Dinar earthquake, SW Turkey, *Terra Nova* 8: 479-485.

GLOVER, C. and ROBERTSON, A.H.F. (1998) Neotectonic intersection of the Aegean and Cyprus tectonic arcs: extensional and strike-slip faulting in the Isparta Angle, SW Turkey, *Tectonophysics* 298: 103-132.

GOLDSWORTHY, M. and JACKSON, J. (2000) Active normal fault evolution in Greece revealed by geomorphology and drainage patterns, *Journal of the Geological Society, London* 157: 967-981.

GOLDSWORTHY, M. and JACKSON, J. (2001) Migration of activity within normal faults systems: examples from the Quaternary of mainland Greece, *Journal of Structural Geology* 23: 489-506.

JACKSON, J.A. and LEEDER, M.R. (1994) Drainage systems and the development of normal faults: an example from Pleasant Valley, Nevada, *Journal of Structural Geology* 16: 1041-1059.

KORAL, H. (2000) Surface rupture and rupture mechanism of the October 1, 1995 (M_w = 6.2) Dinar earthquake, SW Turkey, *Tectonophysics* 327: 15-24.

LEEDER, M.R. and ALEXANDER, J. (1987) The origin and tectonic significance of asymmetrical meander-belts, *Sedimentology* 34: 217-226.

LEEDER, M.R. and GAWTHORPE, R.L. (1987) Sedimentary models for extensional tilt-block/half-graben basins, In: M.P. COWARD, J.F. DEWEY and P.L. HANCOCK (eds.) *Continental Extensional Tectonics, Special Publications 28*. Geological Society, London: 139-152.

LEEDER, M.R. and JACKSON, J.A. (1993) The interaction between normal faulting drainage in active extensional basins, with examples from the western United States and central Greece, *Basin Research* 5: 79-102.

LEEDER, M.R., SEGER, M.J. and STARK, C.P. (1991) Sedimentation and tectonic geomorphology adjacent to major active and inactive normal faults, southern Greece, *Journal of the Geological Society, London* 148: 331-343.

MICHETTI, A.M., AUDEMARD M., F.A. and MARCO, S. (2005) Future trends in paleoseismology: Integrated study of the seismic landscape as a vital tool in seismic hazard analyses, *Tectonophysics* 408: 3-21.

MICHETTI, A.M. and HANCOCK, P.L. (1997) Paleoseismology: understanding past earthquakes using Quaternary geology, *Journal of Geodynamics* 24: 3-10.

NEMEC, W. and KAZANCI, N. (1999) Quaternary colluvium in west-central Anatolia: sedimentary facies and palaeo-climatic significance, *Sedimentology* 46: 139-170.

PATON, S. (1992) Active normal faulting, drainage patterns and sedimentation in southwestern Turkey, *Journal of the Geological Society, London* 149: 1031-1044.

PRICE, S.P. and SCOTT, B. (1991) Pliocene Burdur basin, SW Turkey: tectonics, seismicity and sedimentation, *Journal of the Geological Society, London* 148: 345-354.

PRICE, S.P. and SCOTT, B. (1994) Fault-block rotations at the edge of a zone of continental extension: southwest Turkey, *Journal of Structural Geology* 16(3): 381-392.

ROBERTS, S. and JACKSON, J.A. (1991) Active normal faulting in central Greece: an overview, In: A.M. ROBERTS, G. YIELDING and B. FREEMAN (eds.) *The Geometry of Normal Faults, Special Publications 56.* Geological Society, London: 125-142.

ROBERTSON, A.H.F. (1993) Mesozoic-Tertiary sedimentary and tectonic evolution of Neotethyan carbonate platforms, margins and small ocean basins in the Antalya Complex, southwest Turkey, *Spec. Publs Int. Ass. Sediment.* 20: 415-465.

SENEL, M. (1997a) *1:100 000 geological map of the Isparta – J10 Quadrangle,* General Directorate of Mineral Research and Exploration, Ankara.

SENEL, M. (1997b) *1:250 000 geological maps of Turkey – Isparta No. 4,* General Directorate of Mineral Research and Exploration, Ankara.

SIMILOX-TOHON, D., FERNANDEZ-ALONSO, M., VANNESTE, K., WAELKENS, M., MUCHEZ, P. and SINTUBIN, M. (this volume b) Identifying active normal faults in the Burdur-Isparta region (SW Turkey): remote sensing, surface geology and near-surface geophysics, In: P. DEGRYSE and M. WAELKENS (eds.) *Sagalassos VI. Geo- and Bio-Archaeology at Sagalassos and in its Territory,* Leuven University Press, Leuven: 75-130.

SIMILOX-TOHON, D., FERNANDEZ-ALONSO, M., VANNESTE, K., WAELKENS, M., MUCHEZ, P. and SINTUBIN, M. (this volume c) An integrated neotectonic study of the Çanaklı basin (SW Turkey): remote sensing, surface geology and near-surface geophysics, In: P. DEGRYSE and M. WAELKENS (eds.) *Sagalassos VI. Geo- and Bio-Archaeology at*

Sagalassos and in its Territory, Leuven University Press, Leuven: 131-153.

SINTUBIN, M., MUCHEZ, P., SIMILOX-TOHON, D., VERHAERT, G., PAULISSEN, E. and WAELKENS, M. (2003) Seismic catastrophes at the ancient city of Sagalassos (SW Turkey) and their implications for the seismotectonics in the Burdur-Isparta area, *Geological Journal* 38: 359-374.

STEWART, I.S. and HANCOCK, P.L. (1991) Scales of structural heterogeneity within neotectonic normal fault zones in the Aegean region, *Journal of Structural Geology* 13(2): 191-204.

STEWART, I.S. and HANCOCK, P.L. (1994) Neotectonics, In: P.L. HANCOCK (ed.) *Continental Deformation,* Pergamon Press, Oxford: 370-409.

STIROS, S.C. (1996) Identification of earthquakes from archaeological data: methodology, criteria and limitations, In: S.C. STIROS and R.E. JONES (eds.), *Archaeoseismology, Fitch Laboratory Occasional Paper 7,* Institute of Geology and Mineral Exploration and The British Scholl at Athens, Athens: 129-152.

TAYMAZ, T. and PRICE, S.P. (1992) The 1971 May 12 Burdur earthquake sequence, SW Turkey: a synthesis of seismological observations, *Geophysical Journal International* 108: 589-603.

TEMIZ, H., POISSON, A., ANDRIEUX, J. and BARKA, A.A. (1997) Kinematics of the Plio-Quaternary Burdur-Dinar cross-fault system in SW Anatolia (Turkey), *Annales Tectonicae* 11: 102-113.

TEN VEEN, J.H. (2004) Extension of Hellenic forearc shear zones in SW Turkey: the Pliocene-quaternary deformation of the Ersen Çayı Basin, *Journal of Geodynamics* 37(2): 181-204.

TEN VEEN, J.H. and KLEINSPEHN, K.L. (2002) Geodynamics along an increasingly curved convergent plate margin: Late Miocene-Pleistocene Rhodes, Greece, *Tectonics* 21(3), 10.1029/2001TC001287.

TEN VEEN, J.H. and KLEINSPEHN, K.L. (2003) Incipient continental collision and plate-boundary curvature: Late Pliocene-Holocene transtensional Hellenic forearc, Crete, Greece, *Journal of the Geological Society, London* 160: 161-181.

VERHAERT, G., SIMILOX-TOHON, D., VANDYCKE, S., SINTUBIN, M. and MUCHEZ, P. (2006) Different stress states in the Burdur-Isparta region (SW Turkey) since Late Miocene times: a reflection of a transient stress regime, *Journal of Structural Geology* 28: 1067-1083.

WAELKENS, M., SINTUBIN, M., MUCHEZ, P. and PAULISSEN, E. (2000a) Archeological, geomorphological and geological evidence for a major earthquake at Sagalassos (SW Turkey) around the middle of the seventh century AD, In: W.J. McGUIRE, D.R. GRIFFITHS, P.L. HANCOCK and

I.S. Stewart (eds.) *The Archaeology of Geological Catastrophes, Special Publications 171*. Geological Society, London: 373-383.

Yagmurlu, F., Savaşçın, Y. and Ergün, M. (1997) Relation of Alkaline Volcanism and Active Tectonism within the Evolution of the Isparta Angle, SW Turkey, *Journal of Geology* 105: 717-728.

IDENTIFYING ACTIVE NORMAL FAULTS IN THE BURDUR-ISPARTA REGION (SW TURKEY): REMOTE SENSING, SURFACE GEOLOGY AND NEAR-SURFACE GEOPHYSICS

Dominique SIMILOX-TOHON, Max FERNANDEZ-ALONSO, Kris VANNESTE, Marc WAELKENS, Philippe MUCHEZ and Manuel SINTUBIN

1. INTRODUCTION

The Lake Region in SW Turkey, centred on the cities of Burdur and Isparta, is situated in the first-degree seismic hazard zone (Global Seismic Hazard Assessment Program – www.seismo.ethz.ch/GSHAP/), inferring a relatively high risk for major earthquakes. The wider Burdur-Isparta region has indeed been struck by a number of large damaging earthquakes in the last century. Based on archaeological evidence (Waelkens *et al.*, 2000) at the archaeological site of Sagalassos, situated some 10 km SSW of Isparta and some 20 km ESE of Burdur, it could be inferred that the ancient city has been struck by a number of earthquakes during its history. The last earthquake(s), during the late Roman and early Byzantine periods (6th to 7th Century AD), turned out to have caused major damage to the city. Based on archaeoseismological evidence (type of damage, extensive and widespread nature of damage) (Sintubin *et al.*, 2003), an intensity of at least VIII (MSK) is attributed to these earthquakes. Therefore, an epicentre in the direct proximity of the ancient city, i.e. within a radius of less than 20 km, should be considered (cf. Stiros, 1996). Within this radius around the archaeological site of Sagalassos no active fault is, however, known to date (Figure 1).

A first step in the search for the causative fault(s) for the Sagalassos earthquake(s) is a remote sensing analysis in order to identify all structures in the wider surroundings of Sagalassos that may be active faults. Remote Sensing involves gathering data and information from the earth by detecting and measuring radiation, particles, and fields associated with objects located beyond the immediate vicinity of the sensor device(s). We want to gather information about active faults in the Burdur-Isparta area, particularly large ones capable of generating substantial earthquakes (≥ Ms 5.5), using satellite images, aerial photographs and a digital elevation model (DEM). The remote sensing analysis should help us to identify previously unknown active faults within a radius of 20 km of the archaeological site of Sagalassos. It is therefore not our goal to make a detailed cartography of all the faults in the target area but only to describe the major structures which may represent major active faults, relevant for the seismotectonics in the Burdur-Isparta area.

We emphasise that we are concerned only with large active faults, defined as those with dimensions comparable to or greater than the thickness of the seismogenic upper crust. In the Aegean region these are normal fault segments that typically reach maximum lengths of 15 to 20 km, extend to depths of 10 to 15 km, and generate earthquakes of magnitude (Ms) 6.0 to 6.8 (Goldsworthy and Jackson, 2000). An important feature of normal faults on this scale is that they produce vertical motions in their footwalls and hanging walls, i.e. tilting, that die away from the surface rupture over distances of typically 10 to 15 km from the fault, i.e. measured normal to the fault strike (Goldsworthy and Jackson, 2000). These normal faults, moreover, dominated the landscape as mountain-range fronts (Figure 2) and are thus obvious features to be recognized in a remote sensing analysis.

Therefore, the geomorphology and drainage patterns of the known major active faults in the Burdur-Isparta area as seen on remote sensing images have been analyzed first (Similox-Tohon *et al.*, this volume a). The diagnostic criteria with respect to the geomorphology and drainage patterns of these active normal faults are now used as a guideline in a remote sensing analysis of the direct surroundings of the archaeological site of Sagalassos to identify previously unknown active normal faults. The presence of such (a) fault(s) is indeed suggested by the archaeoseismological studies (Sintubin *et al.*, 2003). These faults may potentially be hazardous and are possible candidates to be the causative fault(s) for the Sagalassos earthquake(s) in the 6th to 7th century AD (Waelkens *et al.*, 2000).

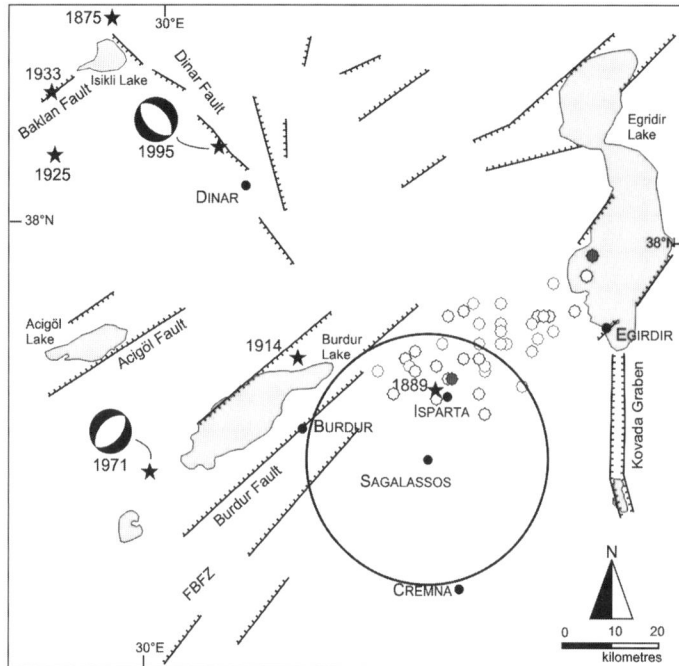

Figure 1: Simplified active fault map of the region of the lakes centred on Burdur and Isparta at the northeastern extremity of the Fethiye-Burdur fault zone (FBFZ) (after Bozkurt, 2001; Eyidoğan and Barka, 1996; Senel, 1997), with indication of the epicentres of recent large earthquakes (stars), available focal mechanisms (after Eyidoğan and Barka, 1996; Taymaz and Price, 1992) and the microseismic activity in the Isparta-Eğirdir region (white circles are Md 3.0-3.9 events; gray circles are Md 4.0-4.9 events) (KOERI, 2002). Also marked is the target area within a radius of 20 km around the archaeological site of Sagalassos.

Figure 2: The Gokova mountain-range front (SW Turkey), an impressive example of a typical 'seismic landscape' (sensu Michetti and Hancock, 1997) related to an Aegean-type active normal fault, showing a prominent relatively undissected footwall ridge.

2. GEODYNAMIC SETTING

The Burdur-Isparta region is situated at the northeastern extremity of the **Fethiye-Burdur fault zone** (FBFZ). This NE-SW trending tectonic feature, running from Fethiye to Burdur, is commonly considered to be the northeastern on-land continuation of the left-lateral transform system of the Pliny-Strabo trench off the coast of Rhodes, linking it with the Hellenic arc (Barka *et al.*, 1995; Bozkurt, 2001; ten Veen, 2004; ten Veen and Kleinspehn, 2002; 2003). Left-lateral motion of the FBFZ is corroborated with GPS measurements showing a movement of at least 15 mm/yr (Barka and Reilinger, 1997). This has, however, not been demonstrated by fault plane solutions of recent earthquakes in the Burdur-Isparta region (Figure 1).

The current geodynamic setting of the Burdur-Isparta region started in Late Miocene to Early Pliocene times (ca. 5 Ma) (Bozkurt, 2001). The extensional regime is expressed by three NE-SW trending half-graben systems (Figure 1), bounded to the southeast by major NW dipping, slightly listric normal faults, the **Burdur**, **Acıgöl** and **Baklan faults** (Price and Scott, 1991; 1994). Quaternary basins developed within these graben depressions, occupying the central part of wider, fault-bounded Pliocene basins (Price and Scott, 1991). To the northeast, the graben system terminates against the NW-SE trending **Dinar fault**.

Although it is generally accepted that the **Burdur graben system** is located at the diffuse eastern edge of the Aegean-Western Anatolian extensional province (Glover and Robertson, 1998), tectonic interpretations differ. Glover and Robertson (1998) consider the Burdur area as part of the N-S trending right-lateral Isparta angle suture zone. Clockwise rotation of fault blocks within this right-lateral shear zone generated NE-SW trending left-lateral faults (Price and Scott, 1994). Barka *et al.* (1995) locate the Burdur graben system at the northeastern extremity of the left-lateral FBFZ. The Dinar fault is considered as a breakaway fault in this graben system.

East of the city of Isparta, the neotectonic setting of the apex of the Isparta angle (Blumenthal, 1963) is dominated by the N-S trending **Kovada graben** and subparallel lineaments (Glover and Robertson, 1998) (Figure 1). The Kovada graben is 25 km long and 2 to 3 km wide, running south from Eğirdir lake, with a small Kovada lake filling the southern end of the graben. Subordinate Quaternary N-S trending faults are mapped to the east of the Kovada graben over a distance of more than 20 km (Robertson, 1993), showing that extensional deformation is affecting a wider area. The graben itself is rather symmetrical, bounded by prominent faults on both sides, and developed in Mesozoic carbonates.

There is, however, little evidence of active faulting (Glover and Robertson, 1998).

In recent history, seismic activity on a number of these faults has been recorded. The Burdur 1914 earthquake (Ms 7.0) and the Burdur 1971 earthquake (Ms 6.2) occurred on the Burdur fault (Ambraseys and Jackson, 1998; Eyidoğan and Barka, 1996) (Figure 1). A surface rupture of 23 km with a maximum offset of 150 cm (Ambraseys and Jackson, 1998) has been observed for the first event, while the second event ruptured the surface over 4 km with a maximum displacement of 30 cm (Ambraseys and Jackson, 1998). Fault-plane solution of the 1971 earthquake indicates pure normal faulting (Eyidoğan and Barka, 1996; Taymaz and Price, 1992). The Dinar 1933 earthquake (Ms 5.8) is considered to have occurred on the Baklan fault (Eyidoğan and Barka, 1996; Koral, 2000) (Figure 1). Eyidoğan and Barka (1996) also consider that the Dinar 1925 (Md 6.0) earthquake occurred on the Baklan fault, although its epicentre is located in the footwall of this fault. The Dinar 1995 earthquake (Ms 6.2) occurred on the Dinar fault (Ambraseys and Jackson, 1998) (Figure 1). The total length of surface rupture was 10 km with a maximum vertical offset of 50 cm (Altunel *et al.*, 1999) and a maximum lateral offset of 10 cm (Ambraseys and Jackson, 1998). Fault-plane solution indicates pure normal faulting (Eyidoğan and Barka, 1996; Taymaz and Price, 1992).

A medium magnitude earthquake has furthermore been reported in 1889 to have caused local damage concentrated at Isparta, located near Sagalassos on the other side of the Ağlasun Dağları mountains, and the nearby village of Deregümü, a few km northwest of Isparta (Ambraseys, pers. comm., 2002). It is unknown which fault has caused this seismic event.

Finally, an inventory of the seismicity in the region in the last century (Kandili Observatory and Earthquake Research Institute earthquake catalogue 1900-2000) reveals three clusters of microseismic activity: (1) associated with the Burdur 1971 earhtquake; (2) associated with the Dinar 1995 earthquake and (3) a cluster in the region between Isparta and Eğirdir. This ENE-WSW trending elongated cluster extends over a region of 41 by 17 km (Figure 1).

3. IDENTIFYING ACTIVE NORMAL FAULTS

An **active fault** is a fault that is likely to have another earthquake sometime in the near future. Faults are commonly considered to be active if they have moved one or more times in the last 10.000 years.

Seismogenic faults rarely cut through the earth's surface. A surface rupture can only be generated by strong earthquakes of which the depth of the focus does not exceed the upper crust (10 to 20 km depth). Earthquakes associated with co-seismic surface faulting are called **morphogenic earthquakes** (Caputo, 1993). Based on a quantitative correlation between magnitude and the surface parameters of a fault, i.e. surface rupture length, maximum vertical displacement, etc., for historical and recent seismic data in the wider Aegean region, Pavlides and Caputo (2004) infer for normal faults in the Aegean region that earthquakes of Ms 5.5 or above may be considered morphogenic. The length of seismogenic fault traces commonly does not exceed 15 to 25 km. A fault capable of generating a moderate to strong earthquake (Ms 5.5 or above) should therefore have a clear surface expression detectable in the landscape. Assuming that a seismogenic fault has been active in the past over a time span of several tens of thousands of years, it is very likely that, depending on the style of faulting and rate of activity, comparable events repeatedly occurred in the past, and produced similar ground effects. Even if partially obliterated or masked by climatically driven or anthromorphic processes, the results of such past activity can be recognized in today's environment (Michetti and Hancock, 1997). In other words, it should always be possible to recognize a **'seismic landscape'** (*sensu* Michetti and Hancock, 1997) that can be considered to be the result of one or more earthquakes that resulted in ground deformation, including surface faulting (Michetti *et al.*, 2005). A classic illustration of this concept is provided by a fault-generated mountain-range front, regarded as the sum over time of the evolution of the free-face of a fault scarp (Stewart and Hancock, 1991; 1994). In many cases the high escarpments associated with active normal faults in the Aegean region dominate the landscape (Figure 2) and can subsequently be identified by a remote sensing analysis, displaying a set of diagnostic characteristics.

Similox *et al.* (this volume a) tested these diagnostic criteria with respect to geomorphology and drainage pattern to the known active normal faults in the wider Burdur-Isparta region. The key features associated with normal faults in hard limestone are a prominent relatively undissected footwall ridge, exposed fault surfaces along the top of the scree cones, and a footwall drainage controlled by the segmentation of the faults (Figure 3a). The most useful characteristics of faults in relatively soft sediments are the abrupt change of the drainage from incision to deposition along a linear scarp bounding the topography, and the generally roughly linear drainage divide set back by upstream incision hundreds of metres to a few km from the fault (Figure 3b). Moreover, the study area is characterized by an extensional half-graben/tilt-block system. The predictable

surface effects of such a system can provide supplementary criteria for the identification of active normal faults. The most useful characteristic of half-graben basins are the relatively low gradient hanging wall dip slope with broad alluvial cones and the relatively high gradient footwall scarp slope, which sources small alluvial fans whose depositional loci occur at the foot of the scarp on the lower hanging wall dip slope (Figure 3c). When local climatic conditions allow, permanent or playa lake bodies will form in the basin as close to the locus of maximum subsidence as the footwall-sourced fans allow.

Aegean-type active normal faults, moreover, show a typical internal fault-zone architecture that can be used to identify them in the field (Hancock and Barka, 1987; Stewart and Hancock, 1988; 1990; 1991). Scarps formed during neotectonic normal faulting of Mesozoic carbonates in mainland Greece and western Turkey, display a varied pattern of degradation related to the history of fault development and variations in fault zone architecture (Figure 4):

(1) Alternating zone-parallel **compact breccia sheets** and **incohesive breccia belts**, of contrasting resistance to erosion, underlie scarps comprising multiple slip planes (Figure 4d).
(2) The contrasting breccia types record different stages of fault zone evolution at shallow (< 500 m) crustal levels. Initial blind faulting at depth produces a **near-surface shatter zone**. Locally, blocks within the shatter zone become increasingly disorganized as slip planes advancing through the zone, create incohesive breccia belts ahead of propagating tips. Cementation and frictional wear accompanying fault movement form narrow compact breccia sheets adjacent to slip planes (Figure 4g). In some major fault zones, fault movement is concentrated along metre-wide zones of intensely deformed **stylobreccia**. When slip planes reach the free surface, post-seismic stress release initiates a new fracture network that is superimposed on and restricted to breccia belts and sheets.
(3) Mesoscale slip-plane phenomena and kinematic indicators, such as corrugations, gutters, comb fractures, and pluck holes (Figure 4e), together with geomorphological features, such as subsurface solution pipes, and vegetation cover, result in initial variations in the denudability of erosionally resistant compact breccia sheets. **Corrugations**, characterized by sinusoidal profiles normal to their long axes (Figure 4c) and, less commonly, culminations and depression along their axis possibly developed as a result of upwards-propagating slip planes seeking undemanding pathways through heterogeneous fault-precursor breccias that formed in advance of tip lines. Parallel to corrugation long axis **gutters**, i.e.

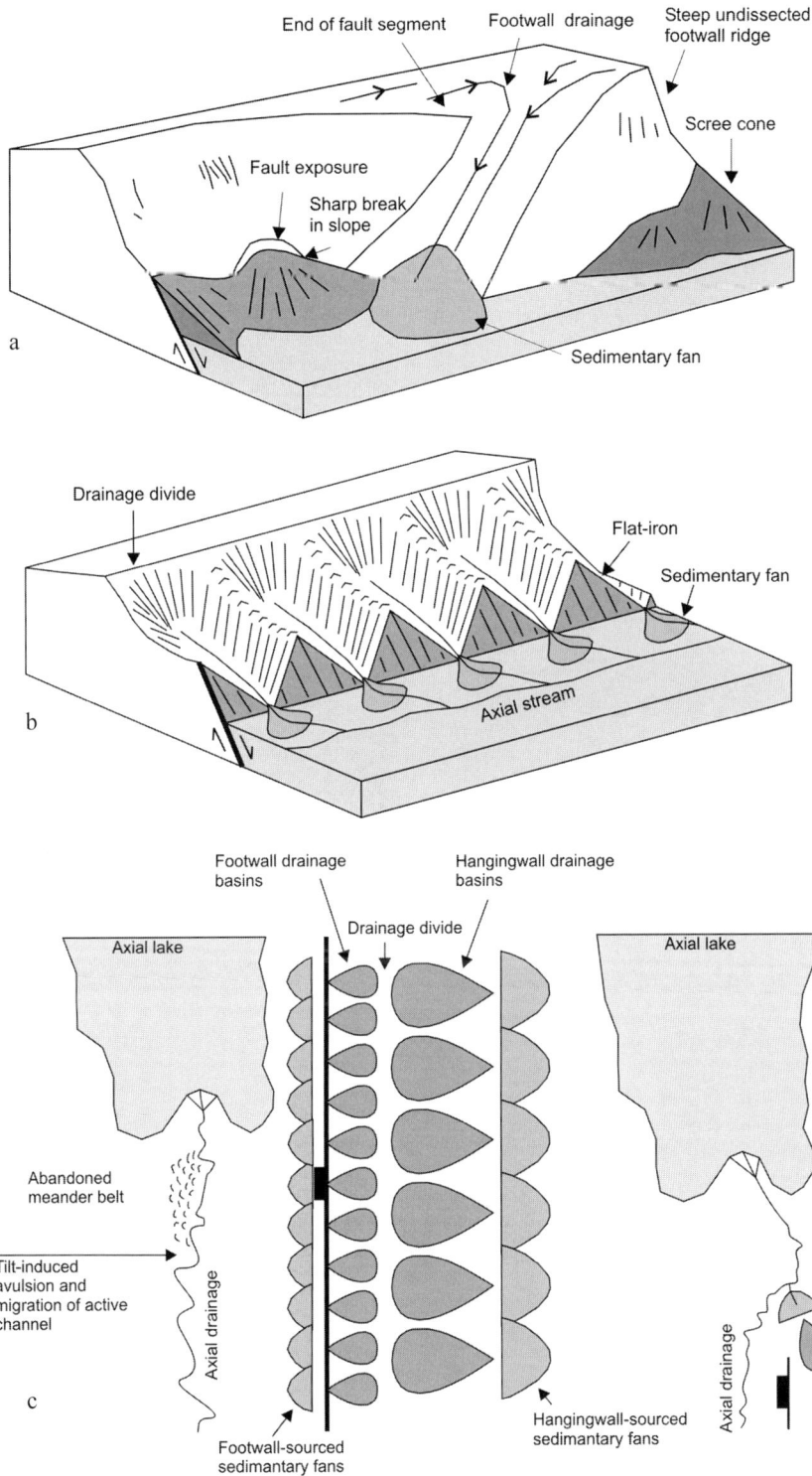

Figure 3: Schematic diagrams (not to scale) summarizing the geomorphological features and drainage pattern generated by active normal faulting in (a) resistant lithology, i.e. Mesozoic limestone (modified after Goldsworthy and Jackson, 2000; Jackson and Leeder, 1994) and (b) less-resistant lithology, i.e. Neogene deposits (modified after Burbank and Anderson, 2001; Goldsworthy and Jackson, 2000). (c) Idealized schematic diagram summarizing the characteristics related to extensional half-graben basins (modified after Leeder and Jackson, 1993) developing in resistant lithology, and developing in less-resistant lithology (Similox-Tohon et al., this volume a).

Figure 4: Some morphological characteristics of Aegean-type active normal faults. (a) Typical fault scarp (Crete, Greece). (b) Highly polished limestone fault scarp with Quaternary deposits in hanging wall (Muğla, SW Turkey). (c) Corrugated fault plane with tool tracks (Arhanes, Crete, Greece). (d) Compact breccia sheet (Lastros, Crete, Greece). (e) Gutters and pluck holes on a corrugated fault surface (Arhanes, Crete, Greece). (f) Comb fractures in limestone footwall of a fault surface (Arhanes, Crete, Greece). (g) Polished fault surface with compact breccia sheet (Lastros, Crete, Greece).

flat-floored, steep-sided channels a few centimetres wide, are probably related to the abrasion of subslip-plane breccia sheets (Figure 4e). Centimetre-scale **tool tracks**, scored in the uppermost subslip-plane breccia sheet by resistant colluvial clasts, are irregular at their proximal ends but distally swing into alignment with corrugation axes (Figure 4e). **Frictional-wear striae**, centimetre long but only a few millimetres wide are superimposed on the other slip-parallel lineations. **Comb fractures**, nearly perpendicular to slip planes, define an intersection lineation, which is normal to corrugation axes (Figure 4f).

Migration with time of slip-plane activity within a fault zone into its hanging wall, i.e. **intrafault-zone hanging wall collapse**, adds to the structural heterogeneity of fault scarp footwalls. Migration of the active slip plane towards the hanging wall results in a distributed network of high-angle faults and a range front, which is stepped in profile.

Quaternary talus, whether offset across a fault (type 1 of faulted bedrock/Quaternary contact according to Stewart and Hancock, 1988), banked unconformably against a slip plane (type 2 of faulted bedrock/Quaternary contact according to Stewart and Hancock, 1988), or faulted against a reactivated slip plane (type 3 of faulted bedrock/Quaternary contact according to Stewart and Hancock, 1988), has a dampening effect on degradation.

The complexities of fault zone architecture, combined with a history of hanging wall collapse, lead in the Aegean region to non-uniform degradation and scarps, which are commonly stepped and occasionally cavitated. Still, variations in rock weathering between different height levels of limestone fault scarps may relate to palaeoseismic activity (Stewart, 1996). Increasing degradation of scarps with height is found to discriminate between parts of the fault surfaces exposed during successive earthquakes.

Once formed, fault scarps caused by a morphogenic, surface-rupturing earthquake, are subject to degradation and are eventually obliterated, in particular when erosion rate exceeds displacement rate, i.e. recurrence of surface rupturing seismic events. In an environment dominated by sediments, active faults may therefore be no longer detectable in the landscape. **Near-surface geophysics**, exploring the direct subsurface, may in these particular cases provide substantial evidence, in particular by identifying **colluvial wedges** that are the sedimentological expression of a degraded fault scarp. These techniques have indeed proven very successful in palaeoseismological studies of active faults (e.g. Camelbeeck and Meghraoui, 1998; Caputo et al., 2004; Caputo et al., 2003; Vanneste et al., 2001).

4. METHODOLOGY

Remote sensing has been performed on a Landsat 7 Enhanced Thematic Mapper + tape, an Aster tape (Figure 5) and a digital elevation model (DEM) (Figure 6). Processing was done using ENVI.

The Landsat 7 tape dates from 9 December 1999 and has a resolution of 30 m for the visible, near-IR and IR bands (1, 2, 3, 4, 5 and 7) and a resolution of 15 m for the panchromatic band (8). The data were contrast-stretched and filtered. Various combinations of bands were used to try to pick out different features. A combination of bands 4, 5 and 7 for red, green and blue respectively was most widely used as this combination clearly showed the known major active faults (Similox-Tohon et al., this volume a). A fusion of bands 4, 5, 7 and 8 was carried out for an even more detailed image, with the colours of bands 4, 5 and 7 (30 m resolution) and the detail of band 8 (15 m resolution).

The Aster tape date from 18 October 2001 and has a resolution of 90 m for the thermal bands (10, 11, 12, 13, and 14), 30 m resolution for the IR bands (4, 5, 6, 7, 8, and 9) and 15 m resolution for the visible bands (1, 2, and 3). The data were contrast-stretched and filtered. Various combinations of bands were used to pick out different features. A combination of thermal bands 14, 12, 10, of IR bands 4, 7, 9 and of visible bands 1, 2, 3, each for red, green and blue respectively provided satisfactory images and were most commonly used. The Aster images with the thermal bands were used in the same way as the Landsat 5 images, while Aster images with the IR and visible bands were used in the same way as the Landsat 7 images. The visible area is however somewhat smaller (70 by 60 km) than that of the Landsat tapes (Figure 5). No fusion of bands with different resolution has been carried out on the Aster data.

A DEM (Figure 6) was obtained by manually digitising 1:25000-scale topographic maps (performed by the team of E. Paulissen, K.U.Leuven) of a 70 by 30 km large area (Figures 2 and 3). The accuracy resulting from digitising is 10 m. Six shaded relief views were computed, using ENVI, with a sun angle of 60° and different values for sun azimuth (270°, 315°, 0°, 45° and 90°). A lineament analysis has been carried out on these images. The shaded relief view with a sun azimuth of 315° appeared to be one of the most useful images as this is subperpendicular to most lineament trends. Topographic profiles were made across some lineaments for a better geomorphological understanding of these lineaments. Moreover, the DEM was combined with the Landsat 7 fusion image to obtain a 3D view of the area.

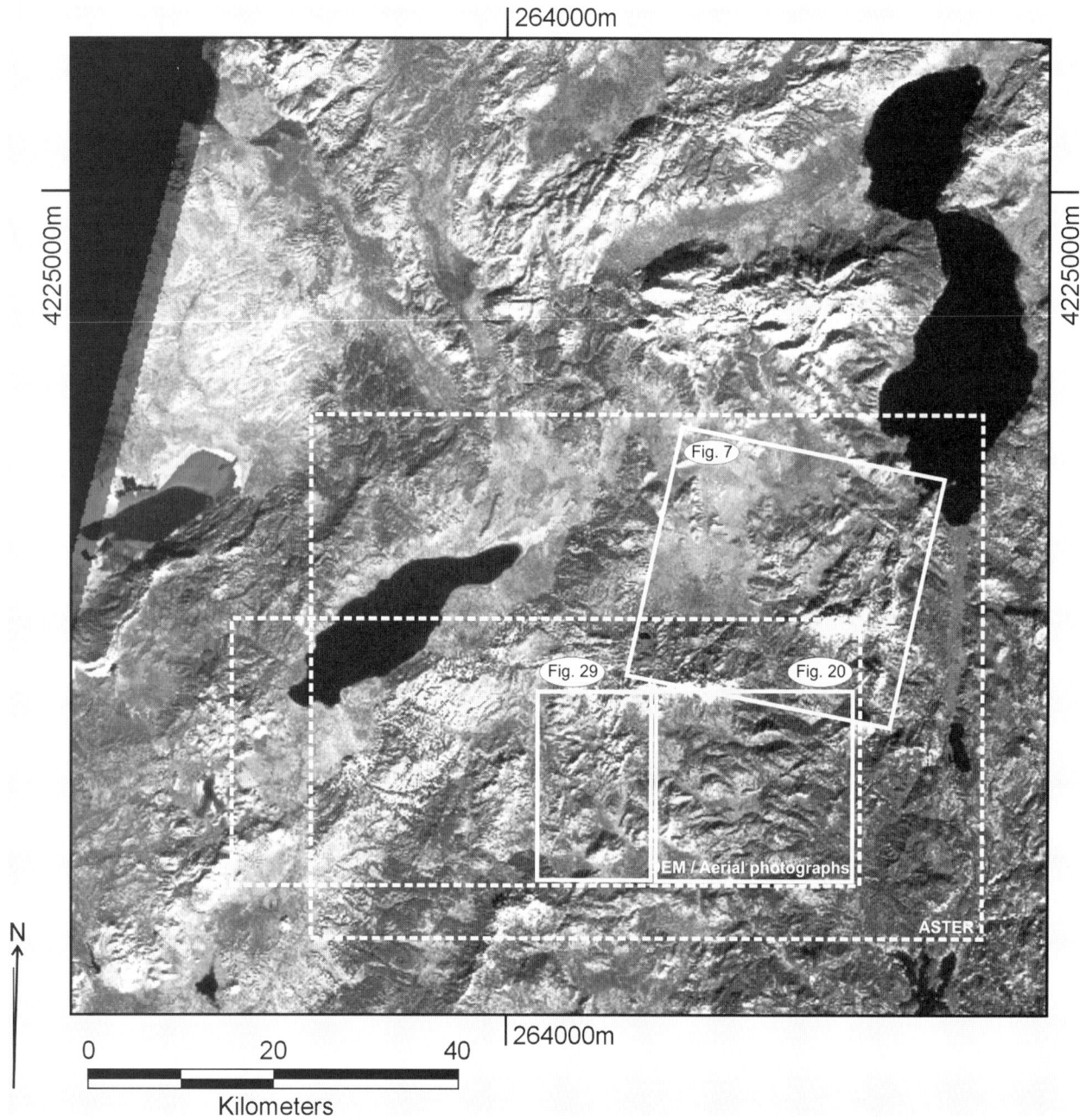

Figure 5: Landsat 7 Enhanced Thematic Mapper + image of the Lake Region with a combination of bands 4, 5 and 7 for red, green and blue respectively. Projection is UTM Zone 36, Northern Hemisphere (WGS 84). Location of the used remote sensing imagery (boxes). Landsat 7 image used in figures 7, 20 and 29. Aster image used in figure 11. DEM used in figures 21 and 29. Areas discussed in the paper: Isparta-Eğirdir area (Figure 7), Çanaklı-Isparta Çayı area (Figure 20), Bağsaray-Başköy area (Figure 29).

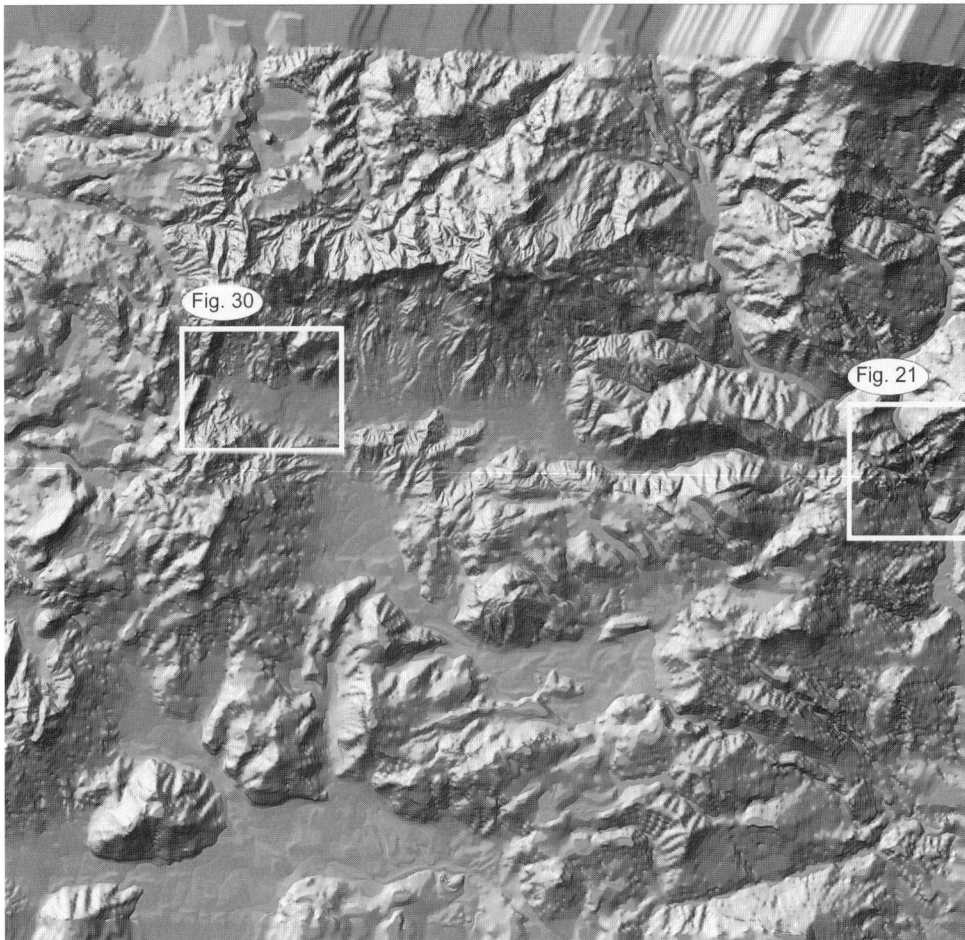

Figure 6: DEM image with shaded relief view of the territory of Sagalassos, illuminated from the NW. See figure 5 for location. Areas discussed in this paper: the Isparta Çayı valley to the east (Figure 21), the Başköy valley to the west (Figures 29 and 30).

2D-resistivity imaging has been chosen as the preferred method, not only because this method is reasonably fast, cost-effective and easy to apply in rough terrains, but also because it proved successful in palaeoseismological research (e.g. Camelbeeck and Meghraoui, 1998; Caputo *et al.*, 2004; Caputo *et al.*, 2003; Vanneste *et al.*, 2001) and in archaeo-seismological research (Similox-Tohon *et al.*, 2004). The resistivity measurements were carried out with the LUND Imaging System of ABEM, which consists of 4 cables of 16 electrodes, branched to a resistivity meter (Terrameter SAS-1000) through an electrode selector (ES-464). Using a roll-along technique, the length of the profile can easily be extended by a multiple of 32 electrodes. All profiles were measured with the standard 64 electrodes. The electrode layout used is a Wenner-Schlumberger layout. This layout is moderately sensitive to both horizontal and vertical structures. It has a rather good penetration and signal/noise

ratio but a rather narrow horizontal data coverage (Loke and Barker, 1996). The electrode spacing along the survey line, i.e. the minimum interelectrode spacing, has been chosen to ensure the required resolution and penetration depth, and was in function of the position of the suspected fault along the profile and the space available. The majority of the profiles were measured with the maximum electrode spacing (5 m) that is possible with the LUND Imaging system, enabling large distances to be surveyed and a large penetration depth (50 m). For each data point, the resistivity meter performed a stack of minimum two and maximum four measurements. The standard deviation for each stack is a good indicator of the quality of the data. The quality of most profiles is relatively good to excellent with standard deviations generally below 2.5%. Before proceeding with the inversion, the data set was reduced, i.e. all negative resistivity values were rejected, as well as all data points with a standard deviation above a certain threshold. The filtered data were subsequently re-evaluated visually, and any remaining isolated extreme value was removed. The measured resistivity values do not represent the true subsurface resistivity, but an 'apparent' resistivity, corresponding to the resistivity of a homogeneous subsurface that would produce the same resistance value for the given electrode arrangement (Loke and Barker, 1996). Pseudosections plotting the apparent resistivity as a point at the mid-point of the array with respect to depth do not give an accurate image of the true subsurface resistivity. These plots do not take into account that the signal of each value measured originates form a volume of the subsurface that depends on the type of array used. The true subsurface resistivity is eventually determined by an inversion. We inverted our data with the commercial Res2Dlnv software from GEOELECTRICAL. This program iteratively calculates a resistivity model section, trying to minimize the difference between the observed and calculated 'apparent' resistivity. A conventional smoothness-constrained least-squares method has been used. This approach gives optimal results where the subsurface geology shows a smooth variation. It tends, however, to smooth sharp boundaries and to under- or overshoot true resistivities (Loke *et al.*, 2001). The inversions were carried out taking into account the topography along the profile. A more detailed description of the method can be found in Similox-Tohon *et al.* (2004).

5. NEW FAULT ZONES IN THE BURDUR-ISPARTA AREA

Based on the different diagnostic criteria to identify active normal faults, using geomorphological features on remote sensing images (Figure 3) (Similox-Tohon *et al.*, this volume a), fabric characteristics in the field (Figure 4), and typical subsurface features in 2D-resistivity measurements, a number of to date unknown, possibly active and potentially hazardous normal faults and fault zones could be identified in the target area centred on the archaeological site of Sagalassos.

The newly identified faults and fault zones are all situated E and ENE of the already known northeastern extremity of the Fethiye-Burdur fault zone (FBFZ). In this paper we will discuss the **Isparta-Eğirdir fault zone** (IEFZ), the **Çanaklı-Isparta Çayı Fault Zone** (CICFZ) and the **Bağsaray-Başköy fault zone** (BBFZ). Part of the CICFZ, more in particular in the Çanaklı basin, is discussed in more detail by Similox-Tohon *et al.* (this volume c), identifying the **Çanaklı fault**. Finally, the newly identified **Sagalassos fault**, running underneath the archaeological site, is

extensively discussed by Similox-Tohon *et al.* (2005; 2006; 2007; 2004) and Sintubin *et al.* (2003).

5.1. Isparta-Eğirdir Fault Zone

5.1.1. Remote sensing

Between Isparta and Eğirdir several NE-SW trending normal faults cross-cut limestone (Senel, 1997). Some of these faults can be seen on the satellite images (Figure 7a). The faults near the Davras Dağı are characterized by undissected slopes and large scree deposits in front of these slopes, indicating active faulting. The major ca. 13 km long and NW-dipping fault west of the Davras Dağı is, moreover, situated in the southwestern continuation of the active normal fault that bounds the southern limit of Lake Eğirdir (Similox-Tohon *et al.*, this volume a). At its southwestern limit a smaller fault exposes Quaternary slope deposits in its footwall (Senel, 1997). An abrupt change of the drainage from incision to deposition along this linear scarp bounding the topography and narrow wine-glass canyons between truncated spurs with triangular facets indicates its Quaternary activity (Figure 7b).

The Darıdere stream flows along a straight NE-SW trending line for ca. 8 km (Figure 7a). This portion of the stream is in line with a major ca. 13 km long and SE dipping normal fault (Savköy fault; Figure 8). Hence, this portion of the stream is believed to be fault-controlled.

5.1.2. Surface geology

Field work focused on two lineaments: (1) the Darıdere lineament in the southwestern part of the IEFZ (Figure 7a) and (2) small lineaments at the northeastern extremity of the IEFZ near Eğirdir, exposed in a road section and in an adjacent quarry.

5.1.2.1. Isparta-Eğirdir road section

West of the city of Eğirdir, a ca. 9 km long valley runs normal to the Isparta-Eğirdir fault zone (Figure 8). The road between Isparta and Eğirdir follows this valley. At about 5 km west of Eğirdir and 23 km northeast of Isparta, a quarry and two cross-sections along the N73WE trending road were investigated (Figures 8 to 11).

The area between Isparta and Eğirdir is characterized by the Bey Dağları autochthonous units, which are mainly composed of Jurassic to Cenomanian neritic limestone of the Bey Dağları formation (Senel, 1997). The Bey Dağları autochthonous units are overthrusted by the Antalya nappes

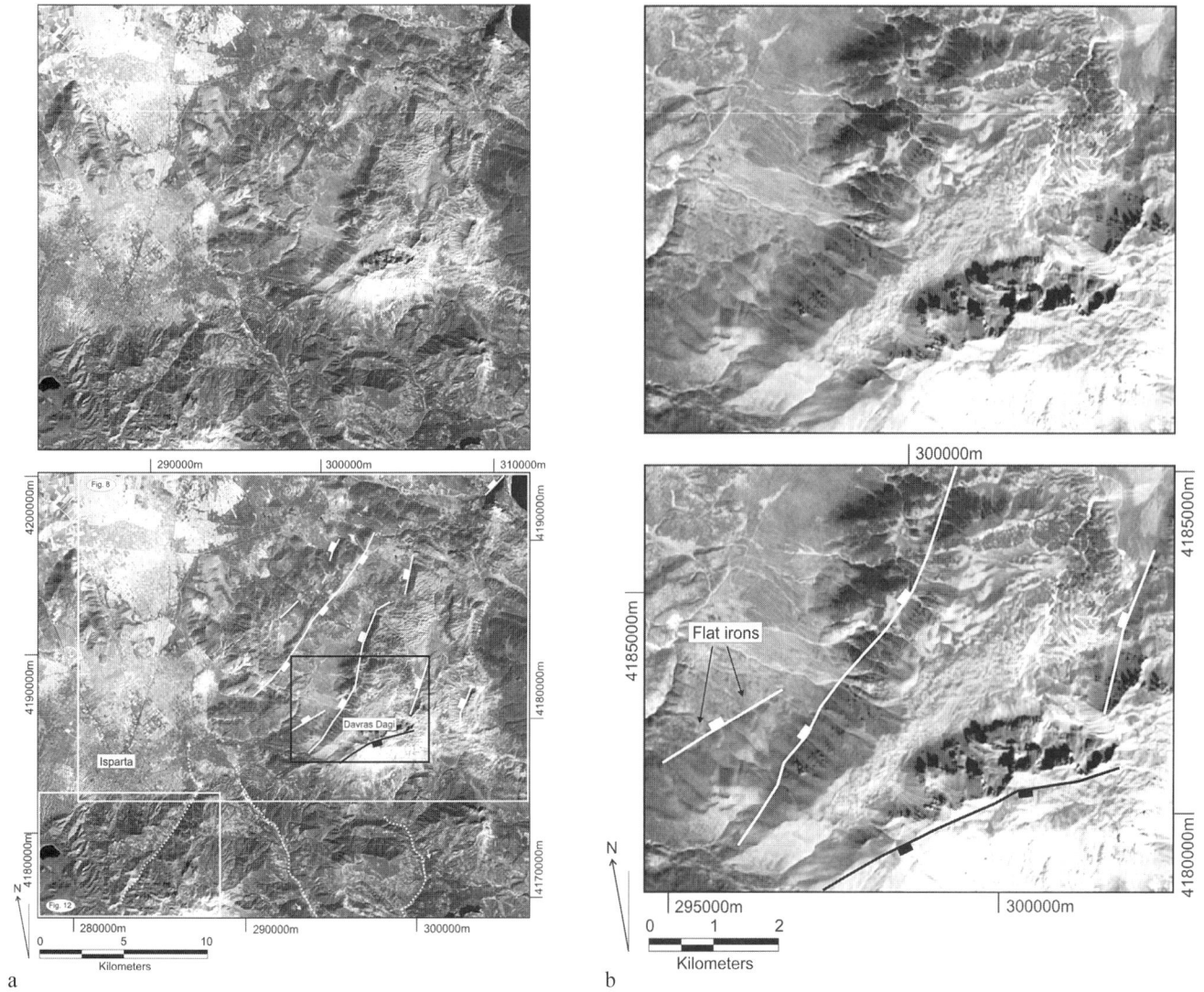

Figure 7: Isparta-Eğirdir area. (a) Aster image with a combination of bands 1, 2, and 3, for red, green and blue respectively, showing active normal faults and major drainage systems. Projection is UTM Zone 36, Northern Hemisphere (WGS 84). See figure 5 for location. (b) Enlarged Aster image of the area near Davras Dağı (see box in a).

85

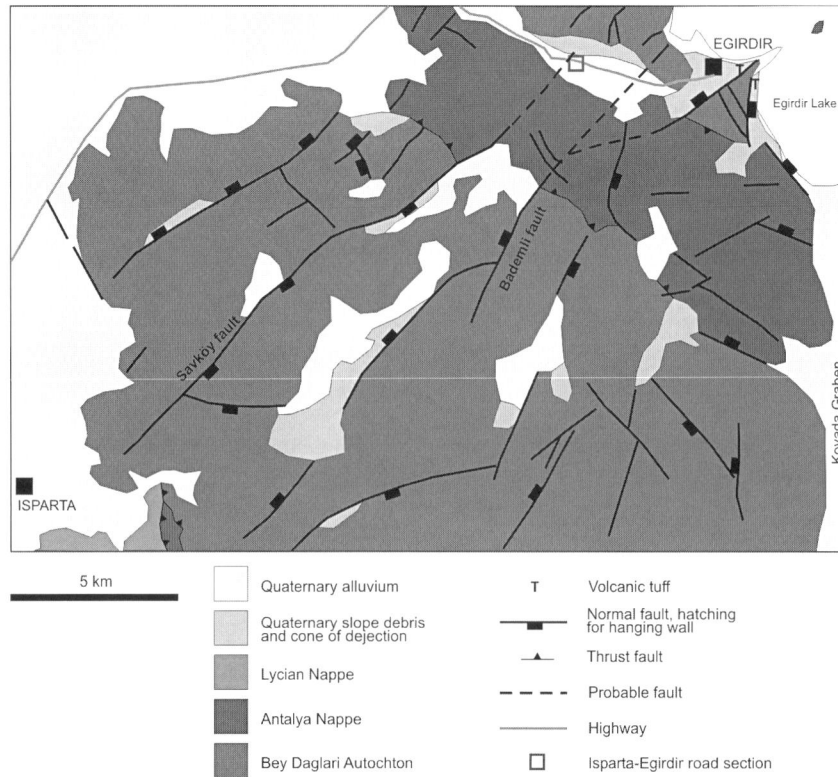

Figure 8: Isparta-Eğirdir area. Simplified geological map after Senel (1997). Location of the Isparta-Eğirdir road section (red square), with indication of the possible continuation to the northeast of the Bademlı and Savköy faults. See figure 7 for location.

in Danian times. To the west of Eğirdir, the Antalya nappes are composed of two distinct nappes. The lower nappe, the Alakırçay nappe, is characterized by the Upper Anisian to Norian rocks (sandstone with plant fragments, shale, radiolarite, chert, limestone with halobia, spilite, basalt, etc.). The upper nappe, the Tahtalıdağ nappe, is mainly composed of Rhaetian to Cenomanian neritic limestone of the Tekedağı formation (Senel, 1997). Volcanic tuff was deposited in the Isparta region during the Upper Pliocene to Pleistocene. The tuff originates from the Gölçük volcano, located 7 km SW of Isparta (Senel, 1997). The volcano is a very large maar with a ca. 500 m thick tephra rim. The maar's tephra succession is split in the middle by a well-developed palaeosoil unit, 1-1.5 m thick, which indicates at least two main phases of explosive activity separated by a relatively long period of quiescence (Nemec *et al.*, 1998). Alici *et al.* (1998) identified three eruptive phases within the phraetomagmatic deposits. The products of these eruptions are separated by erosion and palaeosoils (Alici *et al.*, 1998). Only four occurrences of these pyroclastic deposits were documented so far in the maar's wider surroundings. Firstly, fine-grained waterlain tephra layers in Late Pliocene

lacustrine deposits were encountered in the adjacent Burdur graben, ca. 20 km to the west (Scott and Price, 1988), corresponding to the early explosions (tephra unit below the Gölçük rim's palaeosoil) (Nemec *et al.*, 1998). Secondly, two Early Pleistocene tephra units, 130 and 30 cm thick, were discovered in outcrop sections of Quaternary colluvial aprons near Lake Eğirdir (Figure 8) with K-Ar dates of respectively 1.50 ± 0.18 and 1.38 ± 0.13 Ma BP (Nemec *et al.*, 1998). They represent two separate strong eruptions and associated NE-directed pyroclastic currents. These currents were fully turbulent and carried unusually large lithic clasts (up to 2 to 3 cm in diameter) in suspension (Nemec *et al.*, 1998). It is likely that the Early Pleistocene tephra near Eğirdir represents some of the latest explosive events (tephra unit above the Gölçük rim's palaeosoil) (Nemec *et al.*, 1998). Thirdly, volcanic tuff layers were identified in sondages on the Upper Agora at Sagalassos (Waelkens, 1998). Fourthly, volcanic tuff layers were discovered in an outcrop section a few km east of Ağlasun (Six, 2004) and a reworked volcanic tuff layer was identified behind the brickyard of Çanaklı. These valleys are filled with Quaternary alluvium, wherein reworked volcanic layers are present.

The bedrock of the Isparta-Eğirdir road section corresponds to rocks belonging to the Alakırçay nappe (Senel, 1997). These deep water sediments are strongly deformed, as can be observed in the quarry just south of the cross-section (Figure 9). An at least 9 m thick succession of volcanic tuff and clay layers are unconformably overlying the folded basement. Their lithostratigraphic succession can be divided into five parts, from bottom to top (Figure 10):

(1) 'volcanic tuff 1', an at least 1.8 m thick, planar-bedded, greyish-white volcanic tuff unit;
(2) 'clay 1', an ca. 1.4 m thick red-brown clay unit;
(3) 'volcanic tuff 2', an up to 3.2 m thick, clear alternation of planar-bedded, greyish-white to yellowish-white volcanic tuff and red-brown clay; bed thickness varies from 4 to 50 cm;
(4) 'volcanic tuff 3', an ca. 2.3 m thick, planar-bedded, greyish-white volcanic tuff unit with some intercalations of red-brown clay layers; the base of the unit is characterized by two distinct 7 cm thick, red-brown clay layers (layers X and Y);
(5) 'clay 2', an at least 0.4 m thick red-brown clay unit.

The thickness of 'volcanic tuff 2' and 'volcanic tuff 3' units increase towards the east. Some layers also tend to pinch out towards the west as e.g. the two distinct red-brown clay layers at the base of the 'volcanic tuff 3' unit and layer X within the same unit (Figure 10). As the Isparta-Eğirdir road section is located between the Gölçük volcano and the Early Pleistocene pyroclastic deposits near Lake Eğirdir (Figure 8), the observed tuff layers are interpreted as Gölçük tephras and form a new place of occurrence in the maar's wider surroundings. However, the volcanic tuff layers do not display sedimentological evidence for deposition by pyroclastic currents, as is the case 5 km more eastwards at Lake Eğirdir. The stratigraphy of the observed deposits (Figure 10) is clearly different from the tephra at the Gölçük maar and near Lake Eğirdir (Nemec et al., 1998). The succession of volcanic tuff and clay layers resemble both flood-plain deposits and lake deposits (Paulissen pers. comm.; Swennen pers. comm.). No conclusive determination could yet be made. However, we favour the interpretation of flood-plain deposits since layers of lake deposits are homogeneous and are not likely to pinch out as is the case in the Isparta-Eğirdir road section (Figure 9). Moreover, Lake Eğirdir is at the present situated 916 m a.s.l., while the Isparta-Eğirdir road section is situated ca. 100 m above Lake Eğirdir's level. If the sediments belonged to the Lake Eğirdir deposits, the lake must have been at least 100 m higher and deposition must have occurred in a wider area. As we are not aware of other places of occurrence of such lake deposits, it is more likely that the tuff and clay layers were deposited in a smaller lake, if they would represent lacustrine deposits. Such depositional environment could be compared with the valleys of Çanaklı and Gravgaz, ca. 40 km to the SE, which at present are still characterized by a periodical lake/swamp (Six, 2004). In the case of flood-plain deposits, the light-coloured tuff layers represent the coarser sediments of crevasse splay and the clay layers represent the finer sediments that stayed longer in suspense. The reddish colour of the clay layers could indicate the development of palaeosoils between successive floods. The succession of volcanic tuff and clay layers is important for the age of the sediments. In the case of flood-plain deposits, lots of material has been washed out and reworked. Therefore, the deposition age of the volcanic tuff layers should be younger than that of the associated volcanic eruptions. No correlation can be made with the Early Pleistocene tephra units near Lake Eğirdir and no absolute age can be postulated for the volcanic tuff and clay layers of the Isparta-Eğirdir road section.

The succession of volcanic tuff and clay layers along the cross-sections is incised by river gullies, which may reach a thickness of up to 4 m (Figure 11). In the quarry (Figure 9), these river gullies may be more than 10 m deep and are in direct contact with bedrock. Hence, the gullies have completely eroded the volcanic tuff and clay layers in the southern part of the study area. The river deposits display bedding sequences and are composed of sections characterized by coarse, badly sorted, cm to dm large limestone clasts and sections of mainly red-brown clays. The sections of coarse, badly sorted, cm to dm large limestone clasts must be deposited during high-flow rates and may indicate sheet flows within a wadi system (Swennen pers. comm.). Several gullies display at their base the largest pebbles while the gully infill is made of badly sorted and reworked material, again inferring high-flow rates (Figure 11). In contrast with the coarse sediments, the sections of red-brown clays most likely represent the finer sediments, which stayed longer in suspension in the flood plain. Subsequent periods of drying of the clays and pedogenesis are inferred. The presence of desiccation cracks in the clays, filled by over lying fine-grained sediments, indicates this drying process (Figure 11). In the quarry, some very sharp and narrow V-shaped gullies are also believed to be the result of the drying process (Figure 9). If desiccation cracks lie close to each other, they may intersect and a V-shaped piece of clay may be taken into transport by water flow. Fine-grained sediments were subsequently deposited in the created space (Swennen pers. comm.). Also the presence of pot-holes in the clay indicates that the clays must have been dry and hence very hard and erosion resistant to enable pot-hole formation (Figure 11). Within the clays of the quarry, several thin white layers possibly represent calcrete layers and hence indicate pedogenesis under semi-arid

Sub-crop map from base of alluvium

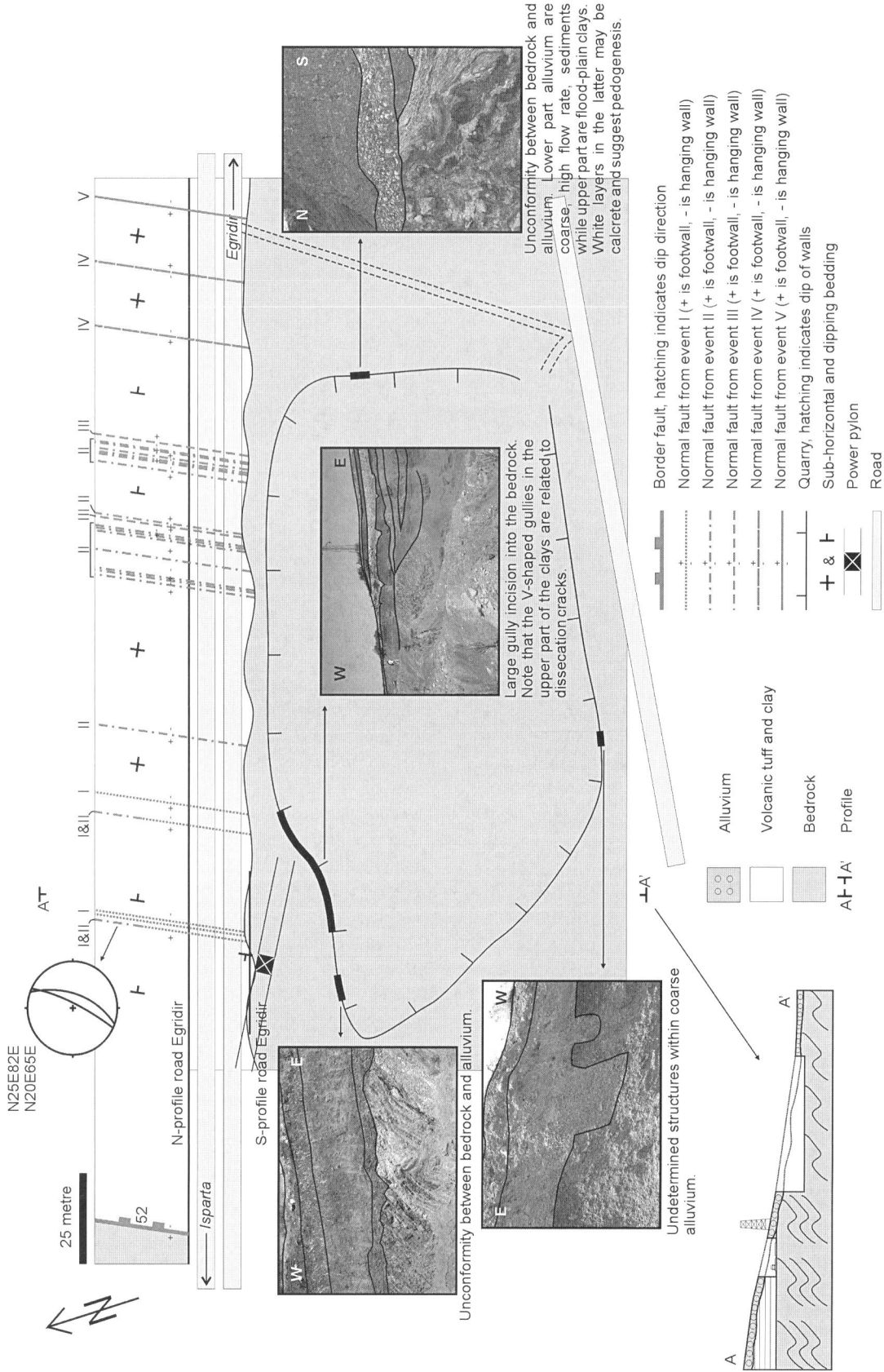

N25E82E
N20E65E

N-profile road Egridir

S-profile road Egridir

25 metre

52

Isparta

Egridir

Unconformity between bedrock and alluvium.

Undetermined structures within coarse alluvium.

Large gully incision into the bedrock. Note that the V-shaped gullies in the upper part of the clays are related to dissecation cracks.

Unconformity between bedrock and alluvium. Lower part alluvium are coarse, high flow rate, sediments while upper part are flood-plain clays. White layers in the latter may be calcrete and suggest pedogenesis.

Border fault, hatching indicates dip direction

Normal fault from event I (+ is footwall, - is hanging wall)

Normal fault from event II (+ is footwall, - is hanging wall)

Normal fault from event III (+ is footwall, - is hanging wall)

Normal fault from event IV (+ is footwall, - is hanging wall)

Normal fault from event V (+ is footwall, - is hanging wall)

Quarry, hatching indicates dip of walls

Sub-horizontal and dipping bedding

Power pylon

Road

Alluvium

Volcanic tuff and clay

Bedrock

Profile

Figure 9: Isparta-Eğirdir road section. Subcrop map of the base of the most recent alluvium. Photographs from the quarry walls show the unconformity between the strongly folded bedrock and the most recent alluvium.

88

Stratigraphy of N-cross-section road Egridir

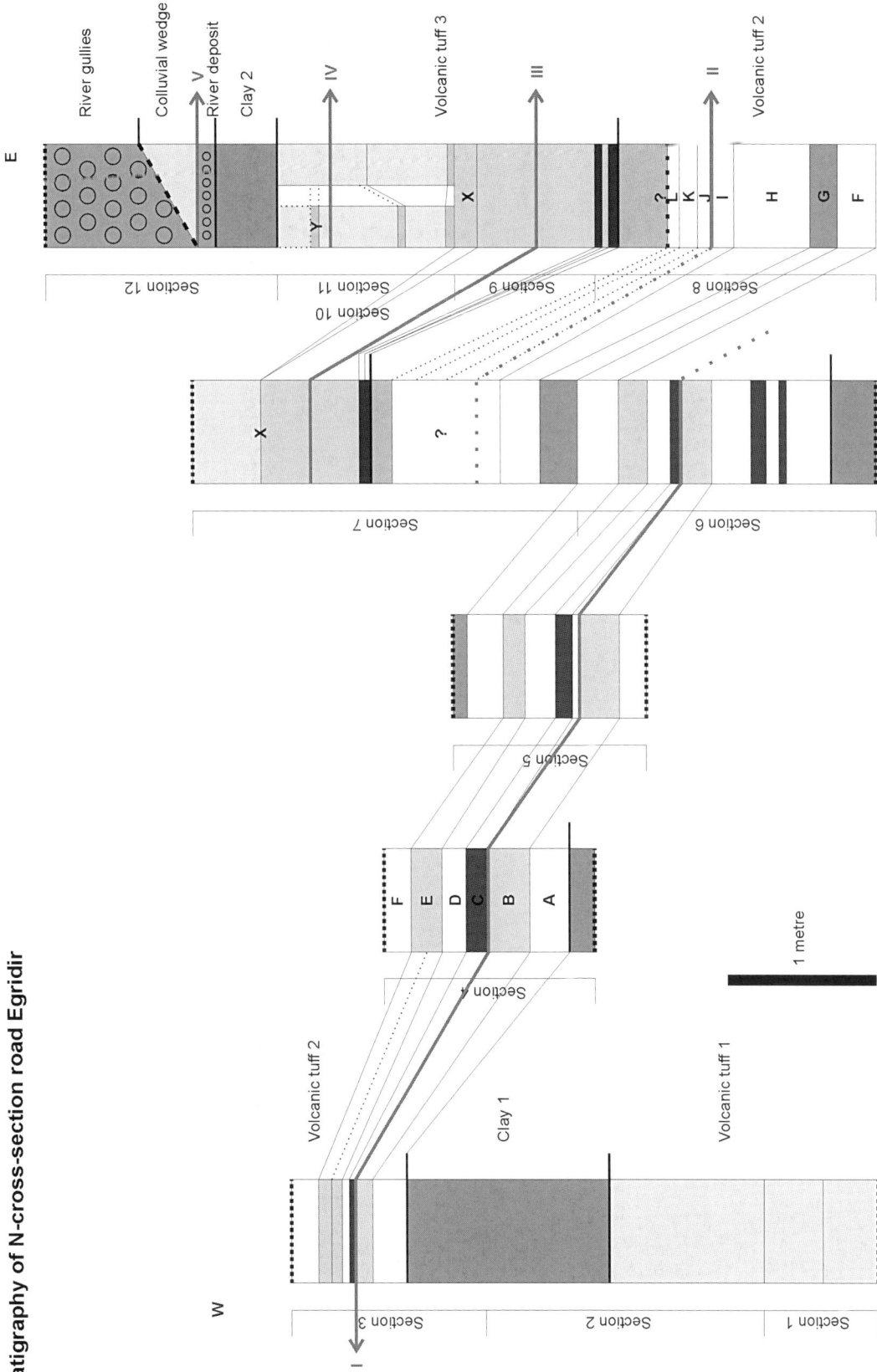

Figure 10: Isparta-Eğirdir road section: Stratigraphy of the succession of volcanic tuff and clay layers as deduced from 12 sections along the northern cross-section (see figure 11). The 5 faulting events are indicated as red lines. Letters indicate individually defined lithostratigraphic units.

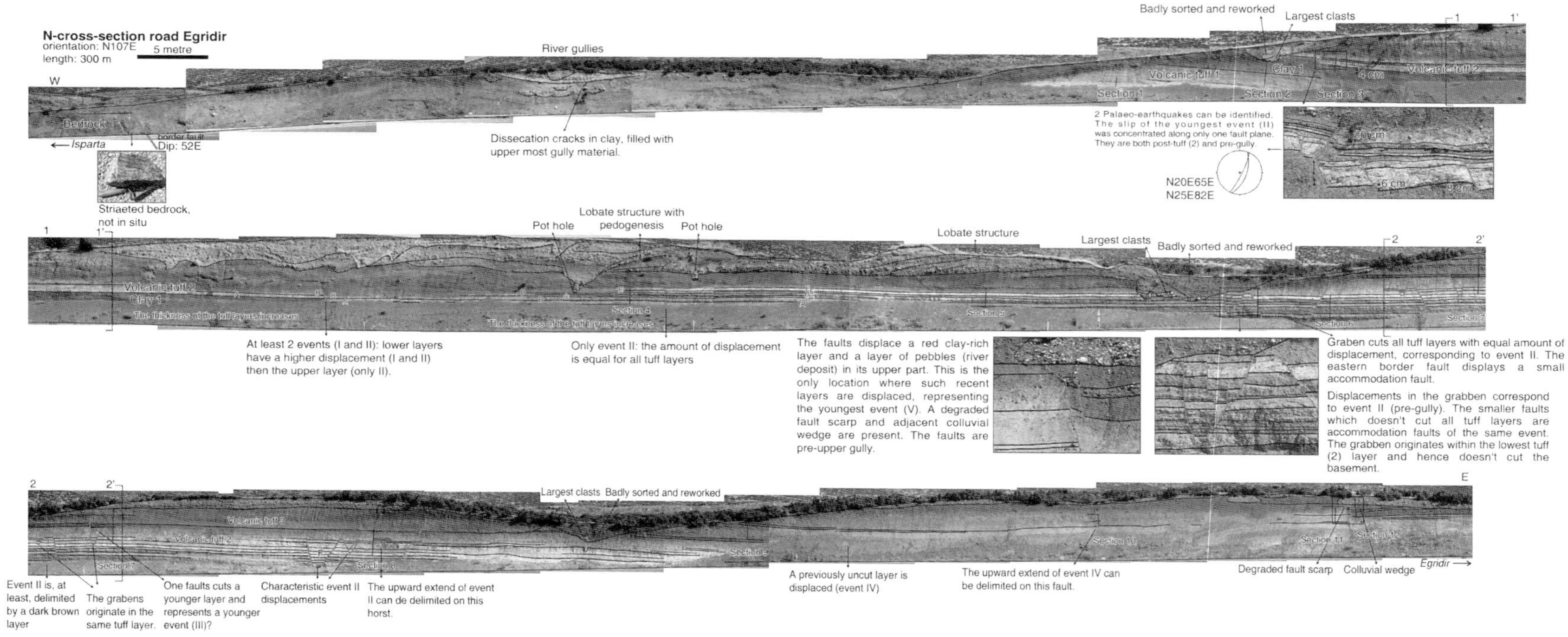

Figure 11: Isparta-Eğirdir road section. The northern cross-section with interpretation.

climate conditions (Swennen pers. comm.) (Figure 11). At certain places, the superposition of several sections, i.e. coarse-grained and fine-grained units, is not horizontal but displays an angle and forms a lobate geometry (Figure 11). Within such lobate structures, sequences of high water flows, represented by coarse sediments, are overlain by red coloured flood plain clays (Figure 11). All previous described features of the river deposits are characteristic for a braided river system on distal alluvial fan(s) where short periods of high-flow rate alternated with subsequent drier periods. The succession of volcanic tuff and clay layers and these braided river gullies represent two clear contrasting deposition environments through time, with an evolution towards a period of higher-flow rates.

An E-dipping border fault delimits the bedrock and the succession of volcanic tuff and clay layers at the western edge of the Isparta-Eğirdir road section (Figures 9 and 11). Several NNE trending normal faults were identified within the volcanic tuff and clay layers, outcropping in the northern cross-section (Figures 9 and 11). The displacement of the volcanic tuff and clay layers ranges between a few cm and a few dm. Most of the faults are dipping to the east and several horst-and-graben structures are present. The grabens often do not cut the entire volcanic tuff and clay succession but start within a layer of the stratigraphical section (mainly in layer F in 'volcanic tuff 2' unit). Moreover, the faults that apparently cut all the volcanic tuff and clay layers could not be followed within the basement, outcropping in the quarry (Figure 9). This suggests that the observed faults, except the border fault, are restricted to the volcanic tuff and clay layers and are no basement faults. The tilt and increase in thickness of the volcanic tuff and clay layers towards the east and the pinching out of some layers to the west suggest differential movements which may be related to faults. Such a fault could be the E-dipping border fault delimiting the bedrock and the succession of volcanic tuff and clay layers at the western edge of the Isparta-Eğirdir road section. Another candidate could be a non-identified active W-dipping border fault cutting through the basement bedrock, more to the east of the Isparta-Eğirdir road section. Based on the geographical position of the Isparta-Eğirdir road section, the two border faults can tentatively be correlated with the NE trending, W-dipping Bademlı fault and the E-dipping Savköy fault, both cutting through the Bey Dağları autochthonous units more to the southwest (Senel, 1997) (Figure 8). The faults within the volcanic tuff and clay layers may be earthquake-induced. The fact that the faults and grabens always start within a tuff layer and not in a clay layer may indicate that earthquakes could be responsible for the liquefaction of water-saturated tuff layers, above which faults and grabens were formed. Layer F in 'volcanic tuff 2' unit represents such a tuff layer.

Based on the hypothesis that the faults within the volcanic tuff and clay layers may be earthquake-induced, five palaeoearthquakes are postulated based on the stratigraphical position of the youngest displaced layers along the different faults (Figure 10). Subsequent reactivation of the same fault could be identified by differences in the amount of offset along the fault (Figure 11). However, the different events resulted mostly in the generation of new fault planes instead of reactivating existing faults. Moreover, each event resulted in an eastward migration of fault location. This is possibly due to the fact that the faults are the result of liquefying tuff layers during an earthquake. Each earthquake may have resulted in the liquefaction of a tuff layer at another locality or the liquefaction of another tuff layer. Most of the identified fault displacements are attributed to event II. This event possibly represents the strongest earthquake, as liquefaction may have been more widespread. This event is characterized by many graben structures. The four oldest events postdate unit 'clay 1' and predate deposition of unit 'clay 2' and the river gullies. The youngest event displaces a layer of river pebbles but does not reach the present surface. A degraded fault scarp and an adjacent colluvial wedge (Figure 10) are present for this event (V). The upper river sediments truncate this degraded fault scarp. Nothing can be said in detail about the magnitude, timing and recurrence of the earthquakes. The earthquakes can only be constrained as post-Upper Pliocene/Pleistocene (cf. tuff layers) and pre-historical. Soil liquefaction is, moreover, generally characterized by limited phenomena that occurred within the epicentral areas of events having intensity $I \geq$ IX MCS at the site (Berrardi et al., 1991; Serva, 1994). Earthquake magnitude less than 5 causes little or no liquefaction, whilst magnitude 6 may cause liquefaction within a radius of 4 km and magnitude 7 in a radius of 20 km (Kuribayashı and Tatsuoka, 1975).

Tuff layers along the Isparta-Eğirdir road section form a new place of occurrence of Gölçük tephras in the maar's wider surroundings. A displaced succession of these waterlain Gölçük tephra layers and clay layers and displaced braided river deposits possibly indicate that the Isparta-Eğirdir fault zone was active in Pliocene-Quaternary times and was capable of generating large earthquakes. Instrumentally recorded microseismic activity near the Isparta-Eğirdir fault zone and the presence of faults up to ca. 13 km long, i.e. the Savköy fault, in the fault zone are additional evidence that it may be capable of generating large earthquakes. It is therefore postulated that the 1889 Isparta earthquake, for which no causative fault has been identified (Ambraseys and Jackson, 1998), may possibly be generated by an active fault of the Isparta-Eğirdir fault zone. This would have implications for the seismic hazard of the Isparta-Eğirdir area as the Isparta-Eğirdir fault zone should then be regarded as a still active fault zone. In our opinion, the Isparta-Eğirdir road section gives an opportunity to investigate the palaeoseismicity of the Isparta-Eğirdir area, in particular by dating the tuff layers.

5.1.2.2. Darıdere lineament

To the northeast of Sagalassos, the Darıdere stream flows to the northeast along a straight NE-SW trending and 8 km long valley (Figures 12 and 13).

The area between Sagalassos and Isparta is characterized by the Lycian nappes, which are here composed of three distinct nappes (Senel, 1997). They comprise, from top to bottom: Middle Triassic-Liassic limestone (Domuz Dağ nappe), the Upper Senonian ophiolitic mélange and olistostrome unit (Marmaris ophiolite nappe) and Upper Lutetian-Lower Burdigalian flysch (Yeşilbarak nappe). The Lycian nappes were thrusted on top of the Bey Dağları autochthonous units, composed of Burdigalian-Lower Langhian flysch. Also Lower Pliocene-Pleistocene volcanic rocks occur in the Gölcük area (Senel, 1997). The development of volcanism can be divided into two major stages (Alici *et al.*, 1998). The oldest stage represents ancient rhyolite lavas/domes and diatremes, which are located in the Darıdere area, east of Gölcük. The youngest stage represents tephriphonelitic, thrachyandesitic to trachytic eruptions (ignimbrites, lava/ dome extrusions, phreatomagmatic deposits and finally, young domes). The ancient lavas/domes are underlain by white to yellow ignimbrites, i.e. the first product of the Gölcük eruptions, but do not represent a direct relation with them (Alici *et al.*, 1998). The Gölcük eruptions can be divided into four main periods such as ignimbrites, lava/ dome extrusions situated in the caldera, prhaetomagmatic deposits (eruptions I, II and III), and young domes in the centre of the caldera (Alici *et al.*, 1998). Surge deposits in the eruptions I and II are characteristic by their block impact structures (Figure 14) (Alici *et al.*, 1998). The Lower Pliocene Gölcük volcanism is interpreted as a response to post-collisional extensional tectonics during the post-Tortonian (Alici *et al.*, 1998).

The Darıdere lineament is described from WSW to ENE (Figure 12):

(1) Firstly, the valley is incised in highly fractured Middle Triassic-Liassic limestone (site 1; Figure 12). A source, which represents a karstic 'resurgence', emerges out of the limestone and is the starting point of the Darıdere stream (Figure 13a).

(2) Secondly, a first widening of the valley is related to the presence of volcanics (rhyolitic layers embedded in white tuff) in its central part, bordered by limestone

(site 2; Figure 12). Where the valley becomes narrow, only limestone crops out.

(3) Thirdly, a second widening of the valley occurs and this widening is characterized by the massive development of volcanics (site 3; Figure 12).

(4) Fourthly, only outcrops of highly deformed flysch, i.e. the basement, are observed in the valley and are seemingly underlying the volcanics (site 4; Figure 12).

(5) Finally, the valley bottom defines a linear border between a 'volcanic region' on the northwestern slopes of the valley and flysch on the southeastern slopes (site 5; Figure 12).

To the southeast of the Darıdere lineament, another NE-SW trending 'volcanic' patch is present (Figures 12 and 13b).

The contacts between the limestone and volcanic rocks (site 2; Figure 11) are characterized by clear limestone scarps (Figure 12). At many places the limestone is completely fractured or brecciated near the tuffs (Figure 15b). Some striated fault planes are observed on limestone debris near the contacts (Figure 15d). A shear zone could be identified at a near-vertical N80W trending contact, where brecciated limestone is juxtaposed to sheared tuffs with lenses of brecciated limestone and lenses of rhyolitic layers, all parallel to the contact (Figure 15). Moreover, the internal foliation of the rhyolites is always steeply dipping and sub-parallel to the closest contact with the limestone (Figures 15f). The limestone breccia is interpreted as fault breccia. The breccia is, indeed, restricted to areas near the contacts, where shear zones and striated fault planes occur. Four such ENE-WSW trending faults are located at the contact between limestone and volcanics. They display fault movement after deposition of the Pliocene volcanics but reveal no sense of fault movement. The parallelism between the contacts, i.e. faults, and the internal foliation in the volcanics suggests a tectonic origin of the 'isolated' volcanic 'basin'. Also in the Pliocene andesite (site; Figure 12) a metre-scale fault plane (040/63 pitch 50)[1] has been observed (Figure 16). Further to the northeast, along the western flank of the Darıdere valley (between sites 4 and 5; Figure 12) a normal fault contact (CN 340/48 pitch 106, CN 340/49 pitch 99; CN: certainly normal fault) is present between flysch and Pliocene andesite (Figure 17). In the footwall of the metre-scale normal fault plane in the Pliocene andesite, both a 'flysch shear zone' (Figure 17b) and sheared andesite rocks (Figure 17c) were encountered in an at least 2 m wide deformed zone. The transition between the 'flysch shear zone' and the sheared

---

[1] Representation of orientation data of planar features uses the '*strike-dip*' and '*azimuth*' conventions; *pitch* is counted within the plane starting from strike direction.

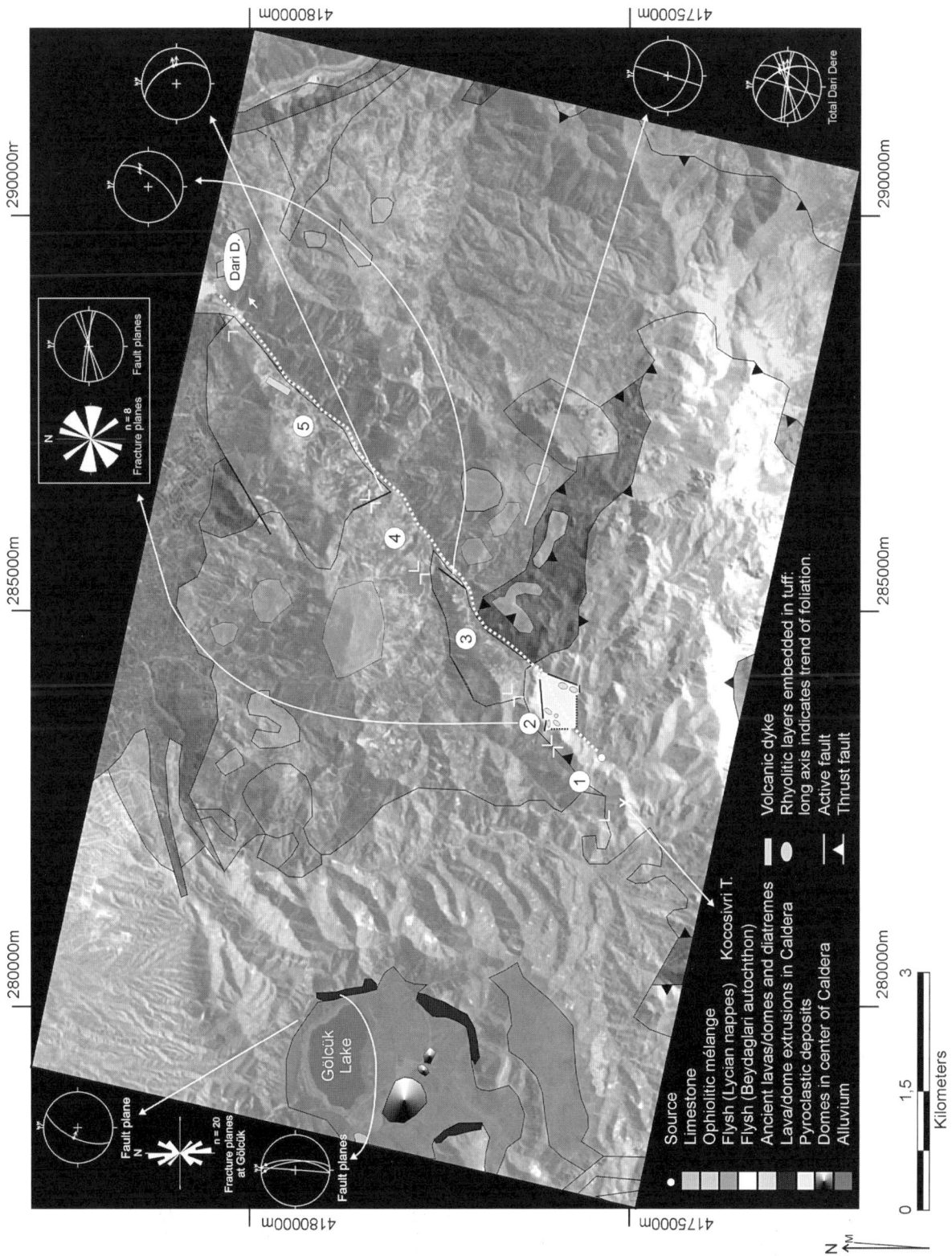

Figure 12: Darıdere lineament. Geological map (modified after Alici *et al.*, 1998; Senel, 1997) with indication of the fault data. Background is Aster satellite image. Stereoplots of fault data are lower-hemisphere equal-area projections. See figure 7 for location.

93

Figure 13: Darıdere lineament. (a) View from Kocosivri Tepe (southwestern extremity of Darıdere lineament) to the north-east (see Figure 12 for location). (b) View from the Darıdere valley towards the east of the NE-SW trending 'volcanic' patch within the Darıdere lineament. This 'volcanic' patch is geomorphologically well-expressed due to its higher erosive resistivity (see Figure 12 for location).

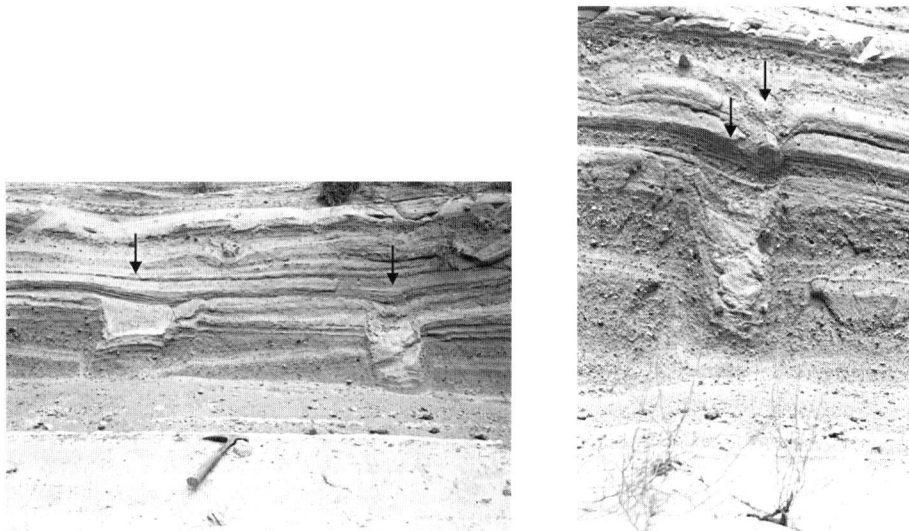

Figure 14: Block impact structures, characteristic for the phreatomagmatic deposits of the Gölçük eruptions I and II (see also Alici *et al.*, 1998) (hammer = 33 cm long).

Figure 15: Darıdere lineament. (a) Schematic representation (not to scale) of a contact between limestone and volcanics on the northwestern slopes of the Darıdere valley (site 2; Figure 12). (b) Fractured limestone (see (a) for location). (c) Brecciated limestone on contact (see (a) for location). (d) Fault with slickenfibres in limestone (see (a) for location). (e) Sheared contact between brecciated limestone and tuff (see (a) for location). (f) Main foliation in rhyolites (see (a) for location) (hammer = 33 cm long).

Figure 16: Darıdere lineament. Slickensides on a fault plane in Pliocene andesite on the western flank of the Darıdere valley (arrow indicates fault movement) (site 3; Figure 12).

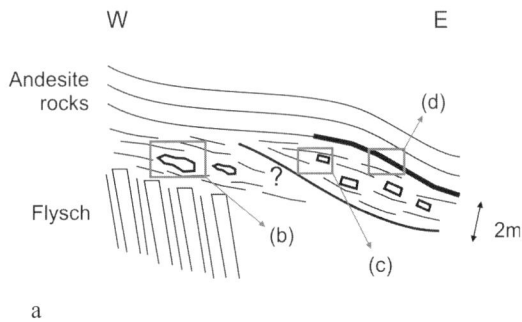

Figure 17: Darıdere lineament. (a) Sketch of fault contact (not to scale) between flysch and andesite on the western flank of the valley (between site 4 and 5; Figure 12). (b) Flysch shear zone (see (a) for location). (c) Sheared andesite (see (a) for location). (d) Slickensides and slickenlines on the hanging wall of a fault plane in Pliocene andesite, with indication of fault movements (lower hemisphere equal-area projection) (see (a) for location) (hammer = 33 cm long).

96

volcanic rocks has not been clearly observed. To the east of the Darıdere valley, flysch and tuff are found in contact along a 020/90 and 120/45 fault plane (Figure 12).

Near Lake Gölçük, the pyroclastic deposits from the Gölçük eruptions are fractured and faulted (Figure 18). Fault movement results in a down-dip displacement (up to ca. 40 cm) of distinct tuff layers, often resulting in horst-and-graben structures. Such faults indicate an extensional regime. Only one reverse fault has been observed (Figures 18b). All faults predate the youngest outcropping pumice layer, composed of coarser clasts. It is not clear whether these faults should be attributed to a tectonic event or to the collapse of the caldera. A few N-S trending striated fault surfaces, indicating a strike-slip motion (Figure 18i), and some fracture planes (180/70 and 220/73) were measured in lava/dome extrusions situated in the caldera (Figure 12). The limestone west of Lake Gölçük displays an intense fracturing (e.g. N40E trending planes).

A conceptual model of the Darıdere lineament development can be proposed (Figure 19). In a first stage, a post-Tortonian NW-SE extension resulted in the break-up of the Lycian nappes along NE-SW trending fracture zones. These fractures form the southwestern part of the Isparta-Eğirdir fault zone. A magma reservoir, underlying the area, is fed by an underlying melting metasomatized and/or enriched lithospheric mantle source during crustal extension in the area (Alici et al., 1998). In a second stage, lava domes, dykes and diatremes are injected along the existing fracture/fault zones, representing the first stage of volcanic development. In a third stage, Gölçük eruptions represent the second phase of volcanic development. In a final stage, some of the NE-SW trending fractures/faults are reactivated and deform both the ancient lava/dome as well as ignimbrites from the first Gölçük eruptions. The normal faults affecting the pyroclastic deposits from the Gölçük eruptions are possibly the result of the collapse of the caldera.

The ca. 8 km long Darıdere lineament northeast of Sagalassos is situated in an area where superposed on the 'basement' structural architecture, consisting of limestone, overthrusted ophiolitic mélange and Tertiary flysch, linear arrays are found of ENE-WSW trending volcanic massifs. These massifs may be interpreted as a sort of 'dyke swarm', consisting of an array of 'eruption centres', along rather pure extensional fracture zones. However, some faulting might already have occurred at that stage, as suggested by the overall rhombic shape of the valley widening, possibly representing a graben or pull-apart (site 2; Figure 12). Extensive, strongly disturbed, tuff deposits surround these volcanic massifs. Often the contacts with the basement

(limestone or flysch) is strongly sheared and brecciated. Therefore, fault activity/reactivation must have occurred after the Gölçük eruptions. It can be concluded that the Darıdere lineament is a neotectonic feature, i.e. postdating the Miocene nappe emplacement, related to a 'recent' stress field (see Verhaert et al., 2006). The Darıdere lineament is defined by the alignment of ENE-WSW trending eruption centres and is therefore considered to have a Pliocene age. It may be related to the Pliocene activity along the Isparta-Eğirdir fault zone. Geodynamically, it may be related to the complex, subduction-related, tectonics in the Eastern Mediterranean. Further, no evidence has been found for post-Pliocene fault activity along the lineament. Historical or recent seismic activity along this lineament can most probably be excluded.

5.2. Çanaklı-Isparta Çayı Fault Zone

In this paper we focus on the northeastern part of this lineament, exposed in the Isparta Çayı valley. The southwestern part, i.e. the Çanaklı basin, located ca. 5 km to the south of the archaeological site of Sagalassos, is extensively discussed by Similox-Tohon et al. (this volume c).

5.2.1. Remote sensing

Several NE-SW trending normal faults, exposing limestone in their footwall, are present along an at least 23 km long and NE-SW trending zone extending from the Isparta Çayı stream up to the south of the village of Çanaklı (Senel, 1997). Some of these faults can be seen on the satellite images, while others, not present on the geological map of Senel (1997), can be inferred (Figure 20). In its upstream part, the Isparta Çayı displays a drainage diversion. The Isparta Çayı and a second parallel stream more to the east at first flow to the SSE. Both rivers abruptly change their course before reaching each other along a 5 km long and NE-SW trending line (Figure 20). This 5 km long portion is believed to be fault-controlled and is parallel to several fault segments of the Çanaklı-Isparta Çayı fault zone 2 km further south. Moreover, this 5 km long river portion is not controlled by lithological contacts since the flow is perpendicular to the stratigraphical contact between Burdigalian-Lower Langhian sandstone from the Bey Dağları autochthon in the east and Scythian-Lower Anisian sandstone from the Antalya nappes in the west (Senel, 1997). Two km south of the previous drainage diversion, the Isparta Çayı crosses the inferred fault zone. Several SE-dipping fault segments are characterized by a prominent relatively undissected footwall ridge, indicating active faulting (Figures 21 and 23). When crossing these segments, the Isparta Çayı flows along some steps/cascades, indicating that tectonic

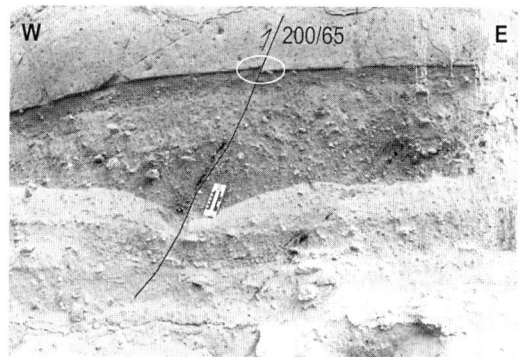

a

b

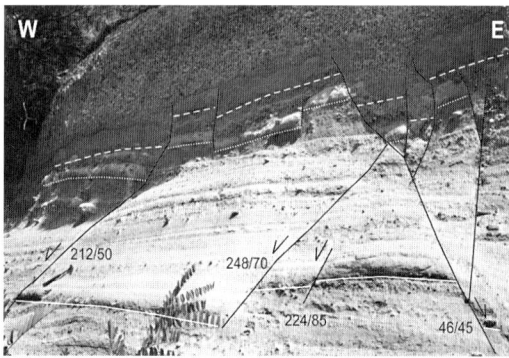

c

d

e

f

g

h

i

Figure 18: Lake Gölçük. (a-h) Fractured and faulted pyroclastic deposits from the Gölçük eruptions. All faults predate the youngest outcropping pumice layer (c-e), composed of coarser clasts. (i) N-S trending striated fault surface indicating a strike-slip motion in lava material situated in the Gölçük caldera (hammer = 33 cm long).

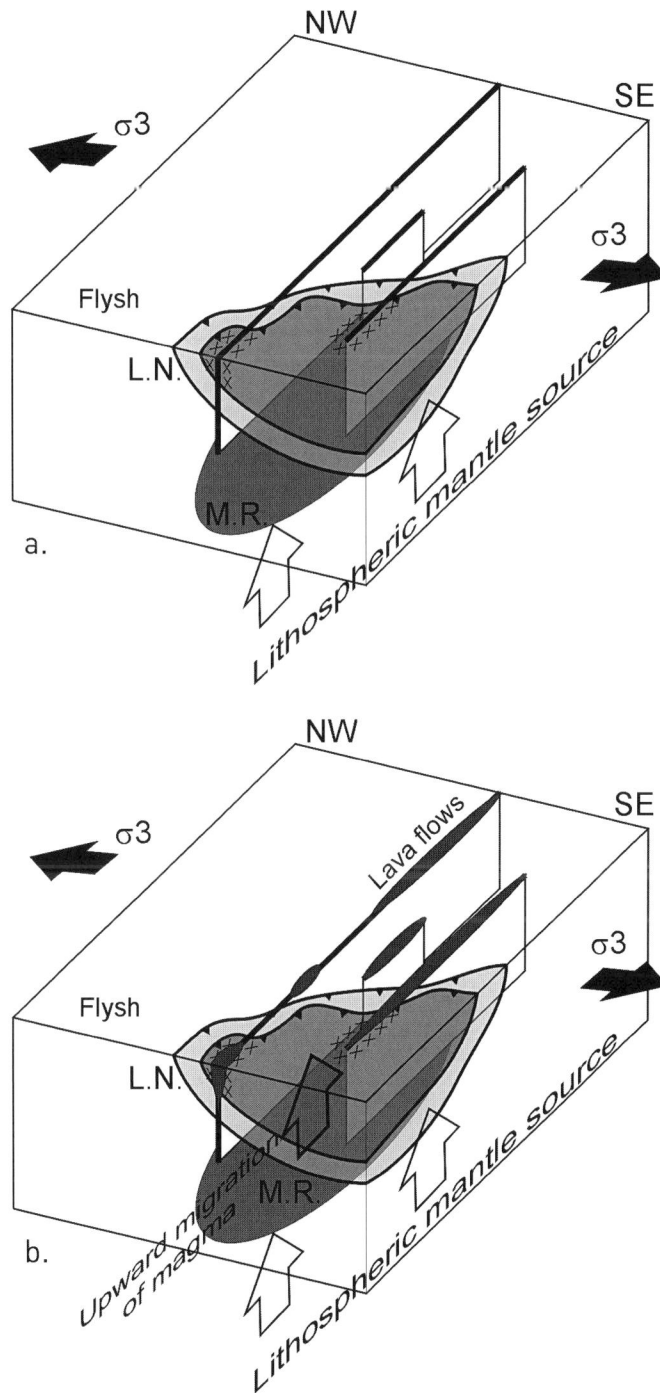

Figure 19: Darıdere lineament. Conceptual model of the geodynamic evolution (not to scale). (a) In a first stage a post-Tortonian NW-SE extension results in the break up of the Lycian nappes (L.N.) along NE-SW trending fracture zones belonging to the IEFZ. A magma reservoir (M.R.) is fed by underlying melting metasomatized and/or enriched lithospheric mantle source during crustal extension in the area (after Alici *et al.*, 1998). (b) In a second stage lava domes, dykes and diatremes are injected along the existing fracture zones.

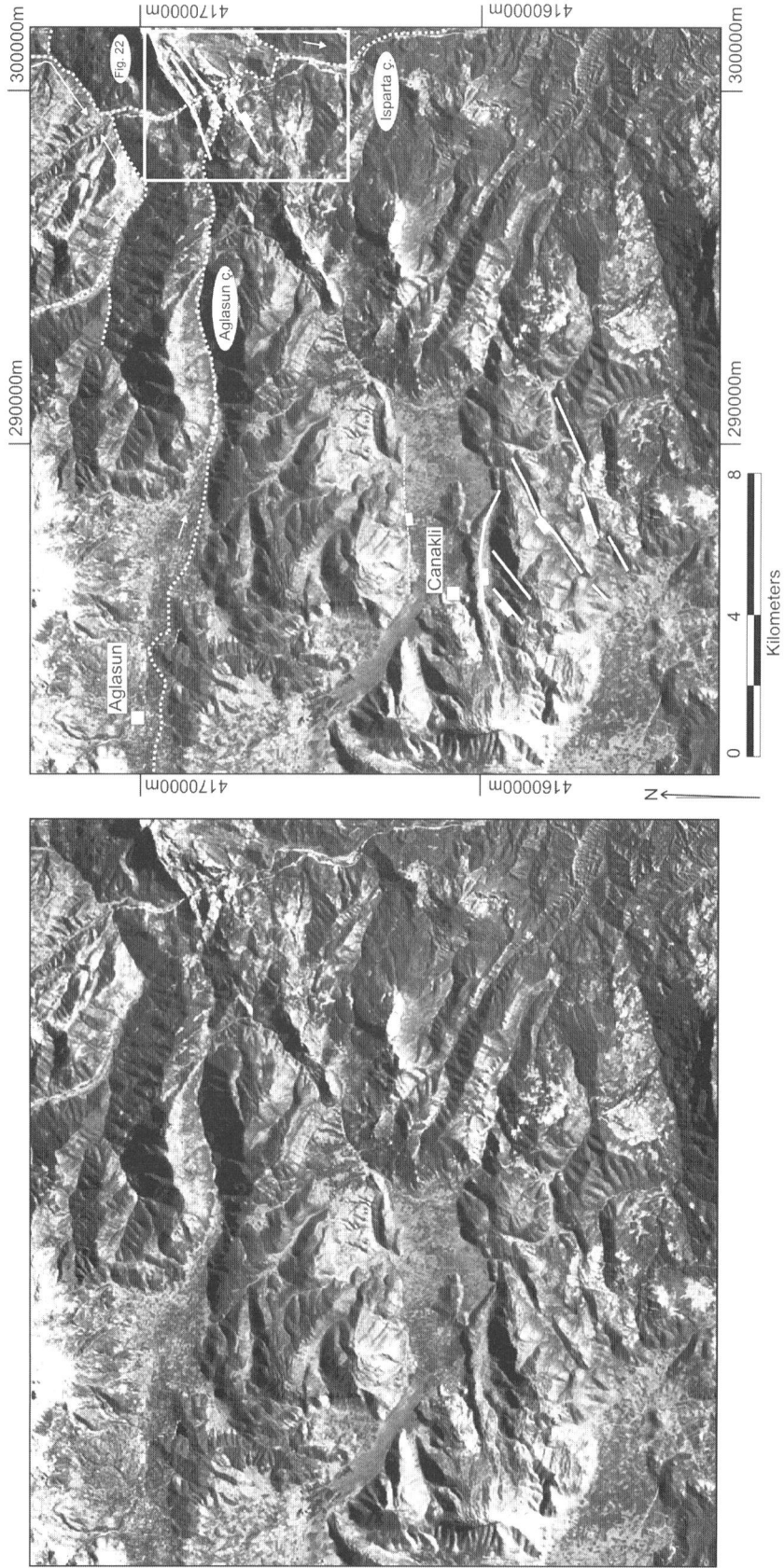

Figure 20: Çanaklı-Isparta Çayı lineament. Landsat 7 Enhanced Thematic Mapper + image with a fusion of bands 4, 5, 7 and 8, showing the location of the major faults and drainage systems. Projection is UTM Zone 36, Northern Hemisphere (WGS 84). See figure 5 for location.

100

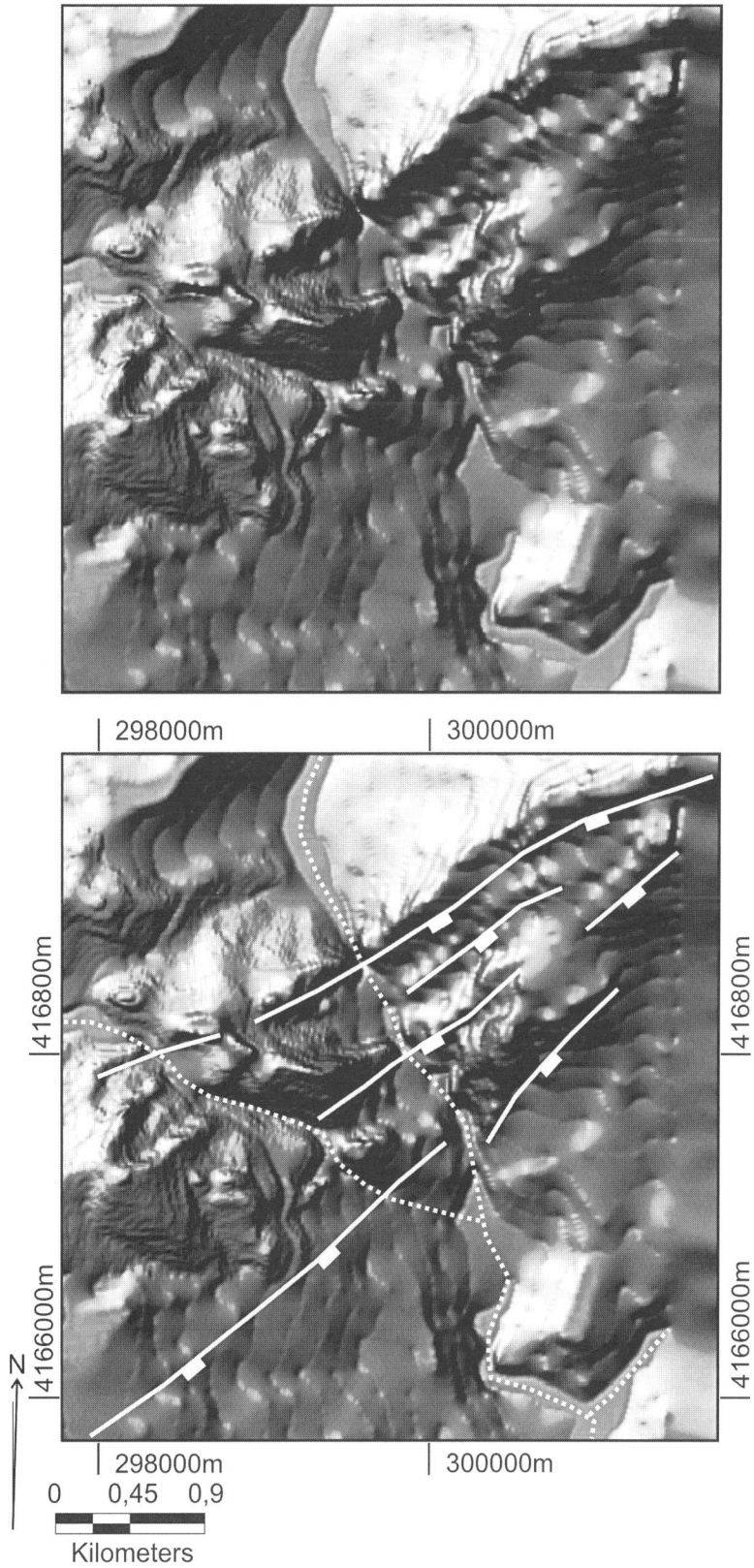

Figure 21: Isparta Çayı area. Enlarged DEM image with shaded relief view of the fault segments, illuminated from the NW. See figure 6 for location.

uplift of the footwall prevails on the erosion rate of the stream (Figure 27).

5.2.2. Surface geology

Some 15 km southeast of Sagalassos, the Isparta Çayı river flows of the footwall of the Isparta Çayı fault zone, as inferred from satellite imagery, to enter the Aksu sub-basin (Figures 22 and 23).

A range of lithologies is present along this portion of the Isparta Çayı valley. They comprize bedrock, belonging to the Lycian nappes, of Middle Triassic-Liassic limestone and the Upper Senonian ophiolitic mélange and olistostrome unit in the northern part (Senel, 1997). Serravallian-Tortonian coastal alluvial fan/fan-delta conglomerates were deposited in the southern part (Karabiyikoglu et al., 2005). The coastal alluvial fan/fan-delta conglomerates, i.e. the Aksuçay conglomerates are one of the Miocene basin fill deposits of the Aksu sub-basin and represent the final stage of terrigeneous sedimentation (Karabiyikoglu et al., 2005). Two lateral facies are distinguished in the Aksuçay conglomerates: (1) a regularly layered (E-dipping), limestone-dominated facies near the limestone range front, with very heterogeneous granulometry, and (2) a very heterogeneous better-sorted facies, with sandstone intercalations (with cross-bedding and fining-upward sequences), gullies and towards the top, thicker and more important conglomerate layers (Figure 22). While the former can be directly related to the degradation of the limestone range front, the latter facies has a composition representative of the Lycian nappes (ophiolitic material, cherts, limestone, etc.). The transition between both facies is seemingly gradual. A number of isolated limestone massifs (with ophiolitic material) are incorporated in the Aksuçay conglomerates (Figure 22). These massifs may represent a palaeorelief within the Aksu sub-basin or could be the result of mass movements The isolated limestone massifs incorporated in the Aksuçay conglomerates are fractured (045/77 and 245/80) (Figures 22 and 24a-b). The joint with a 245/80 orientation is filled by crustiform calcites (see Verhaert et al., 2004). The Aksuçay conglomerates are tilted and possibly folded (S0 005/20, 075/25, 035/15, 355/25, 030/15, 050/20, 000/25, 000/15) (Figure 22). Metre-scale fracture planes (070/65, 145/85, 180/60, 180/85, 220/70) and fault planes (CI 071/80, CN 115/65, 355/35; CN: certainly normal fault, CI: certainly inverse fault) with a limited amount (less than 1 m) of displacement were observed in the Aksuçay conglomerates (Figures 22 and 24c-d-f-g-h). A local concentration of nine, dm- to m-scale, NW-SE to N-S trending conjugate reverse faults affects a layered (S0 005/20) sequence of the limestone-dominated facies of the Aksuçay conglomerates (Figures 22 and 24e). The

limestone-dominated facies of the Aksuçay conglomerates near the Isparta Çayı fault scarp are folded some tens of metres near this scarp (Figure 25). The S-vergent folding may be the expression of an antithetical fault in the direct hanging wall of the main Isparta Çayı normal fault (Figure 25). The contact between the Aksuçay conglomerates (S0 075/25, 035/15) in the south and the limestone in the north forms a clear fault scarp (Figure 23). The fault plane itself is not well defined and no clear evidence of active fault activity was identified. The fault plane (052/49) is characterized by an up-to-2 m wide fault breccia (Figure 26b), typical of Aegean-type normal faults (Hancock and Barka, 1987; Stewart and Hancock, 1988; 1990; 1991). The breccia is matrix-supported and composed of mm to 20 cm large angular limestone clasts in a brown calcite matrix. Some clasts are broken up and recemented by the matrix (Figure 26c). An intense degradation of the fault plane has taken place as evidenced by the presence of rillen karst and pluck holes (Figure 26e) (Hancock and Barka, 1987; Stewart and Hancock, 1988; 1991). In the direct footwall of the fault plane, the limestone is strongly and regularly (ca. 10 m spaced) fractured. Sporadically a (fault) breccia follows the planar fractures (Figure 26d). Also these fracture planes are intensely degraded as evidenced by the dissolution of the mm to 5 cm large limestone breccia clasts (Figure 26e).

The portion of the Isparta Çayı river incising the limestone is characterized by a sudden change in drop between the most northern and central major fault scarp of the Isparta Çayı fault zone (Figure 27). This sudden change in drop may reflect the upstream retreat of the Isparta Çayı river from an active fault scarp. The latter resulted from a footwall uplift caused by a surface rupturing event. Between the most northern and central major fault scarp of the Isparta Çayı fault zone, ophiolitic material is in contact with limestone along a steep ca. N50E trending contact.

The Isparta Çayı lineament, as identified by remote sensing, clearly corresponds to an Aegean-type normal fault zone in the field. The Isparta Çayı fault zone bears Mesozoic to Tertiary limestone in its footwall (to the north), and Tortonian coastal alluvial fan/fan-delta conglomerate in its hanging wall (to the south) (Figure 28). The fault plane itself is characterized by a typical fault breccia. The fault plane is, however, strongly degraded, which implies that recent or historical faulting events did most probably not occur on this segment of the Çanaklı-Isparta Çayı fault zone. In the limestone in the footwall, a steep contact with ophiolitic material is unlikely to be an original tectonic contact (i.e. nappe). The ophiolitic material is rather of secondary origin (e.g. karst filling) and the contact an expression of active tectonics. In the conglomerates, two lateral facies are distinguished:

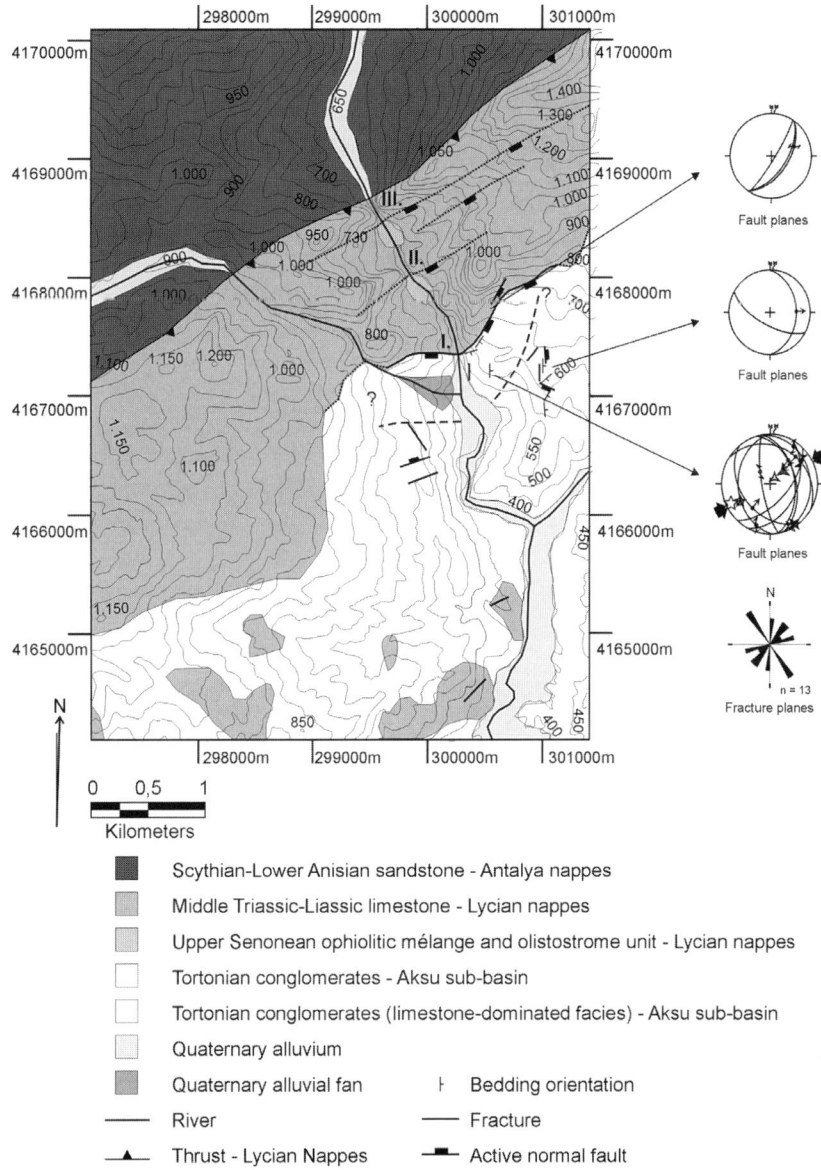

Figure 22: Isparta Çayı area. Geological map with indication of fault data, modified after Senel (1997). Stereoplots of fault data are lower-hemisphere equal-area projections. See figure 20 for location.

Figure 23: Isparta Çayı area. View towards the north of the Isparta Çayı fault scarp, incised by the Isparta Çayı river.

103

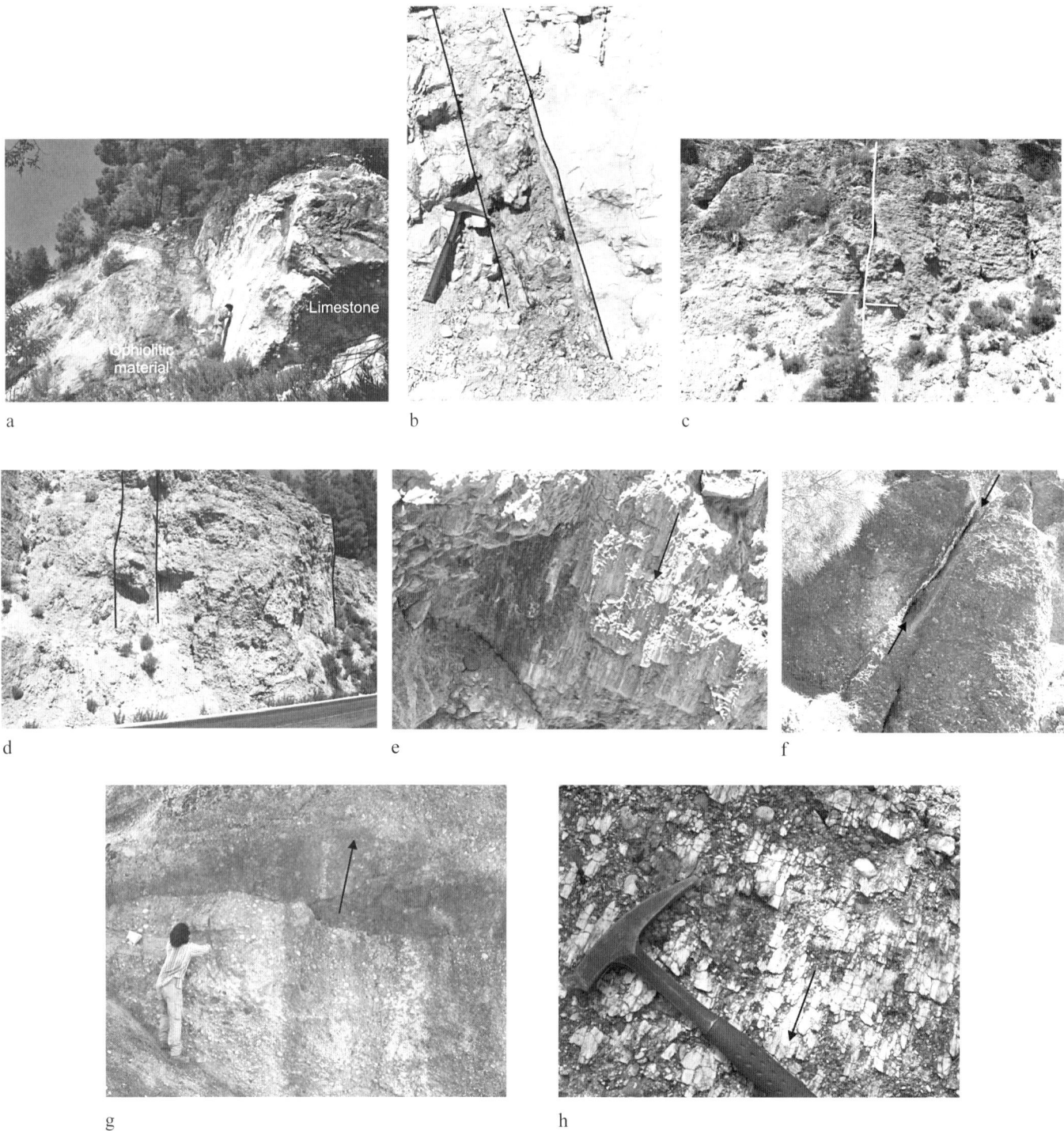

Figure 24: Isparta Çayı area. (a) fracture (orientation 135/77) through the isolated limestone massif. (b) Joint filled by crustiform calcites (orientation 245/80). (c) Metre-scale fault plane (CI 071/80; CI: certainly inverse fault. (d) Metre-scale fracture planes (orientation 145/85). (e) Detail of dm- to m-scale reverse fault plane with slickensides and steps in the limestone-dominated facies of the Aksuçay conglomerates (arrow indicates fault movement). (f) Metre-scale fracture plane (220/70). (g) Metre-scale dip-slip fault plane (CN 355/35; CN: certainly normal fault) with indications of normal faulting (arrow indicates fault movement). (h) Detail of previous fault plane with slickensides and steps (arrow indicates fault movement). (a) to (d) in the Aksuçay conglomerates to the west of the Isparta Çayı river. (e) to (h) in the Aksuçay conglomerates to the east of the Isparta Çayı river (hammer = 33 cm long).

104

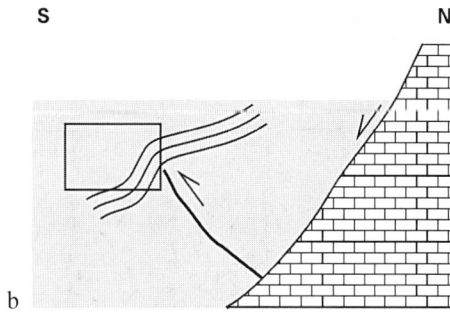

Figure 25: Isparta Çayı area. (a) S-verging folds in the limestone-dominated facies of the Aksuçay conglomerates to the west of the Isparta Çayı river (see box in (b)). (b) Conceptual model to explain the folding (not to scale).

Figure 26: Isparta Çayı area. (a) Strongly degraded fault plane with rillen karst and pluck holes. (b) Fault breccia. (c) Limestone clast from fault breccia which is broken up and recemented by the matrix. (d) Fracture plane in the direct footwall of the limestone range front with sporadic patches of fault breccia. (e) Detail of a fault breccia patch showing dissolution of the limestone clasts (ranging from mm to 5 cm) (hammer = 33 cm long).

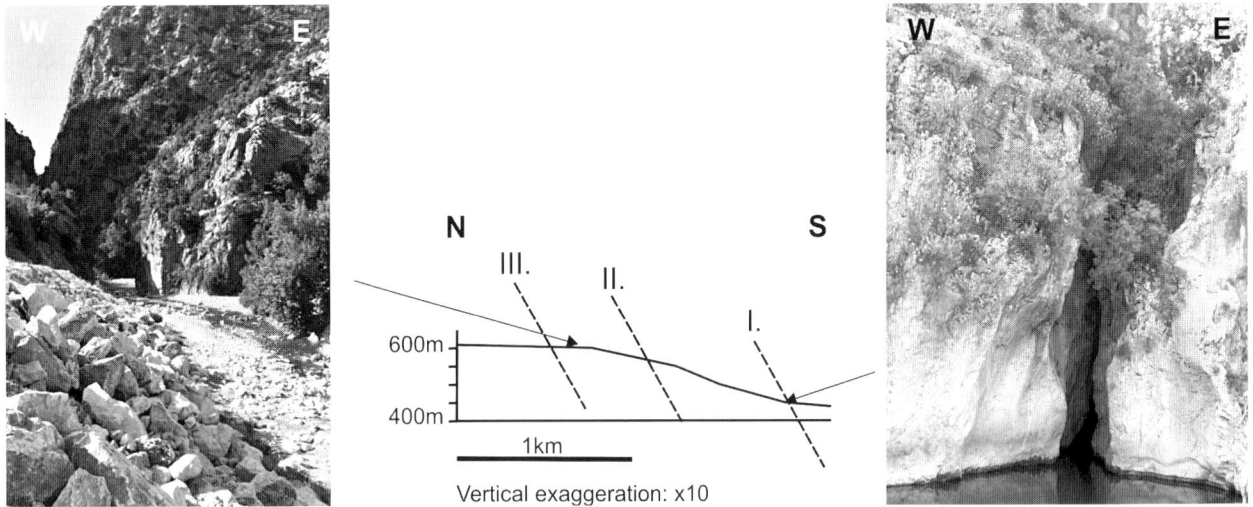

Figure 27: Isparta Çayı area. Elevation profile along the Isparta Çayı river. Photographs show portions of the river where the flow has a constant, relatively low drop. I, II and II are indicated on figure 22.

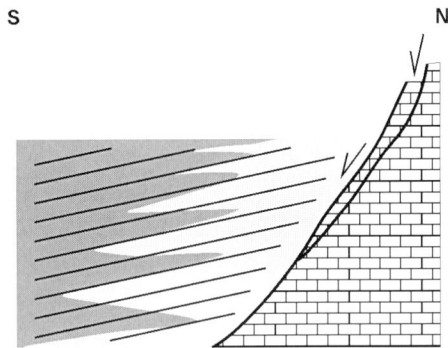

Figure 28: Isparta Çayı area. Conceptual model of the Isparta Çayı fault zone. Not to scale. The transition between light grey and dark grey in the hanging wall represents the two lateral facies in the Aksuçay conglomerates.

(1) a limestone-dominated facies near the fault scarp, and (2) a very heterogeneous facies further away. While the former can be directly related to the degradation of the fault scarp, the latter facies has a composition representative of the Lycian nappes (ophiolitic material, cherts, limestones, etc.). In the conglomerates in the hanging wall, only evidence was found for minor faulting. It can be assumed that in a first stage a NW-SE extension results in the uplift of the Lycian nappes along NE-SW trending normal fault zones. Hence, the limestone fault scarp forms the northern edge of the Aksu sub-basin. During the Serravallian-Tortonian, coastal alluvial fan/fan-delta conglomerates were deposited in the Aksu sub-basin (Karabiyikoglu *et al.*, 2005). Close to the Isparta Çayı fault scarp a limestone dominated facies was deposited. Subsequently, the Tortonian conglomerates were tilted to the east and faulted/fractured. The tilt may partly result from a reactivation of the Isparta Çayı fault zone. In Quaternary times, the Isparta Çayı river started to incise through the Isparta Çayı fault zone. The river profile

crossing the fault system shows a substantial drop (200 m difference in height), suggesting an uplift of the footwall and thus inferring Quaternary faulting. It can therefore be concluded that this segment of the Çanaklı-Isparta Çayı fault system has definitively to be considered as an active normal fault (Quaternary activity), but that no evidence has been found for historical or recent seismic activity.

5.3. Bağsaray-Başköy Fault Zone

5.3.1. Remote sensing

Between Bağsaray and Başköy, located respectively ca. 15 km southwest and 8 km west of the archaelogical site of Sagalassos, several NNE-SSW trending lineaments can be observed on the satellite images along a ca. 22 km long zone (Figure 29). Only some of them are indicated on the geological map of Senel (1997) as faults. The lineaments display the characteristics of active normal faults exposing

106

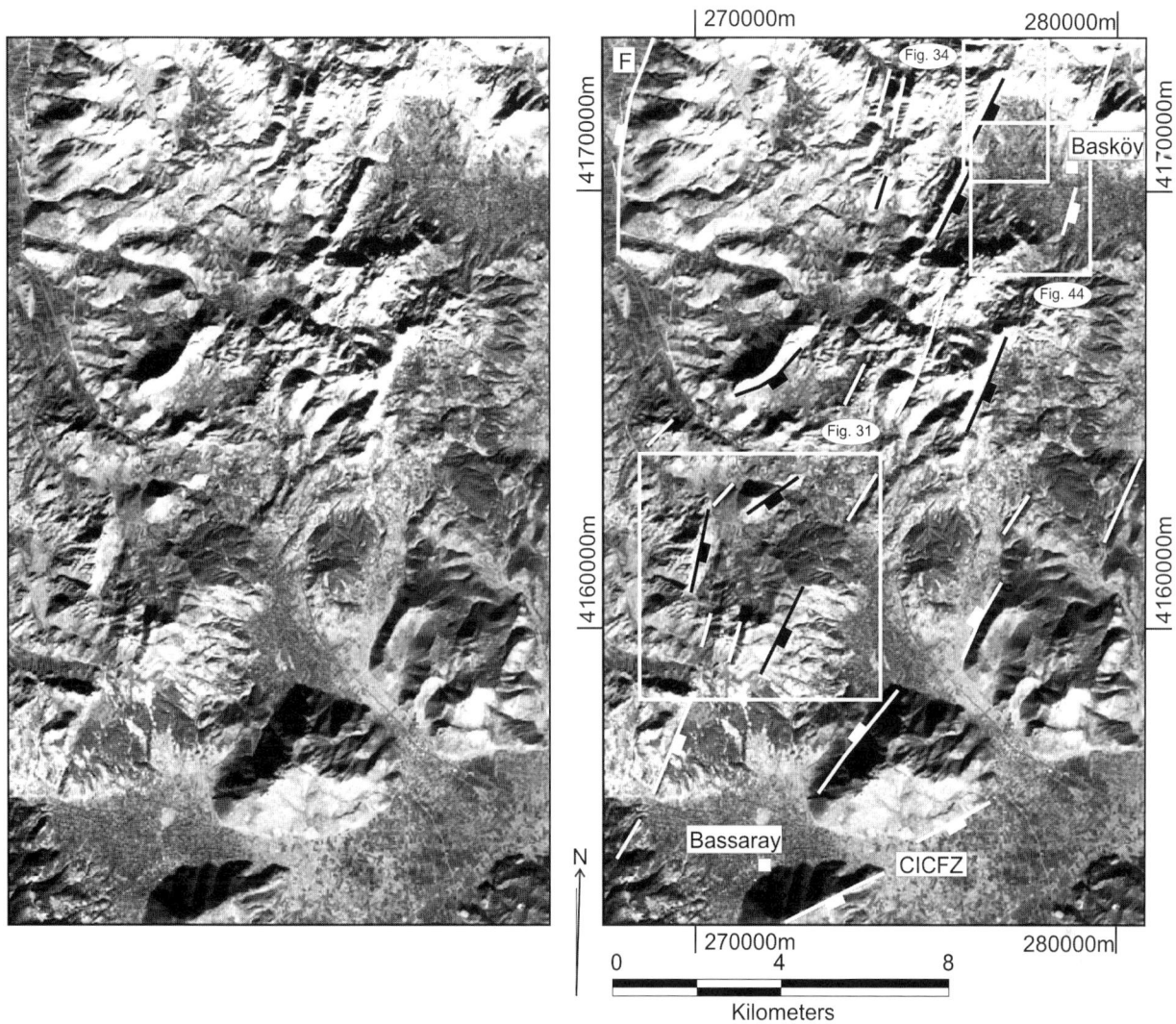

Figure 29: Bağsaray-Başköy lineament. Landsat 7 Enhanced Thematic Mapper + image with a fusion of bands 4, 5, 7 and 8, showing the location of the major faults. Projection is UTM Zone 36, Northern Hemisphere (WGS 84). CICFZ: Çanaklı-Isparta Çayı fault zone. F: unnamed fault (Similox-Tohon *et al.*, (this volume a)). See figure 5 for location.

limestone in their footwall since undissected footwall ridges can be observed (Figures 3 and 29). The fault zone is strongly segmented and bounded in the west by E-dipping faults and in the east by W-dipping faults, forming a graben-like structure (Figure 29). The Kayaaltı fault (Similox-Tohon *et al.*, this volume a) may be interpreted as part of the western border of the fault zone. In the northeastern part of the fault zone a 1.4 km long lineament cross-cuts the E-W trending Başköy valley (Figures 29 and 30). A clear morphological step is observed on the Quaternary alluvial valley floor, suggesting Quaternary fault activity. In the north, the fault zone terminates against volcanic tuff deposits from the Upper Pliocene-Quaternary Gölçük

formation (Senel, 1997). These tuff deposits are not affected by the Bağsaray-Başköy fault zone on the satellite image, suggesting fault activity predates the deposition of the tuff. However, on the geological map of Senel (1997) N-S to NNW-SSE trending normal faults affects both Mesozoic limestone and tuff deposits from the Gölçük formation, indicating Upper Pliocene-Quaternary fault activity. These contrasting views may be due to the fact that the satellite images are not detailed enough to enable the visualization of faults from the Bağsaray-Başköy fault zone within the volcanic tuff deposits.

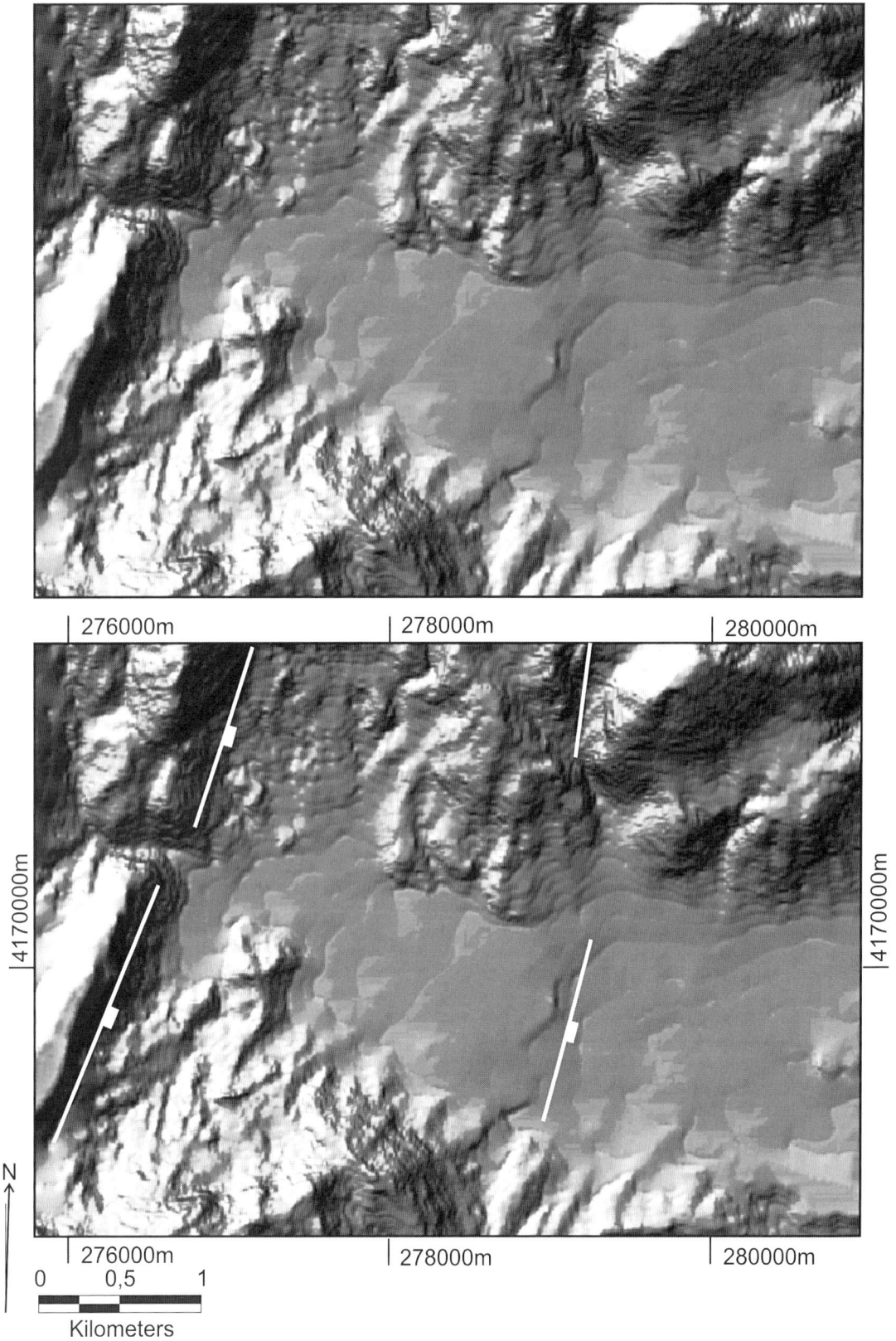

Figure 30: Başköy area. Enlarged DEM image with shaded relief of the Bağsaray-Başköy fault zone near Başköy, illuminated from the NW. See figure 6 for location.

5.3.2. Surface geology

Surface data were collected in three key areas: the Gravgaz valley, Sarıkaya (see also Verhaert *et al.*, 2006) and the Başköy valley.

5.3.2.1. Gravgaz valley

The area around the Gravgaz valley is characterized by the Lycian nappes and comprises bedrock of Middle Triassic-Liassic limestone and the Upper Senonian ophiolitic mélange and olistostrome unit (Senel, 1997). Pliocene lacustrine deposits, Upper Pliocene-Quaternary conglomerates and Quaternary alluvium and slope debris were deposited on top of the Lycian nappes (Figure 31).

Some fault segments belonging to the Bağsaray-Başköy fault zone, as inferred from satellite imagery, cross the Gravgaz valley area (Figures 29 and 31). A fault scarp (CN ca. 200/50 pitch 70; CN: certainly normal fault) with limestone in the footwall and Upper Pliocene-Quaternary conglomeratic deposits in the hanging wall, is present in the southwest of the Gravgaz depression (site b; Figure 31). The exposed part of the slip plane is about 3 m high and 30-35 m long and difficult to trace further in the landscape (Figure 32a). The fault plane itself displays clear characteristics typical of Aegean-type normal faults in carbonates (Hancock and Barka, 1987; Stewart and Hancock, 1988; 1990; 1991), i.e. fault breccia, corrugations, slickensides, comb fractures, remnants of brecciated hanging wall material and pluck holes (Figure 32b). The presence of tectonic breccias in the Upper Pliocene-Quaternary sediments immediately overlying the faulted bedrock/Upper Pliocene-Quaternary contact is evidence for tectonic reactivation. The main fault plane is displaced (30-40 cm) by another fault (PD 330/55 pitch 4; PD: probably dextral fault) with indications of strike-slip slickensides and fault breccia (Figure 32c). The Upper Pliocene-Quaternary conglomerates are delimited to the south from the limestone by a N70W trending and steeply N-dipping corridor of iron-rich material. The iron-rich material shows randomly oriented slickensides. The western border of the Gravgaz depression is dominated by a linear ca. N-S trending limestone escarpment (site a; Figure 31). The limestone is intensely fractured (000/60, 010/65, 165/90, 020/65, 130/90, 165/90) (Figure 31). The joints are often filled with a flowstone-type of calcite. The limit of the 'wet' area (swamp) in the Gravgaz depression (Figure 33) lays in continuation of this limestone escarpment and is seemingly rather rectilinear with a N35E trend (Figure 31). Therefore, the elongated and isolated hill composed of Upper Pliocene-Quaternary conglomerates within the Gravgaz depression may represent deposits of a fault-bounded basin (Figure 33). The presence of tectonic breccias in the Upper Pliocene-Quaternary sediments is clear evidence that some basin faults were reactivated in Upper Pliocene-Quaternary times.

Less direct evidence of basin activity during the Holocene can be retrieved from sediment cores in the central part of the Gravgaz basin, i.e. in the marsh area (Six, 2004). Tectonic (thrust) activity has been put forward by Six (2004) as an explanation for a sedimentary hiatus observed in a core (core SA-96). In our opinion, however, any recent tectonic activity should be related to the basin (normal) faults. From a W-E core profile through the Gravgaz marsh it is clear that in the west (core SA-96) the deepest part of the core consists of Unit I (ca. 4000 cal BC till ca. 930-790 cal BC) below Unit II (ca. 930-790 cal BC till ca. 770-760 cal BC) while in the central and eastern part Unit II is thicker and Unit I is not reached/observed. No anomalies were observed along two S-N core profiles.

A ca. 30 m long, NW-SE trending reverse fault (CI ca. 335/70 pitch 51; CI: certainly inverse fault) (Figure 32d-e) affects the limestone south of the Gravgaz depression (site d; Figure 31). The fault plane itself is characterized by slickensides, corrugations, comb fractures, remnants of a clay gauge and remnants of breccia sheet on the fault plane (Figure 32e). The fault plane was reactivated several times as evidenced by different generations of breccia and slickensides on the breccia. The limestone south of the Gravgaz depression is also intensely fractured by ca. dip-slip normal faults characterized by fault breccia, slickensides and corrugations (site c; Figure 31). These fault planes are highly degraded. On a NE-SW trending fault plane, a clear distinction can be made between the upper part of the fault plane that is fully degraded and the lower part of the fault plane on which corrugations and fault breccia are still visible (Figure 32f-g). This means that the lower part has been exhumed more recently.

An active fault scarp has thus been identified in the Gravgaz valley area. The fault scarp may represent the eastern border of a ca. N-S trending fault-bounded basin, filled up by Upper Pliocene-Quaternary conglomerates. The southern border is characterized by a corridor of iron-rich material and probably represents the alteration product of a fault zone. The northern part of the western border is characterized by a rectilinear swamp, which may be the expression of a fault in the subsurface. The eastern border fault has been reactivated after deposition of the conglomerates, implying an activity during the Upper Pliocene-Quaternary. Basin activity during the Holocene may be evidenced by a sedimentary hiatus observed in sediment cores in the central part of the Gravgaz depression. Holocene vertical movement along a ca. N-S trending active normal fault during Unit I

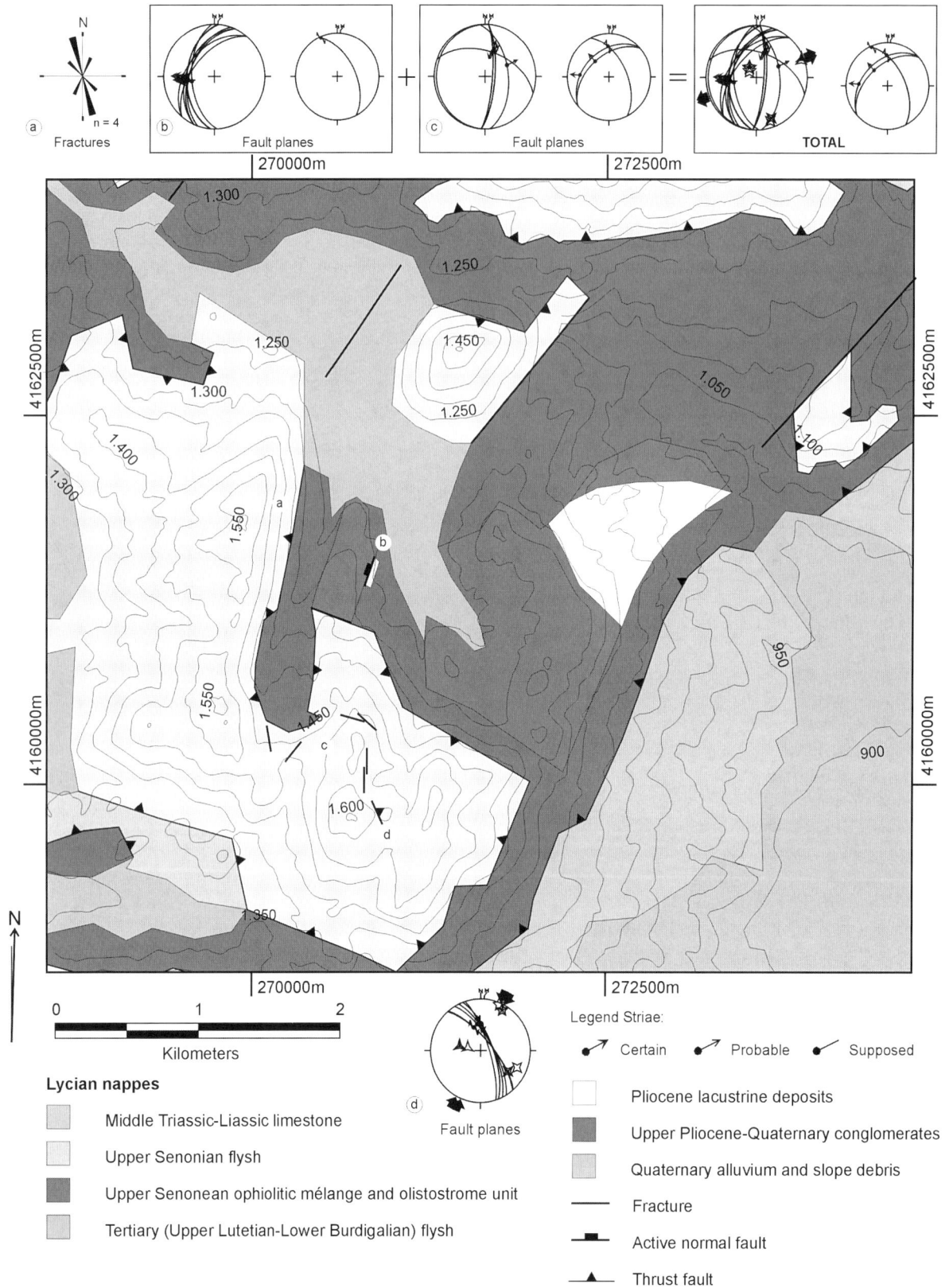

Figure 31: Gravgaz valley. Geological map with indication of fault data, modified after Senel (1997). Stereoplots of fault data are lower-hemisphere equal-area projections. See figure 29 for location.

110

Figure 32: Gravgaz valley. (a) Fault scarp (CN ~200/50 pitch 70; CN: certainly normal fault) with limestone in the footwall and Upper Pliocene-Quaternary conglomerates in the hanging wall in the southwestern part of the Gravgaz depression (site b; Figure 31). (b) Detail of the fault plane in (a) with slickensides and corrugations (arrow indicates fault movement). (c) Displacement of the main fault plane by another fault (PD 330/55 pitch 4; PD: probably dextral fault movement) (arrow indicates fault movement). (d) ca. 30 m long, NW-SE trending reverse fault (CI ~335/70 pitch 51; CI: certainly inverse fault) affects the limestone south of the Gravgaz depression (arrow indicates fault movement) (site d; Figure 31). (e) Detail of fault plane in (d) with slickensides and remnants of breccia sheet on the fault plane (arrow indicates fault movement). (f) A clear distinction (dotted line) between the upper part of the fault plane that is fully degraded and the lower part of the fault plane on which corrugations and fault breccia are still visible (arrow indicates fault movement) (site c; Figure 31) (hammer = 33 cm long). (g) Detail of currugations and fault breccia (arrow indicates fault movement).

111

Figure 33: Gravgaz valley. Panoramic view toward the east of the Gravgaz depression. The elongated and isolated hill, composed of Upper Pliocene-Quaternary conglomerates may represent a deposit in a fault-bounded basin. Dashed lines represent the possible basin-bounding faults. The linear boundary of the wet area parallels a limestone escarpment (white dashed line).

but before the start of Unit II in the sediment cores may have displaced the sediments in the basin. This fault could either be a fault of which the ca. N-S trending limestone escarpment is the surface expression or a fault of which the rectilinear swamp is the surface expression. However, no evidence has been found for any historical or recent seismic activity, although the 'fresh' fault surface (Figure 32f-g) may suggest otherwise.

5.3.2.2. Sarıkaya area

The Sarıkaya area is an area of 1 km by 800 m, character-ized by the Lycian nappes and comprize bedrock of Middle Triassic-Liassic limestone and the Upper Senonian ophiolitic mélange and olistostrome unit (Senel, 1997). Quaternary slope debris was deposited on top of the Lycian nappes. Four huge limestone blocks are lying underneath the main limestone cliff (Figures 34 and 35). They show a slight anti-slope dip and are surrounded by ophiolitic material with a varying concentration of limestone debris (Verstraeten et al., 2000) (Figures 34 and 35). This morphology has been interpreted by Verstraeten et al. (2000) as a lateral spread of limestone blocks due to a slide or flow of the underlying ophiolitic material. The limestone blocks are dragged with the flowing ophiolitic material and are first rotated causing the anti-slope (Verstraeten et al., 2000). There are some indications that these mass movements are a historic phenomenon. A local farmer explained that after a long period of stability, some 50 years ago, there was a slide of ophiolitic material from above the great cliff, resulting in a debris cone between the cliff and the limestone blocks (Verstraeten et al., 2000) (Figures 34 and 35d). This created a hollow above the cliff. In this hollow, there is now one single tree, a Salix, about 40 to 50 years old, which might corroborate the farmer's story (Verstraeten

et al., 2000) (Figures 34 and 35b). The slide of ophiolitic material from above the cliff resulted from the instability of the slope above the cliff, which in turn was probably due to the prior detachment of the four limestone blocks from the cliff (Verstraeten et al., 2000). The two phenom-ena are thus connected and it is therefore not unrealistic to believe that the displacement of the four limestone blocks occurred in recent or at least historic times (Verstraeten et al., 2000). Moreover, the faces of the limestone blocks and the cliff appear to be quite 'fresh', i.e. they do not yet show a black-grey patina and probably have not been exposed to the atmosphere for a very long period (Vers-traeten et al., 2000). Since part of the cliff wall, which has become exposed by the loss of the limestone blocks, was already exploited as a quarry in Hellenistic to early Imperial times (Degryse et al., this volume b) times, one can attribute a date of at least 2000 years to these mass movements (Verstraeten et al., 2000).

The Sarıkaya area is characterized by seven geomorphologi-cally different fault types (Figure 33):

(1) Wedge-shaped faults (site 4; Figure 34). Cavities in the limestone massif are filled with ophiolitic mélange (mixed with some limestone fragments) (Figure 36). The wedge-shaped contact surfaces between limestone and ophiolitic mélange all show evidence of fault move-ment (slickensides and striae, mostly down-dip). Also the infill is faulted. Within the infill throughgoing faults are observed (Figure 36b). In some of the later faults, a calcite infill is displaced showing small 'pull-apart' features (down-dip motion) (Figure 36c).
(2) Large ca. E-W trending and S-dipping striated fault plane (site 5; Figure 34). The fault plane is irregular with striae in various directions, but dominantly strike-slip

112

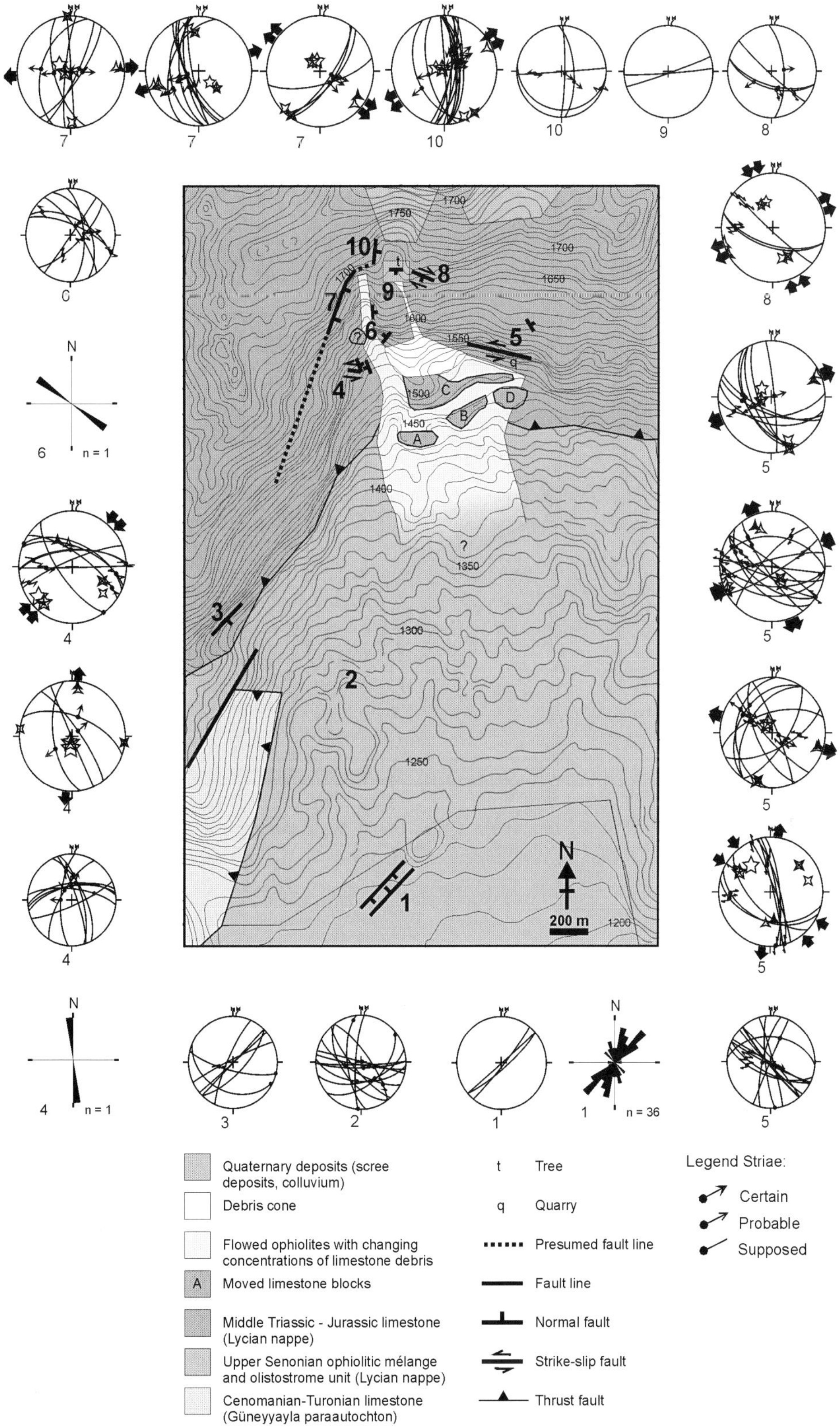

Figure 34: Sarıkaya area. Geological map, modified after Senel (1997) and Verstraeten *et al.* (2000) with fault data (see Verhaert *et al.*, 2006 for extensive discussion). Stereoplots of fault data are lower-hemisphere equal-area projections. See figure 29 for location.

113

Figure 35: Sarıkaya area. (a) View of the debris cone between the cliff and limestone blocks B and C (Figure 34). (b) View of the eastern side of the hollow above the limestone cliff with the 40 to 50 year old tree. Note the fresh surfaces on the limestone behind the tree. (c) View of the western part of the Sarıkaya area with the debris cone and the limestone block A (Figure 34). Fault sites 4, 6, 7 and 8 are indicated (Figure 34). (d) 'Slided' or 'flowed' ophiolitic material with changing concentration of limestone debris (arrow indicates flow direction).

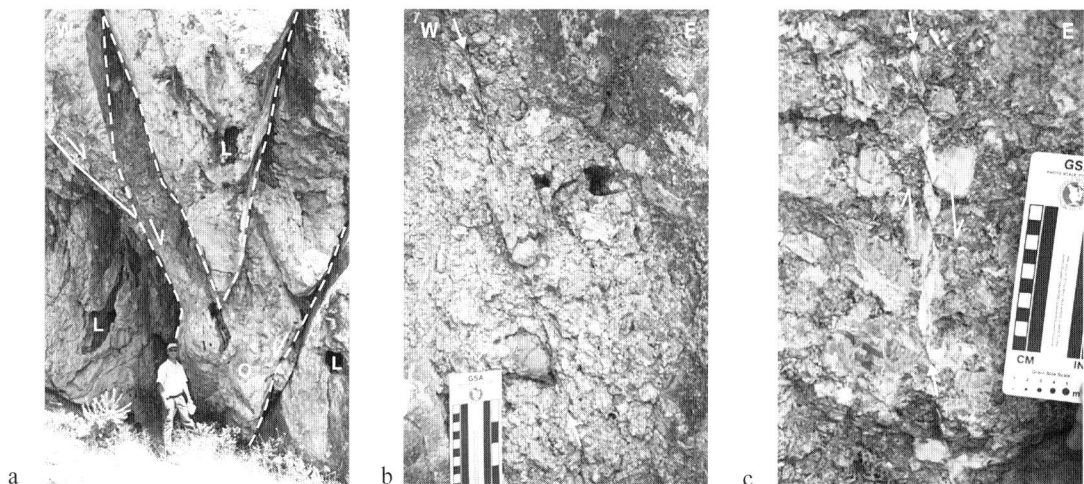

Figure 36: Sarıkaya area. Fault type 1 (site 4; Figure 34). (a) Infill of cavities within the limestone massif (L) with ophiolitic mélange (O). The contact surfaces of limestone and ophiolitic material all show evidence of faulting (slickensides, striae). (b) Detail of ophiolitic infill with a throughgoing fault. (c) Detail of calcite vein within ophiolitic infill displaced showing small 'pull-apart' features.

and sinistral (Figure 37b). Part of the fault plane was already exploited as a quarry, as indicated by man-made stepped extractions (Figure 37a).

(3) Small fault planes along both sides of a gully (site 6; Figure 34). The gully is filled with 'slided or flowed' ophiolitic material (i.e. historical mass movement according Verstraeten *et al.*, 2000). At the eastern border of the gully, a normal fault delimits the ophiolitic material, which is at this location also clearly sheared, from the limestone massif (Figure 38a). The fault plane (CN 000/65 pitch 90; CN: certainly normal faulting) displays striae and comb fractures (Figure 38a), while zone-parallel layers of cohesive (next to the fault plane) and incohesive fault breccia are present within the fractured limestone massif (Figure 38b). At the western border of the gully, the ophiolitic material is also sheared. Striae and a calcite vein are present on the limestone contact (Figure 38d). The limestone most likely belongs to a limestone block which slided down into the ophiolitic material. The in-situ limestone surrounding the gully is also affected by small faults and a single large fault (CN 040/90 pitch 62; CN: certainly normal faulting). This fault is characterized by zone-parallel layers of cohesive breccia next to the fault plane and incohesive breccia further away (Figure 38).

(4) Cohesive, intensely fractured limestones with multiple slip planes (site 7; Figure 34). Site 7 is characterized by a major, m-scale, NE-SW trending and E-dipping throughgoing normal fault plane in limestone with fault breccia, corrugations, slickensides and slickenfibers (Figure 39) and by a multitude of smaller, dm- to m-scale, fault planes with slickensides, slickenfibers, slickensteps and corrugations, indicating multiple fault activity, i.e. multiple striae on calcite coatings. The continuation of the main fault plane of site 7 is not obvious towards the south. A number of steps are present in the slope and may be related to normal faulting and the degradation of a major normal fault zone (Figure 39c).

(5) Large WNW-ESE trending and S-dipping undulating fault plane (site 8; Figure 34). The fault plane displays slickensides and striae, covered at different places by flowstone on which another slickenslide developed (Figure 40). Ophiolitic and limestone fragments were incorporated in the flowstone. The fault affects limestone and the first fault activity (pre-flowstone) indicates dextral movement. The second reactivation (post-flowstone) indicates a normal fault movement.

(6) Faults crosscutting Holocene colluvium (site 9; Figure 34). The colluvium, deposited during the historical slide of ophiolitic material from above the great cliff and/or older events, is characterized by several nearly parallel E-W and ENE-WSW trending faults (n = 10). These faults displace the colluvium down-dip (displacement between 10 and 20 cm) (Figure 41). Since their competence is low no sense of fault movement could be observed.

(7) Non-cohesive limestone fault breccia, crosscut by several N-S trending and E-dipping parallel normal fault zones (site 10; Figure 34). This fault zone affects fractured limestone and forms the western edge of an ophiolitic material infill, i.e. a karst depression (?), within the limestone (Figure 42). The fault planes contain oblique to dip slip corrugations, comb fractures and slickensides (Figure 42b-c). The damage zone of this fault zone is composed of non-cohesive limestone breccia (Figure 42), crosscut by the several parallel faults (Figure 42). The breccia consists of limestone fragments ranging in size from 2 mm to 10 cm. Stewart and Hancock (1991) describe this fault rock as an incohesive breccia belt, typical of shallow, active normal faults crosscutting limestone substrate in the Aegean region. An intense degradation of the fault planes has taken place as evidenced by the presence of pluck holes (Figure 42g) (Hancock and Barka, 1987; Stewart and Hancock, 1988; 1991).

The Sarıkaya area is, in comparison to other areas, characterized by many 'fresh' fault surfaces in the limestone. South of this area, Quaternary consolidated screes (site 1; Figure 34) are crosscut by a NE-SW trending corridor (Figure 43a-b). Many small-scale faults (< 1 m) crosscut the ophiolitic mélange (site 2; Figure 34), and a limestone fault breccia is crosscut by a m-scale NE-SW trending fault plane with clear slickensides (Figure 43c) (site 3; Figure 34).

Different types of ophiolitic material have been observed in the Sarıkaya area: ophiolite *in situ*, i.e. the Upper Senonian ophiolitic mélange and olistostrome unit of the Lycian nappes (Senel, 1997), 'slided' or 'flowed' ophiolitic material, and ophiolitic material that may represent a karstic infill. Also different fault types occur, some of them indicating multiple fault activity. A sequence of multiple fault activity can be postulated for the wedge-shaped faults (site 4; Figure 34): firstly, infill with ophiolitic mélange in karstic cavities, probably fault-related, secondary, faulting or fracturing of ophiolitic mélange with calcite precipitation and finally, displacement of veins. Multiple slip planes in the cohesive, intensely fractured limestone (site 7; Figure 34) and the large undulating fault plane (site 8; Figure 34) indicate multiple fault activity based on the multiple striae on calcite coatings or flowstone. The fault zones composed of multiple-slip planes and zone-parallel layers of noncohesive limestone fault breccia (site 10; Figure 34), also indicate several faulting events. Although, several faulting events could be identified in the area, clear evidence of historical or recent tectonic fault activity could not be found. At site 1 (Figure 34)

Figure 37: Sarıkaya area. Fault type 2 (site 5; Figure 34). (a) View of the major ca. E-W trending fault plane in the Sarıkaya quarry. Note man-made exploitation steps. (b) Detail of fault plane with slickensides and slickensteps indicating sinistral strike-slip movement (arrow indicates fault movement) (hammer = 33 cm long).

Figure 38: Sarıkaya area. Fault type 3 (site 6; Figure 34). (a) Fault (CN 000/65 pitch 90; CN: certainly normal fault) between limestone and ophiolitic material at the eastern border of the 'slided' or 'flowed' ophiolitic gully (arrow indicates fault movement). (b) Detail of the hanging wall with cohesive breccia next to the fault plane and incohesive breccia further away. (c) Fault between limestone and ophiolitic material at the western border of the gully. The limestone most likely belongs to a limestone block which slided down into the ophiolitic mélange. (d) Large fault (CN 040/90 pitch 62; CN: certainly normal fault) east of the gully within the limestone massif (arrow indicates fault movement) (pencil = 14 cm).

116

Figure 39: Sarıkaya area. Fault type 4 (site 7; Figure 34). (a) Major throughgoing normal fault in limestone with slicken-sides and slickenfibers (arrow indicates fault movement). (b) Detail of slickensides and slickensteps on a small limestone fault in the hanging wall (arrow indicates fault movement). (c) Steps in the slope that may be related to normal fault-ing and the degradation of a major normal fault zone. (d) Multiple slip planes and zone-parallel layers of fault breccia (pencil = 14 cm).

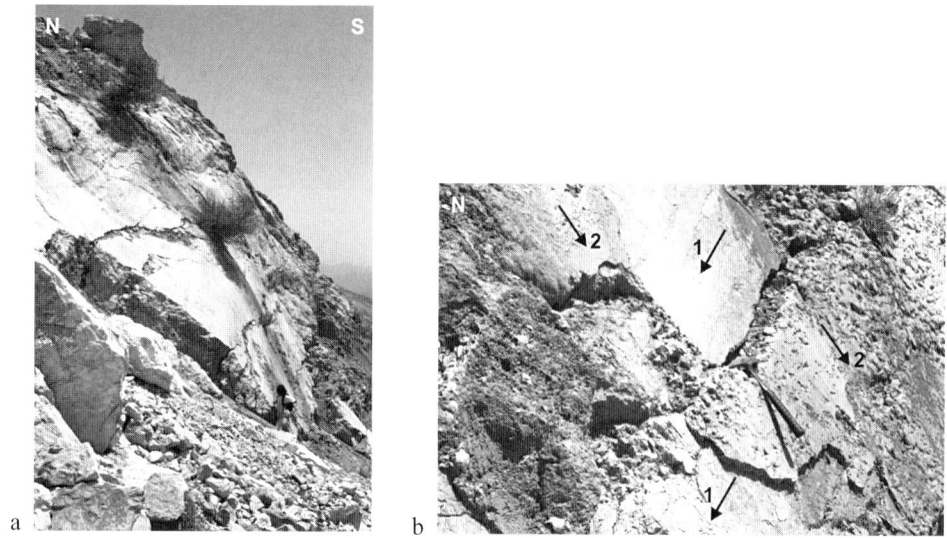

Figure 40: Sarıkaya area. Fault type 5 (site 8; Figure 34). (a) Major fresh fault plane. (b) Detail with arrow 1 indicating first fault movement (before precipitation of flow stone) and arrow 2 indicating second fault movement (after precipitation of flow stone) (hammer = 33 cm long).

Figure 41: Sarıkaya area. Fault type 6 (site 9; Figure 34). Normal faulting in recent Holocene colluvium (hammer = 33 cm long).

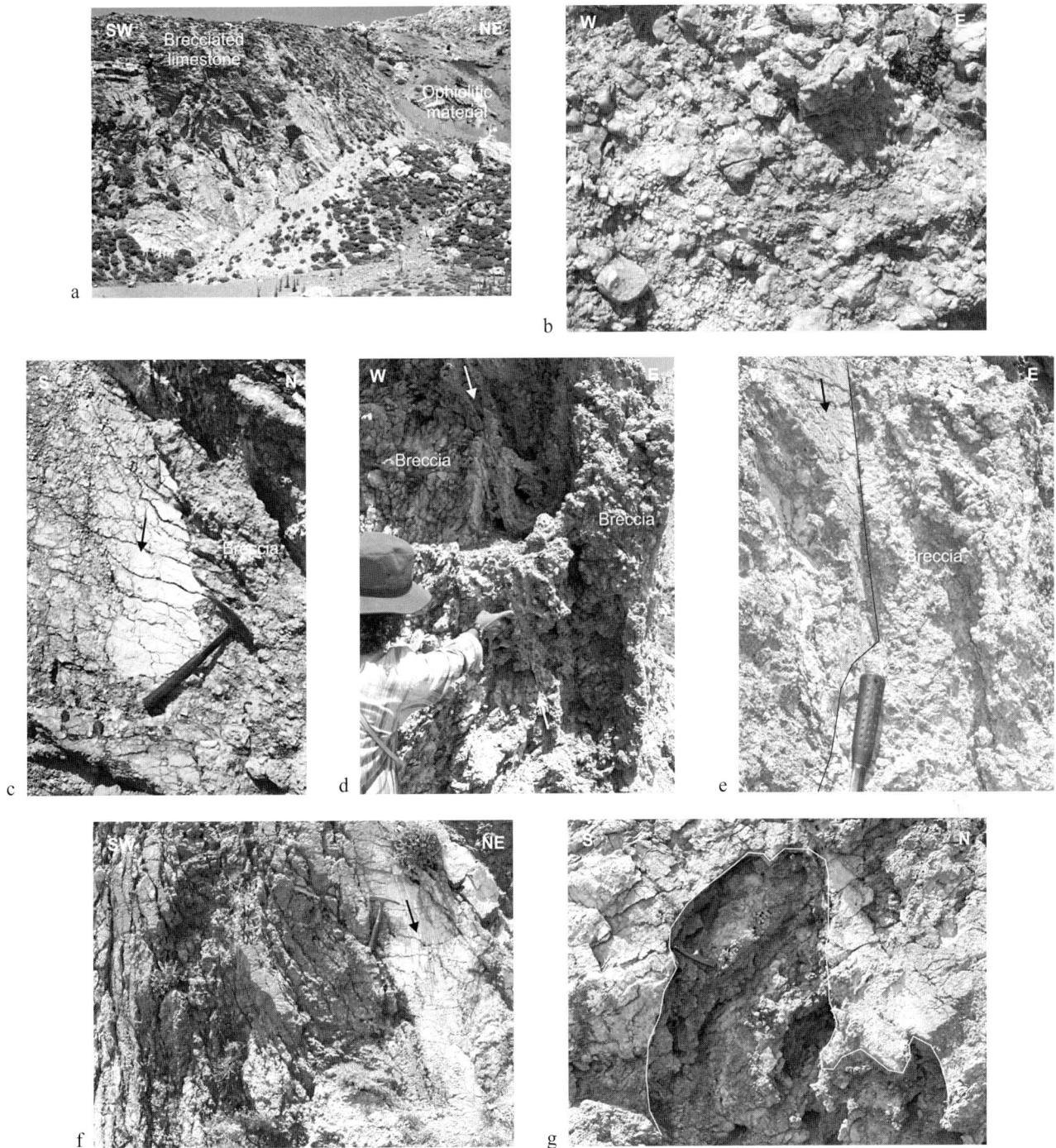

Figure 42: Sarıkaya area. Fault type 7 (site 10; Figure 34). (a) Overview of major fault. (b) Non-cohesive limestone breccia, consisting of limestone fragments ranging in size from 2 mm to 10 cm. (c) Detail of a fault plane with comb fractures within non-cohesive limestone breccia (arrow indicates fault movement). (d) Fault plane within the non-cohesive breccia. (e) Detail of fault plane with comb fractures within non-cohesive limestone breccia (arrow indicates fault movement). (f) Fault plane with comb fractures within non-cohesive limestone breccia (arrow indicates fault movement). (g) Strongly degraded fault plane with pluck holes (hammer = 33 cm long).

Figure 43: Sarıkaya area. (a) View of the NE-SW trending corridor in Quaternary consolidated scree deposits (site 1; Figure 34). (b) Fault plane, bordering the corridor in (a) at its southern extremity. (c) NE-SW trending fault plane with clear slickensides in a limestone fault breccia (site 3; Figure 34) (arrow indicates fault movement).

tectonic activity could only be constrained as Quaternary. The faults displacing the colluvium down-dip at site 9 (Figure 34) are probably the result of mass movements and not of a morphogenic earthquake because the surface ruptures could not be followed laterally. The Sarıkaya area forms a complex zone where fault/fracture systems intersect (see also Verhaert et al., 2006). In the western part, ca. N-S trending normal faults affect the Lycian nappes, while in the eastern part ca. E-W trending strike-slip faults are dominant. The intersection of both orthogonal fault/fracture systems results in an intensely fractured area. Therefore, it is not exceptional that this area is sensitive to mass movements. Mass movements occurred up to recent times. The mass movements could be seismically triggered but non-seismic causes are equally possible. The fault surfaces are relatively 'fresh'. This is likely because the fault planes have not been exposed to the atmosphere for a very long period since their exposure results from very recent mass movements along the existing fractures. No conclusive evidence for historical or recent surface-rupturing seismic events could be identified.

5.3.2.3. Başköy valley

The Başköy valley is characterized by Holocene cool water tufa (Degryse et al., this volume a; Vermoere et al., 1999) (Figure 44). U/Th dating of the upper part of the Başköy tufa suggests an early Holocene age of 9000 ± 600 yr B.P. (ca. 7600-6400 cal BC) (Degryse et al., this volume a; Vermoere et al., 1999). Based on the occurrence and association of different tufa facies (phytotherm framestone, finely laminated tufa and detrital tufa) Degryse et al. (this volume a) and Vermoere et al. (1999) conclude that the tufa were deposited in an alternating fluvial-barrage and paludal system (see also Ford and Pedley, 1996; Pedley, 1990). Today both systems no longer exist at Başköy. They must have largely disappeared 1350 yr ago, since by that time (ca. 650 AD) graves were being cut into the tufa walls (Degryse et al., this volume a).

To the E of the village of Başköy, some 4 km southwest of Sagalassos, a clear NNE-SSW trending and E-dipping escarpment can be observed crosscutting the E-W trending Başköy valley (site b; Figure 44). This lineament can partly be followed, to the north and south, into the limestone

120

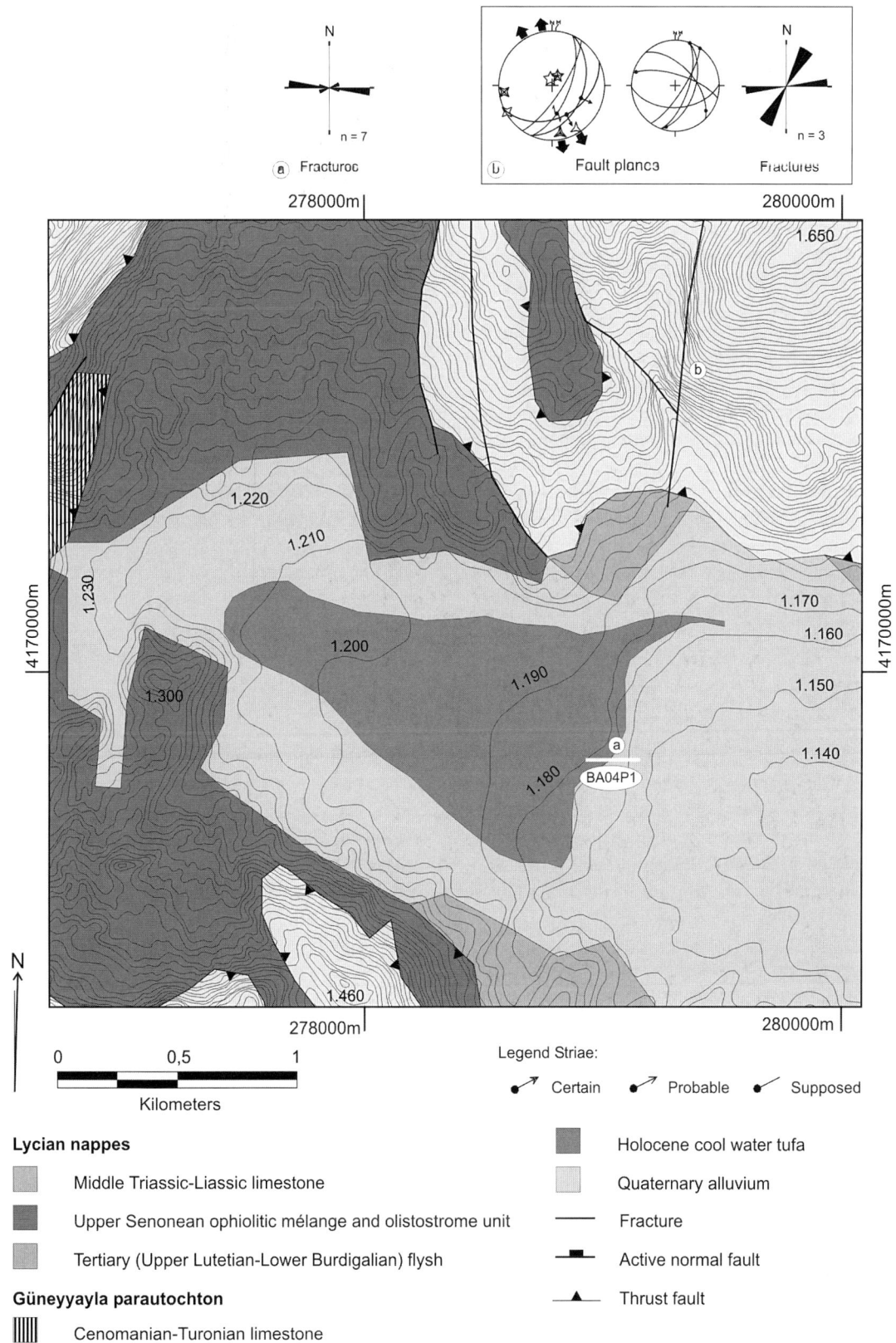

Figure 44: Başköy area. Geological map after Senel (1997) and Degryse *et al.* (this volume c) with indication of fault data. See figure 29 for location.

basement and displays a similar geomorphology as the mountain front north of Sagalassos. In the limestone massif northeast of Başköy, ca. NE-SW trending fault planes with ca. down-dip slickensides developed in a limestone fault breccia (Figure 45). Occasionally flowstone precipitated on these striated fault surfaces (Figure 45c). A second population of strike-slip faults with slickensides and corrugations are present in the limestone massif northeast of Başköy (Figure 45e). The tufa deposits are bordered to the east by a tufa cliff more than 10 m high, which corresponds to the major escarpment crossing the Başköy valley (site a; Figure 44). The tufa step has artificially been steepened by exploitation of the tufa stones (Six, 2004) for use at Sagalassos as a building material in late Roman to early Byzantine times (6th to 7th century AD). Fracture planes developed perpendicular to the tufa step (Figure 45f). Different models can explain the occurrence of this 10 m high tufa cliff. Firstly, the cliff may represent the principal barrage within the fluvial-barrage tufa environment (Ford and Pedley, 1996). Damming may have been initiated at a constriction point in the valley system or by log jams causing ponding. Secondly, the cliff also represents the principal barrage within the fluvial-barrage tufa environment, but in this case damming may have been initiated by fault blocks. Such depositional-tectonic model has been postulated for the Antalya tufa, less than 100 km southeast of Başköy (Glover and Robertson, 2003). Subsequent reactivation of the fault blocks, during tufa deposition, is still possible in this model. Thirdly, the cliff may represent a fault scarp, indicating normal fault activity after deposition of the tufa. Because the Başköy valley is a rather open valley, the tufa cliff lies in the continuation of lineaments and faults within the limestone basement and because of the presence of fracture planes in the tufa cliff one of the two tectonic models may be favoured.

Başköy is the only site in the close proximity of Sagalassos where such an extensive production of tufa has occurred. For some reasons this site must have particular properties, which enabled tufa production. An essential feature in the tufa production at Başköy is the great difference in conductivity, pH, hardness and temperature between tufa- and non-tufa-forming waters (Schroyen et al., 2000). The tufa-forming waters typically have greater hardness, temperature and conductivity (Schroyen et al., 2000). According to Schroyen et al. (2000) this suggests a more prolonged interaction with the limestone aquifers and possibly a deeper circulation of the fluids. Tectonic features may very well have served as conduits for this deeper circulation of the fluids.

The main lineament inferred from the remote sensing in the Başköy area corresponds to a 10 m-high cool water tufa escarpments in the field. The tufa cliff is fractured

and faults were observed in the northern continuation of the tufa cliff within the limestone massif. The tufa has a Holocene age and, in our opinion, a tectonic origin may be favoured instead of a sedimentary origin. Either the cliff represents the principal barrage within a fluvial-barrage tufa environment where damming has been initiated by fault blocks, either the cliff represents a fault scarp, indicating normal fault activity. In the first case fault activity occurred prior to (and possibly also during) the tufa deposition, in the second case fault activity occurred after deposition of the tufa which largely ended 1350 yr ago. It should be noted that the end of tufa production coincides with the period of the Sagalassos earthquake(s) in the 6th to 7th century AD (Sintubin et al., 2003; Waelkens et al., 2000).

5.3.3. 2D-resistivity imaging

Two profiles (BA03P1/b and BA04P1) have been measured across the NNE-SSW trending Holocene cool water tufa escarpment near Başköy (Figure 44), trying to answer the question whether these tufa deposits represents the principle barrage within a fluvial-barrage tufa environment where damming has been initiated by fault blocks, or whether the cliff represents an (active) fault scarp. The profiles were partly shot along a steep irrigation channel that crosses the tufa cliff (Figure 46). Profile BA03P1 (Figure 47) provides a detailed view of the eastern part of the tufa, below the tufa cliff, while profile BA04P1 (Figure 48) provides a general view of the subsurface architecture of the tufa more to the west. Even though many electrodes were located within the solid and high-resistivity (>700 .m) tufa, the measurements were of good quality, with only some data points with standard deviation above 2.5%. The deeper architecture of the eastern part of the tufa corresponds with a wedge-shaped high-resistivity body (Figure 47). The wedge can be subdivided in two zones, inclined to the east (Figure 47). The eastern zone has rather homogeneous resistivity values, while the western zone has lower and heterogeneously organized resistivity values. They are interpreted as solid and loose tufa respectively (Figure 47). The presence of aquifers within the tufa (Degryse pers. comm., 2004) results in lower resistivity values for loose tufa as water flows preferentially in these tufa. Two small steps, a few metres high, can be recognized at the top of the eastern part of the tufa (Figure 47). However, they are not observed at the bottom of the tufa deposits, around a depth of 15 m (Figure 47). The depth of the eastern part of the tufa wedge is in good agreement with the observation of a local farmer, who performed a drilling just down-slope of the tufa wall, and recognized 17 m of tufa below the surface, before reaching peat (Six, 2004). The bottom of the eastern part of the tufa is nearly horizontal, but seems

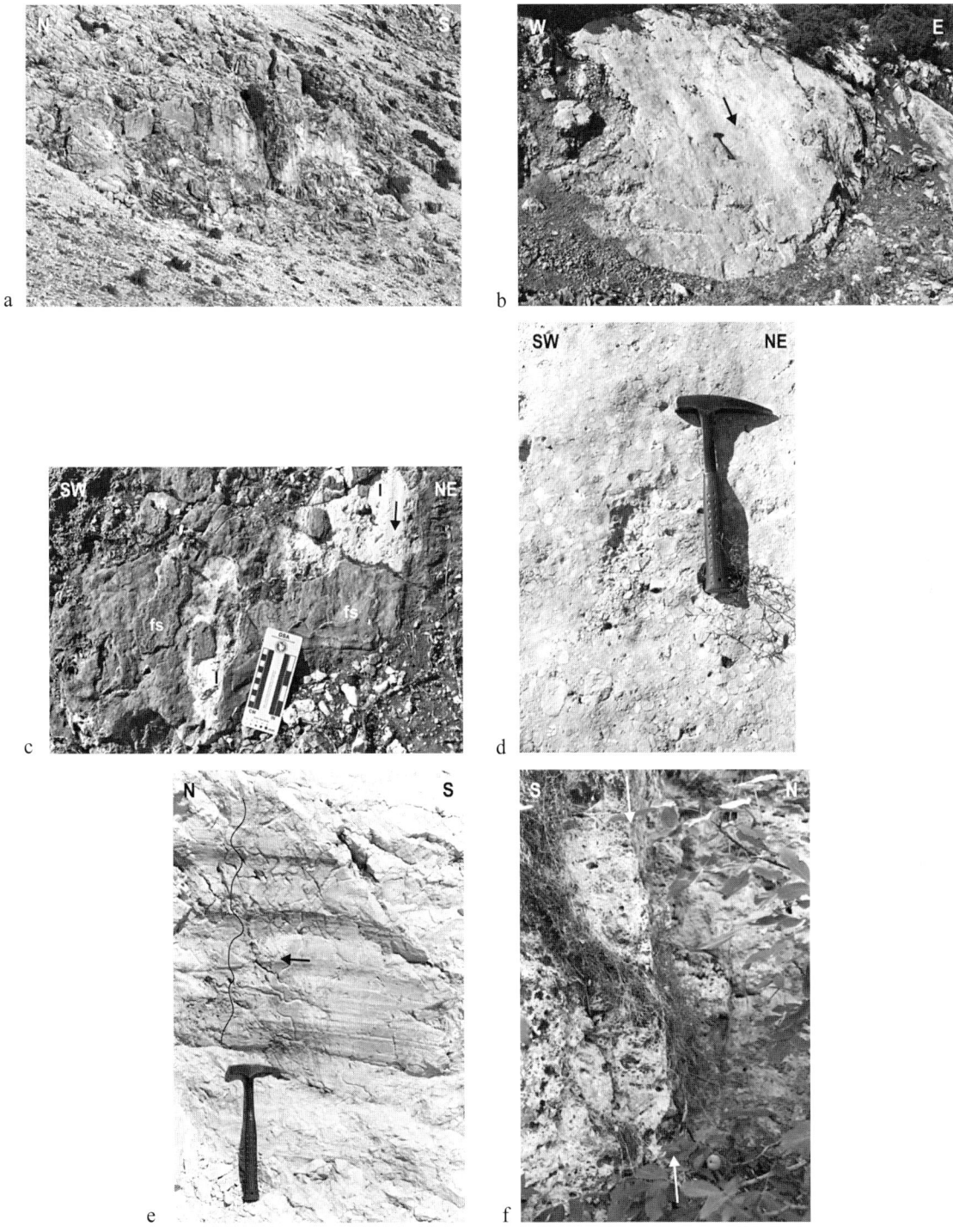

Figure 45: Başköy area. (a) Major fault plane (CN 019/63 pitch 125; CN: certainly normal fault) in the limestone massif NE of Başköy, in the prolongation of the tufa cliff (site b; Figure 44). (b) Fault plane (CN 020/40 pitch 90; CN: certainly normal fault) with slickenside developed in a limestone breccia, northeast of Başköy (arrow indicates fault movement) (site b; Figure 44). (c) Flowstone (fs) precipitation on striated fault plane (CN 060/40 pitch 90; CN: certainly normal fault) in limestone (I) northeast of Başköy (arrow indicates fault movement) (site b; Figure 44). (d) Detail of breccia in (b). (e) Corrugations and slickensides on a strike-slip fault plane (CF 015/53 pitch 170; CF: certainly strike-slip fault) in limestone (site b; Figure 44). (f) Fracture plane (arrow) within the tufa scarp south of Başköy (site a; Figure 44) (hammer = 33 cm long).

Figure 46: Başköy area. Site of the western part of the 2D-resistivity profile BA03P1, which is partly the same as the eastern part of profile BA04P1, laid out along a steep irrigation channel. See figure 44 for location.

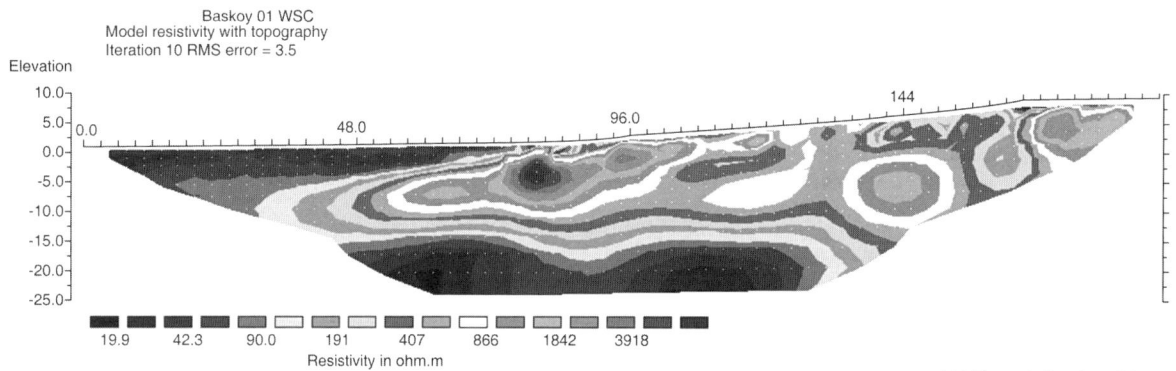

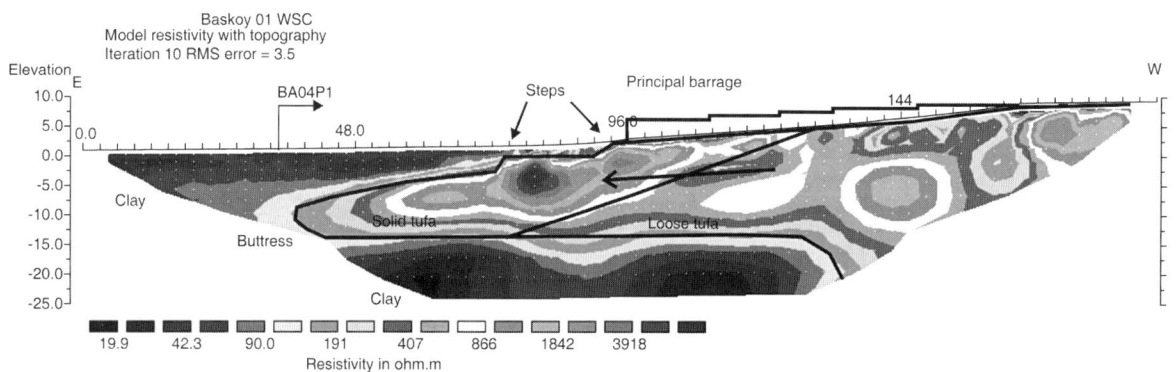

Figure 47: Başköy area. Conventional inversion for 2D resistivity profile BA03P1 with an optimized colour scale. Wenner-Schlumberger layout. Number of electrodes: 64; electrode spacing: 3 m; total length: 189 m; investigated depth: 30; data quality: excellent.

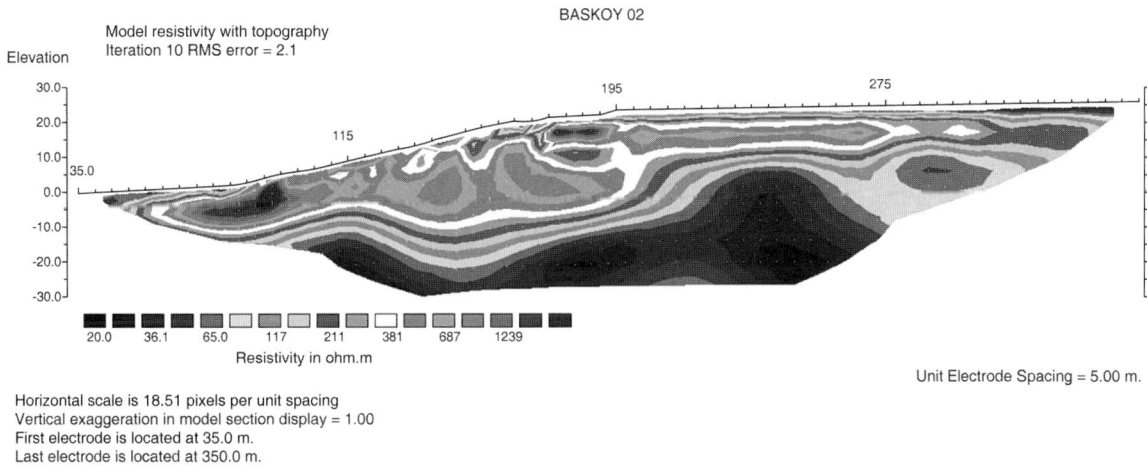

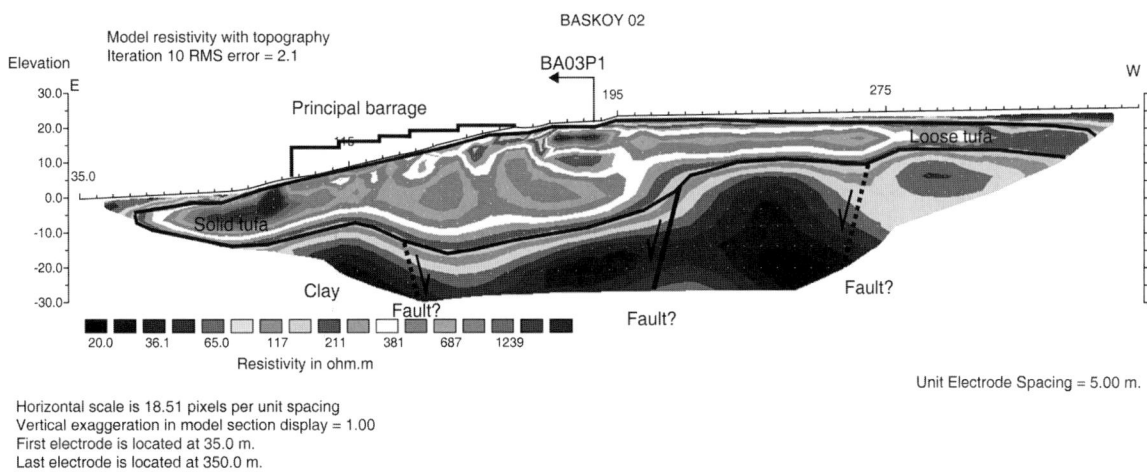

Figure 48: Başköy area. Conventional inversion for 2D resistivity profile BA04P1 with an optimized colour scale. Wenner-Schlumberger layout. Number of electrodes: 64; electrode spacing: 5 m; total length: 315 m; investigated depth: 50; data quality: excellent.

to thicken abruptly in the western part (Figure 47). The subsurface geometry of the tufa further to the west can be depicted on profile BA04P1 (Figure 48). The tufa body, showing high resistivity values, is clearly delimited within low resistivity values (Figure 48). The tufa in the eastern part has higher resistivity values than in the western part. A difference in height is present between the eastern and western part: the top of the eastern part of the tufa is lower than the bottom of the western part of the tufa. In its central part the tufa clearly increases in thickness. The bottom of both eastern and western part of the tufa is nearly horizontal. Between both ends, the bottom of the tufa is characterized by a minor W-dipping slope in the east and a major E-dipping slope in the west (Figure 48).

The wedge shape and small steps in the eastern part of the tufa (Figure 47) are interpreted as the subsurface expression

of the transgrading fluvial-barrage tufa system (Ford and Pedley, 1996). Accordingly, the tufa cliff corresponds with a principal barrage of a fluvial-barrage tufa system and not to a fault scarp. A buttress is present in front of this principal barrage (Figure 47). A downflow-inclined tabular stratification is observed (Figure 47). Lower resistivity values within the tufa may correspond with loose tufa able to act as an aquifer. The difference in height between the eastern and western part of the tufa bottom, the increase in thickness in its central part and the bottom slopes between the two horizontal ends (Figure 48) suggest that tufa deposition was initiated on a palaeosurface (Degryse pers. comm., 2004). This palaeosurface may be the expression of normal fault activity (Figure 48). In this tectonic model normal fault activity results firstly in a palaeosurface along the whole width of the valley. Secondly, tufa deposition is initiated on the most prominent E-dipping escarpment. Finally, tufa deposition advances down flow. It resulted in an increase in thickness of the tufa and in a displacement of the most prominent escarpment. No fault activity since deposition of the tufa could be observed since no displacement of both the top and bottom of the tufa has been evidenced on the profiles. The fact that the end of tufa production coincides with the period of the Sagalassos earthquake(s) is therefore not related to fault activity on this part of the Bağsaray-Başköy fault zone. However, the reactivation of another, nearby, fault can still be postulated as a possible cause for the end of tufa production.

6. DISCUSSION AND CONCLUSIONS

Based on diagnostic criteria with respect to geomorphology and drainage pattern of known active normal faults in the Burdur-Isparta area (Similox-Tohon *et al.*, this volume a) (Figure 3), the remote sensing analysis proved to be an efficient way to identify previously unknown active normal faults within the target area centred on the archaeological site of Sagalassos. A large area could be investigated without time-consuming field work. Previously unknown or undescribed, active fault zones could be postulated: i.e. the **Isparta-Eğirdir fault zone**, the **Çanaklı-Isparta Çayı fault zone**, the **Bağsaray-Başköy fault zone** and the **Sagalassos fault**. The latter lineament is already extensively discussed by Similox-Tohon (2005; 2006; 2004) and falls outside the scope of this paper. All these newly identified active normal fault systems fall within the target area, i.e. within a radius of 20 km around the archaeological site of Sagalassos, and could be considered possible candidates to be the causative fault(s) of the late Roman to early Byzantine Sagalassos earthquakes.

The remote sensing analysis indicates (1) that the NE-SW trending Isparta-Eğirdir fault zone is at least 35 km long and that some of the faults seems to have been active in Quaternary times, (2) that the NE-SW trending Çanaklı-Isparta Çayı fault zone is at least 23 km long and that tectonic uplift of some footwalls prevails on the erosion rate of the Isparta Çayı river, and (3) that the NNE-SSW trending Bağsaray-Başköy fault zone is at least 22 km long and that some of the faults were probably active in Quaternary times.

Surface geology indicates that there is sufficient evidence to consider these fault zones as 'active', thus potentially hazardous. These active fault zones are expressed in different ways: fault scarps, magmatism, river incision, mass movements, etc. Many faults often display architectural elements and fabrics typical of Aegean-type normal faults (e.g. zone-parallel fault breccia, multiple slip-planes, and

varied pattern of degradation). Even though the identified fault zones have definitively known a geologically recent activity, i.e. since Late Miocene times, no distinct historical or recent activity could be argued on any of the faults. It is therefore inferred that the area is seismically not really highly active. This is corroborated by the high degree of degradation of these fault planes (in limestone), seriously hampering any conclusive interpretation with respect to historical or recent fault activity. Also 2D-resistivity imaging confirms this conclusion (Similox-Tohon *et al.*, this volume c). Moreover, with respect to the tufa escarpment in the Başköy area the 2D-resistivity imaging proved that this escarpment is no fault scarp at all, which does not exclude that the end of the tufa production may still be related to the period of the Sagalassos earthquake(s) in the 6th to 7th century AD.

Nevertheless, a quantitative estimation of the stress field evolution in the Burdur-Isparta area (Verhaert *et al.*, 2006) is in concordance with fault plane solutions of 20th century earthquakes in the area. The identified active faults fit into the current stress field and should therefore be considered potentially hazardous faults. This applies certainly for certain faults in the IEFZ, more in particular in the Davras Dağı area, and in the CICFZ, more in particular the **Çanaklı fault** (Similox-Tohon *et al.*, this volume c). To date, there is, however, no evidence that these faults show any historical activity that could be related to the Roman and Early Byzantine Sagalassos earthquakes.

Finally, the identification of these active fault zones allows to proposed a new geodynamic model for the entire Lake Region (Sintubin *et al.*, in prep) (Figure 49). Both the ca. NE-SW trending IEFZ and the CICFZ are largely parallel to the FBFZ. In particular the IEFZ can be considered as the northeastern continuation of the FBFZ. These two fault zones show a right-stepping en-echelon configuration and can therefore be considered kinematically linked. Within the transfer zone the WSW-ENE trending Sagalassos fault is situated (Similox-Tohon *et al.*, 2006). Left-lateral movement on the Sagalassos fault system is indicated by the en-echelon arrangement of its fault segments (Similox-Tohon *et al.*, 2006). Also the microseismic activity in the wider Isparta region is clearly related to this transfer zone. This kinematically linked fault system suggests a propagation to the northeast of a tectonic feature 'cutting into' the Anatolian plate, as already suggested in recent research on Crete, Rhodes and in the Fethiye area on mainland Turkey (ten Veen, 2004; ten Veen and Kleinspehn, 2002; 2003).

The NE-SW trending CICFZ is situated at a certain distance with respect to both the FBFZ and the IEFZ. It is

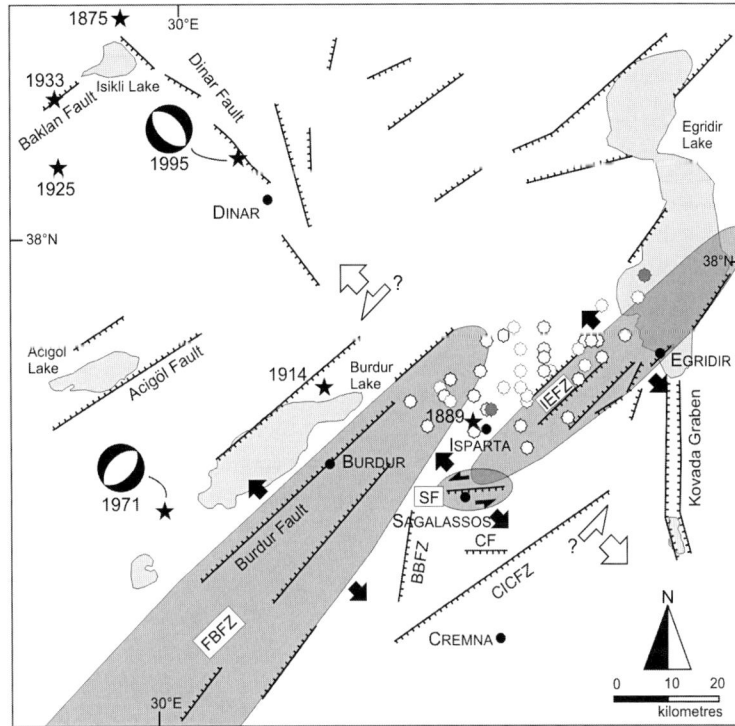

Figure 49: New geodynamic model for the Burdur-Isparta region (Sintubin *et al.*, in prep). Open arrows indicate the overall NW-SE trending extensional deformation. Black arrows show the deformation for the individual fault and fault zones. SF: Sagalassos fault. FBFZ: Fethiye-Burdur fault zone. CICFZ: Çanaklı-Isparta Çayı fault zone. CF: Çanaklı fault. BBFZ: Bağsaray-Başköy fault zone. IEFZ: Isparta-Eğirdir fault zone. Epicentres of recent large earthquakes (stars), available focal mechanisms (after Eyidoğan and Barka, 1996; Taymaz and Price, 1992) and the microseismic activity in the Isparta-Eğirdir region (white circles are Md 3.0-3.9 events; gray circles are Md 4.0-4.9 events) (KOERI, 2002).

therefore less obvious to consider the CICFZ kinematically linked to one of them. Regionally, it forms, however, part of the overall geodynamically active system. The BBFZ, finally, may play a role in linking the CICFZ with the FBFZ-IEFZ system.

The superior number of NE-SW trending active faults in comparison to NW-SE trending active faults (e.g. Dinar fault) might indicate a growing importance of a NW-SE extension in the overall biaxial extension regime in the region (Temiz *et al.*, 1997). An extensive palaeostress analysis and reconstruction of the stress field evolution since Pliocene times (Verhaert *et al.*, 2006) confirms the growing dominance of the so-called 'Burdur stress regime' since Quaternary times. Taking into account the prevailing stress field, as well as the assumed north-eastward propagation of the global tectonic feature, an increased seismic activity within the transfer zone and the IEFZ can be predicted.

7. ACKNOWLEDGMENTS

A version of this article in full colour is available from the authors. The research was supported by the Belgian Programme on Interuniversitary Poles of Attraction (IAP V/9) and the Research Fund of the K.U.Leuven (BOF-GOA02/2). The satellite images were provided by Prof. Dr. E. Paulissen (K.U.Leuven). Processing using ENVI was performed at the Royal Museum of Central Africa at Tervuren (Belgium). We thank the Akdemiz University of Antalya for the opportunity to study the aerial photographs. Manuel Sintubin is Research Professor of the Research Fund K.U.Leuven. Marc Waelkens, the excavation director of the archaeological site of Sagalassos, is acknowledged for enabling our research in and around the archaeological site. We are grateful to Patrick Degryse for taking this initiative and giving us the opportunity to publish results of our research in SW Turkey.

127

8. REFERENCES

ALICI, P., TEMEL, A., GOAURGAUD, A., KIEFFER, G. and GÜNDOGDU, M.N. (1998) Petrology and geochemistry of potassic rocks in the Gölçük area (Isparta, SW Turkey): genesis of enriched alkaline magmas, *Journal of Volcanology and Geothermal Research* 85: 423-446.

ALTUNEL, E., BARKA, A.A. and AKYÜZ, S. (1999) Palaeoseismicity of the Dinar fault, SW Turkey, *Terra Nova* 11: 297-302.

AMBRASEYS, N.N. and JACKSON, J.A. (1998) Faulting associated with historical and recent earthquakes in the eastern Mediterranean region, *Geophysical Journal International* 133: 390-406.

BARKA, A.A. and REILINGER, R. (1997) Active tectonics of the eastern Mediterranean region: deduced from GPS, neotectonics and seismicity data, *Annali di Geofisica* 40: 587-610.

BARKA, A.A., REILINGER, R., SAROGLU, F. and SENGÖR, A.M.C. (1995) The Isparta Angle: Its importance in the neotectonics of the Eastern Mediterranean Region, *International Earth Sciences Colloqium on the Aegean Region* 1: 3-17.

BERRARDI, R., MARGOTTINI, C. and PARISI, A. (1991) Soil liquefaction: case histories in Italy, *Tectonophysics* 193: 141-164.

BLUMENTHAL, M.M. (1963) Le système structural du Taurus sud Anatolien, *Mémoire de la Société Géologique de France* 1(2): 611-662.

BOZKURT, E. (2001) Neotectonics of Turkey – a synthesis, *Geodinamica Acta* 14: 3-30.

BURBANK, D.W. and ANDERSON, R.S. (2001) *Tectonic Geomorphology*, Blackwell Science, Malden, Massachusetts.

CAMELBEECK, T. and MEGHRAOUI, M. (1998) Geological and geophysical evidence for large palaeo-earthquakes with surface faulting in the Roer Graben (northwest Europe), *Geophysical Journal International* 132: 347-362.

CAPUTO, R. (1993) Morphogenic earthquakes: a proposal, *Bulletin INQUA-NC* 16: 24.

CAPUTO, R., HELLY, B., PAVLIDES, S.B. and PAPADOPOULOS, G.A. (2004) Palaeoseismological investigation of the Tyrnavos Fault (Thessaly, Central Greece), *Tectonophysics* 394: 1-20.

CAPUTO, R., PSCITELLI, S., OLIVETO, A., RIZZO, E. and LAPENNA, V. (2003) The use of electrical resistivity tomographies in active tectonics: examples from the Tyrnavos Basin, Greece, *Journal of Geodynamics* 36: 19-35.

DEGRYSE, P., MUCHEZ, P., VIAENE, W., QUINIF, Y. and WAELKENS, M. (this volume a). Depositional environment and climatic implications of Holocene travertines in the valley of Başköy (SW Turkey), In: P. DEGRYSE and M. WAELKENS (eds.) *Sagalassos VI. Geo- and Bio-Archaeology at Sagalassos and in its Territory*, Leuven University Press, Leuven: 211-214.

DEGRYSE, P., HELDAL, T., BLOXAM, E., STOREMYR, P., WAELKENS, M. and MUCHEZ, PH. (this volume b) The Sagalassos quarry landscape: bringing stone quarries in context, in: P. DEGRYSE and M. WAELKENS (eds.) *Sagalassos VI. Geo- and Bio-Archaeology at Sagalassos and in its Territory*, Leuven University Press, Leuven: 261-290.

DEGRYSE, P., MUCHEZ, PH., SINTUBIN, M., CLIJSTERS, A., VIAENE, W., DEDEREN, M., SCHROOTEN, P. and WAELKENS, M. (this volume c) Geological mapping of the area around Sagalassos, in: P. DEGRYSE and M. WAELKENS (eds.) *Sagalassos VI. Geo- and Bio-Archaeology at Sagalassos and in its Territory*, Leuven University Press, Leuven: 17-24.

EYIDOĞAN, H. and BARKA, A.A. (1996) The 1 October 1995 Dinar earthquake, SW Turkey, *Terra Nova* 8: 479-485.

FORD, T.D. and PEDLEY, H.M. (1996) A review of tufa and travertine deposits of the world, *Earth-Science Reviews* 41: 117-175.

GLOVER, C. and ROBERTSON, A.H.F. (1998) Neotectonic intersection of the Aegean and Cyprus tectonic arcs: extensional and strike-slip faulting in the Isparta Angle, SW Turkey, *Tectonophysics* 298: 103-132.

GLOVER, C. and ROBERTSON, A.H.F. (2003) Origin of tufa (cool-water carbonates) and related terraces in the Antalya area, SW Turkey, *Geological Journal* 38: 329-358.

GOLDSWORTHY, M. and JACKSON, J. (2000) Active normal fault evolution in Greece revealed by geomorphology and drainage patterns, *Journal of the Geological Society, London* 157: 967-981.

HANCOCK, P.L. and BARKA, A.A. (1987) Kinematic indicators on active normal faults in western Turkey, *Journal of Structural Geology* 9(5/6): 573-584.

JACKSON, J.A. and LEEDER, M.R. (1994) Drainage systems and the development of normal faults: an example from Pleasant Valley, Nevada, *Journal of Structural Geology* 16: 1041-1059.

KARABIYIKOGLU, M., TUZCU, S., CINER, A., DEYNOUX, M., ÖRÇEN, S. and HAKYEMEZ, A. (2005) Facies and environmental setting of the Miocene coral reefs in the late-orogenic fill of the Antalya Basin, western Taurides, Turkey: implications for tectonic control and sea-level changes, *Sedimentary Geology* 173: 345-371.

KORAL, H. (2000) Surface rupture and rupture mechanism of the October 1, 1995 (M_w = 6.2) Dinar earthquake, SW Turkey, *Tectonophysics* 327: 15-24.

KURIBAYASHI, E. and TATSUOKA, F. (1975) Brief review of liquefaction during earthquakes in Japan, *Soils and Foundations* 15: 81-92.

LEEDER, M.R. and JACKSON, J.A. (1993) The interaction between normal faulting drainage in active extensional basins, with examples from the western United States and central Greece, *Basin Research* 5: 79-102.

LOKE, M.H., ACWORTH, I. and DAHLIN, T. (2001) A comparison of smooth and blocky inversion methods in 2-D electrical imaging surveys, *ASEG 15th Geophysical Conference and Exhibition*, Brisbane: 4.

LOKE, M.H. and BARKER, R.D. (1996) Practical techniques for 3-D resistivity surveys and data inversion, *Geophysical Prospecting* 44: 499-523.

MICHETTI, A.M., AUDEMARD M., F.A. and MARCO, S. (2005) Future trends in paleoseismology: Integrated study of the seismic landscape as a vital tool in seismic hazard analyses, *Tectonophysics* 408: 3-21.

MICHETTI, A.M. and HANCOCK, P.L. (1997) Paleoseismology: understanding past earthquakes using quaternary geology, *Journal of Geodynamics* 24: 3-10.

NEMEC, W., KAZANCI, N. and MITCHEL, J.G. (1998) Pleistocene explosions and pyroclastic currents in west-central Anatolia, *Boreas* 27: 311-332.

PAVLIDES, S.B. and CAPUTO, R. (2004) Magnitude versus faults' surface parameters: quantitative relationships from the Aegean Region, *Tectonophysics* 380: 159-188.

PEDLEY, H.M. (1990) Classification and environmental models of cool freshwater tufas, *Sedimentary Geology* 68: 143-154.

PRICE, S.P. and SCOTT, B. (1991) Pliocene Burdur basin, SW Turkey: tectonics, seismicity and sedimentation, *Journal of the Geological Society, London* 148: 345-354.

PRICE, S.P. and SCOTT, B. (1994) Fault-block rotations at the edge of a zone of continental extension: southwest Turkey, *Journal of Structural Geology* 16(3): 381-392.

ROBERTSON, A.H.F. (1993) Mesozoic-Tertiary sedimentary and tectonic evolution of Neotethyan carbonate platforms, margins and small ocean basins in the Antalya Complex, southwest Turkey, *Spec. Publs Int. Ass. Sediment.* 20: 415-465.

SCHROYEN, K., VERMOERE, M., DEGRYSE, P., LIBRECHT, I., MUCHEZ, P., VIAENE, W., SMETS, E., PAULISSEN, E., KEPPENS, E. and WAELKENS, M. (2000) Preliminary study of travertine deposits in the vicinity of Sagalassos: petrography, geochemistry, geomorphology and palynology. In: M. WAELKENS and L. LOOTS (eds.) *Sagalassos V. Report on the Survey and Excavation Campaigns of 1996 and 1997, (Acta Archaeologica Lovaniensia Monographiae 11)*, Leuven University Press, Leuven: 755-780.

SCOTT, B. and PRICE, S.P. (1988) Earthquake-induced structures in young sediments, *Tectonophysics* 147: 165-170.

SENEL, M. (1997) *1:100 000 geological map of the Isparta – J11 Quadrangle,* General Directorate of Mineral Research and Exploration, Ankara.

SERVA, L. (1994) Ground effects in intensity scales, *Terra Nova* 6(4): 414-416.

SIMILOX-TOHON, D., FERNANDEZ-ALONSO, M., WAELKENS, M., MUCHEZ, P. and SINTUBIN, M. (this volume a) Testing diagnostic geomorphological criteria of active normal faults in the Burdur-Isparta region (SW Turkey), In: P. DEGRYSE and M. WAELKENS (eds.) *Sagalassos VI. Geo- and Bio-Archaeology at Sagalassos and in its Territory*, Leuven University Press, Leuven: 53-74.

SIMILOX-TOHON, D., FERNANDEZ-ALONSO, M., VANNESTE, K., WAELKENS, M., MUCHEZ, P. and SINTUBIN, M. (this volume c) An integrated neotectonic study of the Çanaklı basin (SW Turkey): remote sensing, surface geology and near-surface geophysics, In: P. DEGRYSE and M. WAELKENS (eds.) *Sagalassos VI. Geo- and Bio-Archaeology at Sagalassos and in its Territory*, Leuven University Press, Leuven: 131-153.

SIMILOX-TOHON, D., SINTUBIN, M., MUCHEZ, P., VANHAVERBEKE, H., VERHAERT, G. and WAELKENS, M. (2005) Identification of a historical morphogenic earthquake through trenching at ancient Sagalassos (SW Turkey), *Journal of Geodynamics* 40: 279-293.

SIMILOX-TOHON, D., SINTUBIN, M., MUCHEZ, P., VERHAERT, G., VANNESTE, K., FERNANDEZ-ALONSO, M., VANDYCKE, S., VANHAVERBEKE, H. and WAELKENS, M. (2006) The identification of an active fault by a multidisciplinary study at the archaeological site of Sagalassos (SW Turkey), *Tectonophysics* 420: 371-387.

SIMILOX-TOHON, D., SINTUBIN, M., MUCHEZ, P., VERHAERT, G., VANNESTE, K., FERNANDEZ-ALONSO, M., VANDYCKE, S., VANHAVERBEKE, H. and WAELKENS, M. (2007) Erratum to "The identification of an active fault by a multidisciplinary study at the archaeological site of Sagalassos (SW Turkey)" [Tectonophysics Volume 420 (2006) 371-387], *Tectonophysics* 435: 55-62.

SIMILOX-TOHON, D., VANNESTE, K., SINTUBIN, M., MUCHEZ, P. and WAELKENS, M. (2004) Two-dimensional Resistivity Imaging: a Tool in Archaeoseismology. An Example from Ancient Sagalassos (Southwest Turkey), *Archaeological Prospection* 11: 1-18.

SINTUBIN, M., MUCHEZ, P., SIMILOX-TOHON, D., VERHAERT, G., PAULISSEN, E. and WAELKENS, M. (2003) Seismic catastrophes at the ancient city of Sagalassos (SW Turkey) and their implications for the seismotectonics in the Burdur-Isparta area, *Geological Journal* 38: 359-374.

SINTUBIN, M., SIMILOX-TOHON, D., VERHAERT, G. and MUCHEZ, P. (in prep) New geodynamic model for the region of the lakes (SW Turkey) based on remote sensing, surface geology, archaeoseismology and near-surface geophysics, *Turkish Journal of Earth Sciences*.

SIX, S. (2004) *Holocene Geomorphological Evolution of the Territory of Sagalassos*, Unpublished Ph.D. thesis, Katholieke Universiteit Leuven.

STEWART, I.S. (1996) A rough guid to limestone fault scarps, *Journal of Structural Geology* 18: 1259-1264.

STEWART, I.S. and HANCOCK, P.L. (1988) Normal fault zone evolution and fault scarp degradation in the Aegean region, *Basin Research* 1: 139-153.

STEWART, I.S. and HANCOCK, P.L. (1990) Brecciation and fracturing within neotectonic normal fault zones in the Aegean region. In: R.J. KNIPE and E.H. RUTTER (eds.) *Deformation Mechanisms, Rheology and Tectonics*, Specal Publications 54. Geological Society, London: 105-112.

STEWART, I.S. and HANCOCK, P.L. (1991) Scales of structural heterogeneity within neotectonic normal fault zones in the Aegean region, *Journal of Structural Geology* 13(2): 191-204.

STEWART, I.S. and HANCOCK, P.L. (1994) Neotectonics, In: P. L. HANCOCK (ed.) *Continental Deformation*, Pergamon Press, Oxford: 370-409.

STIROS, S.C. (1996) Identification of Earthquakes from Archaeological Data: Methodology, Criteria and Limitations, In: S.C. STIROS and R.E. JONES (eds.), *Archaeoseismology (Fitch Laboratory Occasional Paper 7)*, Institute of Geology and Mineral Exploration and The British Scholl at Athens, Athens: 129-152.

TAYMAZ, T. and PRICE, S.P. (1992) The 1971 May 12 Burdur earthquake sequence, SW Turkey: a synthesis of seismological observations, *Geophysical Journal International* 108: 589-603.

TEMIZ, H., POISSON, A., ANDRIEUX, J. and BARKA, A.A. (1997) Kinematics of the Plio-Quaternary Burdur-Dinar cross-fault system in SW Anatolia (Turkey), *Annales Tectonicae* 11: 102-113.

TEN VEEN, J.H. (2004) Extension of Hellenic forearc shear zones in SW Turkey: the Pliocene-quaternary deformation of the Esen Cay Basin, *Journal of Geodynamics* 37(2): 181-204.

TEN VEEN, J.H. and KLEINSPEHN, K.L. (2002) Geodynamics along an increasingly curved convergent plate margin: Late Miocene-Pleistocene Rhodes, Greece, *Tectonics* 21(3), 10.1029/2001TC001287.

TEN VEEN, J.H. and KLEINSPEHN, K.L. (2003) Incipient continental collision and plate-boundary curvature: Late Pliocene-Holocene transtensional Hellenic forearc, Crete, Greece, *Journal of the Geological Society, London* 160: 161-181.

VANNESTE, K., VERBEECK, K., CAMELBEECK, T., PAULISSEN, E., MEGHRAOUI, M., RENARDY, F., JONGMANS, D. and FRECHEN, M. (2001) Surface-rupturing history of the Bree fault scarp, Roer Valley graben: Evidence for six events since the late Pleistocene, *Journal of Seismology* 5: 329-359.

VERHAERT, G., MUCHEZ, P., SINTUBIN, M., SIMILOX-TOHON, D., VANDYCKE, S., KEPPENS, E., HODGE, E.J. and RICHARDS, D.A. (2004) Origin of palaeofluids in a normal fault setting in the Aegean region, *Geofluids* 4: 300-314.

VERHAERT, G., SIMILOX-TOHON, D., VANDYCKE, S., SINTUBIN, M. and MUCHEZ, P. (2006) Different stress states in the Burdur-Isparta region (SW Turkey) since Late Miocene times: a reflection of a transient stress regime, *Journal of Structural Geology* 28: 1067-1083.

VERMOERE, M., DEGRYSE, P., VANHECKE, L., MUCHEZ, P., PAULISSEN, E., SMETS, E. and WAELKENS, M. (1999) Pollen analysis of two travertine sections in Başköy (southwestern Turkey): implications for environmental conditions during the early Holocene, *Review of Palaeobotany and Palynology* 105: 93-110.

VERSTRAETEN, G., PAULISSEN, E., LIBRECHT, I. and WAELKENS, M. (2000) Limestone platforms around Sagalassos resulting from giant mass movements. In: M. WAELKENS and L. LOOTS (eds.) *Sagalassos V. Report on the Survey and Excavation Campaigns of 1996 and 1997 (Acta Archaeologica Lovaniensia Monographiae 11)*, Leuven University Press, Leuven: 783-798.

WAELKENS, M. (1998) *The 1998 excavation and restoration activities at Sagalassos*, Unpublished annual report, Ankara.

WAELKENS, M., SINTUBIN, M., MUCHEZ, P. and PAULISSEN, E. (2000) Archeological, geomorphological and geological evidence for a major earthquake at Sagalassos (SW Turkey) around the middle of the seventh century AD, In: W.J. MCGUIRE, D.R. GRIFFITHS, P.L. HANCOCK and I.S. STEWART (eds.) *The Archaeology of Geological Catastrophes*, Special Publications 171. Geological Society, London: 373-383.

AN INTEGRATED NEOTECTONIC STUDY OF THE ÇANAKLI BASIN (SW TURKEY): REMOTE SENSING, SURFACE GEOLOGY AND NEAR-SURFACE GEOPHYSICS

Dominique SIMILOX-TOHON, Max FERNANDEZ-ALONSO, Kris VANNESTE, Marc WAELKENS, Philippe MUCHEZ and Manuel SINTUBIN

1. INTRODUCTION

Archaeological evidence (Waelkens *et al.*, 2000) has demonstrated that the ancient city of Sagalassos has been struck by a number of earthquakes during its occupation history. Archaeoseismological evidence (type of damage, extensive and widespread nature of damage) (Sintubin *et al.*, 2003) suggests an intensity of at least VIII (MSK) for the last earthquake(s), causing major damage in the city. An epicentre in the direct proximity, i.e. within a radius of less than 20 km, of the site should be considered (cf. Stiros, 1996). Epicentres of recent and historical earthquakes in the wider area are all located further away from the site (Figure 1). All known active faults in the wider region (Similox-Tohon *et al.*, this volume a) are thus located too far to be considered responsible for the most destructive earthquakes.

In the Aegean region, surface rupturing occurs on normal faults for earthquakes of Ms 5.5 or above (Pavlides and Caputo, 2004). It is fair to assume that the fault(s), responsible for the most destructive earthquakes at the ancient city of Sagalassos, are morphogenic, i.e. have a geomorphological expression. Using diagnostic geomorphological features for active normal faults (Similox-Tohon *et al.*, this volume a) a search for active normal faults within a radius of 20 km from the site has been performed, primarily using remote sensing (Similox-Tohon *et al.*, this volume b). In a number of areas, where active normal faults were positively identified, the remote sensing results have been complemented with surface data and date resulting from near-surface geophysics (Similox-Tohon *et al.*, this volume b).

Similox-Tohon *et al.* (2006) discusses the results of an integrated study on the immediate environment of the archaeological site of Sagalassos, identifying the Sagalassos fault, an active normal fault that may have been the causative fault of the earthquake(s) affecting the city during the late Roman and early Byzantine periods (6th to 7th century AD). In this paper, we discuss the results of an integrated study of the Çanaklı basin, situated some 10 km south of the ancient city of Sagalassos, where a number of lineaments (Similox-Tohon *et al.*, this volume b) may also be potential candidates for the fault(s) causing the destructive earthquakes at Sagalassos (Figures 1 and 2).

2. GEOLOGICAL SETTING

With respect to active geodynamics and seismotectonics the target area is situated at the outskirts of the northeastern extremity of the Fethiye-Burdur fault zone (FBFZ) (Figure 1), a major tectonic feature in SW Turkey (Barka *et al.*, 1995; Bozkurt, 2001; ten Veen, 2004; ten Veen and Kleinspehn, 2002; 2003). Based on recent surveys in the area (Similox-Tohon *et al.*, this volume b; Similox-Tohon *et al.*, 2006; 2007) a new overall, active geodynamic model is proposed in which the study area is situated in a diffuse transfer zone between the Fethiye-Burdur fault zone and the newly defined Isparta-Eğirdir fault zone (IEFZ) (Sintubin *et al.*, in prep).

On the geological map of Senel (1997a; 1997b) (Figures 3 and 4) it is clear that a wide range of lithologies is present in and around the Çanaklı basin (see also Degryse *et al.*, this volume). The subsurface of the area primarily consists of rocks belonging to the Bey Dağları autochthonous units, which are mainly composed of Jurassic to Cenomanian neritic limestone of the Bey Dağları formation, covered by Tertiary flysch deposits (Burdigalian to Lower Langhian). In the northeastern extremity of the area Scynthian to Lower Anisian sandstones crop out, belonging to the Antalya nappes (Figure 4). These nappes are emplaced on top of the Bey Dağları autochthonous domain in Danian times, reflected in the Danian olistostrome unit (Senel, 1997a). Both in the northwest of the area and around the village of Çanaklı rocks belonging to the Lycian nappes are exposed (Figure 4). The Lycian nappes comprise bedrock of Middle Triassic-Liassic limestone, an Upper Senonian ophiolitic mélange and olistostrome unit, covered by Tertiary flysch (Upper Lutetian to Lower Burdigalian) (Senel, 1997a).

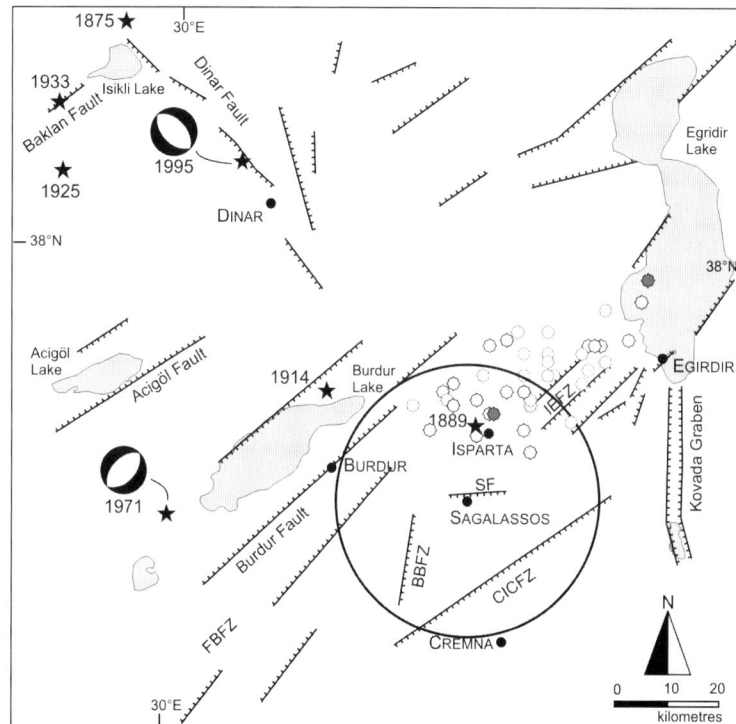

Figure 1: Simplified active fault map of the Lake District centred on Burdur and Isparta at the northeastern extremity of the Fethiye-Burdur fault zone (FBFZ) (after Bozkurt, 2001; Eyidoğan and Barka, 1996; Senel, 1997b), with indication of the epicentres of recent large earthquakes (stars), available focal mechanisms (after Eyidoğan and Barka, 1996; Taymaz and Price, 1992), the microseismic activity in the Isparta-Eğirdir region (white circles are Md 3.0-3.9 events; gray circles are Md 4.0-4.9 events) (KOERI, 2002), and the newly identified fault zones (Similox-Tohon et al., this volume b; Similox-Tohon et al., 2006): the Isparta-Eğirdir fault zone (IEFZ), the Bağsaray-Başköy fault zone (BBFZ), the Çanaklı-Isparta Çayı fault zone (CICFZ), and the Sagalassos fault (SF). Also marked is the target area within a radius of 20 km around the archaeological site of Sagalassos.

The central flat area of the valley is filled by Quaternary alluvial, colluvial and lake deposits (Six, 2004). They are composed of mainly clays and pebbles, gravel and tufa, which originated from weathering and erosion of the surrounding lithologies, i.e. flysch, limestone, ophiolitic mélange, shales, olistostromes and marl with cherts. Soils have vertic properties (Six, 2004).

3. METHODOLOGY

Remote sensing has been performed on a Landsat 7 Enhanced Thematic Mapper + tape and an Ikonos tape. Processing was done using ENVI.

The Landsat 7 tape dates from 9 December 1999 and has a resolution of 30 m for the visible, near-IR and IR bands (1, 2, 3, 4, 5 and 7) and a resolution of 15 m for the panchromatic band (8) (Figure 2). The data were contrast-stretched and filtered. Various combinations of bands were used to try to pick out different features. A combination of bands 4, 5 and 7 for red, green and blue respectively was most widely used as this combination clearly showed the known major active faults (Similox-Tohon et al., this volume a). A fusion of bands 4, 5, 7 and 8 was carried out for an even more detailed image, with the colours of bands 4, 5 and 7 (30 m resolution) and the detail of band 8 (15 m resolution).

The Ikonos tape has a resolution of 4 m for the visible and near-IR bands and of 1 m for the panchromatic band. It covers an area of 8 by 7 km west of the village of Çanaklı (Figure 2). The data were contrast-stretched and filtered. Various combinations of bands were again used to pick out different features. A combination of bands red, green and blue has been used.

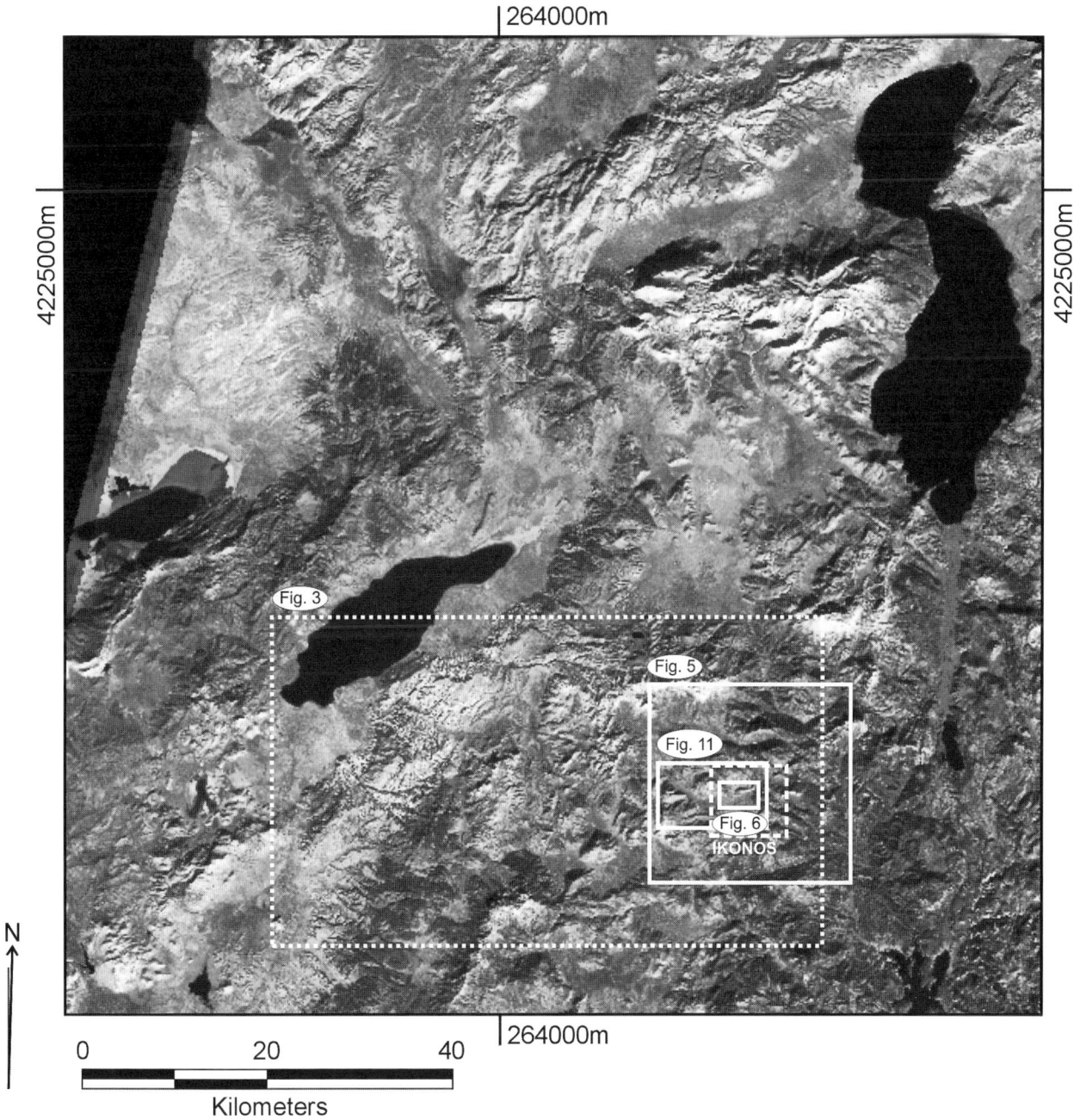

Figure 2: Landsat 7 Enhanced Thematic Mapper + image of the Lake District with a combination of bands 4, 5 and 7 for red, green and blue respectively. Projection is UTM Zone 36, Northern Hemisphere (WGS 84). Location of the Ikonos image. Landsat 7 image used in figures 5 and 11. Ikonos image used in figures 6, 11 and 21.

Figure 3: Geological map of the territory of Sagalassos (after Şenel, 1997b). Active faults, identified based on remote sensing analysis (Similox-Tohon et al., this volume a; Similox-Tohon et al., this volume b) are indicated in red. See figure 2 for location.

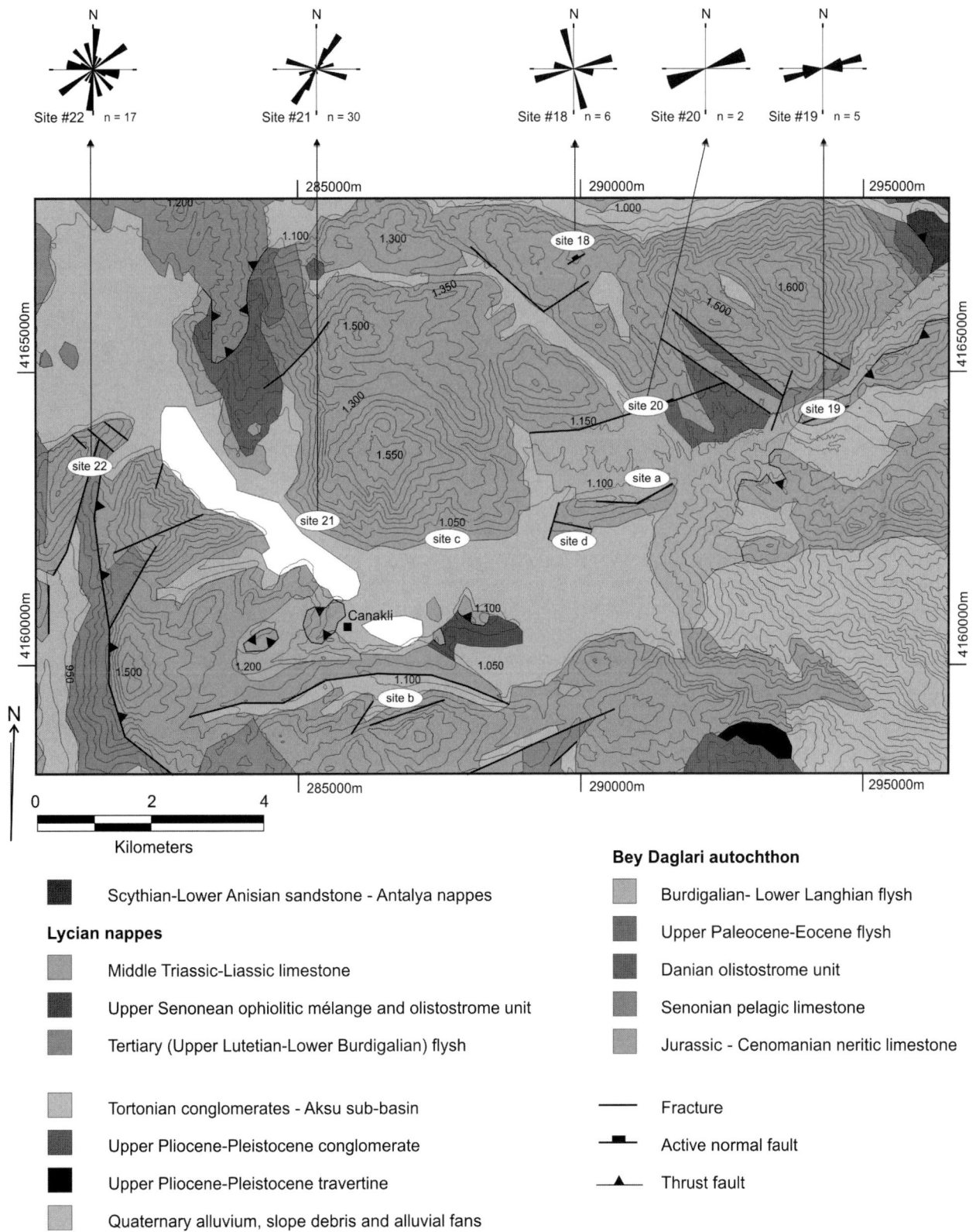

Figure 4: Geological map of the Çanaklı basin and surroundings (Senel, 1997a) with indication of fault and fracture data measured at different sites. See figure 3 for location.

2D-resistivity imaging has been chosen as the preferred method, not only because this method is reasonably fast, cost-effective and easy to apply in rough terrains, but also because it proved successful in palaeoseismological research (e.g. Camelbeeck and Meghraoui, 1998; Caputo et al., 2004; Caputo et al., 2003; Vanneste et al., 2001) and in archaeoseismological research (e.g. Similox-Tohon et al., 2004).

The resistivity measurements were carried out with the LUND Imaging System of ABEM, which consists of 4 cables of 16 electrodes, branched to a resistivity meter (Terrameter SAS-1000) through an electrode selector (ES-464). Using a roll-along technique, the length of the profile can easily be extended by a multiple of 32 electrodes. All profiles were measured with the standard 64 electrodes. Only profile CA03P01 was extended by roll-along to a total of 96 electrodes. The electrode layout used is a Wenner-Schlumberger layout. This layout is moderately sensitive to both horizontal and vertical structures. It has a rather good penetration and signal/noise ratio but a rather narrow horizontal data coverage (Loke and Barker, 1996). The electrode spacing along the survey line, i.e. the minimum interelectrode spacing, has been chosen to ensure the required resolution and penetration depth, and was in function of the position of the suspected fault along the profile and the space available. The majority of the profiles were measured with the maximum electrode spacing (5 m) that is possible with the LUND Imaging system, enabling large distances to be surveyed and a large penetration depth (50 m). Profile CA03P1 has a spacing of 4 m and profile CA03P5 of 3 m, with penetration depths of 40 m, respectively 30 m. For each data point, the resistivity meter performed a stack of minimum two and maximum four measurements. The standard deviation for each stack is a good indicator of the quality of the data. The quality of most profiles is relatively good to excellent with standard deviations generally below 2.5%. Before proceeding with the inversion, the data set was reduced, i.e. all negative resistivity values were rejected, as well as all data points with a standard deviation above a certain threshold. The filtered data were subsequently re-evaluated visually, and any remaining isolated extreme value was removed. The measured resistivity values do not represent the true subsurface resistivity, but an 'apparent' resistivity, corresponding to the resistivity of a homogeneous subsurface that would produce the same resistance value for the given electrode arrangement (Loke and Barker, 1996). Pseudo-sections plotting the apparent resistivity as a point at the mid-point of the array with respect to depth do not give an accurate image of the true subsurface resistivity, because these plots do not take into account that the signal of each value measured originates form a volume of the subsurface that depends on the type of array used. The true subsurface resistivity is eventually determined by an inversion. We inverted our data with the commercial Res-2Dlnv software from GEOELECTRICAL. This program iteratively calculates a resistivity model section, trying to minimize the difference between the observed and calculated 'apparent' resistivity. A conventional smoothness-constrained least-squares method has been used for sections CA03P2, CA03P3, and CA03P5. This approach gives optimal results where the subsurface geology shows a smooth variation. It tends, however, to smooth sharp boundaries and to under- or overshoot true resistivity (Loke et al., 2001). The robust or blocky inversion method, on the other hand, has been applied to sections CA03P4, CA03P5 and CA03P6. This approach tends to produce internally homogeneous bodies with sharp boundaries. All inversions were carried out taking into account the topography along the profile. A more detailed description of the method can be found in Similox-Tohon et al. (2004).

4. REMOTE SENSING

Based on the analysis of the Landsat 7 Enhanced Thematic Mapper + image (Figure 5), it can be inferred that the Çanaklı basin is situated on a NE-SW trending lineament extending from the Isparta Çayı valley in the northeast to south of the village of Çanaklı over a distance of at least 23 km (cf. Senel, 1997b). This lineament is interpreted to be composed of a series of normal faults, defining the Çanaklı-Isparta Çayı fault zone (CICFZ) (Similox-Tohon et al., this volume b). Contrary to the Isparta Çayı area (Similox-Tohon et al., this volume b) the geomorphological features in and around the Çanaklı basin are not at all obvious.

Northeast of the village of Çanaklı two ca. E-W trending normal faults with opposite dip (F1 and F2; Figure 5) are inferred, exposing in their common hanging wall Burdigalian-Lower Langhian flysch deposits (Bey Dağları formation) from the Bey Dağları autochthonous domain (Senel, 1997b). The sandstone is heavily dissected by a drainage system flowing to the south (Figure 5). Such dissection is considered characteristic for the footwall of an active normal fault since relative uplift is needed to start the dissection process (Similox-Tohon et al., this volume a). Therefore, another active normal fault should be present to the south, in which footwall the sandstone is located. A possible candidate would be the ca. E-W trending northern border of the Çanaklı basin (C1; Figure 5) or a NE-SW trending lineament (C2; Figure 5) crossing the Çanaklı basin. The latter lineament is aligned with the NE-SW trending, SE-dipping fault segments towards the Isparta Çayı valley

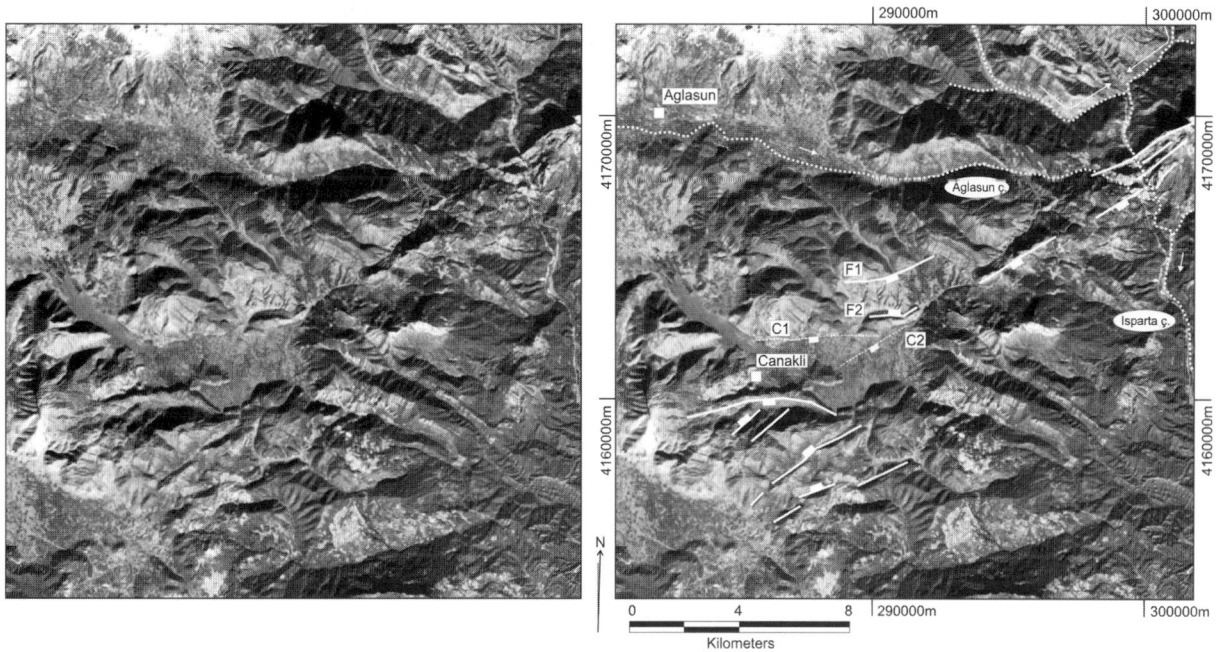

Figure 5: Landsat 7 enhanced Thematic Mapper + image with a fusion of bands 4, 5, 7 and 8 of the area centred on the Çanaklı basin in the southwest and the Isparta Çayı in the northeast, showing the traces of the major faults and drainage systems. Projection is UTM Zone 36, Northern Hemisphere (WGS 84). See figure 2 for location.

(Figure 5) (Similox-Tohon *et al.*, this volume b). Both lineaments (C1 and C2) are also apparent on the Ikonos image (Figure 6). The NE-SW trending lineament (C2) is expressed by a slight difference in soil colour, possibly reflecting the presence of different facies on both sides of the lineament. Furthermore, two large alluvial fans entering the Çanaklı basin at its northeastern end can be outlined on this satellite image (Figure 6).

5. SURFACE GEOLOGY

In the wider area in and around the Çanaklı basin a number of sites are investigated looking for evidence of active faulting. The limestones of the Bey Dağları autochthonous domain north and west of the valley (sites 18, 21 and 22; Figure 4) display an intense fracturing (N70E, N30E and N70W trending fracture sets) (Figure 7a). These fractures are often filled with a flowstone-type of calcite precipitate (Figure 7b and c). The limestone escarpment (240/75)[1] at site 18 (Figure 4) juxtaposes limestone and cemented scree (bedding

290/70) (Figure 8). Flowstone-type of calcite precipitated along this contact. In one of the isolated depressions (a few 100 m SE of site 18; Figure 4), conjugate fracture sets were also observed in Quaternary alluvial deposits (Figure 9). Brecciated calcite veins and limestone are abundantly present at the contact. NE of the Çanaklı basin (site 19; Figure 4) a clear limestone escarpment (070/60) (Figure 10a) has been identified. This escarpment aligns with the Isparta Çayı fault scarp to the northeast (Figure 5). No evidence (e.g. fault breccia) has been found for (active) faulting along the escarpment. To the west (site 20; Figure 4), another, less pronounced in height but longer, linear limestone escarpment (N70E) forms the contact between limestone (with thick palisade calcite precipitation) in the north and reddish shales in the south (Figure 10b). Also in this case, no evidence (e.g. fault breccia) has been found for (active) faulting along the escarpment. The isolated limestone massif at the northeastern border of the Çanaklı basin (site a; Figure 4) is limited to the north by an escarpment (240/80) (Figure 10c). This escarpment forms the contact between limestone in the south and a chaotic mélange in the north. Again, no evidence was found for (active) faulting. A limestone mountain range is present south of the Çanaklı basin (site b; Figure 4). In front of the mountain range, a less than 100 year old cedar forest has been planted on slope debris (screes) originating from

---

[1] Representation of orientation data of planar features uses the '*strike-dip*' and '*azimuth*' conventions; *pitch* is counted within the plane starting from strike direction.

Figure 6: Enlarged Ikonos image with a combination of bands red, green and blue of the northern part of the **Çanaklı basin**, showing the lineaments, interpreted as normal fault traces, and alluvial fans. Geological background is taken from figure 4 (Senel, 1997a). See figure 2 for location.

138

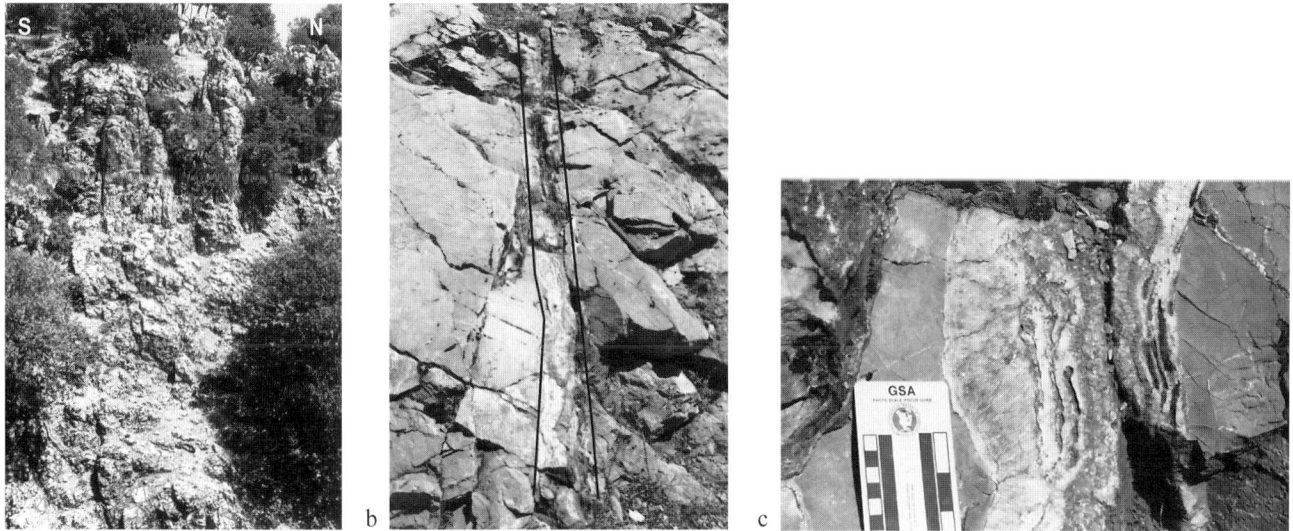

Figure 7: (a) Intense N70E fracture set in Bey Dağları limestone north of the Çanaklı basin (site 18, Figure 4). (b) Large, wide extension vein in limestone with calcite precipitates (hammer = 33 cm long) (site 21, Figure 4). (c) Extension veins filled with crustiform calcites, built up of several, individual parallel calcite layers (site 21, Figure 4).

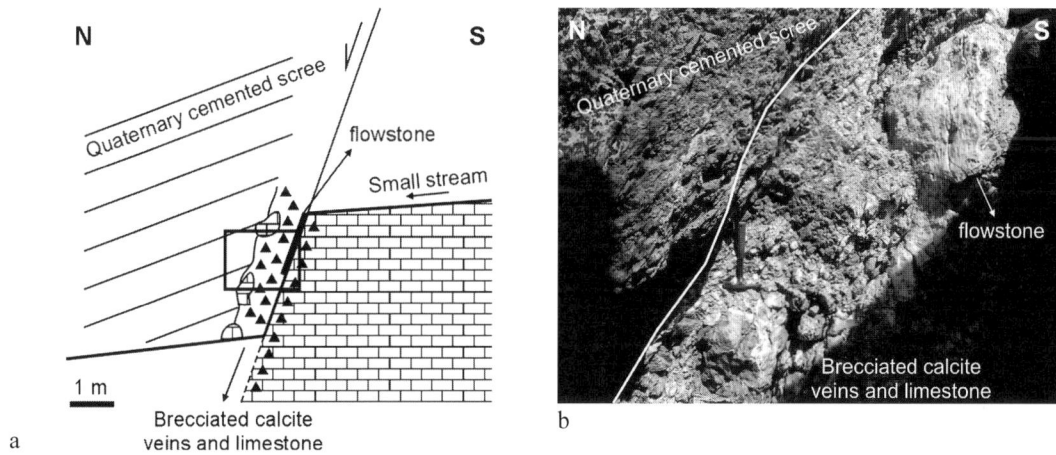

Figure 8: (a) Palaeo-fault scarp (240/75) at the Bey Dağları massif's northern extremity (site 18, Figure 4). (b) Detail of fault zone (see box in a).

Figure 9: Conjugate fracture set, filled with sandy material in the Quaternary alluvial deposits (hammer = 33 cm long) (site situated some 100 m SE of site 18; Figure 4).

Figure 10: (a) Limestone escarpment (070/60) (site 19; Figure 4). (b) Limestone escarpment (N70E) (site 20; Figure 4). (c) Limestone escarpment (240/80) (site a; Figure 4). (d) Limestone mountain range south of the Çanaklı basin (site b; Figure 4). (e) Fault breccia along the E-W trending limestone front (site c; Figure 4). (f) Small elevated (ca. 10 m above valley floor) terrace in the footwall part of the E-W trending limestone front (site d; Figure 4).

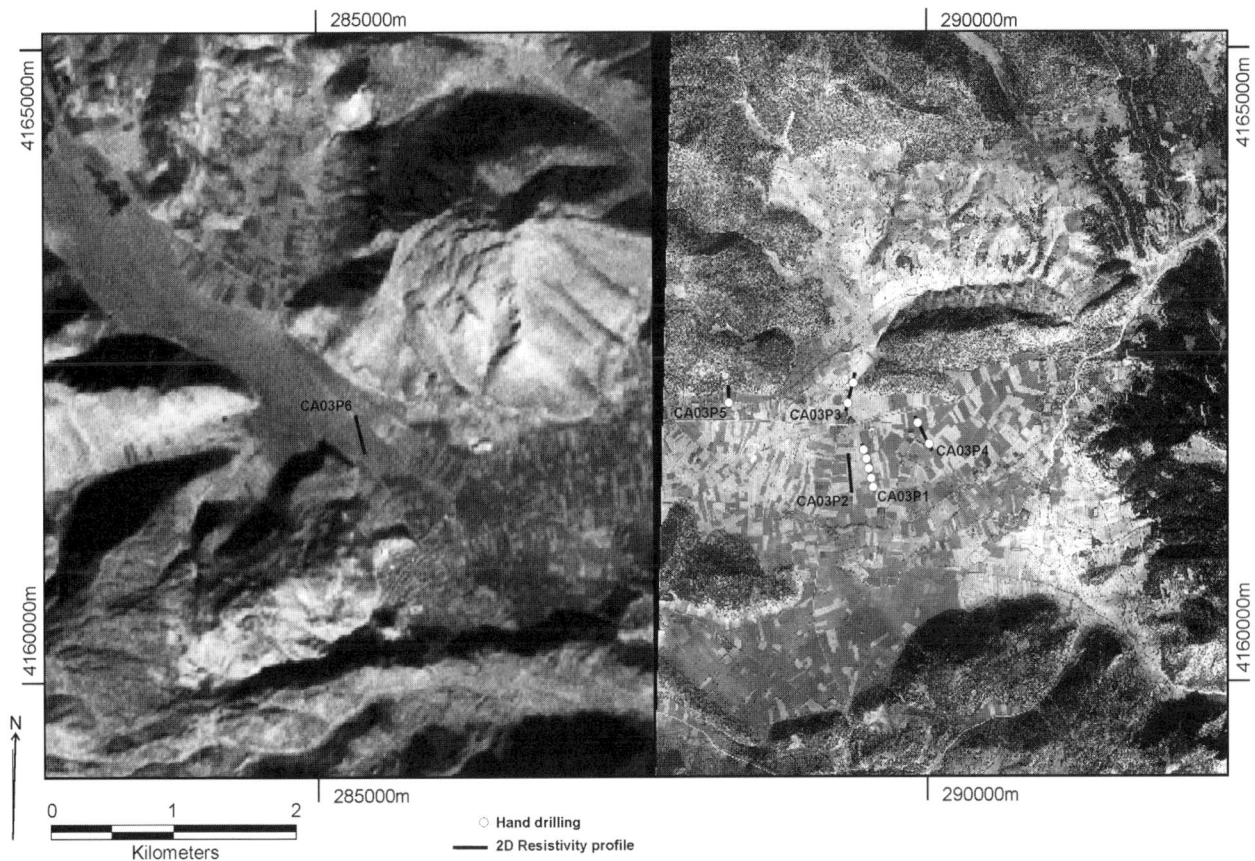

Figure 11: Combined satellite image of the Çanaklı basin with location of the six 2D-resistivity profiles and the ten hand drillings along the profiles. Left part of the image is a Landsat 7 Enhanced Thematic Mapper + image with a fusion of bands 4, 5, 7 and 8. Right part of the image is an Ikonos image with a combination of bands red, green and blue. Projection is UTM Zone 36, Northern Hemisphere (WGS 84). See figure 2 for location.

the mountain range (Figure 10d). In front of the forest and screes, reddish clay deposits, until recently used for producing local ceramics, are present in very irregular hills in the depression between the surrounding limestone outcrops. Again, there is no evidence of (active) faulting. A distinct E-W-trending front also occurs north of the Çanaklı basin (site c; Figure 4), also apparent as a clear lineament (C1; Figure 6) on satellite images. Here a fault breccia has been encountered on the E-W-trending limestone front, suggesting the presence of a(n) (active) (normal) fault (Figure 10e) (cf. Stewart and Hancock, 1990). Small elevated (alluvial?) terraces were observed in the footwall part of this lineament (site d; Figure 4). However, these steps could equally be man-made terraces and/or ancient walk levels to by-pass a swamp or periodical lake (Paulissen pers. comm., 2004) (Figure 10f).

6. NEAR-SURFACE GEOPHYSICS: 2D RESISTIVITY IMAGING

The geophysical analysis focuses on two lineaments: (1) the E-W trending lineament (C1) delimiting the Çanaklı basin to the north, apparent on both satellite images (Figure 6) and in the landscape as a clear escarpment bearing indications of active faulting (Figure 10e-f); and (2) the NE-SW trending lineament (C2) crossing the valley (Figure 6), lacking any geomorphological expression. 2D-resistivity imaging is used to image the subsurface, eventually to detect any evidence of historical or recent fault activity.

In total 6 profiles were measured, 1 of 380 m (using a roll-along technique), 1 of 189 m and 4 of 315 m (Figure 11). The relevant acquisition parameters can be found in Table 1. The topography has been taken into account for each profile. An impression of different settings is given

Nr.	Locality	Nel	dE(m)	Layout	Length	Orientation	Investigation depth	Data quality
CA03P1	Çanaklı	96	4	WSC	380	S-N	40	bad
CA03P2	Çanaklı	64	5	WSC	315	S-N	50	good
CA03P3	Çanaklı	64	5	WSC	315	S-N	50	excellent
CA03P4	Çanaklı	64	5	WSC	315	S-N	50	good
CA03P5	Çanaklı	64	3	WSC	189	S-N	30	medium-good
CA03P6	Çanaklı	64	5	WSC	315	S-N	50	good

Table 1: Relevant acquisition parameters for the 2D-resistivity profiles. Nel = number of electrodes. dE (m) = electrode spacing in meters. WSC = Wenner-Schlumberger layout.

Figure 12: (a) View of profile CA03P4. (b) View of profile CA03P5. (c) View of profile CA03P6. Arrows indicate direction of cable layout. See figure 11 for location of profiles.

in figure 12. In total 10 hand drillings (up to 4 m depth) were performed to constrain the lithological composition of the upper part of several profiles (Figures 11 and 13). Profiles CA03P3, CA03P5 and CA03P6 concern lineament C1. While profiles CA03P3 and CA03P5 are located in front of the limestone escarpment and are oriented nearly perpendicular to the escarpment approximately down-slope, the profile CA03P6 is located on the valley floor, potentially crossing the western continuation of the lineament. Profiles CA03P1, CA03P2 and CA03P4 concern lineament C2 and are oriented nearly perpendicular to this lineament.

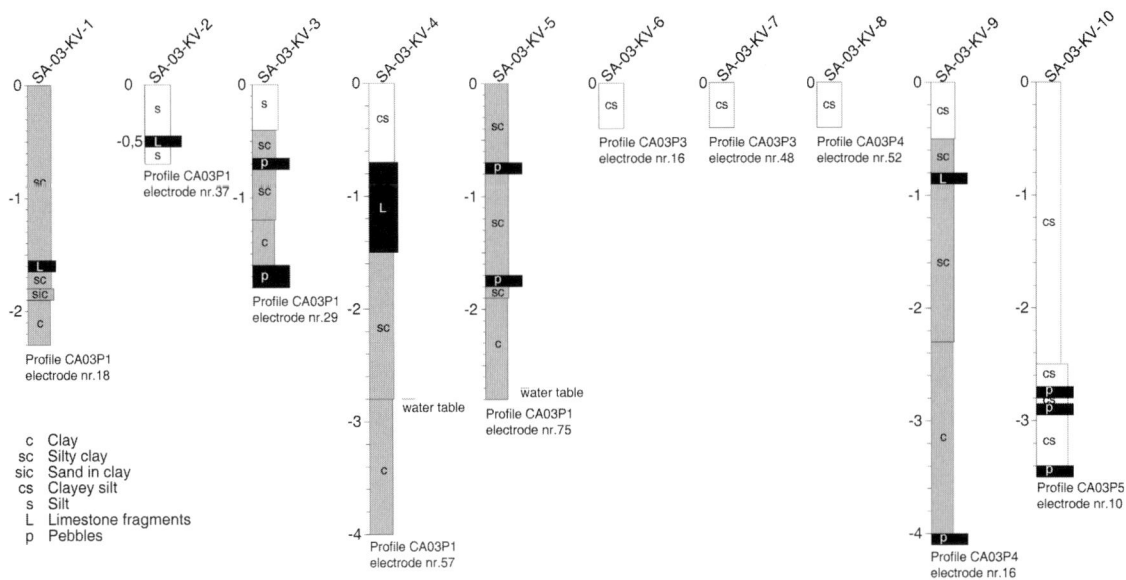

Figure 13: Overview of hand drillings in the Çanaklı basin. SA-03-KV-1 to SA-03-KV-5 are five drillings located along profile CA03P1. Drillings SA-03-KV-6 and SA-03-KV-7 are located along profile CA03P3 (Figure 15). Drillings SA-03-KV-8 and SA-03-KV-9 are located along profile CA03P4 (Figure 16). Drillings SA-03-KV-10 is located along profile CA03P5 (Figure 17 and 18). The electrode number is indicated each time. The location of the profiles is indicated on figure 11.

6.1. Profile CA03P1

Extreme high error % (standard deviation between the same measurements) occurred during several measuring slices. This problem is due to an overheating of the ABEM resistivity meter. The data can be considered to be useless. To overcome this problem the next days, the measuring device was put in the shade and Imax was lowered. Five hand drillings were carried out, with a maximum depth of 4 m (Figures 11 and 13). The first metres consist of silt and silty clays (Figure 13), below which pure wet and compact clays are present. According to a local farmer a phreatic zone is reached at 8 m depth around electrode nr. 1.

6.2. Profile CA03P2

The lowest resistivity (1-40 Ωm) is believed to represent (wet) clay (up to 45 m depth) (Figure 14). It corresponds with the Quaternary fill of the Çanaklı basin. These clays may have accumulated in periodical lakes and/or by clay supported alluvial fans originating from the surrounding hills (Paulissen pers. comm., 2004). Higher-resistivity zones (80 Ωm) are incised in the low-resistivity material (Figure 14). They are interpreted as river gullies. The gully at metre mark 70 (Figure 14) corresponds with one of the secondary lineaments on the Ikonos image (Figure 6). We therefore assume that those lineaments do not correspond with

secondary faults but represent abandoned river beds. The most northern higher-resistivity zone can correspond to the alluvium north of the main lineament (C2), as defined on the Ikonos image (Figure 6). This main lineament crosses the profile around electrode nr. 40 at metre mark 200 (Figure 14). No evidence of a fault is observed at this point. The spectral difference on the Ikonos image between the alluvium north and south of the main lineament (Figure 6), can thus be attributed to a different origin of the deposits and not to fault activity (Paulissen pers. comm., 2004). The alluvium north of the main lineament is a direct result of weathering and erosion of the surrounding limestone. The alluvium south of the main lineament can be interpreted as major debris cones originating from flysch hills in the NE. Its direction of transport corresponds to the small actual topographic inclination. However, no subsurface morphological features of such a cone were observed on the resistivity profiles (Figure 14). The abandoned riverbeds are located within and parallel to the debris cone. They may attest of a more active (ephemeral) river system in earlier times, as already suggested by Six (2004) for the western part of the valley. No drillings were carried out along this profile.

6.3. Profile CA03P3

This profile lies nearly perpendicular to the limestone escarpment bordering the valley to the north and is centred with

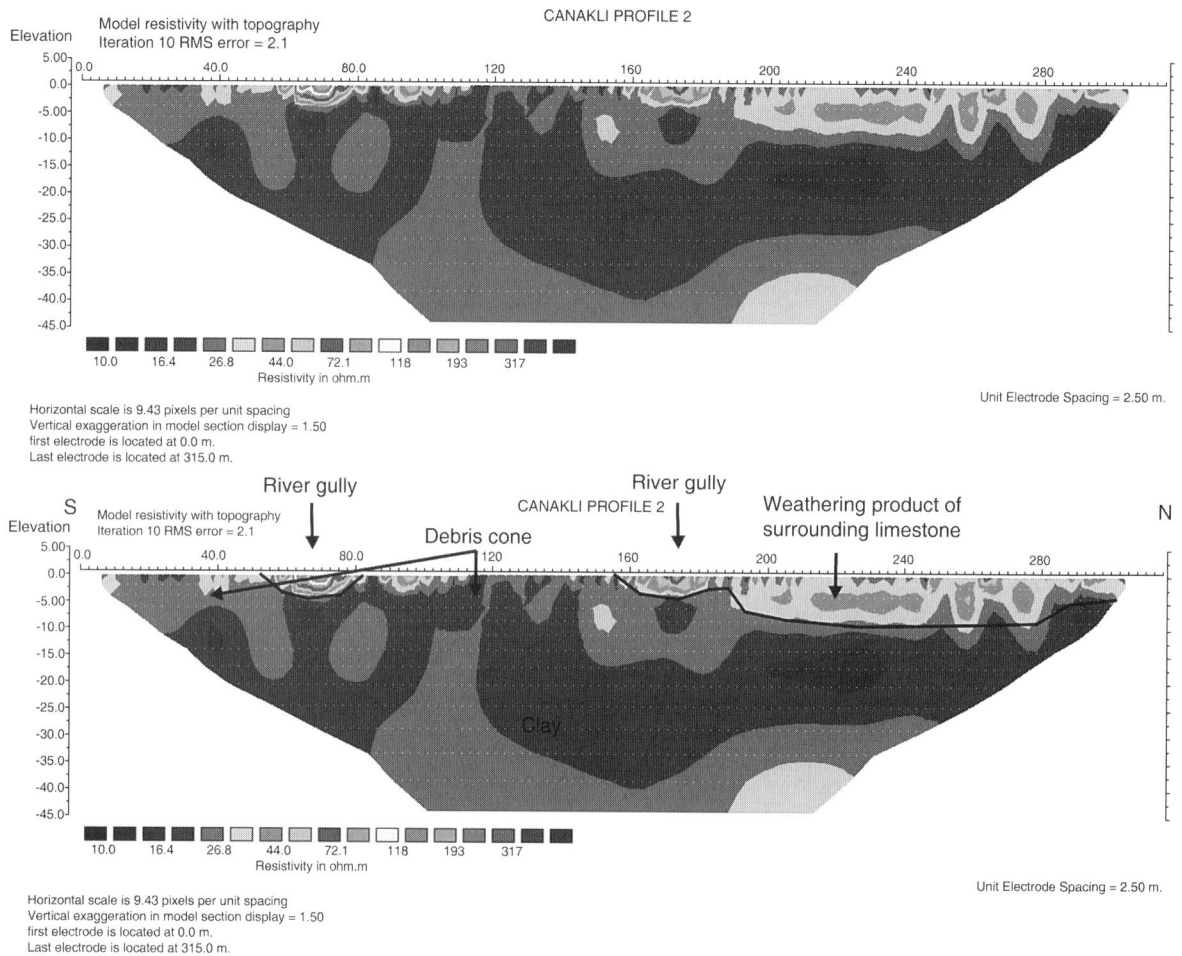

Figure 14: Conventional inversion for profile CA03P2 with a uniform colour scale for all Çanaklı profiles, and with interpretation. See figure 11 for location.

respect to this lineament. The limestone front, at metre mark 130 (Figure 15), north of the depression is apparent as a very sharp and straight, steeply S-dipping contact between high-resistivity material (limestone) to the N and low-resistivity material (clay/silt) to the S. The northern border of the depression seems clearly fault controlled. Some evidence is present on the resistivity profile that may infer an active normal fault: (1) in the hanging wall, a wedge-shaped body (Figure 15) is observed, which is probably related to surface faulting, i.e. colluvial wedge(s); and (2) resistivity layers in the hanging wall block seem to be vertically displaced by a set of subsidiary 'antithetic' normal faults (Figure 15). Quaternary activity on these faults may have occurred. As no topographical scarp is present, faulting must be older than the most recent deposits. These deposits are possible very young as indicated in Six (2004), which dates the upper 4.6 m sediments in a sediment core near profile CA03P6 as Late Holocene (< 1000 BC). The

resistivity values of the deepest layer in the hanging wall (Figure 15) correspond with those of the weathering product of the surrounding limestone observed in the CA03P02 profile (Figure 14), which lies in the southern prolongation of the CA03P03 profile (Figure 11). However, the thickness of this layer extends here up to a depth of 45 m. The resistivity values near the surface cannot well be correlated with the observations on the Ikonos image (Figure 6). The resistivity profile crosses the contact between a debris cone originating from the NE, in the north, and alluvium corresponding to the erosion product from the limestone, in the south. No evidence of such a cone can be seen on the resistivity profiles (Figure 15). Moreover, the surface resistivity values can be divided in three, instead of two zones. The central zone with higher resistivity values can be linked to the proximity of the outcropping limestone to the east and may be interpreted as a colluvium originating from this limestone. Two hand drillings were carried out,

144

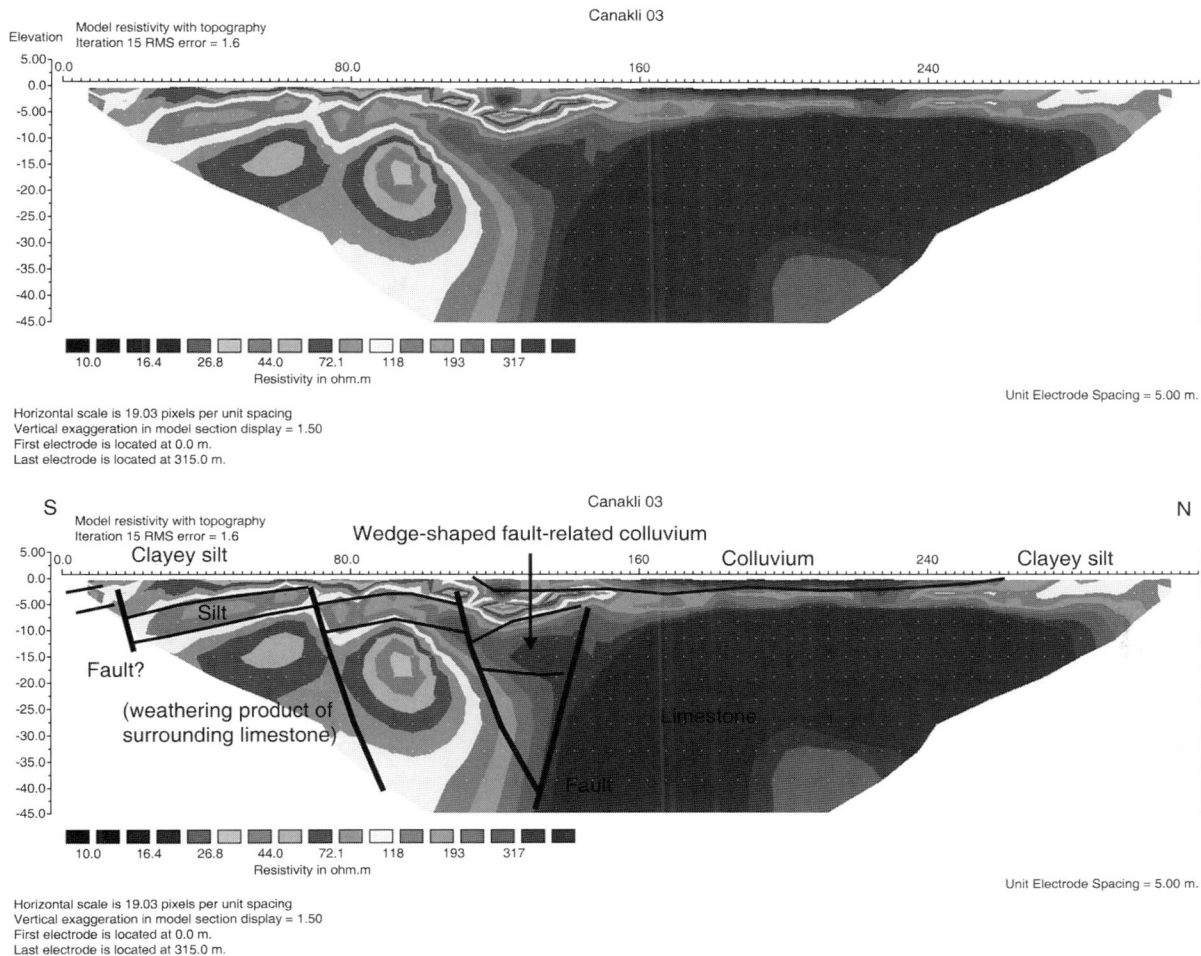

Figure 15: Conventional inversion for profile CA03P3 with a uniform colour scale for all Çanaklı profiles, and with interpretation. See figure 11 for location.

with a maximum depth of 40 cm (Figure 13). The upper 40 cm consist of clayey silt with small limestone fragments. No water table was reached.

6.4. Profile CA03P4

This profile lies perpendicular to lineament C2, to the east of profile CA03P2. It is somewhat similar to the profile CA03P2. Very low resistivity values are dominant up to a depth of 45 m (Figure 16). A surface layer with slightly higher resistivity values is present (Figure 16). This layer is more than 5 m thick in the N and gradually dies out to the S. A high-resistivity body is present around electrode nr. 40-41 / metre mark 202 in this surface layer (Figure 16). At this location a secondary lineament was observed on the Ikonos image (Figure 6). This high-resistivity body is interpreted as a river gully. No evidence of faulting is

observed at the contact between the alluvium type N of the main lineament and the alluvium type S of the main lineament. Two hand drillings with a maximum depth of 4 m (Figure 13) indicate that the surface layer is composed of clays and silt with limestone fragments, while the lower resistivity values represent rather pure clays. The water table has not been reached.

6.5. Profile CA03P5

This profile is located along the northern border of the Çanaklı basin, to the W of profile CA03P3. It is also similar to it. A very sharp and straight, steeply S-dipping contact between high-resistivity material (limestone) to the north and low-resistivity material (clay/silt) to the south is observed (Figures 17 and 18). This is a clearly fault-controlled contact. This fault, around metre mark 80 (Figures 17 and 18),

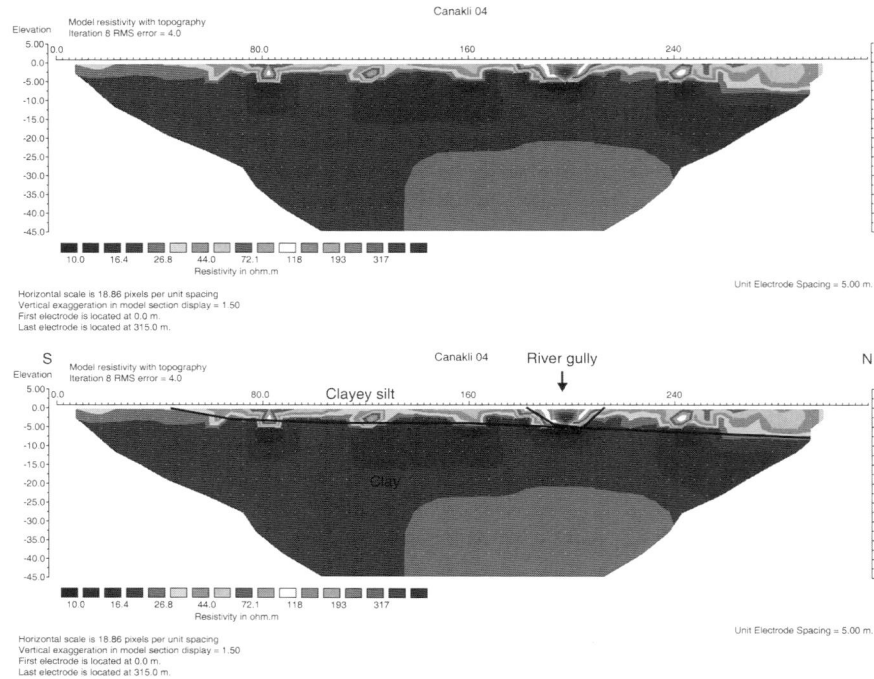

Figure 16: Robust inversion for profile CA03P4 with a uniform colour scale for all Çanaklı profiles, and with interpretation. See figure 11 for location.

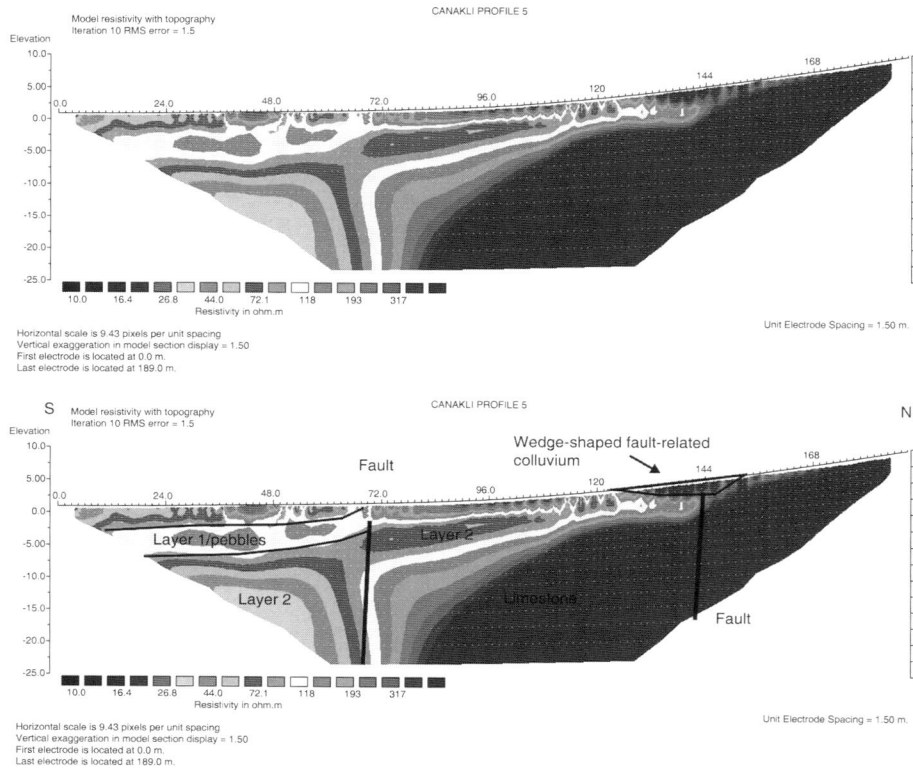

Figure 17: Conventional inversion for profile CA03P5 with a uniform colour scale for all Çanaklı profiles, and with interpretation. See figure 11 for location.

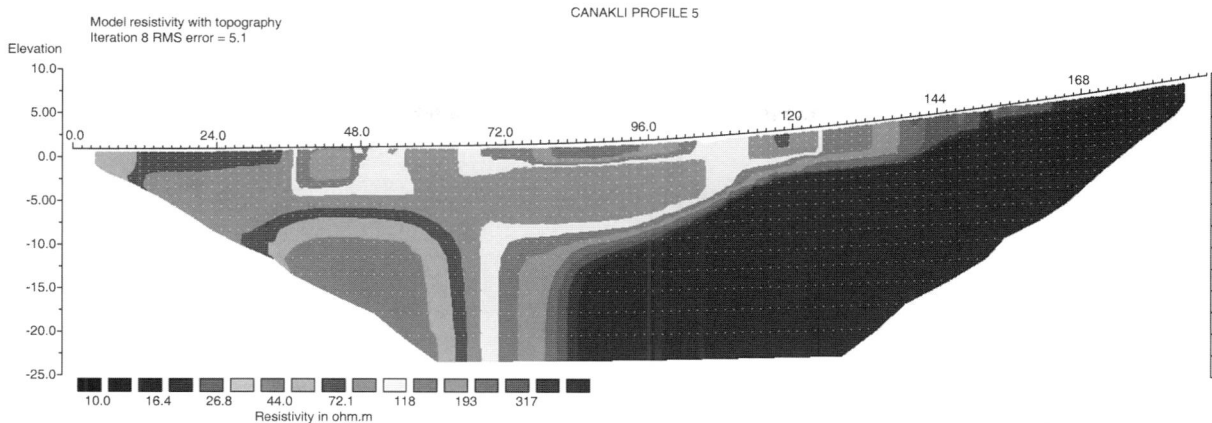

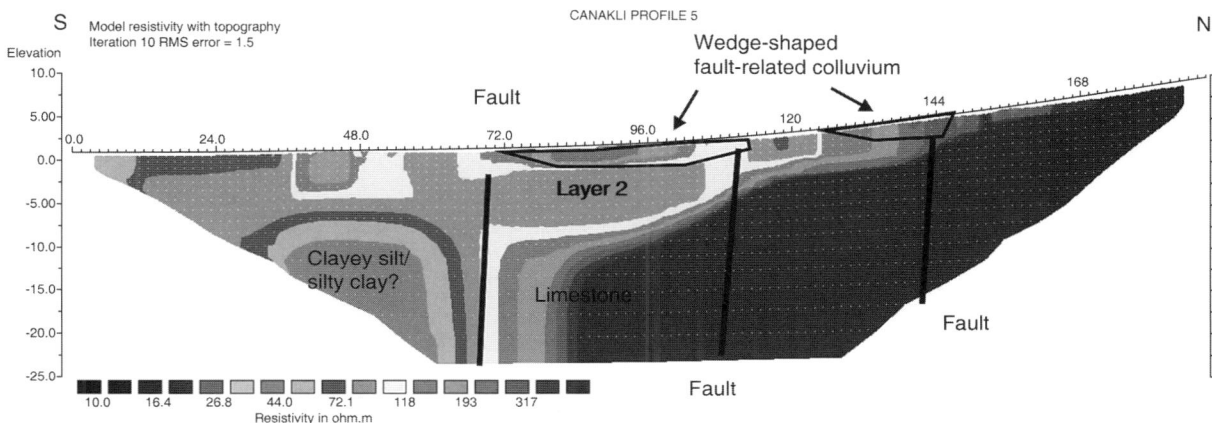

Figure 18: Robust inversion for profile CA03P5 with a uniform colour scale for all Çanaklı profiles, and with interpretation. See figure 11 for location.

corresponds with the location of the limestone front at the surface. Two additional 'synthetic ' normal faults can be observed in the footwall, as the top of the limestone bedrock displays vertical offsets (Figures 17 and 18). Some evidence is present that these faults may be interpreted as active normal faults: (1) in the hanging wall of the two most northern faults, wedge-shaped bodies are observed, which are probably related to surface faulting (Figures 17 and 18), i.e. colluvial wedges; (2) a knick-point is present in the topography, between electrode nr. 43 and 47, above the most northern wedge-shaped body and could represent a small degraded fault scarp (Figures 17 and 18); and (3) on the conventional inversion (Figures 17) a resistivity layer in the hanging wall seems to be vertically displaced

at the main fault. The resistivity values of the deepest part of the hanging wall correspond with those of the weathering product of the surrounding limestone observed in the CA03P2 and CA03P3 profile. One hand drilling has been carried out around electrode nr. 10 (Figures 13 and 17). The upper most drilled material consists of brown clayey silt with rounded limestone fragments (up to 7 cm) and small pebbles. Layer 1 on the conventional inversion (Figure 17) corresponds with an increase in pebbles and sand (cf. drilling SA03KV10). These fluviatile pebbles and sands may also testify to a more active (ephemeral) river system in earlier times, as already suggested by Six (2004) for the western part of the valley.

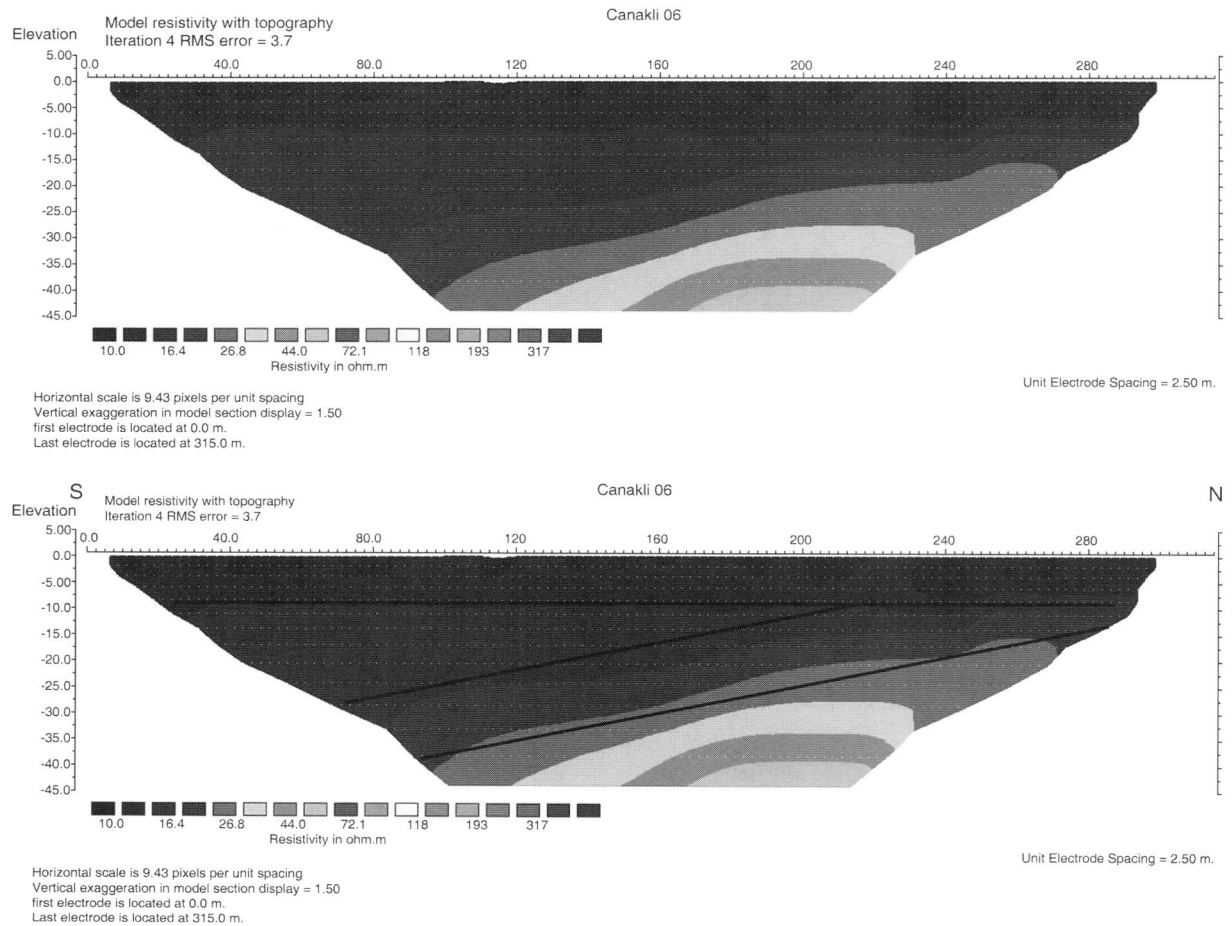

Figure 19: Robust inversion for profile CA03P6 with a uniform colour scale for all Çanaklı profiles, and with interpretation. See figure 11 for location.

6.6. Profile CA03P6

The CA03P6 profile was laid out at the western continuation of the normal fault detected on the profiles CA03P3 and CA03P5. This profile lies totally within the Çanaklı basin and allows us to investigate if this fault affects the Quaternary sediments within this basin. On the resistivity profiles we observe that a very thick sequence of clay is present (Figure 19). A surface layer displays a horizontal stratification, while the deeper layers show a tilted stratification towards the south and an increase in resistivity value (Figure 19). The small variation in resistivity does not allow to exclude or to prove the presence of a fault. However, there is no surface evidence for a fault scarp. This excludes fault reactivation since the youngest sediments are not affected. These deposits are very young, as indicated by Six (2004), who dates the upper 4.6 m sediments in a sediment core near profile CA03P6 as Late Holocene

(< 1000 BC). Hence, there is no evidence of recent (< 1000 BC) reactivation. The sedimentary fill of the valley is supposed to be subhorizontal or has a small slope basin inwards (Paulissen pers. comm., 2004). The tilted stratification (11°) of the deeper layers (Figure 19) is, however, too high and may reflect older tectonic activity. This is e.g. the case for the Burdur Formation which dips 10-15° as a result of basin-controlling fault activity (cf. Price and Scott, 1991). The location of any active fault can not be deduced based on these observations alone. The presence of a major antithetic fault to the south of the CA03P6 profile, responsible for the observed (back-)tilt, is highly hypothetical. No additional drillings were carried out along the profile.

6.7. Interpretation of 2D resistivity imaging

Clay deposits characterize the Çanaklı basin. Hand drillings show the presence of a water table at shallow depth.

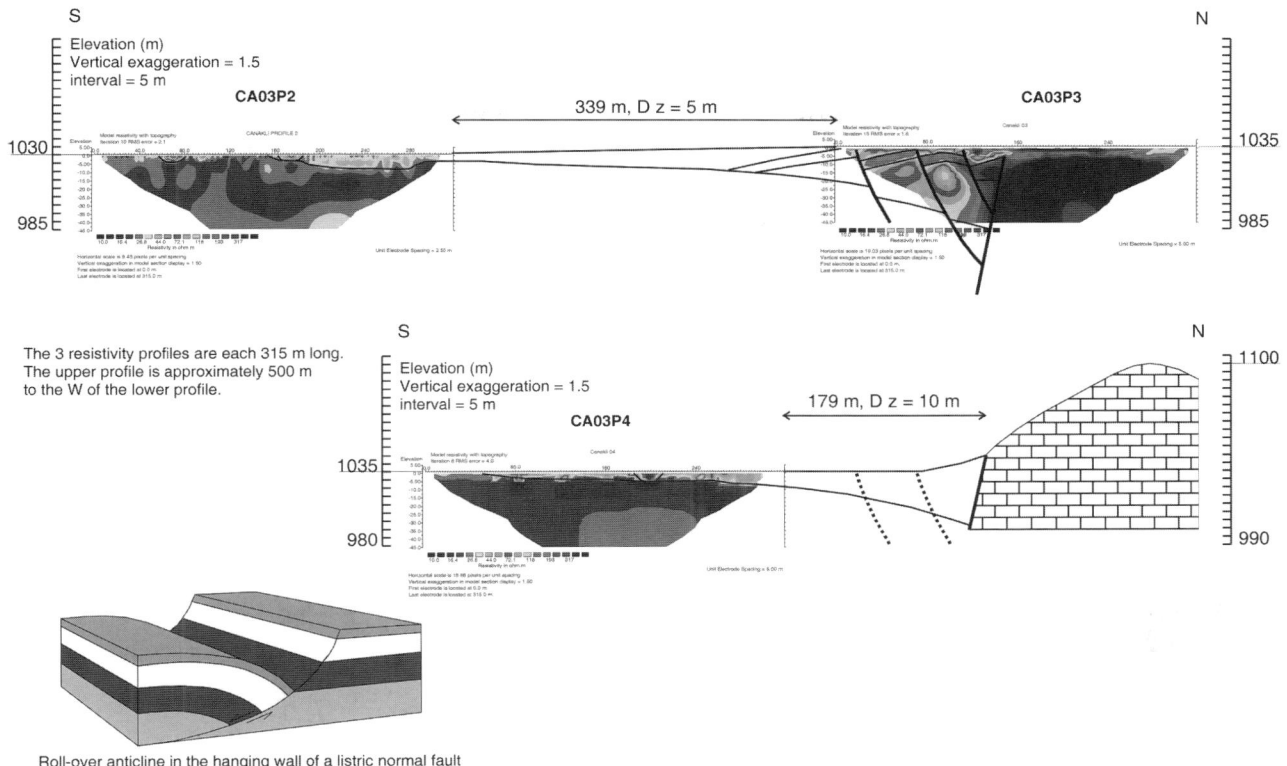

S   N

Elevation (m)
Vertical exaggeration = 1.5
interval = 5 m

CA03P2   339 m, D z = 5 m   CA03P3

The 3 resistivity profiles are each 315 m long.
The upper profile is approximately 500 m
to the W of the lower profile.

Elevation (m)
Vertical exaggeration = 1.5
interval = 5 m

CA03P4   179 m, D z = 10 m

Roll-over anticline in the hanging wall of a listric normal fault

Figure 20: Correlation of the N-S profiles (CA03P2, CA03P3 and CA03P4) along the northern edge of the Çanaklı basin, possibly inferring a roll-over anticlinal architecture in the hanging wall of a listric normal fault.

The resistivity profiles demonstrate that the basin is filled with at least 45 m of (wet) clays. This extremely thick sequence of low-resistivity (1-60 Ωm) material did not affect the quality of the measurements (standard deviation mostly below 2.5%). Near the surface, a more silt-rich layer can be observed, which displays slightly higher resistivity values. This surface layer is not more than 10 m thick in the depression, but represents a layer of at least 45 m close to the fault-controlled northern border of the valley. The contrast in thickness may be due to a roll-over anticline in the hanging wall of this normal fault (Figure 20). In areas where flat-lying beds are deformed by normal faults, roll-over folds in the hanging wall block are common. In these folds, the beds in the hanging wall block tilt down into the fault. They form on listric normal faults. As the hanging wall block slips on the fault, it deforms to maintain contact with the footwall block across the fault, thereby producing a bend in the layering. The presence of a rollover anticline, subsidiary 'antithetic' normal faults and wedge-shaped fault-related colluvium in the basin deposits suggest that displacement on the listric normal fault occurred during sedimentation, i.e. a growth fault (Figure 20). However,

there is no evidence on the profiles that this fault affected the youngest (Late Holocene) sedimentary filling of the valley. Still, Six (2004) invokes tectonic activity to explain the much more pronounced recent accumulation in a core near profile CA03P6 in comparison to 2 other cores more northwards. A listric fault geometry for the Burdur fault is also pointed out by Price and Scott (1991) based on the difference in plunge at surface and at the hypocentre of the 1971 Burdur earthquake (fault-plane solution).

The continuation of the Isparta Çayı lineament into the Quaternary Çanaklı basin did not show up at all in the resistivity profiles. No evidence of faulting is present within the Çanaklı basin. The spectral differences of the basin on the Ikonos image are due to a different origin of the deposits. Some of the secondary lineaments observed by the remote sensing correspond with river gullies that display a higher resistivity (Figure 21). The presence of these gullies, the 2 debris cones originating from the flysch hills in the northeast (Figure 21) and the fluviatile pebbles and sand observed in hand drillings, suggest the presence of a more active river system in earlier times.

149

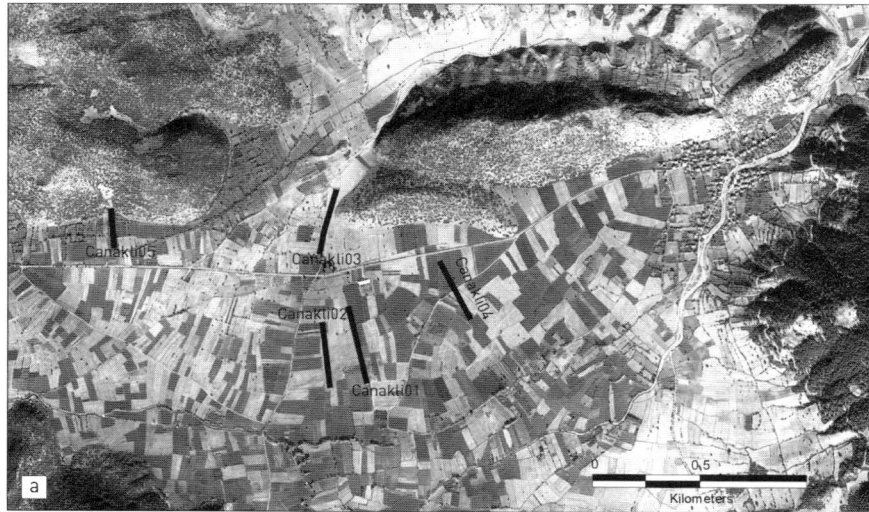

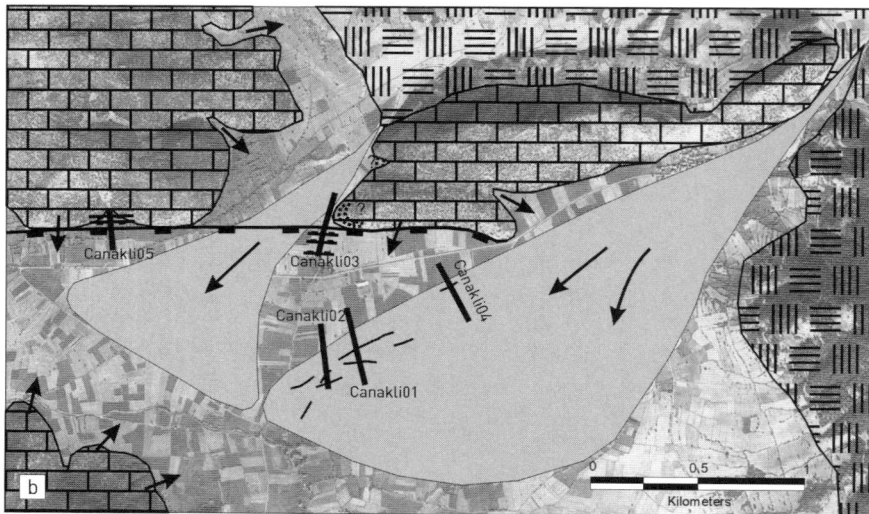

Figure 21: Active faulting in the Çanaklı basin as inferred from the 2D-resistivity imagery. (a) Ikonos image with a combination of bands near-infrared, green and blue. See figure 2 for location. (b) Interpretation. Compare to original working hypothesis in figure 6.

7. DISCUSSION AND CONCLUSIONS

Remote sensing analysis of the wider area around the Çanaklı basin revealed heavily dissected and hence uplifted sandstones (Burdigalian to Langhian in age) north of the valley, inferring active normal faulting within the area. Moreover, the Çanaklı basin is the southwestern portion of a lineament, interpreted as the Çanaklı-Isparta Çayı fault zone (Similox-Tohon et al., this volume b).

Subsequent research focused on two lineaments, an EW trending lineament (C1), limiting the basin to the north, and an NE-SW trending lineament (C2) within the valley (Figure 21). The latter lineament has no geomorphological expression, apart from some slight colour difference of the soil. Inversion results, moreover, show that this lineament does not show up at all in the profiles. The Çanaklı basin seemingly consists of a very thick (> 45 m) sequence of low-resistivity material, probably Quaternary clays, as evidenced by hand drillings. There is no evidence for any tectonic disturbance.

Field evidence, however, demonstrates that the limestone front, which is the geomorphological expression of the EW trending lineament (C1), bears the characteristics of an Aegean-type normal fault (Hancock and Barka, 1987; Stewart and Hancock, 1988; 1990; 1991). The degradation of the limestone fault scarp, however, hampers to identify conclusive evidence for historical fault activity. Moreover, the time resolution of the available surface material is too poor to enable identifying historical or recent surface-rupturing events. The fault scarp clearly shows up on two of the resistivity profiles as a very sharp and straight, steeply S-dipping contact between high-resistivity material, i.e. the limestone in the footwall, in the north and low-resistivity material in the south, i.e. the clays in the hanging wall of the fault. Taking into account the minimum thickness of the low-resistivity material, a minimum finite displacement of 45 m can be inferred. On a third resistivity profile within the depression, but along strike with respect to the inferred EW trending normal fault, the presence of the fault within the Quaternary deposits can not be proven or excluded due to the small variation in resistivity.

Although this fault bears no evidence of historical or recent activity the overall interpretation of the 2D-resistivity profiles in the Çanaklı basin (Figures 20 and 21) suggests Quaternary fault activity. We, therefore, consider this newly identified fault, the **Çanaklı fault**, as an active fault. The fault scarp is EW trending and has a length of ca. 3 km. The identified active fault has, moreover, an appropriated orientation with respect to the current dominant stress field (Verhaert et al., 2006) to be considered potentially hazardous.

The Çanaklı fault is the second active fault we thus have identified in the territory of Sagalassos, besides the Sagalassos fault (Similox-Tohon et al., 2005; Similox-Tohon et al., 2006; 2007; Similox-Tohon et al., 2004). It is striking that both faults have a very similar orientation, different from the overall NE-SW trend of the majority of active faults within the Fethiye-Burdur fault zone. To date, only the Sagalassos fault bears evidence of historical surface rupturing (Similox-Tohon et al., 2005; Similox-Tohon et al., 2006; Similox-Tohon et al., 2004; Sintubin et al., 2003). Although the Çanaklı fault is only situated 10 km to the south of the ancient city of Sagalassos, there is currently no reason to retain this active fault as a potential candidate for the causative fault for the destructive Sagalassos earthquake(s) during the 6th to 7th century AD (Waelkens et al., 2000). Therefore, the most likely candidate remains the 'Sagalassos fault' itself.

8. ACKNOWLEDGMENTS

A version of this article in full colour is available from the authors. The research was supported by the Belgian Programme on Interuniversity Poles of Attraction (IAP V/9) and the Research Fund of the K.U.Leuven (BOF-GOA02/2). The satellite images were provided by Prof. Dr. E. Paulissen (K.U.Leuven). Processing using ENVI was performed at the Royal Museum of Central Africa at Tervuren (Belgium). Manuel Sintubin is Research Professor of the Research Fund K.U.Leuven. Etienne Paulissen is acknowledged for stimulating discussions. We are grateful to Patrick Degryse for taking this initiative and giving us the opportunity to publish results of our research in SW Turkey.

9. REFERENCES

BARKA, A.A., REILINGER, R., SAROGLU, F. and SENGÖR, A.M.C. (1995) The Isparta Angle: Its importance in the neotectonics of the Eastern Mediterranean Region, *International Earth Sciences Colloqium on the Aegean Region* 1: 3-17.

BOZKURT, E. (2001) Neotectonics of Turkey – a synthesis, *Geodinamica Acta* 14: 3-30.

BURBANK, D.W. and ANDERSON, R.S. (2001) *Tectonic Geomorphology*, Blackwell Science, Malden, Massachusetts.

CAMELBEECK, T. and MEGHRAOUI, M. (1998) Geological and geophysical evidence for large palaeo-earthquakes with surface faulting in the Roer Graben (northwest Europe), *Geophysical Journal International* 132: 347-362.

CAPUTO, R., HELLY, B., PAVLIDES, S.B. and PAPADOPOULOS, G.A. (2004) Palaeoseismological investigation of the Tyrnavos Fault (Thessaly, Central Greece), *Tectonophysics* 394: 1-20.

CAPUTO, R., PSCITELLI, S., OLIVETO, A., RIZZO, E. and LAPENNA, V. (2003) The use of electrical resistivity tomographies in active tectonics: examples from the Tyrnavos Basin, Greece, *Journal of Geodynamics* 36: 19-35.

DEGRYSE, P., MUCHEZ, P., SINTUBIN, M., CLIJSTERS, A., VIAENE, W., DEDEREN, M., SCHROOTEN, P. and WAELKENS, M. (this volume). Geological mapping of the area around Sagalassos (SW Turkey), In: P. DEGRYSE and M. WAELKENS (eds.) *Sagalassos VI. Geo- and Bio-Archaeology at Sagalassos and in its Territory*, Leuven University Press, Leuven: 17-24.

EYIDOĞAN, H. and BARKA, A.A. (1996) The 1 October 1995 Dinar earthquake, SW Turkey, *Terra Nova* 8: 479-485.

HANCOCK, P.L. and BARKA, A.A. (1987) Kinematic indicators on active normal faults in western Turkey, *Journal of Structural Geology* 9(5/6): 573-584.

LOKE, M.H., ACWORTH, I. and DAHLIN, T. (2001) A comparison of smooth and blocky inversion methods in 2-D electrical imaging surveys, *ASEG 15th Geophysical Conference and Exhibition*, Brisbane: 4.

LOKE, M.H. and BARKER, R.D. (1996) Practical techniques for 3-D resistivity surveys and data inversion, *Geophysical Prospecting* 44: 499-523.

PAVLIDES, S.B. and CAPUTO, R. (2004) Magnitude versus faults' surface parameters: quantitative relationships from the Aegean Region, *Tectonophysics* 380: 159-188.

PRICE, S.P. and SCOTT, B. (1991) Pliocene Burdur basin, SW Turkey: tectonics, seismicity and sedimentation, *Journal of the Geological Society, London* 148: 345-354.

SENEL, M. (1997a) *1:100 000 geological map of the Isparta – J11 Quadrangle*, General Directorate of Mineral Research and Exploration, Ankara.

SENEL, M. (1997b) *1:250 000 geological maps of Turkey – Isparta No. 4*, General Directorate of Mineral Research and Exploration, Ankara.

SIMILOX-TOHON, D., FERNANDEZ-ALONSO, M., WAELKENS, M., MUCHEZ, P. and SINTUBIN, M. (this volume a) Testing diagnostic geomorphological criteria of active normal faults in the Burdur-Isparta region (SW Turkey), In: P. DEGRYSE and M. WAELKENS (eds.) *Sagalassos VI. Geo- and Bio-Archaeology at Sagalassos and in its Territory*, Leuven University Press, Leuven: 53-74.

SIMILOX-TOHON, D., FERNANDEZ-ALONSO, M., VANNESTE, K., WAELKENS, M., MUCHEZ, P. and SINTUBIN, M. (this volume b) Identifying active normal faults in the Burdur-Isparta region (SW Turkey): remote sensing, surface geology and near-surface geophysics, In: P. DEGRYSE and M. WAELKENS (eds.) *Sagalassos VI. Geo- and Bio-Archaeology at Sagalassos and in its Territory*, Leuven University Press, Leuven: 75-130.

SIMILOX-TOHON, D., SINTUBIN, M., MUCHEZ, P., VANHAVERBEKE, H., VERHAERT, G. and WAELKENS, M. (2005) Identification of a historical morphogenic earthquake through trenching at ancient Sagalassos (SW Turkey), *Journal of Geodynamics* 40: 279-293.

SIMILOX-TOHON, D., SINTUBIN, M., MUCHEZ, P., VERHAERT, G., VANNESTE, K., FERNANDEZ-ALONSO, M., VANDYCKE, S., VANHAVERBEKE, H. and WAELKENS, M. (2006) The identification of an active fault by a multidisciplinary study at the archaeological site of Sagalassos (SW Turkey), *Tectonophysics* 420: 371-387.

SIMILOX-TOHON, D., SINTUBIN, M., MUCHEZ, P., VERHAERT, G., VANNESTE, K., FERNANDEZ-ALONSO, M., VANDYCKE, S., VANHAVERBEKE, H. and WAELKENS, M. (2007) Erratum to "The identification of an active fault by a multidisciplinary study at the archaeological site of Sagalassos (SW Turkey)" [Tectonophysics Volume 420 (2006) 371-387], *Tectonophysics* 435: 55-62.

SIMILOX-TOHON, D., VANNESTE, K., SINTUBIN, M., MUCHEZ, P. and WAELKENS, M. (2004) Two-dimensional Resistivity Imaging: a Tool in Archaeoseismology. An Example from Ancient Sagalassos (Southwest Turkey), *Archaeological Prospection* 11: 1-18.

SINTUBIN, M., MUCHEZ, P., SIMILOX-TOHON, D., VERHAERT, G., PAULISSEN, E. and WAELKENS, M. (2003) Seismic catastrophes at the ancient city of Sagalassos (SW Turkey) and their implications for the seismotectonics in the Burdur-Isparta area, *Geological Journal* 38: 359-374.

SINTUBIN, M., SIMILOX-TOHON, D., VERHAERT, G. and MUCHEZ, P. (in prep) New geodynamic model for the region of the lakes (SW Turkey) based on remote sensing, surface geology, archaeoseismology and near-surface geophysics, *Turkish Journal of Earth Sciences*.

SIX, S. (2004) *Holocene Geomorphological Evolution of the Territory of Sagalassos*, Unpublished Ph.D. thesis, Katholieke Universiteit Leuven.

STEWART, I.S. and HANCOCK, P.L. (1988) Normal fault zone evolution and fault scarp degradation in the Aegean region, *Basin Research* 1: 139-153.

STEWART, I.S. and HANCOCK, P.L. (1990) Brecciation and fracturing within neotectonic normal fault zones in the Aegean region. In: R.J. KNIPE and E.H. RUTTER (eds.) *Deformation Mechanisms, Rheology and Tectonics, Specal Publications 54*. Geological Society, London: 105-112.

STEWART, I.S. and HANCOCK, P.L. (1991) Scales of structural heterogeneity within neotectonic normal fault zones in the Aegean region, *Journal of Structural Geology* 13(2): 191-204.

STIROS, S.C. (1996) Identification of Earthquakes from Archaeological Data: Methodology, Criteria and Limitations, In: S.C. STIROS and R.E. JONES (eds.), *Archaeoseismology (Fitch Laboratory Occasional Paper 7)*. Institute of Geology and Mineral Exploration and The British Scholl at Athens, Athens: 129-152.

TAYMAZ, T. and PRICE, S.P. (1992) The 1971 May 12 Burdur earthquake sequence, SW Turkey: a synthesis of seismological observations, *Geophysical Journal International* 108: 589-603.

TEN VEEN, J.H. (2004) Extension of Hellenic forearc shear zones in SW Turkey: the Pliocene-quaternary deformation of the Esen Cay Basin, *Journal of Geodynamics* 37(2): 181-204.

TEN VEEN, J.H. and KLEINSPEHN, K.L. (2002) Geodynamics along an increasingly curved convergent plate margin: Late Miocene-Pleistocene Rhodes, Greece, *Tectonics* 21(3), 10.1029/2001TC001287.

TEN VEEN, J.H. and KLEINSPEHN, K.L. (2003) Incipient continental collision and plate-boundary curvature: Late Pliocene-Holocene transtensional Hellenic forearc, Crete, Greece, *Journal of the Geological Society, London* 160: 161-181.

VANNESTE, K., VERBEECK, K., CAMELBEECK, T., PAULISSEN, E., MEGHRAOUI, M., RENARDY, F., JONGMANS, D. and FRECHEN, M. (2001) Surface-rupturing history of the Bree fault scarp, Roer Valley graben: Evidence for six events since the late Pleistocene, *Journal of Seismology* 5: 329-359.

VERHAERT, G., SIMILOX-TOHON, D., VANDYCKE, S., SINTUBIN, M. and MUCHEZ, P. (2006) Different stress states in the Burdur-Isparta region (SW Turkey) since Late Miocene times: a reflection of a transient stress regime, *Journal of Structural Geology* 28: 1067-1083.

WAELKENS, M., SINTUBIN, M., MUCHEZ, P. and PAULISSEN, E. (2000) Archeological, geomorphological and geological evidence for a major earthquake at Sagalassos (SW Turkey) around the middle of the seventh century AD, In: W.J. MCGUIRE, D.R. GRIFFITHS, P.L. HANCOCK and I.S. STEWART (eds.) *The Archaeology of Geological Catastrophes* (*Special Publications 171*). Geological Society, London: 373-383.

PART II

THE GEOMORPHOLOGICAL SETTING

EXTRACTING ARCHAEOLOGICAL FEATURES FROM VERY HIGH RESOLUTION QUICKBIRD-2 REMOTE SENSING IMAGERY: A METHODOLOGICAL APPROACH BASED ON THE TOWN OF SAGALASSOS

Veronique DE LAET, Branco MUŠIČ, Etienne PAULISSEN and Marc WAELKENS

1. INTRODUCTION AND AIMS

Remote sensing is the acquisition of information about an object without touching it (Jensen, 2000). This broad definition encompasses all types of remote sensing, including geophysical prospecting, aerial photography, aerial spectroscopy and satellite remote sensing. In relation to archaeology, remote sensing encompasses methods to discover and map remnants of past civilisations above or below ground level (e.g. crop marks, buried archaeological remains, traces of ancient industrial activity and above ground architectural structures). Remote sensing is very useful in preparing an intensive survey campaign or to direct other fieldwork. In several cases observing archaeological structures from ground level does not clearly identify their spatial characteristics or the relationship to surrounding sites and landscape.

Since the beginning of the 20th century, aerial photography has been applied in archaeology primarily to view features on the earth's surface, which are difficult, if not impossible to visualize from ground level (Sever, 1995; Vermeulen and Verhoeven, 2004). With the launch of the first Landsat satellite in 1972 (*http://landsat7.usgs.gov/*), satellite remote sensing also became accessible to the archaeological community (Clark *et al.*, 1998). Due to ground resolution constraints, much of these images provide less information than aerial photography. Indeed, even the most recent Landsat ETM+ images (launched in 1999) have a resolution of 15 m for the panchromatic band, which is not detailed enough for the identification of most archaeological structures. Therefore, the launch of the first commercial very high-resolution satellite Ikonos-2 in 1999 was a major step forward. This satellite platform provides panchromatic images with 1 m and multispectral images with 4 m spatial resolution. Fusing the 1 m panchromatic and 4 m multispectral bands, a 1 m false or natural colour image can be generated. Since 2001 also Quickbird-2 imagery with a spatial resolution of 0.61 m for the panchromatic band and 2.44 m for the multispectral bands is available. Recently, aerial hyperspectral imagery

has also been used in archaeology (Emmolo *et al.*, 2004). It is characterized by its enormous number of wavebands and possibly very high spatial resolution, defined by the operator (Richards and Xiuping, 1999). Until now, very few geoarchaeological studies have applied these type of images (Changlin *et al.*, 2004; Emmolo *et al.*, 2004; Georgoula *et al.*, 2004; Pavlidis, 2005).

In general, visual as well as automatic methods are applied to analyze very high resolution satellite imagery. Within this study Quickbird-2 imagery of the monumental centre of Sagalassos is examined in order to test its potential for the automatic extraction of archaeological features with different characteristics ranging from excavated monuments towards discrete features, by means of GIS-, pixel- and object-based methods. Subsequently the obtained results are compared with a visual interpretation and the detailed map of the ancient town. A second objective is to evaluate to what extend Quickbird-2 imagery is able to detect previously unknown features.

2. STUDY AREA

The study area covers the ancient town of Sagalassos (Figures 1a and 1b). The site is chosen for its large size and its dense pattern of well visible buildings with regular vertical walls in the monumental quarter as well as large unexcavated areas that are prospected by intensive archaeological and detailed geophysical exploration, applying several physically independent and therefore complementary methods.

Sagalassos is situated on the south-facing slopes of the east-west orientated Akdağ (Turkish for 'white mountain') mountain range (Figure 1b) – at an altitude between 1450 and 1600 m a.s.l – and overlooks the fertile intermountaneous Ağlasun Cayı valley. The substrate of the area is composed of limestone overlaying respectively less permeable ophiolitic mélange and flysch formations (Şenel, 1997). The succession of limestone and ophiolitic mélange in combination

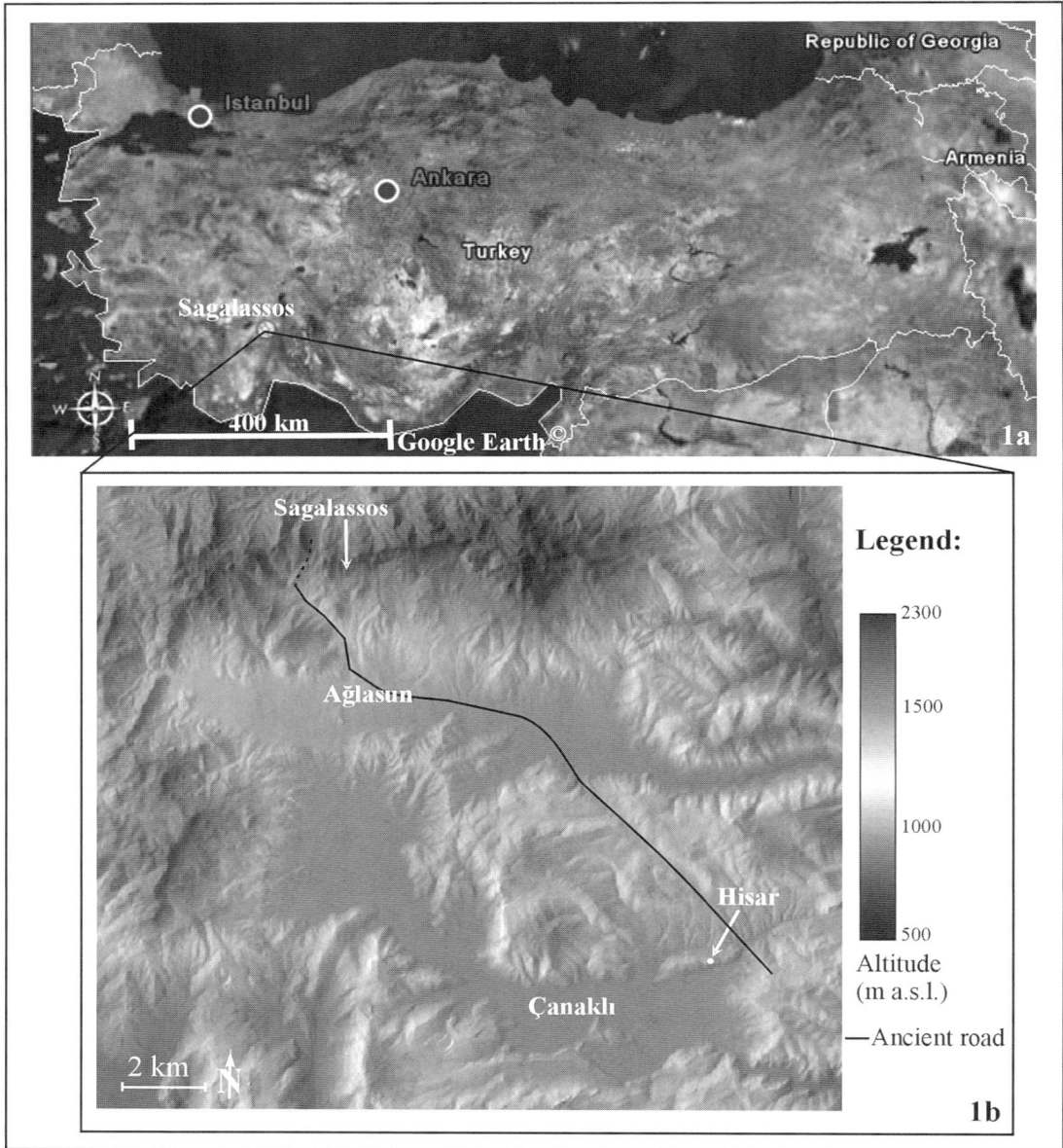

Figure 1: Location of the study area (A) situation of the study area in Turkey (B) physical setting of the archaeological site of Sagalassos (20 m resolution DEM derived from 1:25.000 topographic map).

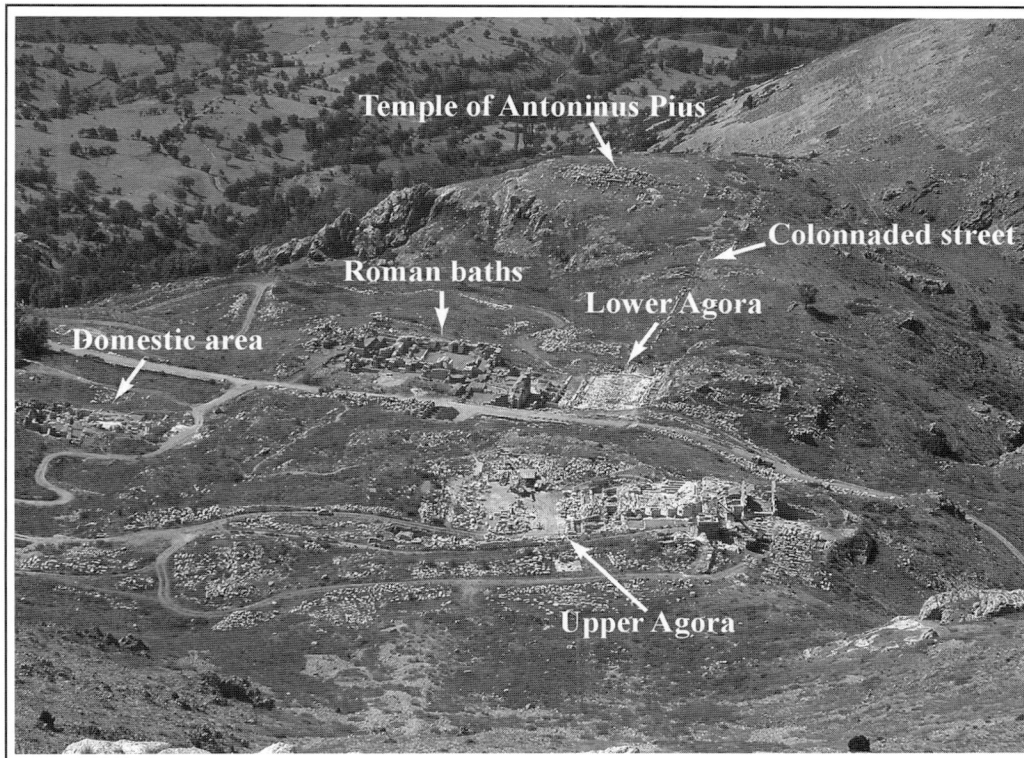

Figure 2: The archaeological site of Sagalassos seen from the North.

with catastrophic earthquakes, provide the ideal situation for the generation of many large mass movements. The relief of the entire mountain range including the monumental town is entirely transformed by large mass movements of different ages (Paulissen *et al.*, 1993; Verstraeten *et al.*, 2000). The vegetation in the area consists of pastures and needle-leaved tree zones on the more elevated mountain slopes and agricultural terraces on slopes below 40% (95% confidence level).

Literary sources and excavations in the monumental town centre show that Sagalassos was occupied from the 4th century BC till at least the 7th century AD. The most recent campaigns, however, have established that perhaps for a very short hiatus after the 540-620 AD earthquake, parts of the site remained inhabited until the 12th to 15th century AD, whereas an early Iron Age predecessor (Ur-Sagalassos) was discovered at Tepe Düzen, ca. 1.8 km southwest of the current site. Within the monumental centre a theatre, a library, a palatial late Roman mansion, an odeon, four magnificent Imperial nympheae and a late Hellenistic fountain house, some beautiful temples, two large market places (agora's) surrounded by shops and porticoes, a Roman bathhouse, a Hellenistic Bouleuterion, a stadium,

a gymnasium and an industrial potters' quarter are present (Figure 2; Waelkens, 1993; Waelkens and Poblome, 1993, 1995, 1997; Waelkens and Loots, 2000). During Hellenistic, Imperial and late Roman to early Byzantine times, the site covered respectively an area of 12.8, 23.5 and 31.5 hectares (Martens, 2005).

3. METHODS

The applied methodology is identical to the methodology applied in De Laet *et al.* (2007) and will be briefly outlined here.

3.1. Quality of the satellite imagery

De Laet *et al.* (2007) have shown that a minimum spatial resolution of 1 m of the satellite imagery is required for adequate visual interpretation and inferred automatic extraction of archaeological features. For this study covering Sagalassos and surroundings a Quickbird-2 image, acquired on 19 September 2003 at 8.34 am, was used (see Table 1 for the image characteristics).

	Bandwidth (μm)	Spatial resolution (m)
Panchromatic	0.45 – 0.90	0.61
Band 1	0.45 – 0.52 (blue)	2.44
Band 2	0.52 – 0.60 (green)	2.44
Band 3	0.63 – 0.69 (red)	2.44
Band 4	0.76 – 0.90 (near infrared)	2.44

Table 1: Spectral characteristics of Quickbird-2 imagery (http://www.digitalglobe.com/product/basic_imagery.shtml).

Attributes	Archaeological Description
Tone	Tonal differences in soil may indicate buried structures (crop marks)
Texture	Different vegetation textures may indicate buried features (crop marks)
Shape	Knowledge of shape of archaeological features can assist with determining whether a feature can be recognised as archaeological or not
Size	The dimensions of the feature are also important in order to regard the feature as archaeological or not
Spatial patterns	The spatial patterns among different features may represent an ancient settlement
Orientation	Some archaeological features are consistently orientated in a certain direction
Shadows	Positive archaeological features appear in an imagery through the shadows they cast
Spatial relationships	Ruins which have been abandoned for hundreds or thousands of years are sometimes located in isolated areas. Depending on the state of the ruins, they may still be associated with other nearby ancient features

Table 2: Quickbird-2 attributes for visual interpretation of archaeological remnants (modified after Pavlidis, 2005).

Before data extraction, a pan-sharpened colour image is produced and further rectified by combining the Image Support Data files and ground control points derived from a 1:25.000 topographical map, in order to accurately locate objects within a 3 to 4 m range. No radiometric corrections are applied.

3.2. Extraction of excavated structures

3.2.1. Visual interpretation of excavated structures

Visual interpretation is a multifaceted method combining in a subjective way visible elements outlined in Table 2. In this study, the visual interpretation is used to evaluate the information gathered by the different automatic extraction techniques on the same Quickbird-2 imagery (see 3.2.2). The antique site of Sagalassos is an adequate location since large areas of its monumental centre are already excavated so that the results can be confronted with reality.

The advantage of a visual interpretation derived from VHRS imagery is the ability to integrate archaeological structures in an initial city ground plan. These data form a meaningful document for guiding different types of fieldwork, particularly for designing efficient archaeological prospection strategies.

3.2.2. Automatic extraction of excavated structures

As for proto-urban Hisar, a late Iron Age site within the territory of Sagalassos to the north of Çanaklı (De Laet et al., 2007), three different automatic extraction methods were applied: a GIS-based, a pixel-based and an object-based method. GIS-based filtering techniques involve methods for increasing the visual distinctions between features in a scene (Lillesand et al., 2004). Since De Laet et al. (2007) showed that edge enhancement filtering provided the best results, this technique is also used to classify the ancient remains at Sagalassos.

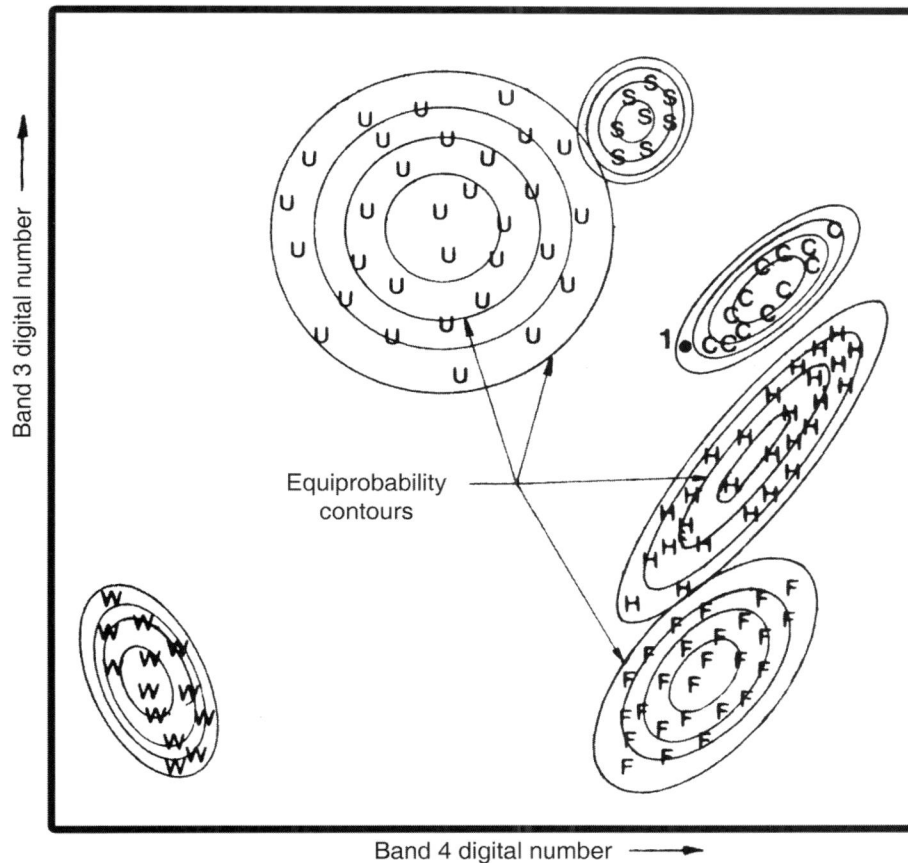

Figure 3: Class division defined by a maximum likelihood classifier (after Lillesand *et al.*, 2004).

As pixel-based method, a maximum likelihood classification was selected, because of the incorporation of both variance and covariance of the spectral classes (Figure 3; Lillesand *et al.*, 2004). This classification method evaluates for each pixel the spectral probability of being a member of a particular predefined class based on training samples. Training samples for different types of land cover are based on field observations and are characterized by a unique spectral composition. A class separability index, ranging between 0 and 2 (Swain and Davis, 1978), indicates to what extent the various training classes can be separated. Class-combinations with values higher than 1.9 are easy to separate, values between 1.9 and 1.7 are difficult to distinguish, while values lower than 1.7 are impossible to differentiate (Jensen, 1996).

For the Quickbird-2 imagery at Sagalassos, pixel-based classifications are not carried out at a spatial resolution of 0.61 m, but of 2.44 m due to the restricted spectral diversity of the panchromatic band.

As archaeological remains of monumental Sagalassos mainly consist of limestone walls with various heights, their shadows can also be used for detection. Two classes (walls and shadows of walls) supplemented with a class, representing floor surfaces were selected for the extraction. Because it was impossible to differentiate between shadows of walls and other types of shadows, one large "shadow" class was used. Once classified, shadows of walls became recognisable by their position adjacent and parallel to wall remains. Floor surfaces represent areas paved with limestone slabs or mosaic floors currently covered with a protecting gravel layer. Within the walls a distinction was made between excavated features and unexcavated features, which were often partly covered with vegetation. To enhance the extraction results, also other classes were added: vegetation, actual roads, anthropogenic steppe and natural limestone outcrops.

For all class-combinations, except for the combination natural limestone outcrops – unexcavated archaeological features

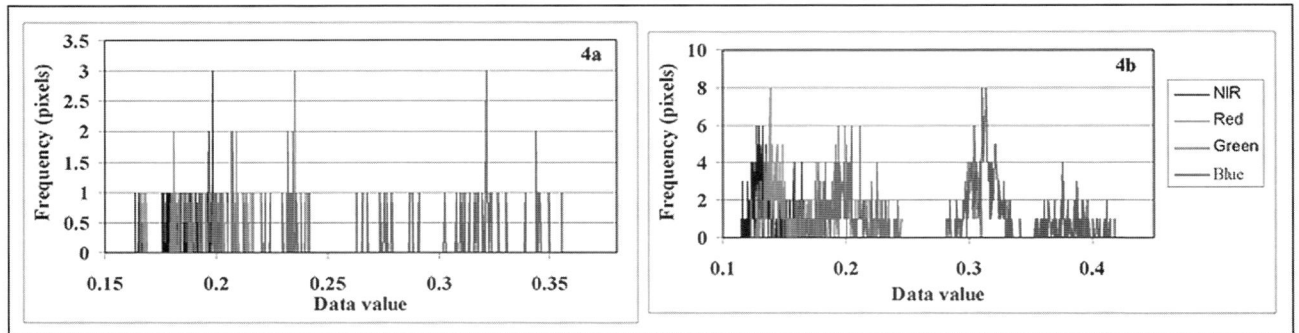

Figure 4: (A) signature distribution of unexcavated archaeological features and (B) anthropogenic steppe.

Homogeneity criteria				
Level	Scale factor	Shape factor	Compactness factor	Smoothness factor
1	80	0.1	0.1	0.9

Table 3: Segmentation parameters.

the separability index is higher than the critical threshold. As a result adequate classification results are expected for excavated features, such as floor/slabs surfaces, shadows of walls and other landscape features, and less accurate results are to be expected for unexcavated features. Classification problems arise because for some land cover classes no normality can be achieved – a requirement for applying a maximum likelihood classification. For instance, unexcavated limestone signatures do not show a normal distribution in contrast with an anthropogenic steppe (Figure 4).

Object-based remote sensing takes into account spectral as well as shape characteristics and is very useful for heterogeneous land covers (Giada *et al.*, 2003; Thomas *et al.*, 2003; Laliberte *et al.*, 2004). It treats the image as a set of meaningful objects rather than as pixels and spectral, shape and hierarchical parameters are taken into account (Table 3). An object-based technique, particularly developed for very high-resolution imagery, is applied (Blaschke and Strobl, 2001; Kiema, 2002; Giada *et al.*, 2003).

3.3. Identification of unexcavated features

For recovering unknown features, a visual examination of the Quickbird-2 image was carried out in an unexcavated area of the ancient town where already 'intensive' archaeological and geophysical prospecting had taken place. Newly detected features were compared with geophysical data, prior to fieldwork.

The multi-method geophysical research strategy applied at Sagalassos thus incorporates advanced magnetic interpretative procedures such as direct and inverse 2D and 3D magnetic modelling, Upward Continuation, Residual anomalies and To the Pole transformation (Dobrin and Savit, 1988; Telford *et al.*, 1990; Mušič *et al.*, 2004). Upward Continuation of the magnetic potential field eliminates small anomalies from near surface objects to enhance response from deeply buried sources (Tchernychev, 1998). Therefore, the aim of magnetic prospecting is locating architectural remains built mainly with non-magnetic limestone blocks, the identification of strongly magnetic potter's kilns, streets made of limestone slabs and some architectural elements made of brick (Clark, 1990; Mušič, 2001). The reliability of magnetic method results is undoubted. Results were confirmed by the excavation of workshops in the industrial area, a gymnasium near the theatre and houses and streets in the residential area (Martens, 2004, 2005).

4. RESULTS

4.1. Excavated archaeological structures in the monumental town

4.1.1. Visual interpretation

A visual interpretation of the Quickbird-2 image was made on the monumental centre of the town. These data as well as the Sagalassos city map were used to evaluate the results of

162

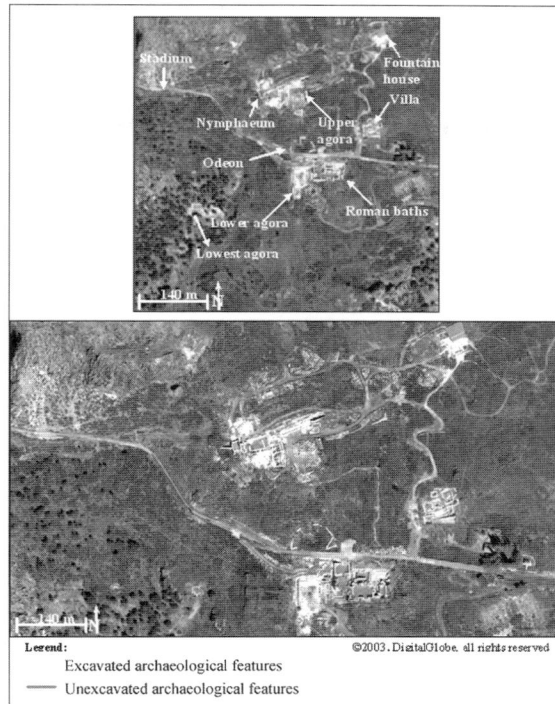

Legend:
      Excavated archaeological features
—   Unexcavated archaeological features

Figure 5: Visual interpretation of archaeological features on Quickbird-2 imagery.

the automatic extractions. One distinguished between excavated and unexcavated archaeological structures, which have less specific colour and shape characteristics. In Figure 5 only the main visual structures are represented. In the excavated areas, the remains of two agora's, the Roman baths, different fountain houses, the odeon, the stadium, areas with floors and the palatial mansion can be recognized. The contours of these buildings are visible, as well as elements of their internal structure. Because slabs have a very specific visual signature, spectral signatures for ancient floors and slabs were sampled separately, to enhance the automatic extraction results. Most of the unexcavated structures were already inventoried by the archaeological survey.

4.1.2. Edge enhancement filtering

The initial result of this GIS-based method is a greyscale image (Figure 6a). This image is reclassified according to values based on the visual interpretation of the Quickbird-2 image: >5000 for walls and <–5000 for shadows of walls (Figure 6b). Compared to the visual interpretation results, all linear structures are extracted very well. As was already the case for the Ikonos image at the Hisar site (De Laet et al., 2007), edge enhancement filtering of the Sagalassos Quickbird-2 image does neither provide a unique class for archaeological remains, which is at least partly due to their

intermingling with other linear features such as rows of trees and shrubs. Although the Quickbird-2 results of the filtering technique for ancient features are acceptable (an accuracy of ca. 85%), we suggest that filtering is probably not the best extraction method, since the overall accuracy of this technique solely amounts to ca. 40%.

4.1.3. Pixel-based classification

The maximum likelihood classification accuracy for Sagalassos on Quickbird-2 (Figure 7) amounts to 50%. Large excavated structures, such as limestone slabs of the lower and upper agora, some parts of the mansion, a nymphaeum, the Hellenistic fountain house in the northeast and the Roman baths are correctly classified. Striking is that this approach succeeds to extract very well all floor areas and slabs, a result we could not achieve with the edge enhancement filtering technique. This technique is neither able to classify the individual limestone blocks that have been assembled in certain areas for anastylosis. Also a number of unexcavated structures are extracted, although the attempt failed to classify them in a single class. Some of the fractured limestone areas are for instance designated to the category "unexcavated archaeological features". Although the overall accuracy of the pixel-based classification is superior to the GIS-based method, the results for excavated remains

163

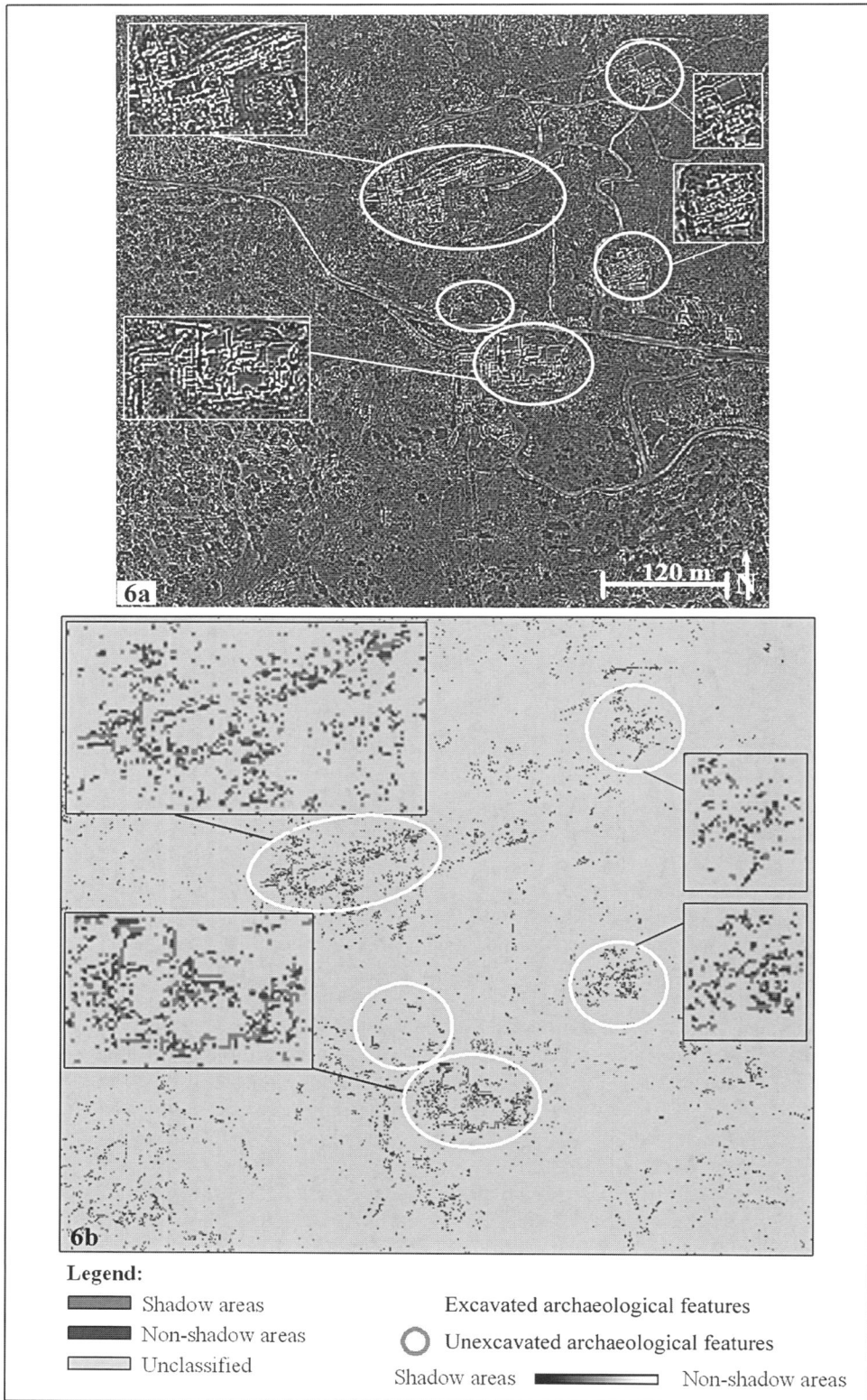

Figure 6: Result edge enhancement filtering technique (A) initial result edge enhancement (B) final result edge enhancement filtering.

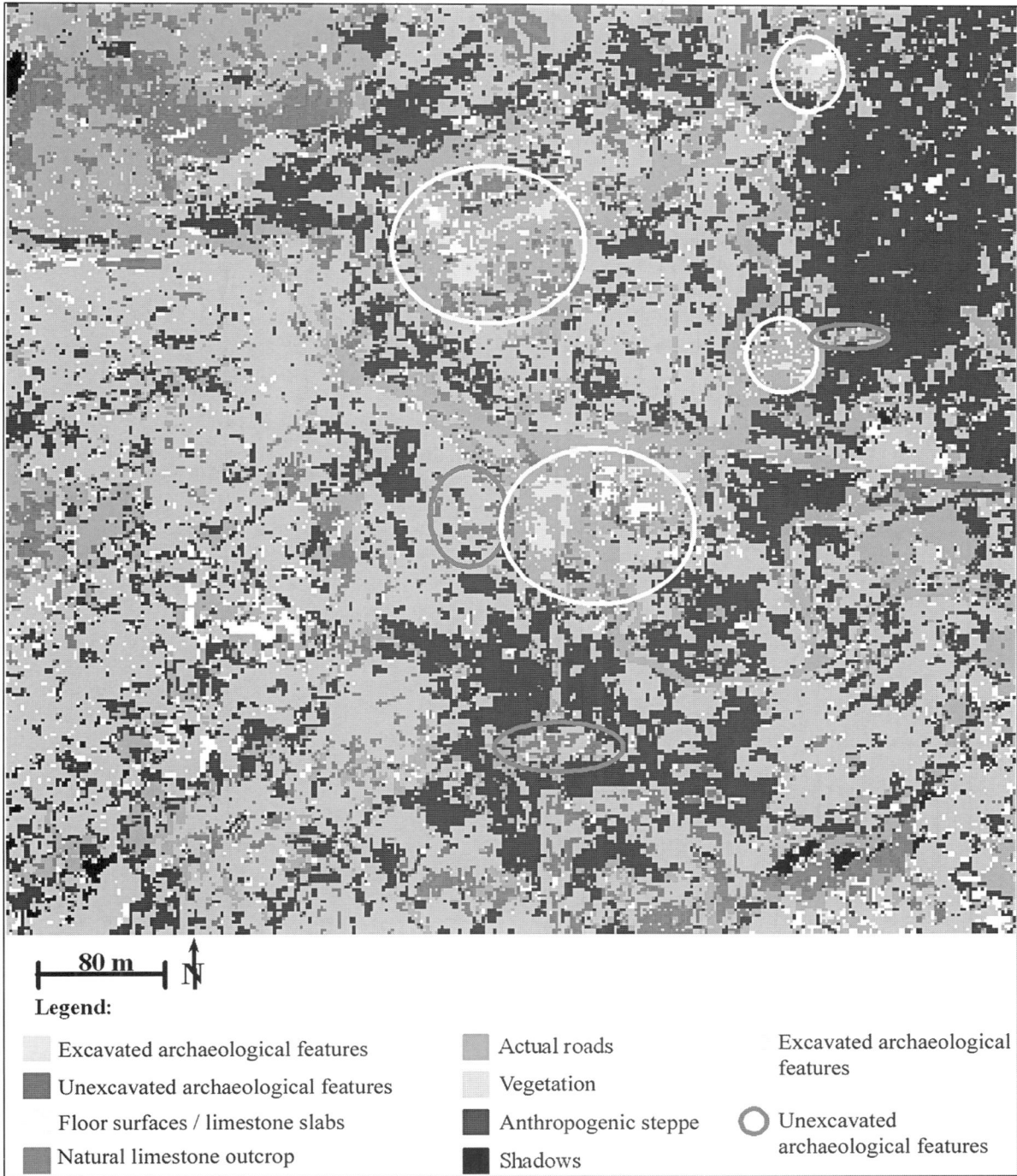

Legend:

▢ Excavated archaeological features	▢ Actual roads		Excavated archaeological features
▢ Unexcavated archaeological features	▢ Vegetation		
Floor surfaces / limestone slabs	▢ Anthropogenic steppe	◯	Unexcavated archaeological features
▢ Natural limestone outcrop	▢ Shadows		

80 m   N

Figure 7: Pixel-based maximum likelihood classification result.

and shadows of walls are less accurate compared to edge enhancement filtering.

4.1.4. Object-based classification

Analogous to the pixel-based method, limestone outcrops, excavated and unexcavated structures, floor surfaces, slabs, shadows of walls and other landscape features were selected. The segmentation parameters at one segmentation level applied to segment antique remnants built with limestone blocks are given in Table 3. Figure 8 shows the results of the object-based classification for the monumental centre of Sagalassos, with the results of the segmentation procedure (Figure 8a), the signature samples for the various landscape categories (Figure 8b) and the results of the classification procedure are visualized (Figure 8c). These data make clear that many ancient structures are well segmented and appear as separate objects.

All monumental buildings, even the less obvious odeon and lowest agora, were accurately mapped. These results, with an accuracy of 75%, are significantly better than those of both the pixel-based classification and edge enhancement filtering technique. An important advantage of this technique is that excavated ancient structures are classified as a separate category. Even though the category "floor surfaces / limestone slabs" contains floor areas as well as excavated structures, the contours of floors and slabs surfaces are correctly delimited.

The classification of unexcavated structures, on the contrary, remains problematic. Unexcavated structures, composed of limestone and often covered with a sparse vegetation cover, were categorized as anthropogenic steppe or limestone outcrops. Also some shadows of walls and the scattered presence of building blocks are not accurately classified and assigned to natural limestone outcrops. Though, within a perimeter around the archaeological site the results for the individualization of shadows of walls within the class shadows are promising.

Due to the non-unique spectrum or shape characteristics of archaeological remains, the success of an object-based classification varies. The segmentation procedure within the object-based method is, however, a valuable approach to limit the digitalisation of individual structures as performed in a visual interpretation.

4.2. Visual interpretation of unexcavated features outside the monumental town

In spite of the large number of excavations and intensive surveys within the Sagalassos' urban and industrial areas, a visual interpretation of Quickbird-2 imagery revealed some remarkable features (Figure 9).

In the potters' quarter the variation of surface marks was rather large and a distinction could be made between recent and non-recent surface marks (Figure 9a). This figure only shows a few examples of surface marks visible on the Quickbird-2 imagery. Although most of the structures visualized in Figure 9a are easily recognizable in the field, none of the N-S lineaments clearly visible on the Quickbird-2 image could be identified during an intensive field survey of the area. Since processing errors in satellite imagery express itself as a continuous array of very low/high Digital Number (DN) values (i.e. black/white colour) in either a N-S or E-W direction or a systematic grey colour striping of the imagery (Simpson et al., 1998; Corsini et al., 2000; Goodenough et al., 2003), the N-S lineaments recognizable in the Quickbird-2 image have a non-error character.

In order to reveal the significance of these N-S lineaments, the Quickbird-2 image was geographically linked with geophysical data. The intersection of red lines in Figure 9a and the intersection of white lines in Figure 9b point to the same topographic location. Magnetic prospecting with optically pumped caesium magnetometer (Geometrics G-858) in gradient configuration (Smith, 1997) clearly showed the subsurface presence of different architectural remains associated with streets and numerous workshops (kilns) in the potters' quarter, but did not portray the remarkable N-S lineaments visible on the Quickbird-2 image, as is visualized by the yellow line in Figure 9b. At the position of these N-S lineaments, geophysical data show the presence of an alternation of colluvial deposits, wall remains and kilns, which were abandoned from the 5th to 7th century AD onwards (Poblome, 2006; Figure 9b). Consequently, we suggest that these linear features are situated on the very top of archaeological remains. Aerial photographs taken with a kite by M. Waelkens clearly identified these lineaments as well and moreover showed that they were subdivided by numerous parallel lineaments perpendicular to the above mentioned ones. Based on palynological data, Vermoere (2004) suggested that from the Roman period onwards, grapes were most likely cultivated on the south facing slopes of the potters' quarter. As a result, these N-S lineaments and E-W subdivisions may correspond with agricultural activities and represent the delineation of ancient field plots. In the future trenches have to be made to clarify the actual meaning of these N-S and E-W lineaments. As for the date of this land use, it must be clear that they postdate the main occupation period of Sagalassos, which came to an end by an earthquake dated to the 7th century AD. As a result, they probably represent land use corresponding with the recently identified hamlets of the 'kastron' type, living

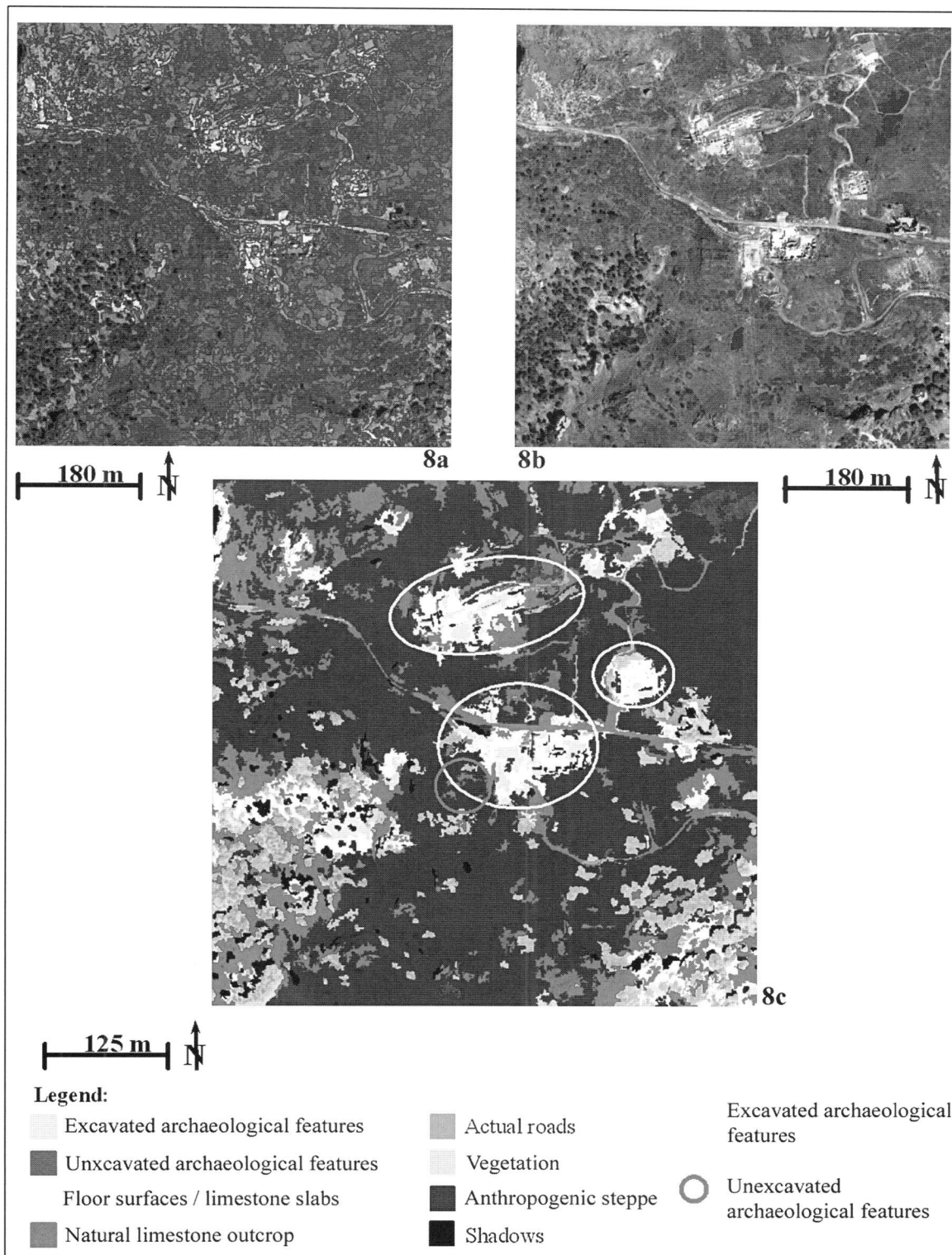

Figure 8: Object-based segmentation and image classification results (A) segmentation level 1: archaeological remnants (B) classification signatures for the various landscape categories (C) classification results.

Legend:

- Excavated archaeological features
- Unxcavated archaeological features
- Floor surfaces / limestone slabs
- Natural limestone outcrop
- Actual roads
- Vegetation
- Anthropogenic steppe
- Shadows
- Excavated archaeological features
- ⭕ Unexcavated archaeological features

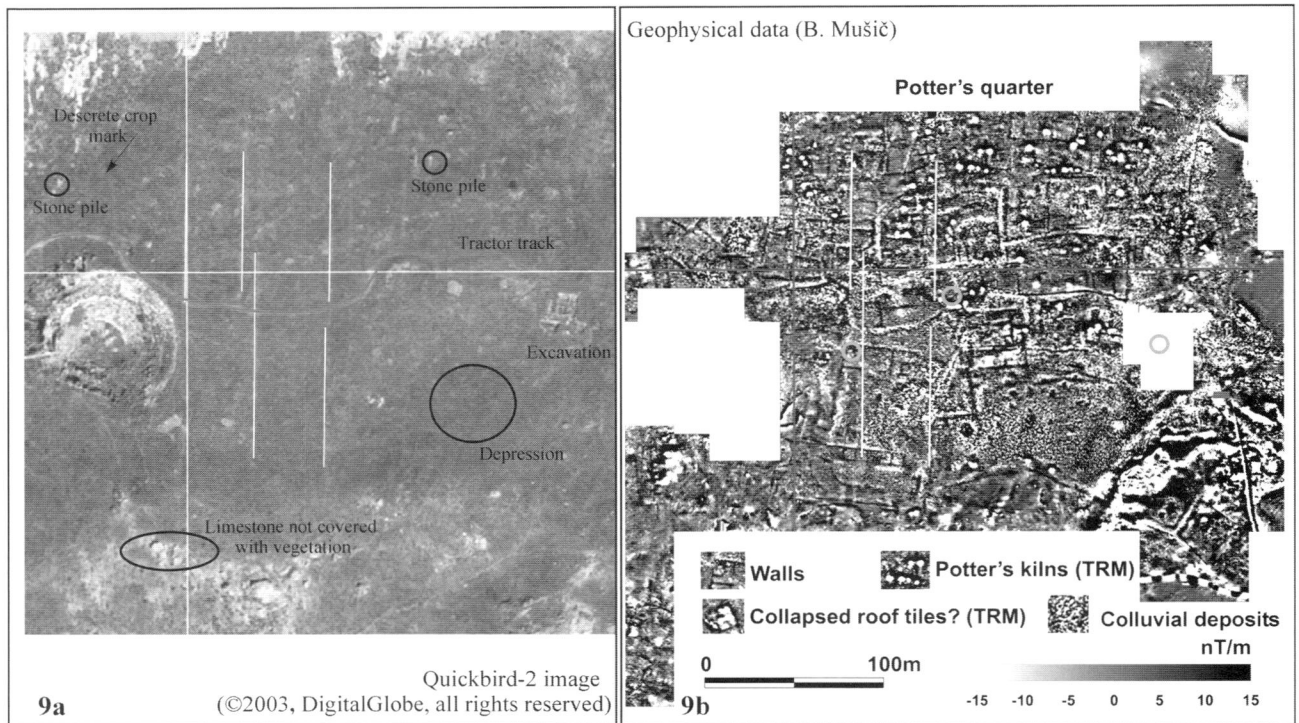

9a

Geophysical data (B. Mušič)

Potter's quarter

9b

Legend:

—— Recent surface marks   Remarkable N-S lineaments

—— Not-recent surface marks   ○ Excavated areas

Figure 9: (A) Unexcavated features visible on Quickbird-2 imagery but (B) lacking on geophysical data.

on at Sagalassos until the 11th century AD, or with the occupation of the mid Byzantine fortress on the Alexander Hill, dated to the 12th to 15th century AD.

5. DISCUSSION AND CONCLUSION

The automatic classification methods applied in this paper are able to recognize archaeological features with variable success on a Quickbird-2 image. High-quality results for most landscape elements are obtained especially by the object-based classification technique. For excavated structures edge enhancement filtering provides reasonable results, when only a limited perimeter around excavated building remains is taken into account. This technique enables to very accurately extract the inner structure of the buildings. In all other cases, filtering does not provide a unique class for ancient features and its overall contribution is not better than any other applied technique. This is due to the complexity of the landscape with many other types of linear

features. Floor surfaces and areas paved with limestone slabs are most accurately extracted using an object-based classification technique.

Considering the overall classification accuracy, solely object-based classification of well-preserved archaeological structures presents valuable results. For all other archaeological remains, a visual interpretation supplemented with a GIS, pixel- and/or object-based classification is obligatory to accurately extract excavated features. The unsatisfactory overall classification results of the pixel-based technique are primarily due to the spectral similarity between archaeological remains and the surrounding limestone substrate, a coincidence that is seldom an issue for other landscape elements. With building materials different from the limestone substrate in the immediate vicinity, it is expected that their automatic extraction would be more successful. Since the Sagalassos site is protected, shrubs and trees are expanding due to the interdiction of herding flocks. Without shrubs and trees, much of the areas actually under shadow would disappear and the classification of archaeological structures would be more straightforward.

A visual interpretation presents excellent results and is therefore recommended before automatic extraction. It provides information on site location, site extension or site planning. Automatic extraction techniques should be further refined because they are less subjective than visual interpretation and less time consuming when applied on large areas and on sites with well visible structures. Satellite imagery has revealed previously unknown features, situated on the very top of subsurface architectural remains, mapped in detail by geophysical prospecting and intensive surveying. The interpretation of surface marks is, however, very much dependent on the time of acquisition and the type of imagery applied. Satellite remote sensing, aerial photography, geophysical prospecting and field walking are therefore complementary techniques.

6. ACKNOWLEDGEMENTS

A version of this article in full colour is available from the authors. The research was supported by the Belgian Programme on Interuniversitary Poles of Attraction (IAP V/9) and the Research Fund of the K.U.Leuven (BOF-GOA02/2) and S&T Cooperation Belgium – Central and Eastern Europe Programme of Belgian Science Policy. The authors would like to thank the entire archaeological team of the Sagalassos project for providing sufficient archaeological information in order to carry out this research. We also would like to thank the RMCA for their collaboration.

7. REFERENCES

BAATZ, M. and SCHÄPE, A. (2000) Multiresolution segmentation: an optimization Approach for high quality multi-scale image segmentation, in: J. STROBL and T. BLASCHKE (eds.) *Angewandte Geographische Informations Verarbeitung XII*, Wichmann-Verlag, Heidelberg: 12-23.

BAATZ, M., HEYNEN, M., HOFMANN, P., LINGENFELDER, I., MILMER, M., SCHAEPE, A., WEBER, M. and WILLHAUCK, G. (2002) eCognition. *Object Oriented Image Analysis. User guide 3.0*, Definiens AG, Munich.

BLASCHKE, T.S. and STROBL, J. (2001) What's wrong with pixels? Some recent developments interfacing remote sensing and GIS, *GIS – Zeitschrift für Geoinformationssysteme* 6: 12-17.

CHANGLIN, W., NING, Y., YUEPING, N. and LIN, Y. (2004) Environmental study and information extraction of archaeological features with remote sensing imagery in

arid area of western China, *Proceedings of the International Conference on Remote Sensing Archaeology*, Beijing, 17-21 October 2004.

CLARK, A. (1990) *Seeing Beneath the Soil – Prospecting Methods in Archaeology*, Batsford, London.

CLARK, C.D., GARROD, S.M. and PEARSON, M.P. (1998) Landscape archaeology and remote sensing in southern Madagascar, *International Journal of Remote Sensing* 19 (8): 1461-1477.

CORSINI, G., DIANI, M. and WALZEL, T. (2000) Striping removal in MOS-B data, *IEEE Transactions on Geoscience and Remote Sensing* 38 (3): 1439-1446.

DE LAET, V., PAULISSEN, E. and WAELKENS, M. (in press) Methods for the extraction of archaeological features from very high-resolution Ikonos-2 remote sensing imagery, Hisar (southwest Turkey), *Journal of Archaeological Science*.

DOBRIN, M.B. and SAVIT, C.H. (1988). *Introduction to Geophysical Prospecting*, McGraw-Hill International editions, New York.

EMMOLO, D., FRANCO, V., LO BRUTTO, M., ORLANDO, P. and VILLA, B. (2004) Hyperspectral techniques and GIS for archaeological investigation, *Proceedings of the XXth ISPRS congress on Geo-imagery Bridging Continents*, Istanbul, Turkey, 12-23 July 2004.

GEORGOULA, O., KAIMARIS, D., TSAKIRI, M. and PATIAS, P. (2004) From the aerial photo to high resolution satellite image. Tools for the archaeological research, *Proceedings of XXth ISPRS congress on Geo-imagery Bridging Continents*, Istanbul, Turkey, 12-23 July 2004.

GIADA, S., DE GROEVE, T. and EHRLICH, D. (2003) Information extraction from very high resolution satellite imagery over Lukole refugee camp, Tanzania, *International Journal of Remote Sensing* 24 (22): 4251-4266.

GOODENOUGH, D.G., DYK, A., NIEMANN, K.O., PEARLMAN, J.S., HAO CHEN, HAN, T., MURDOCH, M. and WEST, C. (2003) Processing Hyperion and ALI for forest classification, *IEEE Transactions on Geoscience and Remote Sensing* 41 (6): 1321-1331.

HOFMANN, P. (2001) Detecting informal settlements from Ikonos image data using methods of object oriented image analysis – an example from Cape Town (South Africa), in: C. JÜRGENS (ed.) *Remote Sensing of Urban Areas/ Fernerkundung in urbanen Räumen, Regensburger Geographische Schriften*: 107-118.

JENSEN, J.R. (1996) *Introductory Digital Image Processing: A Remote Sensing Perspective*, Prentice Hall, New Jersey.

JENSEN, J.R. (2000) *Remote Sensing of the Environment. An Earth Resource perspective*, Prentice Hall, New Jersey.

JORDAN, G., MEIJNINGER, B.M.L., VAN HINSBERGEN, D.J.J., MEULENKAMP, J.E. and VAN DIJK, P.M. (2005) Extraction of morphotectonic features from DEMs: Development and applications for study areas in Hungary and NW Greece, *International Journal of Applied Earth Observation and Geoinformation* 7 (3): 163-182.

KIEMA, J.B.K. (2002) Texture analysis and data fusion in the extraction of topographic objects from satellite imagery, *International Journal of Remote Sensing* 23 (4): 767-776.

LALIBERTE, A.S., RANGO, A., HAVSTAD, K.M., PARIS, J.F., BECK, R.F., MCNEELY, R. and GONZALEZ, A.L. (2004) Object-oriented image analysis for mapping shrub encroachment from 1937 to 2003 in southern New Mexico, *Remote Sensing of Environment* 93 (1-2): 198-210.

LEICA (2002) *Erdas Field Guide, sixth ed.*, Leica Geosystems, Atlanta.

LILLESAND, T.M., KIEFER, R.W. and CHIPMAN, J.W. (2004) *Remote Sensing and Image Interpretation*, John Wiley & Sons, New York.

MARTENS, F. (2004) *Interdisciplinary Research Concerning the Urban Development of Sagalassos: Settlement Development, Urban Layout and Infrastructure*, Unpublished Ph D thesis, Katholieke Universiteit Leuven.

MARTENS, F. (2005) The archaeological urban survey of Sagalassos (South-West Turkey): The possibilities and limitations of surveying a 'non-typical' classical site, *Oxford Journal of Archaeology* 24 (3): 229-254.

MASSALABI, A., HE, D.C., BÉNIÉ, G.B. and BEAUDRY, E. (2004) Restitution of information under shadow in remote sensing high space resolution images: Application to Ikonos data of Sherbrooke City, *XXth ISPRS congress on Geo-Imagery Bridging Continents*, Istanbul, Turkey, 12-23 July.

MASUOKA, P.M., CLABORN, D.M., ANDRE, R.G., NIGRO, J., GORDON, S.W., KLEIN, T.A. and KIM, H. (2003) Use of Ikonos and Landsat for malaria control in the Republic of Korea, *Remote Sensing of Environment* 88 (1-2): 187-194.

MATHER, P.M. (2004) *Computer Processing of Remotely-Sensed Images: An Introduction*, John Wiley & Sons, Chichester.

MUŠIČ, B. (2001) An evaluation of the potential of geophysical prospections in difficult environments: The silent presence of GIS, in: B. SLAPSAK (ed.) *On the Good Use of Geographic Information Systems in Archaeological Landscape Studies, Proceedings of the COST G2*, Luxembourg: 127-144.

MUŠIČ, B., SLAPSAK, B. and FARINETTI, E. (2004) Ancient Tanagra (Grimadha): Geophysical prospection and modelling for understanding of urban plan and on-site activity areas, in: K. FISCHER AUSSERER (ed.) *The e-way into the four dimensions of cultural heritage, Proceedings of the 30th conference [Enter the past] (BAR international series 1227)*, Archaeopress, Oxford: 317-320.

PAVLIDIS, L. (2005) High resolution satellite imagery for archaeological application: *www.fungis.org/files/news_mar05_archaeology.pdf*

PAULISSEN, E., POESEN, J., GOVERS, G. and DE PLOEY, J. (1993) The physical environment at Sagalassos (Western Taurus, Turkey). A reconnaissance survey, in: M. Waelkens and J. Poblome (eds.) *Sagalassos II. Report on the third excavation campaign of 1992 (Acta Archaeologica Lovaniensia Monographiae 9)*, Leuven University Press, Leuven: 229-240.

PCI GEOMATICS (1998) *OrthoEngine Reference Manual*, PCI geomatics, Ontario.

POBLOME, J. (2006) Mixed feelings on Greece and Asia Minor in the third century AD, in: D. MALFITANA, J. POBLOME and J. LUND (eds.), *Old Pottery in a New Century. Innovating perspectives in Roman pottery studies* (Monografie dell Istituto per I Beni Archeologici e Monumentali-CNR 1), Catania, 22-24 April 2004.

RICHARDS, J.A. and XIUPING, J. (1999) *Remote Sensing Digital Image Analysis, An Introduction*, Springer Verlag, New York.

RYHERD, S. and WOODCOCK, C.E. (1996) Combining spectral and texture data in the segmentation of remotely sensed images, *Photogrammetric Engineering and Remote Sensing* 62 (2): 181-194.

ŞENEL, M. (1997) *1:100 000 scale geological maps of Isparta – J11 Quadrangle*. General Directorate of Mineral Research and Exploitation, Ankara.

SEVER, T.L. (1995) Remote sensing, *American Journal of Archaeology* 99 (1): 83-84.

SIMPSON, J.J., STITT, J.R. and LEATH, D.M. (1998) Improved finite impulse response filters for enhanced destriping of geostationary satellite data, *Remote Sensing of Environment* 66 (3): 235-249.

SMITH, K. (1997) *Cesium optically pumped magnetometers, Technical report M-TR91, Geometrics ltd.* (www.geometrics.com).

SWAIN, P.H. and DAVIS, S.M. (1978) *Remote Sensing: The Quantitative Approach*, McGraw Hill Book Company, New York.

TCHERNYCHEV, M. (1998) *MAGPICK – magnetic map & profile processing, User Guide,* Geometrics ltd. (www.geometrics.com).

TELFORD, W.M., GELDART, L.P. and SHERIFF, R.E. (1990) *Applied Geophysics, second ed.*, Cambridge University Press, Cambridge.

THOMAS, N., HENDRIX, C. and CONGALTON, R.G. (2003) A comparison of urban mapping methods using high-resolution digital imagery, *Photogrammetric Engineering and Remote Sensing* 69 (9): 963-972.

VAN DER MEER, F.D. and DE JONG, S. (2003) *Imaging Spectrometry. Basic Principles and Prospective Applications*, Kluwer Academic Publishers, Dordrecht.

VANHAVERBEKE, H. and WAELKENS, M. (2003) *The Chora of Sagalassos (Pisidia, southwest Turkey). The Evolution of the Settlement Pattern from Prehistory until Recent Times* (*Studies in Eastern Mediterranean Archaeology VIII*), Brepols Publishers, Turnhout.

VERMEULEN, F. and VERHOEVEN, G. (2004) The contribution of aerial photography and field survey to the study of urbanization in the Potenza valley (Picenum), *Journal of Roman Archaeology* 17 (1): 57-82.

VERMOERE, M. (2004) *Holocene Vegetation History in the Territory of Sagalassos (southwest Turkey) A Palynological Approach* (*Studies in Eastern Mediterranean Archaeology VI*), Brepols Publishers, Turnhout.

VERSTRAETEN, G., PAULISSEN, E., LIBRECHT, I. and WAELKENS, M. (2000) Limestone platforms around Sagalassos resulting from giant mass movements, in: M. WAELKENS and L. LOOTS (eds.), *Sagalassos V, Report on the survey and excavation campaigns of 1996 and 1997* (*Acta Archaeologica Lovaniensia 11/B*), Leuven University Press, Leuven: 783-798.

WAELKENS, M. (ed.) (1993) *Sagalassos I. First General Report on the Survey (1986-1989) and Excavations (1990-1991)* (*Acta Archaeologica Lovaniensia Monographiae 5*), Leuven University Press, Leuven.

WAELKENS, M. and POBLOME, J. (eds.) (1993) *Sagalassos II. Report on the Third Excavation Campaign of 1992* (*Acta Archaeologica Lovaniensia Monographiae 6*), Leuven University Press, Leuven.

WAELKENS, M. and POBLOME, J. (eds.) (1995) *Sagalassos III. Report on the Fourth Excavation Campaign of 1993* (*Acta Archaeologica Lovaniensia Monographiae 7*), Leuven University Press, Leuven.

WAELKENS, M. and POBLOME, J. (eds.) (1997) *Sagalassos IV. Report on the Survey and Excavation Campaigns of 1994 and 1995* (*Acta Archaeologica Lovaniensia Monographiae 9*), Leuven University Press, Leuven.

WAELKENS, M. and THE SAGALASSOS TEAM (1997) Interdisciplinarity in classical archaeology. A case study: the Sagalassos Archaeological Research Project (Southwest Turkey), in: M. WAELKENS and J. POBLOME (eds.) *Sagalassos IV. Report on the Survey and Excavation Campaings of 1994 and 1995* (*Acta Archaeologica Lovaniensia Monographiae 9*), Leuven University Press: 225-252.

WAELKENS, M. and LOOTS, L. (eds.) (2000) *Sagalassos V. Report on the Survey and Excavation Campaigns of 1996 and 1997* (*Acta Archaeologica Lovaniensia Monographiae 11*), Leuven University Press, Leuven.

WAELKENS, M., PAULISSEN, E., VAN HAVERBEKE, H., ÖZTÜRK, I., DE CUPERE, B., EKINCI, H.A., VERMEERSCH, P., POBLOME, J. and DEGEEST, R. (1997) The 1994 and 1995 Surveys on the territory of Sagalassos, in: M. WAELKENS and J. POBLOME (eds.), *Sagalassos IV, Report on the survey and excavation campaigns of 1994 and 1995* (*Acta Archaeologica Lovaniensia Monographiae 9*), Leuven University Press: 11-103.

WILLHAUCK, G. (2000) Comparison of object oriented classification techniques and standard image analysis for the use of change detection between SPOT multispectral satellite images and aerial photos, *Proceedings of the XIXth ISPRS Congress*, Amsterdam, 16-22 July 2000.

TEPHRA FROM THE MINOAN ERUPTION OF SANTORINI IN THE TERRITORY OF SAGALASSOS

Simon SIX, Patrick DEGRYSE, Etienne PAULISSEN, Wouter HEIJLEN, Marleen VERMOERE and Marc WAELKENS

1. INTRODUCTION

The marsh of Gravgaz (N37°34', E30°24') is located 20km southeast of Burdur and 15 km southwest of the ancient city of Sagalassos. A few kilometres to the southeast of the marsh, the ruins (with a well-preserved circuit wall) of an unidentified early Iron Age proto-urban site, part of the Hellenistic territory of Sagalassos, occupying the rock promontory of Kepez Kalesi (Vanhaverbeke and Waelkens, 2003). The marsh at an elevation of 1215 m a.s.l. forms the lowest parts of a closed basin of 10.6 km² surrounded by limestone mountains towards the south and the west reaching altitudes of 1550 m a.s.l. The Gravgaz basin is closed and characterized by endorheic drainage fed by springs at the base of the western limestone slopes. Because of its closed structure nearly all eroded material is preserved within the basin. The marsh has been the subject of detailed Late Holocene palaeoenvironmental research (Vermoere *et al.*, 2000, 2002a, 2002b, 2004; Six, 2004).

This paper reports the discovery of a 2 cm thick layer of tephra recovered in one of the cores in the Gravgaz basin. This ash layer has been identified as the distal fallout of the 'Minoan' or Z-2 tephra from the Santorini (Thera) volcano in the Aegean located at 460 km SW from Gravgaz. Its geochemical composition is indeed identical with the tephra from Gölhisar Gölü, Santorini and Crete (Eastwood *et al.*, 1999a). For Anatolia, it is the first time that the Thera tephra has been recovered from alluvial fan deposits. The sedimentological and geochemical characteristics of this tephra layer are presented. In this paper, we also briefly discuss the state of the art concerning the age of the Minoan Thera explosion and the impact of the distal Thera tephra deposits on the local environment.

2. FIELDWORK AND ANALYTICAL METHODS

A north-south transect from the middle of the marsh towards the gentle colluvial slopes under cultivation is presented in figure 2 (for location see figure 1). The cores are drilled with an end filling Dachnowsky core in the soft deposits and with an end filling percussion core in the stiff deposits. The lithological succession in core SA-00-02 can be correlated with the very organic lithological succession in the core SA-00-03 and the marsh deposits in general (Six, 2004).

Core SA-00-EP-01, situated in colluvial deposits 140m upslope from the marsh, is different as it totally lacks organics and carbonates. The top 7 m is homogeneous clayey silt. Between 7 and 10 m the lithology is heterogeneous with an alternation of sandy and clayey layers. A 2 cm thick, pale tephra layer of ash and glass shards has been recovered at a depth of 8.73-8.75 m (Figure 2 and 3). This volcanic layer is not pure as it contained streaks of dark clayey components, suggesting a slightly reworked condition. The core was sampled with a 5 cm interval between 6-10 m for grain size, palynological, mineralogical and geochemical analyses, except for the depth interval 7.0–7.5 m where sandy sediments were lost during coring. The tephra layer was sampled as SAEP28. Core SA-00-EP-2 was also sampled in detail, but no visible traces of a tephra layer were observed in the field.

Part of the samples of core 1 was used for grain size analyses. After oxidation of the organic matter with H_2O_2 (30% solution) the grain size distribution was obtained for the fraction >500 μm by wet sieving and for the fraction <500 μm with laser diffractometry using a Malvern Mastersizer. Larger quantities of samples from both cores (for core 1 between 8.50 and 10.00 m; for core 2 between 9 and 10 m) were sieved over a 62 μm mesh and studied with the binocular and the microscope in search for volcanic glass shards and plant remains or charcoal fragments for radiocarbon dating.

For optical and mineralogical analysis of the glass shards present in samples SAEP28 and SAEP29, a representative quantity of these samples were washed with deionized water and sieved over a 36 μm mesh to remove the greater part of the clay minerals present. The fraction larger than 36 μm was subsequently cleaned with 1N HCl, 30% H_2O_2 and 2N Na(OH), applying the chemicals for one hour and washing and sieving over a 36 μm mesh in between each

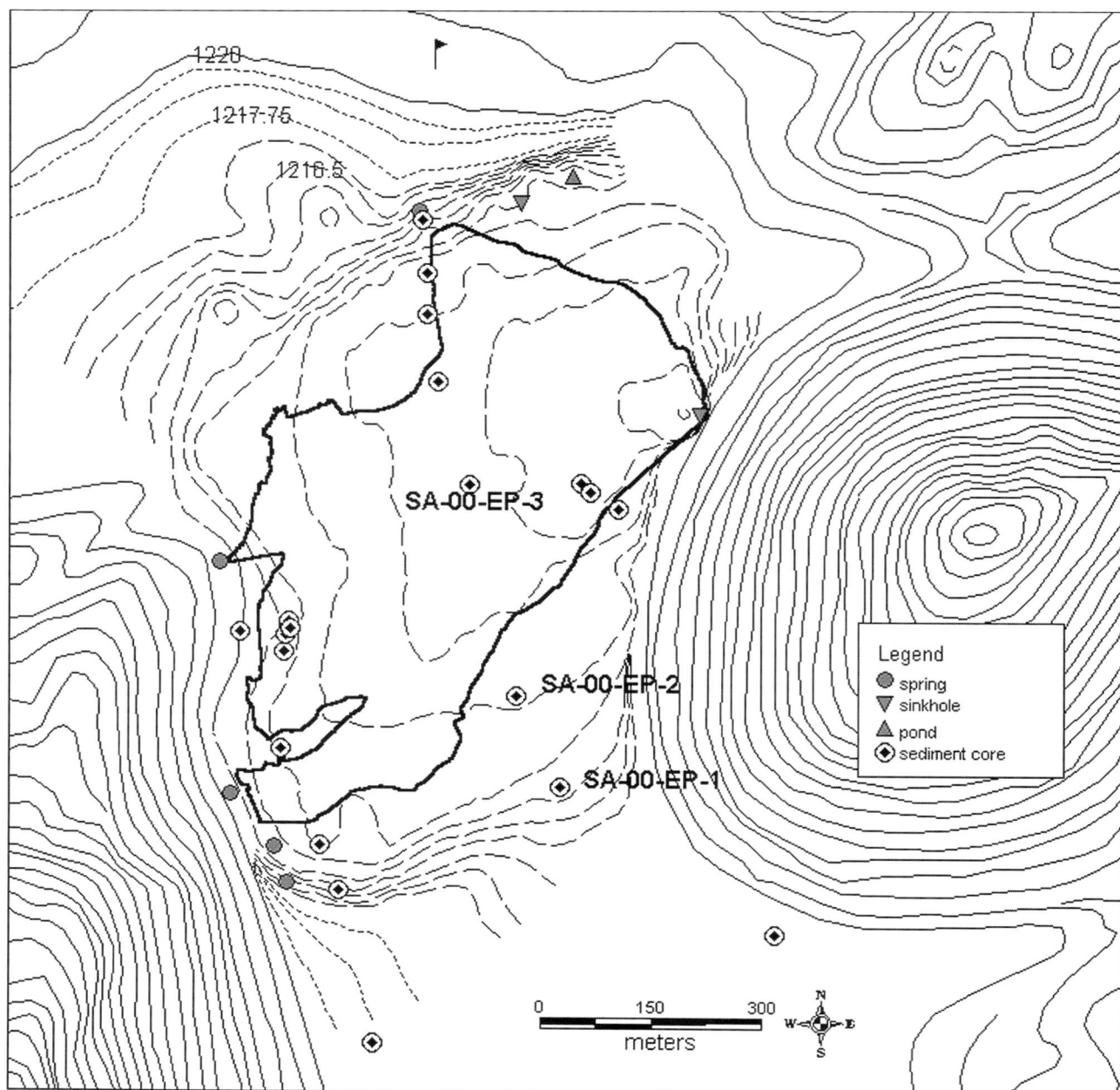

Figure 1: Situation of cores SA-00-EP-1 (N37°580459, E30°404987), SA-00-EP-2 (N37°581593, E30°404307) and SA-00-EP-3 (N37°584248 and E30°403578) in the Gravgaz basin plotted on a contour map. The bold line indicates the extent of the marsh during the summer of 1999, while the marsh was nearly totally dry during the years 2000-2006. The contour intervals are: 10 m for medium lines, 1 m for the small dashed lines and 0.25 m for the long dashed lines. Altitudes are in meters above sea level (m a.s.l.).

S SA-00-EP-1   SA-00-EP-2   SA-00-EP-3   N
   1215.38 m a.s.l.   1214.97 m a.s.l.   1214.59 m a.s.l.

140m

300m

STL

3720 +/- 45 BP   2700 +/- 45 BP
4655 +/- 45 BP   Reworked Santorini
                                  Shards

S : 0.85%

Legend

pure detritals

carbonate rich detritals

organic and carbonate
rich detritals

organic rich detritals

peat

STL   Santorini Tephra Layer

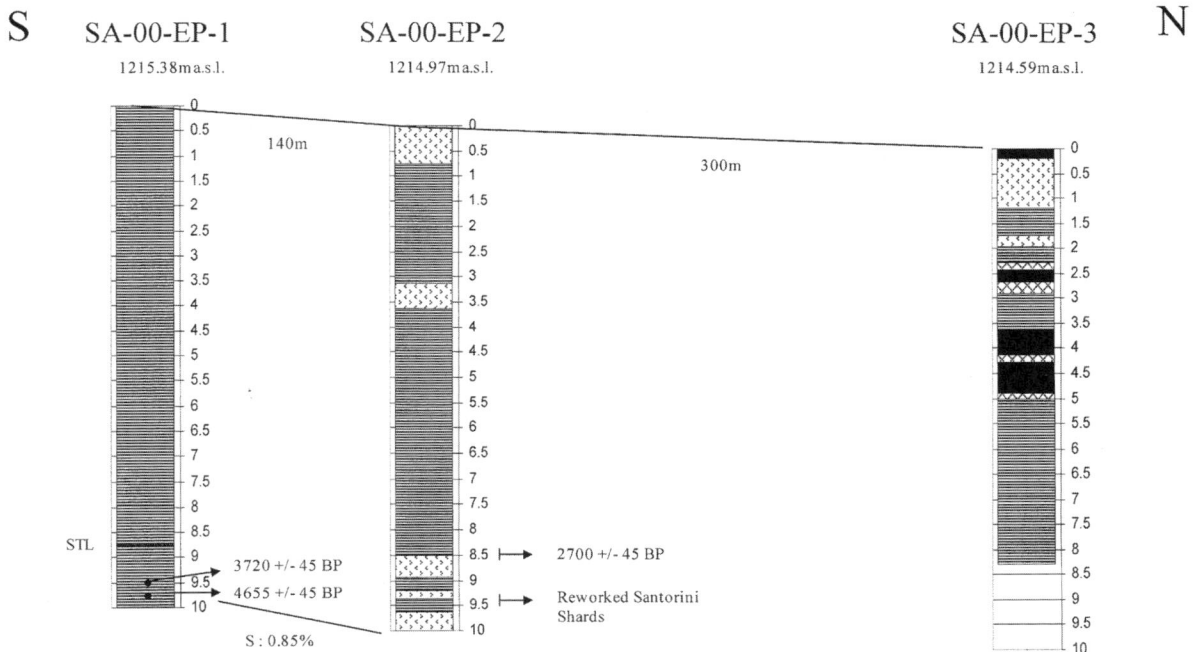

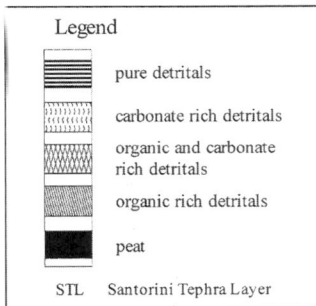

Figure 2: North-South profile of cores SA-00-EP-1, SA-00-EP-2, south of the Gravgaz marsh and SA-00-EP-3, in the centre of the marsh.

Figure 3: Photo of the disturbed pale ash layer in core SA-00-EP-1 at 8.73-8.75 m, indicated by arrows.

step. Samples were finally dried at 105°C and magnetically separated. The non-magnetic fraction was used for optical analysis on an Olympus ® optical microscope. The mineralogical composition of this fraction was also determined with X-ray diffractometry (XRD) on a Philips® PW3710. Operational parameters were: Cu-K$_\alpha$ radiation, graphite monochromator, 45 kV, 30 mA, automatic divergence slit and receiving slit of 0.1°. Laser ablation inductively coupled plasma-mass spectrometric (LA-ICP-MS) analyses of volcanic glass shards was performed using a 266 nm Cetac LSX200 Laser Ablation unit, coupled to a Hewlett Packard (Agilent) 4500 ICP-MS. The frequency quadrupled Nd:YAG laser delivers 5 mJ laser pulses with a pulse duration < 6 ns. After acquisition of the background signal for 60 seconds, the samples were ablated with a spot size of 50 μm during 20 seconds (at a repetition rate of 5 pulses per second). Calibration of the obtained signals was carried out using NIST612 calibration glass standards. Concentration data for this material were taken from Pearce et al. (1997). ^{29}Si was taken as internal standard. Quantification of the calibrated signals was obtained using a Si concentration of 73.624 wt% for the glasses (Pearce et al., 2002). Reproducibility was checked through analyses of NIST612 glass, and is better than 10% for most elements.

The volcanic material identified in core SA-00-EP-1 was compared with a reference sample of the tephra layer collected at Gölhisar Gölü (SW Turkey, 88 km SW of Gravgaz and kindly provided by W.J. Eastwood). The mineralogy and rare earth elements of the Gölhisar tephra have been analyzed in detail by Eastwood et al. (1998a; 1999a). These authors have shown that the geochemical composition of the Gölhisar tephra is identical to the tephra deposits of the Minoan volcanic eruption of Santorini (Thera), found in the Black Sea (Guichard et al., 1993), in Gölçük Gölü (Sullivan, 1988), in Köycegiz (Sullivan, 1990) and in the Eastern Mediterranean Sea (Federman and Carey, 1980; Vinci, 1985). We have named this sample henceforth Thera tephra or Santorini tephra layer (STL).

In order to contribute to the study of the environmental impact of these distal tephra deposits, a palynological study of the lower part of coring SA-00-EP-1 was carried out, according to a methodology described in Vermoere (2004).

3. SEDIMENTOLOGICAL AND GEOCHEMICAL CHARACTERISTICS OF THE GRAVGAZ TEPHRA

The comparison of the grain size characteristics of the STL in core SA-00-EP-1 at Gravgaz with those of the surrounding deposits (Figure 4 and 5) shows that the STL-layer (SAEP28)

is clearly coarser than the surrounding fan deposits. It is a well sorted silt (50% in the fine silt fraction 31.2-3.9 μm and 20% in the coarse silt fraction 31.2-63 μm) with a sand fraction of about 10 %. The mean grain size characteristics are: arithmetic mean: 29 μm, mode: 26 μm and median: 18 μm; the distribution is positively skewed. The coarsest glass shards are very platy and coarser than 200 μm. Part of the fraction <3.90 μm is due to local admixture of dark clay particles. The high silt content is also present in one sample just below (SAEP29 – see also Figure 4) and two samples above STL. Sample SAEP25 is the first superposed fan deposit of local origin with higher clay contents reflected in a lower median grain size of about 5 μm. Between 7.5 and 10m, the sand content of the deposits is variable suggesting a stratification.

In core SA-00-EP-1 no volcanic glass shards were recovered beneath sample SAEP29, suggesting that bioturbation has been very limited and that the tephra layer had been covered quite soon after deposition. Above the STL volcanic glass shards are present in samples SAEP26 (at 8.62 m) and 27 (at 8.68 m) but are not recovered in SAEP25 (at 8.56 m). In core SA-00-EP-2 the tephra layer was visually absent, but volcanic glass shards have been recovered at depths from 9.53 m till 9.26 m, indicating reworking and redeposition of the original tephra layer.

The glass shards present in the washed fraction of sample SAEP28 and the reference sample of the Thera tephra from Gölhisar Gölü were optically compared. The glass shards from Gölhisar are very fresh and very angular and mainly subangular to subrounded in the Gravgaz sample (compare Figure 6 A and B). Other grains in the Gravgaz sample consist of detrital quartz and chert, derived from the limestone and the Lycian ophiolitic mélange underneath (Degryse et al., this volume; Muchez et al., this volume). The difference in the glass shards morphology and the admixture of detritic quartz and chert grains (detritic admixture also visible in the sediment core) are considered consistent arguments for the not fully in situ character of the Gravgaz tephra, which is therefore interpreted as locally reworked but in original stratigraphic position.

The refraction index of the Gravgaz glass shards is 1.510 +/– 0.002, which is identical to the refraction index reported by most authors (see Sullivan, 1988). The XRD analysis of the Gravgaz tephra and the reference sample of Gölhisar indicate their identical mineralogy, apart from the admixture of quartz and chert grains in the Gravgaz sample (Figure 7).

It is clear from the LA-ICP-MS analyses that all grains analyzed from the Gölhisar reference sample and the

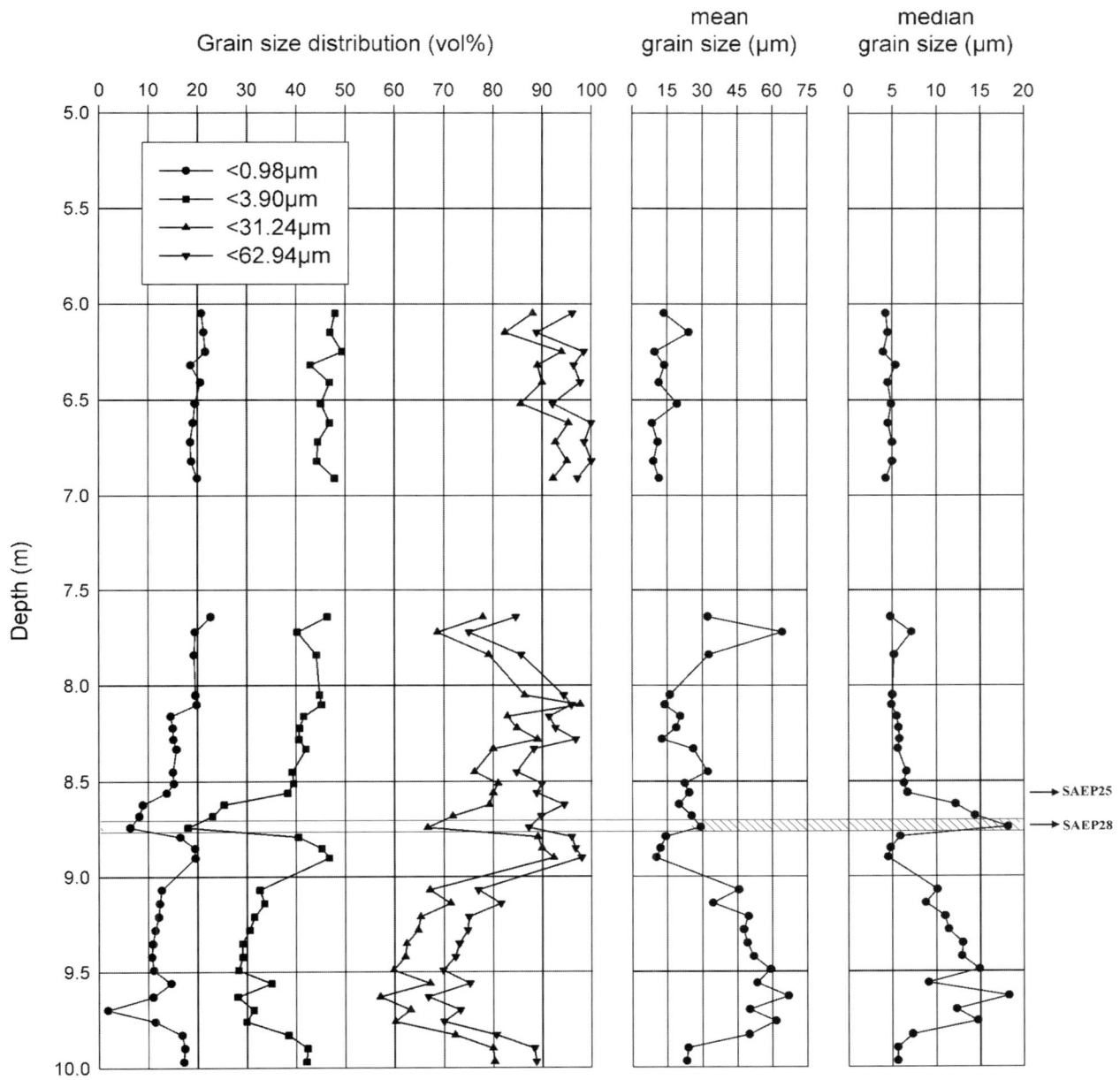

Figure 4: Grain size distribution with the mean and median grain size values of core SA-00-EP-1. The Santorini tephra is shaded.

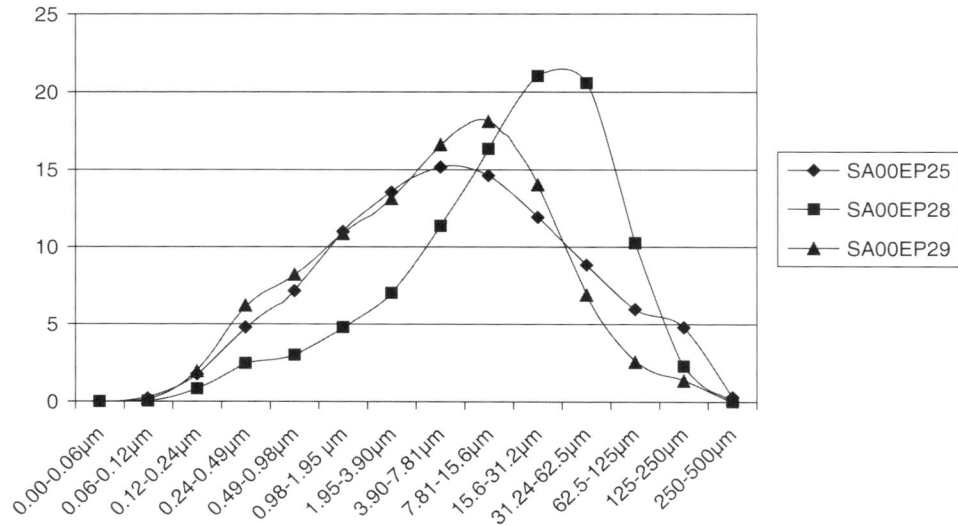

Figure 5: Grain size distribution of the Santorini tephra layer at 8.74 m (SA EP28), compared with the sediment sample immediately below (SA EP29) and with the sediments at 8.56 m (SA EP25).

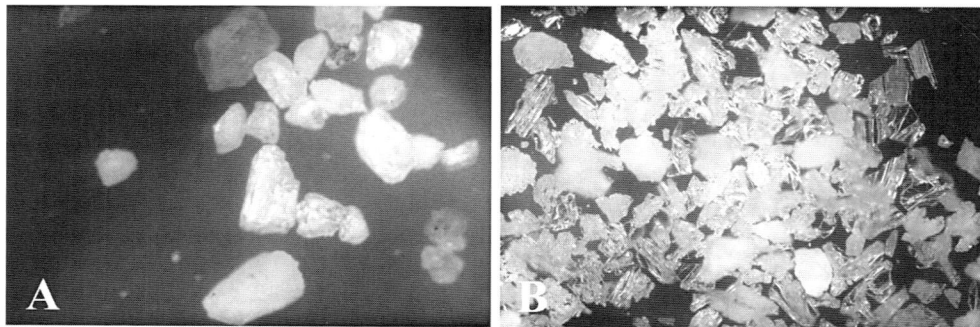

Figure 6: (A) Photo of the non-magnetic washed fraction of sample SAEP28 from the Gravgaz marsh (magnified 20 times). The white grains are volcanic glass shards, the dark grains consist of detrital quartz and chert (B) Photo of the Thera tephra from Gölhisar Gölü (magnified 10 times).

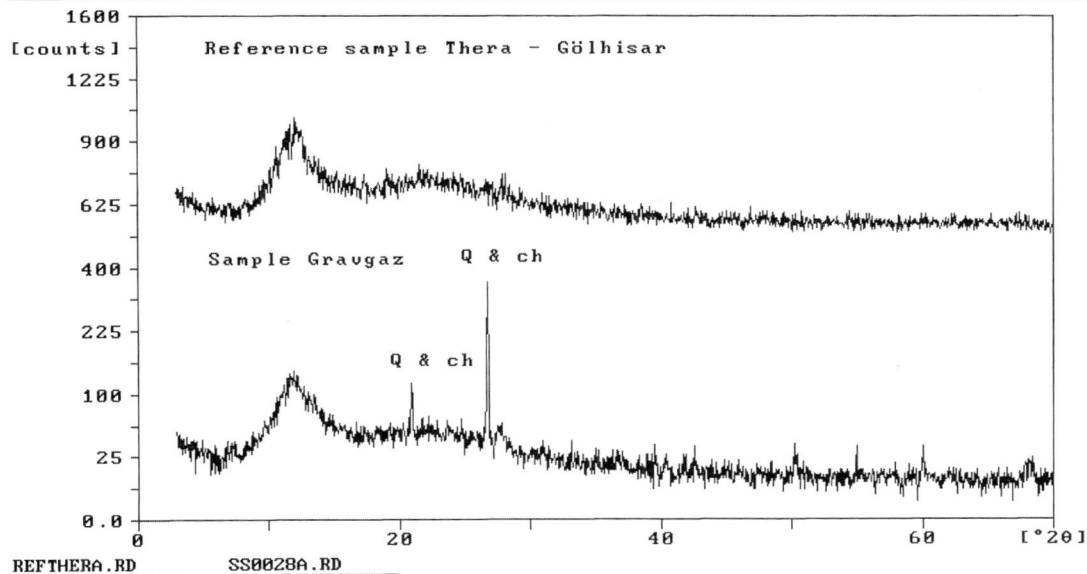

Figure 7: Comparative XRD-analysis of the glass shards from Gravgaz and a reference sample of the Thera tephra from Gölhisar Gölü.

volcanic glass shards in the Gravgaz basin are practically identical in chemical composition (Table 1 and Figure 8). Moreover, the chemical analysis of the material from Gravgaz corresponds well to the range of composition of the Gölhisar Minoan tephra as defined by Eastwood et al. (1998a; 1999a) and Pearce et al. (1999; 2002). This range of elemental compositions combined with the consistency of many trace element ratios are characteristic of the Minoan Thera glass and provide a trace element signature that can be used to distinguish the Minoan tephra from other Mediterranean tephra deposits (Pearce et al., 2002). Hence, the occurrence of tephra from the Minoan eruption of Thera at Gravgaz is established.

4. THE LOCAL CHRONOLOGY AND THE AGE OF THE MINOAN THERA ERUPTION

Precise dating of this Thera eruption is extremely important because the tephra layer acts as a very important geologic time marker as well as a universal time marker of Late Bronze Age contexts in the Eastern Mediterranean region. There exists an abundant literature and a lot of controversy about the precise timing of the Minoan Santorini eruption (see a.o. Manning, 1999). Some archaeologists have traditionally placed the Minoan eruption around the mid- to late 16th century BC but for almost 30 years ^{14}C ages have yielded earlier ages around 100 years older, leading to controversies.

Recently, precise and direct dating of the Minoan eruption has been possible by the unique find of an olive tree, buried alive in life position by tephra on Santorini and of which the last preserved ring provides the best current date for the eruption (Friedrich et al., 2006). Wiggle-matching of ^{14}C-sequence of tree-ring segments is applied to constrain the eruptions date to the range 1627-1600 cal yr BC with 95.4% probability (1621-1605 cal yr BC at 1 sigma). It is the first accurately defined sequence based on an object buried alive by the eruption. The age is consonant but more precise than the independent and consistent age of 3344.9 +/- 7.5 ^{14}C years BP, or 1683-1611 cal yr BC at 2 sigma confidence with the use of IntCal04 (Manning et al., 2006). This date is based on 13 different short-lived samples (groups of seeds) from four larger seed samples recovered in situ from prehistoric storage containers found in the volcanic destruction level on Santorini. This age is in the range of previous, less precise and less direct results, but are a century earlier than the date derived from a comparison with traditional Egyptian chronologies.

For the construction of a timeframe for the deposits in Gravgaz cores SA-00-EP-1 and SA-00-EP-2, some small charred particles and/or plant remains found in three samples below 8.00 m were ^{14}C-dated. The AMS ages (Table 2) were calibrated on a two sigma level with INTCAL04 (Reimer et al., 2004). At Gravgaz the tephra layer in core SA-00-EP-1 is dated younger than 2275 to 1980 cal yr BC, while the reworked glass shards in core SA-00-EP-2 have been

Isotope	24	43	45	49	55	57	85	88	89	90	93	133	137	139	140	141	146	147	153	157	159	163	165	166	169	172	175	178	181	232	238
Element	Mg	Ca	Sc	Ti	Mn	Fe	Rb	Sr	Y	Zr	Nb	Cs	Ba	La	Ce	Pr	Nd	Sm	Eu	Gd	Tb	Dy	Ho	Er	Tm	Yb	Lu	Hf	Ta	Th	U
LOD	0.4	713	0.8	2.6	0.7	55	0.7	0.2	0.2	0.3	0.4	0.4	1.1	0.2	0.2	0.2	0.6	1.4	0.3	1.0	0.2	0.7	0.3	0.5	0.2	0.6	0.2	0.7	0.2	0.2	0.2
Ref.																															
a	1569	12306	9.5	2119	446	7125	82	56	44	309	9	bd	473	28	48	4.9	22	bd	bd	4.6	0.4	6.6	1.3	3.3	0.6	3.4	0.7	8.3	0.9	18	4.8
b	1479	13235	9.1	2065	402	6700	78	55	41	302	13	3.9	489	28	50	6.0	24	5.7	0.8	4.6	0.7	5.8	1.7	4.4	1.0	5.1	0.8	7.5	0.9	20	4.6
c	1945	15505	10.0	2236	449	7123	88	84	53	400	11	3.2	574	35	53	6.9	30	bd	bd	9.1	1.43	8.9	2.0	6.0	0.8	5.6	1.6	9.5	1.3	25	5.0
d	1636	11127	7.9	2221	444	6832	82	63	43	322	10	3.7	519	32	52	7.0	26	bd	bd	bd	1.43	8.2	1.8	5.8	bd	5.6	bd	10.3	bd	21	4.5
e	2014	8753	8.8	1828	402	6518	78	54	46	300	11	1.9	547	31	54	6.4	24	bd	bd	5.8	1.0	7.6	1.1	3.6	1.0	4.7	1.0	9.1	1.5	23	4.6
f	1094	9239	8.1	1664	389	6078	85	45	38	251	12	2.5	498	31	51	5.6	22	bd	0.6	4.6	0.8	5.4	1.8	4.5	0.5	4.8	0.7	7.1	0.8	18	4.3
g	1594	9683	9.0	2228	428	7068	87	66	46	354	12	2.5	560	32	57	7.0	25	bd	bd	6.4	1.1	8.0	2.0	5.6	1.0	5.4	0.8	9.1	1.3	22	5.2
h	1677	8498	7.9	2053	450	7246	84	64	46	339	11	3.2	541	34	54	6.4	29	bd	bd	5.3	1.0	8.9	1.9	5.2	1.1	6.0	1.0	9.1	1.1	22	4.4
SAEP28																															
a	1101	12222	11.0	2227	402	8261	89	60	46	339	12	2.7	519	31	52	7.1	27	6.5	0.8	6.5	1.0	6.6	1.6	4.7	0.8	6.1	0.7	9.3	1.0	21	4.7
b	3308	16142	15.6	3011	515	12953	90	76	53	338	12	3.5	535	34	58	7.1	31	7.4	1.0	7.3	1.2	8.0	1.7	5.2	0.9	7.2	1.0	8.3	1.0	22	4.3
c	1107	12044	10.8	2115	408	8239	85	58	44	319	11	2.4	508	30	52	6.8	25	5.4	1.2	6.7	1.0	7.0	1.4	4.7	0.7	5.9	1.0	9.2	1.0	21	4.6
d	1373	11384	12.1	2471	437	8878	91	66	52	375	12	bd	562	34	59	7.3	30	7.0	0.6	7.3	1.1	7.7	1.5	5.7	1.0	7.7	1.1	9.9	1.2	25	6.4
e	1019	10220	9.4	2076	406	7814	80	56	41	306	12	bd	510	29	51	5.8	25	4.7	0.7	5.7	0.9	6.2	1.5	4.8	0.8	5.1	1.0	9.4	1.0	21	4.7
f	1328	10820	8.6	2281	429	8151	88	73	53	359	12	bd	568	35	54	8.2	32	bd	1.2	7.5	1.3	8.1	2.1	5.0	0.8	5.7	.07	10.1	1.5	25	4.2
g	1705	14252	11.7	2905	497	10001	87	101	46	309	13	bd	698	41	64	8.4	30	5.7	0.9	5.8	1.1	7.4	1.7	4.9	0.5	5.7	0.8	7.9	1.2	24	3.8
h	1222	11436	8.4	1779	371	7048	88	53	44	295	11	2.4	509	30	52	6.5	25	6.4	0.6	4.9	0.9	6.8	1.6	4.4	0.8	5.7	0.7	9.2	1.1	21	5.3
i	1057	10221	8.5	2070	404	8409	82	53	40	275	12	2.5	461	28	50	5.9	22	6.0	0.8	6.0	0.8	5.6	1.5	4.4	0.7	4.8	0.7	7.3	0.9	16	4.7
j	1043	9699	8.5	2147	442	8832	94	59	41	303	12	3.1	510	29	54	6.6	26	7.3	bd	7.4	1.0	8.0	1.3	5.3	1.0	5.1	0.9	8.3	1.0	20	5.3
SAEP29																															
a	1422	10996	9.9	2439	505	11693	95	65	43	316	12	3.1	529	32	57	6.6	26	5.4	0.6	6.1	1.1	8.5	1.6	4.9	0.7	4.8	0.8	8.2	1.0	20	5.3
b	1503	10513	9.9	2345	462	10606	82	56	36	288	10	2.8	489	27	50	5.8	21	4.2	0.9	5.4	0.8	6.9	1.6	4.0	0.8	5.2	0.7	8.1	1.0	19	5.0

All values in ppm; LOD: detection limit; bd: below detection limit

Table 1: LA-ICP-MS chemical analysis results of Thera tephra from Gölhisar (= Ref.) and Gravgaz.

180

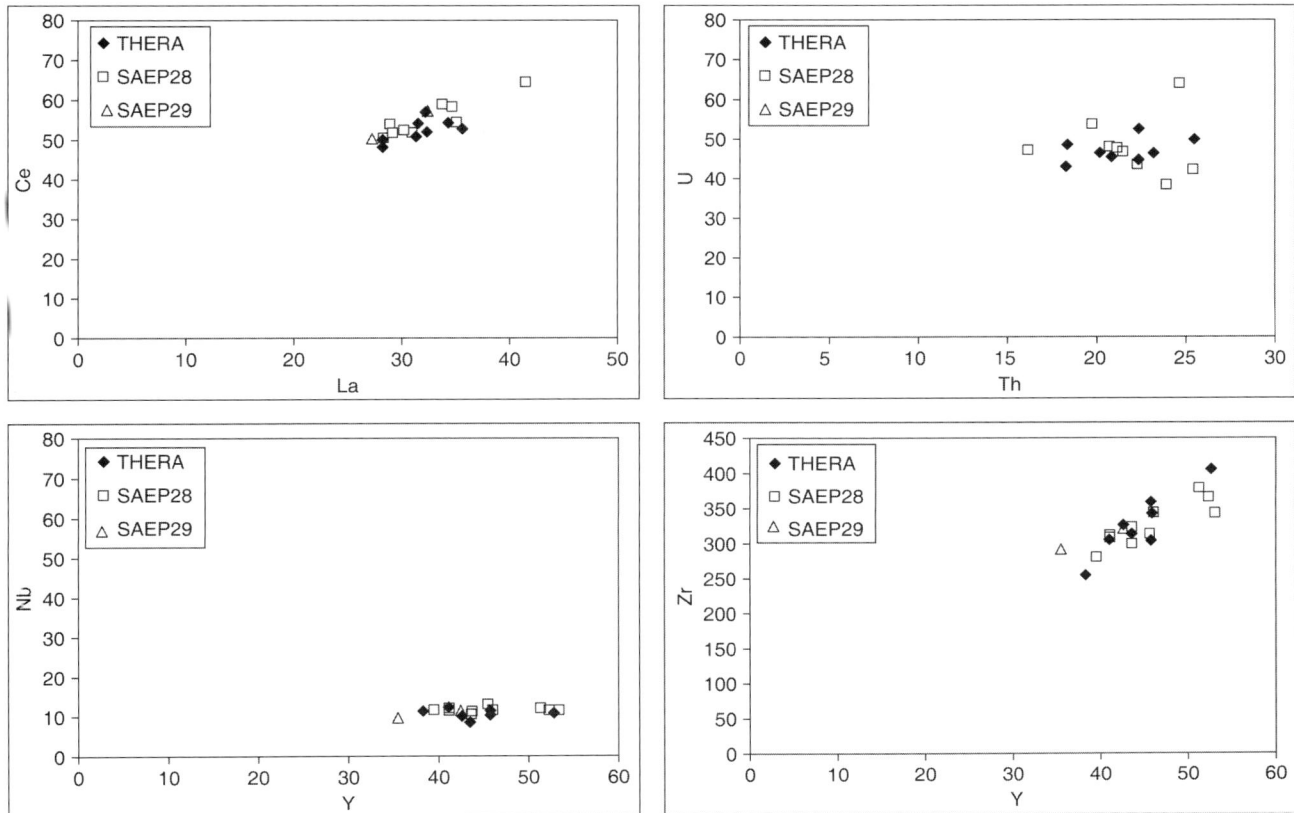

Figure 8: Biplots of the chemical analysis results of Thera tephra from Gölhisar and Gravgaz.

deposited before 925 – 795 cal yr BC (both calibrations on the 2 sigma level).

The number of radiocarbon dates directly related to the distal Minoan Santorini tephra layer in Anatolia is still limited (Table 2 – all calibrated ages at 2 sigma level). The two youngest dates from just below the tephra layer from Gölhisar are: 1765 to 1450 cal yr BC (3330 +/– 70 BP) and 1610 to 1415 cal yr BC (3225 +/– 45 BP) (Eastwood et al. 1999a). The oldest dates above the tephra layer are 1440 to 1195 cal yr BC (3070 +/– 55 BP) and 1740 to 925 cal yr BC (3111 +/– 160 BP), respectively from Köycegiz and Gölçük Gölü near Izmir. These time ranges confirm the chronostratigraphical positions of the STL in Anatolia, but are far too broad to contribute to the debate on the precise date of the Minoan eruption.

In the Anatolian dendrochronology from the second millennium BC, there is a unique and extraordinary growth anomaly starting in relative Ring 854 and lasting about 3 to 5 years (Kuniholm et al., 1996). This growth anomaly was interpreted as a climatic excursion thought to be caused by the impact of the Thera eruption. A correlation was proposed with major growth anomalies at 1628/1627 cal yr BC known in the absolutely dated dendrochronologies of Europe and the United States. Further refinement of the Anatolian tree ring chronology resulted in an older date for Ring 854: 1650 + 4/–7 BC (Manning et al., 2001). This positive growth anomaly now seems a little too early to be associated with Thera.

5. THE DIRECT REGIONAL IMPACT OF THE THERA TEPHRA

The Santorini Minoan tephra has already been detected in lake sediments from west and southwest Turkey in Gölçük east of Izmir (Sullivan, 1988), Köycegiz, Gölhisar and Söğüt (Eastwood et al., 1998b). More to the east in Pinarbaşı (west of the lake of Burdur) and in Beyşehir the ash was not identified (Eastwood et al., 1998a). To the northeast the tephra has been found as far as the Black Sea (Guichard et al., 1993) and to the southeast possibly as far as the Nile delta (Stanley and Sheng, 1986). Indeed, according to Eastwood et al. (1999a), solely on the basis of major-element analyses the provenance of the Nile delta

Coring	Sample depth (m)	Laboratory sample number	Conventional Radiocarbon Age (BP)	INTCAL04 RADIOCARBON AGE CALIBRATION – 2 sigma in cal yr BC	Dated material type	Stratigraphical position
SA00EP1	9.49-9.63	GrA-19298	3720 +/- 45	2275 to 2250 and 2225 to 2015 and 1995 to 1980 cal yr BC	charcoal	0.75-0.84 m below STL
SA00EP1	9.70-9.83	GrA-19300	4655 +/- 45	3625 to 3595 and 3525 to 3355 cal yr BC	charcoal	0.97-1.09 m below STL
SA00EP2	8.36-8.86	GrA-19297	2700 +/- 45	925 to 795 cal yr BC	seeds	above reworked STL
Gölhisar (Eastwood et al. 1999)						
GHA.92-3	2.69-2.73	Beta 56673	3330 +/- 70	1765 to 1450 cal yr BC	peat	just below STL
GHE.93-7	2.50-2.62	SRR-5188	3225 +/- 45	1610 to 1415 cal yr BC	peat	just below STL
Gölçük Gölü (Sullivan 1988)						
n.i.	~8.70	n.i.	3110 +/- 160	1740 to 925 cal yr BC	peat	30 cm above STL
Köycegiz (van Zeist et al. 1975)						
n.i.	3.89-4.01	GrN-6451	3070 +/- 55	1440 to 1205 and 1200 to 1195 and 1135 to 1130 cal yr BC	gyttja	20 cm above STL
Söğüt (van Zeist et al. 1975)						
n.i.	2.05-2.20	GrN-6452	2885 +/- 35	1190 to 1140 and 1130 to 975 and 955 to 940 cal yr BC	organic fraction	10 cm above STL

n.i.= not indicated

Table 2: Radiocarbon ages from Gravgaz cores SA-00-EP-1 and 2 and from Gölhisar Gölü, Gölçük Gölü, Köycegiz and Söğüt, sampled just below or above the Santorini tephra layer. INTCAL04 Calibration on a two sigma level.

tephra cannot be assigned unequivocally as some of their compositional data are not consistent with the Minoan eruption. Rare earth element data are needed. The characteristics of the sites containing the Santorini tephra are summarized in Figure 9 and Table 3. All these observations together with the finding of the tephra in Gravgaz lead to a more detailed reconstruction of the fallout area. As the STL at Gravgaz becomes very thin and has been found only once in spite of intensive coring in recent deposition centres and fieldwork during many seasons, we suggest that we are close to the eastern limit where the STL still can be found by the naked eye. More to the east, the STL will most probably be found as traces.

As suggested by the STL distribution map, the greatest extension of the STL is towards the NNE-NE, so that this key horizon may be also present in NW Anatolia and connected to late Bronze Age environments.

6. THE DIRECT IMPACT OF THE THERA TEPHRA ON THE ENVIRONMENT SURROUNDING GRAVGAZ

Only the direct impacts – impacts due to the direct deposition of tephra and other pyroclastics, including gaseous compounds – will be discussed here. Effects on vegetation are based on observations reviewed by Walker (2001). Damage to vegetation and soils will vary with the thickness and composition of the ash. The consequences of a moderate (5-25 mm) tephra burial – eventually the case in Gravgaz – can be summarized as follows: buried microphytes could survive and recover, larger grasses were damaged but not killed, the tephra layer remained nearly intact on the soil surface after one year, while the soil remained viable and was not so deprived of oxygen or water that it ceased to act as a topsoil.

For distal areas, the danger is mostly caused by the aerosols transported by the tephra. These experiences are gained in Iceland during 1100 years of settlement (Thorarinsson, 1979). Especially acid sulphur and fluorine compounds can affect vegetation and animals through grazing. Most dangerous for the grazing animals is a layer of fluorine-contaminated tephra that is so thin that it does not hinder grazing. Fine grained tephra particles stick easily to the vegetation and go into the digestive organs of the animals. Fluorosis (i.e. poisoning with fluorine) in grazing animals is therefore usually more severe farther away from the erupting volcano (Thorarinsson, 1979). The zone of potential fluorine poisoning of grazing animals is likely to occur, where the fluorine content of dried grass exceeds 250 ppm (Walker, 2001). In an archaeological context evidence for fluorine poisoning can be detected by outgrowth on the molars or by characteristic coating of a porous and brittle, osseous tissue on the bones (Thorarinsson, 1979).

The effects of the distal Minoan tephra deposits on the environment have been studied for the first time by Eastwood et al. (2002) at Gölhisar. According to this study the impact of this 4 cm thick tephra layer on regional vegetation was minimal over decade-to-century scales, as any clear, discernible change in the terrestrial pollen composition following tephra deposition was lacking. There is however clear evidence that the Thera tephra may have had an impact on Gölhisar lake system: the lake productivity was enhanced due to accelerated input of silica and other nutrients following tephra dissolution.

For Gravgaz core SA-00-EP-1 we dispose of a pollen diagram with 15 spectra between 8.05 and 9.05 m for the deposits surrounding the STL (Figure 10). The period covered by this diagram is new for Gravgaz, as the published pollen diagrams cover younger periods (Vermoere et al., 2000, 2002a, 2002b, 2004). The exact time range of this diagram is unknown, but we suggest that it covers a relatively short period around 1627-1600 cal yr BC, the most probable age of the STL layer (see above). This hypothesis is based on the presence of stratification and the lack of bioturbation suggesting tephra fall out in an area characterized by active colluviation.

One of the main characteristics of the diagram is that the AP-pollen percentage is seldom higher than 50%, with between 8.90 and 8.05 m a clear decrease till 33% at 8.56 m, best reflected in a decrease in Pinus pollen (as low as 10% at 8.22 m). The main AP types are: Pinus (10-30%), Quercus coccifera-tp (7-12%) and Quercus cerris-tp (5-10%). Low percentages of Olea and the sporadic presence of Juglans are also noted below as well as above the STL layer. In the non-arboreal pollen (NAP) types, the dryland herbs largely dominate with several continuous pollen curves on both sides of STL: Poaceae, Cerealia-tp, Plantago lanceolata, Silene-tp, Centaurea solstitialis-tp, Artemisia-tp, Lactuceae, etc.

In the STL-layer, situated within the phase of lower AP content, AP % increases till 57%, a percentage about 20% higher than the immediate neighbours with resp. 37 and 34%. Part of this increase is due to decreases of some herbs, such as Centaurea solstitialis-tp and Silene-tp, probably suffering from the tephra fallout. Within the AP pollen (= 100%), clear relative increases are noted of (windblown?) pollen of Quercus cerris-tp (from 18 till 26%) and Pinus (from 42 till 54%). Some of the herb pollen curves, such as Silene-tp, Cerealia-tp and Poaceae show a slight increase

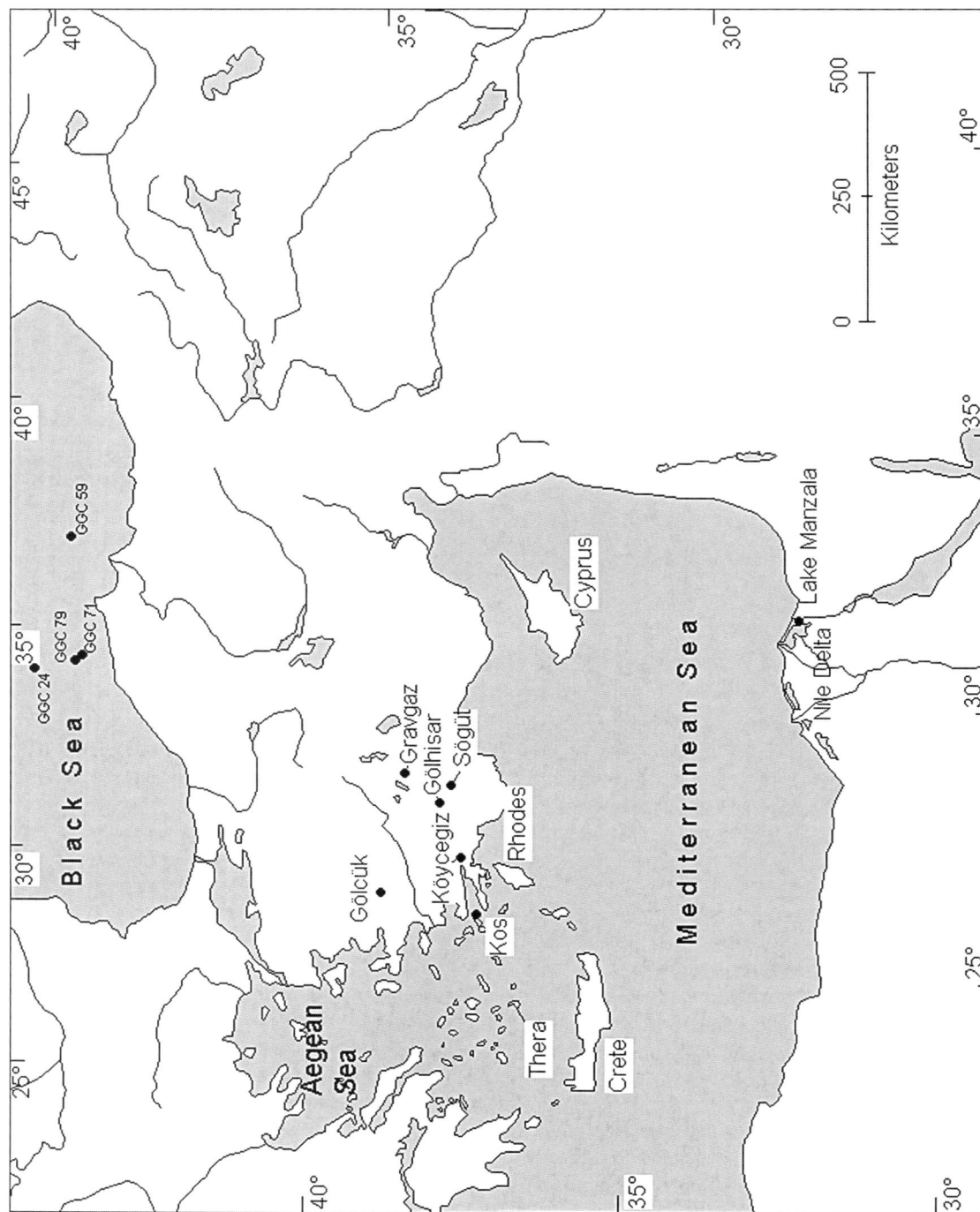

Figure 9: Map of the Eastern Mediterranean showing the sites, where tephra from the Thera eruption of Santorini has been found (see also table 3).

Site	Elevation (m a.s.l.)	Thickness of tephra layer (cm)	Depth of tephra layer (m below surface)	Environment	Distance (km) and direction from Thera	Characteristics of the Santorini Tephra Layer	Reference
Köycegiz	1	9	4.14-4.23	lake deposits	270 km ENE	in situ	Sullivan et al. 1990
Sögüt	1393	1	2.29-2.30	lake deposits	430 km ENE	in situ	Eastwood et al. 1998a
Kos	n.i.	30	n.i.	terrestrial deposits	190 km ENE	probably in situ	Keller 1980 in: Sullivan 1988
Rhodes (Triada)	n.i.	10	1.80	terrestrial deposits	225 km E	probably in situ	Doumas and Papazoglou 1980
Rhodes (Airport)	n.i.	50	n.i.	n.i.	n.i.	probably in situ	Sullivan 1988
Nile Delta (Lake Manzala)	sea level	n.i.	5.00-7.00	Nile Delta sediments	890 km SE	some dispersed tephra grains	Stanley and Sheng 1986
Gölçük Gölü (Izmir area)	1050	12	~ 8.90	lake deposits	310 km NE	in situ	Sullivan 1988
Black Sea – GGC79	−707	0,015	0.74	marine laminated deposits	1043 km NE	in situ	Guichard et al. 1993
Black Sea – GGC71	−411	0,0188	0.92	marine laminated deposits	1041 km NE	in situ	Guichard et al. 1993
Black Sea – GGC24	−2195	0,0122	0.48	marine laminated deposits	1096 km NE	in situ	Guichard et al. 1993
Black Sea – GGC59	−600	n.m.	0.77	marine laminated deposits	1201 km NE	in situ	Guichard et al. 1993
Gölhisar – A	930	1-4	2.69-2.73	lake deposits	380 km ENE	in situ	Eastwood et al. 1998a
Gölhisar – B	930	3	2.74-2.77	lake deposits	380 km ENE	in situ	Eastwood et al. 1998a
Gravgaz (near Burdur)	1215	2	8.73-8.75	Colluvial deposits	460 km NE	slightly disturbed	this paper

Table 3: Characteristics of the sites in the Eastern Mediterranean and the Black Sea, where the tephra of the Thera eruption of Santorini has been found. For the exact location of these sites, see figure 9. Negative elevation values indicate the depth below sea level at which the sediment cores were taken. (n.i. = not indicated; n.m. = not measured). Distances for Turkish sites are from Google Earth.

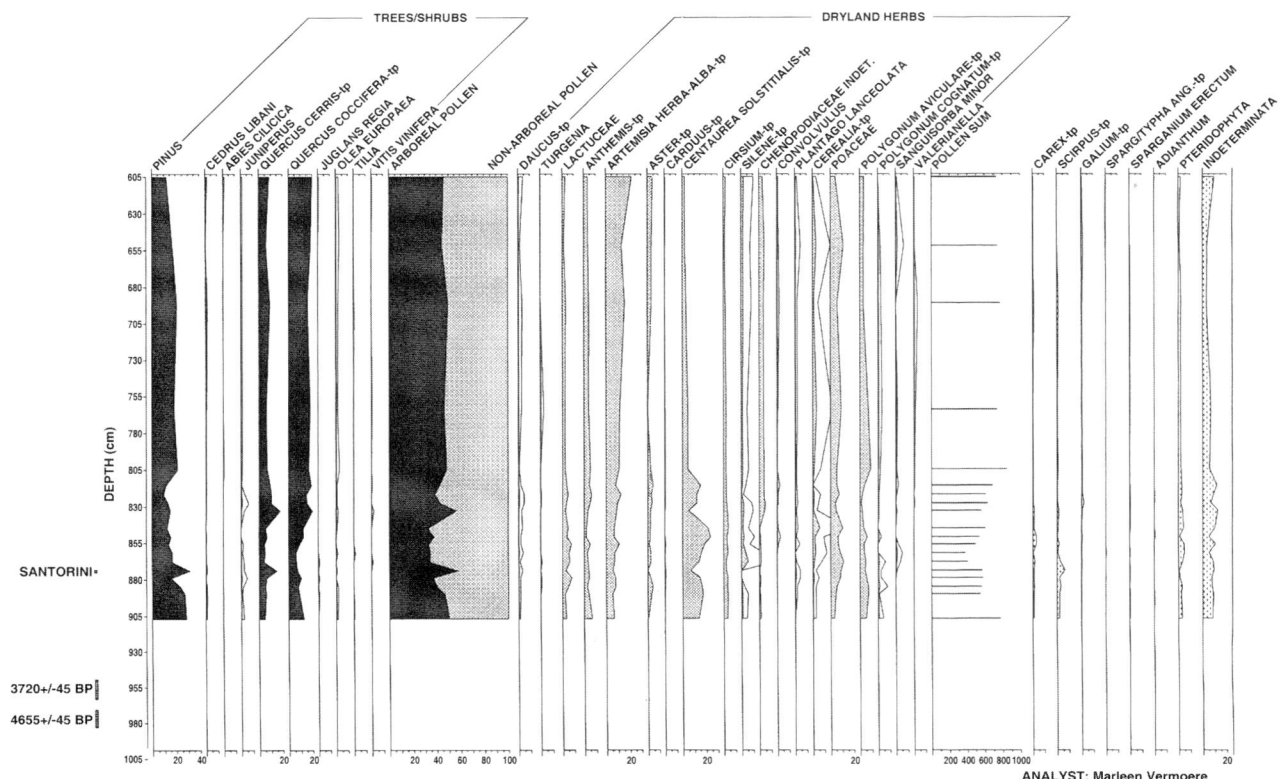

Figure 10: Simplified pollen diagram of part of core SA-00-EP-1.

immediately after the STL-deposition. While discussing this pollen spectrum we have to be aware of the fact that the tephra layer has been deposited during a short period of time, probably in the order of days or weeks. This pollen spectrum may therefore reflect the pollen shedding during a (part of a) season. If so, the high pollen percentage of *Quercus cerris*-tp could correspond with the flowering period which is late spring.

These data confirm the conclusion by Eastwood *et al.* (2002) that the percentage pollen data do not suggest any significant effect on terrestrial vegetation. In the Gölhisar catchment area the eruption occurred prior to major human-induced deforestation, which means that any volcanic impacts would have been registered on what was a largely natural landscape dominated by pine forests (Eastwood *et al.*, 1999b; Eastwood *et al.*, 2002). The pollen derived vegetation at Gravgaz at the time of the Minoan eruption was however very different from that of Gölhisar. In Gravgaz the AP-content points to a more open landscape succeeding an environment where pine has prevailed and oak trees and shrubs were not very important. The latter vegetation cover is suggested by pollen zone G0 in core 1996 (Vermoere *et al.*, 2002a, 2002b). This zone is characterized by high AP percentages

till 76%. *Pinus* largely prevailed and *Cedrus libani* reached 6%, while *Quercus cerris*-type and *Quercus coccifera*-type were of secondary importance. There were no indications of cultivation in the landscape. An AMS date on seeds from a depth of 7.91 m in core 1996-zone G0 is now available: 5240 ± 60 BP (GrA-20027), or 4250 – 3950 cal yr BC at 2 sigma level. The pine forest of zone G0 dates thus from an older age than calculated by linear extrapolation in Vermoere *et al.* (2002a, 2002b). It is tempting to consider the vegetation cover represented by G0 at Gravgaz as the natural vegetation that had already been deforested by man before the STL deposition. Primary indicators of human presence are however rare and may also occur in the natural environment. Forest clearings favoured the expansion of herbaceous taxa, such as *Artemisia*, Gramineae. *Plantago lanceolata* and Cerealia-type pollen are also represented in a continuous curve, but in the Middle East they go together with Poaceae so that their presence as such cannot be considered as sure indicators for cultivation.

Human presence in the fertile Gravgaz basin is evidenced by the Early Bronze Age site Yüksek Yurt (Vanhaverbeke and Waelkens, 2003). Some of the archaeological sites in the immediate surroundings show evidences of a Late

186

Bronze Age occupation: Kale at Taşkapı, Kale Kayış and Kale Kökez, resp. at 6.5 km NE, 6 km SW and 8.5 km W from Gravgaz marsh (Vanhaverbeke and Waelkens, 2003). These sites could provide arguments for human impact on the Gravgaz environment during the STL deposition.

The fallout of the Thera tephra in the opened landscape of Gravgaz can be summarized as follows. During dry weather a thin layer of tephra – mainly of silt size – was deposited on leafs and needles of trees and shrubs, on lower herbs and eventually on bare soil. The particles deposited on the plants were blown away as particles by the first winds or washed away as slurry by the first rains.

7. CONCLUSION

The 2 cm thick tephra layer, found in the Gravgaz basin at an altitude of 1215 m a.s.l. originates from the atmospheric fallout of the Minoan eruption of the Santorini (Thera) volcano dated 1627-1600 cal yr BC (Friedrich et al., 2006). The geochemical characteristics of this layer are proven to be identical to a reference sample of the Thera eruption from Gölhisar (Eastwood et al., 1998a). The Gravgaz find at 460 km from Santorini extends the fall out zone of the Minoan Thera eruption with 80 km towards the NE. The potential effects on terrestrial vegetation resulting from this thin distal STL fallout are estimated to be low, as is suggested from the pollen data.

It is the first time that the distal tephra layer is found in fan deposits on a gentle foot slope and not in a lake or marine environment. There are several arguments suggesting that this tephra layer is not completely in situ, but is slightly reworked. It must be indeed extremely difficult to have distal tephra deposits completely in situ on land, because the tephra fallout covered mainly the existing vegetation and is redistributed later on the soil surface.

The Thera tephra remains are one of the main late Holocene key horizons for SW Turkey and very probably also for NW Turkey as is suggested by ash deposits in the Black Sea.

8. REFERENCES

DEGRYSE, P., MUCHEZ, PH., SINTUBIN, M., CLIJSTERS, A., VIAENE, W., DEDEREN, M., SCHROOTEN, P. and WAELKENS, M. (this volume) Geological mapping of the area around Sagalassos, in: P. DEGRYSE and M. WAELKENS (eds.) Sagalassos VI. Geo- and Bio-Archaeology at Sagalassos and in its Territory, Leuven University Press, Leuven: 17-24.

EASTWOOD, W.J., ROBERTS, N. and LAMB, H.F. (1998a) Palaeoecological and archaeological evidence for human occupance in southwest Turkey: the Beysehir occupation phase, Anatolian Studies 48: 69-86.

EASTWOOD, W.J. and PEARCE, N.J.G. (1998b) Recognition of Santorini (Minoan) Tephra in Lake Sediments from Gölhisar Gölü, Southwest Turkey by Laser Ablation ICP-MS, Journal of Archaeological Science 25: 677-687.

EASTWOOD, W.J., PEARCE, N.J.G., WESTGATE, J.A., PERKINS, W.T., LAMB, H.F. and ROBERTS, N. (1999a) Geochemistry of Santorini tephra in lake sediments from Southwest Turkey, Global and Planetary Change 21: 17-29.

EASTWOOD, W.J., ROBERTS, N., LAMB, H.F. and TIBBY, J.C. (1999b) Holocene environmental change in southwest Turkey: a palaeoecological record of lake and catchment-related changes, Quaternary Science Reviews 18: 671-695.

EASTWOOD, W.J., TIBBY, J., ROBERTS, N., BIRKS, H.J.B. and LAMB, H.F. (2002) The environmental impact of the Minoan eruption of Santorini (Thera): statistical analysis of palaeoecological data from Gölhisar, southwest Turkey, The Holocene 12(4): 431-444.

FEDERMAN, A.N. and CAREY, S.N. (1980) Electron microprobe correlation of tephra layers from Eastern Mediterranean abyssal sediments and the island of Santorini, Quaternary Research 13: 160-171.

FRIEDRICH, W.L., KROMER, B., FRIEDRICH, M., HEINEMEIER, J., PFEIFFER, T. and TALAMO, S. (2006) Santorini Eruption Radiocarbon Dated to 1627-1600 B.C., Science 312: 548.

GUICHARD, F., CAREY, S., ARTHUR, M.A., SIGURDSSON, H. and RANOLD, N. (1993) Tephra from the Minoan eruption of Santorini in sediments of the Black Sea, Nature 363: 610-612.

KUNIHOLM, P.I., KROMER, B., MANNING, S.W., NEWTON, M., LATINI, C.E. and BRUCE, M.J. (1996) Anatolian tree-rings and the absolute chronology of the eastern Mediterranean 2220-718 B.C., Nature 307: 780-783.

MANNING, S.W. (1999) A Test of Time. The Volcano of Thera and the Chronology and History of the Aegean and East Mediterranean in the Mid Second Millennium BC. Oxbow Books, Oxford and Oakville.

MANNING, S.W., KROMER, B., KUNIHOLM, P.I. and NEWTON, M.W. (2001) Anatolian Tree Rings and a New Chronology for the East Mediterranean Bronze-Iron Ages, Science 294: 2532-2536.

MANNING, S.W., RAMSEY, C.B., KUTSCHERA, W., HIGHAM, T., KROMER, B., STEIER, P. and WILD, E.M. (2006) Chronology for the Aegean Late Bronze Age 1700-1400 BC, Science 312: 565-569.

MUCHEZ, PH., LENS, S., DEGRYSE, P., CALLEBAUT, K., DEDEREN, M., HERTOGEN, J., JOACHIMSKI, M., KEPPENS, E., OTTENBURGS, R., SCHROYEN, K. and WAELKENS, M. (this volume)

Petrography, mineralogy and geochemistry of the rocks in the area of the archaeological site of Sagalassos, in: P. DEGRYSE and M. WAELKENS (eds.) *Sagalassos VI. Geo- and Bio-Archaeology at Sagalassos and in its Territory*, Leuven University Press, Leuven: 25-52.

PEARCE, N.J.G., PERKINS, W.T., WESTGATE, J.A., GORTON, M.P., JACKSON, S.E., NEAL, C.R. and CHENERY, S.E. (1997) A compilation of new and published major and minor trace element data for NIST 610 and NIST 612 glass reference materials, *Geostandards Newsletter* 21: 115-144.

PEARCE, N.J.G., WESTGATE, J.A., PERKINS, W.T., EASTWOOD, W.J. and SHANE, P. (1999) The application of laser abla-tion ICP-MS to the analysis of volcanic glass shards from tephra deposits : bulk glass and single shard analysis, *Global and Planetary Change* 21: 151-171.

PEARCE, N.J.G., EASTWOOD, W.J., WESTGATE, J.A. and PERKINS, W.T. (2002) Trace-element composition of single glass shards in distal Minoan tephra from SW Turkey, *Journal of the Geological Society of London* 159: 545-556.

REIMER, P.J. *et al.* (29 authors) (2004) INTCAL04 terres-trial radiocarbon age calibration, 0-26 CAL KYR B.P., Radiocarbon 46: 1029-1058.

SIX, S. (2004) *Holocene Geomorphological Evolution of the Territory of Sagalassos. Contribution to the Palaeoenvi-ronmental Reconstruction of Southwest Turkey*, Unpub-lished Ph.D. Thesis, Katholieke Universiteit Leuven.

STANLEY, D.J. and SHENG, H. (1986) Volcanic shards from Santorini (Upper Minoan ash) in the Nile Delta, Egypt, *Nature* 320: 733-735.

SULLIVAN, G.D. (1988) The discovery of Santorini Minoan tephra in western Turkey, *Nature* 333: 552-554.

SULLIVAN, G.D. (1990) Minoan tephra in lake sediments in western Turkey, dating eruption and assessing the atmospheric dispersal of ash, in: D.A. HARDY and A.C. RENFREW (eds.) *Thera and the Aegean World III. Volume Three: Chronology* (*Proceedings of the Third International Congress*, Santorini, Greece), The Thera Foundation, London: 114-119.

THORARINSSON, S. (1979) On the damage caused by volcanic eruptions with special reference to tephra and gases, in: P.D. SHEETS and D.K. GRAYSON (eds.) *Volcanic Activity and Human Ecology*, Academic Press, New York: 125-160.

VANHAVERBEKE, H. and WAELKENS, M. (2003) *The Chora of Sagalassos. The Evolution of the Settlement Pattern from Prehistoric until Recent Times* (*Studies in Eastern Mediterranean Archaeology 5*), Brepols Publishers, Turnhout.

VERMOERE, M. (2004) *Holocene Vegetation History in the Ter-ritory of Sagalassos (southwest Turkey) A Palynological Approach (Studies in Eastern Mediterranean Archaeology VI)*, Brepols Publishers, Turnhout.

VERMOERE, M., SMETS, E., WAELKENS, M., VANHAVERBEKE, H., LIBRECHT, I., PAULISSEN, E. and VANHECKE, L. (2000) Late Holocene Environmental Change and the Record of Human Impact at Gravgaz near Sagalassos, Southwest Tur-key, *Journal of Archaeological Science* 27: 571-595.

VERMOERE, M., VAN THUYNE, T., SIX, S., VANHECKE, L., WAELKENS, M., PAULISSEN, E. and SMETS, E. (2002a) Late Holocene local vegetation dynamics in the marsh of Gravgaz (SW Turkey), *Journal of Palaeolimnology* 27(4): 429-451.

VERMOERE, M., BOTTEMA, S., VANHECKE, L., PAULISSEN, E., WAELKENS, M. and SMETS, E. (2002b) Palynological evi-dence for late Holocene human occupation in two wetlands in southwest Turkey, *The Holocene* 12(5): 569-588.

VINCI, A. (1985) Distribution and chemical composition of tephra layers from Eastern Mediterranean abyssal sedi-ments, *Marine Geology* 64: 143-155.

WALKER, A. (2001) Impacts of ash fall on animal and plants, in: A. WALKER (ed.) *Impact of a Volcanic Eruption on Agriculture and Forestry in New Zealand*, Ministry of Agriculture and Forestry (MAF), New Zealand.

LATE HOLOCENE SEDIMENT CHARACTERISTICS AND SEDIMENT ACCUMULATION IN THE MARSH OF GRAVGAZ: EVIDENCE FOR ABRUPT ENVIRONMENTAL CHANGES

Simon SIX, Etienne PAULISSEN, Thijs VAN THUYNE, Joachim LAMBRECHTS, Marleen VERMOERE , Véronique DE LAET and Marc WAELKENS

1. INTRODUCTION

Detailed sediment analysis is often used for the reconstruction of the palaeoenvironment (Lowe and Walker, 1984). The interpretation and combination of different sediment characteristics (used as proxy-records) can lead towards a regional ecological history (Bell and Walker, 1992). For Southwest Turkey pollen analysis has been performed on lake sediments from Beyşehir, Söğüt and Köycegiz (van Zeist *et al.* 1975), Pinarbaşı (Bottema and Woldring 1984), Gölhisar (Eastwood *et al.* 1999), Gravgaz and Canakli (Vermoere, 2000; 2002a, b), Eski Acıgöl (Roberts *et al.* 2001). These publications give an overview on the regional Holocene vegetation evolution and clearly indicate the presence of human activity during the Late Holocene as a phase of land clearing and occupation. Data upon Holocene soil erosion and evolution of erosion intensities however, such as collected by Pope and van Andel (1984) and by van Andel *et al.* (1990) for Greece, are scarce for Southwest Turkey. Eastwood *et al.* (1998, 1999) and Roberts *et al.* (1997, 2001) used a detailed multi-proxy method to describe the sedimentation pattern of Lake Gölhisar and Lake Eski Acıgöl. Some other Holocene sediment studies on a large resolution are present for the Konya basin (Roberts *et al.* (1995, 1999), Reed *et al.* (1999), Karabiyikoğlu *et al.* (1999)), for the Gediz and Büyük Menderes grabens (Hakyemez *et al.* (1999)) and for Acıgöl, central Anatolia (Kazancı, 1995). The general aim of this study is to provide an overview of the detailed sedimentation and erosion history of the Gravgaz basin, situated on the territory of the ancient city of Sagalassos, and to relate the sedimentation with the known evolution of human occupation and of climate.

The marsh of Gravgaz (+/– 15 km southwest of Sagalassos) was studied a first time during the field campaign of 1996 as part of the inter-disciplinary project '*Ecology and Economy of Sagalassos*'. A contour map of the Gravgaz basin is shown in Figure 1. The Gravgaz area was found highly suitable for palaeoenvironmental research because of a few reasons: first, the Gravgaz basin is a closed basin, so all eroded material is preserved within the basin and second,

the lower parts of the basin are covered by a marsh due to springs in the western limestone mountains. In the marsh water is always present and this could be indicative for the presence of peat forming conditions during the formation of the Quaternary deposits. Peat layers are formed under stable, wet conditions and because of its high organic carbon-content, ^{14}C- ages are possible. Further environmental settings are presented in Vermoere (2000; 2002a, b). A first sediment core (SA-96) was taken in 1996. Sedimentological parameters were determined and the data were processed by Lambrechts (1998). During the following years sediment cores were taken spread over the lower parts of the Gravgaz basin. Core SA-99-EP-3 was analyzed on sedimentological characteristics as a dissertation by Van Thuyne (2000). These two sediment cores (SA-96 and SA-99-EP-3) were analyzed for pollen (Vermoere, 2000; 2002a, b). This article focuses on the general sediment characteristics and on the timeframe of the sedimentation in the lowest parts of the basin. The sediment accumulation rates will be calculated and important changes in the sedimentation pattern will be discussed. Finally the sedimentological data will be correlated with the regional pollen evolution (Vermoere, 2000; 2002a, b).

2. METHODOLOGY

Three types of cores were used for the sampling of the sediments: an Edelmann sampler was used for taking shallow test cores, while a Dachnowsky corer was used for collecting undisturbed samples of soft sediments. Harsh sediments were cored with a Ramguts sampler driven by an electric hammer. At the moment we have 22 cores (17 undisturbed and 5 Ramguts cores) in the marsh at our disposal with a minimum depth of 0.70 and a maximum of 10.00 m (Figure 1 and Table 1). The sediment cores were analyzed in the laboratory for dry bulk density, organic matter content and carbonate content. The organic matter content is calculated using the weight loss after oxidation with H_2O_2 and is expressed as a weight percentage. Carbonates were removed from the samples with HCl and

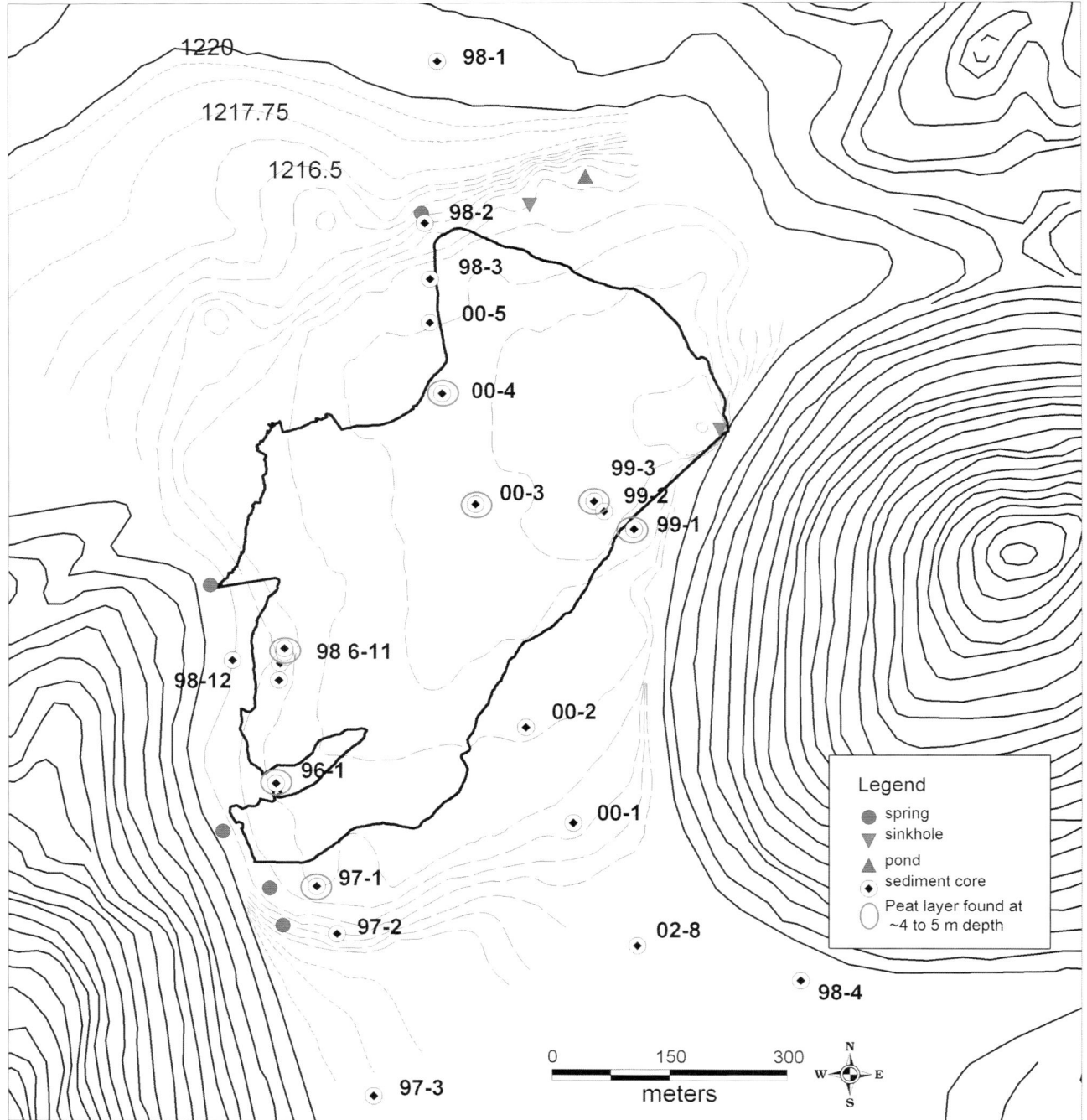

Figure 1: Situation of the cores in the Gravgaz basin plotted on a contour map. The bold line indicates the position of the marsh during the summer of 1999. The medium lines are contours with an interval of 10 m, the small dashed lines have an interval of 1 m and the long dashed lines of 0.25 m. Altitude values are added in meters above sea level (m a.s.l.) The prefixes SA-EP and SA-MV are left out from the core numbering.

Boring	Core type	Coring Depth (m)	Absolute Altitude (m a.s.l.)	Relative altitude (m)
SA-96	Dachnowsky	8.00	1215.19	0.22
SA-97-EP-1	Dachnowsky	5.00	1215.25	0.28
SA-97-EP-2	Dachnowsky	6.00	1216.18	1.20
SA-97-EP-3	Dachnowsky	2.20	1218.99	4.02
SA-98-MV-1	Dachnowsky	0.70	1224.78	9.80
SA-98-MV-2	Dachnowsky	5.00	1215.86	0.89
SA-98-MV-3	Dachnowsky	3.00	1214.94	−0.03
SA-98-MV-4	Dachnowsky	2.00	1218.05	3.08
SA-98-MV-6	Dachnowsky	1.38	1215.38	0.40
SA-98-MV-7	Dachnowsky	8.16	1215.38	0.40
SA-98-MV-8/9	Dachnowsky	8.00	1215.36	0.39
SA-98-MV-10	Edelmann	2.25	1215.44	0.46
SA-98-MV-11	Edelmann	1.25	1215.38	0.40
SA-98-MV-12	Edelmann	2.60	1216.58	1.60
SA-99-EP-1	Ramguts/Dachnowsky	8.00	1214.61	−0.36
SA-99-EP-2	Edelmann	1.00	1214.35	−0.62
SA-99-EP-3	Dachnowsky	7.79	1214.39	−0.59
SA-00-EP-1	Ramguts	10.00	1215.38	0.40
SA-00-EP-2	Ramguts	10.00	1214.97	0.00
SA-00-EP-3	Dachnowsky	8.30	1214.59	−0.38
SA-00-EP-4	Ramguts	9.00	1214.64	−0.34
SA-00-EP-5	Ramguts	5.00	1214.83	−0.14

Table 1: Coring depth (m), absolute height (m a.s.l.), altitude relative to SA00EP1 (m) and coring type of the borings in the Gravgaz marsh.

carbonate content is also expressed as weight percentage. The detrital matter content is calculated as the amount of non-organic and non-carbonate matter and is expressed as a weight percentage. The dry bulk density shows the amount of material per unit weight (g/cm³) and is interpreted as a function of the organic matter content (Gosselink et al. 1984) and of the hydrological conditions (Verstraeten and Poesen, 2001). This parameter could only be calculated for the cores taken with the Dachnowsky sampler. The analyzed parameters are plotted for core SA-96 in Figure 2. Based on these parameters the lithology of the cores was subdivided into 5 categories : peat (organic matter >20%), organic rich detritals (organic matter <20%, >10% and carbonate content <16%), carbonate rich detritals (organic matter <10%, carbonate content >16%), organic and carbonate rich detritals (organic matter <20%, >10% and carbonate content >16%) and pure detritals (organic matter content <10% and carbonate content <16%). These categories are presented in Figure 3 for four dated cores in a west-east profile and in Figure 4 for a south-north profile. The harshness of the sediments and limitations of the core equipment (maximum drilling depth = 10.00 m) were the limiting factors for sediment retrieval on the coring sites.

During the field campaign of 2000 detailed topographical information of the lowest parts of the Gravgaz basin

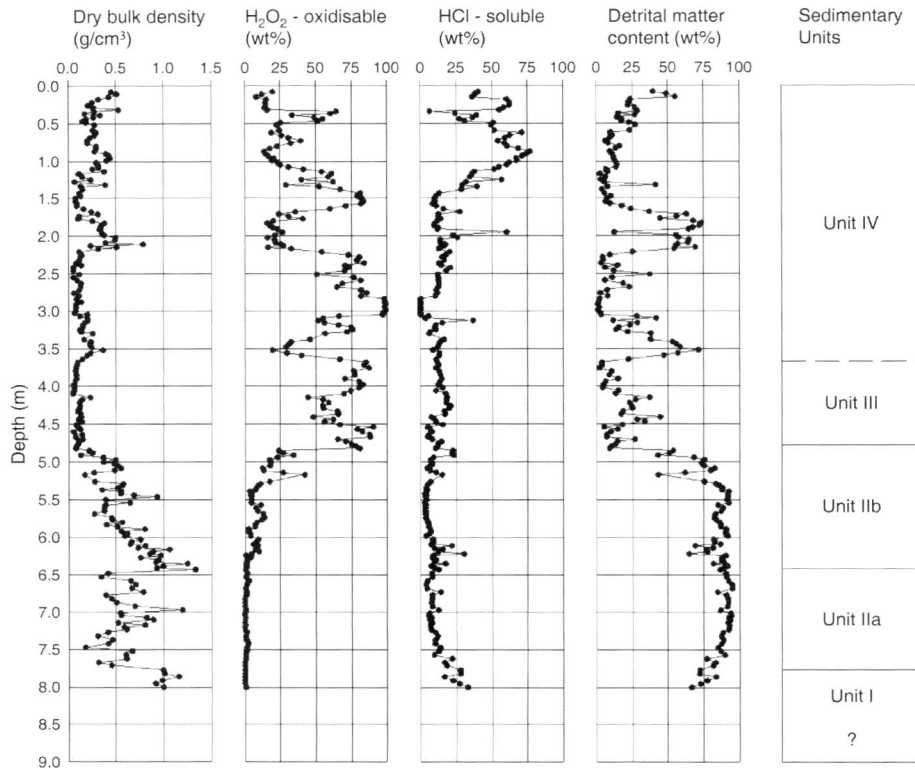

Figure 2: Detailed sedimentological characteristics of core SA-96. Dry bulk density is expressed as the amount of material (g) in a volumetric unit (cm³), the other parameters are expressed as a weight percentage (wt%). The sedimentological subdivisions in this core and in the Gravgaz basin are added. The local and regional pollen zones were adopted from Vermoere *et al.* (2000).

was obtained with an automatic theodolite. The measured coordinates and altitude values were used to construct a detailed digital terrain model (DTM) of the basin in Idrisi®. Contour lines were extracted from this DTM and were fitted in the contours of the topographical map (Figure 1). From the DTM altitude values (in m a.s.l.) were extracted for all the coring sites (Table 1).

3. TIME OF SEDIMENTATION

At the moment 9 cores are placed within a timeframe using 30 ^{14}C ages from 4 laboratories:

– 18 ages are from the *Groningen Isotope Research Centre*, The Netherlands (GrN, GrA – radiometric and AMS ages).
– 6 ages are from *Beta Analytic Inc.*, Miami, USA (Beta – AMS ages).

– 3 ages are from *Nosams Institute*, Massachusetts, USA (OS – AMS ages)
– 3 ages are from the *R.J. Van de Graaff Lab*, Utrecht, The Netherlands (UtC – AMS ages).

The ^{14}C ages were calibrated and analyzed with Oxcal V3.5-software (Bronk Ramsey, 1995). The results of the calibration are summarized in Table 2. Mean, minimum and maximum sedimentation rates (mm/yr) for every core were calculated using a linear interpolation between the calibrated dates (Table 3). To exclude the influence of the present topography, all ages were plotted versus their depth relative to the absolute height of the top of each core SA-00-EP-01 (top at 1215.38 m a.s.l.). This calculated depth will be referred to as the relative depth of the dating. The depth below the surface is named the sample depth.

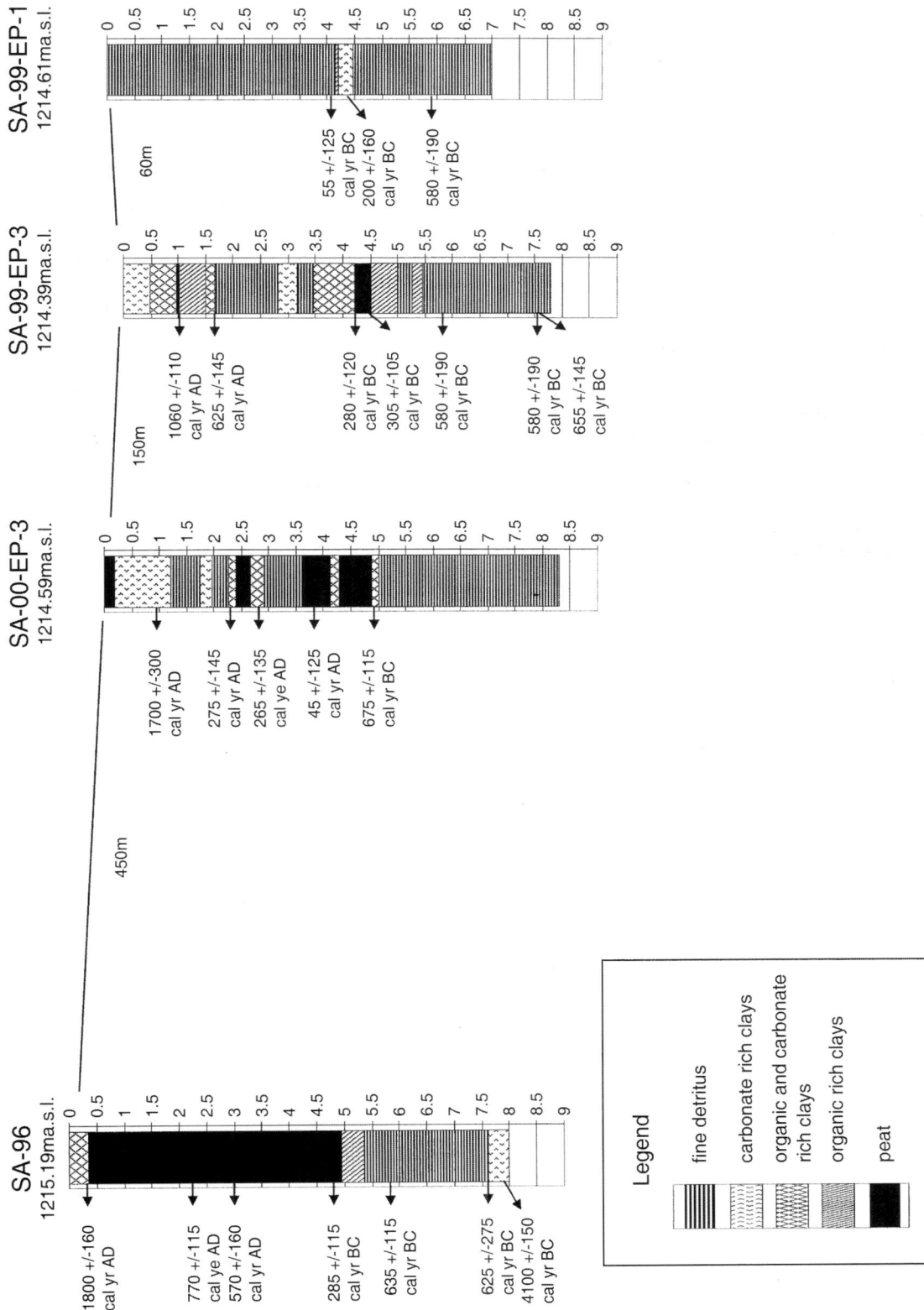

Figure 3: West to east classified core profile through the Gravgaz marsh. The absolute altitude of every core (m a.s.l.) and the absolute distance (in m) between the cores are added.

193

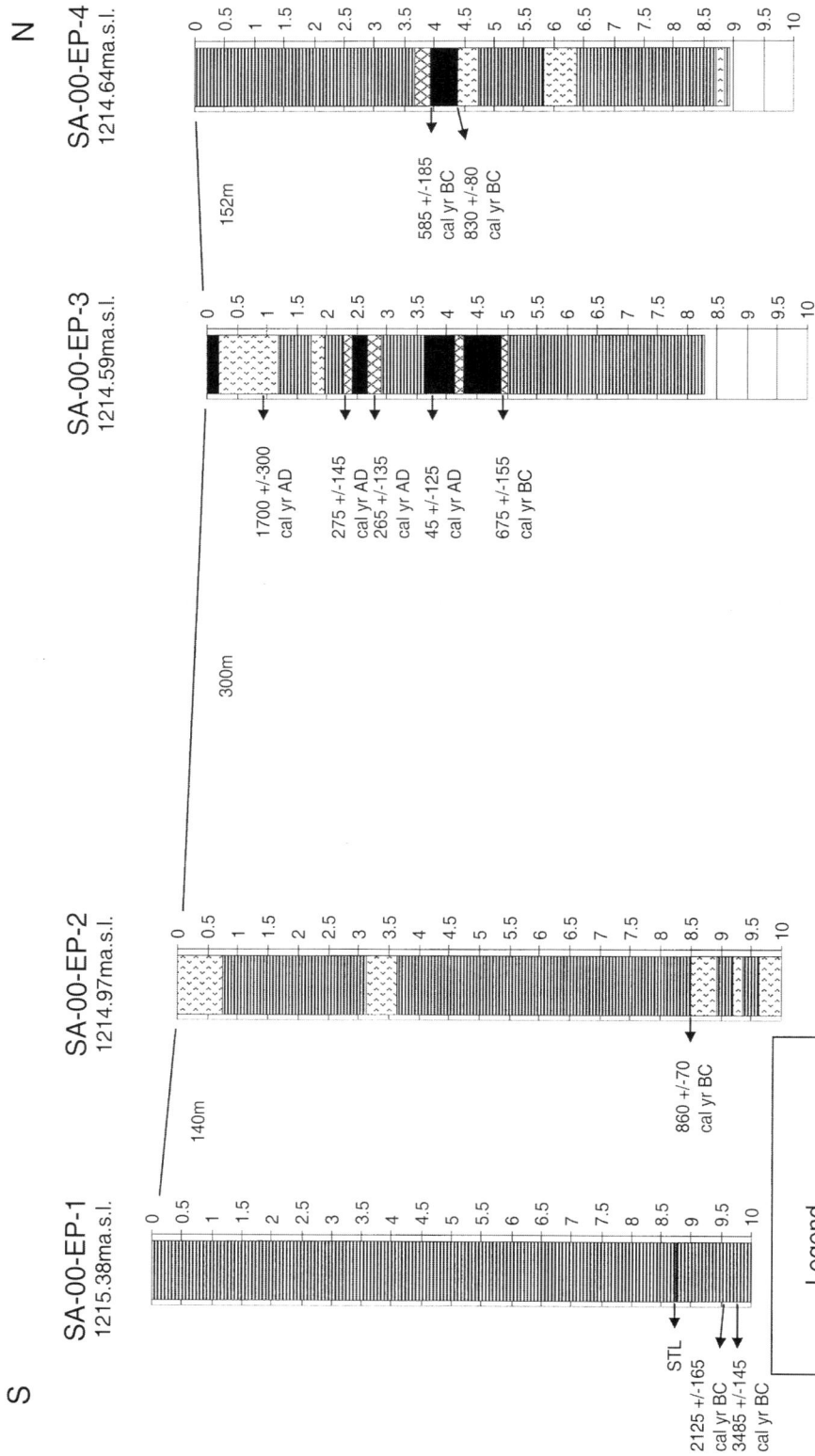

Figure 4: South to north classified core profile through the Gravgaz marsh. The absolute elevation (in m a.s.l.) of every core and the absolute distance (in m) between the cores are added. STL indicates the position of the Santorini Tephra Layer in core SA-00-EP-1.

194

Boring	Sample depth (m)	Relative depth (m)	Sample number	Laboratory sample number	Conventional ^{14}C date (BP)	Calibrated ^{14}C age (cal yr BC/AD) – 2 sigma	Material
SA-96	0.37	0.56	SA-96-EP-36b	GrA-19721	200 +/– 60	1520 (3.3%) 1560 cal yr AD and 1630 (92.1%) 1960 cal yr AD	peat
SA-96	0.37	0.56	SA-96-EP-36b (duplo)	GrA-19876	180 +/– 45	1640 (79.9%) 1890 cal yr AD and 1910 (15.5%) 1960 cal yr AD	peat
SA-96	2.25	2.44	SA-96-EP-43b	GrA-19878	1280 +/– 50	650 (95.4%) 890 cal yr AD	peat
SA-96	2.98	3.17	SA-96-EP-46e	utc-6738	1460 +/– 90	410 (93.4%) 730 cal yr AD and 740 (2.0%) 770 cal yr AD	peat
SA-96	4.82	5.01	SA-96-EP-53e	GrA-19892	2240 +/– 50	400 (95.4%) 170 cal yr BC	peat
SA-96	5.83	6.02	SA-96-EP-58d	utc-6739	2495 +/– 40	790 (88.8%) 480 cal yr BC and 470 (6.6%) 410 cal yr BC	plant remains
SA-96	7.71	7.90	SA-96-EP-65e	utc-6741	2480 +/– 120	900 (94.3%) 350 cal yr BC and 300 (1.1%) 200 cal yr BC	humics
SA-96	7.91	8.10	SA-96-EP-65d1	GrA-20027	5240 +/– 60	4250 (95.4%) 3950 cal yr BC	seeds
SA-97-EP-1	2.56	2.69	SA-97-EP-169A	GrN-26335	1500 +/– 30	430 (95.4%) 650 cal yr AD	peat
SA-97-E-P1	4.93	5.06	SA-97-EP-173K	GrN-26336	2570 +/– 50	830 (95.4%) 520 cal yr BC	peat
SA-98-MV-9	3.81	3.82	SA-98-MV-17	GrN-26683	2060 +/– 40	180 cal yr BC (95.4%) 30 cal yr AD	peat
SA-98-MV-9	5.05	5.06	SA-98-MV-20	GrN-26684	2650 +/– 60	980 (1.0%) 950 cal yr BC and 940 (88.1%) 750 cal yr BC and 690 (1.9%) 660 cal yr BC and 640 (4.3%) 550 cal yr BC	peat
SA-99-E-P1	4.1	4.86	SA-99-EP-135V1	Beta-142071	2040 +/– 50	180 cal yr BC (95.4%) 70 cal yr AD	peat
SA-99-EP-1	4.34	5.10	SA-99-EP-135V3	Beta-142072	2140 +/– 50	360 (22.5%) 270 cal yr BC and 260 (72.9%) cal yr 40 BC	peat
SA-99-EP-1	5.91	6.67	SA-99-EP-132p	Beta-142074	2410 +/– 40	770 (22.1%) 680 cal yr BC and 670 (4.9%) 630 cal yr BC and 600 (1.8%) 570 cal yr BC and 560 (66.5%) 390 cal yr BC	plant remains
SA-99-EP-3	1.02	2.01	SA-99-EP-122e	GrA-19895	1010 +/– 50	890 (4.8%) 930 cal yr AD and 950 (90.6%) 1170 cal yr AD	peat
SA-99-EP-3	1.61	2.60	SA-99-EP-107e	OS-25651	1410 +/– 55	530 (93.5%) 720 cal yr AD and 740 (1.9%) 770 cal yr AD	seeds
SA-99-EP-3	4.21	5.20	SA-99-EP-113c	Beta-142070	2220 +/– 50	400 (95.4%) 160 cal yr BC	peat
SA-99-EP-3	4.45	5.44	SA-99-EP-113k	Beta-142069	2270 +/– 50	410 (95.4%) 200 cal yr BC	peat
SA-99-E-P3	5.79	6.78	SA-99-EP-116k	OS-25652	2400 +/– 45	770 (21.3%) 680 cal yr BC and 670 (5.0%) 630 cal yr BC and 600 (69.1%) 390 cal yr BC	seeds
SA-99-EP-3	7.52	8.51	SA-99-EP-120f	OS25653	2400 +/– 50	770 (28.6%) 610 cal yr BC and 600 (66.8%) 390 cal yr BC	seeds

Table 2: Data of the ^{14}C ages in the Gravgaz marsh. Calibration is performed on a two sigma level.

SA-99-EP-3	7.55	8.54	SA-99-EP-120g	Beta-142073	2520 +/– 40	800 (94.4%) 510 cal yr BC and 470 (1.0%) 450 cal yr BC	seeds
SA-00-EP-1	9.49-9.63	9.49-9.63	SA-00-EP-213	GrA-19298	3720 +/– 45	2290 (95.4%) 1960 cal yr BC	charcoal
SA-00-EP-1	9.70-9.83	9.70-9.83	SA-00-EP-214	GrA-19300	4655 +/– 45	3630 (4.4%) 3580 cal yr BC and 3530 (89.3%) 3350 cal yr BC	charcoal
SA-00-E-P2	8.36-8.86	8.76-9.26	SA-00-EP-160	GrA-19297	2700 +/– 45	970 (1.3%) 960 cal yr BC and 930 (94.1%) 790 cal yr BC	seed
SA-00-EP-3	0.91	1.69	SA-00-EP-216g	GrN-26686	270 +/– 100	1400 (95.4%) 2000 cal yr BC	peat
SA-00-EP-3	2.33	3.11	SA-00-EP-219L	GrN-26339	1760 +/– 60	130 (95.4%) 420 cal yr AD	peat
SA-00-EP-3	2.82	3.6	SA-00-EP-220L	GrA-19896	1760 +/– 50	130 (95.4%) 400 cal yr AD	peat
SA-00-EP-3	3.86	4.46	SA-00-EP-222h	GrA-19898	2020 +/– 50	170 cal yr BC (95.4%) 80 cal yr AD	peat
SA-00-EP-3	4.92	5.7	SA-00-EP-224M	GrN-26340	2570 +/– 50	830 (95.4%) 520 cal yr BC	peat
SA-00-EP-4	3.94	4.68	SA-00-EP-238	GrN-26689	2450 +/– 50	770 (95.4%) 400 cal yr BC	peat
SA-00-EP-4	4.41	5.15	SA-00-EP-245	GrN-26690	2630 +/– 50	910 (87.3%) 750 cal yr BC and 690 (2.8%) 660 cal yr BC and 640 (3.7%) 590 cal yr BC and 580 (1.6%) 550 cal yr BC	peat

Table 2 (*cont.*)

4. RESULTS

4.1. Sediment description

Figure 3 shows the sediment cores with the calibrated ages in a W (near the sources) to E (near the swallet) profile. The gentle inclination from southwest to northeast is visible in the absolute and relative altitude of the cores (Table 1). Core SA-96 has an absolute altitude of 1215.19 m a.s.l. and is situated 0.59 m higher than core SA-00-EP-3 in the middle of the marsh. Core SA-99-EP-3 is situated near the eastern border of the marsh and lies 0.21 m lower than core SA-00-EP-3. Core SA-97-EP-1 and core SA-99-EP-1 are situated on debris slopes near the borders of the marsh and have an absolute altitude of respectively 1215.25 m a.s.l. and 1214.61 m a.s.l. It is noticed that the relative differences in altitude of the coring sites in and near the marsh are very small, describing the flat topography of the area. The detailed contour lines show the presence of a small wall delineating the flat basin floor in the north near core SA-98-MV-2 and in the south near core SA-97-EP-2 and core SA-00-EP-1. The lowest point in the basin is situated near the swallet at an altitude of 1214.00 m a.s.l.

In the S to N profile (Figure 4) a decrease of the influence of the springs on the sediment composition is visible as colluvial deposits become more important near the swallet. In core SA-96 colluvium dominates the lower part (>5.34 m) except for a calcareous rich layer at the bottom (7.62 m-8.00 m) and peat deposits dominate the upper part (<5.34 m). The same peat layer is found in core SA-97-EP-1 from a depth of 5.00 m to 2.52 m and in core SA-98-MV-9 at 5.05 m to 3.81 m. Core SA-97-EP-1 was ended at 5.00 m because a layer of hard material hampered the coring. This depth is interpreted as the transition to more compact colluvial deposits such as found in other cores. In the centre of the basin (core SA-00-EP-3) and near the eastern border (core SA-99-EP-3) a change in the sedimentation towards peat deposits is found at respectively 5.02 and 4.75 m. In these two cores, a pattern of interfingering layers of peat, organic and carbonate rich sediments and detritus is found above the peat layer. This pattern disappears in core SA-99-EP-01 where clay deposits are present in the entire core except for a small disturbance at 4.48-4.14 m (organic and carbonate rich material).

Cores SA-00-EP-1 and 2 (Figure 4) were drilled in a field southeast of the marsh in order to delineate the peat layer at a depth of around 4 meter found in the marsh. However, no organic rich material was found in these two cores. Core SA-00-EP-1 was completely composed of detrital matter except for a small pale layer of glass shards and clays at 8.73-8.75 m.

Accumulation rates in Core SA-96 (mm/yr)					
Depth interval (m)	Mean time interval (yr)	Sedimentological unit	Mean	Min	Max
0.00 – 2.25	1225	IV	1.84	1.68	2.03
2.25 – 2.98	200	IV	3.65	1.54	/
2.98 – 4.82	285	III (1.26m) – IV (0.58m)	2.15	1.63	3.17
4.82 – 5.83	350	II	2.89	1.63	12.63
5.83 – 7.71	0	II	/	4.48	/
Accumulation rates in Core SA-97-EP-1 (mm/yr)					
Depth interval (m)	Mean time interval (yr)	Sedimentological unit	Mean	Min	Max
0.00 – 2.56	1410	IV	1.82	1.68	1.97
2.56 – 4.93	1215	III (1.19m) – IV (1.18m)	1.95	1.60	2.49
Accumulation rates in Core SA-98-MV-9 (mm/yr)					
Depth interval (m)	Mean time interval (yr)	Sedimentological unit	Mean	Min	Max
0.00 – 3.81	2075	III (0.24m) – IV (3.57m)	1.84	1.75	1.93
3.81 – 5.05	770	III	1.61	1.28	2.18
Accumulation rates in Core SA-99-EP-1 (mm/yr)					
Depth interval (m)	Mean time interval (yr)	Sedimentological unit	Mean	Min	Max
0.00 – 4.10	2005	III (0.14m) – IV (3.96m)	2.04	1.92	2.18
4.10 – 4.34	145	III	1.66	0.56	/
4.34–5.91	380	II (1.43m) – III (0.14m)	4.13	2.15	52.33
Accumulation rates in Core SA-99-EP-3 (mm/yr)					
Depth interval (m)	Mean time interval (yr)	Sedimentological unit	Mean	Min	Max
0.00 – 1.61	1350	IV	1.19	1.09	1.30
1.61 – 4.21	900	IV	2.88	2.23	4.11
4.21 – 4.45	25	III	9.60	0.96	/
4.45 – 5.79	275	II	4.87	2.35	67.00
5.79 – 7.55	75	II	23.47	14.67	58.67
Accumulation rates in Core SA-00-EP-1 (mm/yr)					
Depth interval (m)	Mean time interval (yr)	Sedimentological unit	Mean	Min	Max
0.00 – 8.75	3628	I – II – III – IV	2.41	/	/
8.75 – 9.56	497	I	1.63	1.22	2.44
9.56 – 9.76	1330	I	0.15	0.13	0.19

Table 3: Mean, minimum and maximum calculated accumulation rates in different cores from the Gravgaz marsh. The mean time interval and the sedimentological unit of every depth interval are added. The contribution of a sedimentological unit is indicated in m, when it partly occurs in a depth interval.

Accumulation rates in Core SA-00-EP-2 (mm/yr)					
Depth interval (m)	Mean time interval (yr)	Sedimentological unit	Mean	Min	Max
0.00 – 8.50	2860	II – III – IV	2.97	2.86	3.05
Accumulation rates in Core SA-00-EP-3 (mm/yr)					
Depth interval (m)	Mean time interval (yr)	Sedimentological unit	Mean	Min	Max
0.00 – 0.91	300	IV	3.03	0.65	/
0.00 – 2.33	1725	IV	1.35	1.25	1.47
2.33 – 2.82	0	IV	/	1.26	/
2.82 – 3.86	310	IV	3.35	1.82	20.80
3.86 – 4.92	630	III	1.68	1.16	3.03
Accumulation rates in Core SA-00-EP-4 (mm/yr)					
Depth interval (m)	Mean time interval (yr)	Sedimentological unit	Mean	Min	Max
0.00 – 3.94	2585	III (0.35m) – IV (3.59m)	1.52	1.42	1.64
3.94 – 4.41	245	III	1.92	0.92	/

Table 3 (*cont.*)

This layer originated from the fallout of tephra from the Minoan eruption on Santorini and so forms an important stratigraphical marker (Six *et al.*, this volume). Detritals also dominate core SA-00-EP-2 to a depth of 8.57 m. Clays and sand are situated below alternating layers of calcareous material. Traces of the tephra from the Thera eruption, highly mixed with detrital minerals, were found in this core from 9.26-9.53 m (Six *et al.*, this volume). At the northern border of the marsh, in core SA-00-EP-4 the previously mentioned peat layer is present from 3.94 m to 4.41 m and separates two colluvial layers (8.95-4.41 m and 3.94-0.00 m). In the lowest detrital layer two calcareous rich units occur (5.82-6.37 m and 8.70-8.85 m).

An overall observation shows an increase of the carbonate content in the uppermost ~1.5 m of the cores probably related to recent precipitation from the spring waters after drying of the area. Indeed, during the field campaigns of 1996-1999 the area covered by the marsh was inaccessible because of a water level of +/– 0.5 m, but the marsh was completely dry during the summer of 2000 when core SA-00-EP-3 was taken in the centre of the former marsh and remained dry till at least 2007.

In general, the sedimentation pattern in the lowest parts of the basin shows 4 distinctive units. The transition of one phase to another reflects changes of the environmental conditions:

4.1.1. Unit I

This unit has only been recovered in a few deep cores and the sediment characteristics depend on the position of the cores in the basin. Core SA-00-EP-1 is generally characterized by compacted clays which shows a sandy character between 10.00 and 9.00 m and a fining up sequence above the Santorini tephra layer towards a depth of ~7.5 m. SA-00-EP-2 shows an alternation of detrital deposits (sand and clays) and calcareous rich layers, and SA-96 has calcareous rich and harsh clays at its deepest level (8.00-7.62 m). Probably the calcareous deposits from core SA-00-EP-04 (8.85-8.70 m) must also be added to this unit. Because little and scattered data is available on these sediments, unit I groups all the deposits below the sediments of unit II.

4.1.2. Unit II

Unit two groups the large amounts of detrital material situated between ~8.00 and ~5.00 m in different cores. These deposits are poor in organic and calcareous matter, except for a small layer in core SA-00-EP-4 (5.82-6.37 m).

Based on the evolution of the dry bulk density (e.g. Figure 2) this unit is subdivided into two parts: a lower part (Unit IIa) where the sediments are deposited and preserved under wet conditions, which resulted in a relative low dry bulk density. This subunit is separated from the upper part

(Unit IIb) by a level of harsh compacted clays. Towards the top of Unit IIb a trend towards wetter conditions is observed where the dry bulk density gradually decreases and the organic matter slowly increases. On the overall, the deposits of Unit II depict instability of the slopes resulting in increased soil erosion.

4.1.3. Unit III

This unit is characterized by wet and stable conditions (constant high water level) in the lowest parts of the basin. Peat with a varying thickness, function of the distance to the springs, has accumulated, starting between ~5.00 and ~4.50 m. The low detrital content is a result of an increased slope stability which leads to a reduced erosion intensity.

4.1.4. Unit IV

The upper part of this unit is characterized by very wet conditions and maintained peat growth near the springs in the southwest of the marsh. Towards the northeast however these wet conditions disappear gradually and fine detritus dominates more and more, resulting in a complex pattern of organic and carbonate rich layers and detritals. Compared with phase III, the slopes became unstable with soil erosion as a consequence, but the deepest parts of the basin remained relatively wet. Significant differences in carbonate content occur in the most recent colluvial deposits until ~1.5 m below the surface.

4.2. Timeframe of the sedimentation and calculation of sediment accumulation rates

4.2.1. Unit I

Two small charred particles and/or seeds at a depth of 9.56 +/– 0.07 m and 9.76 +/– 0.07 m from core SA-00-EP-1 were dated (Table 2). These two samples revealed the oldest ages of the basin, respectively 2125 +/– 165 cal yr BC and 3485 +/– 145 cal yr. It is assumed that these ages are representative for the sedimentation period of unit I. Slow deposition characterized the sedimentary environment with a calculated mean accumulation rate of 0.15 mm/yr (Table 3). A somewhat higher accumulation rate of 1.63 mm/yr is found between 9.56 m and the tephra layer at 8.75 m if an age of 1628 cal yr BC is assumed for the Minoan Thera eruption (Manning, 1999). More recently, Friedrich et al. established this date with 95.4% probability at 1623 – 1600 cal yr BC (Six et al., this volume). This observation indicates that the accumulation rate might have already intensified before the tephra layer in unit I. Whether this

accumulation phenomenon is just local or related to the entire basin could not be determined.

4.2.2. Unit II

A dating in core SA-00-EP-2 taken from the interval 8.36-8.86 m shows an age of 860 +/– 70 cal yr BC (Table 2). This sample was taken at the transition from calcareous rich samples towards pure detrital deposits, and so it gives a rough estimate of the start of unit II. All dated material in the +/– 3 m detritus of unit II has been deposited during the same period indicating a very rapid accumulation. Core SA-96 has statistically the same age at 7.71 m (~625 +/– 275 cal yr BC) and at 5.83 m (~635 +/– 155 cal yr BC). Also core SA-99-EP-3 is dated ~580 +/– 190 cal yr BC at 5.79 m as well as at 7.52 m. In the same core organic material at 7.55 m is dated ~655 +/– 145 cal yr BC. There are no indications that the sediments below 7.71 m are of an older phase, so the start of unit II could not be dated in this core. This same period of accumulation is found for the fan deposits outside the marsh in core SA-99-EP-1 at 5.91 m (~580 +/– 190 cal yr BC). All these ages are statistically the same but have relative large deviations. Dating around the period 760-420 cal yr BC is problematic due to the presence of a 'plateau' in the calibration curve known as the « Hallstatt-plateau » (Kilian et al., 1995). This change in the calibration curve is related to a decrease in solar activity which caused an increase in the production of ^{14}C in the atmosphere (Speranza et al., 2000). A combination of all the ages below ~5.00 m in Oxcal gives a date of 2452 +/– 19 BP or ~585 + /– 185 cal yr BC, which corresponds with the Hallstatt-plateau. This phenomenon is correlated with the Subboreal/Subatlantic transition or a climatic change towards cooler, moister conditions (Speranza et al., 2000) and so a climatic influence on the sedimentation pattern is not excluded. In this perspective a shift in climate towards a more humid regime from about ~1600 cal yr BC to ~600 cal AD has also been suggested for northern Turkey by Bottema et al. (1993). An interval was calculated between the oldest (2700 +/– 45 BP) and the youngest date (2400 +/– 50 BP) of unit II to estimate its duration (Figure 5). At a two sigma level this calculation revealed a possible time range of 60-510 years. This broad result reflects the difficulty of exact dating in the vicinity of the Hallstatt-plateau (see also Figures 9A and B).

Accumulation rates in these lowest detrital deposits could be calculated in three cores: SA-96, SA-99-EP-3 and SA-99-EP-1 (Table 3). Because of the large deviations of the ages the accumulation rates have broad ranges. A high mean value of 23.5 mm/yr was calculated in core SA-99-

Interval unit II

68.2% probability
100 (13.7%) 180
300 (54.5%) 490
95.4% probability
60 (95.4%) 510

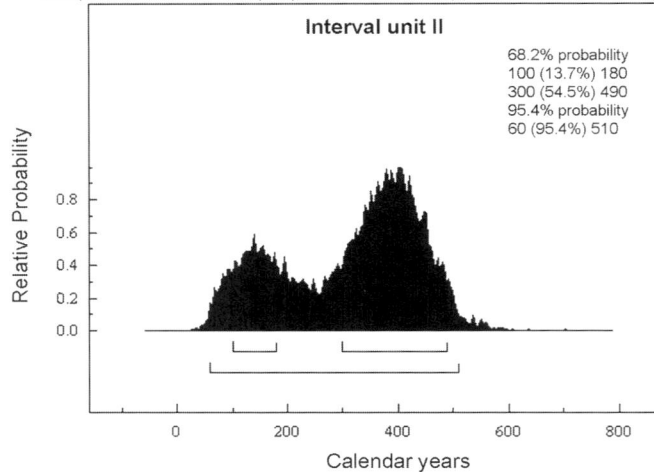

Figure 5: Probability curve of the calculated interval between the oldest (2700 +/− 45 BP) and the youngest ages (2400 +/− 50 BP) of Unit II. The interval expresses the possible duration of Unit II.

EP-3 between 5.79 m and 7.55 m. This value decreases to 9.6 mm/yr between 4.45 m and 5.79 m in the same core. Because of the similarity of the two ages below 5.00 m in core SA-96 only a minimum accumulation rate of 4.1 mm/yr could be calculated but the real accumulation was probably faster. Also core SA-99-EP-1 shows a relative high sediment accumulation rate of 4.1 mm/yr (2.2-52.3 mm/yr) between 4.34 and 5.91 m. A detail of the oldest ages plotted versus its relative depth, sorted by sedimentary unit, is given in Figure 6. Further research is necessary to elucidate whether this unit of rapid accumulation is a local or a regional phenomenon. Also Eastwood *et al.* (1998) deduced a phase of rapid accumulation between 2830 +/− 50 BP (1024-910 cal yr BC (1 sigma)) and 2480 +/− 55 BP (770-416 cal yr BC (1 sigma)) for Lake Gölhisar, situated ~100 km southwest of the Gravgaz basin.

4.2.3. Units III and IV

The base of the peat layer and so the start of the wet conditions (start of unit III) is dated in 7 cores (Figures 6 and 7). The western core (SA-97-EP-1) and the core in the middle of the marsh (SA-00-EP-3) show the same age for the start of the stable period (~675 +/− 155 cal yr BC). Also in core SA-98-MV-9 (~845 +/− 95 cal yr BC) and in SA-00-EP-4 (~830 +/− 80 cal yr BC) a relative old age was obtained for the start of this third phase (Table 2). These four ages are statistically the same and a combination gives an age of 2602 +/− 26 BP (~793 +/− 33 cal yr BC), which corresponds with the steeper part of the calibration curve preceding the Hallstatt-plateau. The age of the start

of unit III does not statistically differ from the ages of unit II because of the presence of the plateau in the calibration curve (Figure 6). This fact confirms that the very rapid accumulation of unit II and the start of unit III occurred in the time period of ~770-400 yr BC, with a preference for the first part of the interval.

In the east of the marsh the start of the peat forming conditions is dated significantly later: ~305 +/− 105 cal yr BC in core SA-99-EP-3 and ~200 +/− 160 cal yr BC for the organic rich layer in core SA-99-EP-1. This observation points to a diachronic extension of the marsh to the east. As a consequence, the ages in core SA-99-EP-1 describe the period of the largest extension of the wet conditions in the marsh. The duration of the largest extension of the peat forming conditions was estimated in core SA-99-EP-3 to be shorter than 140 years (Van Thuyne, 2000). Taken into account the age of the start of the peat layer in the other parts of the marsh, unit III in total must have lasted longer. Also in core SA-96 a younger date was obtained (285 +/− 115 cal yr BC) for the start of the peat layer. A possible explanation for this younger date is that the topography at that coring place was somewhat higher during the period of increasing moisture so that it took some time to initiate the peat forming here. It is also possible that because of its position near the springs a permanent water flow at that spot hampered peat formation.

The very wet conditions of unit III ended at the latest around ~55 +/− 125 cal yr BC in the eastern part of the basin (core SA-99-EP-1) and is expected to be diachronic

200

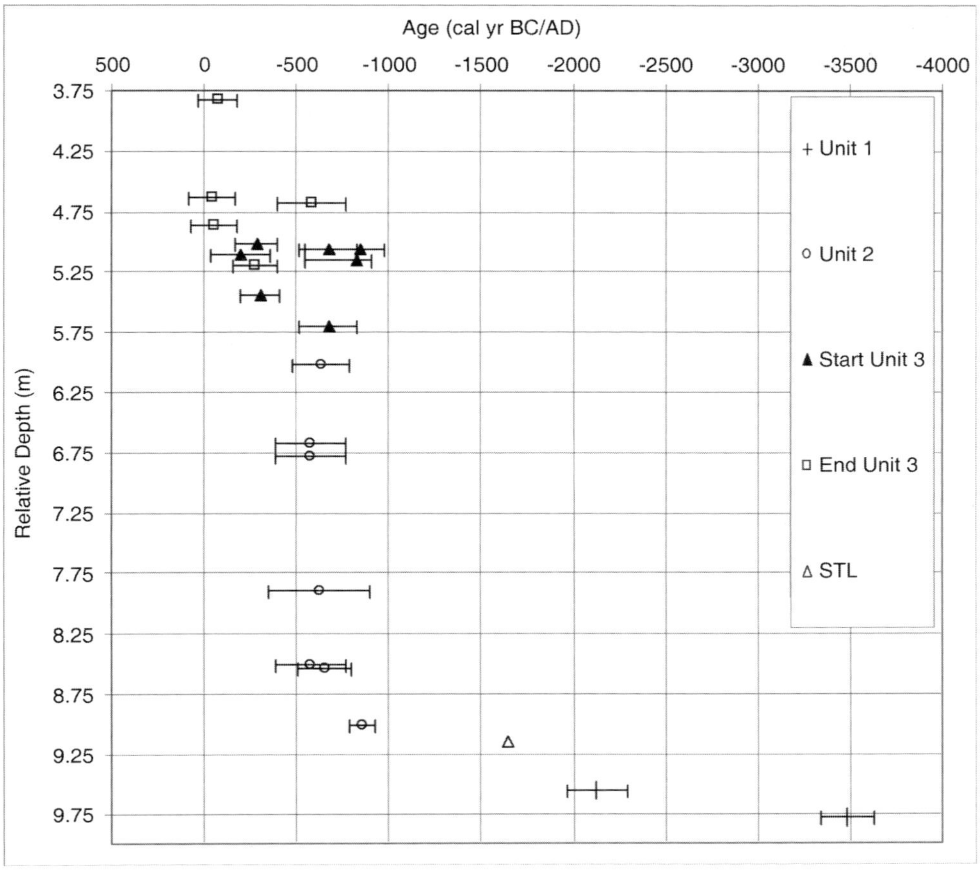

Figure 6: Calibrated ^{14}C ages versus relative depth (relative to the top of core SA-00-EP-01) – period 4000 cal yr BC – 500 cal yr AD for units 1, 2 and 3.

with younger ages towards the spring zone. Also in core SA-98-MV-9 and core SA-00-EP-3 the end of the peat growth has similar ages of respectively 75 +/– 105 cal yr BC and 45 +/– 125 cal yr BC.

After ~55 +/– 125 cal yr BC until nowadays the basin is marked by the sedimentological characteristics of unit IV. All the ages of this last unit plotted versus their relative depth fit very well and describe the gradual filling of the basin (Figures 7 and 8).

Towards the top of the cores (phase III and IV), the sediment accumulation rates decrease to mean values around 2.00 mm/yr (Table 3). The rate of the peat growth is estimated to mean values of 2.37 mm/yr in core SA-96, 1.61 mm/yr in core SA-98-MV-9, 1.66 mm/yr in core SA-99-EP-1 and

1.92 mm/yr in core SA-00-EP-4 which is significantly slower than the accumulation rates of phase II. The upper 1.61 m in core SA-99-EP-3 even shows a mean accumulation value of 1.19 mm/yr.

A summary of the accumulation history of the Gravgaz basin (Table 4) shows a slow deposition during phase I (before ~860 +/– 70 cal yr) followed by a very fast accumulation of detritals in units IIa and IIb from a sample depth of ~8.00 m to ~5.00 m (~585 +/– 185 cal yr BC) and a decrease of the accumulation rates from the start of the peat layer around ~5.00 m towards the top of the cores (unit III and IV). This pattern is depicted in Figure 8 where the ages are sorted by coring and plotted versus their relative depth. The slope of the mean curve through the ages represents the accumulation rate.

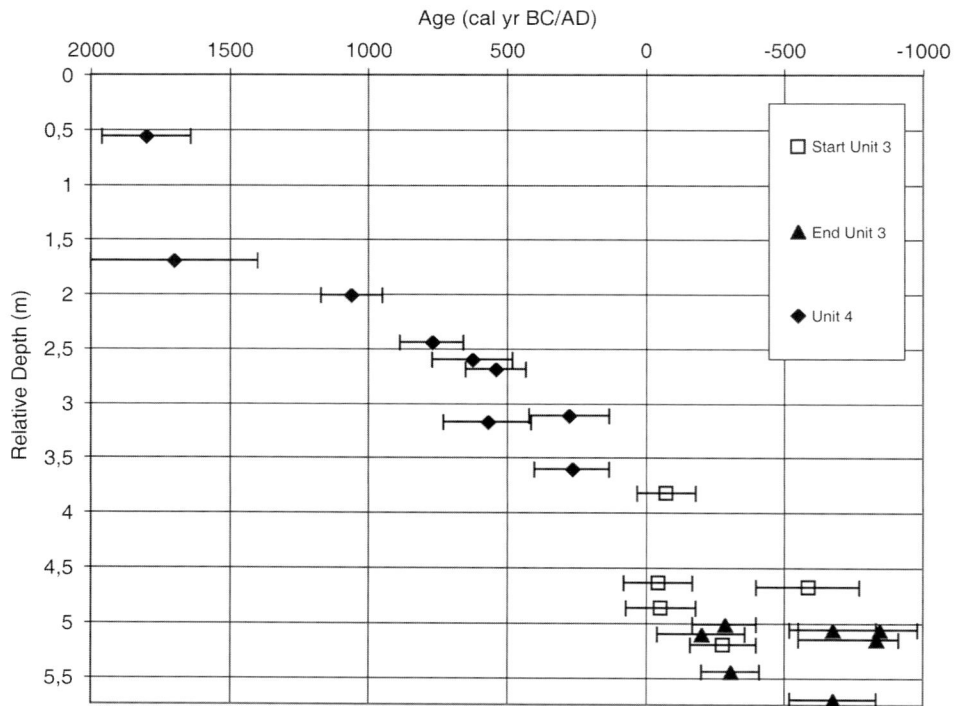

Figure 7: Calibrated ^{14}C ages versus relative depth (relative to the top of core SA-00-EP-01) – period 1000 cal yr BC – 2000 cal yr AD for units 3 and 4.

Boring	Basis unit III (m)	Top unit III (m)	Thickness (m)	Start unit III (cal yr BC – 2 sigma)	End unit III (cal yr BC/AD – 2 sigma)
SA-96	5.13	3.75	1.38	400 – 170 cal yr BC	Not dated
SA-97-EP-1	5.13	3.87	1.26	830 – 520 cal yr BC	Not dated
SA-98-MV-9	5.23	3.58	1.65	940 – 750 cal yr BC	180 cal yr BC – 30 cal yr AD
SA-99-EP-1	5.24	4.72	0.52	360 – 40 cal yr BC	180 cal yr BC – 70 cal yr AD
SA-99-EP-3	5.49	5.20	0.29	410 – 200 cal yr BC	400 – 160 cal yr BC
SA-00-EP-3	6.10	4.54	1.56	830 – 520 cal yr BC	170 cal yr BC – 80 cal yr AD
SA-00-EP-4	5.34	4.33	1.01	910 – 750 cal yr BC	770 – 400 cal yr BC

Table 4: Characteristics of sedimentological unit III. The basis and top are expressed as the depth relative to the top of core SA-00-EP-1 and the start and the end are indicated at a two sigma calibration level.

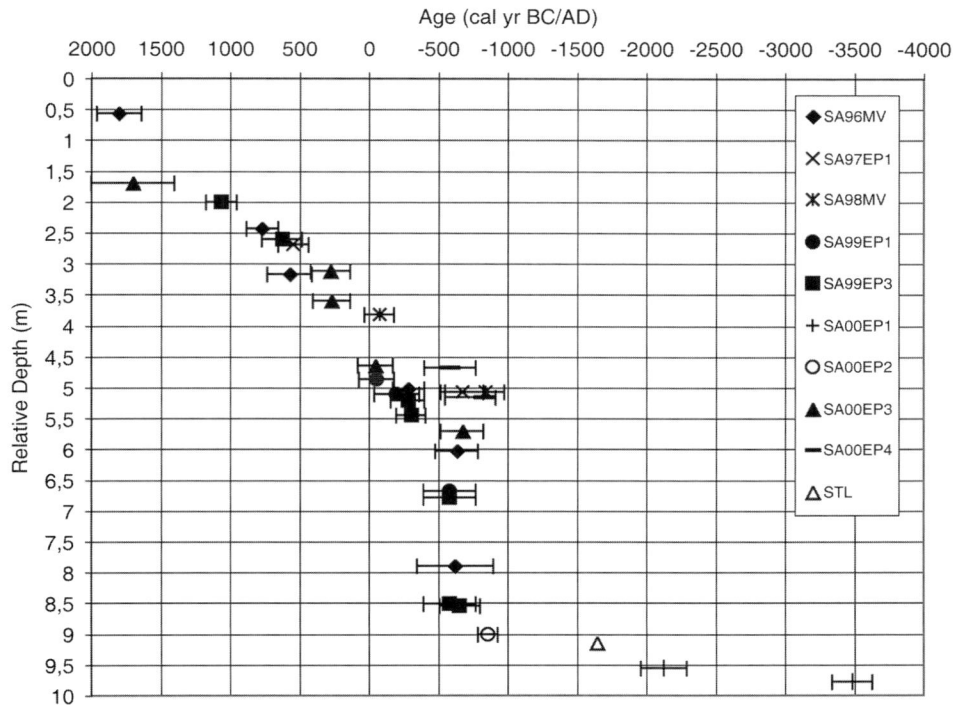

Figure 8: Calibrated ^{14}C ages versus relative depth (relative to the top of core SA-00-EP-01) sorted by boring.

5. CORRELATION OF SEDIMENTOLOGICAL AND POLLEN DATA

The pollen profiles of cores SA-96 and SA-99-EP-3, that describe the change in regional and local vegetation cover (Vermoere *et al.* 2000; 2002a, b) are clearly correlated with the sedimentation pattern presented above (Table 5). The calcareous samples of unit I in core SA-96 between 8.00 m and 7.62 m are grouped in pollen zone G0 (8.00-7.67 m). This zone shows high percentages of arboreal pollen with a dominance of Pinus. Plant species requiring marshy habitats are not present. During pollen zone A and sedimentological unit I a slow deposition of clays in calm waters without the development of a marsh is noted (Vermoere *et al.*, 2000).

The unit of rapid accumulation (unit II) between ~8.30 m and ~5.00 m is characterized by high percentages of *Artemisia* and the establishment of secondary anthropogenic indicators characteristic for grazed, cultivated or degraded areas in pollen zone G1. Because marsh vegetation was already present in the pollen diagram during this period, it is suspected that the springs in the west were already active. The very fast accumulation of detritus is interpreted as an adaptation of the catchment to the wetter conditions at the onset of the Subatlantic. In combination with a defor-

estation, which was deduced from the pollen diagram, the highly unstable conditions in the basin can be explained. *Artemisia* then is interpreted here a colonizer on the highly active fresh deposits. During these highly unstable conditions with very fast sediment accumulation it is suggested that the pollen diagram gives mainly very local information while during phases of slow sediment the pollen diagram provides a more regional picture of the vegetation cover. This local information may reflect the mergence of a large proto-urban site, needing both timber (*Pinus*) or farming or grazing land, with much Archaic to early Imperial surface sherds, an impressive defensive wall with five towers, probably to be dated to the post-Classical period (early 4th century BC) at Kepez Kalesi, located ca. 3.5 km to the northeast of the Gravgaz marshes. The 'Pisidian' architecture of that period, as revealed by ongoing excavations at the early Iron Age predecessor of Sagalassos (Ur-Sagalassos) located at Tepe Düzen, ca. 1.8 km to the southwest of the current site, in the 4th to 6th century BC, was composed of rubble socles supporting a wood and mudbrick architecture.

The pollen profiles of SA-96 and SA-99-EP-3 (Vermoere *et al.*, 2000; 2002) show a break in the vegetation cover at a depth around 5.20 m in core SA-96 and around 4.50 m in core SA-99-EP-3, where the percentages of *Artemisia* decrease. Here the pollen diagrams indicate the start of a

Units	Sample depth (m)	Period of deposition (cal yr BC/AD)	Characteristics of the deposits	Mean Accumulation Rate (mm/yr)	Regional Vegetation (*)
Unit IV	0.00 – ~ 4.00	2000 cal yr AD – (160cal yr BC-30 cal yr AD)	Peat growth near the springs and deposition of calcareous and organic rich clays elsewhere. The end of the occupation phase leaves no imprint in the sediments	~ 2.0	Continuation and end of occupation phase followed by a domination of pine pollen – Disappearance of oaks and cultivation indicators
Unit III	~ 4.00 – ~ 5.00	(160 cal yr BC-30 cal yr AD) – 770-760 cal yr BC	Peat growth in the lowest parts of the basin; reduced input of detritus	~ 1.6	Start of occupation phase with arboriculture of olives, walnuts and manna ashes – Widespread presence of oaks and *Artemisia*
Unit IIb	~ 5.00 – ~ 6.50	770-760 cal yr BC – 930-790 cal yr BC	Deposition of stratified fine detritus; dry period followed by a trend towards wetter conditions	~ 17.6	Dominance of *Artemisia* – Widespread presence of oaks
Unit IIa	~ 6.50 – ~ 8.00		Deposition of stratified fine detritus under wet conditions		
Unit I	8.50 – ?	930-790 cal yr BC – ?	Stratified deposition of calcareous sediments and clays	~ 0.15	Coniferous forest

Table 5: Summary of the sedimentological units with their approximate sample depth, approximate period of deposition, sediment characteristics, mean accumulation rate and pollen characteristics ((*) based on Vermoere et al., 2000).

cultivation phase (known as the Beyşehir Occupation Phase – BO Phase) in the Gravgaz basin (pollen zone G2-A). It appears that the start of this cultivation phase, the stabilization of the environment and the start of the peat growth are synchronous. Here the hypothesis is formulated that the people cultivating the slopes controlled the water erosion processes by soil conservation measurements. Also an exhaustion of erodible material (as is observed nowadays on the limestone slopes) and the achievement of a natural equilibrium could have played a role in the stabilisation of the environment.

After ~55 +/– 125 cal yr BC (the utmost date of the largest extension of the peat growth), colluviation restarted in the marsh under relative wet conditions (unit IV), with local peat formation near the springs and in the central parts of the basin. The erosion intensity is lower than in unit II. These conditions are maintained during the remaining period of the BO Phase visible in pollen zone G2-B (end at ~715 +/– 55 cal yr AD) until now (pollen zone G3). It is tempting to correlate the onset of this second colluviation phase with

the beginning of the Roman domination in 129 BC, when the area became part of the Roman province of Asia lasting until 35 BC (Waelkens, 1993: 45; Poblome, 1999: 17). In another valley of Sagalassos, the Bereket basin, a similar start of arboriculture (vine, ash, walnut…) commenced around 180 BC, whereas after a human-induced palaeofire had cleared the pine forest, an intensive cultivation phase coinciding with the start of a three century long warmer and dryer climate, started ca. 20 BC with the introduction of olive-yards at an altitude of 1410 m a.s.l. At Bereket as well, a wetter and possibly colder climate put an end to olive and other arbocultures from ca. 300 AD onwards (Kaniewski et al., 2007, 2008) The destabilisation and the renewed detrital input could be due to a degradation of the soil conservation measurements and/or a more intensive use of the landscape under Roman rule. Indeed the pollen profiles show a higher pollen percentage of species representing the cultivation in the upper part of the cultivation phase (pollen zone G2-B). The end of the cultivation phase did not leave a clear imprint in the characteristics of the contemporaneous deposits.

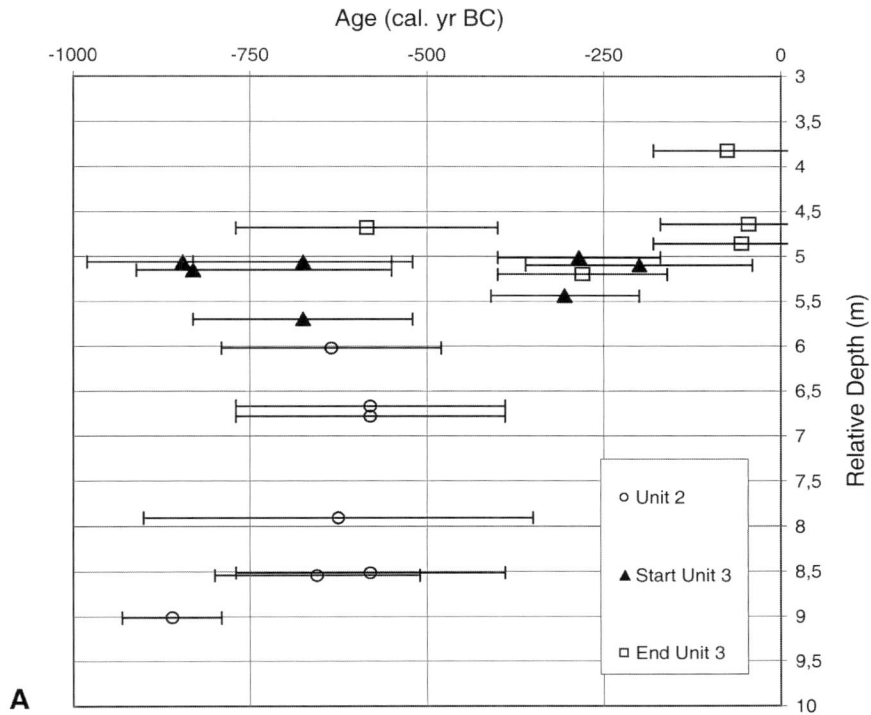

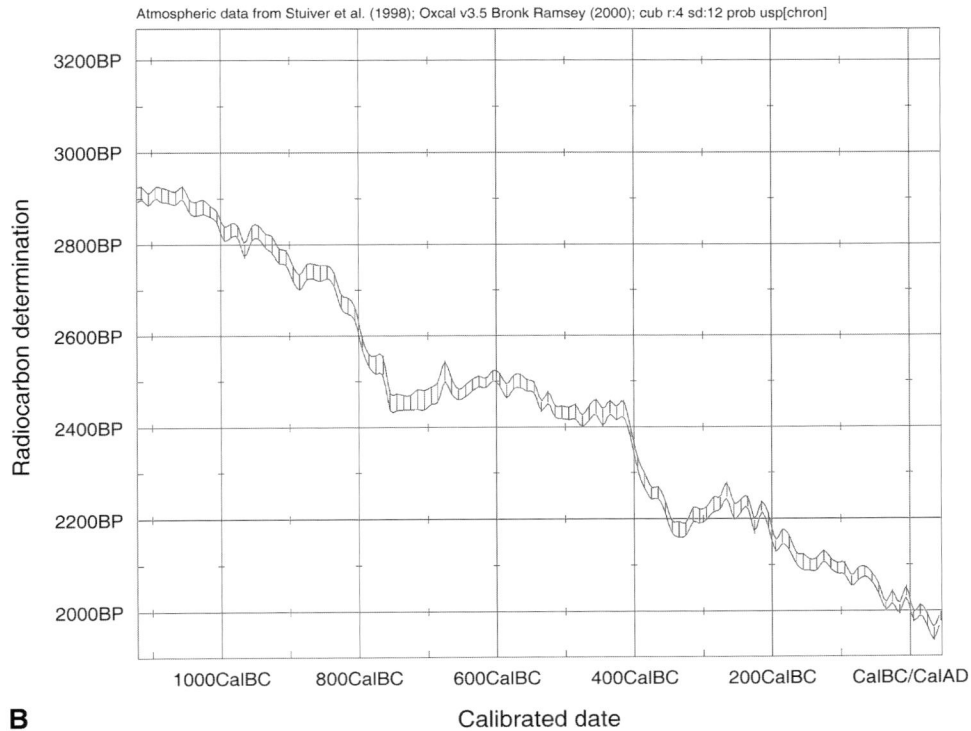

Figure 9: (A) Calibrated ^{14}C ages versus relative depth (relative to the top of core SA-00-EP-01) for the time interval 1000-0 cal yr BC (B) ^{14}C-Calibration curve for the time interval 1000-0 cal yr BC (based on Stuiver *et al.* 1998). The flat area on the curve between 760 and 400 cal yr BC is called the Hallstatt plateau.

6. CONCLUSIONS

Based on sediment description and accumulation rates, the infilling of the Gravgaz basin is divided into four sedimentological units (Table 5). The first unit is only recovered in a few cores and is characterized by a slow sedimentation probably under wet conditions without the formation of peat and by the deposition of clay rich detritus with or without interfingering calcareous rich layers. A detailed characterisation is not yet possible because of a lack of data on the thickness and extension of this unit. The end of these settings is dated around 860 +/– 70 cal yr BC. The second unit shows a very fast accumulation of ~3.00 m clay rich detritals at the Subboreal/Subatlantic transition (~ 585 +/– 185 cal yr BC) which may be caused by a climatic event towards wetter conditions (Fig. 9A). The calculated accumulation rates vary between 2.4 mm/yr and a maximum value of >67 mm/yr. This unit II corresponds with pollen zone II characterized by high *Artemisia* content and the introduction of secondary anthropogenic indicators. Those may be caused by the emergence of a proto-urban settlement at Kepez Kalesi, which needed both timber and arable land (Vanhaverbeke and Waelkens, 2003; Vermoere, 2004). These environmental settings stop suddenly. The environment became stable and wet resulting in the formation of a peat layer with reduced detritus content. This peat growth gradually covered the lower parts of the basin. This event occurs at a sample depth varying between 5.00 and 4.50 m and marks the start of unit III. During this unit, the accumulation rate decreases drastically. The peat growth is diachronic: the start of the wet conditions is dated in the western and central part of the marsh to ~675 +/– 155 cal yr BC. This age is statistically identical to the ages corresponding with the very rapid accumulation of unit II. In the east the lowest parts of the peat layer are dated significantly later to ~305 +/– 105 cal yr BC (in core SA-99-EP-3) and ~200 +/– 160 cal yr BC (in core SA-99-EP-1). Correlated with the pollen data, this phase of environmental stability corresponds to the start of a cultivation period (known as the 'Beyşehir Occupation Phase'). It is therefore suggested that the people cultivating the landscape took soil conservation measurements to control the erosion, but the role of natural changes is not excluded. The utmost age of these stable and wet conditions is dated at ~55 +/– 125 cal yr BC. At that moment deposition of fine detritus restarts in the fourth unit at a lower intensity as in unit II, with a mean accumulation rate of ~2.0 mm/yr. In the central part of the basin sedimentation persists under wet conditions with interfingering layers of peat, organic rich and/or carbonate rich clays, and organic poor detrital material. Because the start of phase IV is still situated in the cultivation phase, the colluviation probably restarted because of a degradation of the soil conservation measurements and/or a more intensive use of the landscape. The ending of cultivation did not drastically change the environmental settings and so the sedimentological conditions of this last phase persist until nowadays. An overall observation is that during the sedimentation of phase III and IV, a gradient of the damp conditions clearly exists from the wetter western part of the basin near the springs to the dryer eastern part near the swallet.

7. REFERENCES

Bell, M. and Walker, M.J.C. (1992) *Late Quaternary Environmental Change*, Longman, Essex.

Bottema, S. and Woldring, H. (1984) Late Quaternary vegetation and climate of Southwest Turkey II, *Palaeohistoria* 26: 123-149.

Bottema, S., Woldring, H. and Aytug, B. (1993) Late Quaternary vegetation history and climate in northern Turkey, *Palaeohistoria* 35/36: 13-72.

Bronk Ramsey, C. (1995) Radiocarbon Calibration and analysis of stratigraphy: the OxCal program, *Radiocarbon* 37(2): 425-430.

Eastwood, W.J., Roberts, N. and Lamb, H.F. (1998) Palaeoecological and archaeological evidence for human occupance in southwest Turkey: the Beyşehir occupation phase, *Anatolian Studies* 48: 69-86.

Eastwood, W.J., Roberts, N., Lamb, H.F. and Tibby, J.C. (1999) Holocene environmental change in southwest Turkey: a palaeoecological record of lake and catchment-related changes, *Quaternary Science Reviews* 18: 671-695.

Friedrich, W.L., Kromer, B. Friedrich, M. Heinemeier, J., Pfeifer, T. and Talamo, S. (2006) Santorini Eruption Radiocarbon dated to 1627-1600 B.C., *Science* 312: 548.

Gosselink, J.G., Hatton, R. and Hopkinson, C.S. (1984) Relationship of organic carbon and mineral content to bulk density in Louisiana marsh soils, *Soil Science* 3: 177-180.

Hakyemez, H.Y., Erkal, T. and Göktas, F. (1999) Late Quaternary evolution of the Gediz and Büyük Menderes grabens, Western Anatolia, Turkey, *Quaternary Science Reviews*, 18, 549-554.

Kaniewski, D., Paulissen, E., De Laet, V., Dossche, K., Waelkens, M. (2007) 3000 years BP high-resolution physical landscape history inferred from an intramontane basin in the Western Taurus Mountains, Turkey, *Quaternary Science Reviews* 26 (17-18): 2201-2218.

Kaniewski, D., Paulissen, E., De Laet, V., and Waelkens, M. (2008) Late Holocene fire impacts and post-fire regeneration dynamics in a western Taurus Mountains watershed, southwest Turkey, *Quaternary Research* 70 (in press).

KAZANCI, N., GEVREK, A.I. and VAROL, B. (1995) Facies changes and high calorific peat formation in a Quaternary maar lake, central Anatolia, Turkey: the possible role of geothermal processes in a closed lacustrine basin, *Sedimentary Geology* 94: 255-266.

KARABIYIKOGLU, M., KUZUCUOGLU, C., FONTUGNE, M., KAISER, B. and MOURALIS, D. (1999) Facies and depositional sequences of the Late Pleistocene Göçü shoreline system, Konya basin, Central Anatolia: Implications for reconstructing lake level changes, *Quaternary Science Reviews* 18: 593-609.

KILIAN, M.R., VAN DER PLICHT, J. and VAN GEEL, B. (1995) Dating raised bogs: new aspects of AMS ^{14}C wiggle matching, a reservoir effect and climatic change, *Quaternary Science Reviews* 14: 959-966.

LAMBRECHTS, J. (1998) *Bijdrage tot de studie van de evolutie van paleo-meren in de omgeving van Sagalassos (S-W Turkije) met het bekken van Gravgaz als case-study*, Unpublished Licenciate Thesis (in Dutch), Katholieke University Leuven.

LOWE, J.J. and WALKER, M.J.C. (1984) *Reconstructing Quaternary Environments*, Longman, Essex.

MANNING, S.W. (1999) *A Test of Time. The Volcano of Thera and the Chronology and History of the Aegean and East Mediterranean in the Mid Second Millennium BC.* Oxbow Books, Oxford and Oakville.

POBLOME, J. (1999) *Red slip ware produced at Sagalassos (Southern Turkey). Typology and chronology (Studies in Eastern Mediterranean Archaeology II)*, Brepols, Turnhout.

POPE, K.O. and VAN ANDEL, T.H. (1984) Late Quaternary alluviation and soil formation in the southern argolid: its history, causes and archaeological implications, *Journal of Archaeological Science* 11: 281-306.

REED, J.M., ROBERTS, N. and LENG, M.J. (1999) An evaluation of the diatom response to Late Quaternary environmental change in two lakes in the Konya Basin, Turkey, by comparison with stable isotope data, *Quaternary Science Reviews* 18: 631-646.

ROBERTS, N. (1995) Climatic forcing of alluvial fan regimes during the Late Quaternary in the Konya basin, south central Turkey, in: J. LEWIN, M.G. MACKLIN and J.C. WOODWARD (eds.) *Mediterranean Quaternary River Environments*, A.A. Balkema, Rotterdam: 207-217.

ROBERTS, N., EASTWOOD, W.J., LAMB, H.F. and TIBBY, J. (1997) The age and causes of mid-Holocene environmental change in Southwest Turkey, in: H.N. ZHET DALFES, G. KUKLA and H. WEISS (eds.) *Third Millenium BC Climatic Change and Old World Collapse (NATO ASI series 149)*, Springer, Heidelberg: 409-429.

ROBERTS, N., BLACK, S., BOYER, P., EASTWOOD, W.J., GRIFFITHS, H.I., LAMB, H.F., LENG, M.J., PARISH, R., REED, J.M.,

TWIGG, D. and YIGITBASIOGLU, H. (1999) Chronology and stratigraphy of Late Quaternary sediments in the Konya Basin, Turkey: Results from the KOPAL Project, *Quaternary Science Reviews* 18: 611-630.

ROBERTS, N., REED, J.M., LENG, M.J., KUZUCUOGLU, C., FONTUGNE, M., BERTAUX, J., WOLDRING, H., BOTTEMA, S., BLACK, S., HUNT, E. and KARABIYIKOĞLU, M. (2001) The tempo of Holocene climatic change in the eastern Mediterranean region: new high-resolution crater lake sediment data from central Turkey, *The Holocene* 11(6): 721-736.

SIX, S., DEGRYSE, P., PAULISSEN, E., HEIJLEN, W., VERMOERE, M. and WAELKENS, M. (THIS VOLUME) Tephra from the Minoan eruption of Santorini in the territory of Sagalassos, in: P. DEGRYSE and M. WAELKENS (eds.) *Sagalassos VI. Geo- and Bio-Archaeology at Sagalassos and in its Territory*, Leuven University Press, Leuven: 173-188.

SPERANZA, A., VAN DER PLICHT, J. and VAN GEEL, B. (2000) Improving the time control of the Subboreal/Subatlantic transition in a Czech peat sequence by ^{14}C wiggle-matching, *Quaternary Science Reviews* 19: 1589-1604.

STUIVER, M., REIMER, P.J., BARD, E., BECK, J.W., BURR, G.S., HUGHEN, K.A., KROMER, B., MCCORMAC, G., VAN DER PLICHT, J. and SPURK, M. (1998) Radiocarbon age calibration, 24.000-0 Cal.BP, *Radiocarbon* 40: 1041-1083.

VAN ANDEL, T.H., ZANGGER, E. and DEMITRACK, A. (1990) Land use and soil erosion in prehistoric and historical Greece, *Journal of Field Archaeology* 17: 379-396.

VANHAVERBEKE, H. and WAELKENS, M. (2003) *The Chora of Sagalassos. The Evolution of the Settlement Pattern from Prehistoric until Recent Times (Studies in Eastern Mediterranean Archaeology 5)*, Brepols Publishers, Turnhout.

VAN THUYNE, T. (2000) *Laat-Holocene accumulatiegeschiedenis van het bekken van Gravgaz (Sagalassos Territorium, Z-W Turkije)*, Unpublished Licenciate Thesis (in Dutch), Katholieke Universiteit Leuven.

VAN ZEIST, W., WOLDRING, H. and STAPERT, D. (1975) Late Quaternary vegetation and climate of southwestern Turkey, *Palaeohistorial* 17: 55-143

VERMOERE, M. (2004) *Holocene Vegetation History in the Territory of Sagalassos (southwest Turkey) A Palynological Approach (Studies in Eastern Mediterranean Archaeology VI)*, Brepols Publishers, Turnhout.

VERMOERE, M., SMETS, E., WAELKENS, M., VANHAVERBEKE, H., LIBRECHT, I., PAULISSEN, E. and VANHECKE, L. (2000) Late Holocene Environmental Change and the Record of Human Impact at Gravgaz near Sagalassos, Southwest Turkey, *Journal of Archaeological Science* 27: 571-595.

VERMOERE, M., VAN THUYNE, T., SIX, S., VANHECKE, L., PAULISSEN, E. and SMETS, E. (2002a) Late Holocene local vegetation dynamics in the marsh of Gravgaz, *Journal of Palaeolimnology* 27: 428-451.

207

VERMOERE, M., BOTTEMA, S., VANHECKE, L., PAULISSEN, E., WAELKENS, M. and SMETS, E. (2002b) Palynological evidence for late Holocene human occupation in two wetlands in southwest Turkey, *The Holocene* 12(5): 569-548.

VERSTRAETEN, G. and POESEN, J. (2001) Variability of dry sediment bulk density between and within retention ponds and its impact on the calculation of sediment yield, *Earth Surf. Process. Landforms* 26: 375-394.

WAELKENS, M. (1993) Sagalassos. History and archaeology, in: M. WAELKENS (ed.) *Sagalassos I* (*Acta Archaeologica Lovaniensia Monographiae 5*), Leuven University Press, Leuven: 37-50.

PART III

THE CLIMATIC SETTING

DEPOSITIONAL ENVIRONMENT OF HOLOCENE COOL WATER TRAVERTINES IN THE VALLEY OF BAŞKÖY

Patrick DEGRYSE, Philippe MUCHEZ, Willy VIAENE[†], Yves QUINIF and Marc WAELKENS

1. INTRODUCTION

The study of cool water travertines in the village of Başköy, located some 5 km to the west of Sagalassos, forms part of an interdisciplinary research carried out at the territory of the archaeological site of Sagalassos. This site was occupied from prehistoric times until the 7th century A.D. The aim of this interdisciplinary study is to reconstruct the physical, biological and socio-economical environment of the ancient city (Waelkens *et al.*, 1999). Within the present paper, a reconstruction of the environment in the valley of Başköy has been made based on travertine deposits.

2. MODERN ENVIRONMENT

2.1. Geomorphology and geology

The valley of Başköy is surrounded to the north, west and south by the slopes of the Taurus Mountains and opens towards the east to the valley of Ağlasun. The flanks of this valley consist of Tertiary allochthonous nappes, built up by limestone and ophiolites and of Tertiary flysch deposits. These nappes are thrusted over the allochthonous Mesozoic limestone massif of the Bey Dağları (Robertson, 1993). The limestone acts as an aquifer for travertine depositing waters in the area. In the valley itself we find alluvial, lake and travertine deposits of Quaternary age.

2.2. Climate

The area studied is characterized by a relatively short dry, hot period in summer, and a long wet, cold period from autumn until spring. Most of the precipitation falls as snow in December and January. The area has an oro-mediterranean climate (Poesen *et al.*, 1995). The valley of Başköy, where the travertines are situated, lies at an altitude between 1000 and 1200m a.s.l.

3. FIELD INVESTIGATION

A field study was carried out to map different types of travertine deposits and to collect samples for a further petrographical investigation. Within the field, three major types of travertine have been distinguished: phytoherm framestone (Figure 1A), finely laminated (Figure 1B) and detrital travertine. The phytoherm framestone consists of coarse-grained radial and concentric calcites encrusting plants. The finely laminated travertine is composed of thin calcite layers, in which different morphologies are present. Detrital travertine is characterized by rounded sand to cobble sized carbonates. In addition to the mapping of the different travertine types on a regional scale, three sections have been studied.

4. PETROGRAPHY

4.1. Description and interpretation

Microscopically, the phytoherm framestone (Figure 1A) consists of equidimensional to acicular calcite crystals. The crystals grew perpendicular on a plant stem. The detrital travertine deposits are built up by reworked fragments of earlier deposited travertine and siliciclastics. Sometimes the relic structures of the older, original deposits can be seen. In the finely laminated travertine, several biological features can be observed. Firstly, the calcites may show a three-dimensional network of spheres composed of a micritic nucleus surrounded by irregular concentric laminae (Figure 1B). This structure is identical to the 3D network of bacterial shrubs described by Chafetz and Folk (1984) and Guo *et al.* (1996). Since the growth period of these bacteria is dominantly from spring until summer, these calcites are likely to have been precipitated during these seasons. However, they can also grow in zones of slow flow throughout the year. Secondly, acicular sparitic calcite crystals radiating from a central line may build up mm- to cm-thick layers (Figure 1C). This structure closely resembles that of colonies of Rivulariacea (Caudwell, 1983; Obenlüneschloß, 1991). Gastropods belonging to the families Succineidea and Zonitidae, occur within the mm to cm-thick layers. Thirdly, calcite encrusting half circular to oval pores (Figure 1D) consists of three layers. The latter are composed of a white microsparitic layer of 5μm, a brown micritic layer of 10μm and a layer of acicular crystals in which there are remains of tubes. These structures are biomediated

211

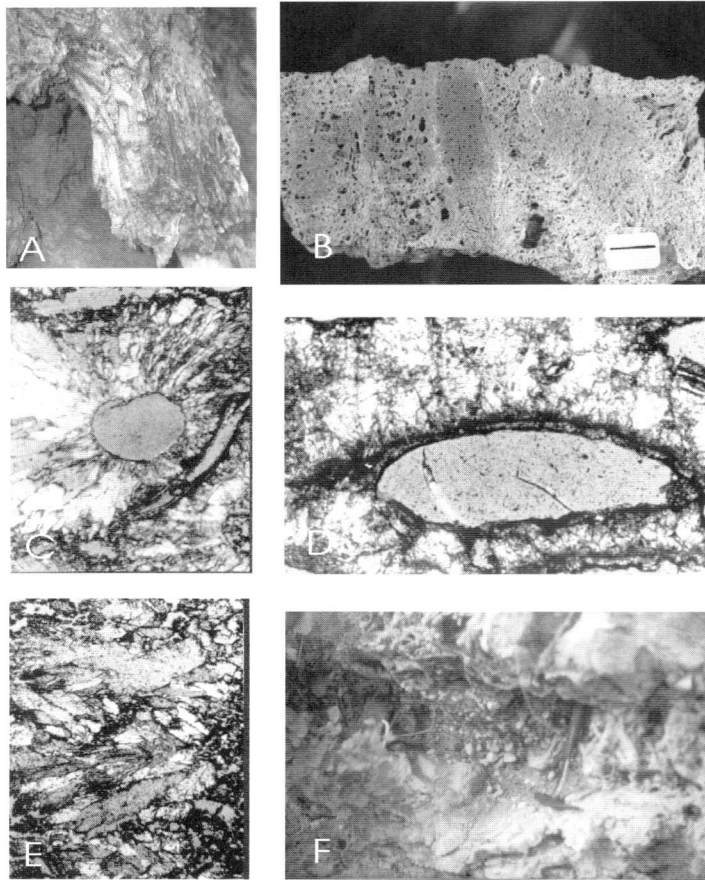

Figure 1: Photographs of the different travertine structures recognized and of a palaeochannel. A. Phytoherm framestone (scale is 10 cm) Calcite crystals encrusting an original plant stem. B. Finely laminated travertine (scale is 2 cm). Network of calcite composed of a micritic nucleus surrounded by irregular concentric laminae. This structure is interpreted as bacterial shrubs. C. Acicular calcite crystals radiating from a central line. They closely resemble colonies of Rivulariacea. D. Calcite encrusting half circular to oval pores, consisting of three layers: a white microsparitic layer of 5 μm, a brown micritic layer of 10 μm and a layer of acicular crystals. This structure is biomediated by algae colonising on larvae of Chironomida. E. Compact layer of acicular calcite crystals, with micritic particles enclosed in and between them. F. Remains of a palaeochannel with rounded pebbles of travertine and lithic fragments from the mountain flanks (hammer = 30 cm).

by algae colonizing on larvae of Chironomida, encrusting themselves with calcite, as described by Thienemann (1954) and Golubic et al. (1993). The larvae of Chironimus only live in April and May in this region (Thienemann, 1954). The finely laminated travertine is also composed of white to brown, compact layers of acicular calcite crystals with micritic particles enclosed in and between them (Figure 1E). The acicular calcite crystals are interpreted to represent recrystallized lime mud (see also Guo and Riding, 1994). Such micritic sediments represent microdetrital travertine (Pedley, 1990) and are ubiquitous in lakes, ponds and marshes. They are likely deposited in summer, when the system enters a dry period. During summer, water supply drops and the ponds are no longer fed with fresh water.

This allows micritic particles to settle at the bottom of the pond. In addition, the increase in temperature during summer and subsequent in water saturation, plays an important role in this process.

4.2. Discussion

The petrographical characteristics of the finely laminated travertine correspond with those of travertine forming in ponds (e.g. Rouchy et al., 1996), within a fluvial induced travertine system and more specifically the barrage model (Ford and Pedley, 1996). The gastropods Succineidea and Zonitidae present in the finely laminated travertine live near the margin of such ponds. A paludal setting can be

212

excluded in these deposits, since in the finely laminated travertine no incrustation by macrophytes or lichens has been observed. In addition, coarse lithic fragments are not incorporated, humus-rich layers are not present and lime mud is less abundant than in a paludal setting. In the fluvial barrage model, we have the damming of flowing water by transverse barrages. Behind these barrages, ponds are formed that favour organically induced travertine precipitation by algae and bacteria (Emeis *et al.*, 1987). The chain of ponds is typically connected with falls and streams. In the falls and in the turbulent mountain-streams that feed the valley with water, inorganic precipitation of travertine through CO_2-degassing could have occurred.

The detrital travertine has probably been reworked to the present location, since these deposits are located on the highest point of the valley. In the valley of Başköy, the remains of a palaeochannel filled with rounded pebbles were found at several locations and at different elevations in the travertine deposits (Figure 1F). The phytoherm framestone below and above the finely laminated travertine in sections 1A and 1B may reflect the development of a marshy environment in the pools, when the latter dried out or were filled with travertine deposits. These levels are also associated with a rise in macrophytal remains, coarse lithic fragments and lime mud. This suggests an alternation of the system from fluvial to paludal. The palaeochannel filled with rounded pebbles may thus represent a stage of increased run-off under wetter climatic conditions. An analogue system for travertine deposition, with the combination and alteration of fluvial and paludal settings, can be found in the nearby Aksu basin around the city of Antalya (Glover and Robertson, 1998). The fluvial system that formed the travertine deposits has now disappeared in the valley of Başköy. Nowadays, only small streams provide water flowing into the valley, much of which is consumed by irrigation of fields. A possible explanation for the disappearance of river recharge would be a change in climate towards more arid conditions. Other possibilities for the disappearance of the fluvial system are karstification or tectonic activity (earthquakes), which can create pathways allowing large amounts of water to disappear into the subsurface.

5. DATING OF THE TRAVERTINES

The dating of the travertines was done by the U/Th method. The U and Th isotopic ratios were determined by mass-spectrometry. The activities were calibrated by addition of known quantities of artificial radioactive spikes ($^{232}U - ^{228}Th$ in radioactive equilibrium). Chemical preparation followed the standard methods described in Bernat (1969) and Gascoyne (1977).

Sample	1A20
U (ppm)	0.301 ± 0.003
$^{234}U/^{238}U$	1.217 ± 0.014
$^{230}Th/^{234}U$	0.080 ± 0.006
$^{230}Th/^{232}Th$	3.4 ± 0.5
$[^{234}U/^{238}U]_{t=0}$	1.223
Age	9.0 (+0.7/–0.6) ka

Table 1: Results of the U/Th dating.

In a section through a travertine wall, a Roman potsherd of type 1A100 was found and was dated to the 1st-2nd century AD (Poblome, 1999). The travertine, in which this sherd was found, is therefore younger than 1800 yr. Some travertine sections were used for rock-cut tombs dated to the 4th to 6/7th century A.D. (Waelkens *et al.*, 1997). Hence, the fluvial system that formed these travertines probably was largely abandoned by this time. Section 1A was dated as being 9000 ± 600 yr old by the U/Th dating method (Table 1). We can conclude that travertine deposits were at least present in the valley of Başköy during the early Holocene, and that travertine precipitation was still active 1800 yr ago. Active deposition of travertine in this fluvial system had terminated 1350 yr ago.

6. CONCLUSION

A combined paludal and fluvial-barrage system can be recognized within the travertine deposits of Başköy. The travertine facies deposited in this system can be divided into three groups. Firstly, phytoherm framestone in which calcite precipitated inorganically around plants by degassing of turbulent waters in mountain streams or falls. Secondly, finely laminated travertine built up by calcite precipitates related to the activity of bacteria, blue-green algae, and larvae and by microdetrital calcite. They formed in ponds mainly during spring and summer. The ponds in which this travertine accumulated, were created by the damming of a stream through travertine precipitation and hence the formation of barrages. Other sections above and under such fluvial-barrage deposits show more the characteristics of paludal environments. Because of reworking of earlier deposited travertine, the third type, consisting of detrital travertine, was formed. Probably, the travertine formation was largely abandoned between 1550 and 1350 years ago. The existence of a larger fluvial system in the Başköy valley, still active in Imperial times, in the location of what is now the Ağlasun Çayı, a tributary of the Aksu river, the ancient Kestros river, may explain the depiction of this ancient Kestros on Imperial city coins. The Kestros formed the eastern boundary of the territory of Sagalassos from at the latest Hellenistic to early Byzantine times. It is not unlikely that the Sagalassians considered a major stream flowing in the Başköy and Ağlasun valleys already a part of this Kestros.

7. ACKNOWLEDGEMENTS

The research was supported by the Belgian Programme on Interuniversitary Poles of Attraction (IAP V/9) and the Research Fund of the K.U.Leuven (BOF-GOA02/2). We are grateful to Dr. M. Pedley and Dr. A. Janssen for constructive comments and suggestions.

8. REFERENCES

BERNAT, M. (1969) Utilisation des methodes basées sur le déséquilibre radioactive dans la géologie du Quaternaire. *Cahiers de l'ORSTOM, Série Géologique I* 2: 3-27.

CAUDWELL, C. (1983) Les rivulariacées actuelles: interprétation possible de la structure zonée des concrétions stromatolitiques à *Rivularia haematites*, *Geobios* 16: 169-177.

CHAFETZ, H.S. and FOLK, R.L. (1984) Travertines: depositional morphology and the bacterially constructed constituents, *Journal of Sedimentary Petrology* 54: 289-314.

EMEIS, K.L., RICHNOW, H.H. and KEMPE, S. (1987) Travertine formation in Plitvice National Park, Yugoslavia: chemical versus biological controls, *Sedimentology* 34: 595-609.

FORD, T.D. and PEDLEY, H.M. (1996) A review of tufa and travertine deposits of the world, *Earth Science Reviews* 41: 117-175.

GASCOYNE, G. (1977) *Uranium Series Dating of Speleothems: Analytical Procedure.* Department of Geology, McMaster University, Hamilton, Ontario, Canada.

GLOVER, C.P. and ROBERTSON, H.F. (1998) Role of regional extension and uplift in the Plio-Pleistocene evolution of the Aksu basin, SW Turkey, *Journal of the Geological Society* 155: 365-387.

GOLUBIC, S., VIOLANTE, C., FERRERI, V. and D'ARGENIO, B. (1993) Algal control and early diagenesis in Quaternary travertine formations, Rochetta a Volturno, Central Apennines, *Bollettino della Societa Paleontologica Italiana*, 1: 231-247.

GUO, L. and RIDING, R. (1994) Origin and diagenesis of Quaternary travertine shrub fabrics, Rapolano Terme, Central Italy, *Sedimentology* 41: 499-520.

GUO, L., ANDREWS, J., RIDING, R., DENNIS, P. and DRESSER, Q. (1996) Possible microbial effects on stable carbon isotopes in hot spring travertines, *Journal of Sedimentary Research* 66: 468-473.

OBENLÜNESCHLOB, J. (1991) *Biologie und Ökologie von drei rezenten Süßwasser-Rivularien (Cyanobakterien) – Übertragbarkeit artspezifischer Verkalkungsstrukturen auf fossile Formen, Göttinger Arbeitsblätter Geologie Paläontologie 50.*

PEDLEY, H.M. (1990) Classification and environmental models of cool freshwater tufas, *Sedimentary Geology* 68: 143-154.

POBLOME, J. (1999) *Red Slip Ware Produced at Sagalassos (southern Turkey). Typology and Chronology (Studies in Eastern Mediterranean Archaeology II)*, Brepols, Turnhout.

POESEN, J., GOVERS, G., PAULISSEN, E. and VANDAELE, K. (1995) A geomorphological evaluation of erosion risk at Sagalassos, in: M. WAELKENS and J. POBLOME (eds.) *Sagalassos III (Acta Archaeologica Lovaniensia Monographiae 7)*, Leuven University Press, Leuven, 341-355.

ROBERTSON, A.H.F. (1993) Mesozoic-Tertiary sedimentary and tectonic evolution of Neotethyan carbonate platforms, margins and small ocean basins in the Antalya Complex, southwest Turkey, in: L.E. FROSTICK and R.J. STEEL (eds.) *Tectonic Controls and Signatures in Sedimentary Successions (Special Publication of the International Association of Sedimentologists 20)*, Blackwell Scientific Publications, Oxford: 415-465.

ROUCHY, J.M., SERVANT, M., FOURNIER, M. and CAUSSE, C. (1996) Extensive carbonate algal bioherms in upper Pleistocene saline lakes of the Central Altiplano of Bolivia, *Sedimentology* 43: 973-993.

THIENEMANN, A. (1954) *Chironimus: Leben, Verbreitung und wirtschaftliche Bedeutung der Chironomiden*, Schweizerbartsche Verlagsbuchhandlung, Stuttgart.

WAELKENS, M., PAULISSEN, E., VANHAVERBEKE, H., ÖZTÜRK, I., DE CUPERE, B., EKINCI, H.A., VERMEERSCH, P.M., POBLOME, J. and DEGEEST R. (1997) The 1994 and 1995 surveys on the territory of Sagalassos, in: M. WAELKENS and J. POBLOME (eds.) *Sagalassos IV (Acta Archaeologica Lovaniensia Monographiae 9)*, Leuven University Press, Leuven: 11-102.

WAELKENS, M., PAULISSEN, E., VERMOERE, M., DEGRYSE, P., CELIS, D., SCHROYEN, K., DE CUPERE, B., LIBRECHT, I., NACKAERTS, K., VANHAVERBEKE, H., VIAENE, W., MUCHEZ, P., OTTENBURGS, R., DECKERS, S., VAN NEER, W., SMETS, E., GOVERS, G., VERSTRAETEN, G., STEEGEN, A. and CAUWENBERGHS, K. (1999) Man and Environment in the territory of Sagalassos, a classical city in SW Turkey, *Quaternary Science Reviews* 18: 697-709.

WEATHERING OF LIMESTONE IN THE HISTORICAL BUILDINGS OF SAGALASSOS

Patrick DEGRYSE, Marc WAELKENS, Peter VANDEVELDE, Philippe MUCHEZ
and Willy VIAENE[†]

1. INTRODUCTION

The historical buildings of the ancient city of Sagalassos are mainly constructed with local limestone that has been, more or less, weathered in the course of time. The topic of this paper handles the dependency of this weathering on burial conditions, the nature of the limestone, atmospheric circumstances and biological factors. Only limestone building stones are regarded in this study. To investigate the above mentioned relationships, it is necessary to obtain insight into the different weathering mechanisms, the nature of the surface and the weathering layers of limestone and the stability of the different types of limestone under different conditions.

2. MECHANISMS OF WEATHERING

2.1. Physical weathering

With physical weathering, the breaking down of rock through internal and external tension, caused by weathering factors, is meant. The latter can be frost wedging, exfoliation, grain disintegration and unloading (Wittow, 1988). With frost and thaw, water inside the pores of the rock appears either in a solid (ice) or a liquid phase. The freezing of pore water causes a volumetric expansion of about 9%. Together with the pressure increase caused by the decrease of the gas volume (air) in the capillaries behind the ice, this may fissure the stone or make it more susceptible to further weathering. Exfoliation is the process of pealing off the top layer of the stone. This is caused by the crystallization of salts from capillary groundwater through evapotranspiration of the rock. Identical pressures as with frost/thaw can be obtained during this process (Scott, 1996). Grain disintegration is caused by differential expansion and contraction of grains in the stone due to a different heat transfer capacity (Wittow, 1988). Unloading causes the expansion of rocks through a decrease in pressure on them. Due to climate conditions present at Sagalassos (Paulissen *et al.*, 1993), frost and thaw is the far most important factor in physical

weathering. Also the impact of grains carried by the wind may abrade the buildings.

2.2. Chemical weathering

Chemical weathering leads to the decomposition of solid rock through chemical reactions. This occurs through the decomposition of the constituting minerals or cements or through the formation of secondary minerals. Hydrolysis is a type of reaction in which the H^+ or OH^- ions of water replace ions of a mineral. Dissolution and dehydration are two simple reactions during which either minerals are dissolved or water is added to form hydrates (Krauskopf, 1979). Dissolution is the most important reaction in limestone, leading to so-called karstic phenomena of different sizes (Zonneveld, 1981). Karstic phenomena occurring in the area around Sagalassos are illustrated in Figures 1 to 3. Such phenomena may be responsible for the 4th century BC abandonment of the much larger Ur-Sagalassos, identified in 2005 at Tepe Düzen, in favour of the much smaller Hellenistic Sagalassos, and also other locations such as Kepez Kalesi, foritified during this period. Finally, oxidation is the process whereby oxygen reacts with (especially iron-bearing) minerals to form oxides and hydroxides.

2.3. Biological weathering

Organic or biological weathering comprises the deterioration of rock through the activity of fauna and flora. Examples are the mechanical disintegration caused by trees and their roots and the working of organic acids of plant materials. In our case, special attention is given to lichen on limestone.

Lichen are composed of two organisms in symbiosis: photosynthetic algae and a *fungus*. The body of the lichen is called the *thallus*. In the case of Sagalassos, only the crust shaped organisms are relevant. They live in close contact with the limestone, either epilithic (on the stone surface) or endolithic (attached with penetrating roots). The *thallus* is composed of three layers (Figure 4). The cortex is a protecting cover of gelatinous hyphen. The *medulla* is the

215

Figure 1: Karstic phenomena around the city of Sagalassos: rills of 1 cm deep and with a 2 cm spacing. Limestone surface at Çanaklı. Compass is 10 cm.

Figure 2: Karstic phenomena around the city of Sagalassos: limestone peak at Sarıkaya. Hammer is 30 cm.

Figure 3: Karstic phenomena around the city of Sagalassos: 'deckenkarren' on limestone at Sagalassos. Compass is 10 cm.

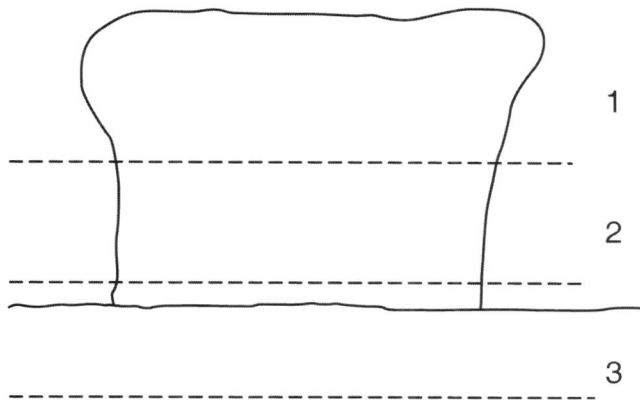

Figure 4: Structure of the thallus of lichen. 1: cortex, 2: algal layer, 3: medulla. The solid line represents the limestone surface.

main part of the body composed of interwoven hyphen of the fungus. The algal layer is composed of fungi-hyphen surrounding the algae. The three layers together are attached to the stone through roots or through hyphen on the stone surface.

The way lichen influence their substrate is a matter of discussion. Both mechanical and chemical processes act on the substrate. The biomechanical action consists of two mechanisms: root penetration in the substrate and expansion/contraction of the *thallus*. In dry conditions, the upper cortex of the lichen will contract, putting a tension on their entire body, which can rupture the *thallus* and disintegrate the rock surface. The biochemical weathering is induced by the chemical agent CO_2, oxalic acid and lichen-complexes. Since lichen hold water in their *thallus*, the normal chemical weathering processes can act longer. On top of this, CO_2 produced by lichen will influence the pH of the fluids acting, thus determining the solubility of limestone. The oxalic acid produced by the lichen, binds with calcium from the limestone, forming calcium-oxalates such as weddelite and whewellite (Blazquez *et al.*, 1995). According to Franzini (1995), oxalates rather protect than deteriorate buildings, keeping the stone from weathering through exfoliation or acid rain.

3. WEATHERING OF THE BUILDING STONES AT SAGALASSOS

The fact that some recently excavated limestone architectural fragments after a very short period already show severe frost damage is an acute problem at Sagalassos. Four buildings were studied: the late Antonine Nymphaeum (ca. 160-180 AD), the east side of the late Roman defence wall (ca. 400 AD), the Doric temple (late 1st century BC) and the theatre (late 2nd century AD). Microfissures and large cracks and fissures were investigated in several building elements.

3.1. The late Antonine nymphaeum

This building was erected during the reign of Marcus Aurelius, forming the northern extremity of the Upper Agora, thus exposing it to the sun the larger part of the day (Waelkens, 2002). As a result, the difference in temperature to which the monumental fountain was exposed during the summer and winter months was very high. Moreover, during the latter period, due to its location, on sunny but cold days, temperature differences may have fluctuated much. Corner stone 80, which formed the upper socle moulding of the podium of one of the aediculae (Figure 5), was investigated as it could be studied from two sides (east and south). The stone is a locally quarried beige limestone, to be found all around monumental Sagalassos in quarries in the Lycean nappes (Degryse *et al.*, this volume). It showed already severe damage after just one year of *in situ* exposure. The fissures measured are shown in Figure 6 and Table 1.

It is clear that most fissures are situated around the same N70E direction in the building block. This is probably a direction proper to the stone, in which water preferentially penetrated and which was a mechanical weakness in the block.

Number	Orientation
1	EW48N
2	N64E48S
3	N48E50N and N72E46S
4	N66E18S
5	N66E32S
6	N66E38S
7	N68W36N
8	N50E60N
9	N78W90
10	EW40N
11	N80E38N
12	EW46S
13	EW56N
14	N76E38N
15	NS60W
16	EW44N
17	N56E34N
18	N52W34N
19	N82W34N
20	N64W44N
21	N58E90
22	N64W3N

Table 1: Measurements of the fissures in block 80 of the late Antonine nymphaeum.

3.2. The late Roman defence wall

The Hellenistic circuit wall surrounding the city most likely was built during the late 3rd century BC (Waelkens, 2004). Only the western section of its northern stretch and part of the western half of the south wall, near the Hellenistic South Gate, were left standing. When ca. 400 AD a new wall had to be built to defend the city against Isaurian raids, the still standing wall sections of the Hellenistic defence wall were incorporated into its late Roman successor, which most probably used as much as possible the foundations of the Hellenistic predecessor and was mainly built of *spolia* or in other places mortared rubble (Waelkens, 2002). The campaign of 2007 even made clear that parts of the late Roman wall, e.g. near the Hellenistic South Gate were still rebuilt in the course of the 7th century AD, after the 540-620 AD earthquake, most probably as part of the fortified hamlet (7/8th-9th century AD) installed inside the former shrine of the Imperial cult. The wall section that was studied, was the east face of the late Roman circuit, built of *spolia*, between the northern part of the Northwest Gate and the northwest corner of the Northwest Heroon, incorporated and transformed into a tower, just like the Doric Temple near it. The nature of the monument that was spoliated to deliver the building material of this part of the structure is unknown. The stone, however, is a locally quarried beige limestone, to be found all around monumental Sagalassos in quarries in the Lycean nappes (Degryse *et al.*, this volume). The fissure pattern in the studied section of the defence wall, is shown in Figure 7 and Table 2. Here again, most fissures are related to the geological properties of the building stone: all cracks are situated around diaclase patterns and stylolites.

3.3. The Doric temple

This sanctuary was most probably built during the late 1st century BC (perhaps under the short rule of the Galatian King Amyntas) and dedicated to Zeus. It occupies a klippe at the highest point in the northwestern part of the city. This location made its limestone building material, originating from the Sarıkaya quarry near the village of Başköy (Degryse *et al.*, this volume), extremely vulnerable to changing temperatures and to wind erosion. This explains why the intense pattern of cracks on the west face of the temple was initially thought to be frost damage. However, since the cracks continue through adjoining stones, this cannot be the result of frost damage, as structural weaknesses in the stones involved will have a random orientation in the building. Moreover, the fissure pattern is located at one specific place in the outer face of the wall, whereas its interior is almost not affected by damage at all. This is never the case in buildings where frost damage can be clearly

Number	Orientation
1	N80E90
2	N6E90
3	Subhorizontal
4	N52E56N
5	N22W80S
6	N54E56N
7	N28W85S
8	N80W3S
9	N30E90
10	N60E90
11	N58E90 and N50W90
12	N60E90
13	N52W65N
14	N58E72N
15	N60W
16	EW50N
17	EW10S
18	N85W60S

Table 2: Measurements of the fissures in the late Hellenistic defense wall.

identified. Therefore, the most straightforward explanation for the fissures is a fire, affecting the surface of the wall. It is known that for example stones in a campfire will be affected by the flames and will fissure through the action of the heat. As in contrast with the opposite eastern face of the building, where early Byzantine structures abutted the temple, no structure except the late Roman wall itself, in which the temple was incorporated, ever existed against the west face of the sanctuary, the nature of such fire is uncertain. The most plausible explanation seems that part of the upper structure of the tower into which the temple was transformed ca. 400 AD collapsed along the western face of the building, possible during the 540-620 AD earthquake. The excavations of the Doric Temple revealed that during its transformation into a tower the original roof was removed, whereas eight pilasters made of volcanic tuff blocks and brick layers were built against the inner side of the lateral walls. These pilasters must have supported a timber floor for defendants of the tower, possible located above the original entablature of the temple. The latter is

	Sector 1	Sector 2	Sector 3	Sector 4
Number of benches	17	6	9	9
chert height (mm)				
Mean height	12.7	12.1	10.0	7.3
Mean of maximum	15.9	13.3	12.9	9.5
Range	3.4-21.1	4.2-18.5	4.7-17.4	3.2-18.1

Table 3: Elevation of the cherts above the limestone surface of the benches.

still preserved to the course of blocks just below the original triglyph and metope frieze. As no holes for a floor structure in timber are visible up to this height, the original height of the shrine may have been reused considerably using *spolia*. One may also assume the presence of a roof above the tower, using much timber as well. If parts of these new additions collapsed to the west side of the temple, a fire may have destroyed this collapse and affected the adjoining outer face of the remaining part of the west wall.

3.4. The theatre

The theatre of Sagalassos occupies the highest point of the settlement in the northeastern part of it. The stage building must have been completed in the late Antonine to early Severan period (Waelkens, 2002), but the actual *cavea* or *auditorium* must be older. As the seats of this *cavea* were supported by Roman concrete, in its western part in its turn supported by large arcaded and vaulted exposed wall sections, and as the first known concrete thus far was used at Sagalassos in the Trajanic nymphaeum on the Lower Agora, a 2nd century AD date for the *cavea* seems most likely. Although it could have been completely installed into a natural (?) cavity in the hill slope it was turned towards the southwest, so that the above mentioned enormous vaulted wall sections made of ashlars became necessary. The reason for this clearly was the intention to make the hill upon which Alexander the Great had defeated the Sagalassians in 333 BC would be visible above the exceptionally only one storied stage building. These two unusual architectural features included this flat conical hill, which perhaps carried a commemorative monument, next to a shrine for a female goddess as part of the *vista* for those occupying the upper *maenianum* of the seats. Due to its location and the fact that the stage building was only half the height of the *cavea*, the upper part of the latter was totally unprotected against severe weather conditions. The limestone used for its seats represented two different types of local limestone. In fact, the western part of the *cavea* is constructed using limestone building blocks with chert fragments, while in

the eastern part of the theatre limestone without cherts is used. Both types originate from the local Lycean nappes around the monumental city (Degryse *et al.*, this volume; Muchez *et al.*, this volume). The chert fragments (mainly silica), weather much slower than the limestone (mainly calcite) in which they occur. The cherts form outstanding knots on the limestone. The height of the cherts was measured, to obtain an insight in the rate of weathering since the construction of the building. The building blocks in which the cherts were measured, are indicated on Figure 8. The data are presented in Table 3. The building blocks are recorded into different sectors, to study the influence of their orientation on the weathering process.

Analysis of the data in Table 3 shows that the cherts have different characteristics in different sectors. Only sectors one and two are similar. A gradual increase in height of the cherts, and thus in amount of calcite weathered away, can be seen from sector four to one. This can be partly due to the predominant direction of the wind at Sagalassos, coming from the east and carrying dust which may weather limestone.

This wind has a direct impact in sectors one and two, while its influence is less in sectors three and four. This wind erosion was one factor, erosion from rain another. The results of the latter can be seen on the blocks as small pits of 2 cm diameter in the stone.

The choice of two different types of limestone for the theatre seats, whereby those of the eastern half of the *cavea*, that were rather well protected against the wind, did not contain any chert at all, and where in the western half of the *cavea*, that was totally exposed to the wind, a type of limestone was chosen containing chert fragments that are more resistant to wind erosion than the calcite matrix in which they are set, may have been deliberate. Such choice would bear testimony to the skill and knowledge of the architects who planned the structure and must have chosen in the quarries different types of limestone that were best

Figure 5: Photograph of the east (A) and south (B) side of building block 80 from the late Antonine Nymphaeum.

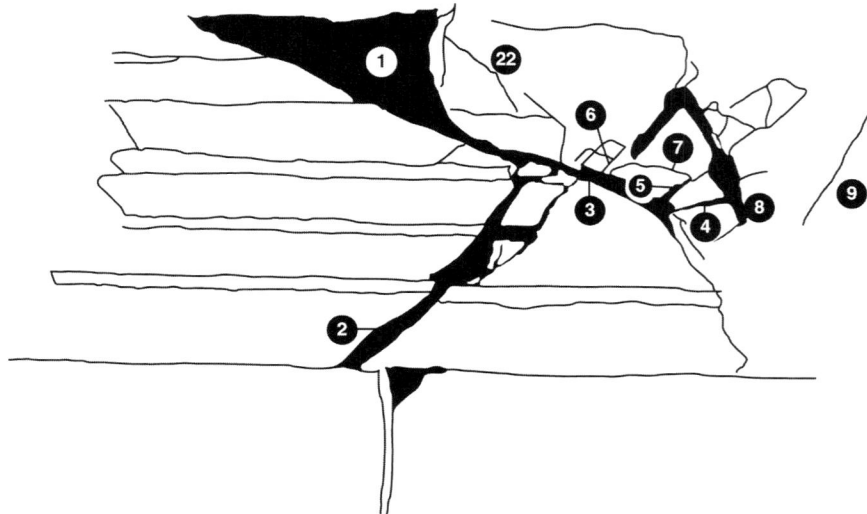

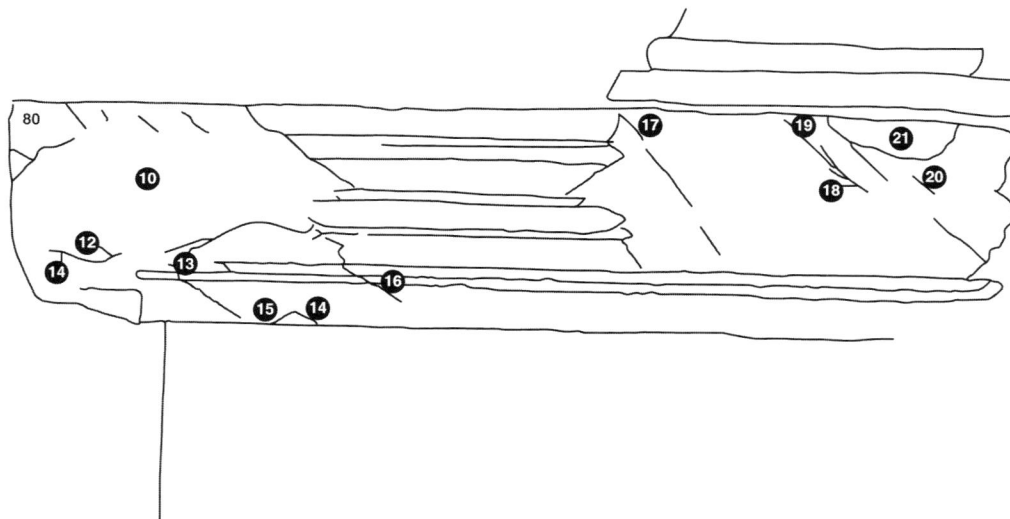

Figure 6: Drawing of the fissures in the east (A) and south (B) side of block 80.

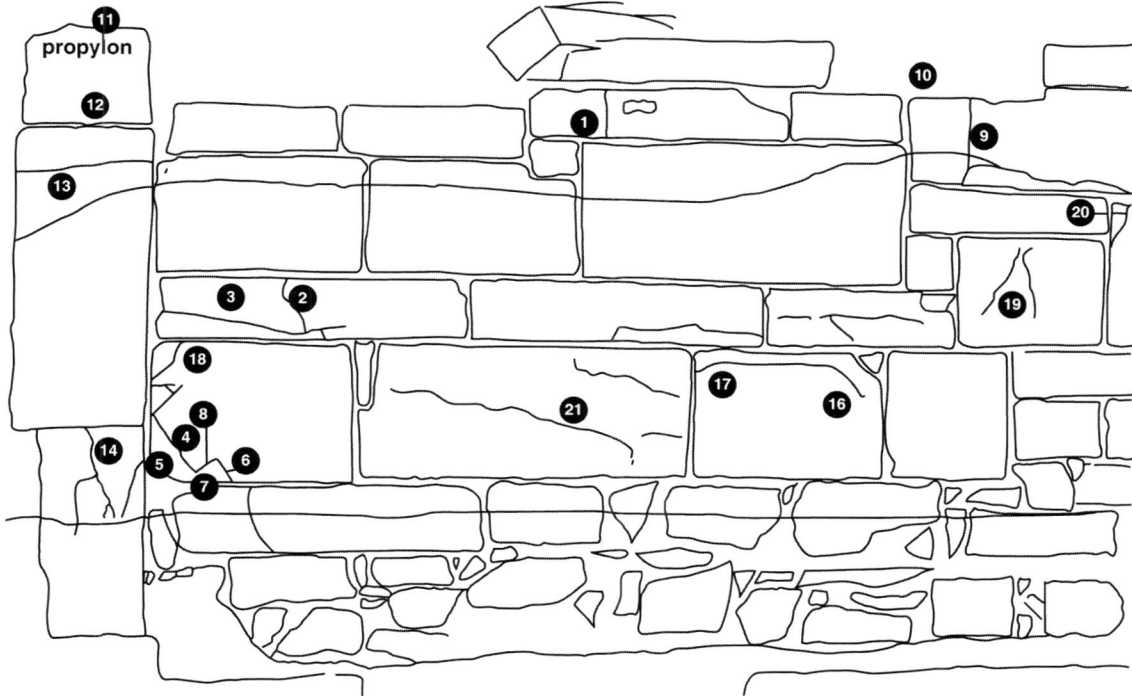

Figure 7: Drawing of the fissures in the late Roman defense wall.

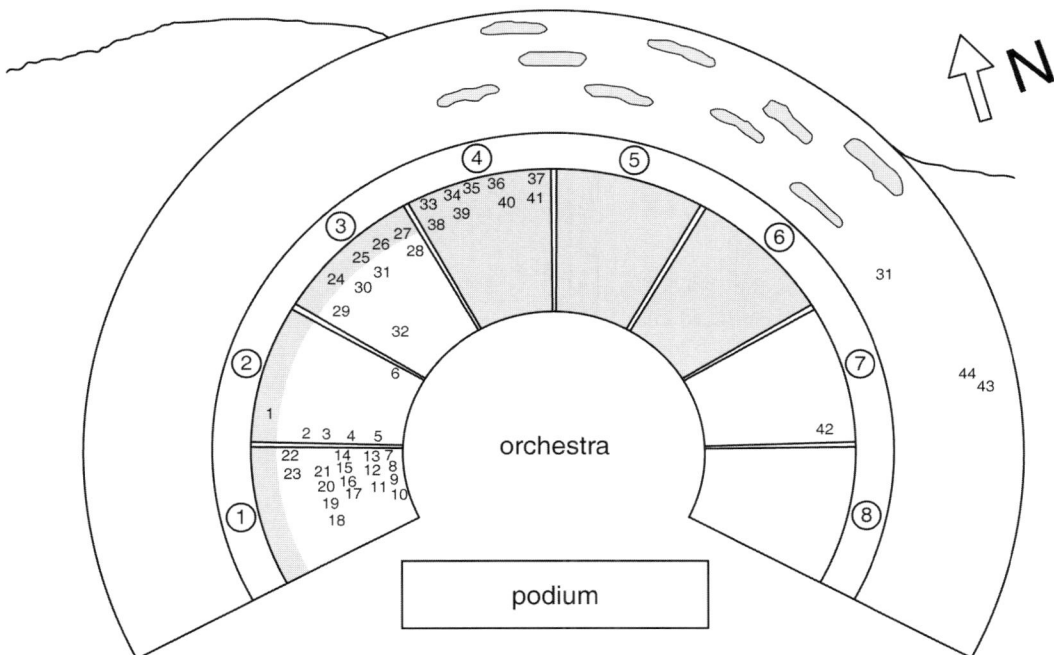

Figure 8: Drawing and identification of the building blocks of the theatre in which the height of the cherts was measured as given in Table 3. Circled numbers define the sectors of the theatre.

suited for the position which they would eventually occupy in the theatre.

4. MINERALOGY AND PETROGRAPHY OF THE WEATHERING PRODUCTS

4.1. Weathering residues from stylolites and fissures

Weathering residues from fissures in building blocks in the limestone of the late Antonine nymphaeum were studied using X-ray diffractometry. The operational parameters of the Philips diffractometer were: Cu K_α radiation, 45 kV, 30 mA, automatic divergence slit. The weathering residue from corner stone 80 of the nymphaeum, the upper moulding of the podium supporting an aedicula, contained smectite, chlorite and kaolinite. Also quartz, calcite and feldspars can be identified. As clays are abundant in the fissures of the limestone building elements, the retention of water in these blocks is enhanced. At the same time, swelling clays such as smectite may also contribute to pressures needed to crack limestone. The clay residues in the limestone are similar in mineralogy to 'terra rossa'. The presence of 'terra rossa' in the Mediterranean is widely described (Atalay, 1997; Darwish and Zurayk, 1997). The red colour is attributed to the presence of fine hematite (Yaalon, 1997). The abundance of kaolinite is regarded as the remains of palaeo-soil formation during the Tertiary and the warm, humid periods of the Quaternary (Atalay, 1997; Darwish and Zurayk, 1997). The importance of karstic phenomena for the formation of such 'terra rossa' is stressed by Atalay (1997), as the broken structure of the limestone leads to abnormal circulations of water and air, favouring the strong weathering of the limestone material. Karstic phenomena are abundant in the territory of Sagalassos.

4.2. Oxalates and lichen

Samples of building elements from the Late Antonine Nympaeum, the late Roman defence wall and the *cavea* of the theatre, covered with lichen, were impregnated with a resin, avoiding damaging the weathering surface. Subsequently, polished sections were made from the impregnated samples. These were studied under incident, polarized light with an Olympus BX 60 microscope. Both epilithic and endolithic lichen could be identified. The former do not have any significant effect on the substrate, whereas the latter clearly show a weathering zone of up to 800 um thick into the limestone. This layer is very porous and the lichen preferentially grow in stylolites or small fissures (e.g. Blazquez *et al.*, 1995), which characterize the above mentioned structures. A mineralogical study of the weathering layer around the lichen was made with X-ray

Test object	E-modulus (Gpa)	Sample
1	49.8	37
2	32.6	37
3	80.8	34
4	89.5	N387
5	82.1	N387
6	70.6	29
7	78.4	29
8	51.6	27a
9	57.4	27a
10	73.3	27a
11	67.8	27a
12	75.4	27a

Table 4: Elastic modulus of the building stone test objects.

diffractometry. The oxalates whewellite ($CaC_2O_4.H_2O$) and weddellite ($CaC_2O_4.2H_2O$) are clearly present. An increase in the abundance of weddelitte towards the unweathered rock can be seen. This can be explained through the higher temperatures and thus dehydration that occurs on the surface of the stone. It has been proposed by Franzini (1995) that these oxalate layers rather protect than damage the stone, as this layer preserves the stone from further physical and chemical weathering.

5. PHYSICAL TESTING OF LIMESTONE BUILDING ELEMENTS

5.1. Elastic modulus

The elastic modulus (E-modulus) of limestone building elements from the Late Antonine Nympaeum and the late Roman defence wall is determined using a Grindo-Sonic device. This measures the resonance-oscillation of the object and compares it to a reference quartz crystal. The test objects should be minimal 6 cm long and at least three times longer than the height of the test object. This method is further explained by Ottenburgs *et al.* (1993). Five different building elements were tested using different test blocks from the same stone (Table 4). It was striking that different test objects from the same sample sometimes showed a large difference in E-modulus. This is due to inherent weaknesses in the building stones, such as stylolites and small fissures.

Stone type	Porosity	E-modulus
Sagalassos limestone (this study)	–	67GPa
Sagalassos limestone (Viaene et al., 1993)	1%	72GPa
Visean Meuse-limestone	1%	70GPa
Visean Longpré-limestone	1%	70GPa
Carrara Bianco marble	0.3%	60GPa
White Naxos marble	0.3%	36GPa

Table 5: Comparison of the elastic modulus of ancient building stone test objects with modern building stone.

The porosity of several limestone building elements and samples of the limestone outcrops around the monumental centre at Sagalassos was determined by Viaene *et al.* (1993) and measured on average 1 percent. If we compare the E-modulus and porosity of the test objects to that of several excellent modern building stones (Table 5; WTCB, 1997), we can conclude that the Lycean limestone of Sagalassos is in general, on a micro- to meso-scale, a good, frost resistant building stone. However, the presence of fissures and stylolites on a macro-scale, noticed in many buildings and structures, will weaken it and make it susceptible to frost damage.

5.2. Heating tests

Test blocks of the same samples studied for their E-modulus were heated in a Prolabo-oven to a temperature of 500° C in one hour time and then cooled to room temperature. This cycle was repeated 20 times. After each cycle, the E-modulus of the test objects was measured. All samples showed a decrease in E-modulus, most of all in the first cycle (Table 6). Thereafter the decrease in E-modulus stabilized. All test objects remained intact after heating.

5.3. Frost and thaw cycles

Test objects of the same samples previously studied were saturated with water, frozen to -20° C for one night and then defrosted at room temperature. This cycle was repeated 25 times. After all cycles were complete, the E-modulus of the test objects was measured (Table 7). No objects were destroyed in this testing. Only a slight change in E-modulus could be observed. Thus, on the scale of the test objects, the Lycean limestone used as building elements, are frost resistant. The currently visible frost damage in the building stones is hence caused by the presence of fissures (possibly filled with clays) or stylolites, retaining water in the stone and thus representing a weak spot in the limestone that is very sensitive to frost weathering.

6. CONCLUSION

In the vicinity of the city of Sagalassos, many karstic phenomena can be observed in the limestone bedrock. In the city of Sagalassos itself, frost damage in limestone building blocks can be observed, mainly along weaknesses such as stylolites and fissures, inherent to the stone proper. This frost damage is caused by pressure build-up, when water partly retained by clays in the fissures freezes and the volumetric expansion of the ice and the pressure of the gasses trapped behind the latter make the stone crack. Other forms of weathering observed on building stones of Sagalassos were mainly of biological nature. The growth of lichen on building stones exposed for centuries, forms a weathering layer of maximum 800 um thick, in which oxalates are formed. This oxalate weathering layer is thought to protect the stone from further physical and chemical weathering rather than to damage it. The effect of wind erosion can be seen in the theatre, where building blocks were abraded by wind carrying dust. The physical properties of the Lycean limestone show that of a generally good, frost-resistant material on a micro- to meso-scale. However, on a larger scale, weaknesses such as stylolites and fissures, may weaken the stone and form a basis for weathering of the building blocks, as was the case with excavated structures such as the late Antonine nymphaeum and the late Roman city wall. Yet, the careful selection of different types of limestone for carving the seats of the *cavea* of the theatre, whereby the selected stone was well suited to withstand the wind erosion according to the exact location where it would be used in the enormous structure, seems to indicate that at least some architects were aware of the weathering weakness of the limestone, which they eventually selected. For such a massive structure, a long-distance import of bulky building elements was impossible. Yet, by carefully selecting the locally available types of limestone, they made the best of the situation, taking into account the kind of erosion that the stone would be submitted to in its final location.

Cycle	Test object 1	Test object 7	Test object 9	Test object 11
0	49.8	70.6	51.6	74.9
1	22.5	48.6	21.3	61.8
2	21.4	47.1	24.0	60.7
3	20.5	45.4	18.2	58.5
4	19.7	45.1	22.9	56.5
5	19.2	44.8	18.5	53.6
6	18.7	44.4	20.0	53.6
7	18.7	44.1	19.3	53.6
8	18.7	43.5	17.7	53.6
9	18.3	43.2	18.3	52.7
10	18.3	42.9	18.0	52.7
11	18.0	42.0	18.0	52.7
12	17.3	40.8	18.0	51.8
13	16.9	40.5	17.4	51.8
14	16.9	38.6	15.0	51.0
15	16.7	38.9	15.4	50.1
16	16.3	38.9	15.3	50.1
17	16.2	38.6	14.8	50.1
18	15.9	37.9	14.3	50.1
19	15.5	37.6	15.1	49.3
20	15.3	37.4	14.4	48.5

Table 6: Elastic modulus of the test objects during the heating test cycles.

Sample	E-modulus (Before frost in GPa)	E-modulus (After frost in GPa)
N387	86.8	81.9
N387b	82.2	80.5
27a	71.1	69.8
29	72.5	74.4
34	73.5	72.7
37	61.6	60.7

Table 7: Elastic modulus of the test objects after all cycles of frost-thaw testing.

7. ACKNOWLEDGEMENTS

This research was supported through the QuarryScapes project (contract no. 015416 of EU FP6 STREP-INCO programme) and by the Belgian Programme on Interuniversitary Poles of Attraction (IAP V/9 and VI/22). The text also presents the results of projects of the Special Research Fund of the K.U.Leuven (BOF-GOA02/2 and GOA07/2). The authors would like to thank Raoul Ottenburgs, Etienne Paulissen and Lieven Loots for stimulating discussions on various aspects of this research. Herman Nijs kindly prepared the thin sections.

8. REFERENCES

ATALAY, I. (1997) Red Mediterranean soils in some karstic regions of the Taurus mountains, Turkey, *Catena* 28: 247-260.

BLAZQUEZ, F., CALVET, F. and VENDRELL, M. (1995) Lichenic alteration and mineralization in calcareous monuments of northeastern Spain, *Geomicrobiology Journal* 13: 223-247.

DARWISH, T.M. and ZURAYK, R.A. (1997) Distribution and nature of Red Mediterranean soils in Lebanon along an altitudinal sequence, *Catena* 28: 191-202.

DEGRYSE, P., HELDAL, T., BLOXAM, E., STOREMYR, P., WAELKENS, M. and MUCHEZ, PH. (this volume) The Sagalassos quarry landscape: bringing stone quarries in context, in: P. DEGRYSE and M. WAELKENS (eds.) *Sagalassos VI. Geo- and Bio-Archaeology at Sagalassos and in its Territory*, Leuven University Press, Leuven: 261-290.

EASTON, R.M. (1996) Lichen-rock mineral interactions: an overview, in: J.M. MC INTOSH and L.A. GROAT (eds.) *Biological-Mineralogical Interactions (Mineralogical Association of Canada Short Course 25)*, 209-230.

FRANZINI, M. (1995) Stones in monuments: natural and anthropogenic deterioration of marble artifacts, *European Journal of Mineralogy* 7: 735-743.

KRAUSKOPF, K.B. (1979) *Introduction to Geochemistry*, McGraw-Hill.

MUCHEZ, PH., LENS, S., DEGRYSE, P., CALLEBAUT, K., DEDEREN, M., HERTOGEN, J., JOACHIMSKI, M., KEPPENS, E., OTTENBURGS, R., SCHROYEN, K. and WAELKENS, M. (this volume) Petrography, mineralogy and geochemistry of the rocks in the area of the archaeological site of Sagalassos, in: P. DEGRYSE and M. WAELKENS (eds.) *Sagalassos VI. Geo- and Bio-Archaeology at Sagalassos and in its Territory*, Leuven University Press, Leuven: 25-52.

OTTENBURGS, R., VIAENE, W. and JORISSEN, C. (1993) Mineralogy and firing properties of clays at and near the archaeological site of Sagalassos, in: M. WAELKENS and J. POBLOME (eds.) *Sagalassos II (Acta Archaeologica Lovaniensia Monographiae 6)*, Leuven University Press, Leuven: 209-220.

PAULISSEN, E., POESEN, J., GOVERS, G. and DE PLOEY, J. (1993) The physical environment at Sagalassos (Western Taurus, Turkey). A reconnaissance survey, in: M. WAELKENS and J. POBLOME (eds.) *Sagalassos II (Acta Archaeologica Lovaniensia Monographiae 6)*, Leuven University Press, Leuven: 229-248.

SCOTT, R.C. (1996) *Physical Geography*, West Publishing Company, London.

VIAENE, W., OTTENBURGS, R., MUCHEZ, PH. and WAELKENS, M. (1993) The building stones of Sagalassos, in: M. WAELKENS (ed.) *Sagalassos I (Acta Archaeologica Lovaniensia Monographiae 5)*, Leuven University Press, Leuven: 85-92.

WAELKENS, M. (2002) Romanization in the East. A case study: Sagalassos and Pisidia (SW Turkey), *Istanbuler Mitteilungen* 52: 311-368.

WAELKENS, M. (2004) Ein blick von der Ferne. Seleukiden und Attaliden in Pisidien, *Istanbuler Mitteilungen* 54: 435-471.

WHITTOW, J. (1998) *Dictionary of Physical Geography*, Penguin Books, London.

WTCB (1997) *Natuursteen (Technische Voorlichtingen 205)*, WTCB, Brussel.

YAALON, D.H. (1997) Soils in the Mediterranean region: what makes them differ? *Catena* 28: 157-169.

ZONNEVELD, J.I.S. (1981) *Vormen in het Landschap. Hoofdlijnen van de Geomorfologie*, Het Spectrum, Antwerpen.

PART IV

EXPLOITATION OF LOCAL RESOURCES AND THE IMPORT OF SUBSISTENCE GOODS

CLAYS FOR MASS PRODUCTION OF TABLE AND COMMON WARES, AMPHORAE AND ARCHITECTURAL CERAMICS AT SAGALASSOS

Patrick DEGRYSE and Jeroen POBLOME

1. INTRODUCTION

An exploration of the eastern part of Sagalassos in 1987, revealed the artisanal quarter of the town (Mitchell and Waelkens, 1988). The so-called potters' quarter (Figure 1), located between the theatre in the west and a Hellenistic tower in the east, comprises an area of several hectares, still littered with ceramic waste. It forms one of the few located artisanal quarters in the Roman East still accessible for modern research.

One concentration of dumped material was studied on the surface in 1988 (Mitchell *et al.*, 1989). That season, the first samples were collected for preliminary archaeometrical analyses. A small-scale rescue excavation was undertaken in 1989 at Site D in the western part of the potters' quarter (Waelkens *et al.*, 1990). Site F, in the northern part of the quarter, was one of the three sites where regular, planned excavations started in 1990 (Waelkens *et al.*, 1991). This excavation was continued in 1991 (Waelkens *et al.*, 1992). The excavations at sites D and F confirmed the existence of a local pottery industry through the finding of large quantities of dumped material. The classification, identification and dating of these products followed immediately. The typo-chronological studies of both the table and common wares were largely based on the excavations in the urban centre of Sagalassos (Poblome, 1999; Degeest, 2000). At the same time, a complementary full-scale archaeometrical programme was initiated with the aim of fingerprinting the local production and reconstructing the production technology (Ottenburgs *et al.*, 1993a, b; Viaene *et al.*, 1993, 1995a, b). While initial research was mainly aimed at finding the resources of the local table ware or Sagalassos red slip ware (SRSW), later research also investigated predecessors of SRSW (Poblome *et al.*, 2002) as well as the raw materials for common wares (Degryse *et al.*, 2000, 2003).

2. CHARACTERISATION OF WARE GROUPS

Fabric classification of the excavated pottery followed the system introduced by Peacock (1977). Six fabrics (at Saga-lassos) were considered, on archaeological grounds, to be locally made (Poblome, 1999; Degeest, 2000). A provenance study was carried out by archaeometrical analysis. Other, non-local ware groups were also characterised (Poblome, 1999; Degeest, 2000), but form no part this study. The different fabrics were related to different functional groups. Fabrics 1 and 11 were used for the local tableware or SRSW, including a series of closed vessels. Fabric 2 was mainly used for medium to large size storage vessels, fabric 3 for architectural ceramics such as bricks, tiles and water pipes, fabric 4 for cooking vessels, jars and amphorae and fabric 5 for large storage vats or pithoi. Mass production of pottery began (at Sagalassos) in the early Imperial period and continued without interruption, albeit possibly on a different scale from the end of the sixth century AD onwards, into the eighth century AD. A late Hellenistic predecessor of SRSW was identified (Poblome, 1999), whereas other ware groups, which are mostly residual in later contexts, can be attributed to the early Hellenistic period (Poblome, 2006). The following macroscopic descriptions were made by Poblome (1999) for fabrics 1 and 11 and by Degeest (2000) for the other fabrics.

The fabric of SRSW, or fabric group 1 (Poblome, 1999 and Degeest, 2000: 79), can be described macroscopically as follows. The colour of the core is usually 2.5R 5/6 red on the Munsell soil colour chart. If margins are present, which is the case only with larger vessels, the colour is 5YR 6/6 reddish yellow. The fabric is normally hard, i.e. it cannot be scratched with a fingernail. The feel is smooth and the fracture is conchoidal to smooth. No inclusions are visible, with the exception of very small voids and occasionally white limestone inclusions for larger vessels. The slip varies considerably in colour.

Macroscopically the late Hellenistic fabric 11 (Poblome *et al.*, 2000, 2002) is hard to distinguish from the mass produced fabric 1. The distinction is based on the appearance of the slip, which is very thin with a watery appearance, varying in colour from a darker reddish-brown to reddish orange. The exterior bottom part is occasionally not slipped, while a part on the rim can be accentuated

SAGALASSOS

100m

Necropolis

Potters' quarter

1. Theater
2. Doric fountain
3. Neon library
4. Upper Agora
5. Lower Agora
6. Doric temple
7. Antonine nymphaeum
8. North-West Heroon
9. Tiberian Gate
10. Bouleuterion
11. Early-Byzantine basilica
12. Roman baths
13. Odeon
14. Macellum
15. Domestic Area 1
16. Temple of Apollo Klarios
17. Colonnaded street
18. Temple of Hadrian and Antoninus Pius
19. Basilica E1 in the former stadion
20. Hadrianic nymphaeum

Alexander's Hill

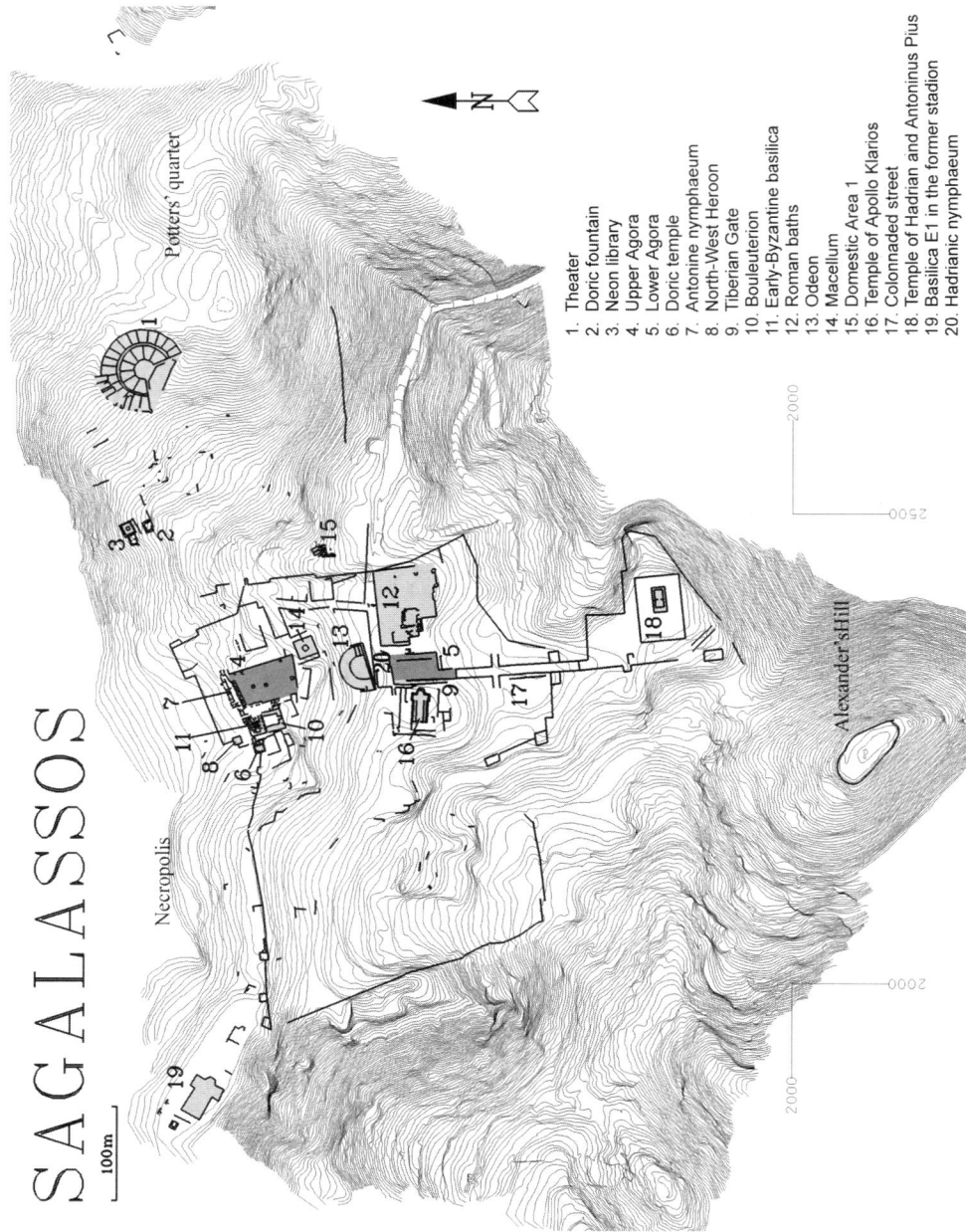

Figure 1: Location of the potters' quarter within the city of Sagalassos (Figure F. Martens).

by a band of a darker slip. The slip of fabric 1 is much thicker and more uniform, with a typical bright orange-red colour during Imperial times. Fabric 11 tends to be softer and more buff than fabric 1.

Fabric group 2 (Degeest, 2000: 81), the buff wares, is limited to storage containers of medium to large size, and basins, often *mortaria* of some kind. The main fabric colour is a homogeneous 5YR 6/6 reddish yellow on the Munsell Soil Colour Charts. The paste is sometimes powdery. Due to the inclusions the feel is rough and the fracture is hackly. The surface of these vessels is normally wiped.

Fabric group 3 (Degeest, 2000: 83) comprises the architectural ceramics. The core colour is 5YR 6/6 reddish yellow to 10R 6/6 light red, and occasionally even 10R 5/6 red. The consistency varies between soft and hard. The feel is generally rough and the fracture is hackly. Inclusions are characteristically dull white and grey with an average size of 1mm in diameter, but larger ones, up to 5 mm, are not rare. The frequency of the inclusions is moderate and the filler is well sorted. The inclusions are angular. A partial slip is sometimes present on the exterior. If present, the slip colour is 10R 5/8 red to 2.5YR 5/6 red. Even when slipped, the filler remains normally visible on the exterior and interior surface. The exterior is often smoothed.

After fabric 1, fabrics 3 and 4 are the most common ones in Sagalassos. The essential types of this fabric can be classified under building ceramics for fabric 3 and two headings for fabric 4, namely kitchen wares of all kinds and amphorae (Poblome *et al.*, 2008). The core colour varies between 2.5R 4/8 red and 5YR 5/6 yellowish red. Surfaces are between 2.5YR 5/8 red and 5YR 6/6 reddish yellow. The consistency can be described as hard to very hard. The feel is rough to harsh, sometimes powdery. The fracture is always hackly. The frequency of the inclusions is sparse to moderate. The inclusions are mostly dull white and dark red, but on rare occasions there are also shiny yellow or shiny black ones. Surface treatment can be wiped or smoothed.

Fabric 5 (Degeest, 2000: 86) is mostly limited to large dolia or *pithoi* or storage vessels. Chronologically this fabric is found throughout the Roman period, but with a concentration from the fifth to the seventh centuries. The ware has a distinctive reddish brown colour. The core is normally 2.5YR 5/6 red, while the surface is often 2.5YR 5/4 reddish brown.

3. CERAMIC THEORY AND CLAY RESOURCES

The availability of clay resources is the most obvious factor favouring the development of pottery production. The essential resources needed for pottery are clay, water and fuel for firing. Temper is not as necessary since most naturally occurring clays contain some non-plastics. If the raw material is too plastic however, the potter may need to add some non-plastics to improve workability, to counteract shrinkage, to facilitate drying and to manipulate firing properties (Shepard, 1956; Rye, 1976).

A close relationship exists between the ability of a population to exploit a resource profitably and the amount of energy necessary for this exploitation (Jarman, 1972). Energy expenditure is closely related to the distance of the resource. Several authors (Jarman, 1972; Higgs and Vita-Finzi, 1972; Jarman *et al.*, 1972) developed the concept that an archaeological site occupies a position within an exploitable territory and has certain economic possibilities according to its location. How does this model apply to ceramic resources? Arnold (1985), using ethnological evidence, showed that the geodesic distance from settlements to clay resources is between 1 and 50 km. The preferred territory of exploitation most probably occurs at 1 km because the most distances to clay resources in his set of cases is 1 km or less. Eighty-four percent of these distances are within 7 km and this probably represents the upper limit of the range of profitable exploitation (Arnold, 1985). The distances to temper resources are very similar. These range from less than 1 km to 25 km. The 1 km range is probably the preferred exploitation distance. Ninety-seven percent of the set of case-studies obtain their temper within 7 to 9 km around the production site, suggesting that this is the upper limit of the range of profitable temper exploitation (Arnold, 1985). As for the slip, the potters needed smaller quantities compared to the quantity of clay for the body and could therefore expend more energy obtaining the required resources. 57% of the case studies of Arnold (1985) obtain their slip resources at 30 km or less. Pheric distance (the distance to be crossed effectively – not as the crow flies) is probably a more useful measure of distance because it includes some correction for different factors such as topography and more closely reflects energy costs. Thus, in mountain areas, such as in the case of Sagalassos, more time is needed to traverse a certain geodesic distance than in a fluvial plain. The type of transportation available may also affect the distances for profitable exploitation. Transportation such as pack animals or oxen carts would reduce the total energy cost by greatly increasing the amount of clay or temper obtained in one journey (Arnold, 1985).

Based on this theoretical model, the area around Sagalassos was surveyed for likely clay sources for body and slip of the local wares. Several promising sources were sampled in an area of approximately 15 km around (the city centre of) Sagalassos (Figure 2). All interesting and relevant (large enough) clay deposits present were sampled and investigated. For the locally produced ware fabric groups, the ceramics were compared to the locally available clay raw materials identified in the geological survey. The comparison between the ceramics and the clay raw materials is based on a mineralogical and geochemical study of the clay and ceramics as a bulk material and a similar study of their constituent minerals.

The mineral content of the ceramics and the clays was determined by X-Ray Diffractometry (XRD) and the study of thin sections. The amounts of the different minerals were determined by image analysis and by visual estimation. Chemical components SiO_2, Al_2O_3, Fe_2O_3, MgO, CaO, P_2O_5 and TiO_2 were determined by Atomic Emission Spectrometry (AES). Na_2O and K_2O contents were measured from the same solution through Atomic Absorption Spectrometry (AAS). With the exception of the Loss On Ignition (LOI), all results are expressed as weight percentage of oxides. Trace element analysis was performed by X-Ray Fluorescence (XRF) or Neutron Activation Analysis (NAA as described by Hertogen and Gijbels, 1971). To enable a valid comparison between clays and sherds, the chemical composition of the clays was rescaled by putting the sum of the non-volatile oxides equal to one hundred percent, since a large part of the volatile components of the clays disappear during firing and the resulting ceramics no longer contain them (Ottenburgs et al., 1993a).

4. THE CLAY RAW MATERIALS

The different sources sampled around Sagalassos are indicated on Figure 2. Samples taken by Ottenburgs et al. (1993a) are specified in the text. The remainder was sampled within the framework of this study. Three of the six sets of samples fall within the 7 to 9 km ranges proposed by Arnold (1985) as the threshold for profitable raw material exploitation. A first set of samples was taken in several boreholes and sondages in the potters' quarter of Sagalassos. The 13 samples were taken at a depth of 0.5 m in the weathering horizon of the ophiolitic bedrock for the boreholes and on the ophiolitic rock for the sondages. Below the upper layers containing limestone and pottery fragments, indicating disturbance of the layers, a weathered red to green shale to red sticky clay is present (Ottenburgs et al., 1993a). These lower layers are residual material from the weathering of the ophiolitic bedrock present at this location. A second

set of 8 samples was taken from detrital clays present in and around the area of Köyünü and in the valleys of Ağlasun and Yazır. These clays are red to yellow detrital clays resulting from the weathering of the flysch deposits in the area. They consist of clays from alluvial fans and terraces of a palaeo-river. A third set of samples was taken from three promising sites in the Çanaklı valley which is situated at some 11 km to the south-east of Sagalassos. Pottery is still being produced in the village. 11 samples were collected from clay layers on the slopes south-east in this area. They consisted of brown-yellow to dark red sedimentary-residual clays from weathered shales, with a poor plasticity (Ottenburgs et al., 1993a). Another site for sampling was closer to Sagalassos at about 8 km south of it, in the intramontane valley north-west of the village of Çanaklı which is filled with lake-deposited clays (Ottenburgs et al., 1993a). Brown, green and red detrital clays (11 samples) with sandy intercalations and some pebbles were collected from the plain. About two km north of this plain, still in the valley of Çanaklı, a red to yellow clay (3 samples) with sandy intercalations was sampled. Fourth and fifth sets of respectively 12 and 6 samples were taken from the weathered material of ophiolitic bedrock, located outside Sagalassos in the villages of Başköy and Taşkapı. In both sets the samples consist of weathered green to red shales with only a small amount of clay material. A sixth and last set of two samples contained clays from the south banks of Lake Burdur. They consisted of green to black clays, rich in salt crusts and organic matter.

4.1. Geochemistry

A general overview of the chemical composition of the different possible clay raw materials sampled is given in Table 1 for main element analysis and Table 2 for the trace elements. Analyses are given comprising Loss on Ignition and on an LOI-free basis. In general (excluding many other possible Al-containing minerals), the Al_2O_3 content is a measure of the clay content of the raw material, MgO a measure for the chlorite and smectite content (among other minerals) and K_2O a measure for the illite content of the clay (again among others). Na_2O, together with K_2O and CaO, suggests feldspars. CaO is mainly found in calcite. Fe_2O_3 and SiO_2 are found in silica or quartz and iron oxides/hydroxides as well as pyroxenes, amphiboles, feldspars and clays.

As the clay raw materials consist mainly of clay minerals, the differences in chemistry between the different clays will mainly be due to differences in clay content (Al_2O_3 content) and clay mineralogy (MgO and K_2O content). These, together with the content of other minerals (SiO_2 is the best measure), will determine the characteristic parameters

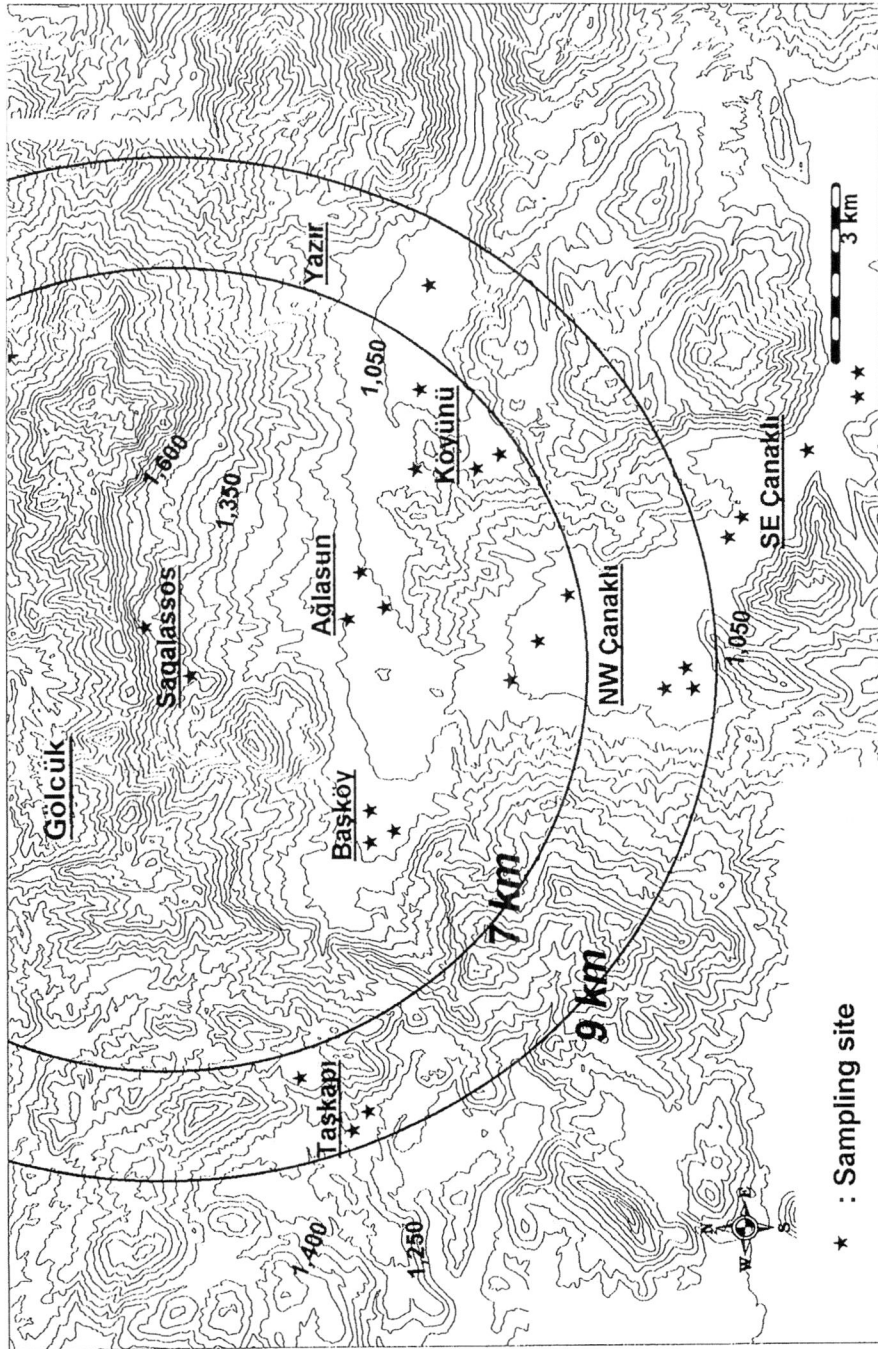

Figure 2: The area of Sagalassos with the clay sampling sites indicated. The sampling site at the south bank of Lake Burdur is situated some 15 km to the SW of this map.

235

	SiO$_2$	Al$_2$O$_3$	Fe$_2$O$_3$	MnO	MgO	CaO	Na$_2$O	K$_2$O	TiO$_2$	P$_2$O$_5$	LOI
Sagalassos ophiolitic clay (n = 13)											
mean	54.59	16.03	7.03	0.17	3.58	3.58	1.22	1.35	0.90	0.23	8.39
st.dev.	3.03	3.68	1.31	0.05	1.81	2.65	1.02	1.06	0.23	0.10	3.29
LOI free basis	59.56	17.49	7.67	0.19	3.91	3.91	1.33	1.47	0.98	0.25	–
Ağlasun-Köyünü-Yazır flysch clay (n = 8)											
mean	58.70	14.20	6.28	0.16	2.41	4.59	1.73	2.96	0.71	0.18	7.37
st.dev.	3.33	2.17	0.64	0.06	0.58	2.93	0.87	0.93	0.04	0.03	2.61
LOI free basis	63.81	15.44	6.83	0.17	2.62	4.99	1.88	3.22	0.77	0.20	–
Çanaklı clay detrital North location A (n = 3)											
mean	57.58	13.11	6.77	0.14	2.62	6.10	1.79	2.70	0.73	0.15	7.65
st.dev.	3.91	1.89	0.17	0.04	0.84	3.11	0.69	0.92	0.02	0.02	3.67
LOI free basis	62.30	14.19	7.33	0.15	2.83	6.60	1.94	2.92	0.79	0.16	8.28
Çanaklı clay detrital NW location B (n = 2)											
mean	50.92	15.90	7.36	0.13	4.18	5.11	0.92	2.55	0.83	0.11	11.32
st.dev.	4.65	0.65	1.18	0.02	1.61	0.08	0.45	0.05	0.01	0.02	1.70
LOI free basis	57.44	17.94	8.30	0.15	4.72	5.76	1.04	2.88	0.94	0.12	–
location C (n = 9)											
mean	49.00	15.11	7.34	0.11	4.51	6.90	1.03	2.60	0.79	0.27	11.90
st.dev.	3.23	1.95	0.46	0.01	1.28	2.00	0.57	0.60	0.10	0.19	3.62
LOI free basis	55.62	17.15	8.33	0.12	5.12	7.83	1.17	2.95	0.90	0.31	–
Çanaklı clay residual SE (n = 11)											
mean	54.22	19.72	7.65	0.18	1.68	2.76	2.00	3.52	0.93	0.33	6.28
st.dev.	2.90	2.28	1.58	0.03	0.93	2.09	0.50	0.74	0.11	0.24	1.56
LOI free basis	58.29	21.20	8.22	0.19	1.81	2.97	2.15	3.78	1.00	0.35	–
Başköy clay (n = 12)											
mean	48.67	10.36	6.64	0.13	6.82	11.12	2.01	1.26	0.62	0.40	11.25
st.dev.	15.79	4.08	2.65	0.06	8.39	10.32	1.85	0.96	0.51	0.48	8.58
LOI free basis	55.24	11.76	7.54	0.15	7.74	12.62	2.28	1.43	0.70	0.45	–
Taşkapı clay (n = 6)											
mean	48.88	14.04	6.85	0.14	5.20	14.28	2.05	0.88	0.54	1.66	4.74
st.dev.	5.43	6.12	4.24	0.06	3.50	7.21	1.83	1.35	0.59	3.61	5.18
LOI free basis	51.67	14.84	7.24	0.15	5.50	15.09	2.17	0.93	0.57	1.75	–
Burdur clay (n = 2)											
mean	33.90	6.54	3.76	0.08	8.01	20.40	2.24	0.95	0.45	0.29	23.85

Table 1: Main element analysis of the clays around Sagalassos.

	Ba	Sr	Cr	Ni	Zr	Zn	Cu	
Sagalassos ophiolitic clay (n = 5)								
mean	2023	2726	95	65	320	231	32	
st.dev.	991	1219	34	25	78	59	16	
Çanaklı clay detrital northwest								
mean	371	130	120	82	206	127	30	
Çanaklı clay residual southeast								
mean	736	668	312	–	–	–	–	
	Th	La	Co	Rb	Ce	Sc	Nb	Y
Sagalassos ophiolitic clay (n = 5)								
mean	56	312	17	201	398	14	60	45
st.dev.	12	96	10	58	246	0	20	22
Çanaklı clay detrital northwest (n = 1)								
mean	27	71	38	136	96	22	–	–
Çanaklı clay residual southeast (n = 2)								
mean	23	80	33	127	138	20	–	–

Table 2: Trace element analysis of the clays around Sagalassos (ppm).

if ceramics are grouped on the basis of a certain clay raw material. The CaO content of a certain clay raw material will not be as relevant for chemical comparison, as it is mainly due to small fragments of limestone and calcite in the raw materials and these amounts can vary enormously according to the geomorphological and geological situations of the direct environment of the deposit. The chemical composition of the clays is recalculated on an LOI-free basis for comparison with ceramics groups.

The trace element contents are normal, considering the dominant relation of all the clays (directly for the ophiolitic clay, indirectly for the Çanaklı clays) to basic rocks. The lower contents of most trace elements in the NW Çanaklı clays can be explained through the influence of more than one source rock on the formation of these clay deposits (e.g. the limestone). The high chromium and nickel contents can be related to the chemical resistance of the minerals bearing these elements and to the affinity of clay minerals for nickel. Trace element contents of the flysch and the other clay resources were not determined.

4.2. Mineralogy

A general mineralogical characterization was made of all the clays. For the ophiolitic clays of the site of Sagalassos, the main clay mineral present is smectite with a smaller amount of chlorite and illite. The feldspars are mainly K-feldspar and plagioclase poor in Na. High amounts of large, idiomorphic amphibole minerals (ferro-hornblende, ferro-richterite and ferro-pargasite, determined by XRD) and biotite crystals are present, together with small amounts of idiomorphic ferro-augite. Magnetite, ilmenite, chromite, hematite, diopside, apatite, perovskite and monazite are common as minor constituents. This clay is a good raw material for ceramics production: it shows a good plasticity and a large content in clay minerals. However, these ophiolitic clays also contain a fair amount of other minerals, which will make a coarser fabric, if fired without washing.

For the clays from the flysch deposits in the area of Köyünü, Ağlasun and Yazır, the main clay mineral is illite, with small amounts of smectite and kaolinite. Feldspars are mainly K-feldspar with lesser amounts of plagioclase. Rounded, small amphiboles and biotites are present in much smaller amounts than pyroxenes (small, rounded augite). Quartz is omnipresent. Magnetite, chromite and ilmenite are minor or accessory minerals in these clays. In fact, the Tertiary flysch is a weathering product of the Mesozoic limestones and ophiolitic sequences in the area. These clays are suitable for ceramics production, but are poorer in clay content than the ophiolitic clay.

The clay deposits from the north of the valley of Çanaklı have the same mineralogical composition and physical properties as the flysch clays of Köyünü, Ağlasun and Yazır. Also these deposits comprise clays derived from the flysch.

In the detrital clays from the NW-Çanaklı plain (Ottenburgs et al., 1993a) the main clay minerals present are chlorite and mixed layers chlorite/smectite with smaller amounts of illite and kaolinite. The feldspars are mainly plagioclases poor in Na, with a smaller amount of K-feldspar. An important quartz fraction is present. Magnetite, hematite, calcite and dolomite are minor constituents. The clay here is very suitable for ceramics production, as it is fat with a good plasticity. Modern clay pits are being exploited for the production of roofing tiles and bricks.

The residual clays from the SE-Çanaklı plain mainly consist of the clay minerals illite and kaolinite with lesser amounts of smectite and of chlorite-smectite mixed layers. Feldspars and quartz are also present in considerable amounts. Goethite and hematite appear in lesser quantities. This is a poor clay with low plasticity, less suitable for ceramics production.

The clays of Taşkapı and Başköy show a similar mineralogy, comprising very little clay fraction. The main clay minerals are smectite and chlorite, with lesser amounts of illite. Feldspars, amphiboles and magnetite are present, together with micas and some quartz. These clays are totally unsuitable for ceramics production as they are too poor.

The main clay mineral present in the lake sediments of the south bank of Lake Burdur is chlorite, together with smaller amounts of smectite and illite. Many salts from the evaporation of lake water occur, including hydromagnesite ($Mg_5(CO_3)_4(OH)_2.4H_2O$) and halite (NaCl). The mica's muscovite and lepidolite and the metamorphic minerals allanite and lawsonite together with the minerals calcite, dolomite, quartz and some feldspar are present in the lake sediments. These clays are an unlikely raw material for the ceramics studied here.

5. SAGALASSOS RED SLIP WARE AND PREDECESSOR (FABRICS 1 AND 11)

Ottenburgs et al. (1993a, b) pointed out that the clays found in the plain NW of the village of Çanaklı were suitable for the production of SRSW (fabric 1). This was based on chemical and mineralogical correspondence between the clays sampled in Çanaklı and the ceramics, which were practically identical. The technological parameters further supported this hypothesis (Ottenburgs et al., 1993b). In the framework of the present study, the archaeometry of the predecessors of the mass produced Sagalassos red slip ware was investigated. Another important element in the study of the table ware discussed here is the thin slip layer applied on this type of ceramic (Poblome et al., 1993). Thin sections were prepared and examined with a polarising microscope. Areas where the slip was well preserved were selected for microprobe analysis. In this way, the composition of the slip was determined and a correlation made with the possible raw materials.

A first group of samples of the table ware contains 21 sherd of ware fabric group 11 (Chronological group 1 of the table wares in Table 3). Nine of these were collected during the 1996 survey just beyond the territory of Sagalassos at the site of Kozluca höyük (Poblome et al., 2002). This höyük is situated some 20 km south of Burdur and about 50 km southwest of Sagalassos, near the site of Kormasa (Waelkens et al., 1998 and 2000). The material belongs to the later part of the Hellenistic period. During the excavation seasons, several deposits were discovered containing similar late Hellenistic pottery (Poblome, 1999; Poblome et al., 1998, 2002): the deposits behind the northeastern corner of the late Hellenistic fountain-house (site NON), the deposits to the east of the same building (site EON), the west basin of this fountain-house, the deposist to the north of the library (site L), the sondage behind the north terrace wall of the upper agora (site UAN), the deposits underneath and predating the roman baths (site RB, room 2 and room 3), the deposits to the south of the NW-Heroon (site H), the deposits below the eastern portico of the lower agora (site LA) and the sondages executed in the 1999 and 2000 campaigns respectively located along the colonnaded street and the slopes around the theatre (sites SSC1, TSW 1 and 2). A total of 12 sherds was selected from these deposits. The deposits are, in fact, early Imperial in date, but each contained a significant amount of late Hellenistic residual material (Poblome et al., 2002). Except for the cremational burials of Site F, only a limited number of genuine Hellenistic deposits was discovered in 2007, underneath the Odeion and the Macellum. The samples of the latter sites are currently being analysed.

Chronological group											
	SiO_2	$Al2O_3$	Fe_2O_3	MnO	MgO	CaO	Na_2O	K_2O	TiO_2	P_2O_5	LOI
Ophiolite 1 (n = 10)											
mean	52.82	19.06	7.69	0.10	3.55	8.11	0.82	3.64	0.91	0.27	2.25
st.dev.	3.27	1.62	0.53	0.01	1.46	2.80	0.19	0.70	0.07	0.03	0.73
Çanaklı 1 (n = 11)											
mean	49.10	13.70	8.07	0.10	6.95	9.41	0.79	2.70	0.80	0.40	13.20
st.dev.	4.20	2.38	1.37	0.01	1.33	5.53	0.19	0.30	0.10	0.20	2.39
Ophiolite 2 (n = 6)											
mean	54.10	15.15	7.55	0.11	5.27	8.07	1.05	3.01	0.81	0.34	3.88
st.dev.	3.54	1.62	0.73	0.02	2.01	2.48	0.40	0.54	0.07	0.22	3.01
Çanaklı 2 (n = 1)											
mean	43.40	11.70	7.17	0.10	6.27	14.30	0.50	2.00	0.60	0.30	13.40
3 (n = 20)											
mean	51.74	15.00	8.10	0.10	6.32	9.03	0.97	2.60	0.83	0.32	4.43
st.dev.	2.20	1.21	0.57	0.01	1.69	2.78	0.20	0.32	0.06	0.11	1.79
4 (n = 6)											
mean	52.27	16.16	8.20	0.10	6.92	8.11	0.99	2.68	0.87	0.22	2.85
st.dev.	1.73	0.49	0.23	0.01	0.58	1.29	0.07	0.07	0.04	0.04	0.48
5 (n = 16)											
mean	54.27	16.33	8.40	0.10	6.59	6.07	1.01	2.79	0.90	0.20	2.71
st.dev.	1.40	0.87	0.38	0.01	0.68	1.82	0.10	0.27	0.04	0.04	1.43
6 (n = 2)											
mean	51.68	16.46	8.23	0.08	6.61	8.54	0.98	2.66	0.88	0.21	2.96
st.dev.	0.14	0.05	0.03	0.01	1.03	0.59	0.05	0.08	0.01	0.02	0.54
7 (n = 12)											
mean	52.11	15.95	7.94	0.10	6.66	8.05	1.00	2.81	0.86	0.32	3.53
st.dev.	2.05	1.10	0.63	0.01	0.73	1.64	0.10	0.12	0.04	0.11	1.82
8 (n = 4)											
mean	51.57	16.21	8.14	0.09	6.54	7.00	1.07	2.72	0.86	0.27	4.82
st.dev.	2.00	1.00	0.64	0.01	1.11	2.12	0.11	0.25	0.03	0.05	2.42
9 (n = 4)											
mean	52.04	16.09	8.49	0.10	6.60	7.93	1.07	2.81	0.91	0.26	3.16
st.dev.	2.96	1.10	0.11	0.01	1.13	1.25	0.24	0.03	0.06	0.05	2.46

Table 3: Main element analysis of the fine wares.

10 (n = 16)										
mean	52.62	15.83	8.32	0.10	6.92	7.40	1.05	2.76	0.88	0.28	3.29
st.dev.	1.41	0.75	0.57	0.01	0.81	1.53	0.07	0.19	0.05	0.11	1.92
11 (n = 11)										
mean	52.19	15.97	8.41	0.09	6.79	8.48	1.13	2.82	0.89	0.28	2.44
st.dev.	1.33	0.66	0.28	0.01	0.64	1.29	0.17	0.18	0.04	0.07	1.91
12 (n = 30)										
mean	52.68	16.39	8.48	0.09	6.86	7.55	0.97	2.71	0.90	0.23	2.52
st.dev.	1.36	0.92	0.57	0.01	0.81	1.21	0.11	0.23	0.08	0.05	1.82

Table 3 (*cont.*)

The second group of samples contains 7 sherds (named chronological group 2 in Table 3). The samples were selected from early Imperial deposits and probably represent residual Hellenistic material in Augustan contexts at Sagalassos, dating from 25 BC to 25 AD (Poblome, 1999). The basics of the later morphological series are already recognisable, but the finish of the ceramics and the standardisation in form typical for the mass production lack. The typology of the samples is defined in Poblome *et al.* (2002).

The third group, investigated by Ottenburgs *et al.* (1993a, b), contains 121 samples of Sagalassos red slip ware (groups 3-12 in Table 3). These were selected from a series of well-dated stratigraphical deposits excavated at Sagalassos. Their chronology was defined by Poblome (1999). A selection of 18 samples from these 121 sherds was made in order to analyze the composition of the slip layer of the tableware of Sagalassos (Degryse *et al.*, this volume). The samples were collected at six different sites: two ceramic dumps in the potters' quarter (sites D and F), the house north of the library (site L), the library itself, the esplanade in front of the library (all site N) and the waste dump to the west of the Doric temple (site WDT). Also the fabrics 4 and 5 of the common wares sometimes show such a slip (Degeest and Waelkens, 1993). Four common wares were further analysed for their slip composition. They were selected from the sherds found at the fountain-house (site N; Degeest, 2000).

5.1. Geochemistry

The mean chemical composition of the table wares is given in Table 3. Trace elements are given in Table 4. The table wares are divided into twelve chronological groups, ranging from the Hellenistic antecedent of the mass production phase (group 1; fabric 11), through the initial mass production phase

(group 2; fabric 1) to the 10 chronological phases of mass production of the table ware (groups 3 to 12; fabric 1). The chemical data of the mass production phases (groups 3 to 12) show a very small variability throughout the chronology of the ceramics, indicating that the clay raw material must have been derived from a large, homogeneous deposit and that the same clay was used throughout centuries of mass production. It has been shown (Poblome *et al.*, 1997) that the potters achieved and retained this high level of quality over a period of at least seven centuries, and possible longer. However, the chemical composition (especially the K_2O and MgO contents) of some sherds from the Hellenistic antecedent of the mass production (group 1) and of the initial mass production (group 2) differs from the mean composition of the mass production, as can be seen in Table 5 and Figure 3.

5.2. Mineralogy

All samples from chronological groups 3 to 12 and half of the samples from groups 1 and 2 have a homogeneous fabric, orange to brown in colour. These samples correspond to the chemical signature of the Çanaklı clay. In some samples a few large shaping pores are present, otherwise minute pores are homogeneously distributed (Figure 4a). Almost no mineral inclusions can be seen in the table ware. Only very small pyroxene and amphibole crystals were identified. In half of the samples from group 1 and 2 a dark brown homogeneous matrix can be seen, coarser than the former fabric, with larger pores. These samples correspond to the chemical signature of the ophiolitic clays. Small inclusions of biotite, amphibole, feldspar, limestone, pyroxenes and volcanic rock fragments were identified (Figure 4b). The slip layer varies from orange-red to brown and dark brown. It is less porous than the paste and its thickness is mostly between 5 and 10 µm (Viaene *et al.*, 1993). The

	Ba	Sr	Cr	Ni	Zr	Zn	Cu	
Ophiolite 1 (n = 2)								
mean	327	178	119	73	207	127	45	
Çanaklı 1 (n = 1)								
mean	371	130	120	82	206	127	30	
Ophiolite 2 (n = 2)								
mean	1114	720	288	299	260	128	65	
Çanaklı 2 (n = 1)								
mean	391	282	345	310	133	106	55	
Çanaklı 3-12 (n = 14)								
mean	420	209	343	337	160	131	55	
st.dev.	105	32	23	42	26	5	13	
	Th	La	Co	Rb	Ce	Sc	Nb	Y
Ophiolite 1 (n = 2)								
mean	<	65	63	136	<	<	51	49
Çanaklı 1 (n = 1)								
mean	27	<	58	143	<	<	43	47
Ophiolite 2 (n = 2)								
mean	27	132	58	135	<	<	50	45
Çanaklı 2 (n = 1)								
mean	<	<	46	73	<	<	21	33
Çanaklı 3-12 (n = 14)								
mean	19	36	41	111	59	21	14	24
st.dev.	10	3	3	2	5	2	2	3

Table 4: Trace element analysis of fine wares.

thickness of the slip is uniform in only one sample. Minute, brighter inclusions are sometimes observed, representing free hematite, which gives the slip its characteristic red-orange colour. An exception is sample 320, showing a white slip of 40 μm thickness. An XRD study shows that this slip contains a mixture of cordierite and muscovite.

5.3. Discussion

The chemical and mineralogical compositions of the table wares from the mass production phases (groups 3 to 12) can be compared to the clays from the NW plain of Çanaklı, about 8 km from Sagalassos (Ottenburgs et al., 1993a). Ottenburgs et al. (1993 a, b) and Viaene et al. (1995b), based on the main and trace element chemistry and the firing properties of the clays, showed that these were the raw material for the production of SRSW. However, some differences can be seen between these resources and the earlier phases (the predecessor) of Sagalassos red slip ware. The chemical and mineralogical composition of the ophiolitic weathering product clearly conforms with that of most of the samples of the predecessor of SRSW (group 2) and

	SiO$_2$	Al$_2$O$_3$	Fe$_2$O$_3$	MnO	MgO	CaO	Na$_2$O	K$_2$O	TiO$_2$	P$_2$O$_5$	LOI
Sagalassos ophiolitic clay (n = 13)											
mean	54.59	16.03	7.03	0.17	3.58	3.58	1.22	1.35	0.90	0.23	8.39
st.dev.	3.03	3.68	1.31	0.05	1.81	2.65	1.02	1.06	0.23	0.10	3.29
LOI free basis	59.56	17.49	7.67	0.19	3.91	3.91	1.33	1.47	0.98	0.25	–
Çanaklı clay location C (n = 9)											
mean	49.00	15.11	7.34	0.11	4.51	6.90	1.03	2.60	0.79	0.27	11.90
st.dev.	3.23	1.95	0.46	0.01	1.28	2.00	0.57	0.60	0.10	0.19	3.62
LOI free basis	55.62	17.15	8.33	0.12	5.12	7.83	1.17	2.95	0.90	0.31	–
Ophiolite group 1 (n = 10)											
mean	52.82	19.06	7.69	0.10	3.55	8.11	0.82	3.64	0.91	0.27	2.25
st.dev.	3.27	1.62	0.53	0.01	1.46	2.80	0.19	0.70	0.07	0.03	0.73
LOI free basis	54.03	19.50	7.87	0.10	3.63	8.30	0.84	3.72	0.93	0.28	–
Çanaklı group 1 (n = 11)											
mean	49.10	13.70	8.07	0.10	6.95	9.41	0.79	2.70	0.80	0.40	13.20
st.dev.	4.20	2.38	1.37	0.01	1.33	5.53	0.19	0.30	0.10	0.20	2.39
LOI free basis	56.56	15.78	9.30	0.12	8.01	10.84	0.91	3.11	0.92	0.46	–
Ophiolite group 2 (n = 6)											
mean	54.10	15.15	7.55	0.11	5.27	8.07	1.05	3.01	0.81	0.34	3.88
st.dev.	3.54	1.62	0.73	0.02	2.01	2.48	0.40	0.54	0.07	0.22	3.01
LOI free basis	56.26	15.76	7.85	0.11	5.48	8.39	1.09	3.13	0.84	0.35	–
Çanaklı group 2 (n = 1)											
mean	43.40	11.70	7.17	0.10	6.27	14.30	0.50	2.00	0.60	0.30	13.40
st.dev.	–	–	–	–	–	–	–	–	–	–	–
LOI free basis	50.00	13.48	8.26	0.12	7.22	16.47	0.58	2.30	0.69	0.35	–
Group 3 – 12 (n = 121)											
mean	52.40	16.10	8.28	0.10	6.47	8.10	0.97	2.70	0.88	0.27	3.18
st.dev.	2.16	1.31	0.54	0.01	1.04	2.30	0.15	0.30	0.10	0.12	2.09
LOI free basis	54.08	16.62	8.54	0.10	6.68	8.36	1.00	2.79	0.91	0.28	–

Table 5: Fine wares versus clays.

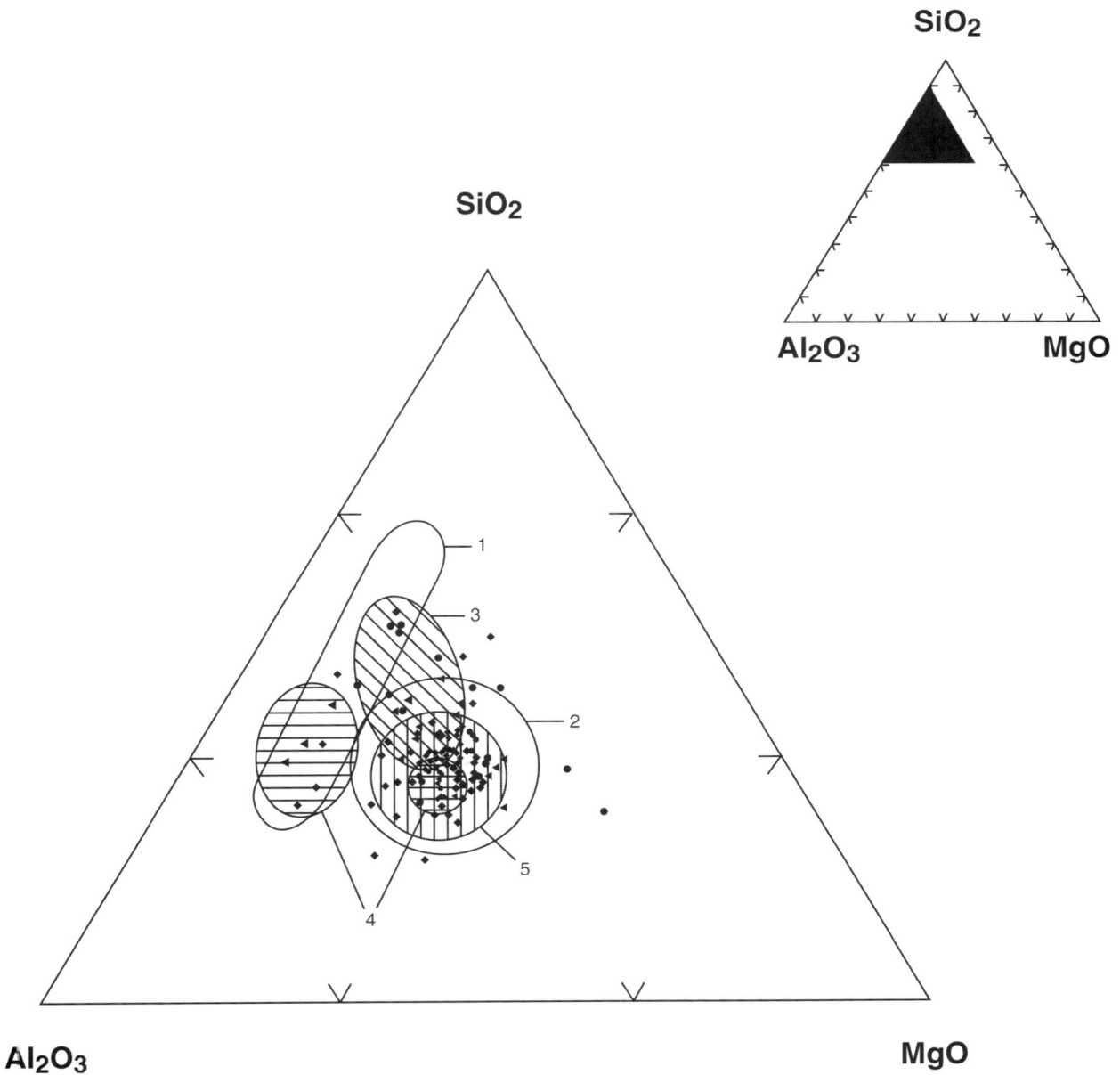

Figure 3: Ternary diagram of the fine tablewares compared to the clay raw materials. **1** the ophiolitic clay of Sagalassos **2** the NW Çanaklı clays **3** chronological group 1 **4** chronological group 2 **5** Sagalassos red slip ware, chronological groups 3 to 12. Triangles are sherds from chronological group 1, dots are sherds of chronological group 2, frames are sherds of chronological groups 3 to 12.

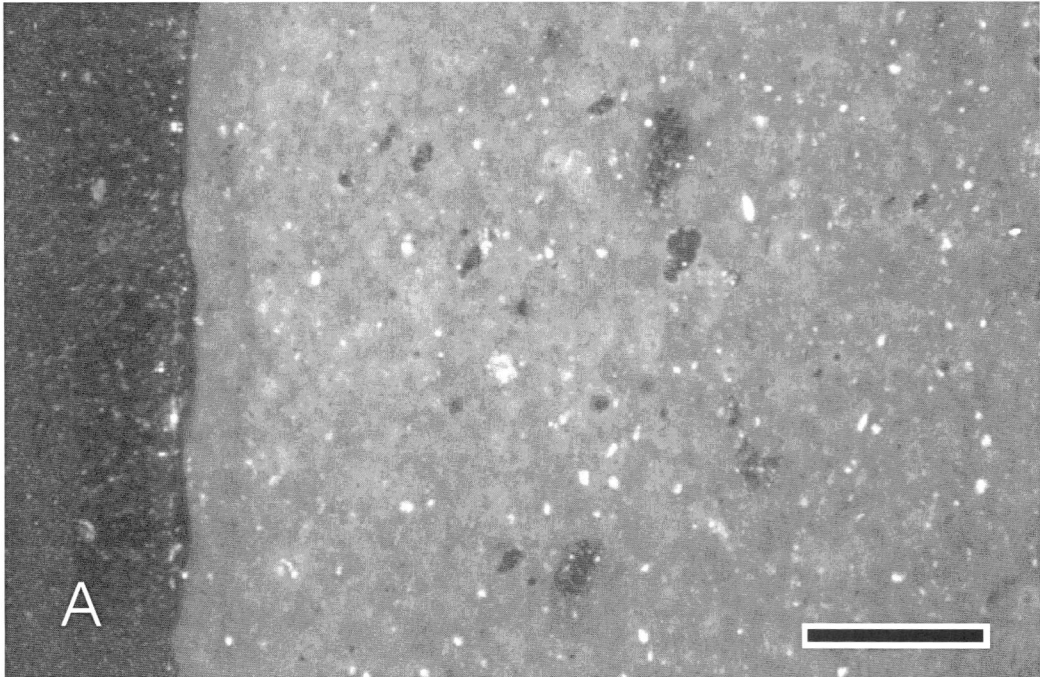

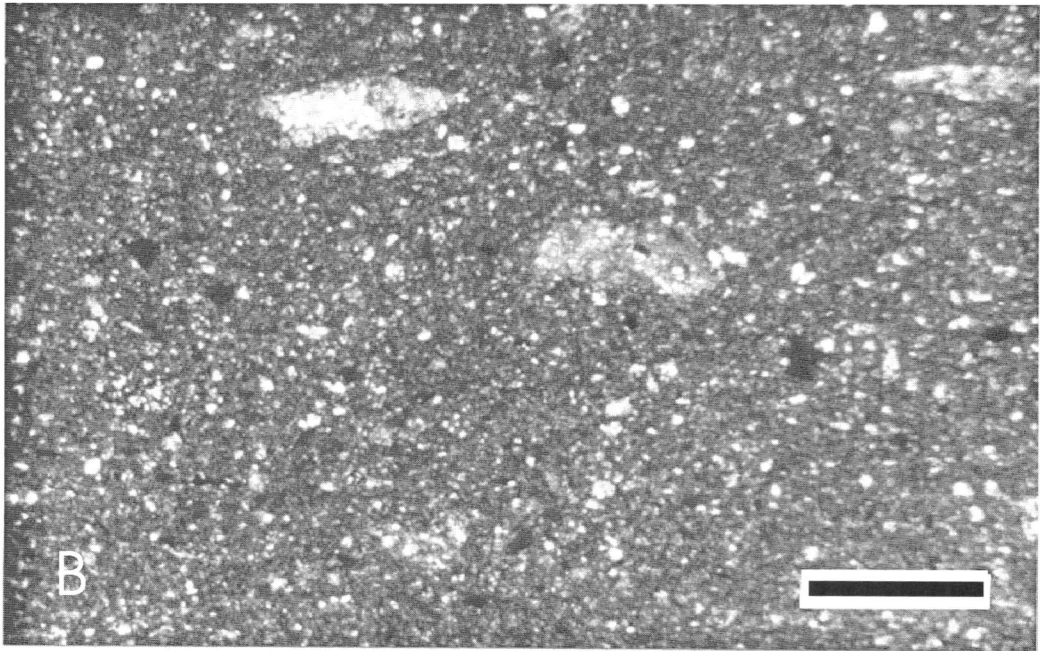

Figure 4: Microphotographs of the fine tableware.

A. Sample SA99JP8 – Hellenistic antecedent. Corresponding to the chemical signature of the ophiolitic clay. Scale bar is 500 µm, crossed Polaroids.
B. Sample SAG 34 – Sagalassos red slip ware. Corresponding to the chemical signature of the NW Çanaklı clay. Scale bar is 250 µm, crossed Polaroids.

also with that of half of the Hellenistic samples collected at Kozluca Höyük and Sagalassos (group 1; Figure 3). These sherds are produced with the ophiolitic clays from Sagalassos as a raw material. The late Hellenistic table ware sherds found at Kozluca Höyük and Sagalassos, which macroscopically looked similar to the later SRSW, can thus be considered to be a Hellenistic antecedent of the imperial mass produced Sagalassos tableware. Eleven late Hellenistic sherds (group 1) and one early Augustan sherd (group 2) are more similar to the clays of the valley northwest of Çanaklı (Figure 3). Differences in the CaO, SiO_2 and Al_2O_3 contents of the sherds are mainly due to the precipitation of $CaCO_3$ in the pores after burial. However, the K_2O and MgO contents, the indicative elements for comparison, are similar to those of the clays of Çanaklı. The latter clays show an elevated MgO content as they comprise a large amount of chlorite as a clay mineral, unlike the ophiolitic clays. However, the MgO content of the sherds made from Çanaklı clays may be slightly elevated compared to the clay itself, as larger fragments of quartz and feldspar were probably removed from the raw material before processing. This can be seen as the SiO_2 and Na_2O is lower in the sherds than in the clays (removal of quartz and feldspar), but the Al_2O_3 content remains comparable as its removal by the removal of feldspar is compensated by the relative enrichment in clay minerals. The same correspondence between clays and sherds applies to the indicative trace elements. The sherds or groups that correspond to the ophiolitic clays have elevated Ba, Sr, Zr, Rb and La contents, while the content in Cr and Ni is lower. The opposite applies for correspondence to the Çanaklı clays.

Mass production of SRSW started in the Augustan period, probably in the second half of his reign (Poblome, 1999). At that time, the local potters already had experience of tableware manufacture. The clay used for the predecessors of the Imperial SRSW could be identified. On the one hand, the potters principally exploited the clayey weathering horizon of the ophiolitic bedrock in the potters' quarter of Sagalassos. This fact further helps to explain the location of the potters' quarter. Yet, at the same time, the potters were already aware of the qualities of the clay found in the valley northwest of Çanaklı. This silt-rich clay can readily be used for ceramics production. It is unclear from the limited analyses how much local clay from the ophiolitic sequence was used and how much was imported from Çanaklı. About half of the analyses of the sherds from chronological groups one and two belong to either clay raw material. During the later Augustan period, a mass production process was initialised and the potters made a deliberate choice to exploit the clays northwest of Çanaklı in a more systematical way to provide the raw material for the fabric of their tableware. The choice of these specific clays clearly had technological advantages, in that they needed less preparation than did the ophiolitic clays of the potters' quarter. No coarser non-clay minerals have to be removed from the Çanaklı clay by washing, as is the case with the ophiolitic clay. The potters required enormous quantities of high quality clays and they apparently preferred the trouble of exploiting and transporting their clays from approximately eight km distance, rather than carrying out the tedious process of preparing the ophiolitic clays on a large scale. Apparently the latter continued to be used for the local production of common wares, for which less pure clay may even be advantageous (see below).

6. THE COMMON WARES, AMPHORAE AND ARCHITECTURAL CERAMICS (FABRICS 2 TO 5)

The same question of raw material provenance as with the table wares was asked with the study of the utilitarian wares (fabric 2, 4 and 5: Figure 5) and the architectural ceramics (fabric 3; Figure 6). Like with the study of the provenance of the raw materials for the table wares, the provenance of the raw materials for the amphorae, cooking and storage vessels on the one hand and for the architectural ceramics on the other hand was based on the chemical and mineralogical correspondence between the clays surveyed around Sagalassos and samples of the ceramics. However, because of the addition of temper to these common ware fabrics, clear from the relation of the constituents of the sherds in the petrography of the ceramics, the mineralogical and geochemical study of the possible raw materials is more complex than for the table ware. Besides the classical approach of chemical comparison, the mineralogy of the raw materials and of the ceramics and the geochemistry of individual minerals will be a conclusive element in determining the raw materials used in the production of common ware fabrics at Sagalassos. It is striking, however, that the amphorae, cooking and storage vessels and the building ceramics show an identical range of chemical compositions and mineralogical constituents, and therefore from an archaeometrical point of view can be treated together as 'the common wares' or 'the coarse ceramics', despite the fact that they are an entirely different type of material from a typological and general archaeological point of view. These fabrics are referred to as the common ware fabrics in the following paragraphs.

6.1. Geochemistry

A summary of the results is given in Tables 6 and 7. 132 sherds of Sagalassos common ware fabrics (groups 2, 3, 4 and 5) were analyzed. A ternary composition diagram of

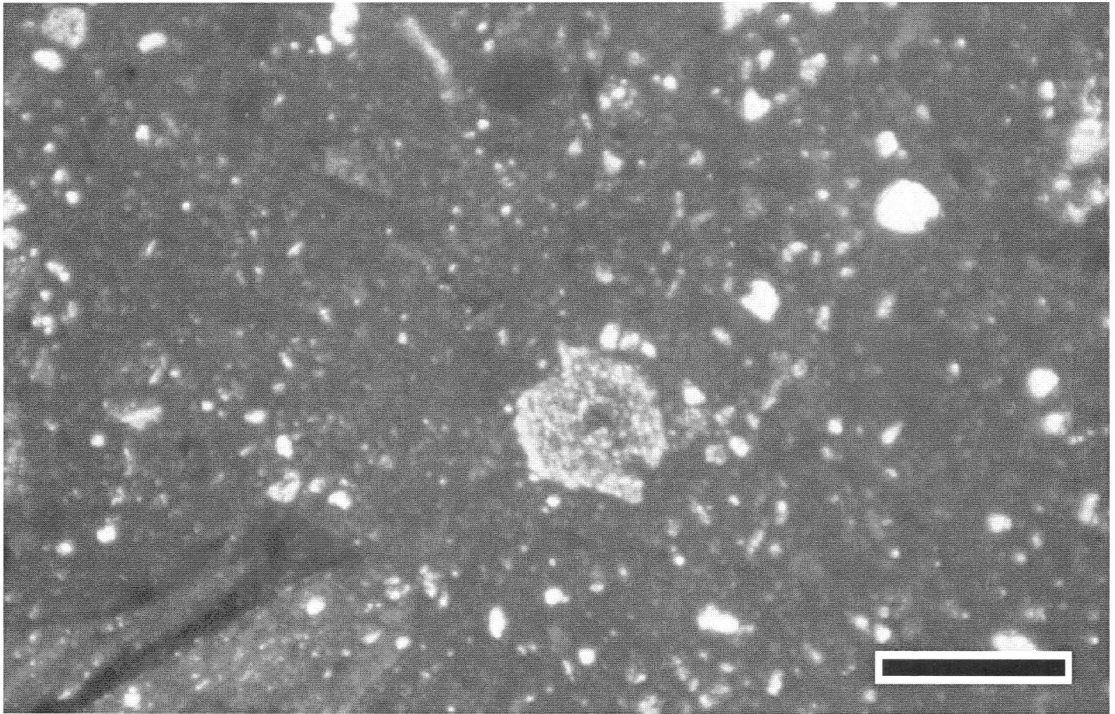

Figure 5: Microphotograph of a cooking/storage vessel, sample SAG 10. Scale bar is 500 μm, crossed Polaroids.

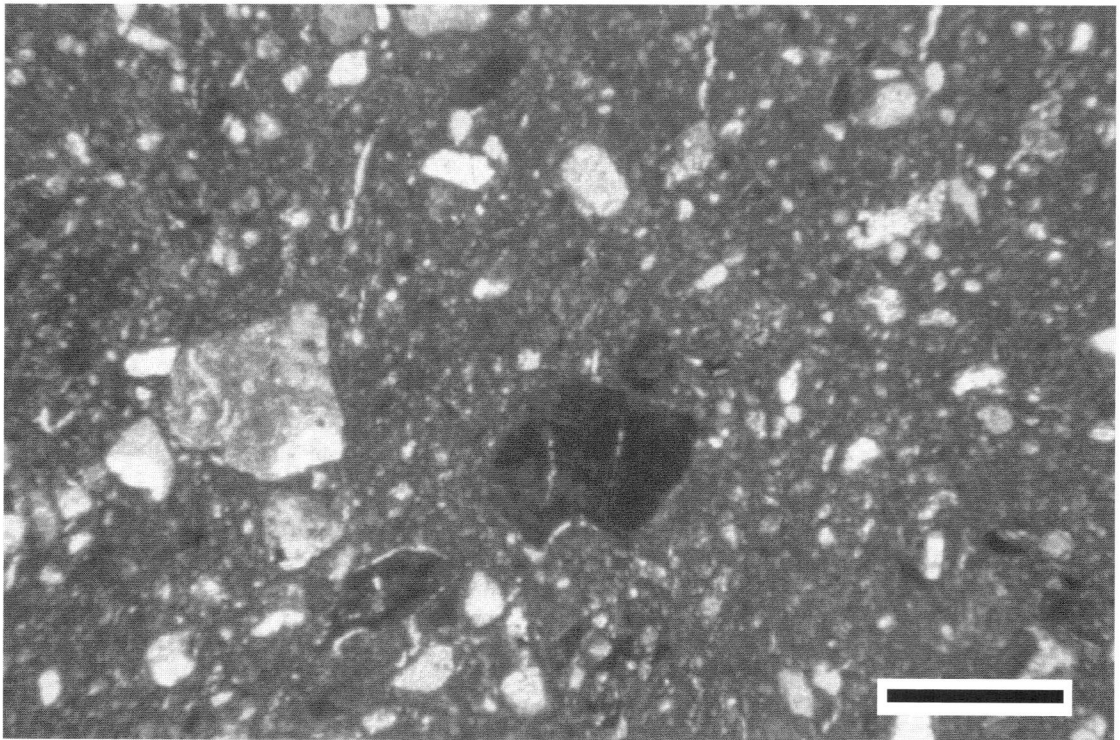

Figure 6: Microphotograph of architectural ceramics, sample SAG 210. Scale bar is 500 μm, crossed Polaroids.

	SiO$_2$	Al$_2$O$_3$	Fe$_2$O$_3$	MnO	MgO	CaO	Na$_2$O	K$_2$O	TiO$_2$	P$_2$O$_5$	LOI
Ware group 2-4-5 (cooking & storage vessels, n = 78)											
mean	58.24	17.04	7.15	0.13	2.92	4.91	1.15	2.85	0.85	0.34	3.75
st.dev.	5.20	2.65	1.24	0.04	1.99	3.59	0.55	0.80	0.14	0.18	2.74
LOI free basis	60.92	17.82	7.48	0.14	3.05	5.14	1.20	2.98	0.89	0.36	–
Ware group 3 (building ceramics, n = 54)											
mean	54.20	15.50	7.15	0.12	4.64	8.19	1.13	2.73	0.83	0.18	4.72
st.dev.	6.54	1.89	1.46	0.03	2.46	4.27	0.37	0.68	0.08	0.11	3.14
LOI free basis	56.85	16.23	7.50	0.13	4.87	8.60	1.19	2.87	0.87	0.19	–

Table 6: Main element analysis of the common wares.

	Ba	Sr	Cr	Ni	Zr	Zn	Cu	
Ware group 2-4-5 (cooking & storage vessels, n = 3)								
mean	574	401	248	196	123	95	43	
st.dev.	201	313	112	91	45	24	20	
Ware group 3 (building ceramics, n = 10)								
mean	730	607	237	197	223	108	62	
st.dev.	395	548	78	89	70	14	15	
	Th	La	Co	Rb	Ce	Sc	Nb	Y
Ware group 2-4-5 (cooking & storage vessels, n = 3)								
mean	<	37	31	101	53	<	24	39
st.dev.	<	11	7	39	29	<	2	11
Ware group 3 (building ceramics, n = 10)								
mean	23	77	31	114	70	<	30	45
st.dev.	10	64	28	40	113	<	11	9

Table 7: Trace element analysis of the common wares.

the common ware fabric chemistry is given in Figure 7. With this diagram the chemistry of the sherds can easily be compared with the chemistry of the possible raw materials, recalculated without the volatile components and LOI. Since no relevant geochemical separation could be made between the four ware groups, no distinction is made between them regarding the geochemical data. However, the amphorae, cooking and storage vessels are treated differently from the architectural ceramics, as the latter show an occasional high addition of limestone as a temper, largely affecting the SiO$_2$ and CaO contents and the LOI. The limestone fragments as a temper can be observed in the larger pieces of the architectural ceramics. This is probably done to reduce the amount of clay needed for the preparation of these pieces. These limestone fragments are largely absent from the amphorae, cooking and storage vessels.

In the ternary diagram we see that the chemical signature of the common ware fabrics does not correspond to the chemical signature of the clays from the villages of Başköy and

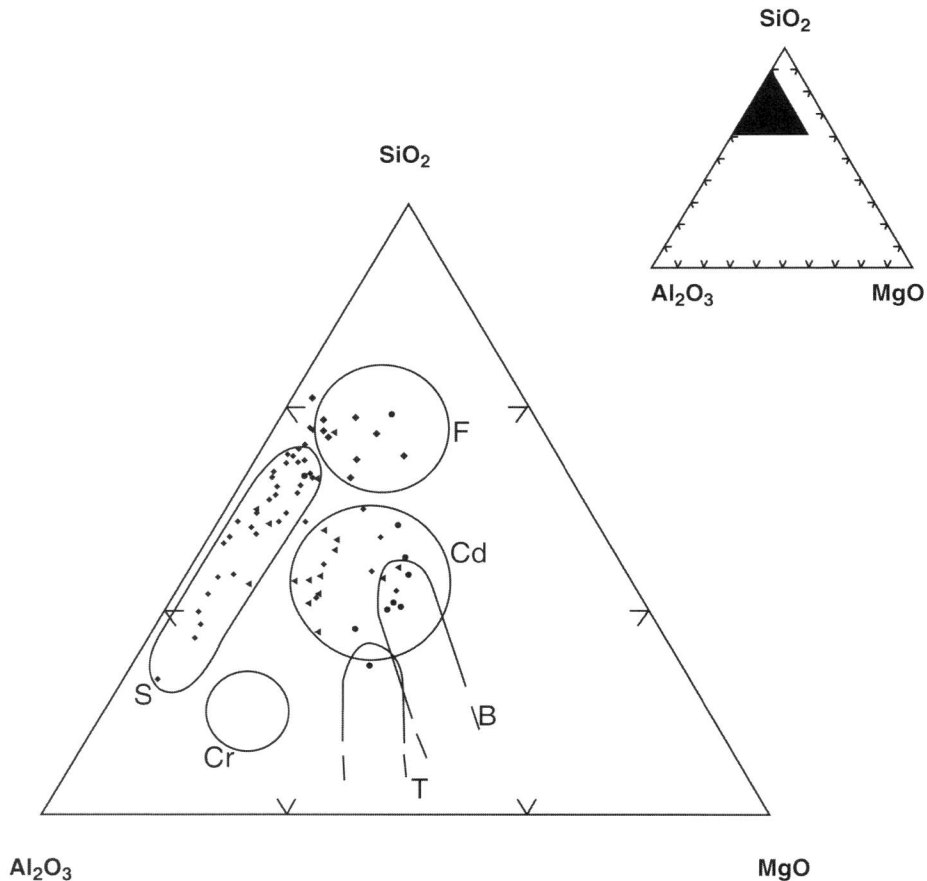

Figure 7: Ternary diagram of the geochemistry of the common wares compared to the clay raw materials. The analysis of common wares are plotted, the fields for the raw materials are labeled. S: ophiolitic clay from Sagalassos, F: flysch and N-Çanaklı clays, Cd: NW-Çanaklı clays, Cr: SE-Çanaklı clays, B: Başköy clays, T: Taşkapı clays. The clays from Burdur are not indicated. Triangles are fabric 2, frames are fabric 4, dots are fabric 5.

Taşkapı. Some clay samples correspond to some sherds of common ware. In general, the clays of Taşkapı and Başköy have a low clay content (the Al_2O_3 content is low). Other differences from the common ware fabrics are the lower K_2O and SiO_2 contents and the higher CaO content (possibly due to calcite veinlets present in the ophiolitic rocks). Hence the correspondence can be regarded as coincidental and the clays of Taşkapı and Başköy are an improbable raw material for common ware fabric production.

On the other hand, identical groups of sherds correspond to the chemical signatures of the clays from Sagalassos, NW-Çanaklı and Köyünü/Ağlasun/Yazır/N-Çanaklı. The same sets of sherds always have the same chemical signature as a certain clay, either the ophiolitic clay of the site itself, the detrital clay from the NW-Çanaklı plain or the clay from the flysch. No sherds correspond to the sedimentary-residual clays of SE-Çanaklı or the clays from Burdur. In addition, the chemical signatures of some sherds always lie between those of the ophiolitic clays of the potters' quarter at the Sagalassos site and those of the detrital clays of Çanaklı and other sherds always lie between the ophiolitic clays of the site and the clays from the flysch. No sherds lie between the detrital clays of Çanaklı and the clays from the flysch. Hence the common ware fabrics can be divided into three groups, each with its own geochemical signature. A group of sherds corresponding geochemically to the clays from the flysch, a group of sherds corresponding to the detrital clays near Çanaklı and a group of sherds corresponding to the ophiolitic clays of the site of Sagalassos can be identified. Moreover, two groups of sherds with a mixed chemical signature occur. The groups here defined contain sherds of all types of ceramics from the three different fabric groups (Fabrics 2, 4 and 5).

Mineral	SiO$_2$	Al$_2$O$_3$	Fe$_2$O$_3$	MnO	MgO	CaO	Na$_2$O	K$_2$O	TiO$_2$
Amphibole (kaersturite, n = 9)									
mean	39.33	12.79	16.95	–	11.47	12.03	1.46	2.24	2.75
st. dev.	0.94	0.91	1.82	–	1.07	0.35	0.53	0.33	0.18
Biotite (n = 6)									
mean	42.92	18.36	14.67	0.34	10.63	0.58	0.18	7.73	3.39
st. dev.	9.07	6.36	5.42	0.43	7.59	0.60	0.13	2.72	1.84

Table 8: Microprobe analysis of biotites and amphiboles in common ware.

Source	Mg	Ca	Fe	Si	Ti	Mn	Al	O
Ophiolitic clay								
magnetite 1	1.09	0.01	66.98	0.01	3.40	0.42	1.83	23.93
magnetite 2	1.09	0.01	66.74	0.01	3.48	0.38	1.85	23.93
magnetite 3	1.08	0.01	66.95	0.01	3.44	0.39	1.82	23.93
Common ware								
magnetite 1	0.50	0.02	66.38	0.01	3.63	0.61	0.80	22.67
magnetite 2	0.42	0.01	66.40	0.01	3.87	0.55	0.71	22.69
magnetite 3	0.53	0.01	66.11	0.01	3.41	0.60	0.85	22.52

Table 9: Microprobe analysis (as elements) of magnetites in common ware and in the ophiolitic clay.

The trace element chemistry of the common ware fabrics points to the relation of these wares to a basic parent rock, as can be seen from the elevated contents in Cr and Ni among other indicators. The chemical composition of the idiomorphic biotites in the sherds, with up to 5% of TiO$_2$ and no more than 0.6% CaO, together with up to 0.5% MnO, points to an ophiolite as a parent rock for the raw materials (H. Kucha, personal communication, Table 8). Analyses of magnetite in the architectural ceramics are given in Table 9, which show that these are similar in chemistry to the magnetites in the ophiolitic clays. Larger differences in the Mg and Al contents can be explained by the miscibility and exchange of these elements with iron at firing temperatures of the ceramics to 900 °C (Sack and Ghiorso, 1991).

6.2. Mineralogy

The mineral content was determined on one representative sample of each group of sherds with a typical chemical signature corresponding to one possible clay raw material. For the group with the chemical signature of the clays from the flysch, the results of image analysis are given in Table 10, column 1. For quartz, large angular 300 µm grains and small, rounded 10 µm grains are present. For amphiboles and biotites large angular 200 to 400 µm grains and small rounded (often heavily weathered) 10 µm grains are present. The feldspars consist of K-feldspar and Ca-plagioclase, poor in Na. The rounded nodules in the sherds are probably balls (pebbles) of clay, formed during the preparation of the clay for shaping. Chert fragments and basalt clasts up to 2 mm are also very abundant, mostly as rounded grains. Magnetite, ilmenite, hematite, chromite, calcite, pyroxene and apatite are present in quantities not more than 5%.

For the group with the chemical signature of the ophiolitic clays of the site of Sagalassos, the results of image analysis are given in Table 10, column 2. For quartz mostly large angular grains up to 800 µm are present. Amphiboles and biotites are present in high amounts as idiomorphic crystals up to 800 µm large. Entire biotite plates are preserved. The feldspar consists mainly of Ca-plagioclase with smaller amounts of K-feldspar. Chert fragments and basalt clasts are

Mineral/phase	Estimated quantity		
	(%)		
Signature	Flysch signature	Ophiolite signature	NW-Çanaklı signature
porosity	25	15	15
(% of temper)	(–): not present		
feldspar	25	35	)
quartz	5	5	)
chert	15	5	) in total 57
basaltic clasts	14	15	)
clay nodules	20	7	)
grog	–	–	28
biotite	1	7	2
pyroxene	5	3	2
amphibole	7	12	7
opaque minerals	3	5	2
calcite	5	5	?
apatite	<1	<1	–
perovskite	–	<1	–

Table 10: Image analysis of common ware.

large (up to 2 mm) and angular. Pyroxene, magnetite, ilmenite, chromite, hematite, calcite, apatite, diopside and perovskite were found in quantities equal or less than 5%.

For the group with the chemical signature of the detrital clays of the NW-Çanaklı plain, the results of image analysis are given in Table 10, column 3. The grog consisting of crushed table ware is up to 2 mm large. No grog of crushed common ware fabrics was observed. Large idiomorphic amphiboles, biotites and pyroxenes of up to 800 µm can be seen. Ca-plagioclase, K-feldspar and chert are present in large amounts. Quartz, magnetite, ilmenite and diopside were found in small amounts.

The general characteristics of the minerals present in the sherds have also been studied. The amphiboles (Figure 8a) in the sherds are always the same varieties: ferro-hornblende, kaersturite and/or ferro-richterite. The amphiboles in sherds with a chemical signature comparable to the ophiolitic clays are always large and idiomorphic. In other sherds smaller, rounded (weathered) crystals occur. The same applies for

the pyroxenes (always belonging to the augite/ferro-augite series; Figure 8b) and the biotites (Figure 8c) in the sherds. The pyroxene/amphibole ratio is lower in the sherds with the chemical signature of the ophiolitic clay than in sherds with another signature. The same situation applies for the pyroxene/biotite ratio. The feldspars present in the sherds are Ca-plagioclases and Na-poor K-feldspars. In all sherds, apatite, magnetite, chromite and hematite are found, and occasionally perovskite, diopside and ilmenite. Clasts with a basaltic appearance are found in high amounts in all sherds. They have the appearance of certain volcanic materials found near the lake of Gölçük, north of the site of Sagalassos. Their provenance, however, remains uncertain, but they might be Gölçük related pyroclastics found all around the region of Sagalassos, such as in the valleys of Ağlasun, Yazır, Köyünü, Çanaklı and Dereköy. They could have been added deliberately, but could equally have been an inherent part of the clay raw materials, incorporated after volcanic activity in the area. Limestone was usually added to the architectural ceramics, often in very large amounts (8e). This was the beige limestone from the nappes around

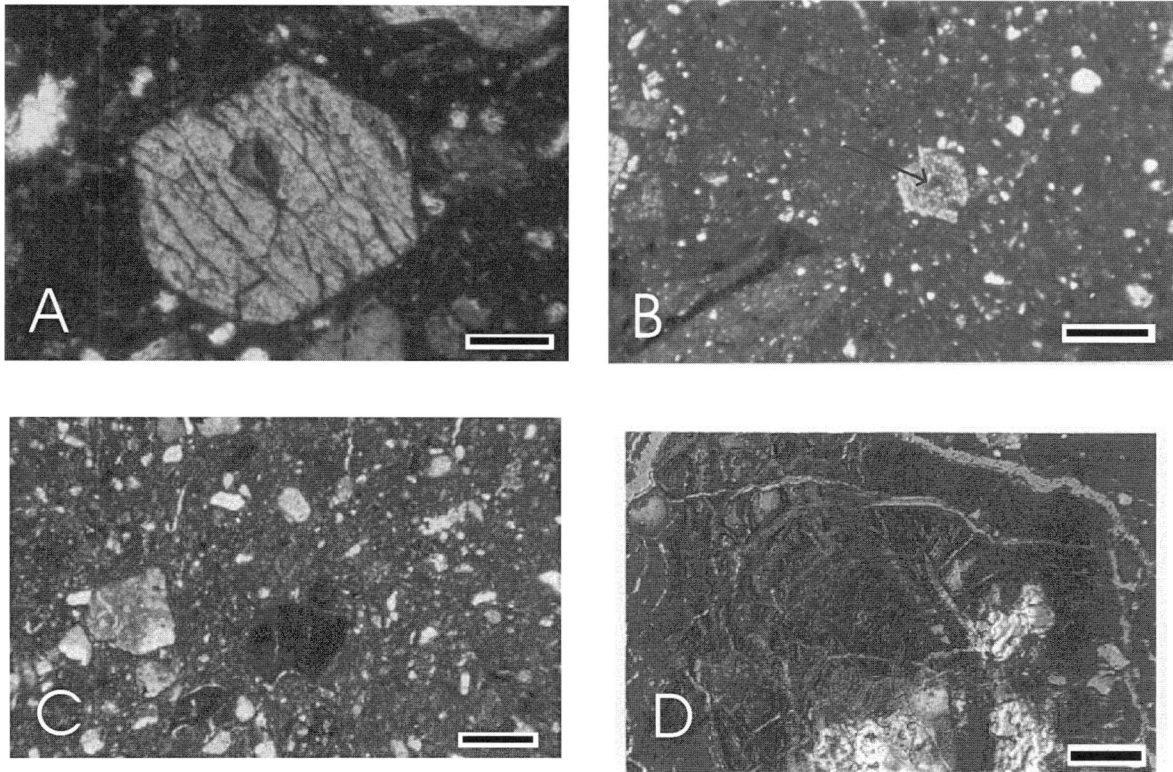

Figure 8: Microphotograph of A: amphibole (arrow) in sample SAG 200. Scale bar is 100 μm, crossed Polars; B: pyroxene (arrow) in sample SAG 210. Scale bar is 250 μm, crossed Polars; C: biotite in sample SAG 210. Scale bar is 250 μm, crossed Polars; D: serpentinite in sample SA97MJ12. Scale bar is 200 μm, parallel Polaroids.

the city itself. The small calcite precipitates present in the sherds are caused by deposition of secondary $CaCO_3$ in the pores of the ceramics. Clay nodules in the sherds can represent the use and mixing of two different clay raw materials or indicate a bad mixture of several layers from the same deposit. The chert fragments present in the sherds probably come from the silicified limestone present around the ophiolites. Fragments of this chert can be present through weathering and transport in the clays derived from the ophiolites. However, cherts were also found in the flysch deposits and in the clays derived from them. Their provenance thus remains unclear.

6.3. Discussion

If we compare the different possible clay resources with the different groups of common ware fabrics (based on chemical signatures), we see that the mineralogy of a particular sherd corresponds to the mineralogy of the clay resource of which it has the chemical signature. In some cases we are probably dealing with mixtures of raw materials. The sherds with the chemical signature of the ophiolitic clay of

Sagalassos have a practically identical mineralogy to the clays: large idiomorphic crystals of biotites, amphiboles and pyroxenes, the presence of apatite and perovskite, a low pyroxene/amphibole ratio (smaller than with other signatures) and a high proportion of plagioclase in the feldspar. This similarity indicates that clays from the site were used in the production of Sagalassos common ware fabrics.

The sherds with the chemical signature of the clays from the flysch possess some mineralogical characteristics of the ophiolitic clays from the site, but also certain characteristics of the clays from the flysch taken at Köyünü, Yazır and Ağlasun. We observe a smaller proportion of plagioclase, a higher pyroxene/amphibole ratio and the presence of small, rounded (weathered) crystals of all minerals together with large idiomorphic crystals of the same minerals. These features point to the mixing of the two clay materials for the production of Sagalassos common ware fabrics.

The sherds with the chemical signature of the detrital clays of Çanaklı have all the mineralogical characteristics of the ophiolitic clays of Sagalassos with the addition of grog in the ceramics. This points to the use of the ophiolitic clays of the site with the addition of large amounts of grog of crushed SRSW. The addition of the grog of the local table ware passes on the chemical signature of the detrital clays of Çanaklı, from which the red slip ware was made (Ottenburgs *et al.*, 1993a). High MgO contents of certain sherds can also be related to the occasional presence of serpentinite fragments in the clays from the tectonized ophiolite sequence (Figure 8d).

The sherds with a mixed chemical signature could have been formed by the addition of more or less grog or flysch clay as a temper. The sherds showing the chemical signature of the flysch clays comprise many more clay nodules, pointing to the mixing of different clays. The addition of volcanic material as a temper or its accidental presence has no clear influence on the chemical signatures, but such an effect cannot be ruled out. It could be the cause of small variations within the different groups of (mixed) chemical signatures. The absence of sherds with a mixed chemical signature between that of the clays from the flysch and that of the detrital clays of Çanaklı points to the continuous use over time of the ophiolitic clay of the site of Sagalassos. This is confirmed by the mineralogy of the pottery. Furthermore, the geochemistry of the large idiomorphic biotites and amphiboles in the sherds and the presence of serpentinite suggests an ophiolitic parent rock such as the bedrock at Saglassos for these minerals.

For all of the three chemical/mineralogical groups, the ware groups 2, 3 and 5 have sherds corresponding to the chemical signatures and mineralogy of these groups. The ceramics of ware group 4 shows only little addition of grog in its chemical signature and mineralogy. No chronological patterns in the use of different clays and tempers throughout the evolution of these ceramics can be seen so far.

7. CONCLUSION

The archaeometrical ceramic research at Sagalassos allowed the identification of most raw materials used in this craft and resulted in the reconstruction of the environmental and socio-economic factors influencing the latter. Mineralogical, petrographical and geochemical techniques were successfully applied in this respect.

8. ACKNOWLEDGEMENTS

This research was supported by the Belgian Programme on Interuniversity Poles of Attraction (IAP V/9) and the Research Fund of the K.U.Leuven (BOF-GOA02/2), next to project G.0152.04 of the Fund for Scientific Research Flanders (FWO).

9. REFERENCES

ARNOLD, D. (1985) *Ceramic theory and cultural process*, Cambridge University Press, Cambridge.

DEGEEST, R. (2000) *The Common Wares of Roman Sagalassos* (*Studies in Eastern Mediterranean Archaeology 3*), Brepols, Turnhout.

DEGEEST, R. and WAELKENS, M. (1993) Sagalassos ware II. The common ware, in: M. WAELKENS (ed.) *Sagalassos I. First General Report on the Survey (1986-1989) and Excavations (1990-1991)* (*Acta Archaeologica Lovaniensia Monographiae 5*), Leuven University Press, Leuven: 131-152.

DEGRYSE, P., DEGEEST, R., POBLOME, J., VIAENE, W., OTTENBURGS, R., KUCHA H. and WAELKENS, M. (2000) Mineralogy and geochemistry of Roman common wares produced at Sagalassos and their possible clay sources, in: M. WAELKENS and L. LOOTS (eds) *Sagalassos V. Report on the Survey and Excavation Campaigns of 1996 and 1997* (*Acta Archaeologica Lovaniensia Monographiae 11*), Leuven University Press, Leuven: 709-722.

DEGRYSE, P., POBLOME, J., DONNERS, K., DECKERS, J. and WAELKENS, M. (2003) Geoarchaeological investigations of the 'potters' quarter' at Sagalassos (SW Turkey), *Geoarchaeology* 18 (2): 255-281.

DEGRYSE, P., POBLOME, J., VIAENE, W., KUCHA, H., OTTENBURGS, R., WAELKENS, M. and NAUD, J. (this volume) Provenancing the slip of Sagalassos red slip ware, in P. Degryse and M. Waelkens (eds.) *Sagalassos VI. Geo- and Bio-archaeology at Sagalassos and in its Territory*, Leuven University Press, Leuven: 255-259.

HERTOGEN, J. and GIJBELS, R. (1971) Instrumental neutron activation analysis of rocks with a low-energy photon detector, *Anal. Chemica Acta* 56: 61-82.

HIGGS, E.S. and VITA-FINZI, C. (1972) Prehistoric economies: a territorial approach, in: E.S. HIGGS (ed.) *Papers in Economic Prehistory*, Cambridge University Press: 27-46.

JARMAN, M.R. (1972) A territorial model for archaeology: a behavioral and geographical approach, in: D.L. CLARKE (ed.) *Models in Archaeology*, Methuen, London: 705-733.

JARMAN, M.R., VITA-FINZI, C. and HIGGS, E.S. (1972) Site catchment analysis in archaeology, in: P.J. UCKO, R. TRINGHAM and G.W. DYMBLEBY (eds.) *Man, Settlement and Urbanism*, Schenkman, Boston: 61-66.

MITCHELL, S. and WAELKENS, M. (1988) Cremna and Sagalassus 1987, *Anatolian Studies* 38: 60-65.

MITCHELL, S., OWENS, E. and WAELKENS, M. (1989) Ariassos and Sagalassos 1988, *Anatolian Studies* 39: 63-77.

OTTENBURGS, R., JORISSEN, C. and VIAENE, W. (1993a) Sagalassos ware IV. Study of the clays, in: M. WAELKENS (ed.) *Sagalassos I. First General Report on the Survey (1986-1989) and Excavations (1990-1991)* (*Acta Archaeologica Lovaniensia Monographiae 5*), Leuven University Press, Leuven: 163-169.

OTTENBURGS, R., VIAENE, W. and JORISSEN, C. (1993b) Mineralogy and firing properties of clays at and near the archaeological site of Sagalassos, in: M. WAELKENS and J. POBLOME (eds.) *Sagalassos II. Report on the Third Excavation Campaign of 1992* (*Acta Archaeologica Lovaniensia Monographiae 6*), Leuven University Press, Leuven: 209-220.

PEACOCK, D.P.S. (1977) Ceramics in Roman and Medieval Archaeology, in: D.P.S. PEACOCK (ed.) *Pottery and Early Commerce*, Academic Press, London: 21-34.

PEACOCK, D.P.S. (1982) *Pottery in the Roman World: an Ethnoarchaeological Approach*, Longmans, London.

POBLOME, J. (1996) Production and distribution of Sagalassos Red Slip Ware. A dialogue with the Roman economy, in: M. HERFORT-KOCH, U. MANDEL and U. SCHÄDLER (eds.) *Hellenistische und kaiserzeitliche Keramik des östlichen Mittelmeergebietes*: 75-103.

POBLOME, J. (1999) *Red slip ware produced at Sagalassos (southern Turkey). Typology and chronology* (*Studies in Eastern Mediterranean Archaeology II*), Brepols, Turnhout.

POBLOME, J. (2006) Made in Sagalassos. Modelling regional potential and constraints, in: S. MENCHELLI and M. PASQUINUCCI (eds.) *Territorio e produzioni ceramiche. Paesaggi, economia e societa in età romana* (*Instrumenta 2*) Pisa University Press: 355-363.

POBLOME, J., DEGEEST, R., WAELKENS, M. and SCHELTENS, E. (1993) Sagalassos ware I. The fine ware, in: M. WAELKENS (ed.) *Sagalassos I. First General Report on the Survey (1986-1989) and Excavations (1990-1991)* (*Acta Archaeologica Lovaniensia Monographiae 5*), Leuven University Press, Leuven: 113-130.

POBLOME, J., DEGRYSE, P., SCHLITZ, M., DEGEEST, R., VIAENE, W., LIBRECHT, I., PAULISSEN, E. and WAELKENS, M. (2000) The ceramic production centre of Sagalassos, *Rei Cretariae Romanae Fautorum Acta* 36: 39-42.

POBLOME, J., EKINCI, H.A., ÖZTÜRK, I., DEGRYSE, P., VIAENE, W. and WAELKENS, M. (2000) An early Byzantine tile and lime kiln on the territory of Sagalassos, in: M. ELKENS and L. LOOTS (eds.) *Sagalassos V. Report on the Survey and Excavation Campaigns of 1996 and 1997* (*Acta Archaeologica Lovaniensia Monographiae 11 and 12*), Leuven University Press, Leuven: 669-683.

POBLOME, J., SCHLITZ, M. and DEGRYSE, P. (1998) Recycling misfired pottery. A standard practice of the potters at ancient Sagalassos? *Forum Archaeologiae, Zeitschrift für klassische Archäologie*, 9/XII/1998 allergy.hno.akh-wien.ac.at/forum/forum1298/09halde.htm.

POBLOME, J., VIAENE, W., KUCHA, H., WAELKENS, M., LADURON, D. and DEPUYDT, F. (1997) The clay raw materials of Sagalassos red slip ware. A chronological evaluation, in: M. WAELKENS and J. POBLOME (eds.) *Sagalassos IV. Report on the Survey and Excavation Campaigns of 1994 and 1995* (*Acta Archaeologica Lovaniensia Monographiae 9*), Leuven University Press, Leuven: 507-518.

POBLOME, J., DEGRYSE, P., VIAENE, W., OTTENBURGS, R., WAELKENS, M., DEGEEST, R. and NAUD, J. (2002) The concept of a pottery production centre. An archaeometrical contribution from ancient Sagalassos, *Journal of Archaeological Science* 29: 873-882.

POBLOME, J., CORREMANS, M., BES, P., ROMANUS, K. and DEGRYSE, P. (2008) It is never too late...The late Roman initiation of amphora production in the territory of Sagalassos, in: I. DELEMEN, S. COKAY-KEPÇE and A. ÖZDIBAY (eds.) *Festschrift for Haluk Abbasoğlu*, 1011-1022.

RICE, P.M. (1987) *Pottery Analysis. A Sourcebook*, The University of Chicago Press, Chicago.

RYE, O.S. (1976) Keeping your temper under controll: materials and the manufacture of Papuan pottery, *Archaeology and Physical Anthropology in Oceania* 11: 106-137.

SACK, R.O. and GHIORSO, M.S. (1991) An internally consistent model for the thermodynamic properties of Fe-Mg–titano magnetite-aluminate spinel, *Contributions to Mineralogy and Petrology* 106: 474-505.

SHEPARD, O. (1956) *Ceramic Technology*, Carnegie Institution of Washington Yearbook 51: 263-266.

VIAENE, W., BOCQUET, A., DEGEEST, R. and POBLOME, J. (1993) Analysis of slip of Sagalassos Ware, in: M. WAELKENS and J. POBLOME (ed.) *Sagalassos II. Report on the third excavation campaign of 1992* (*Acta Archaeologica Lovaniensia Monographiae 6*), Leuven University Press, Leuven: 221-227.

VIAENE, W., OTTENBURGS, R., KUCHA, H., POBLOME, J. and WAELKENS, M. (1995a) Firing temperature of Sagalassos red slip ware, in: M. WAELKENS and J. POBLOME (eds.) *Sagalassos III. Report on the Fourth Excavation Campaign of 1993* (*Acta Archaeologica Lovaniensia Monographiae 7*), Leuven University Press, Leuven: 235-243.

VIAENE, W., POBLOME, J., OTTENBURGS, R., KUCHA, H., HERTOGEN, J., VYNCKIER, C., WAELKENS, M. and LADURON, D. (1995b) Geochemical distribution of trace elements in Sagalassos red slip ware, in: M. WAELKENS and J. POBLOME (eds.) *Sagalassos III. Report on the Fourth Excavation Campaign of 1993* (*Acta Archaeologica Lovaniensia Monographiae 7*), Leuven University Press, Leuven: 245-254.

VIAENE, W., WAELKENS, M., OTTENBURGS, R. and CALLEBAUT, K. (1997) Archaeometric study of mortars used at Sagalassos, in: M. WAELKENS and J. POBLOME (eds.) *Sagalassos IV. Report on the Survey and Excavation Campaigns of 1994 and 1995* (*Acta Archaeologica Lovaniensia Monographiae 9*), Leuven University Press, Leuven: 405-421.

WAELKENS, M., BAŞER, S., LODEWIJCKX, M., VIAENE, W. and DEGEEST, R. (1990) Sagalassos 1989. The rescue excavation in the potter's quarter and the "Sagalassos ware", *Acta Archaeologica Lovaniensia* 28-29: 75-98.

WAELKENS, W., HARMANKAYA, A. and VIAENE, W. (1991) The excavations at Sagalassos 1990, *Anatolian Studies* 41, 197-213.

WAELKENS, M., OWENS, E., HASENDONCKX, A. and ARIKAN, B. (1992) The excavations at Sagalassos 1991, *Anatolian Studies* 42: 79-98.

WAELKENS, M., VANHAVERBEKE, H., PAULISSEN, E., VIAENE, W., DECKERS, J., VAN NEER, W., REYNIERS, J., DE CUPERE, B. and POBLOME, J. (1998) The survey and archaeometrical research at Sagalassos 1996, *The XIIIth International Symposium on Archaeometry*, Ankara: 1-29.

WAELKENS, M., PAULISSEN, E., VERMOERE, M., DEGRYSE, P., CELIS, D., SCHROYEN, K., DE CUPERE, B., LIBRECHT, I., NACKAERTS, K., VANHAVERBEKE, H., VIAENE, W., MUCHEZ, P., OTTENBURGS, R., DECKERS, S., VAN NEER, W., SMETS, E., GOVERS, G., VERSTRAETEN, G., STEEGEN, A. and CAUWENBERGHS, K. (1999) Man and environment in the territory of Sagalassos, a classical city in SW Turkey, *Quaternary Science Reviews* 18: 697-709.

WAELKENS, M., POBLOME, J., PAULISSEN, E., TALLOEN, P., VAN DEN BERGH, J., VANDERGINST, V., ARIKAN, B., VAN DAMME, I., AKYEL, I., MARTENS, F., MARTENS, M., UYTTERHOEVEN, I., DEBRUYNE, T., DEPRAETERE, D., BARAN, K., VANDAELE, B., PARRAS, Z., YILDIRIM, S., BUBEL, S., VANHAVERBEKE, H., LICOPPE, C., LANDUYT, F., DEGEEST, R., VANDEPUT, L., LOOTS, L., PATRICIO, T., ERCAN, S., VAN BALEN, K., SMITS, E., DEPUYDT, F., MOENS, L. and DE PAEPE, P. (2000a) The 1996 and 1997 excavation seasons at Sagalassos, in: M. WAELKENS and L. LOOTS (eds.) *Sagalassos V. Report on the Survey and Excavation Campaigns of 1996 and 1997* (*Acta Archaeologica Lovaniensia Monographiae 11*), Leuven University Press, Leuven: 217-398.

254

PROVENANCING THE SLIP OF SAGALASSOS RED SLIP WARE

Patrick DEGRYSE, Jeroen POBLOME, Willy VIAENE[†], Harry KUCHA, Raoul OTTENBURGS,
Marc WAELKENS and Jean NAUD

1. INTRODUCTION

One of the aims of the new excavation programme in the potters' quarter, which started in 1997, was the integration of archaeometrical knowledge in order to study every single aspect of the pottery manufacturing process of Sagalassos in detail. As a result of this fieldwork, the source of the clays used for the slip of the local tableware or Sagalassos red slip ware (SRSW) was identified. The slip layer was already characterised by Viaene et al. (1993). In this study, the slip layer of 18 samples of SRSW was petrographically and geochemically investigated. The composition of the slip was determined and a correlation made with possible raw materials.

2. MATERIALS AND METHODS

Thin sections of the samples were prepared and examined with a polarising microscope. Areas where the slip was well preserved were selected for microprobe analysis. These were made at the Université Catholique Louvain-la-Neuve with a Cameca Camebax SX 50 microbeam electron microprobe with energy dispersive X-ray analysis system at 15 kV.

Bulk analysis of clay samples was also performed. When dry, the clay samples were gently crushed and sieved. The fraction smaller than 250 μm was used for analysis. A representative part of each sample was dissolved in a lithium metaborate flux, which was then dissolved in diluted HNO_3. Components SiO_2, Al_2O_3, Fe_2O_3, MgO, CaO, P_2O_5 and TiO_2 were determined by AES. Na_2O and K_2O contents were measured from the same solution through AAS. To enable a valid comparison between clays and sherds, the chemical composition of the clays was recalculated by putting the sum of the non-volatile oxides equal to one hundred percent, since a large part of the volatile components of the clays disappear during firing and the resulting ceramics do no longer contain them (Ottenburgs et al., 1993). The results of the microprobe analysis of the slip layers were likewise recalculated to one hundred percent. The mineralogical composition of the clays was determined by X-ray diffractometry (XRD). Operational parameters were as follows: Cu K_a radiation, graphite monochromator, 45 kV, 30 mA, automatic divergence slit, receiving slit of 0.1°.

The 18 sherd samples were collected at six different sites in Sagalassos (Table 1): two ceramic dumps in the potters' quarter (sites D and F), a house to the north of the library (site L), the library itself (Lib), the esplanade in front of the library (Espla) and the waste dump to the west of the Doric temple (site WDT).

Sample	Site	Type
SJ1	Site D	1A140
SJ12	Espla	1C140
Sag 14	Site D	1B233
Sag 15	Site D	1C160
Sag 60	Site F	1C140
Sag 177	Lib	1B190
Sag 178	Site F	1B170
Sag 179	Site D	1B150
Sag 312	Site L	1B170
Sag 313	Site L	1C100
Sag 314	Site L	1F150
Sag 315	Lib	1C180
Sag 316	Site WDT	1B130
Sag 317	Site WDT	1B220
Sag 318	Site WDT	1B230
Sag 319	Site WDT	1C180
Sag 320	Site WDT	1F160
Sag 331	Site F	1B170

Table 1: The samples studied.

Sites D (Waelkens *et al.*, 1990) and F (Waelkens *et al.*, 1991; 1992) were both Roman family tombs, which were plundered in antiquity. In the case of site D, the tomb was filled with a mixture of re-deposited potter's dumps. This was also the case at site F; on a series of terraces in front of the vaulted tomb, a dump composed of several third century AD failed kiln loads was located.

The original construction of the library was dated by an inscribed dedication on the lower part of the back wall to shortly after 120 AD (Waelkens *et al.*, 1995; 1997, for the preliminary excavation reports; Devijver, 1993, for the set of inscriptions). The library, however, was possibly built inside an older, Hellenistic construction, of which only one wall was exposed. By the time the library was built this construction had already been abandoned and another structure had been built on top of it. This construction, presumably a house, contained several rooms of which the northern sides have not been reached. The space between the library and the house was filled intentionally. The house (site L) was abandoned during the third century AD. The library (Lib) was destroyed during the third quarter of the next century and backfilled. Part of this fill swept onto the esplanade, laid out in front of the library, when the front wall of the ruined building was dismantled. Other erosional material mixed into these deposits (Espla).

The stratigraphy excavated in the corner formed by the west wall of the Doric temple and the later Roman fortification wall abutting it (site WDT) has been interpreted as a waste dump datable to the first half of the sixth century AD (Waelkens *et al.*, 1992; 1993). These deposits indicated that the fortification system may not have functioned longer than a century in this area and were abandoned before the town of Sagalassos was.

The 18 samples represented 14 different protagonist types and variants in the chronological evolution of SRSW from early Imperial to early Byzantine times (Poblome, 1999) (Table 1). The general chronological distribution of the types and variants is illustrated in Figure 1 and was determined following the technique established by Fentress and Perkins (1988). Therefore, firstly, the date range of each type and variant was defined. In a next step, the distribution was determined considering it equally probable for a vessel to be made in each year of its range. In other words, a vessel with a date range of 100 years has a probability of 1/100. This figure is multiplied by the total amount of sherds for one type or variant in order to estimate the general relative popularity. Instead of years, longer periods of time may be used as well, 15 or 25 years for instance. In this case, in order to create a general picture, the distribution pattern was not calculated using years or equal periods. We rather opted

to imply the 9 main phases of the chronological evolution of SRSW, as defined in Poblome (1999) and Poblome *et al.* (2005). Clearly, most samples belonged to the late Roman and early Byzantine periods.

3. PETROGRAPHY

All samples had a homogeneous fabric, orange to brown in colour. In some samples few large shaping pores were present, while minute pores were homogeneously distributed. The slip layer varied from orange-red to brown and dark brown. It was less porous than the paste and its thickness mostly 5 to 10 µm (Viaene *et al.*, 1993). The thickness of the slip was uniform in one and the same sample. Minute, brighter inclusions can be observed, representing free hematite giving the slip its characteristic red-orange colour. An exception was sample Sag 320, showing a white slip of 40 µm thickness. An XRD study showed that this slip was composed of a mixture of cordierite and muscovite.

4. CHEMICAL COMPOSITION OF THE SLIP

The chemical analysis results of the slip obtained with microprobe techniques are given in Table 2. Three groups of slip were recognized: the common slip of SRSW (15 samples), a high potassium slip (2 samples) and the exceptional white slip (1 sample). Viaene *et al.* (1993) already demonstrated that the common slip had a higher Al_2O_3 and K_2O content than the body, but a lower MgO and CaO content. The content in Fe_2O_3, Na_2O and TiO_2 was similar. The high potassium slip showed a much higher content in K_2O and MgO but a much lower content in Al_2O_3 and Fe_2O_3. The white slip showed an entirely different chemical composition.

5. GEOCHEMISTRY OF THE CLAYS

W. Viaene *et al.* (1993) ruled out the use of the same clay raw material for the production of the body and slip of SRSW. Ottenburgs *et al.* (1993) pointed out that a Mg-chlorite-rich clay was used for the production of the body. The high Al_2O_3 content of the slip pointed to the use of an enriched clay suspension for the making of the slip layer. As the MgO content of the common slip of SRSW was lower than that of the body, a suspension of the clay used for the body could not have been used for the slip. The use of the same clay raw material would show the opposite, an increase in the MgO content. The analysis of the common slip showed a higher K_2O and lower MgO content, pointing to the use of an illite rich clay suspension for the

	Mean Slip		High K$_2$O		White slip
	mean	st. dev.	mean	st. dev.	
SiO$_2$	50.01	1.67	54.89	2.81	42.74
Al$_2$O$_3$	28.85	1.92	25.44	4.27	26.71
FeO	9.13	1.11	3.66	0.11	10.20
MnO	0.06	0.02	0.05	0.01	0.08
MgO	2.45	0.68	3.64	0.67	6.20
CaO	2.25	1.35	2.31	0.90	8.75
Na$_2$O	1.35	0.50	1.09	0.41	1.91
K$_2$O	5.16	1.03	8.43	0.41	2.79
TiO$_2$	0.74	0.15	0.51	0.20	0.61

Table 2: Chemical composition of the different types of slip layer.

manufacturing of the slip. Such illite rich clay was found in the potters' quarter itself, being the clay derived from the weathered ophiolite sequence.

For the ophiolitic clays from Sagalassos, the main clay minerals present were smectite and illite with a smaller amount of chlorite (Degryse et al., this volume). The feldspars were mainly plagioclase and K-feldspar poor in Na. Magnetite was a common residual mineral in these clays. Also amphiboles and biotite were largely present. The mean chemical composition of these clays is given in Table 3.

As the efforts on behalf of the ancient potters to find a suitable clay for making a slip layer could have been a lot higher than for finding workable clays for the production of the body (Arnold, 1985), clays found at a larger distance from Sagalassos were studied as well. In this way, the lake sediments of the south bank of Lake Burdur were examined. The main clay mineral was chlorite, with smaller amounts of smectite and illite. A lot of salts from the evaporation of lake water were present, comprising bloedite (Na$_2$Mg(SO$_4$)$_2$.4H$_2$O), hydromagnesite (Mg$_5$(CO$_3$)$_4$(OH)$_2$.4H$_2$O), halite (NaCl), natron (Na$_2$CO$_3$.10H$_2$O), gypsum (CaSO$_4$.2H$_2$O) and trona (Na$_3$H(CO$_3$)$_2$.2H$_2$O). Muscovite and lepidolite as micas, some metamorphic minerals such as allanite and lawsonite and the minerals calcite, dolomite, quartz and some feldspar were also present in the lake sediments. The chemistry of these clays is given in Table 3. Notice the high MgO and Na$_2$O content, together with the extremely high CaO and LOI. This can point to salts being present. However, it is clear that these clays had a Mg-rich chloritic nature.

6. DISCUSSION

With the decantation of clays, the coarser fraction of the raw material was removed. For the ophiolitic clays, this meant the removal of amphiboles, biotites and feldspars, leaving behind the illite and smectite with smaller amounts of chlorite. This would lead to an increase in the Fe$_2$O$_3$, Al$_2$O$_3$ and K$_2$O content of the material, while the content in SiO$_2$, MgO and CaO would decrease. Viaene et al. (1993) proved that the fraction <10 μm of the residual clays of the ophiolitic sequence could attain a K$_2$O content of more than 4%. However, in the former study, only partly weathered clays of the ophiolitic sequence were used. The entirely weathered clays recovered from the new sondages and drillings in the potters' quarter showed an even higher K$_2$O content (Table 3: sample WV3). This led to the conclusion that the entirely weathered ophiolitic clays were largely suitable as a raw material for the production of the slip layer on the tableware of Sagalassos, chemically corresponding to the common slip layer composition. A washed fraction of the ophiolitic clays was used for this purpose.

The second group, the high potassium slip, showed a lower Al$_2$O$_3$ and Fe$_2$O$_3$ content, pointing to the use of a raw material poorer in clay but with a higher K$_2$O and MgO content. As the total content in K$_2$O exceeded by large the content of a pure illitic clay (a mean of 7%; Weaver et al., 1975), it is very unlikely that only a pure clay suspension was used for the manufacture of this slip. It is likely that the extra K$_2$O came from potassium feldspar. The high MgO content made it unlikely that the same clay raw material as for the common slip was used, even with the addition of

	ophiolite clay (n = 13)		ophiolite clay (n = 1, WV3)		Burdur clay (n = 2)
	<250μm	LOI-free	<250μm	LOI-free	<250μm
SiO₂	54.60	59.60	55.89	59.17	33.90
Al₂O₃	16.03	17.50	17.42	18.44	6.54
Fe₂O₃	7.03	7.67	5.78	6.12	3.76
MnO	0.17	0.19	0.26	0.28	0.08
MgO	3.58	3.91	3.90	4.13	8.01
CaO	3.60	3.93	2.54	2.69	20.40
Na₂O	1.22	1.33	1.67	1.77	2.24
K₂O	3.50	3.82	5.60	5.93	0.96
TiO₂	0.90	0.98	0.50	0.53	0.45
P₂O₅	0.23	0.25	0.08	0.08	0.29
LOI	8.39	–	5.55	–	23.85

Table 3: Chemical composition of the clays derived from the weathered ophiolitic sequence. Sample WV3 is an entirely weathered ophiolitic clay.

K-feldspar. Such type of clay raw material is unknown in the region of Sagalassos. However, for the purpose of slip manufacturing, raw materials can sometimes be obtained from quite large distances (Arnold, 1985).

It was clear from the mineralogical analysis that the exceptional white slip had an entirely different source material than the common slip. The white slip layer contained the minerals muscovite and cordierite. Minerals such as cordierite readily form in the early stages of metamorphism of argillaceous rocks (Deer et al., 1992), mainly at the expense of chlorite. Therefore, this type of slip was probably formed from a clay suspension enriched in chlorite. The slipped vessels were subsequently fired in reducing conditions resulting in the attested white colour by incorporating iron into the structure of cordierite. The high MgO and chlorite content of the Lake Burdur sediments, together with the presence of metamorphic minerals and suitable micas, make these clays a likely source for the white slip. The raw materials would have been extracted around Lake Burdur and washed in order to retain the small clay fraction and remove the salts and larger constituents.

7. CONCLUSION

The attested variations in the slip chemistry suggested that the main body of slip, the common slip, was manufactured in a standardized way throughout the period of production of SRSW, using residual illite-rich clay suspensions extracted from the weathered ophiolite sequence found in the local potters' quarter. A high-potassium slip and white slip were applied on SRSW as well, indicating the use of other types of clay to obtain a good quality slip. These included unprovenanced illitic clays with undecomposed K-feldspar and Mg-rich chloritic clays from the shores of Lake Burdur. At this stage it is not clear how important both other types of slip were in the production of SRSW. As the differing slip compositions were applied on the standard Fabric 1 of the Sagalassos tableware, it seems reasonable to presume that the unidentified illitic clay and the Burdur clay were transported to Sagalassos and processed in the local potters' quarter. The only attested example of white slip was applied on type 1F160, datable to late Roman times. The high potassium slip was associated with types 1B150 and 1B220 and can therefore have been in use from quite early in the evolution of SRSW to the end of its production. The variation of clay raw materials illustrates the ancient potters' profound knowledge of the potential of raw materials, their efforts to collect the clays and, in the case of the white slip, experience with reducing firing conditions.

8. ACKNOWLEDGEMENTS

This research was supported by the Belgian Programme on Interuniversitary Poles of Attraction (IAP V/9) and the Research Fund of the K.U.Leuven (BOF-GOA02/2), next to project G.0152.04 of the Fund for Scientific Research Flanders (FWO).

9. REFERENCES

ARNOLD, D. (1985) *Ceramic Theory and Cultural Process*, Cambridge.

DEER, W.A., HOWIE, R.A. and ZUSSMAN, J. (1992) *An Introduction to the Rock Forming Minerals*, Hong Kong.

DEGRYSE, P. and POBLOME, J. (this volume) Clays for mass production of table and common wares, amphorae and architectural ceramics at Sagalassos, In: P. Degryse and M. Waelkens (eds.) *Sagalassos VI. Geo- and Bio-Archaeology at Sagalassos and in its Territory*, Leuven University Press, Leuven: 231-254.

DEVIJVER, H. (1993) The inscriptions of the Neon-Library of Roman Sagalassos, in: M. WAELKENS and J. POBLOME (ed.) *Sagalassos II. Report on the third excavation campaign of 1992 (Acta Archaeologica Lovaniensia Monographiae 6)*, Leuven University Press, Leuven: 107-123.

FENTRESS, E. and PERKINS, P. (1988) Counting African Red Slip Ware, in: A. MASTINO (ed.) *L'Africa romana. Atti del V convegno di studio Sassari, 11-13 decembre 1987*, Ozieri: 205-214.

OTTENBURGS, R., JORISSEN, C. and VIAENE, W. (1993) Study of the clays, in: M. WAELKENS (ed.) *Sagalassos I (Acta Archaeologica Monographiae Lovaniensia 5)*, Leuven University Press, Leuven: 163-169.

POBLOME, J. (1999) *Red Slip Ware Produced at Sagalassos (Southern Turkey). Typology and chronology (Studies in Eastern Mediterranean Archaeology II)*, Brepols, Turnhout.

POBLOME, J., BES, P. and DEGRYSE, P. (2005) The decline and fall of Sagalassos. A ceramic perspective, *Rei Cretariae Romanae Fautores Acta* 39: 225-230.

VIAENE, W., BOCQUET, A., DEGEEST, R. and POBLOME, J. (1993) Analysis of slip of Sagalassos Ware, in: M. WAELKENS and J. POBLOME (ed.) *Sagalassos II. Report on the third excavation campaign of 1992 (Acta Archaeologica Lovaniensia Monographiae 6)*, Leuven University Press, Leuven: 221-227.

WAELKENS, M., BAŞER, S., LODEWIJCKX, M., VIAENE, W. and DEGEEST, R. (1990) Sagalassos 1989. The rescue excavation in the potter's quarter and the "Sagalassos ware", *Acta Archaeologica Lovaniensia* 28-29: 75-98.

WAELKENS, W., HARMANKAYA, A. and VIAENE, W. (1991) The excavations at Sagalassos 1990, *Anatolian Studies* 41, 197-213.

WAELKENS, M., OWENS, E., HASENDONCKX, A. and ARIKAN, B. (1992) The excavations at Sagalassos 1991, *Anatolian Studies* 42: 79-98.

WAELKENS, M., PAULISSEN, E., OWENS, E., ARIKAN, B., GIJSEN, L., MARTENS, M., MATAOUCHEK, V. and VANDAELE, K. (1995) The 1993 Excavations in the Fountain House-Library Area, in: M. WAELKENS and J. POBLOME (ed.) *Sagalassos III. Report on the fourth excavation campaign of 1993 (Acta Archaeologica Lovanensia Monographiae 7)*, Leuven University Press, Leuven: 47-89.

WAELKENS, M., VERMEERSCH, P.M., PAULISSEN, E., OWENS, E., ARIKAN, B., MARTENS, M., TALLOEN, P., GIJSEN, L., LOOTS, L., PELEMAN, C., POBLOME, J., DEGEEST, R., PATRICIO, T.C., ERCAN, S. and DEPUYDT, F. (1997) The 1994 and 1995 excavations seasons at Sagalassos, in: M. WAELKENS and J. POBLOME (ed.) *Sagalassos IV. Report on the survey and excavation campaigns of 1994 and 1995 (Acta Archaeologica Lovaniensia Monographiae 9)*, Leuven University Press, Leuven: 103-216.

WEAVER, C.E. and POLLARD, L.D. (1975) *The Chemistry of Clay Minerals (Developments in Sedimentology 15)*, Amsterdam.

THE SAGALASSOS QUARRY LANDSCAPE: BRINGING QUARRIES IN CONTEXT

**Patrick DEGRYSE, Tom HELDAL, Elizabeth BLOXAM, Per STOREMYR, Marc WAELKENS
and Philippe MUCHEZ**

1. INTRODUCTION

Ancient south-western Turkey has always been an area of magnificent white limestone, which was not only extensively used in the local architecture, but was also exported to nearby Pamphylia (Ward-Perkins, 1980; Greenhalgh, 1987; Waelkens *et al.*, 2002). An honorific inscription mentioning the '*local marble of Sagalassos*' shows how closely the polished limestone of the area resembles marble (Waelkens *et al.*, 1997a; Greenhalgh, 1987): "…*Concerning this monument, if it wrongly impresses to be carved in Phrygian stone, it misleads you. The stone originates locally*". In this context, 'Phrygian stone' can only mean marble from ancient Dokimeion (near modern Afyon, 250 km north of Sagalassos) and more specifically the famous purple veined variety, known as 'pavanazetto', that was especially popular for columns, wall veneer and floor pavements in the capital and most of the Imperial provinces, where it was referred to as 'Phrygian marble'. It should not be forgotten, however, that for the ancients (and even today) every stone that could receive a high polish was a 'marble' (Peacock, 1994; Waelkens, 1994). Although Greenhalgh (1987) mentions the polishing qualities of the local limestone, concerning the existence of local marble around Sagalassos, she concludes "whether or not this is true is uncertain, as the stone has not been identified". It is clear that some confusion exists between the geological definition of 'marble' and the ancient use of the term 'marble'. Also the identification by Fleischer (1979) of the building stones of the northwest Heroon at Sagalassos as being marble, shows how well the high quality limestone of Sagalassos resembles this most precious of stones.

The existence of quarries in the neighbourhood of Sagalassos had already been attested before, but a detailed study was never carried out. In his account of the monuments of Sagalassos, Lanckoronski (1893) only mentions the use of (pink) limestone for the construction of the Temple of Antoninus Pius (and the divine Hadrian, as was recently established; Waelkens, 2002), as well as the fact that the theatre of the city was partly built on the bedrock that furnished its building blocks. Of the other eighteenth to twentieth century AD visitors of the city, none seem to have spent any time in the quarries of Sagalassos. Greenhalgh (1987) briefly discusses the stone building materials and mentions the existence of large limestone quarries in the vicinity of Kremna and Sagalassos.

Only recently the quarries of Sagalassos have attracted more interest. From the start of the Sagalassos Archaeological Research Project, geologists have accompanied archaeologists in the field. A preliminary study of the building stones at Sagalassos did not include the quarries proper (Viaene *et al.*, 1993). However, in the context of an extensive survey of the territory of the city during 1994 and 1995, the remains of two large ancient quarries were recorded (Waelkens *et al.*, 1997b). A small scale survey of the quarries on the site and in the immediate vicinity of the city was carried out from 1998 to 2002 (Loots, 2001). After the preliminary study by Viaene *et al.* (1993), which provided a first petrographical and geochemical overview of the building stone used at the site of Sagalassos, all building stones occurring in the city were systematically studied and inventoried, together with the stone material extracted from quarries located in the territory of the city.

A macroscopical description and a lithological-facies analysis of the natural stone in the territory of Sagalassos have been published by Degryse *et al.* (this volume a) and Muchez *et al.* (this volume a). A comparison of the results from a study of the building stones in the city (Degryse *et al.*, 2003) with those from the above-mentioned research in the city's territory, eventually resulted in a provenance determination of most building stones.

The purpose of the present quarry survey was to relate the quarrying of local stone on the territory to specific building projects at Sagalassos. The important research questions were to characterize the quarries according to their individual significance and their role in the development of the city, the recognition of workshops and other quarry related features, a more detailed investigation of the geological features of the individual quarries and quarry groups and questioning the relationship between volumes that were quarried and the volumes that were used. It explores the potential of contextualizing a well-known quarry landscape from site investigation, by studying production and consumption patterns to conservation strategies. The main objectives, however, are to compile an overview of the Sagalassos quarry landscape regarding site characterization, production and consumption patterns and to explore the quarry landscape as being a part of the extended "urban landscape" of Sagalassos.

2. METHODOLOGY

Quarries have been mapped in detail using GPS and satellite photographs. Distinction is made between quarry areas, defined as confined areas where the rock faces display multiple evidence of extraction, which can be assumed to have been one of the main local sources providing stone for the city, and smaller, single extractions. The latter are either trial quarries, looking for building material, or very small extractions meant to produce at the most one or a few objects. Furthermore, areas where subsurface quarries covered by scree deposits or buildings may exist, are also marked.

The determination of the provenance of archaeological materials is an essential part of archaeometry. While the origin of marble and other precious stone is intensely studied, especially in the Mediterranean (e.g. Herz and Waelkens, 1988; Waelkens *et al.*, 1992; Maniatis *et al.*, 1995; Herrmann *et al.*, 2002; Lazzarini, 2002), all too often limestone quarries and building materials are not taken into consideration. However, microfacies analysis of this type of stone has a great potential for differentiating and provenancing local, regional or imported materials (Flügel and Flügel, 1997a; 1997b).

A selection of building stones and quarries was carefully sampled. First, a macroscopical study classified the building stones into categories or types based on mineralogy, colour and the presence of fractures, veins and stylolites. For samples of each category, a complementary petrographical study was carried out and microfacies types were identified. Based on this macroscopical and petrographical study, main- and sub-types of building stones could be defined. Finally, these results were compared with those obtained from macroscopical, petrographical and geochemical analysis of quarries from the territory of the ancient city (e.g. Degryse *et al.*, 2006, this volume a; b).

Thin section petrography was performed and facies were described according to Flügel (1982, 2004). Examples of thin sections and facies descriptions are shown in Figure 1.

The texture of the limestone indicates the depositional environment especially if sedimentation occurred below (mud- and wackestone texture), around (wacke- to packstone texture) or above wave base (pack- to grainstone texture). The biota can reflect sedimentation in an open marine environment (crinoids, bivalves, gastropods, corals, foraminifers…), a restricted (lagoonal) environment (calcispheres, ostracods…) or a deeper shelf to basinal setting (radiolaria, sponge spicules…). Stable isotope analysis of oxygen and carbon was carried out at the University of Erlangen (dr. M. Joachimski). The samples were reacted with 100% phosphoric acid at 75°C in an online carbonate preparation line (Carbo Kiel single sample bath) connected to a Finnigan Mat 252 mass spectrometer. Isotope data are expressed as per mil (‰) deviation from the Vienna Pee Dee Belemnite (VPDB) standard. Reproducibility was checked by replicate analysis of laboratory standards and is better than 0.02‰ for $\delta^{13}C$ (1σ) and 0.03‰ for $\delta^{18}O$ (1σ).

3. GEOLOGICAL BACKGROUND

Sagalassos is geologically located in the Isparta Angle (Robertson, 1993). Rock types and associated structures within this area indicate a progressive evolution from continental rifting and passive margin development to ocean basin formation from Triassic to late Cretaceous times (Dilek and Rowland, 1993). Regional compression began in the latest Cretaceous and led to subduction-accretion. The Antalya nappes were emplaced towards the north onto the Bey Dağları carbonate platform in the latest Cretaceous to Palaeocene. In the late Eocene, this platform was overthrusted from the northeast by the Beyşehir-Hoyran-Hadım nappes. Finally, during the late Miocene, the Lycean nappes were emplaced onto the Bey Dağları platform from the northwest. Sagalassos is situated in the frontal area of the Lycean nappes, on the western flank of the Isparta Angle (Degryse *et al.*, this volume a; Muchez *et al.*, this volume). The geology of the area is described in detail by the latter authors.

For this study, especially the platform carbonates around the city of Sagalassos are important. They consist of six major lithological units, described by Muchez *et al.* (2003; this volume). In some of these units (A and F), quarries were opened around the monumental centre of Sagalassos. The massif beige limestone (unit A) is mainly characterized by bioclastic wackestone with crinoids, foraminifers, bivalves, calpionellids, ostracods, gastropods, sponge spicules, rudist fragments, pellets, micritized grains and clasts. The beige limestone with white chert nodules (unit B) consists of a bioclastic wackestone with abundant radiolaria, sponge spicules, bivalves and occasional gastropods. The thin-bedded, red limestone (unit C) is a bioclastic wackestone with radiolaria,

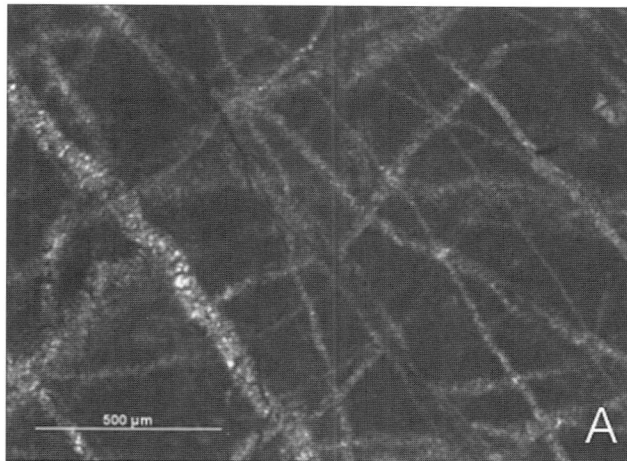

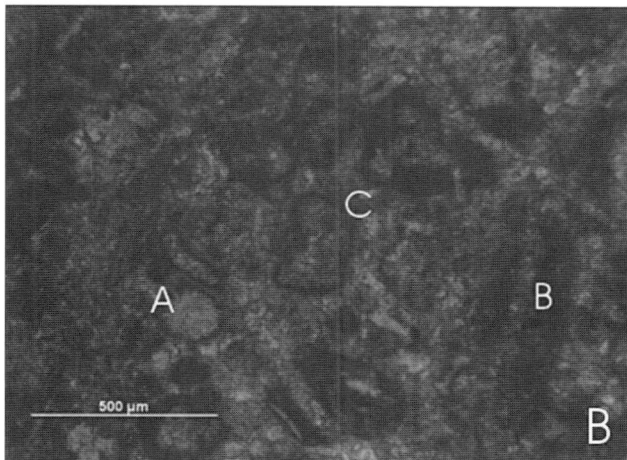

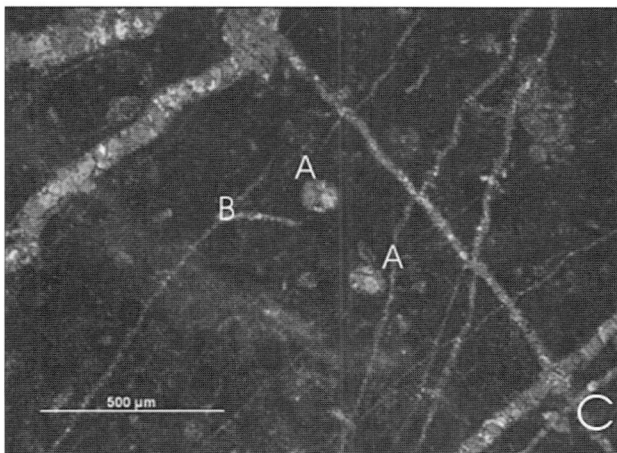

Figure 1: Example of thin sections and facies descriptions a) beige limestone from the Doric temple, a radiolarian mudstone, from a deep shelf to basinal setting b) pink limestone from the temple of Hadrian and Antoninus Pius, a bioclastic packstone with crinoids (A), shell fragments (B) and foraminifera (C), deposited in an open marine environment around wave base c) beige limestone from the late Antonine nymphaeum on the upper agora, a bioclastic wackestone with crinoids (A) and shell fragments (B), originating from an open marine depositional environment below wave base.

263

sponge spicules, bivalves and pellets. A thick, intercalated beige limestone bed is composed of an oolitic grainstone with crinoids, foraminifers, algae, bivalves, lithoclasts, coated and micritized grains and likely represent a sediment gravity flow deposit. The massif beige limestone with white chert (unit D) is made up of bioclastic wackestone and peloidal packstone. The allochems are pellets, radiolaria, sponge spicules, bivalves, foraminifers, crinoids and calpionellids. The overlying beds (unit E) are composed of coarse-grained dolomite and partly dolomitized limestone beds. This type of limestone consists of peloidal pack- to grainstone. The upper massif beige to pink limestone (unit F) is character- ized by bioclastic mud-, wacke- and packstone with pel- lets, micritized grains, clasts, bivalves, foraminifers, algae, crinoids, radiolaria and sponge spicules. The depositional environment of units A and D is that of an open marine environment below wave base. Units B and C represent a deep shelf to basinal setting. The pack- to grainstone of unit E formed in a marine environment above wave base. Unit F reflects an open marine depositional environment varying around wave base. The stable isotopic composition of the Lycian nappe limestone sequence (Figure 2) facing the city shows a relatively narrow range (Muchez *et al.* this volume). $\delta^{13}C$ values are between 1.5‰ and 3.6‰ VPDB and the $\delta^{18}O$ values between –4.1‰ and –0.2‰ VPDB (n = 34).

4. CLASSIFICATION OF THE BUILDING STONE AT SAGALASSOS

The building stones were classified in lithological types, divided in sub-types (Degryse *et al.*, 2003). These are described in Table 1 and are shown in Plate 1 (giving an oversight of some lithological types occurring at Sagalas- sos) and in Plate 2 (showing the petrography of the dif- ferent building stones). An overview of the occurrence of the natural building stones in the different buildings at Sagalassos is presented in chronological order in Table 2. A map of Sagalassos with the main buildings studied is given in Figure 3, a map of the main provenance areas is given in Figure 4.

The beige and pink limestone, the red nodular limestone and the intraformational conglomerate can be found from the early Hellenistic period (late 4th century BC) onwards throughout the building history of the city. As recent research established in 2005 that the current site was only occupied in the course of the 4th century BC, after its much larger predecessor located 1.8 km to the southeast at Tepe Düzen had been abandoned, these types of limestone formed the oldest building material used for monumental structures in the city. They were widely used in all Hellenistic (4th

century BC until 25 BC) and early Imperial (25 BC until 1st century AD) monuments. During the Trajanic (98 AD until 117 AD) and Hadrianic (117 AD until 138 AD) to Severan (193 AD until 235 AD) period, they continued to be widely used, but often in combination with other types of building stones. Mid Imperial buildings (2nd century AD until 3rd century AD) which seem to contain only beige and pink limestone include the Flavian to Hadrianic odeon, the Trajanic rebuilding of the temple of Apollo Klarios, the Hadrianic Dionysos temple, the late Hadrianic nymphaeum above the lower agora, the northeast arch on the upper agora, dated to the middle of the second century AD, the Antonine macellum (meat market), the late second century AD theatre and the early third century AD gate near the bath building.

White recrystallized limestone occurs for the first time in the Tiberian capitals of the southwest gateway on the lower agora and in the columns and capitals of the Flavian west portico of the same square. Several columns which may belong to the Trajanic monument built by Claudia Severa also consist of this type of limestone. The door jambs and lintel of the late Hadrianic to Antonine temple as well as its bases, columns and capitals were also carved from white limestone, as were several of the architraves, friezes and cornices of its propylon. In all these buildings, the white limestone elements were combined with beige and pink limestone in a deliberate effort to obtain poly- chromy. White limestone can be found in the central niche, capitals, architrave-frieze and cornice of the late Antonine nymphaeum on the upper agora, and towards the end of the second century AD in the bases and architrave-frieze of the Severan nymphaeum on the lower agora. In both buildings also beige and pink limestone as well as more exotic types of building stone occur.

Among these exotic building stones is a white recrystal- lized limestone with parallel stylolites which was used for the parapets of the hot water baths of the bath building (caldarium 2 and 3; Waelkens, 2002; Waelkens *et al.*, 2002). This type of stone also occurs in several of the back wall orthostats and four of the columns of the late Antonine nymphaeum on the upper agora. Several other rare stone types were used in this nymphaeum, including a black breccia and a brown-grey limestone in the back wall orthostats, whereas some columns are composed of monomict and polymict breccias. Both the late Antonine nymphaeum on the upper agora and the slightly younger Severan nymphaeum on the lower agora also contain blue 'kaplan postu' marble columns, whereas in the latter structure even white to yellowish 'pavonazetto' columns were used. Both marble types originated from Dokimeion. Docimian marbles (Afyon bal, white to yellowish Afyon şeker as well

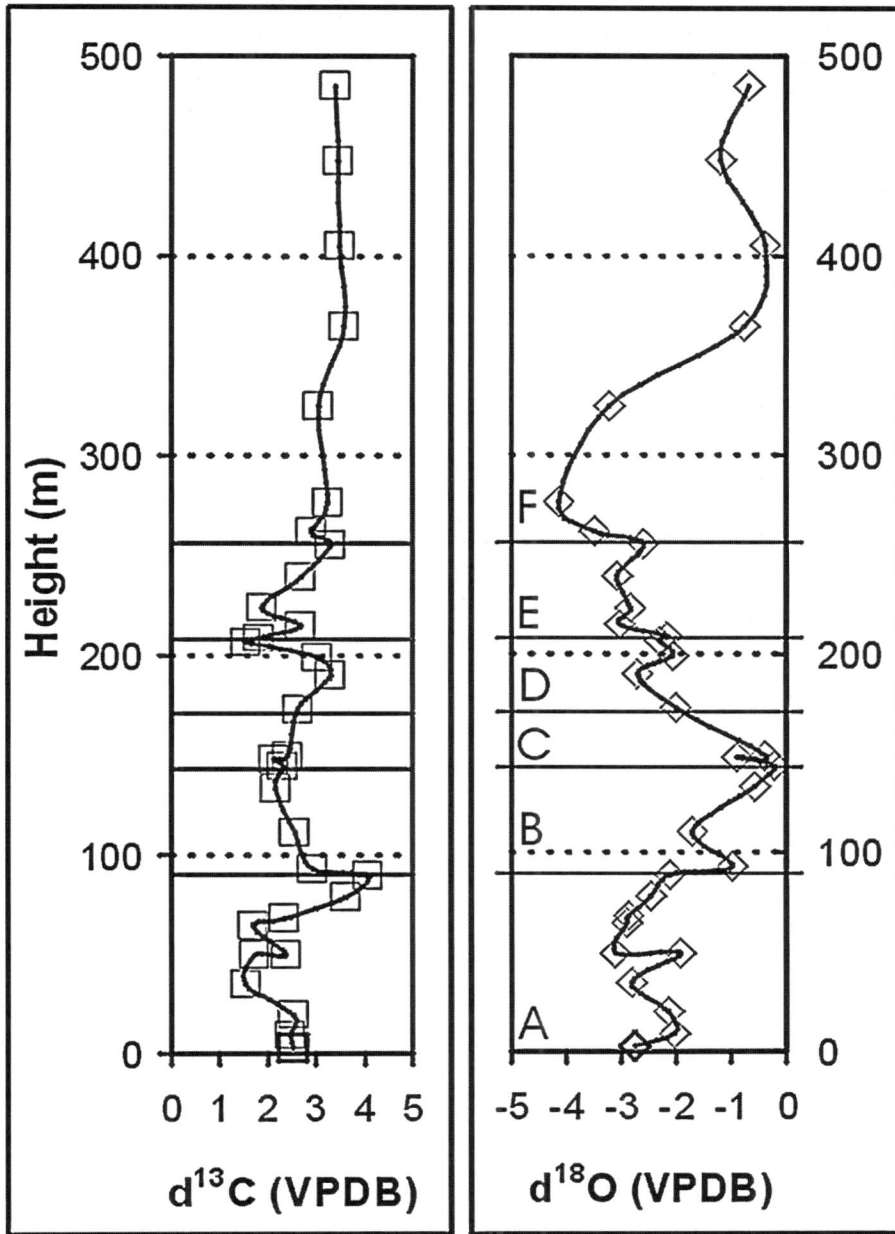

Figure 2: Plot of the oxygen and carbon isotopic composition of the stable isotopic compositions of Unit A and Unit F of the Lycean limestone near the monumental centre of Sagalassos (Muchez *et al.*, 2003).

Lithological type	Macroscopical description	Microscopical description (after Flügel, 1982)
Beige limestone	Beige limestone Limited stylolitization Few veins Beige limestone Abundant stylolitization Intensely veined	Bioclastic peloidal wacke- to grainstone Bioclasts: corals, algae, echinoderms, foraminifers, brachiopods Allochems: pellets and clasts of radiolaria limestone Facies: Open sea shelf or ramp, below to above wave base Bioclastic peloidal mud- to packstones Bioclasts: radiolaria, brachiopods, sponge spicula Allochems: pellets and clasts Facies: Deep marine environment
Pink limestone	Pink to pinkish limestone Abundant stylolitization Intensely veined Pink to pinkish limestone No stylolitization Intensely veined	Bioclastic mud- to wackestones Bioclasts: gastropods, radiolaria, sponge spicula Facies: Deep marine environment and Bioclastic grainstones Bioclasts: crinoids Facies: Open shelf or ramp, above wave base Bioclastic mudstone Bioclasts: crinoids, brachiopods, radiolaria Facies: Deep marine environment
Pink nodular limestone	Pink limestone with chert nodules Abundant stylolitization Intensely veined	Bioclastic mud- to wackestone Bioclasts: foraminifera, moravaminids, corals, crinoids Facies: Open sea shelf or ramp, below wave base
White limestone	White limestone Intensely recrystallized No stylolitization White limestone Intensely recrystallized Parallel black stylolites	Bioclastic grainstones Bioclasts: crinoids Facies: Open sea shelf or ramp, above wave base Bioclastic grainstones Bioclasts: crinoids Facies: Open sea shelf or ramp, above wave base
Breccias (monomict and polymict)	Breccia Intensely recrystallized Breccia Intensely recrystallized Black Breccia Intensely recrystallized	Breccia with red to white micritic to sparitic cement Clasts of beige and pink limestone (type 1 and 2) Breccia with red to white micritic to sparitic cement Clasts of beige and pink limestone (type 1 and 2) Clasts of chert, sandstone, serpentine Breccia with black micritic cement Clasts of beige limestone (type 1 and 2) Bioclasts: foraminifera, algae, corals, crinoids
Conglomerates	Conglomerate	Conglomerate with red to white micritic cement Pink limestone clasts
Intermediate volcanics	Grey tuff and grey-black lava flows	Trachyte to trachyandesite Phenocrysts of feldspar, augite, hornblende, biotite, magnetite
Travertine	Laminated travertine	Phytohermal framestone Biota: algae, bacteria, larvae, plants Layers of acicular sparite
Sand- to siltstone	Calcareous sand- to siltstone Purple shale	
Marbles and other coloured stones	Blue, white and honey marble (Dokimeion) Granite (Troad) porfido verde, porfido rosso (Egypt) antico rosso, giallo antico, verde antico…	Equigranular sparite Phenocrysts of feldspar, quartz and hornblende Porphiry

Table 1: Macroscopical and microscopical description of all lithological types of natural building stones identified at Sagalassos.

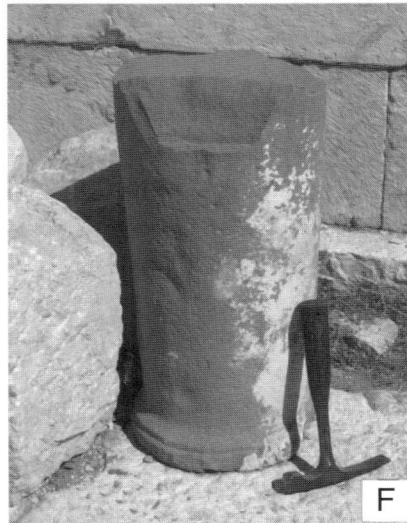

Plate 1: Macroscopical appearance of the natural building stones used at Sagalassos, A: beige limestone in the late Hellenistic bouleuterion, B: sculpted white limestone building block (type 5) from the late Antonine nymphaeum, hammer is 30 cm, C: column of the late Antonine nymphaeum, blue marble ('kaplan postu') from Dokimeion, D: travertine building blocks in the *episkopeion*, height of one block is 1 meter, E: trachy-andesite in the bath building, F: flysch column in the bouleuterion courtyard, from the early 5th century AD transformation into a basilica for St-Michael.

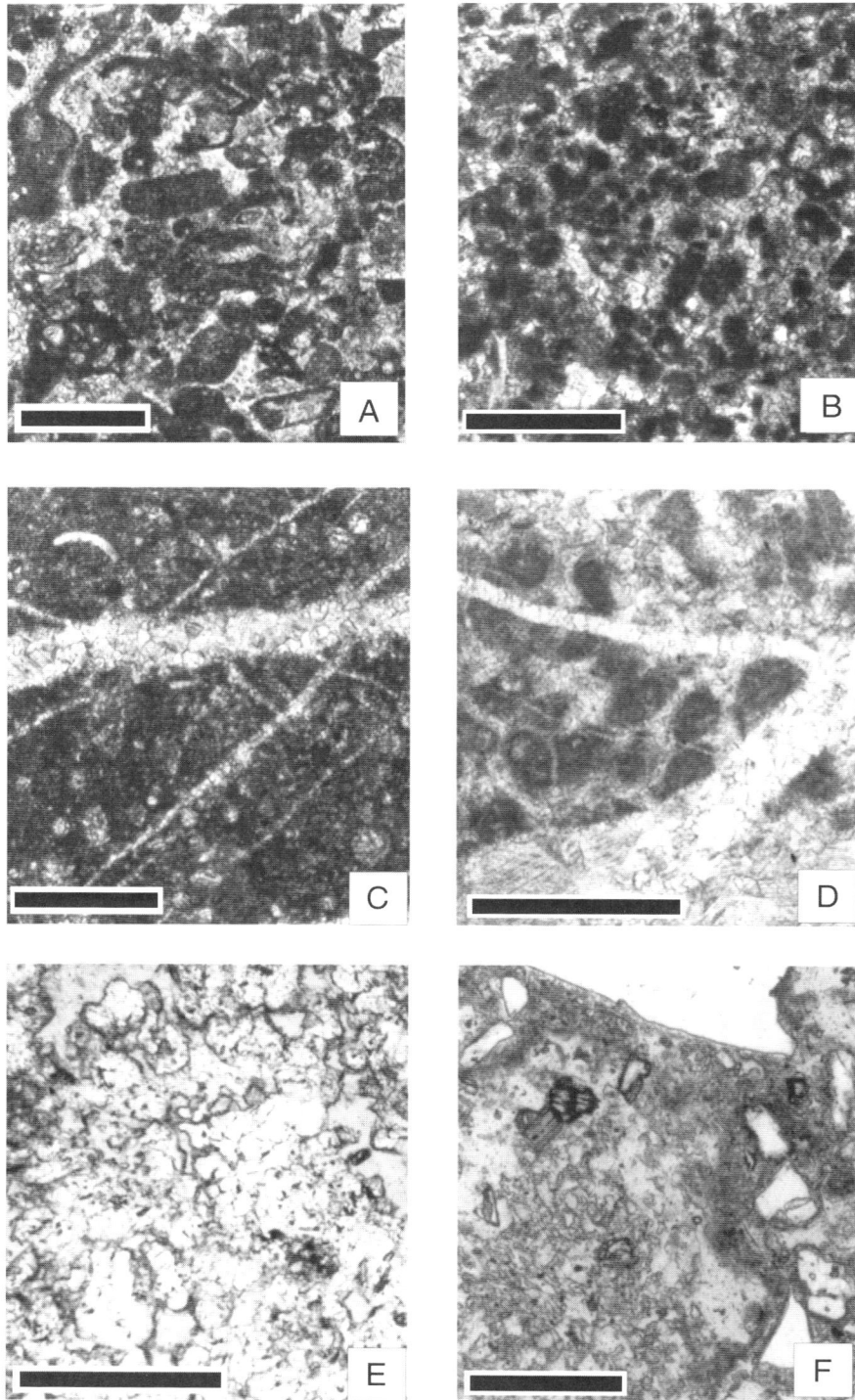

Plate 2: Microscopical facies and biota of the natural building stones used at Sagalassos, A: beige limestone, bioclastic peloidal grainstone, parallel polaroids, scale bar is 250 μm, B: beige limestone, bioclastic peloidal packstone, parallel polaroids, scale bar is 250 μm, C: pink limestone, bioclastic wackestone with radiolaria and sponge specula, parallel polaroids, scale bar is 250 μm, D: beige limestone, peloidal packstone, showing *Thaumatoporella parvovesiculefera RAINERI.* Parallel polaroids, scale bar is 250 μm, E: travertine, phytohermal framestone, parallel polaroids, scale bar is 500 μm, F: hypohalic texture of volcanic tuff, crossed polaroids, scale bar is 250 μm.

period	building	beige limestone	pink limestone	white limestone	marble & coloured stone	travertine & volcanics
Hellenistic	city wall	■				
	bouleuterion	■				
late Hellenistic	fountain house	■				
	Doric temple	■				
Augustan	Heroon	■				
	honorific columns upper agora	■	■			
	Apollo Klarios temple	■	■			
Julio-Claudian	stadion	■				
Tiberian	south gate	■				
	gateway lower agora	■		■		
Flavian	west portico lower agora	■				
Flavian to Hadrianic	odeion	■				
Trajanic	heroon for Trajan	■				
Hadrianic- late Antonine	bath building	■			■	■
	Antoninus Pius temple		■	■	■	
late Antonine	nymphaeum upper agora	■			■	
	macellum					■
	theatre	■				■
Severan	nymphaeum lower agora	■		■		

Table 2: Overview of the different stone types in the monumental buildings of the different periods of building activity.

as purple veined pavanozetto) also occur in the second to fourth century AD wall veneer of the bath building. An inscription mentioning the placement of marble wall veneer in the Trajanic rebuilding of the original temple of Apollo Klarios shows that marble veneer was already used on a large scale two decades earlier (Waelkens et al., 2003). High quality white marble from Dokimeion was also used at Sagalassos for the colossal statue inside the Augustan Northwest Heroon and for most recycled statuary of the late Antonine nymphaeum (Moens et al., 1997). The latter fountain's original statuary was only preserved in the large corner aediculae, and consisted of two double-life-sized statue groups made of Aphrodisian marble (Moens et al., 1997; Waelkens et al., 2000). Next to Docimian marbles, also other imported stones such as cipollino, porfido verde, porfido rosso, rosso antico, verde antico and others were used, especially in the bath building, although many of these stones were recycled here in the 4th to early 5th century AD. Also, a small late Roman fountain to the east of the Northwest Heroon contained onyx wall veneer, the origin of which was macroscopically identified as coming from Pamukkale (ancient Hierapolis; Waelkens et al., 2000a). Re-used white-grey granite columns, most likely 'marmor Troadense', are found in Basilica E1 to the west of the city and in the nymphaea above and on the lower agora, respectively the late Hadrianic and Severan nymphaeum. The walls of the temple of Hadrian and Antoninus Pius also show numerous holes of wall revetment pins, but no remains of the actual veneer have been found. The import of these exotic stones is subject of further research. Finally, next to marbles and limestone, travertine, sand- to siltstone and volcanic (trachy-andesitic) building stones also occur in

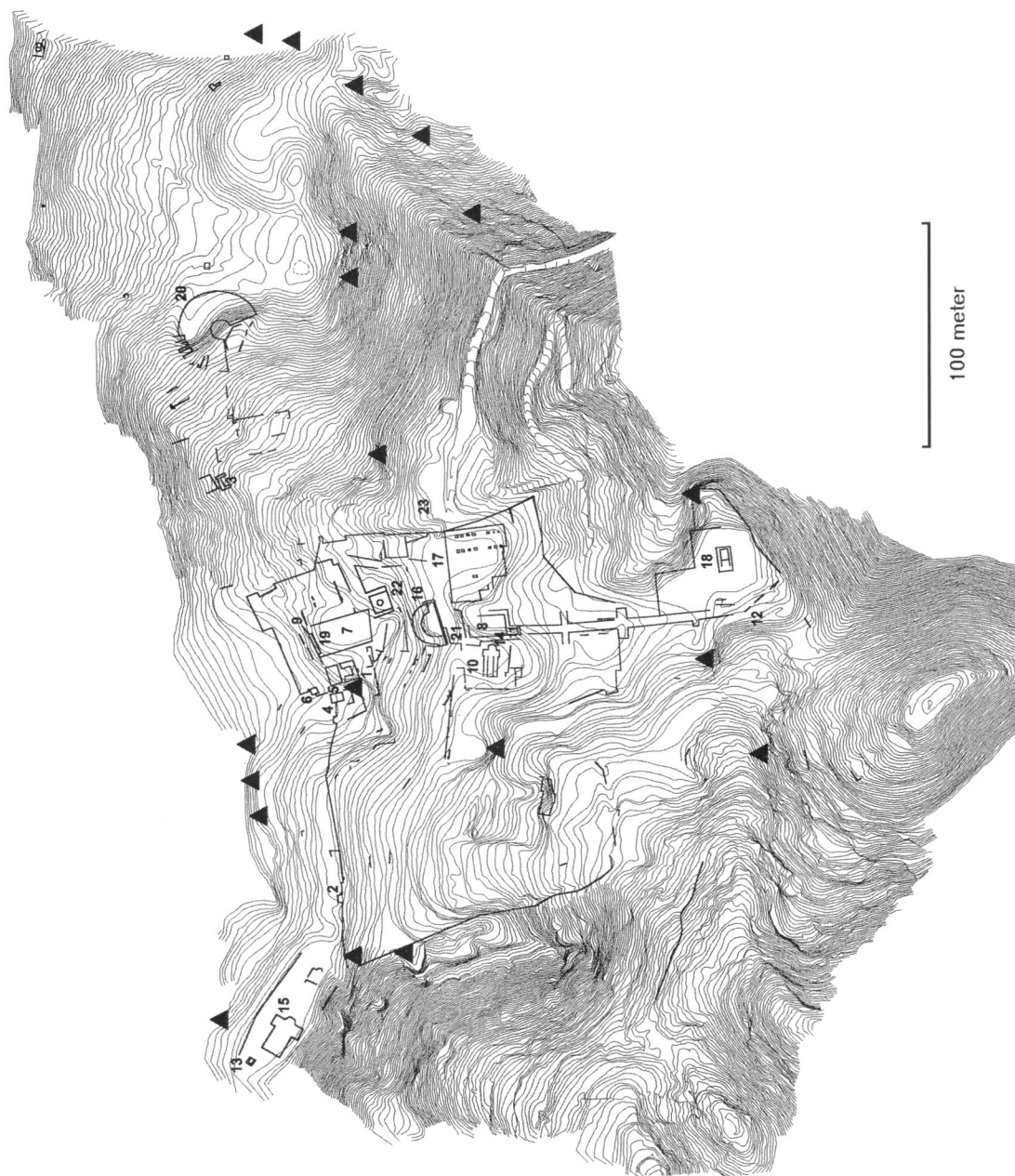

Figure 3: Map of Sagalassos with the main buildings (numbered) and the quarries (triangles) located in the vicinity of the city, as defined by Loots (2001). (1: the bouleuterion, 2: the late Hellenistic city wall, 3: the late Hellenistic fountain house, 4: the Doric temple, 5: the propylon of the Doric temple, 6: the northwest Heroon, 7: the upper agora, 8: the lower agora, 9: the northeast building, 10: the temple of Apollo Klarios, 11: the Tiberian southwest gateway on the lower agora, 12: the Tiberian south gate, 13: the monument for Trajan built by Claudia Severa, 14: the west portico of the lower agora, 15: the temple of Dionysos, 16: the odeon, 17: the bath building, 18: the temple of Hadrian and Antoninus Pius, 19: the late Antonine nymphaeum on the upper agora, 20: the theatre, 21: the Severan nymphaeum on the lower agora, 22: the macellum, 23: the gate near the bath building).

270

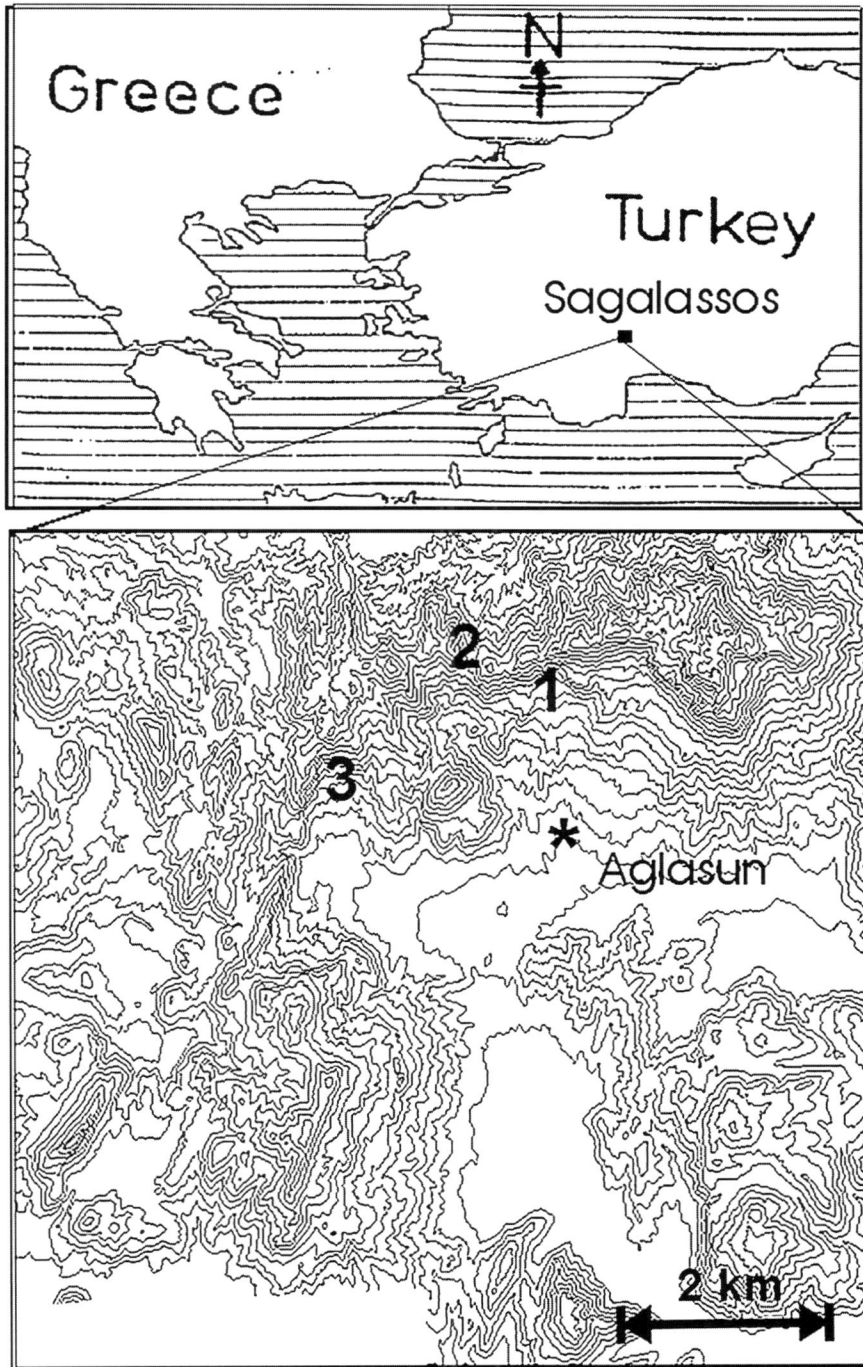

Figure 4: Outline of the central part of the territory of Sagalassos in south-western Turkey, the modern-day village of Ağlasun is indicated. Main quarry locations are 1 – monumental Sagalassos, 2 – the Ağlasun Dağları quarry, 3 – the Sarıkaya quarry.

the bath building, in the theatre and in the 4th to 5th century palatial mansion (most likely the city's bishop's palace or *episkopeion*) in the eastern domestic area.

The main building stones, i.e. the beige and pink limestone, at least partially are local, as indicated by the presence of quarries of this limestone in the Lycean nappes near the site (Degryse *et al.*, this volume a). They show a large variety in appearances: dark beige limestone, beige limestone with beige chert, homogeneous massive beige limestone, beige limestone with red chert, pink limestone and red nodular clayey limestone. The beige limestone can be found all over the region, including many extraction spots in the immediate vicinity of Sagalassos and at Sarıkaya (near the village of Başköy; Waelkens *et al.*, 1997b; Figure 4). Pink limestone and conglomerate are identified along the mountain pass to Isparta and in the valley of Başköy (Figure 4). As the geological substrate, i.e. the Lycean nappes, shows a rapid alternation of these stones over very short distances, these types of stone can be found close together in one and the same place (Muchez *et al.*, this volume). Unfortunately, the limestone breccias could not be attributed to a specific location. The texture of these breccias and the presence of fragments of calcareous sandstone and serpentinite suggest that this type of stone may represent a cemented scree deposit present in large quantities around the city of Sagalassos (Verhaert *et al.*, 2002). Indeed, in front of the propylon of the Doric temple, stone extraction steps were identified in such breccias (Waelkens *et al.*, 2000a). Breccias with a red calcite cement, comparable to those used at Sagalassos, were identified near outcrops with white recrystallized limestone in the region of Burdur, but no traces of ancient quarrying were found there.

The white recrystallized limestone has not been observed in the vicinity of Sagalassos. The modern-day Yarışlı basin quarries are also the possible ancient sources of this crystalline white limestone that today is still extensively quarried under the commercial name "White Antique", illustrating the assumed connection to quarrying of the same stone in Antiquity. The aesthetic "marble-like" appearance, the white colour and the technical qualities of this stone were important reasons for exploiting such a relatively remote source of stone for Sagalassos (Waelkens *et al.*, 2002; 2003). It remains unclear whether the stone had a wider use in Antiquity. During the survey, disputable traces that may represent weathered quarry marks were found in the quarry. Yet, at one location, traces of stepped extraction going back to Antiquity occur. There might be other remains of ancient quarries in the region, but the intensive presence of modern quarries, that usually are started where ancient quarries producing good building stone had been abandoned in most cases during the 3rd century AD (Waelkens,

1994) and during their rapid expansion have destroyed all ancient traces of quarrying activity, as well as the size of the potential provenance area make a survey for ancient exploitation here both time consuming and difficult.

The petrography and biotic context (Table 1, Plate 2) of travertine deposits near the village of Başköy, ca. 5 km to the southwest of Sagalassos (Figure 4) compare very well with travertine building stones that were used at Sagalassos (Vermoere *et al.*, 1999; Schroyen *et al.*, 2000; Degryse *et al.*, this volume b). Indeed, numerous small (<10m wide) and larger (up to 40m wide) quarries were identified in these deposits.

Previous mineralogical and geochemical research made clear that volcanic building stones were quarried in the area of Lake Gölçük (Figure 4), ca. 10 km to the north of Sagalassos (Callebaut *et al.*, 2000). Both consolidated tuff deposits and lava flows can be found in this area. The statigraphically oldest volcanic deposits, which are consolidated and are situated close to the city were quarried for tuff. Suitable lava flows can be found all around the lake proper. No traces of ancient quarrying, which in tuff outcrops can easily be weathered, were identified. The calcareous sandstone and siltstone are present in the flysch deposits around the site of Sagalassos, which consist of an alternation of calcareous sandstone and shale with some conglomerate levels.

5. QUARRY CLASSIFICATION

The quarries around Sagalassos can be grouped according to their location (local or regional), their geology (provenance), morphology (topographical features) and production evidence (quarry marks, extraction sites, partially worked objects – 'Rohlingen' or 'Halb-fabrikaten', spoil heaps etc.). *On-site quarries* are predominantly located within one kilometre from the city centre. *Local and regional quarries* include quarries located 1 to 10 km away from the city centre.

5.1. On-site quarries (Figure 5)

These include limestone and limestone breccia quarries predominantly located within one kilometre from the city centre. The limestone outcrops in and around the city display considerable variations in quality, both regarding use (durability) and quarrying (block size potential). The former is important for preservation of the quarries; particularly, brecciated and nodular limestone varieties are severely weathered and extraction marks are usually strongly deteriorated. Block potential is predominantly related to the

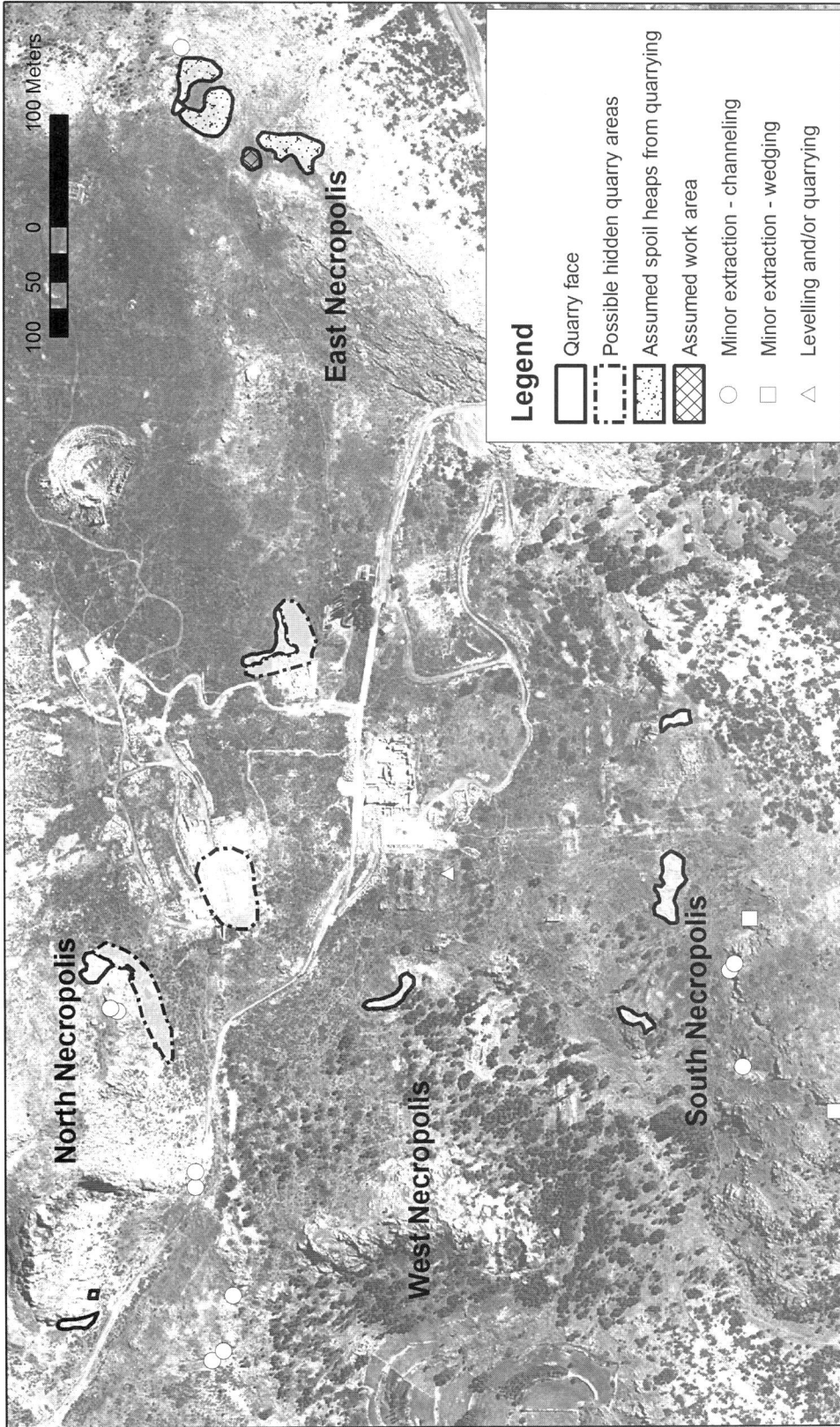

Figure 5: Map of the quarries around Sagalassos.

Legend

- Quarry face
- Possible hidden quarry areas
- Assumed spoil heaps from quarrying
- Assumed work area
- ○ Minor extraction - channeling
- □ Minor extraction - wedging
- △ Levelling and/or quarrying

North Necropolis

West Necropolis

East Necropolis

South Necropolis

100 50 0 100 Meters

degree of fracturing in the limestone deposits. In general, less fractured varieties display abundant extraction marks such as carved walls and quarry trenches, whilst such evidence is rare in fractured limestone. This is due to the fact that extraction of primary blocks bordered by natural fracture surfaces is the main method of quarrying in such quarries. Quarries may be grouped as follows:

5.1.1. Eastern quarries

East of the city, evidence of quarrying is found on top of the hill just to the east of the east necropolis. Little remains of the quarry faces. However, the presence of quite large heaps of limestone chips and fragments, interpreted as quarry spoil heaps, suggest that quite significant quarrying and working of stone took place in this area, and that the quarries were practically exhausted (Figure 6). It is likely to link these quarries to the nearby necropolis, but the quarries may also have supplied building stone to the city. Based on the size and distribution of the spoil heaps, the likely estimate of extracted volumes could be in the thousands rather than the hundreds of cubic metres, thus exceeding the use of stone in the necropolis. Near the quarries is a minor extraction site which perfectly displays stone extraction techniques. The eastern quarries show deposits of a bioclastic mud- to packstone with pellets, shells and crinoids. The depositional environment is that of an open marine to restricted environment around wave base. The oxygen and carbon isotope values of the samples vary between –5,42‰ and –2.44‰ VPDB and between 2.33‰ and 2.60‰ VPDB respectively (n = 5).

5.1.2. Southern quarries

Two quarries and a number of minor extraction sites have been identified near the southern necropolis. The westernmost quarry displays a few tall quarry faces, highly deteriorated due to the poor quality of the stone (nodular limestone; similar types are seen in nearby sarcophagi or their remains). It is difficult to estimate extraction volumes in the quarry, which could range between a few hundred and one thousand m³.

The easternmost quarry can be described as highly irregular, showing several small extraction sites. A few of these are seen as well planned, carved quarry faces. However, scattered quarry marks around the hill suggest that blocks bordered by natural fractures also were extracted, and it is therefore very difficult to estimate extraction volumes. It seems clear however that at least some hundreds cubic metres were quarried. Measurements of the few carved quarry faces indicate that the quarrying targeted sarcophagi which are abundantly present in the necropolis (Köse, 2005).

Furthermore, the scattering of extraction sites in the quarry either indicates a high variation in quality (targeting small "pockets" of sound quality) or non-systematic production, perhaps reflecting smaller operations over a long time. Optimistically viewed, the southern quarries could have supplied raw material for most of the sarcophagi in the area.

In the necropolis itself, there are several minor extraction sites or 'trial quarries'. Particularly interesting is one site, where there is evidence of wedging of stone blocks parallel to natural fracture planes (Figure 7). Outside the necropolis, to the east of the temple of the Imperial cult, is a small quarry displaying some stepped extractions, the size of which is indicative of building-stone production rather than that of sarcophagi. The use of the stone from the quarry is not known.

The southern quarries show deposits of bioclastic wacke- to grainstone with shells, crinoids and foraminifers. The depositional environment is that of an open marine environment around or above wave base. The oxygen and carbon isotope values of the samples vary between –2.68‰ and –3.68‰ VPDB and between 2.07‰ and 3.96‰ VPDB respectively (n = 6).

5.1.3. Northern/western quarries

These include quarries around the northern necropolis and just north of the stadion. In the former case, extraction traces (quarry steps and trenches) are seen at the foot of the cliff below the necropolis. Unfortunately, most of the quarry is probably covered by scree deposits. However, given that such marks are seen through a distance of nearly one hundred metres, it is probable that this quarry could have been a significant source for building stone to the city. Approaching the upper part of the necropolis is a "nonsystematic", shallow quarry with numerous small extraction sites. This may have been the source for the few sarcophagi in the necropolis. Moreover, the upper part of the quarry in Imperial times was used for dozens of rock-cut *arcosolia* tombs (Köse, 2005), which provide a *terminus ante quem* for the beginning of the extraction.

North of the stadion are two quarries and some minor extraction sites along the foot of the hill. The westernmost of these quarries (Figure 8) is of particular interest, due to the extraction techniques displayed. The limestone deposit has frequent oblique fractures, making systematic trenching difficult. The quarry marks thus indicate that these fractures were not only used as primary block boundaries, but that the direction of the existing trenches changed frequently in order to maximize the block yield. Volume estimates are difficult, but it is likely that a gross magnitude of

Figure 6: Photograph of the eastern quarries near the potters' quarter of Sagalassos, showing a quarry face and the spoil heaps in front of the quarry.

Figure 7: Photograph of the southern quarries near the southern necropoleis of Sagalassos, showing wedging near natural fractures.

Figure 8: Photograph of the northern/western quarries near Sagalassos, next to the stadion.

volume close to 1000 m³ was extracted in the area, thus indicating that this was a source for the stone used in the stadion (seats).

The northern and western quarries show deposits of a bioclastic mud- to packstone with pellets, shells, foraminifers and crinoids. The depositional environment is that of an open marine environment below or around wavebase. The oxygen and carbon isotope values of the samples vary between –1.58‰ and –4.61‰ VPDB and between 1.87‰ and 2.81‰ VPDB respectively (n = 6).

5.1.4. Central quarries (Figure 9)

Two, possibly three, quarries exist in the central area of the town. In the eastern part, one possibly major quarry is situated along or even forming the eastern boundary of the palatial mansion, most probably a 4th century *episkopeion* or bishop's palace. Frequent steplike extraction traces, carved walls, combined with the fact that the quarry continues deep below the present soil surface and that the total length of the corner-shaped quarry face is nearly 90 metres, indicate that this could have been a major stone source. A building,

possibly still belonging to the *episkopeion*, has been situated on top of the quarry, so maybe parts of the quarry could have been modified and/or some quarry marks may therefore relate to construction rather than to quarrying alone. The upper part of the quarry displays poor quality, brecciated limestone, but a few metres below the top sound quality of limestone is seen.

To the west of the Augustan Apollo Klarios temple, there is a small hill with traces of quarrying on top of the hill and on its western slope. Partly, the traces seem to be related to levelling rather than stone extracting, and it is difficult to know to what extent extraction did take place, and whether or not it was connected to the buildings at the site. At the southeast corner of the temple, a small outcrop displays some traces of quarrying, most likely related to the levelling of the bedrock beneath the temple.

In the area around the Upper Agora, there are steep quarried walls integrated in the building mass. Given that geological evidence suggests that the area contains (or contained) large volumes of sound quality limestone, one may suggest that stone for building was partially quarried here. Another site,

276

Figure 9: Photograph of the central quarries in Sagalassos, near the palatial mansion or *episkopeion* excavations.

where there might have been limestone resources is the the-atre, however except for geophysical evidence of limestone bedrock, there is no other evidence of quarrying.

The central quarry near the above mentioned palatial mansion shows a deposit of a bioclastic wacke- to packstone with pellets, shells and crinoids. The depositional environment is that of an open marine to restricted environment around wave base. The oxygen and carbon isotope value of this sample is –2.41‰ VPDB and 1.96‰ VPDB respectively (n = 1).

5.2. Local quarries

These include quarries located from 1 to less than 10 km from the city centre.

The **Ağlasun Dağları** quarries (Figure 10) are located on a small plateau at the north side of the Ağlasun Dağları, immediately to the east of the mountain pass northwest of Sagalassos through which an ancient Roman road crossed the mountains. The ca. 100 m wide and 25 m high outcrops have been quarried at several locations, resulting in quarry

faces ca. 10 m high. Beige and pink limestone was quarried here. The pink colour of the stone was probably the reason for undertaking quarrying at such high altitude instead of using more readily available sources. Traces of stepped extraction along natural fractures are still visible, as are many debitages and traces of the use of the pick-hammer. Several roughed out building blocks and sarcophagi are scattered over the slope leading from the quarry faces to the Roman road (Waelkens *et al.*, 1997b: 46). However, the quarry displays few worked quarry faces. Due to overburden it is difficult to estimate extracted volumes. The lack of large spoil heaps indicates that the quarried volumes did not exceed some hundreds cubic metres of usable blocks. The difficult transport over and down the mountain slope may also explain the restricted output.

The Ağlasun Dağları quarry shows deposits of a bioclastic wackestone with crinoids, echinoderms, foraminifers, shell fragments. The depositional environment is that of an open marine environment below wave base. The oxygen and carbon isotope values of the samples vary between –4.27‰ and –3.19‰ VPDB and between –0.08‰ and 3.53‰ VPDB respectively (n = 9). This quarry is located at a level in the

Figure 10: Photograph of a worked entablature block in the Ağlasun Dağları quarry.

Lycean nappes equivalent to unit F around the monumental centre of Sagalassos. However, the petrographic and isotopic characteristics of the stone quarried in the Ağlasun Dağları quarry are different from those of unit F.

The **Sarıkaya Quarry** is located near the village of Yeşilbaşköy, in the western Ağlasun Dağları, on a plateau known as Sarıkaya or 'yellow rock' after the colour of the patina of the stone (Waelkens *et al.*, 1997: 46). A ca. 40 m high cliff face forms the northern border of this plateau, in which the remains of a large limestone quarry are identified. The plateau is easily accessible from the east, where an earth track runs in a northeast direction towards the site of Sagalassos, located ca. 4 km to the northeast (Waelkens *et al.*, 1997b: 46; Waelkens and the Sagalassos Team, 1997a: 241). The main quarry face shows remains of quarry trenches some 25 m above the current ground level. Also, stepped extraction is visible and traces pointing to the use of a heavy pick were observed (Waelkens *et al.*, 1988: 97). In 1994 the remains of a walled structure to the east of the quarry face were recorded. Around this structure, sherds of early imperial *Sagalassos Red Slip Ware* were found (Waelkens *et al.*, 1997b: 46). When the site was revisited in 1997, illegal excavations had obliterated this structure. Sherds of Sagalassos red slip ware were still lying on the surface, as

well as some brick and tile fragments. Heaps of debitages were still apparent in 1994 (Waelkens *et al.*, 1997b: 46), but were no longer noticed during the 1997 visit. The quarry produced beige limestone. Evidence points at this quarry as a main supplier of stone to the city from the Late Hellenistic to the early Imperial Period. This quarry was studied in detail. Its workmen lived in the nearby site of Körustan, ca. 1 km to the south of the quarry (Waelkens *et al.*, 1997b).

The Sarıkaya quarry supplied radiolarian mudstones with foraminifers, calcispheres deposited in a shelf or basinal setting. The stable isotopic composition of the Sarıkaya quarry limestones varies between −1.81‰ and −2.26‰ VPDB for oxygen and between 2.29‰ and 2.44‰ VPDB for carbon (n = 3).

Travertine quarries are located near the village of Başköy. Travertine is applied in the 2nd century AD theatre and especially in 5-6th century AD domestic areas. Based on petrographic evidence, there are reasons to believe that the limited travertine deposit at Başköy was the source for Sagalassos, as well as supplying raw material for buildings in the immediate vicinity of the quarry (Degryse *et al.* this volume b). Remains of quarry faces are still seen, indicating

278

quite significant extraction of travertine. Wherever these observed quarries represent the actual extraction site in antiquity is, however, not clear.

5.3. Regional Quarries

The **Yarışlı limestone quarry**: a crystalline limestone is extensively quarried in the hills southwest of the plain of Burdur under the commercial name "White Antique" – illustrating the assumed connection to quarrying of the same stone in Antiquity. The limestone identified is petrographically identical to the building stone used at Sagalassos, showing recrystallized bioclastic grainstone. At one location, traces of stepped extraction are still preserved.

The Yarışlı quarry supplied bioclastic grainstone with crinoids deposited in an open marine environment above wave base. The stable isotopic composition of the limestone varies between –2.39‰ and –9.54‰ VPDB for oxygen and between 2.09‰ and 3.35‰ VPDB for carbon (n = 8).

5.4. Volume of extraction

5.4.1. Monumental construction

An estimate of the amount of stone (ashlars) used in the monumental architecture of the city was made based on the ground plans and elevations of a number of buildings and streets. As a first result, it can be said that the amount of ashlars used in the northwest Heroon comes to 170 m³, the Bouleuterion contained 280 m³ of stone, the Hadrian and Antoninus Pius temple 500 m³, the pavement of the upper agora 700 m³, the pavement of the lower agora 250 m³, the back wall of the west portico of the lower agora 50 m³ and the pavement of the north-south colon-raded street 600 m³. Though many smaller buildings and a large construction as the theatre have not been taken into account, it seems that paving of streets and agorae constituted a larger investment in terms of volume of stone extracted than that of the monumental architecture. It can also be taken into account that many structures in the city only have a façade of ashlars, and were for the most part constructed with concrete (*opus caementicium*). Also, many building are constructed with mortared rubble walls instead of ashlars. Though speculative, one could suggest that the amount of ashlars needed for entire monumental Sagalassos would not exceed 10.000 m³ of ashlars, but is likely to be as low as 5000 m³.

5.4.2. Burials

During the 2nd cent AD, production of free-standing sarcophagi became integrated into elite burial practices cov-ering a time span of approximately 100 years (see Köse, 2005). These burials, as was intended by their occupants, form highly visible artefacts within the quarry landscape of Sagalassos city. Although the majority of sarcophagi are free-standing, some occur as rectangular rock-cut tombs shaped into the outcrop with lids, some of which might pre-date the more elaborated free-standing variety.

The necropoli described surround the city and in the quest for visibility, can be seen from inside the city and along the approaches to it. In the north and east quarry necropoleis sarcophagi are orientated towards the city and in the south and west would have been clearly visible from the roads approaching it (see Köse, 2005). In some instances, visibility was enhanced by their placement on platforms where the top of the outcrop has been levelled and a shallow groove cut to securely place the sarcophagus. Furthermore, in some instances, particularly in the eastern necropolis, niches appear to have been cut for placing free-standing sarcophagi.

From Köse's (2005) documentation of these burials it is possible to make some estimates as to the volumes of stone used for these purposes over a 100 year period. Stone quarried for the manufacture of sarcophagi could range between 500-1,500 m³ gross volume, this figure varying in relation to the percentage of waste, given that the total net volume used is approximately 300 m³. Yet, as Köse (2005) suggests, such objects were the output of a well-organized and highly specialized workshop which implies that stone quality (see below in relation to the southern quarries and necropolis) would have been a major consideration in such production. As a result, it cannot be discounted that waste percentages could have been reasonably high. Moreover, in a few instances, good quality stone seems to have been acquired from a quarry 2 km east of the city and perhaps from Sarıkaya 3 km away as well as from other sources. Although the volumes of stone extracted for burials over a 100 year period would constitute a significant percentage of stone extraction vis-à-vis that for buildings, it cannot be assumed that this is representative of a sacorphagi production 'industry'.

6. THE SARIKAYA QUARRY – A CASE STUDY

The Sarıkaya quarry shows outcrops of white-beige limestone and red nodular limestone (Degryse *et al.*, 2003). The stone type quarried is unique to the Sarıkaya quarry as it can be microscopically classified as a radiolarian mudstone. This type of stone was used only in late Hellenistic buildings (Bouleuterion, Doric Temple) at Sagalassos. Radiolarian mudstone is not found in quarries elsewhere on the territory and was no longer used in buildings from the Julio-Claudian

Figure 11: Photograph of the Sarıkaya quarry face. The triangular quarry face is 30 meter high.

period onwards. This indicates that the quarry may have been one of the main suppliers of building stones during the late Hellenistic period. *Sagalassos Red Slip Ware* sherds found in front of the main quarry face, date from the early Imperial period and may constitute a *terminus ante quem* for the exploitation of the quarry.

The sub-vertical quarry face is situated in a tall and steep cliffside (Figure 11), which is described by Similox-Tohon (2006) to represent a major fault plane. The fault plane itself, and (towards the east) a minor fault oriented at a steep angle to the cliffside, seem to represent the natural borders of the quarry. Based on the observations of extraction marks (see below) the quarry thus measures 50 metres in length along the cliff, and extends up to 20 metres above the present ground level. By extrapolating the natural cliffside from the east to the west, parallel to the quarry face, it is likely that the extracted volume of rock defined a wedge shaped body, 50 metres long, 20 metres high and 6 metres wide at the base. This gives an estimate of maximum 3000 m³ gross volume extracted rock. The minimal extracted volume of the quarry must have been around 2000 m³ of stone (taking into account a loss of 50% in extraction)

enough to provide several large building projects. Several unfinished ashlars and other objects can be found in the quarry. Dimensions of the blocks range from 30 cm to 120 cm in length, 28 cm to 62 cm in width and 15 cm to 30 cm in height. Wedge marks are 5 cm to 12 cm long, 4 cm wide and 3 cm to 4 cm high.

The extraction marks seen in the quarry face cannot be studied in detail due to their position high above the ground. However, most of them seem to be related to the carving of trenches around blocks, whereas in the eastern part of the wall remains of a step-like extraction can be seen. From their visual appearance, three categories of extraction marks are observed:

1) trenching parallel to the cliffside; straight and slightly curved lines represented stages of work in the carving of these trenches,
2) rectangular grooves perpendicular to the cliffside, probably representing the end of perpendicular trenches,
3) small rectangular or squared grooves in the cliffside – either related to trenching, quality testing or holes for fixing lifting devices.

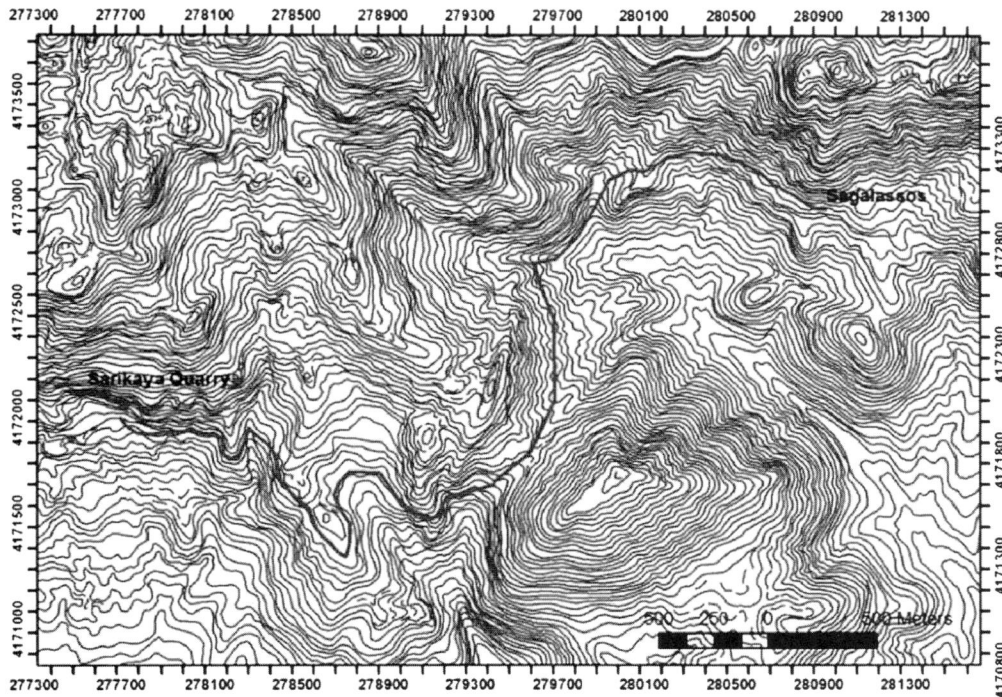

Figure 12: Virtual reconstruction of the road connection between the Sarıkaya quarry and Sagalassos.

Most of the quarry face, however, displays no visible extraction marks. This may partly be explained by the post-quarrying erosion of the quarry face (extraction marks have disappeared) and partly by natural fractures which played an important role in the quarrying; where present, fractures facilitated quarrying since the carving of trenches could be avoided.

South of the quarry face, extraction marks can also be seen in loose blocks, indicating that not only the bedrock but also large limestone blocks in the talus beneath the cliff were exploited. In fact, it seems likely that a talus of such large blocks covered the base of the cliffside before quarrying was initiated, perhaps even making the access to the upper quarrying level easier.

Sarıkaya is located at a distance of approximately 3,5 km from Sagalassos and given that the city was the final destination of the stone the question arises as to how it was transported there. Normally efficient overland stone transport, in the absence of rivers or other waterways, aimed at minimizing the use of steep gradients. In some cases in the Eastern Mediterranean, such gradients have required the building of paved roads or ramps to even-out topographical irregularities, yet at Sarıkaya no traces of paved roads, ramps or tracks have been observed. Hence, drawing any conclusions as to the direction that the stone

was transported from the quarry is subject to speculation. It is likely that draught animals would probably have hauled the loads placed on wooden sledges and that after this first track a possible route (Figure 12) can be suggested that links with a pre-existing road into Sagalassos. The distance to cover would be approximately 5,8 km. The maximum altitude difference along this road is approximately 120m, Sagalassos being the highest point.

Questions as to why the stone from Sarıkaya was particularly sought after, given its potential problems of transporting, are important. Although the quarry is distant from Sagalassos, where there is also good building material available, in general terms, a distance of 5.8 km was not that great when compared to other stone use and transport in Antiquity. One also has to consider that the resource may already have been exploited before it was used for building elements in the city, through already existing networks of stone carvers, producing for instance Hellenistic *ostothecae*, some of which can still be seen at the workman's village of Körustan and in modern Başköy (Waelkens *et al.*, 1997b).

7. CHRONOLOGY OF QUARRYING ACTIVITY

It is still unclear how long the quarries around Sagalassos have produced building stone and how large the produced volumes were. It has been suggested that the Sarıkaya quarry and the Ağlasun Dağları quarry to the northwest of Sagalassos were opened during the late Hellenistic to early Imperial period and during the mid Imperial period respectively (Loots, 2001). At Sagalassos, the quarries seem to have been abandoned from the third century AD onwards, when large building programmes in the city came to an end. From the third century AD onwards, many quarries in the eastern Mediterranean were in decline, and more *spolia* were used (Dworakowska, 1975: 92; Waelkens, 1994). While the petrographical and geochemical studies of the local stone (Degryse *et al.*, 2003, this volume a) identified the geological units from which building stones in general were extracted, the chronology of the quarries is here described by comparing the characteristics of the stone extracted in the quarries (i.e. a facies analysis) to the facies characteristics and chronology of the stone used in monumental Sagalassos (Table 3, Figure 13).

The beige building stone from the Doric Temple (n = 9), representative for the late Hellenistic period, consists of a radiolarian mudstone deposited in a deep shelf or basinal environment. The isotopic composition of this limestone (n = 4) varies between 1.64 and 2.20‰ VPDB for δ^{13}C and between –2.36‰ and –2.81‰ VPDB for δ^{18}O. The building blocks of the bouleuterion, constructed ca. 100 BC (n = 4) are composed of a beige limestone identical to that of the Doric Temple (radiolarian mudstone), but also of bioclastic mud- to wackestone with crinoids, echinoderms and foraminifers, originating from an open marine environment below wave base. A bioclastic wackestone has a δ^{13}C value of 0.19‰ VPDB and a δ^{18}O value of –4.42‰ VPDB. The building stone from the late Hellenistic fountain house (n = 3) consists of a bioclastic wackestone with crinoids deposited in an open marine environment below wave base. The isotopic composition of this limestone (n = 1) is 2.70‰ VPDB for δ^{13}C and –4.77‰ VPDB for δ^{18}O. Beige limestone re-used from the late Hellenistic defence wall consists of a radiolarian mudstone deposited in a deep shelf or basinal environment and but also of bioclastic wackestone with shells, crinoids and radiolarian, originating from an open marine to deeper shelf environment below wave base. The bioclastic wackestone has a δ^{13}C value of 3.32‰ VPDB and a δ^{18}O value of –1.23‰ VPDB. The radiolarian mudstone has a δ^{13}C value of 2.52‰ VPDB and a δ^{18}O value of –1.68‰ VPDB.

The beige building stone from the mid Augustan northwest Heroon (n = 4) representative for the early Imperial period, is made up of a bioclastic packstone with shell fragments, foraminifers, calcispheres, crinoids and pellets, deposited in an open marine environment around wave base. The isotopic composition of this limestone (n = 1) is 0.47‰ VPDB for

δ^{13}C and –4.58‰ VPDB for δ^{18}O. Also representative for the Augustan period, the beige and pink building stone of the northeast honorific column on the upper agora (n = 3) consists of a bioclastic mud- to wackestone with radiolaria, foraminifers, crinoids, pellets and shell fragments from an open marine environment below wave base. The beige building stone from the equally originally Augustan Apollo Klarios temple (n = 2) is a bioclastic wacke- to packstone with crinoids, foraminifers and shell fragments from an open marine environment below or just above wave base.

The beige building stone from the Tiberian south gate (n = 3) is a bioclastic wacke- to packstone with crinoids, foraminifers and algae, deposited in an open marine environment above wave base. The isotopic composition of these limestones (n = 5) vary between 2.34 and 4.34‰ VPDB for δ^{13}C and between –4.98‰ and –2.46‰ VPDB for δ^{18}O. The building stone in the probably Julio-Claudian stadion is a bioclastic wacke- to packstone (n = 3) with crinoids, foraminifers, shell fragments and algae, from an open marine environment above wave base. The isotopic composition of this limestone (n = 1) is –1.58‰ VPDB for δ^{18}O and 2.49‰ VPDB for δ^{13}C.

Representative for the late-Flavian(?) to Trajanic period, the pink building stone from the honorific monument dedicated to Trajan (n = 2) consists of bioclastic mud- to wackestone with echinoderms, foraminifers, radiolarian and crinoids, originating from an open marine environment below wave base. The isotopic composition of this limestone (n = 1) is –4.94‰ VPDB for δ^{18}O and 0.38‰ VPDB for δ^{13}C.

The beige building blocks from the late Antonine nymphaeum on the upper agora (n = 8), built ca. 160-180 AD, have a variable facies, either a bioclastic mud- to wackestone with crinoids, foraminifers, bryozoa, calcispheres and shell fragments from an open marine environment below wave base, or a bioclastic packstone with crinoids, foraminifers, bryozoa and shell fragments from an open marine environment around wave base. The isotopic composition of these limestone (n = 4) vary between 0.66‰ VPDB and 3.36‰ VPDB for δ^{13}C and between –5.47‰ and –1.24‰ VPDB for δ^{18}O. The white recrystallized limestone is a bioclastic grainstone with crinoids deposited in an open marine environment above wave base. The isotopic composition of these limestone (n = 5) vary between 2.45‰ VPDB and 3.35‰ VPDB for δ^{13}C and between –3.79‰ and –9.54‰ VPDB for δ^{18}O.

The beige building stone from the macellum (n = 2, dedicated to Commodus in 180 to 191 AD, is a bioclastic pelloidal grainstone with crinoids, calcispheres, foraminifera and bryozoa, deposited in an open marine environment above

Location	Period	Colour	Facies	δ18O	δ13C
Buildings				VPDB	VPDB
Nymphaeum	Hellenistic	pink	bioclastic wackestone	−4.77	2.70
Bouleuterion	Hellenistic	beige	bioclastic mud- to wackestone	−4.42	0.19
Bouleuterion	Hellenistic	beige	radiolarian mudstone	−	−
Doric Temple	Hellenistic	beige	radiolarian mudstone	−2.49	2.20
Doric Temple	Hellenistic	beige	radiolarian mudstone	−2.36	1.64
Doric Temple	Hellenistic	beige	radiolarian mudstone	−2.81	2.13
Doric Temple	Hellenistic	beige	radiolarian mudstone	−2.65	2.06
Defence Wall	Hellenistic	beige	radiolarian mudstone	−1.68	2.52
Defence Wall	Hellenistic	beige	bioclastic wackestone	−1.23	3.32
NW Heroon	Augustan	beige	bioclastic packstone	−4.58	0.47
NE Honorific Column	Augustan	beige	bioclastic mudstone	−2.95	4.34
NE Honorific Column	Augustan	pink	bioclastic wackestone	−4.08	2.34
NE Honorific Column	Augustan	beige	bioclastic wackestone	−	−
Apollo Klarios Temple	Augustan	beige	bioclastic wacke- to packstone	−3.51	2.49
Apollo Klarios Temple	Augustan	beige	bioclastic wacke- to packstone	−4.98	2.58
South Gate	Tiberian	beige	bioclastic wacke- to packstone	−2.46	3.55
Stadion	Julio-Claudian	beige	bioclastic wacke- to packstone	−1.58	2.49
Monument for Trajan	Trajanic	pink	bioclastic mud- to wackestone	−	−
Monument for Trajan	Trajanic	pink	bioclastic mud- to wackestone	−4.94	0.38
Macellum	Commodus	beige	bioclastic pelloidal grainstone	−4.30	−1.32
Nymph. Lower Agora	Marcus Aurelius	beige	bioclastic wackestone	−2.52	2.74
Nymph. Upper Agora	Marcus Aurelius	beige	bioclastic wackestone	−1.24	1.97
Nymph. Upper Agora	Marcus Aurelius	beige	bioclastic wackestone	−4.61	0.66
Nymph. Upper Agora	Marcus Aurelius	beige	bioclastic packstone	−5.47	3.36
Nymph. Upper Agora	Marcus Aurelius	beige	bioclastic packstone	−5.18	2.73
Nymph. Upper Agora	Marcus Aurelius	beige	bioclastic mud- to wackestone	−	−
Nymph. Upper Agora	Marcus Aurelius	white	bioclastic grainstone	−9.54	2.45
Nymph. Upper Agora	Marcus Aurelius	white	bioclastic grainstone	−5.52	3.19
Nymph. Upper Agora	Marcus Aurelius	white	bioclastic grainstone	−3.79	3.25
Nymph. Upper Agora	Marcus Aurelius	white	bioclastic grainstone	−6.00	3.35
Nymph. Upper Agora	Marcus Aurelius	white	bioclastic grainstone	−6.75	3.21

Table 3: List of the buildings and quarries studied, stating their chronology, the type of limestone found, the facies described in thin section, the oxygen and carbon isotopic composition of the sample.

Antoninus Pius Temple	Antoninus Pius	pink	bioclastic wackestone	−4.42	0.74
Antoninus Pius Temple	Antoninus Pius	pink	bioclastic wackestone	−4.49	1.25
Antoninus Pius Temple	Antoninus Pius	pink	bioclastic wackestone	−4.77	1.38
Antoninus Pius Temple	Antoninus Pius	pink	bioclastic wackestone	−4.97	0.96
Antoninus Pius Temple	Antoninus Pius	white	bioclastic grainstone	−5.84	3.29
Antoninus Pius Temple	Antoninus Pius	white	bioclastic grainstone	−4.74	3.29
Antoninus Pius Temple	Antoninus Pius	pink	bioclastic wackestone	−1.01	2.05
Antoninus Pius Temple	Antoninus Pius	pink	bioclastic wackestone	−0.90	2.15
Antoninus Pius Temple	Antoninus Pius	pink	bioclastic wackestone	−4.97	0.96
Antoninus Pius Temple	Antoninus Pius	beige	bioclastic wacke- to packstone	−4.86	3.46
Theatre	late Antonine	beige	bioclastic packstone	−3.71	2.35

Location	Colour	Facies	d18O	d13C
Quarries			VPDB	VPDB
Ağlasun Dağları Pass	beige	bioclastic wackestone	−3.39	0.13
Ağlasun Dağları Pass	beige	bioclastic wackestone	−4.03	1.38
Ağlasun Dağları Pass	beige	bioclastic wackestone	−3.19	3.53
Ağlasun Dağları Pass	pink	bioclastic wackestone	−3.28	−0.08
Ağlasun Dağları Pass	pink	bioclastic wackestone	−3.74	0.11
Ağlasun Dağları Pass	pink	bioclastic wackestone	−3.33	1.73
Ağlasun Dağları Pass	pink	bioclastic wackestone	−3.78	1.54
Ağlasun Dağları Pass	pink	bioclastic wackestone	−4.27	2.21
Ağlasun Dağları Pass	pink	bioclastic wackestone	−3.76	0.97
Sarıkaya	beige	radiolarian mudstone	−2.26	2.35
Sarıkaya	beige	radiolarian mudstone	−1.81	2.44
Sarıkaya	beige	radiolarian mudstone	−2.03	2.29
Sarıkaya	beige	radiolarian mudstone	−2.37	2.15
Sarıkaya	beige	radiolarian mudstone	−2.64	2.32
Yarışlı	white	bioclastic grainstone	−9.54	2.45
Yarışlı	white	bioclastic grainstone	−5.52	3.19
Yarışlı	white	bioclastic grainstone	−3.79	3.25
Yarışlı	white	bioclastic grainstone	−6.00	3.35
Yarışlı	white	bioclastic grainstone	−6.75	3.21
Yarışlı	white	bioclastic grainstone	−5.84	3.29

Table 3 (*cont.*)

Yarışlı	white	bioclastic grainstone	–4.74	3.29
Yarışlı	white	bioclastic grainstone	–2.39	2.09
Eastern quarries	beige	bioclastic mud- to wackestone	–4.10	2.60
Eastern quarries	beige	bioclastic mud- to wackestone	–5.42	2.36
Eastern quarries	beige	bioclastic mud- to wackestone	–4.13	2.57
Eastern quarries	beige	bioclastic mud- to wackestone	–2.44	2.33
Eastern quarries	beige	bioclastic wacke to packstone	–4.36	2.59
Central quarries	beige	bioclastic wacke to packstone	–2.50	2.72
Northern quarries	beige	bioclastic mud- to wackestone	–2.41	1.96
Northern quarries	beige	bioclastic wacke- to packstone	–2.47	1.87
Northern quarries	beige	bioclastic mud- to wackestone	–2.41	1.96
Western quarries	beige	bioclastic wackestone	–4.60	2.45
Western quarries	beige	bioclastic wackestone	–2.98	2.81
Western quarries	beige	bioclastic wacke- to packstone	–1.58	2.49
Southern quarries	beige	bioclastic grainstone	–2.78	2.62
Southern quarries	beige	bioclastic grainstone	–3.38	3.61
Southern quarries	beige	bioclastic wackestone	–3.06	2.53
Southern quarries	beige	bioclastic wackestone	–2.68	2.07
Southern quarries	beige	bioclastic wackestone	–3.33	2.33
Southern quarries	beige	bioclastic wackestone	–3.09	3.96
Southern quarries	beige	bioclastic wackestone	–3.68	2.56

Table 3 (*cont.*)

wave base. One sample has a $\delta^{13}C$ value of –1.32‰ VPDB and a $\delta^{18}O$ value of –4.30‰ VPDB. The beige building blocks from the early Severan (late 2nd – early 3rd century AD) nymphaeum on the lower agora (n = 4) are bioclastic wackestones with pellets and crinoids from a restricted to open marine environment. One sample has a $\delta^{13}C$ value of 2.74‰ VPDB and a $\delta^{18}O$ value of –2.52‰ VPDB.

The mainly pink building stone from the temple of the divine Hadrian and of Antoninus Pius, started in mid-Hadrianic times (ca. 128-130 AD) but not completed before the beginning of the reign of Antoninus Pius (n = 8) is a bioclastic wacke- to packstone with echinoderms, crinoids, foraminifera, shell fragments and extraclasts, deposited in an open marine environment around wave base. The white recrystallized limestone is a bioclastic grainstone with crinoids deposited in an open marine environment above wave base. The isotopic composition of this limestone

(n = 2) is 3.29‰ VPDB for $\delta^{13}C$ and between –4.74‰ and –5.84‰ VPDB for $\delta^{18}O$. The isotopic composition varies between 0.74‰ and 3.46‰ VPDB for $\delta^{13}C$ and between –4.97‰ and –4.42‰ VPDB for $\delta^{18}O$.

The limestone in the scene of the late Antonine theatre (n = 3) is a bioclastic packstone with shell fragments, foraminifers, calcispheres, crinoids and pellets, deposited in an open marine environment around wave base. The isotopic composition of this limestone (n = 1) is 2.35‰ VPDB for $\delta^{13}C$ and –3.71‰ VPDB for $\delta^{18}O$.

Radiolarian mudstone has only been described in the Sarıkaya quarry and are not found in quarries in the Lycian nappe near Sagalassos. The late Hellenistic building stone of the Doric temple and some of the stone used for the bouleuterion (ca. 100 BC) was clearly quarried at Sarıkaya. It can be observed from the current dataset that stone was

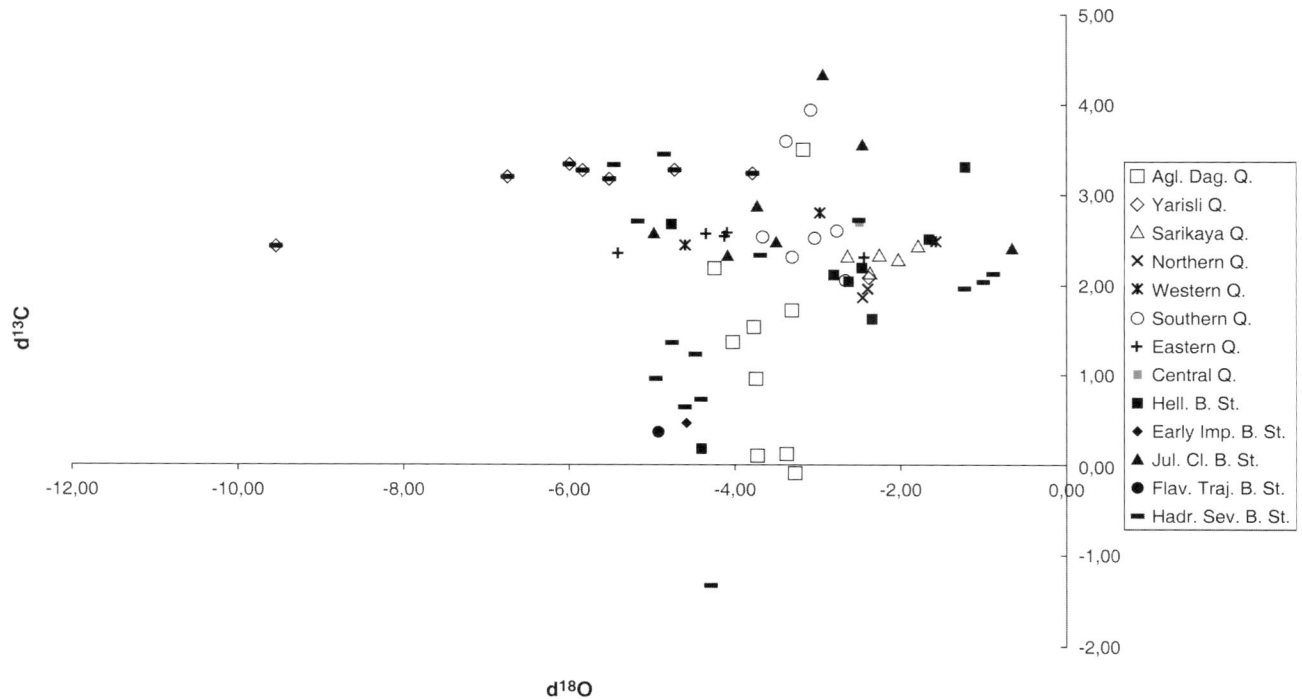

Figure 13: Stable isotope diagram for d^{13}C and d^{18}O of the building stone and quarries investigated in the territory of Sagalassos.

no longer extracted at Sarıkaya after the late Hellenistic period, as it is not used any longer in buildings from the Julio-Claudian period onwards (Degryse *et al.*, 2006).

The Ağlasun Dağları quarry is the only source of pink limestone in the area studied, but it also contains beige limestone. This limestone was already in use in the late Hellenistic bouleuterion. Its use, however, is not necessarily restricted to this period. A pink bioclastic wackestone is proven to have been used in buildings and constructions from the Augustan period (the honorific columns on the upper agora), the Trajanic period (the honorific monument for Trajan) and the Hadrianic to Severan period (late Antonine nymphaeum on the upper agora, the temple for Hadrian and Antoninus Pius). The beige limestone of the Ağlasun Dağları quarry can be distinguished from the beige limestone of unit A and F (with similar petrographical characteristics) by its different isotopic composition (Figure 13).

The isotopic composition of the Ağlasun Dağları stone does, however, not overlap with that of all pink bioclastic wackestone used in the aforementioned buildings. Therefore, the pink limestone was most likely also imported from other locations and quarries in the territory of Sagalassos. Especially the massif pink limestone used in the temple for

the divine Hadrian and Antoninus Pius seems to have different macroscopical characteristics (deep pink colour aspects) than those of the stone quarried in the Ağlasun Dağları quarry, though the petrographic and facies characteristics are the same. Conversely, the oxygen isotopic composition of the pink building stone in the temple for Hadrian and Antoninus Pius matches that of the white recrystallized limestone imported from the wider territory, used in the same building. Both oxygen and carbon isotope values of the beige limestone from the temple for the divine Hadrian and Antoninus Pius and from the late Antonine nymphaeum on the upper agora are similar to the values of the white recrystallized limestone. This makes the import of a pink and beige limestone together with the white limestone all the more likely.

Other stones used in the monumental architecture at Sagalassos can be attributed to the quarries in the different units of the Lycean nappes near the monumental centre. This is the case for building stone from the Augustan period (the honorific columns on the upper agora, the Apollo Klarios temple (?), the Tiberian south gate) as well as from late Antonine to Severan period (the nymphaea on the upper and lower agora).

Some of the beige and pink limestone (the Trajanic re-buildign of the Apollo Klarios temple (?), the late Antonine nymphaeum on the upper agora, the temple for Hadrian and Antoninus Pius) cannot be attributed to the quarries described above. This limestone shows the same isotopic characteristics as the high quality white limestone from the southwest of the territory of the city (Waelkens *et al.*, 2002; Degryse *et al.*, 2003; in press), and was likely imported along with this high quality white limestone. This import can be considered a trend from the Trajanic period (98-117 AD) onwards. The selection of these building stones went hand in hand with the appreciation for their structural strength, their suitability for carving complex architectural ornaments and the desire to obtain a polychrome architecture to imitate the Imperial white marble architecture (Waelkens *et al.*, 2002; Degryse *et al.*, 2003; in press). One sample, from the macellum, according to ongoing research dedicated to Commodus in 180-197 AD, could not be attributed to any known quarry in the area of Sagalassos.

A tentative chronology can now be proposed. The first building stones of Sagalassos were quarried at the site proper. The quarrying of the bedrock on which the bouleuterion was built (Loots, 2001), can be traced to the mid Hellenistic period. The limestone from the Lycian nappe near monumental Sagalassos was extracted throughout the Julio-Claudian and Hadrianic to Severan periods. The unique limestone (radiolarian mudstone) of the Sarıkaya quarry seems to have been used only in late Hellenistic buildings. This indicates that this quarry may have been one of the main suppliers of building stones during this period. The *Sagalassos Red Slip Ware* sherds found in front of the main quarry face, date from the early Imperial period and may constitute a *terminus ante quem* for the exploitation of the quarry. The pink limestone (bioclastic wackestone) was only identified in the Ağlasun Dağları quarry. Although the quarry cannot be dated with certainty, the petrographic and geochemical data indicate that this quarry was at least contemporary to the Sarıkaya quarry, and was still supplying building stone to Sagalassos during the first and second centuries AD, as indicated by some roughed out sarcophagi. Some of the beige and possibly pink limestone used at Sagalassos was likely imported from the Lycian nappes in (or just outside) the south-western territory of the town, along with a high quality white limestone (Waelkens *et al.*, 2002; Degryse *et al.*, 2003). This import can be considered a trend from the Trajanic period (98-117 AD) onwards.

8. GENERAL DISCUSSION AND CONCLUSION

Different types of building stones have been identified at Sagalassos. These include limestones, conglomerates, breccias and sand- to siltstone of different qualities, the provenance of which can be related to the Lycean nappes and flysch deposits, both in the area of the city and further away in the area of Burdur. Travertine and volcanic building stones were brought to the city from a distance of a few kilometres, respectively from the area of Başköy and that of Gölcük. Marbles and coloured stones were transported in substantial quantities from e.g. the Docimian quarries, 250 km to the north of Sagalassos.

Only few buildings at Sagalassos can be attributed to the Hellenistic period. For most of them, no precise date can be given, making it impossible to identify periods of less or more building activity. For the Imperial period, three periods of intensive building activities can be identified (Table 2): these are the Julio-Claudian period (Augustus to Nero: 27 BC to 68 AD), the Flavian(?)-Trajanic period (68 AD to 117 AD) and the period from Hadrian to the Severi (117 AD to 235 AD). Whereas in the past, it was believed that the Flavian period rather was an era of building stagnation, the west and east porticoes of the lower agora as well as the *cavea* of the Odeon can now be firmly attributed to their dynasty.

During the Hellenistic period, the quality of the different local building stones seems not yet to have been appreciated. Also in the early Imperial period, the local limestones were used without regards for their inherent qualities. All buildings of the Hellenistic and Julio-Claudian periods contain only local beige and pink limestone and conglomerate. From the Trajanic and Hadrianic periods onwards, however, a preferential use of good quality building stone became evident, which continued into the late second century AD. This preference went hand in hand with the import of an excellent quality white limestone, which during the Trajanic era, characterized by a rather plain undecorated monumental architecture, seems to have been appreciated for its structural strength. From Hadrian onwards also its suitability for carving complex architectural ornamentation became an additional reason to use it. Its occurrence in some of the wall blocks of the Augustan temple of Apollo Klarios could be considered a result of the Trajanic re-building phase, dated to the years 102-103 AD. It is most probable that the quarries of this type of stone were only opened around the turn of the first century AD as indicated by their first use. Although structural reasons may have played a role in the selection of this white limestone during the Hadrianic era, in the late Hadrianic temple for Hadrian and Antoninus Pius and its propylon, the first attempts to create a polychrome architecture may have been a main incentive for its use (Waelkens *et al.*, 2003). In the temple, white limestone bases, columns and capitals were combined with building elements in pink limestone, while its propylon used several white limestone architraves, friezes and cornices again next to pink limestone elements. During the second half of the second century AD, white limestone continued to be used, this time in combination with even more exotic stone types. In the late Antonine nymphaeum on the upper agora and in the Severan nymphaeum on the lower agora, local beige limestone, white limestone, differently coloured breccias and blue 'kaplan postu' and 'pavanozetto' marbles (both from Dokimeion) were brought together to create polychromatic effects. Although the inherent strength of both the white limestone and the marbles is very high, it is clear that during this period they were in the first place selected for their aesthetic appeal.

A keyword for the quarrying of limestone in the city area seems to be *proximity*; in the immediate vicinity of important stone consuming activities, being construction or funerary use, there are quarries, which in size (at least from an optimistic view) fit the volumes in question. This view is also supported by the integration of possible quarries in buildings. Furthermore, indications of "ad hoc" and non-systematic quarrying around some of the necropoleis indicate quarrying in these areas over time. As overland transport was the main challenge in quarrying and stone commerce, all of this is hardly surprising.

Another interesting aspect of the quarries is the lack of well organized quarries and systematic trenching typical of the Greek and Roman Periods (Waelkens, 1994). From our point of view, this relates to the stone quality; the abundance of natural fractures in the limestone deposit (which of course is to be expected in rocks of such proximity to thrust faults) forced the quarrymen to follow the natural features as best as they could. There is thus reason to believe that quarrying generated quite large amounts of waste rock. Spoil heaps from the quarrying are only found in the eastern quarries. However, the waste material at the other sites may have been carried away by landslides, covered by scree, removed during constructions in the city or even be used as rubble in post-quarrying contexts.

Care needs to be taken when interpreting the necropolis quarries, given that we see a totality of these quarry landscapes. It is problematic to determine whether sarcophagi production was 'made following specific order' or represented a short-term intensive production that was producing prefabricated items. In the case of the latter, it would be expected to find evidence of 'failed' attempts of sarcophagi production from partially worked blocks, although it has to be considered that such evidence might be lost. The evidence that is represented errs towards the former interpretation, as the extractions themselves suggest that quarrying may have

been carried out by skilled artisans exploiting the resource sporadically. Moreover, it is important to recognize that with the 206 sarcophagi documented, if averaged out over a 100 year period, production may only have constituted 2-3 sarcophagi per year.

9. ACKNOWLEDGEMENTS

The research was supported through the QuarryScapes project (contract no. 015416 of EU FP6 STREP-INCO programme) and by the Belgian Programme on Interuniversitary Poles of Attraction (IAP VI/22). The text also presents the results of a project by the Research Fund of the K.U.Leuven (BOF-GOA07/2).

10. REFERENCES

CALLEBAUT, K., VIAENE, W., WAELKENS, M., OTTENBURGS, R. and NAUD, J. (2000) Provenance and characterization of raw materials for lime mortars used at Sagalassos with special reference to the volcanic rocks, in: M. WAELKENS and L. LOOTS (eds) *Sagalassos V. Report on the Survey and Excavation Campaigns of 1996 and 1997 (Acta Archaeologica Lovaniensia Monographiae 11)*, Leuven University Press, Leuven: 651-668.

DEGRYSE P., MUCHEZ PH., LOOTS L., VANDEPUT L. and WAELKENS M. (2003) The building stones of Roman Sagalassos (SW Turkey): Facies analysis and provenance, *Facies* 48: 9-22.

DEGRYSE, P., MUCHEZ, PH. and WAELKENS, M. (2006) Geology and archaeology of late Hellenistic limestone quarries at Sagalassos, *MARMORA* 2: 9-20.

DEGRYSE, P., MUCHEZ, PH., SINTUBIN, M., CLIJSTERS, A., VIAENE, W., DEDEREN, M., SCHROOTEN, P. and WAELKENS, M. (this volume a) Geological mapping of the area around Sagalassos, in: P. DEGRYSE and M. WAELKENS (eds.) *Sagalassos VI. Geo- and Bio-Archaeology at Sagalassos and in its Territory*, Leuven University Press, Leuven, Leuven: 17-24.

DEGRYSE, P., MUCHEZ, PH., VIAENE, W., QUINIF, Y. and WAELKENS, M. (this volume b) Depositional environment and climatic implications of Holocene travertines in the valley of Başköy, in: P. DEGRYSE and M. WAELKENS (eds.) *Sagalassos VI. Geo- and Bio-Archaeology at Sagalassos and in its Territory*, Leuven University Press, Leuven: 211-214.

DEGRYSE P., MUCHEZ PH., TROGH E. and WAELKENS M. (in press) The natural building stones of Hellenistic to Byzantine Sagalassos: provenance determination through stable isotope geochemistry, in: Y. MANNIATIS (ed.) *ASMOSIA*

288

VII, Proceedings of the Seventh International Conference on Interdisciplinary Studies on Ancient Stone, Thassos (Greece), 15-20 September 2003.

DILEK, Y. and ROWLAND, J.C. (1993) Evolution of a conjugate passive margin pair in Mesozoic Southern Turkey, *Tectonics* 12: 954-970.

DWORAKOWSKA, A. (1975) *Quarries in Ancient Greece (Bibliotheca Antiqua, 14)*, Wroclaw.

FLEISCHER, R. (1979) Forschungen in Sagalassos 1972 und 1974, *Istanbuler Mitteilungen* 29: 273-307.

FLÜGEL, E. (1982) *Microfacies Analysis of Limestones*, Berlin.

FLÜGEL, E. (2004) *Microfacies Carbonate Rocks. Analysis, Interpretation and Application*, Berlin.

FLÜGEL, E. and FLÜGEL, C. (1997a) Applied microfacies analysis: provenance studies of Roman mosaic stones, *Facies* 37: 1-48.

FLÜGEL, E. and FLÜGEL, E. (1997b) Der rote Korallenkalk in der Hethiter-Mauer von Boğazköy (Anatolien): Mikrofazies und Herkunft, *Geologische Blätter für Nordost-Bayern* 47: 321-338.

GREENHALGH, J. (1987) *Roman Pisidia. A Study of Development and Change*, Ph.D. Thesis, Univ. Newcastle-upon-Tyne.

HERRMANN, J., HERZ, N. and NEWMAN, R. (2002) *ASMOSIA 5, Interdisciplinary Studies on Ancient Stone (Proceedings of the Fifth International Conference of the Association for the Study of Marble and Other Stones in Antiquity)*, London.

HERZ, N. and WAELKENS, M. (1988) *Classical Marble: Geochemistry, Technology, Trade,* Dordrecht.

KÖSE, V. (2005) *Nekropolen und Grabdenkmäler von Sagalassos in Pisidien in hellenistischer und römischer Zeit (Studies in Eastern Mediterranean Archaeology VII)*, Brepols, Turnhout.

LANCKORONSKI, CH. (1893) *Les villes de la Pamphylie et de la Pisidie 1*, Paris.

LAZZARINI, L. (2002) *Interdisciplinary Studies on Ancient Stone – ASMOSIA VI (Proceedings of the Sixth International Conference of the Association for the Study of Marble and Other Stones in Antiquity)*.

LOOTS, L. (2001) *The Building Materials and Building Techniques at Sagalassos, Turkey*, Ph.D. Thesis, Katholieke Universiteit Leuven.

MANIATIS, Y., HERZ, N. and BASIAKOS, Y. (1995) *The Study of Marble and Other Stones Used in Antiquity*, London.

MOENS, L., DE PAEPE, P. and WAELKENS, M. (1997) An archaeometric study of the provenance of white marble sculptures from an Augustan heroon and a middle Antonine nymphaeum at Sagalassos (Southwest Turkey), in: M. WAELKENS and J. POBLOME (eds.) *Sagalassos IV. Report on the Survey and Excavation Campaigns of 1994 and 1995 (Acta Archaeologica Lovaniensia Monographiae 9)*, Leuven University Press, Leuven: 367-383.

MUCHEZ, PH., NOLLET, S., SINTUBIN, M., LENS, S. and JOACHIMSKI, M. (2003) Fluid flow, alteration and mineralization associated with the emplacement of the Lycian nappes (SW Turkey), *Journal of Geochemical Exploration* 78-79: 553-557.

MUCHEZ, PH., LENS, S., DEGRYSE, P., CALLEBAUT, K., DEDEREN, M., HERTOGEN, J., JOACHIMSKI, M., KEPPENS, E., OTTENBURGS, R., SCHROYEN, K. and WAELKENS, M. (this volume) Petrography, mineralogy and geochemistry of the rocks in the area of the archaeological site of Sagalassos, in: P. DEGRYSE and M. WAELKENS (eds.) *Sagalassos VI. Geo- and Bio-Archaeology at Sagalassos and in its Territory*, Leuven University Press, Leuven: 25-52.

OTA, R. and DINCEL, A. (1975) Volcanic rocks of Turkey, *Bulletin of the Geological Survey of Japan* 26: 393-419.

PEACOCK, D.P.S. (1994) Roman Stones, *Journal of Roman Archaeology* 7: 361-363.

POISSON, A. (1977) *Recherches géologiques dans les Taurides occidentales*, Thèse de Doctorat d'Etat, Orsay.

POISSON, A., AKAY, E., DUMONT, J.F. and UYSAL, S. (1984) The Isparta Angle : a Mesozoic paleorift in the Western Taurides, in: O. TEKELI and C. GONCÜOGLU (eds.) *Geology of the Taurus Belt (Proceedings of the International Symposium on the Geology of the Taurus Belt)*, MTA, Ankara: 11-26.

ROBERTSON, A.H.F. (1993) Mesozoic-Tertiary sedimentary and tectonic evolution of Neotethyan carbonate platforms, margins and small ocean basins in the Antalya Complex, southwest Turkey, in: L.E. FROSTICK and R.J. STEEL (eds.) *Tectonic Controls and Signatures in Sedimentary Successions (Special Publication of the International Association of Sedimentologists 20)*, Blackwell Scientific Publications, Oxford: 415-465.

SCHROYEN, K., VERMOERE, M., DEGRYSE, P., LIBRECHT, I., MUCHEZ, PH., VIAENE, W., SMETS, E., PAULISSEN, E., KEPPENS, E. and WAELKENS, M. (2000) Preliminary study of travertine deposits in the vicinity of Sagalassos: petrography, geochemistry, geomorphology and palynology, in: M. WAELKENS and L. LOOTS (eds.) *Sagalassos V. Report on the Survey and Excavation Campaigns of 1996 and 1997 (Acta Archaeologica Monographiae Lovaniensia 10)* Leuven University Press, Leuven: 755-780.

SIMILOX-TOHON, D. (2006) *An Integrated Geological and Archaeoseismological Approach of the Seismicity in the Territory of Sagalassos (SW Turkey). Towards the Identification of Active Faults in the Burdur-Isparta region,* PhD Thesis, K.U.Leuven.

SINTUBIN, M., MUCHEZ, PH., SIMILOX-TOHON, D., VERHAERT, G., PAULISSEN, E. and WAELKENS, M. (2003) Seismic catastrophes at the ancient city of Sagalassos (SW Turkey) and their implications for the seismotectonics in the Burdur-Isparta area, *Geological Journal* 38 (3-4): 359-374.

VERHAERT, G., MUCHEZ, PH., SINTUBIN, M. and ZEELMAEKERS, E. (2002) Calcite cementation of screes: palaeoclimatic implications, in: P. DEGRYSE and M. SINTUBIN (eds.) *Contributions to the Geology of Belgium and Northwest Europe* (*Proceedings of the first Geologica Belgica International Meeting, Aardkundige Mededelingen 12*): 153-156.

VERMOERE, M., DEGRYSE, P., VANHECKE, L., MUCHEZ, PH., PAULISSEN, E., SMETS, E. and WAELKENS, M. (1999) Pollen analysis of two travertine sections in Başköy (southwestern Turkey): implications for environmental conditions during the early Holocene, *Review of Paleobotany and Palynology* 105: 93-110

VIAENE, W., OTTENBURGS, R., MUCHEZ, PH. and WAELKENS, M. (1993) The building stones of Sagalassos, in: M. WAELKENS (ed.) *Sagalassos I. First General Report on the Survey (1986-1989) and Excavations (1990-1991)* (*Acta Archaeologica Lovaniensia Monographiae 5*), Leuven University Press: 85-92.

WAELKENS, M. (1994) Cave di marmor, in: *Enciclopedia dell' Arte Antica Classica e Orientale. Secondo Supplemento* II: 71-88.

WAELKENS, M. (2002) Romanization in the East. A case study: Sagalassos and Pisidia (SW Turkey), *Istanbuler Mitteilungen* 52: 311-368.

WAELKENS, M., DE PAEPE, P. and MOENS, L. (1988) Quarries and the marble trade in antiquity, in: N. HERZ and M. WAELKENS (eds.) *Classical Marble: Geochemistry, Technology*, Dordrecht: 11-28.

WAELKENS, M., HERZ, N. and MOENS, L. (1992) Ancient Stones: Quarrying, Trade and Provenance, in: *Interdisciplinary Studies on Stones and Stone Technology in Europe and Near East from the Prehistoric to the Early Christian Period*, Leuven.

WAELKENS, M. and THE SAGALASSOS TEAM (1997a) Interdisciplinarity in classical archaeology. A case study: the Sagalassos Archaeological Research Project (Southwest Turkey), in: M. WAELKENS and J. POBLOME (eds.) *Sagalassos IV. Report on the Survey and Excavation Campaigns of 1994 and 1995* (*Acta Archaeologica Lovaniensia Monographiae 9*), Leuven University Press: 225-252.

WAELKENS, M., PAULISSEN, E., VANHAVERBEKE, H., ÖZTÜRK, I., DE CUPERE, B., EKINCI, H.A., VERMEERSCH, P.M., POBLOME, J. and DEGEEST, R. (1997b) The 1994 and 1995 surveys on the territory of Sagalassos), in: M. WAELKENS and J. POBLOME (eds.) *Sagalassos IV. Report on the Survey and Excavation Campaigns of 1994 and 1995* (*Acta Archaeologica Lovaniensia Monographiae 9*), Leuven University Press: 11-102.

WAELKENS, M., PAULISSEN, E., VERMOERE, M., DEGRYSE, P., CELIS, D., SCHROYEN, K., DE CUPERE, B., LIBRECHT, I., NACKAERTS, K., VANHAVERBEKE, H., VIAENE, W., MUCHEZ, P., OTTENBURGS, R., DECKERS, S., VAN NEER, W., SMETS, E., GOVERS, G., VERSTRAETEN, G., STEEGEN, A. and CAUWENBERGHS, K. (1999) Man and Environment in the territory of Sagalassos, a classical city in SW Turkey, *Quaternary Science Reviews* 18: 697-709.

WAELKENS, M., POBLOME, J., PAULISSEN, E., TALLOEN, P., VAN DEN BERGH, J., VANDERGINST, V., ARIKAN, B., VAN DAMME, I., AKYEL, I., MARTENS, F., MARTENS, M., UYTTERHOEVEN, I., DEBRUYNE, T., DEPRAETERE, D., BARAN, K., VANDAELE, B., PARRAS, Z., YILDIRIM, S., BUBEL, S., VANHAVERBEKE, H., LICOPPE, C., LANDUYT, F., DEGEEST, R., VANDEPUT, L., LOOTS, L., PATRICIO, T., ERCAN, S., VAN BALEN, K., SMITS, E., DEPUYDT, F., MOENS, L. and DE PAEPE, P. (2000a) The 1996 and 1997 Excavation Seasons at Sagalassos, in: M. WAELKENS and L. LOOTS (eds.) *Sagalassos V. Report on the Survey and Excavation Campaigns of 1996 and 1997* (*Acta Archaeologica Lovaniensia Monographiae 11*), Leuven University Press: 217-398.

WAELKENS, M., SINTUBIN, M., MUCHEZ, P. and PAULISSEN, E. (2000b) Archeological, geomorphological and geological evidence for a major earthquake at Sagalassos (SW Turkey) around the middle of the seventh century AD, in: W.J. MCGUIRE, D.R. GRIFFITHS, P.L. HANCOCK and I. STEWART (eds.) *The Archaeology of Geological Catastrophes* (*Special Publications*. Geological Society, London): 373-383.

WAELKENS, M., MUCHEZ, PH., LOOTS, L., DEGRYSE, P., MOENS, L. and DE PAEPE, P. (2002) Marble and the marble trade at Sagalassos (Turkey), in: J.J. HERRMANN JR., N. HERZ and R. NEWMAN (eds.) *Asmosia V. Interdisciplinary Studies on Ancient Stone*: 370-380.

WAELKENS, M., DEGRYSE, P., VANDEPUT, L., LOOTS, L. and MUCHEZ, PH. (2003) Polychromy in classical architecture. A case study: Sagalassos (Pisidia), in: L. LAZZARINI (ed.) *Proceedings of the Sixth International Conference of ASMOSIA*, Venice: 517-530.

WARD-PERKINS, J.B. (1980) Nicomedia and the marble trade, *Papers of the British School at Rome* 48: 23-69.

290

IDENTIFYING REMAINS OF ANCIENT FOOD IN THE CERAMICS OF SAGALASSOS: DEVELOPING A METHOD

Katrien KIMPE, Pierre JACOBS and Marc WAELKENS

1. INTRODUCTION

Ancient remains of food are an important source of information to help us understand ancient social and economical systems. Traditional techniques to identify food remains use the morphology of preserved seeds, fruits or roots in the case of plants or preserved bones in the case of animals. The former techniques provide information on the earlier environment, but are inefficient when organic remains are poorly preserved (Jones, 1999). The use of chemical criteria to identify the organic remains can solve these problems. Hereby amorphous residues are identified using specialized analytical techniques. This opens interesting prospects for the research of the encrusted remains in ceramic sherds found in archaeological excavation sites. Ceramics are often abundantly present and possess valuable information hidden in the porous matrix of the sherds. At Sagalassos, which was previously a centre of pottery fabrication, ten thousands of sherds are being excavated. The form and fabric of of coarse ceramics have been well described (Degeest et al., 2000), but relatively little is known about the former contents. The goal of organic residue analysis is to reconstitute the original contents of these ceramics and to find a relation between form and function of the different pots (cooking pots, amphora, dolia, *unguentaria* and jars). This paper will discuss the developing of a method to extract and analyse organic remains in the ceramics of Sagalassos. Because of their favourable characteristics lipids were preferentially extracted and analyzed.

Lipids are in comparison with other food constituents such as proteins, carbohydrates and nucleic acids better preserved due to their hydrophobic nature. Preservation of lipids has been shown in fossil sediments (Eglinton and Logan, 1991; Simoneit, 1977). For example several sterols were found in mature sediments (Mackenzie, 1982). The term lipid covers an extremely diverse range of molecular species. Lipids are classed as being soluble in organic solvents such as chloroform, hydrocarbons and alcohols. Lipids can be classified (Figure 1) into neutral or apolar molecules such as hydrocarbons(e), carotenes, triacylglycerols(a), wax esters(d), sterol esters and other lipids such as fatty acids and sterols(c). The polar lipids contain phospholipids(b),

glycolipis, sulpholipids, some sphingolipids, oxygenated carotenoids and chlorophylls (Berlitz and Grosch, 1986). The most conventional method to extract lipids is based on Folch et al. (1957) with the use of a mixture of chloroform and methanol (2+1 v/v). In the lipid extract two fractions of analytical interest can be distinguished: (1) lipid molecules that are characteristic for one animal or plant species, the 'biomarkers', and (2) common lipid molecules that can be found in a whole range of biological tissues.

Lipids occur widely in foodstuffs, but are also present on the surface of the hands of excavators, in soil (Braids and Miller, 1976), bacteria and in fungi (Ratledge and Wilkinson, 1988). However these sources of contamination can be recognized, as some of these lipids are not or minimally present in foodstuffs. Typical constituents of the lipid fraction of human skin are squalene and cholesterol, with squalene being more abundant (Evershed, 1995). In microbial cells lipids are present, acting as storage materials or responsible for the structure of cell membranes. Yeast can be shown through identification of ergosterol (Figure 1c). Gram positive bacteria are characterized by branched-chain (iso and/or anteiso) fatty acids while Gram negative bacteria contain preferentially common fatty acids (Ratledge and Wilkinson, 1988). Another source of possible contamination is the surrounding burial matrix. The bulk of lipid material in soils is a product of partially or undecomposed plant and animal residues. As the sherds were mostly excavated from domestic contexts, animal and plant residues are abundantly present. Nevertheless it was shown (Kimpe et al., 2004) that contamination from the burial context is reduced to only a small influx of long chain fatty acids and long chain alcohols.

Other contaminants are trace phthalate plasticisers, derived from plastic storage bags, vial caps and para-films. These plasticisers can be readily identified because they exhibit a typical Gas Chromatographic–Mass Spectrometric signal (m/z = 149).

Next to the possibility of contamination, many possibilities exist for the chemical or microbiological alterations occurring to the structures of lipids that complicate interpretations of their origin.

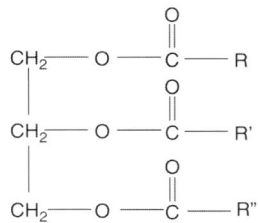

a

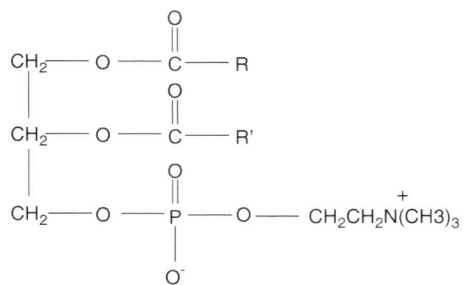

b

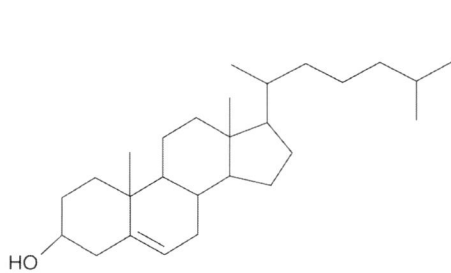

cholesterol

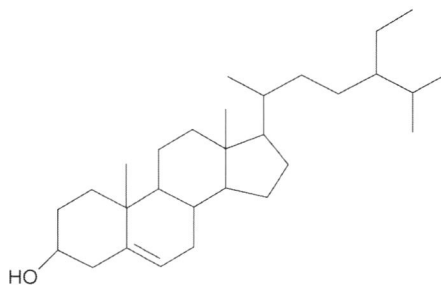

sitosterol

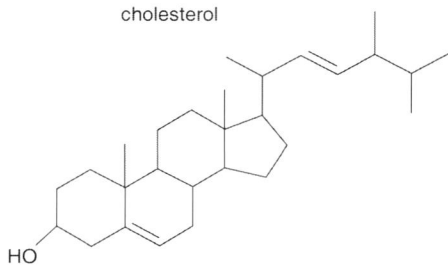

ergosterol

C

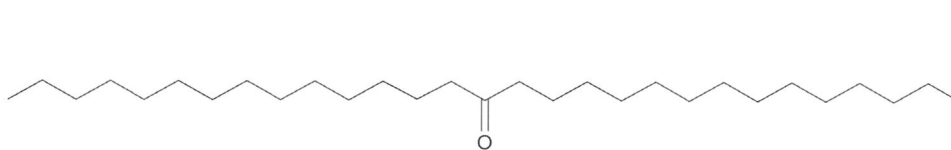

nonacosan-15-one

d

heptacosane

e

Figure 1: Structures of common lipids.

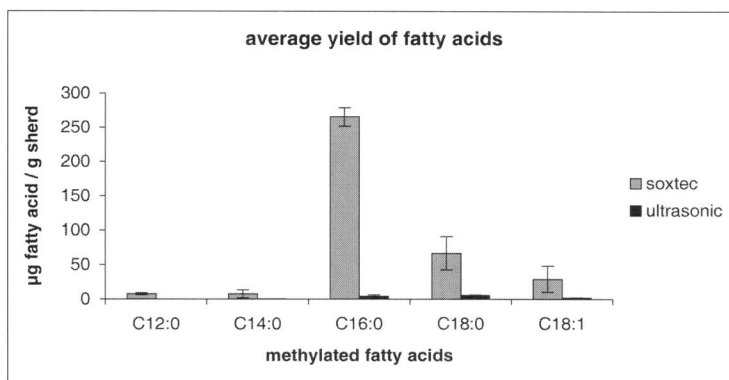

Figure 2: Comparison of the yield of fatty acids obtained with soxtec and ultrasonic extraction.

2. METHODOLOGY

2.1. Preparation of the sherds

The sherds of Sagalassos analyzed here, are sampled from a series of late Roman to early Byzantine (work)shops built along the western edges of the city's two main squares. The sherds are than dried and wrapped in acid-free paper. The wrapped sherd is stored in a plastic bag. Before extracting the lipids, the sherds are cleaned with a spatula and a dentist drill. This is done in order to avoid contamination from the handling of sherds by excavators and lipids from adhering soil. The sherds are then finely ground with pestle and morter, which increases the specific surface for extraction.

2.2. Extraction

Ultrasonic extraction and automated soxhlet extraction (soxtec) of lipids from a cooking potsherd were compared. Ultrasonic extraction is described in the method of Evershed *et al.* (1991) and Malainey *et al.* (1999). Mass exchange in pores of the solid phase is enhanced when exposed to ultrasound. Soxtec extraction uses the same principles of soxhlet extraction, but the extraction time is less than 20% of a soxhlet apparatus. Soxhlet extraction is commonly used in extracting lipid fractions. In soxhlet extraction the lipids are extracted due to a multiple contact with organic solvent. Both methods were applied on three samples of 5 gram of sherd of the same cooking pot (SA-99-RD-38) using a solution of chloroform/methanol (2:1). Before extraction 38 µl of internal standard (heptadecane, 1 µl/ml solution) was added.

With ultrasonic extraction the samples are extracted twice for 10 min using 50 ml of solvent. After each extraction the solvent containing the lipids is separated from the solids through centrifugation and the solvent is poured into a round bottom flask. The surplus of solvent is evaporated with a rotavap.

In the case of soxtec extraction, the system is set on 140°C and 35 ml of solvent is poured in glass extraction cups. The samples are than weighed in the extraction thimbles. When the solvent of all samples (there are six extraction positions) starts to boil, the system is set for one hour in 'boiling mode' and for three hours in the 'rinsing' mode. After that turning the handle that lets the condensed solvent pass to the sample, evaporates the surplus of solvent. After evaporation 1 to 2 ml of solvent remained for both methods, the latter solvent was removed in a vacuum oven on 40°.

A much larger amount of fatty acids was obtained with soxtec extraction (Figure 2). Nevertheless equal yields for ultrasonic and soxhlet extractions are reported in literature (Marvin *et al.*, 1992). The greater yield of lipids with soxtec can be the result of a more efficient evaporation compared to the use of the rotavap when using ultrasonic extraction. It was noticed that sometimes part of the lipid fraction stuck to the walls of the round bottom flask of the rotavap. Also soxtec extraction was found to be more practical and less time consuming. Soxtec can extract six samples at the same time and a minimum of handling is required, while ultrasonic extraction necessitates more actions. Thus soxtec extraction was preferred as the future extraction method.

2.3. Analysis

So far, the approach in residue analysis has been to analyze the total lipid extract or to transesterify the total lipid extract in order to become the total lipid profile. In the first case, one searches for the presence of 'biomarkers' with the help of a gas chromatograph coupled to a mass spectrometer (GC-MS). Most sterols and waxes can be used as biomarkers, since these substances are diagnostic for the nature of a foodstuff (Heron and Evershed, 1993). Nevertheless sterols for example are present in a small percentage in the lipid fraction (usually less than 1%) and often only general specifications can be assigned through the identification of these biomarkers.

When the transesterified extract is analyzed, information can be obtained from the amount of retrieved fatty acids (in the methylated form). Although fatty acid profiles can provide useful information on the origin of residues, their diagnostic potential is limited. Most fats and oils differ in composition according to the relative proportions of a somewhat narrow range of major fatty acids (Belitz and Grosh, 1986). Furthermore, specific fats and oils can exhibit marked variability in composition of individual fatty acids. Factors such as soil type, climate, and method of processing can affect the composition of plant and seed oils, while animal fats may vary in composition as a result of diet and the particular part of the animal from wich the fat is derived (Mills and White, 1994). Moreover, differences between particular types of fats and oils can disappear through oxidative and microbial degradation (Ratledge, 1984; Frankel, 1991). The labile unsaturated fatty acids will be preferentially depleted resulting in an increase of the relative proportions of saturated fatty acids (Frankel, 1991). The survival of polyunsaturated fatty acids in sherds, major constituents of fish and vegetable oils is rare.

Therefore a combination of both methods cited above seems appropriate. Through combining the finding of specific biomarkers with the more general information of fatty acid patterns, substantial information can be obtained. So the decision was made to extract the sherds twice if possible and to saponify one extract. One extract is then silylated and analyzed with a high temperature gas chromatograph coupled to a mass spectrometer. The second lipid extract is transesterified and analyzed with a polar gas chromatograph (GC).

The total lipid extract of archaeological sherds is typical composed of free fatty acids, monoacylglycerols, diacylglycerols and triacylglycerols. Because of the low volatility of the latter lipids a column is needed with temperature programming up to 340°C. In addition, on-column injection and flame ionisation detection is necessitated. The most useful liquid phases are silicone elastomers of high thermal stability, with which separations are achieved solely on the basis of molecular weight. As a result these phases do not permit the separation of saturated and unsaturated

components of the same chain length (Christie, 1981). An immobilised phenylmethyl silicone phase was chosen. In order to reduce analyzing time a short column was selected, as short analyzing times reduce the effect of tailing.

A Hewlett Packard (HP) 5689 gas chromatograph was chosen. The samples are introduced by on-column injection into a 15 m × 0.32 mm internal diameter (i.d.) fused silica capillary, coated with CP Sil 8 stationary phase (immobilized phenylmethyl silicone, 0.25 μm film thickness) provided by SGE. In order to analyze the whole range of lipids the temperature programme starts at 60° with a 5 min isothermal hold followed by a ramp form 60 to 340°C at 10°C/min. The temperature is then held at 340°C for 20 min. Nitrogen is used as a carrier gas and flame ionisation detection is used to monitor the column effluent.

In order to enhance the volality and stability of the lipids with a free alcohol group, the samples are silylated before injection. Silylation replaces the active hydrogen by a silyl group; this decreases the polarity of the product and the possibility of hydrogen bonding (Pierce, 1968). N-methyl-N-trimethylsilyltrifluoroacetamide (MSTFA) was used to derivatize the samples. To the dried extracted lipids, 50 μl of toluene and 50 μl of MSTFA were added and the mixture was heated 1 hr in an oven of 60°C.

An example of the total lipid chromatogram of sherd SA-99-RD-38 can be seen in Figure 3. The common lipids like triacylglycerols can be identified based on their retention time. The amount of lipids of a certain type can be quantified through comparison with an internal standard. The internal standard should be a lipid that is not prevailing in nature, for example heptadecane. When using an internal standard, the sensitivity of the column for a specific lipid molecule has to be calculated. The sensitivity coefficient corrects for the different affinity for the column of various components. The sensitivity coefficients were calculated for the triacylglycerols using following formula:

$$SC = C_{l,s} A_{i,s} / C_{i,s} A_{l,s}$$

SC : sensitivity coefficient
$C_{l,s}$ = concentration of component in standard mixture
$C_{i,s}$ = concentration of internal standard in standard mixture
$A_{i,s}$ = surface of the peak of the component
$A_{l,s}$ = surface of the peak of the internal standard

The amount of the separate triacylglycerols in the sample can be calculated using this formula (Figure 4):

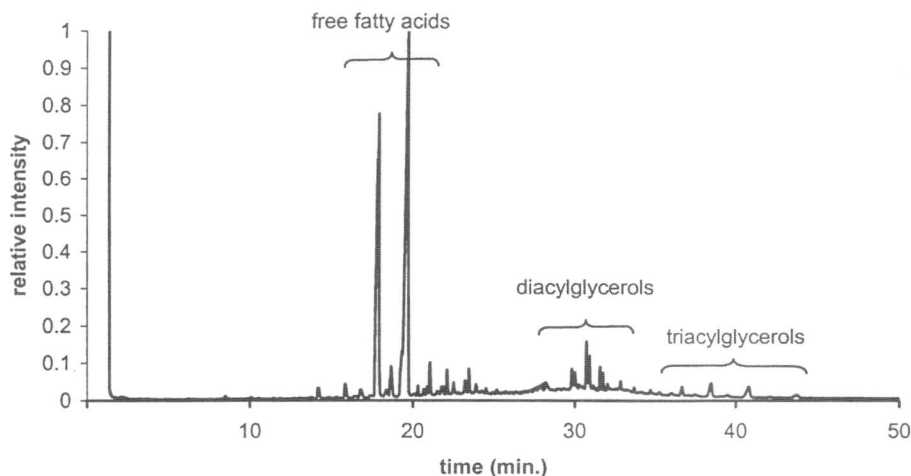

Figure 3: High temperature gas chromatographic profile of cooking potsherd SA-99-RD-38. A typical profile found in archaeological cooking potsherds is seen: free fatty acids, mono-, di- and triglycerols.

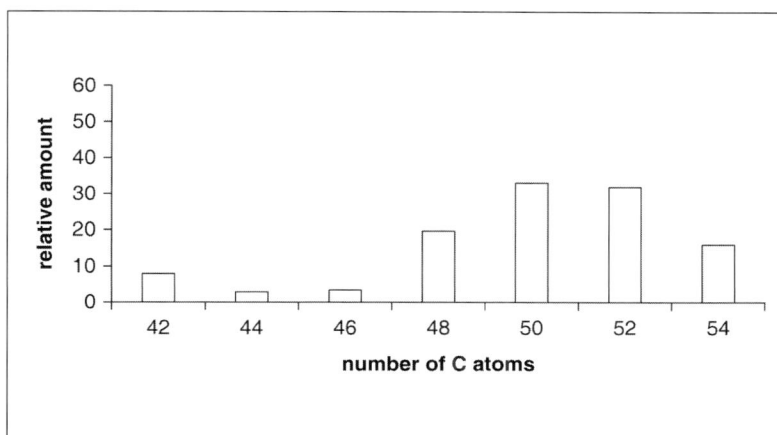

Figure 4: Relative amount of triacylglycerols (on the total amount) in cooking potsherd SA-99-RD-38.

$$m_l = SCA_l/A_i m_i$$

A_l = surface of the component in the sample
A_i = surface of the internal standard in the sample
m_i = weight internal standard added to the sample

In order to identify the less common lipids and more specific the 'biomarkers' the silylated sample was also injected in a gas-chromatograph-mass spectrometer (GC-MS). A mass spectrometer is a powerful detector. In mass spectrometry, gaseous molecules are ionized (usually to make cations), accelerated by an electric field and then separated according to their mass. The ionisation process and especially when electron impact is used, imparts enough energy to the molecule to break it into a variety of characteristic fragments. This pattern of characteristic fragments allows identifying the molecule (Harris, 1999).

The GC-MS analyses are performed using a quadrupole MS of type MD 800 directly coupled to a GC 8000, Fisons instruments. Operating conditions are as follow: ion source 200°C, emission current 400 μA and electron energy 70 eV. The GC-MS interface was maintained at a temperature of 250°C. Spectra were recorded over the range m/z 40-650 every 0.5 s using electron impact ionisation. Data were acquired and processed using the Masslab data system. A longer column with similar packing as in the high-temperature gas chromatograph was installed: CP Sil

8 column (30 m × 0.32 mm i.d., filmthickness 0.25 μm, delivered by SGE). Because especially the components of medium molecurar weight are of interest (mid-chain ketones and sterols) the temperature programme starts at 140° and increases with 15° min. until 340°C. An example of a GC-MS profile and identification of some molecules is given in Figure 5. Because of the use of a longer column (30 m) only spectra are accorded of the substances eluting before the diacyglycerols.

With the purpose of analyzing the fatty acid distribution of the lipid extract, free fatty acids are methylated and mono-, di- and triacylgylcerols are transesterified (base catalyzed). As a catalyst potassium hydroxide is chosen. Potassium hydroxide reacts very rapidly with triacylglycerols and phosphoglycerides, which are completely transesterified in a few minutes at room temperature. Cholesterol esters will only be transesterified very slowly and require reaction times as long as an hour (Christie, 1989). Because our interest is to retrieve the fatty acid profile, a short reaction time is chosen. To the dried total lipid extract 50 μl of toluene and 200 μl methanolic potassium hydroxide (5%) is added. After 5 min the transesterification reaction is stopped with 200 μl bidestilled water. The apolar methylesters are than extracted with cyclohexane. The cyclohexane fraction is dried and once more resolved in 50 μl of cyclohexane and injected on a gas chromatograph. Because it is important that fatty acids with the same chain length, but with various degrees of saturation or with different structural isomers are well separated, a polar column is chosen. The GC analyses are carried out on a Hewlett Packard 5890 gas chromatograph. The injection is introduced on-column into a 60 m × 0.32 mm i.d. fused silica capillary coated with BPX70 stationary phase (delivered by SGE, 70% immobilized bicyanopropyl polysiloxane, filmthickness 0.25 μm). The column was held at 180°C for 40 minutes. Nitrogen functions as a carrier gas and flame ionisation serves as detection system. For the calculation of the amount of retrieved fatty acids the same formula as for the calculation of the triacylglycerols is used (see above). In Figure 6 a chromatogram is given of the different fatty acid methylester of sample SA-99-RD-38. The calculated amounts are than shown in Table 1.

3. CONCLUSION

An appropriate method was found to extract and analyse the lipid fraction of archaeological sherds. After extracting the lipid fraction by a soxtec apparatus, information is gained from the total lipid profile, identified biomarkers and the fatty acid profile. By combining these sources of information it is possible to recognize the former contents of archaeological ceramic pots.

fatty acid	μg/g sherd	%
12:0	2.58	2.8
14:0	3.57	3.8
16:0	61.04	65.5
cis-C16:1	0.00	0.0
17:0	0.00	0.0
18:0	15.53	16.7
trans-C18:1(11)	0.00	0.0
cis-C18:1(9)	8.42	9.0
C18:2	1.32	1.4
C20:0	0.70	0.8

Table 1: μg fatty acids present in transesterified extract of one gram of cooking potsherd SA-99-RD-38. The relative percentages are given in the second column.

4. ACKNOWLEDGEMENTS

This research was supported by the Belgian Programme on Interuniversitary Poles of Attraction (IAP V/9 and VI/22). The text also presents the results of projects by the Research Fund of the K.U.Leuven (BOF-GOA07/2 and GOA07/2).

5. REFERENCES

BELITZ, H.D. and GROSCH, W. (1986) *Food Chemistry*, Springer-Verlag, Berlin.

BRAIDS, O.C. and MILLER, R.H. (1975) Fats, waxes and resins in soil, in: GIESEKING (ed.) *Soil Components, Volume 1, Organic Components*: 343-367.

CHRISTIE, W.W. (1981) The analysis of lipids other than fatty acids, in: W.W. CHRISTIE (ed.) *Gas Chromatography and Lipids*: 187-234.

CHRISTIE, W.W. (1989) *Gas Chromatography and Lipids: a Practical Guide*. The oily press, Dundee.

DEGEEST, R. (2000) *The Common Wares of Roman Sagalassos (Studies in Eastern Mediterranean Archaeology 3)*, Brepols, Turnhout.

EGLINTON, G. and LOGAN, G.A. (1991) Molecular preservation, *Philosophical Transactions of the Royal Society of London B* 333: 315-328.

EVERSHED, R.P., HERON C. and GOAD, L.J. (1991) Analysis of Organic Residues of Archaeological Origin by High-temperature Gas Chromatography and Gas Chromatography-Mass Spectrometry, *Analyst* 115: 1339-1342.

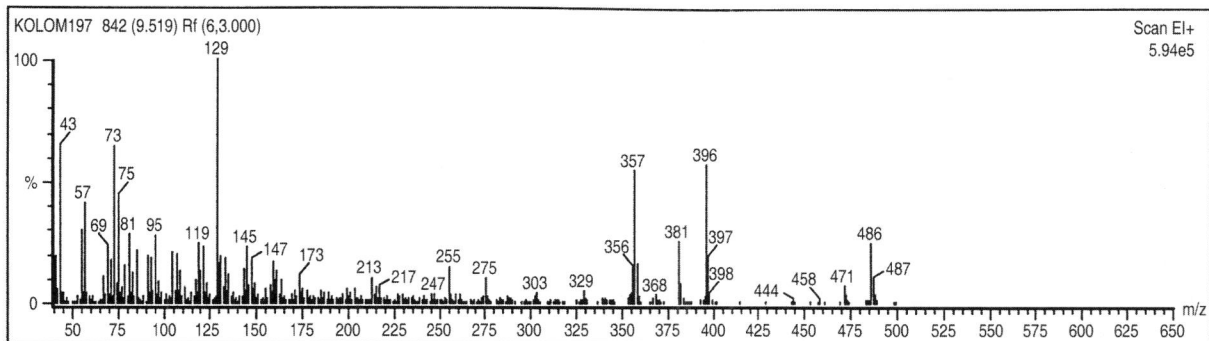

Mass spectrum of trimethylsilyl derivative of β-sitosterol.

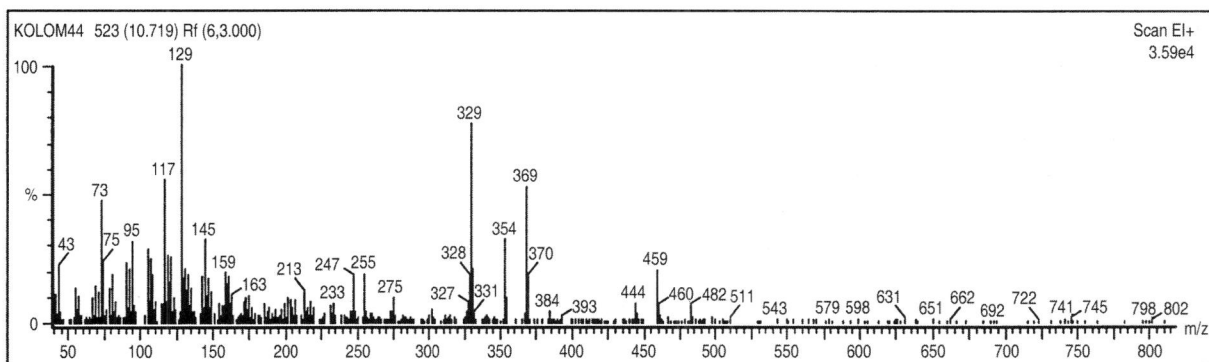

Mass spectrum of trimethylsilyl derivative of cholesterol.

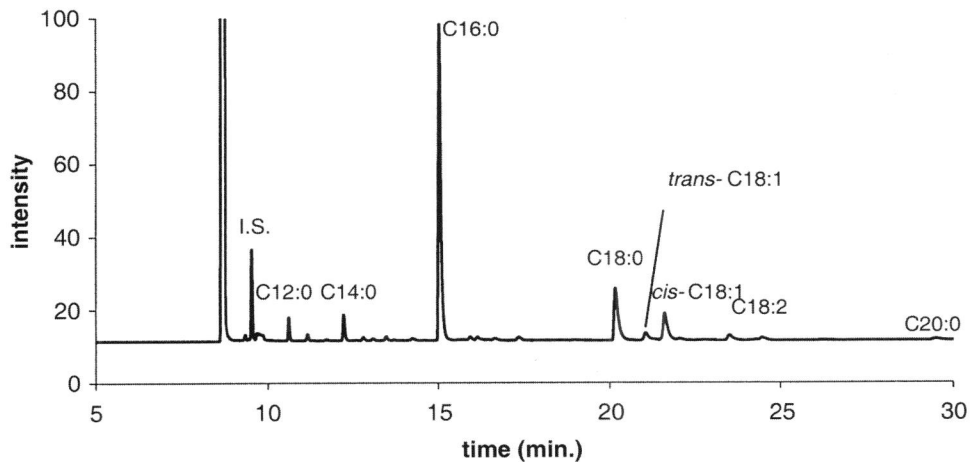

Figure 5: GC-MS profile of cooking potsherd SA-99-RD-38, with mass spectra of cholesterol and β-sitosterol.

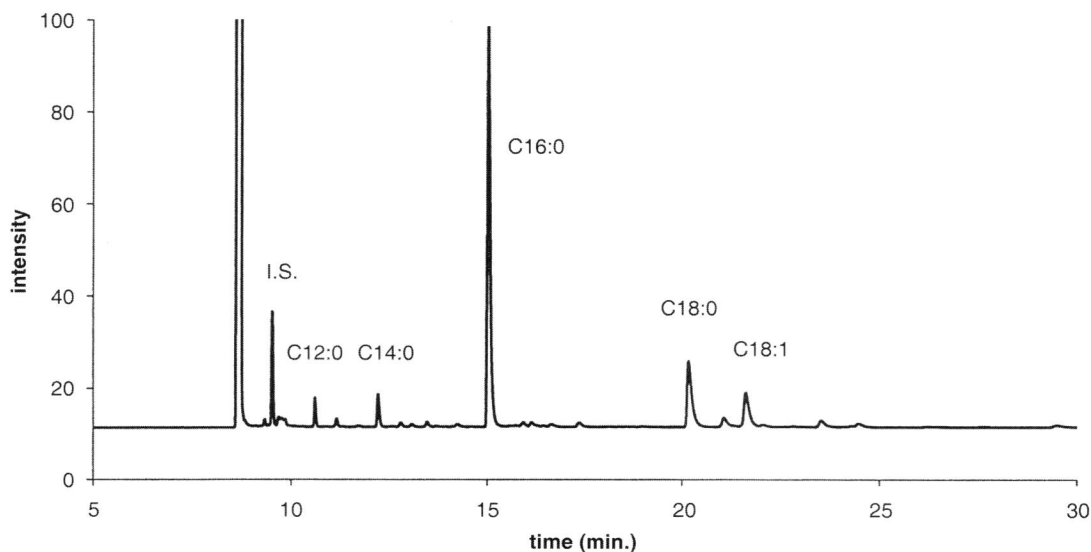

Figure 6: Gas chromatogram of transesterified lipid extract of sample SA-99-RD-38.

EVERSHED, R.P. (1995) Biomolecular archaeology and lipids, *World Archaeology* 25: 74-93.

FOLCH, J., LEES, M. and STANLEY, G.H.S. (1957) A simple method for the isolation and purification of total lipids from animal tissues, *Journal of Biological Chemistry* 226: 497-509.

FRANKEL, E.N. (1991) Review: Recent advances in lipid oxidation, *Journal of Science of Food and Agriculture* 54: 495-511.

HARRIS, D.C. (1999) *Quantitative chemical analysis, fifth edition*, Freeman, New York.

HERON, C. and EVERSHED, R.P. (1993) The analysis of organic residues and the study of pottery use, in: M. SCHIFFER (ed.) *Archaeological Method and Theory 5*, University Press of Arizona, Tucson: 247-284.

JONES, A. (1999) The world on a plate: ceramics, food technology and cosmology in Neolithic Orkney, *World Archaeology* 31(1): 55-77.

KIMPE, K., DRYBOOMS, C., JACOBS, P.A., DEGEEST, R. and WAELKENS, M. (2004) Evidence of processed plant and animal products through lipid analysis and identified biomarkers in ceramic cooking pots, *Journal of Archaeological science* 31: 1503-1510.

MACKENZIE, A.S., BRASSELL, S.C., EGLINTON, G. and MAXWELL, J.R. (1982) Chemical fossils: the geological fate of steroids, *Science* 217: 491-217.

MALAINEY, M.E., PRZYBYLSKI, R. and SHERRIFF, B.L. (1999) Identifying the former contents of late Precontact period pottery vessels from western Canada using gas chromatography, *Journal of Archaeological Science* 26: 425-438.

MARVIN, C.H., ALLAN, L., McCARRY, B.E. and BYRANT D.W. (1992) A comparison of ultrasonic extraction and sowhlet extractioon of polycylclic aromatic hydrocarbons from sediments and air particulate material, *International journal of environmental analytical chemistry* 49(4): 221-230.

MILLS, J.S. and WHITE, R. (1994) *The organic chemistry of museum objects*, Butterworths, London.

PIERCE, A.E. (1968) *Silylation of Organic Compounds: a Technique for Gas-Phase Analysis*, Pierce Chemical Co., Rockford.

RATLEDGE, C. and WILKINSON S.G. (1988) *Microbial Lipids, Volume 1*, Academic press.

RATLEDGE, C. (1984) Microbial conversions of alkanes and fatty acids, *Journal of the American Oil Chemical Society* 61(2): 447-453.

SIMONEIT, B.R.T. (1977) Diterpenoid compounds and other lipids in deep–sea sediments and their geochemical significance, *Geochimica Cosmochimica Acta* 41: 463-476.

THE 1997-1999 SURVEYS OF THE ANATOLIAN FISH FAUNA AND THEIR RELEVANCE TO THE INTERPRETATION OF TRADE AT SAGALASSOS

Wim VAN NEER, Ruud WILDEKAMP, Fahrettin KÜÇÜK, Mustafa ÜNLÜSAYIN

1. INTRODUCTION

The species identified from the fish bones of the Roman and Early Byzantine contexts at Sagalassos show that they came from various regions. Several marine species were identified – of which three occur exclusively in the Mediterranean – as well as Nilotic species such as the Nile perch (*Lates niloticus*), a bagrid catfish (*Bagrus* sp.), tilapia and a clariid catfish (*Clarias gariepinus*) (Van Neer *et al.*, 1997, 2000). The latter two taxa also occur in the Levant, but for *Clarias* it could be demonstrated by mitochondrial DNA-analysis that they originated from Egypt (Arndt *et al.*, 2003). A third category of fishes consumed at Sagalassos are Anatolian freshwater species. The taxa identified thus far are, in descending order of abundance, wild carp (*Cyprinus carpio*), cicek (*Pseudophoxinus handlirschi*), vimba (*Vimba vimba*), *Leuciscus* sp., pike (*Esox lucius*) and European catfish (*Silurus glanis*). The bream (*Abramis brama*) finds previously reported (Van Neer *et al.*, 1997) appear to be misidentifications and are in reality either vimba or unidentifiable cyprinids ("vimba or bream"). Identifying the exact provenance of the Anatolian freshwater fish is hampered by the incomplete knowledge of the modern distribution of the taxa. For this reason, a survey of the waters on the territory of Sagalassos and of some adjacent regions was carried out in 1996 (Van Neer *et al.*, 2000). Emphasis was laid on the region between Sagalassos and the Antalya area because in the past most frequent commercial relationships were maintained with coastal towns such as Perge, Side and Attaleia. The 1996 survey showed that the Ağlasun river, south of the site, is devoid of fishes today except for rainbow trout (*Oncorhynchus mykiss*, an introduced species from northern America) that escaped from a nearby fish farm. Except for its upper reaches, the small river is nowadays seasonally dry as a result of excessive irrigation in the area. However, even in its original state the Ağlasun river would not have been suitable water for the species identified at the site since it is a shallow, fast running body of water as we could observe during spring 1997. Judging from its characteristics, the Ağlasun would be a river typically inhabited by salmonids (river trout *Salmo trutta*) or *Capoeta antalyensis*, a cyprinid that lives in similar waters

in adjacent rivers. Thus far no salmonid bones have been discovered at the site, and *Capoeta antalyensis* has not yet been found among the specifically identified cyprinids. Hence, there is no evidence as of yet that local fishing would have been practised. Of all Anatolian freshwater fishes identified thus far at Sagalassos, only one species was encountered during the 1996 survey: *Vimba vimba* was found in the Aksu river which forms the eastern boundary of the Sagalassos territory. The previous field results hence indicated that all Anatolian freshwater fish, with the possible exception of *Vimba vimba*, must have been brought in from outside the territory. It was therefore necessary to extend the survey of freshwater fishes to a much wider area. Below a detailed account is given of the ichthyological fieldwork conducted between 1997 and 1999. The final aim of these efforts was to obtain a solid data base with the distribution of modern fishes in Anatolia that can serve to determine the geographic origin of the fish identified in the archaeological contexts of Sagalassos.

2. MATERIAL AND METHODS

The surveys summarized here took place between 10 and 22 May 1997, 31 May and 13 June 1998, and between 5 and 13 October 1999. Tables 1-3 give an overview of the 129 localities with their coordinates, that were sampled over the years. Maps of the covered localities are given in Figures 1-5. The sampling gear included electric fishing equipment, castnets, handnets, fish traps, and – during the 1997 campaign – seines with a mesh size of 7 mm and driftnets. Information on the ichthyofauna was also obtained through inspection of the catch of local fishermen and through interviews. Collections have been made in formalin which are kept at the *Fisheries Faculty* in Eğirdir, and subsamples were taken to Belgium for further study. The latter specimens have been registered in the *Royal Museum for Central Africa* as collection numbers MRAC 97033, MRAC 98036 and MRAC 99071. In addition, 124 fish skeletons have been prepared for the reference collection that are registered as collection numbers MRAC 97032, MRAC 98038 and MRAC 99070.

number	name	coordinates	date
97-1	Yalvaç deresi near Madenli	38°11.53'N/31°06.00'E	10-05-97
97-2	Yenice DSİ Canal	38°07.20'N/30°55.22'E	10-05-97
97-3	Karaot, Eğirdir lake	38°08.06'N/30°54.49'E	10-05-97
97-4	Yalvaç deresi rivermouth	38°06.01'N/30°55.93'E	10-05-97
97-5	Köpruçay, Aksu area	37°44.74'N/31°01.67'E	10-05-97
97-6	Çapalı lake at Eldere	38°04.76'N/30°16.28'E	11-05-97
97-7	Dinar Suçıkan	38°04.25'N/30°10.57'E	11-05-97
97-8	Işıklı lake at Beydilli Köyü	38°15.75'N/29°55.59'E	11-05-97
97-9	Karaköprü near Dinar	38°04.80'N/30°09.64'E	11-05-97
97-10	Acıgöl, 1st source from east	37°50.91'N/29°59.42'E	11-05-97
97-11	Acıgöl, 4th source from east	37°50.07'N/29°57.56'E	11-05-97
97-12	Acıgöl, 6th source from east	37°49.85'N/29°57.08'E	11-05-97
97-13	Acıgöl at Gemiş	37°46.02'N/29°50.66'E	11-05-97
97-14	springs at Karamık village	38°22.46'N/30°44.57'E	12-05-97
97-15	Karamık bridge	38°22.81'N/30°44.79'E	12-05-97
97-16	Derekarabağ, Eber lake	38°40.85'N/31°10.89'E	12-05-97
97-17	Gölçayır, Akşehir lake	38°29.13'N/31°20.90'E	12-05-97
97-18	Karabalut Çayı, bridge	38°24.85'N/31°27.76'E	12-05-97
97-19	Karabalut Çayı	38°24.78'N/31°27.88'E	12-05-97
97-20	Gölcük lake	37°43.85'N/30°30.04'E	13-05-97
97-21	Kanlıboğaz, Beyşehir lake	37°48.51'N/31°24.27'E	14-05-97
97-22	springs at Gilet, Beyşehir lake	37°45.34'N/31°24.88'E	14-05-97
97-23	Tol, Gürleviği rivermouth	37°44.47'N/31°26.41'E	14-05-97
97-24	channel towards Beyşehir lake	37°40.89'N/31°26.30'E	14-05-97
97-25	Soğuksu köprüsü at Yeşildağ	37°32.40'N/31°29.79'E	14-05-97
97-26	Beyşehir-Akseki road	37°38.40'N/31°37.70'E	14-05-97
97-27	Eylikler	37°42.67'N/31°44.17'E	14-05-97
97-28	Sarıöz canal	37°42.55'N/31°44.46'E	14-05-97
97-29	Avşar canal	37°41.74'N/31°43.96'E	14-05-97
97-30	small canals east of Sakyatan	37°50.23'N/32°48.13'E 37°49.47'N/32°49.91'E	17-05-97
97-31	Ova Sulaması, Tahliye Kanalı D3	37°48.80'N/32°51.67'E	17-05-97
97-32	Çöğürlü köyü, Asi Nehri	36°04.60'N/36°01.14'E	18-05-97

Table 1: The 1997 sampling localities and their coordinates.

97-33	canal near Medanköyü	36°02.07'N/35°58.86'E	18-05-97
97-34	Yeşilada, Gölcük	36°04.48'N/35°59.26'E	18-05-97
97-35	Yeşilada, Favvar Çayı	36°04.52'N/35°59.62'E	18-05-97
97-36	Demirköprü-Reyhanlı road	36°14.81'N/36°23.17'E	19-05-97
97-37	Acar köyü canal	36°18.80'N/36°24.59'E	19-05-97
97-38	Kanal II and ditch	36°23.48'N/36°24.80'E	19-05-97
97-39	Mersin Çayı	36°40.95'N/36°12.54'E	19-05-97
97-40	Yolçatı bridge	37°03.71'N/36°06.75'E	19-05-97
97-41	Tuzla Gölü	36°40.86'N/35°04.79'E	20-05-97
97-42	Kurukulak Çayı	37°17.71'N/35°42.71'E	20-05-97
97-43	Akgöl	36°18.95'N/33°56.39'E	21-05-97
97-44	Kırkgöz, lakelet near source	37°06.42'N/30°35.00'E	22-05-97
97-45	Terliksir Köyü, canal	36°41.78'N/35°20'29'E	20-05-97

Table 1 (*cont.*)

number	name	coordinates	date
98-1	Acısu Çayı, Kayaburnu	36°55.63'N/31°01.3'E	31-5-98
98-2	Acısu Çayı, Kayaburnu	36°56.02'N/31°01.5'E	31-5-98
98-3	Acısu Çayı	36°56.01'N/31°01.6'E	31-5-98
98-4	Yurtpınar, channel connected to Aksu Çayı	37°00.74'N/30°54.45'E	1-6-98
98-5	Çaybaşı, Tehnelli river	37°01.01'N/30°53.39'E	1-6-98
98-6	Dereboğaz, Tehnelli river	37°01.63'N/30°52.78'E	1-6-98
98-7	Güloluk, swamp of Aksu tributary	37°05.23'N/30°53.72'E	1-6-98
98-8	Güloluk DSİ regulator, Aksu river	37°06.17'N/30°52.42'E	1&2-6-98
98-9	Karakuyu Lake at Çapalı station	38°03.23'N/30°16.36'E	3-6-98
98-10	Karakuyu Lake	38°04.01'N/30°15.71'E	3-6-98
98-11	Karakuyu, at DSİ regulator	38°03.97'N/30°13.01'E	3-6-98
98-12	Dinar Suçıkan, pond near restaurant	38°04.25'N/30°10.57'E	3-6-98
98-13	Bülüçalan	38°03.24'N/30°11.51'E	3-6-98
98-14	Gökgöl	38°11.12'N/30°03.66'E	3-6-98
98-15	Gökgöl, at DSİ pumpstation	38°12.31'N/30°02.81'E	3-6-98
98-16	Işıklı, large spring area and pond near restaurant at Eumeneia	38°19.34'N/29°51.07'E	3-6-98
98-17	Küfü Çayı	38°19.54'N/29°48.45'E	4-6-98
98-18	Küfü Çayı	38°20.31'N/29°48.27'E	4-6-98
98-19	Hasköy Hamam köprüsü, Banaz Çayı	38°22.03'N/29°19.69'E	4-6-98
98-20	Barsakdeğırmeni, Hanönu, Adigüzel barajı	38°14.53'N/29°10.69'E	4-6-98

Table 2: The 1998 sampling localities and their coordinates.

98-21	Yenicekent, DSİ regulator on Büyük Menderes near Tripolis	38°02.30'N/28°57.83'E	4 & 11-6-98
98-22	Tosunlar köyü, drainage canal	37°57.95'N/28°56.70'E	5-6-98
98-23	Ahmetli köyü, Büyük Menderes	37°59.15'N/28°58.50'E	5-6-98
98-24	Yenice Köyü, Dandalas deresi	37°49.94'N/28°34.57'E	5-6-98
98-25	Akçayı regulator, south of Nazilli	37°48.59'N/28°18.91'E	5-6-98
98-26	irrigation channel between Alamut Köyü and Nazilli	37°50.14'N/28°19.84'E	5-6-98
98-27	Çiftlikburnu, Çine Çayı	37°45.87'N/27°50.01'E	6-6-98
98-28	Topçam Barajı, outlet	37°41.28'N/28°00.26'E	6-6-98
98-29	Bağarası, Sarıçay	37°43.02'N/27°33.24'E	6-6-98
98-30	south of Bağarası, flooded area connected to Sarıçayı	37°42.21'N/27°30.01'E	6-6-98
98-31	Bafa Gölü	37°30.60'N/27°22.41'E	6-6-98
98-32	Dalyan, Büyük Menderes	37°30.25'N/27°20.42'E	6-6-98
98-33	Pamucak, canal	37°56.57'N/27°16.82'E	7-6-98
98-34	Ürkmez dam lake	38°05.69'N/26°57.19'E	7-6-98
98-35	Tahtalı Deresı, near Gümüldür	38°04.34'N/27°01.74'E	7-6-98
98-36	Belevi, Küçük Menderes	38°01.57'N/27°26.49'E	7-6-98
98-37	Çamaltı Tuzlası	38°29.29'N/26°55.68'E	8-6-98
98-38	Çamaltı Tuzlası, Homadalyanı	38°30.55'N/26°52.82'E	8-6-98
98-39	Emiralem, DSİ regulator, Gediz river	38°37.75'N/27°10.69'E	8-6-98
98-40	Göksu Kaynakları, near DSİ station	38°41.40'N/27°21.22'E	9-6-98
98-41	Halitpaşa Köprüsü, Gediz river	38°42.14'N/27°35.39'E	9-6-98
98-42	Hacıveliler, Marmara Göl	38°37.31'N/27°56.28'E	9-6-98
98-43	Akpınar at Gölmarmara	38°42.05'N/27°57.99'E	9-6-98
98-44	irrigation canal near Salihli draining Marmara Gölü	38°33.51'N/28°03.15'E	9-6-98
98-45	Demirköprü Barajı near Cevizliköy	38°37.90'N/28°19.21'E 38°37.31'N/28°19.21'E	9-6-98
98-46	near Salihli, Gediz river	38°31.08'N/28°08.21'E	10-6-98
98-47	Yurtbaşı, Gediz river	38°35.46'N/28°48.44'E	10-6-98
98-48	Yenişehir Köprüsü, Gediz river	38°39.67'N/29°01.29'E	10-6-98
98-49	Gümüşlü DSİ regulator, Gediz river	38°57.51'N/29°30.53'E	10-6-98
98-50	Acıgöl, first spring from Gemiş	37°47.97'N/29°53.63'E	11-6-98
98-51	Acıgöl, spring at former teahouse	37°49.06'N/29°55.59'E	11-6-98
98-52	Karapınar near Yeşilova	37°32.53'N/29°46.17'E	11-6-98
98-53	creek emptying in Salda Gölü	37°31.43'N/29°39.25'E	11-6-98
98-54	Burdur Gölü	–	12-6-98
98-55	Yarışlı Gölü	–	12-6-98
98-56	Kırkgöz, lakelet near source	37°06.42'N/30°35.00'E	13-6-98

Table 2 (*cont.*)

number	name	coordinates	date
99-1	Pınarbaşı 1, lake in source area and drainage canal	39°02.89'N/31°19.64'E	5-10-99
99-2	Pınarbaşı 2, small river	39°03.70'N/31°19.61'E	5-10-99
99-3	Küçükhasan river, near bridge	38°57.47'N/31°49.88'E	5-10-99
99-4	Küçükhasan river	38°57.50'N/31°49.45'E	5-10-99
99-5	Ahiler (Sakarya river and floodplain)	39°11.63'N/31°37.28'E	5-10-99
99-6	Seydı çayı, southwest of Yıldızören	39°24.80'N/31°07.29'E	6-10-99
99-7	Sakarya river near Çifteler	39°22.35'N/31°04.18'E	6-10-99
99-8	Seydı çayı at Hamidiye	39°34.60'N/30°54.38'E	6-10-99
99-9	Sarıyar dam lake	40°01.91'N/31°26.50'E	7-10-99
99-10	Çayırhan, Sarıyar dam lake	40°01.90'N/31°26.57'E	7 & 8-10-99
99-11	Kirmir Çayı at Taksir, enfenced part	40°05.29'N/31°53.35'E	7-10-99
99-12	Kirmir Çayı at Taksir, small waterfall	40°05.38'N/31°53.50'E	7-10-99
99-13	Aladağ Çayı at Davutoğlan	40°07.94'N/31°38.36'E	7-10-99
99-14	Nallıdere Çayı at Nallıhan	40°07.16'N/31°19.56'E	7-10-99
99-15	Harmankaya river near Köroğlu	40°37.07'N/30°59.18'E	8-10-99
99-16	Göynükçay at Taraklı	40°23.73'N/30°30.32'E	8-10-99
99-17	Sakarya river at Geyve	40°32.30'N/30°17.93'E	9-10-99
99-18	Sapanca lake at inlet of Kurtköy river	40°42.41'N/30°11.97'E	9-10-99
99-19	Kırandere bridge near Iznik lake	40°24.71'N/29°42.52'E	9-10-99
99-20	Iznik lake near Çakırca	40°28.07'N/29°39.76'E	10-10-99
99-21	Porsuk dam lake	39°36.74'N/30°09.36'E	10-10-99
99-22	Ilıca, branch of Porsuk river	39°34.64'N/30°04.92'E	10-10-99
99-23	Kazanpınarı near Yuva	36°43.40'N/29°49.80'E	12-10-99
99-24	Karapınar near Elmalı	36°41.39'N/29°48.03'E	12-10-99
99-25	canal draining from Avlan lake	36°36.35'N/29°56.77'E	12-10-99
99-26	Yakaçiftlik, canal draining from Avlan lake	36°38.43'N/29°55.89'E	12-10-99
99-27	river near Kestel lake	37°25.28'N/30°25.78'E	12-10-99
99-28A	Salda lake	37°31.62'N/29°43.32'E	13-10-99
99-28B	Salda lake	37°33.87'N/29°42.97'E	13-10-99
99-28C	Salda lake (area with sources)	37°35.01'N/29°41.11'E	13-10-99
99-28D	Salda lake	37°34.46'N/29°38.55'E	13-10-99
99-28E	Salda lake, near inlet river	37°31.80'N/29°39.50'E	13-10-99

Table 3: The 1999 sampling localities and their coordinates.

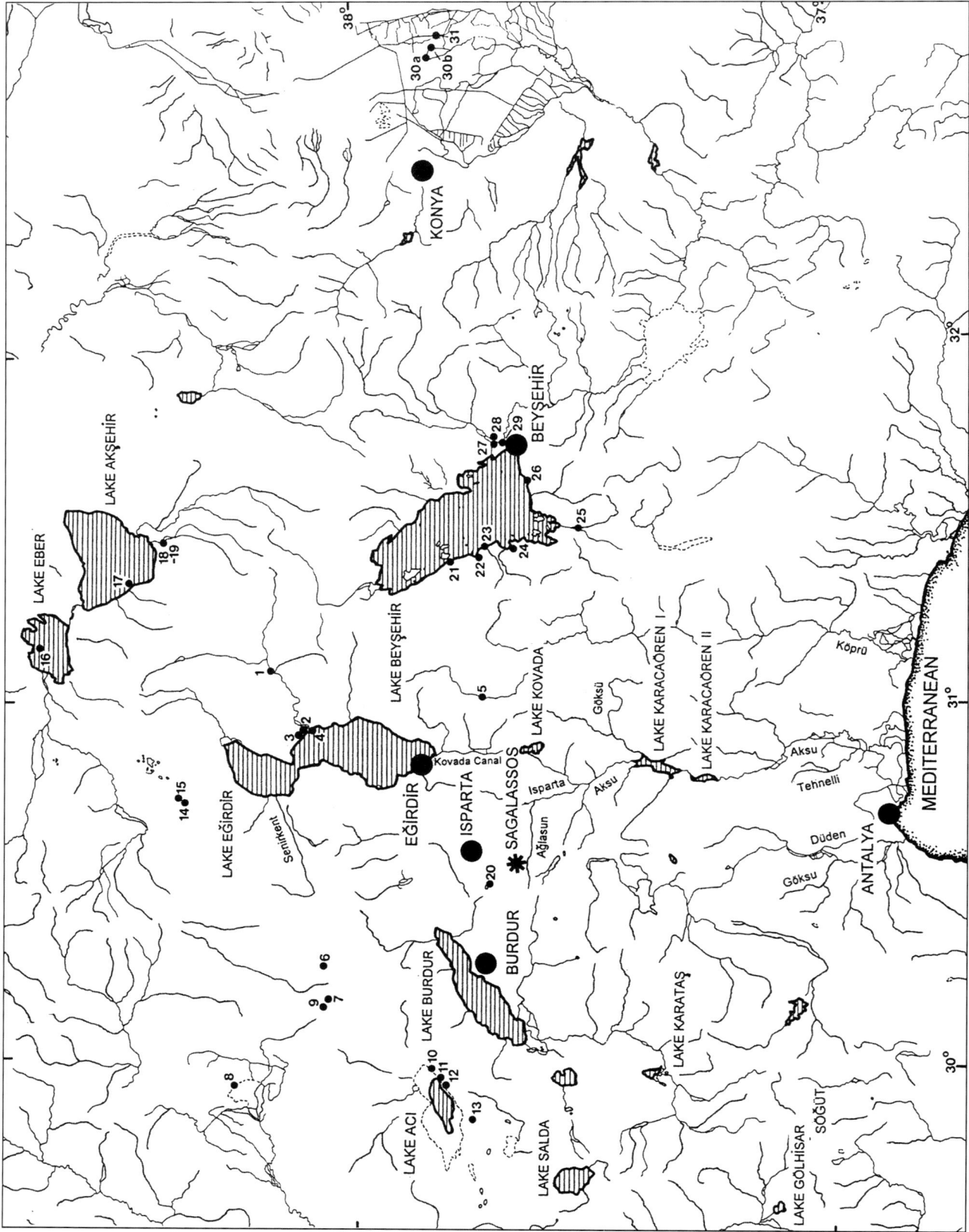

Figure 1: Localities sampled in 1997 (except Adana-Antakya region).

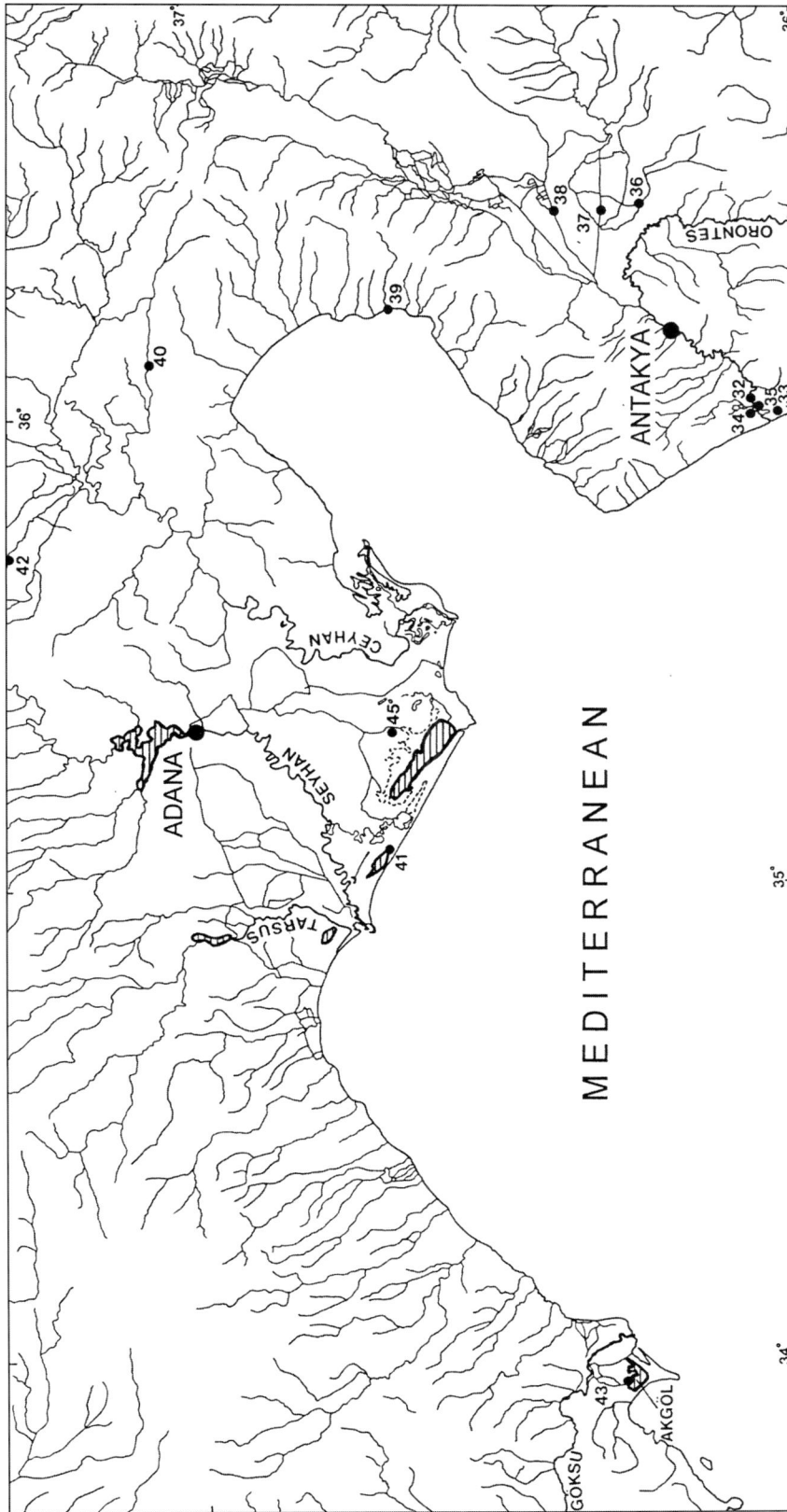

Figure 2: Localities sampled in 1997 (Adana-Antakya region).

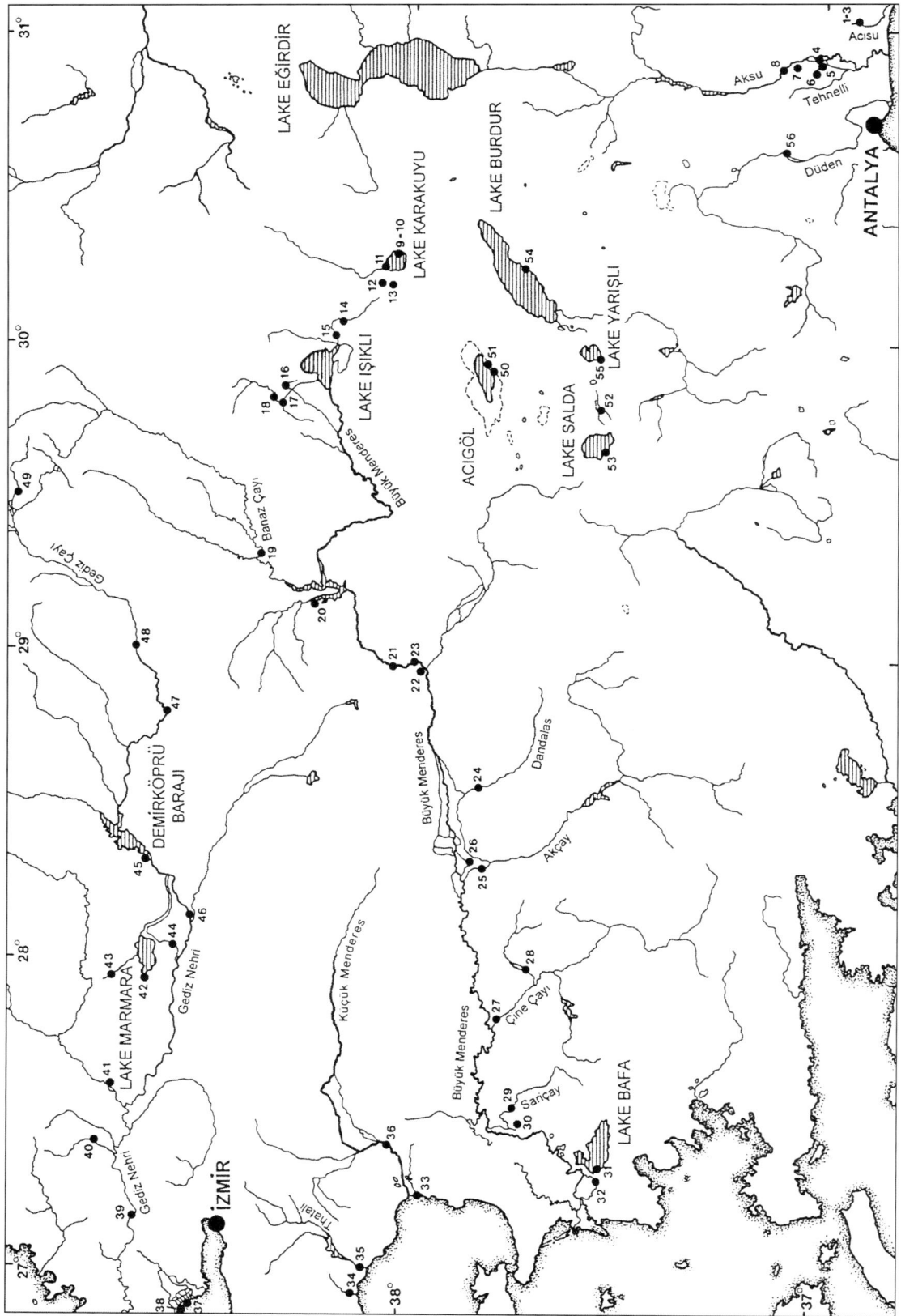

Figure 3: Localities sampled in 1998.

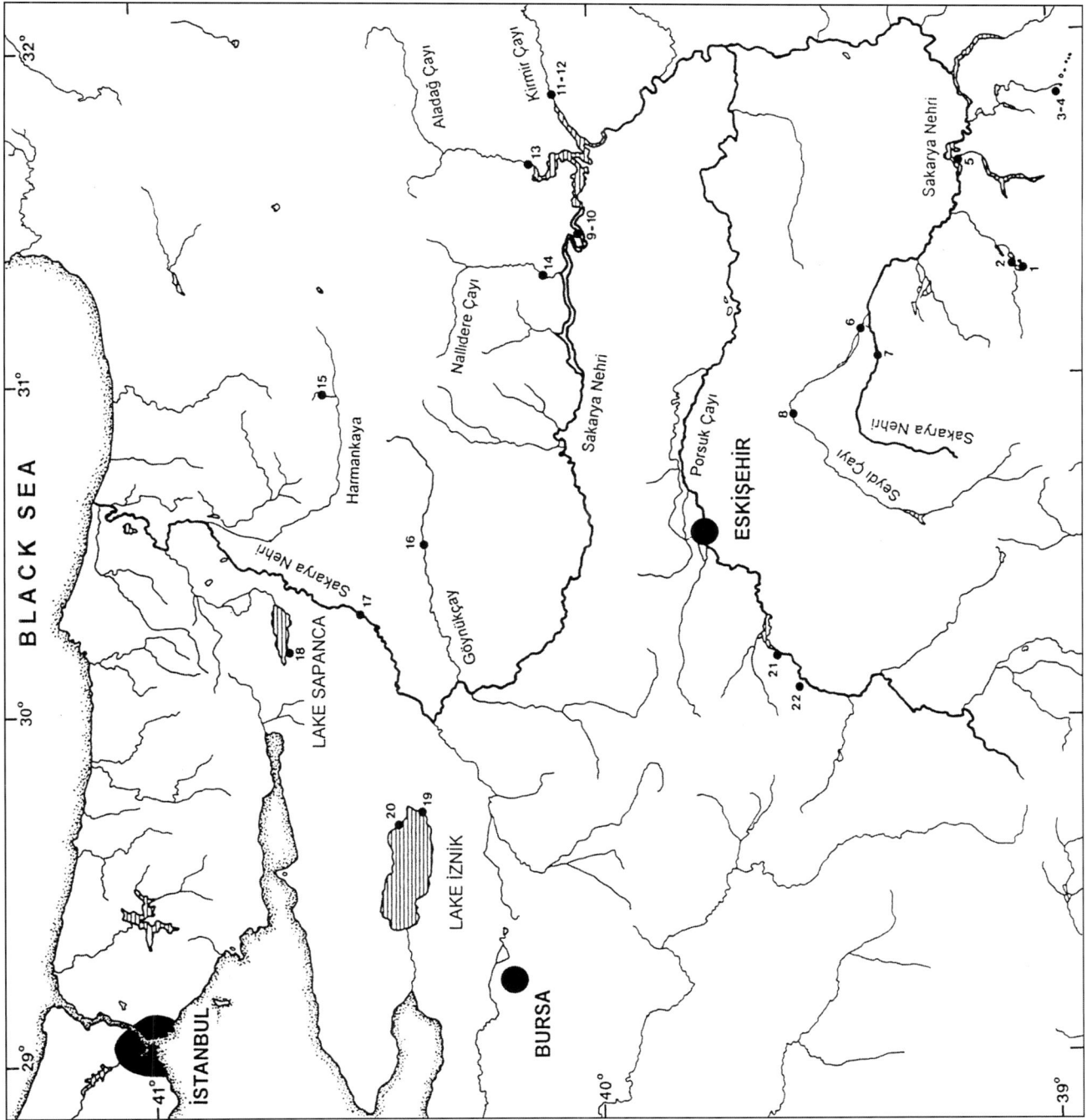

Figure 4: Localities sampled in 1999 (Sakarya basin and İznik lake).

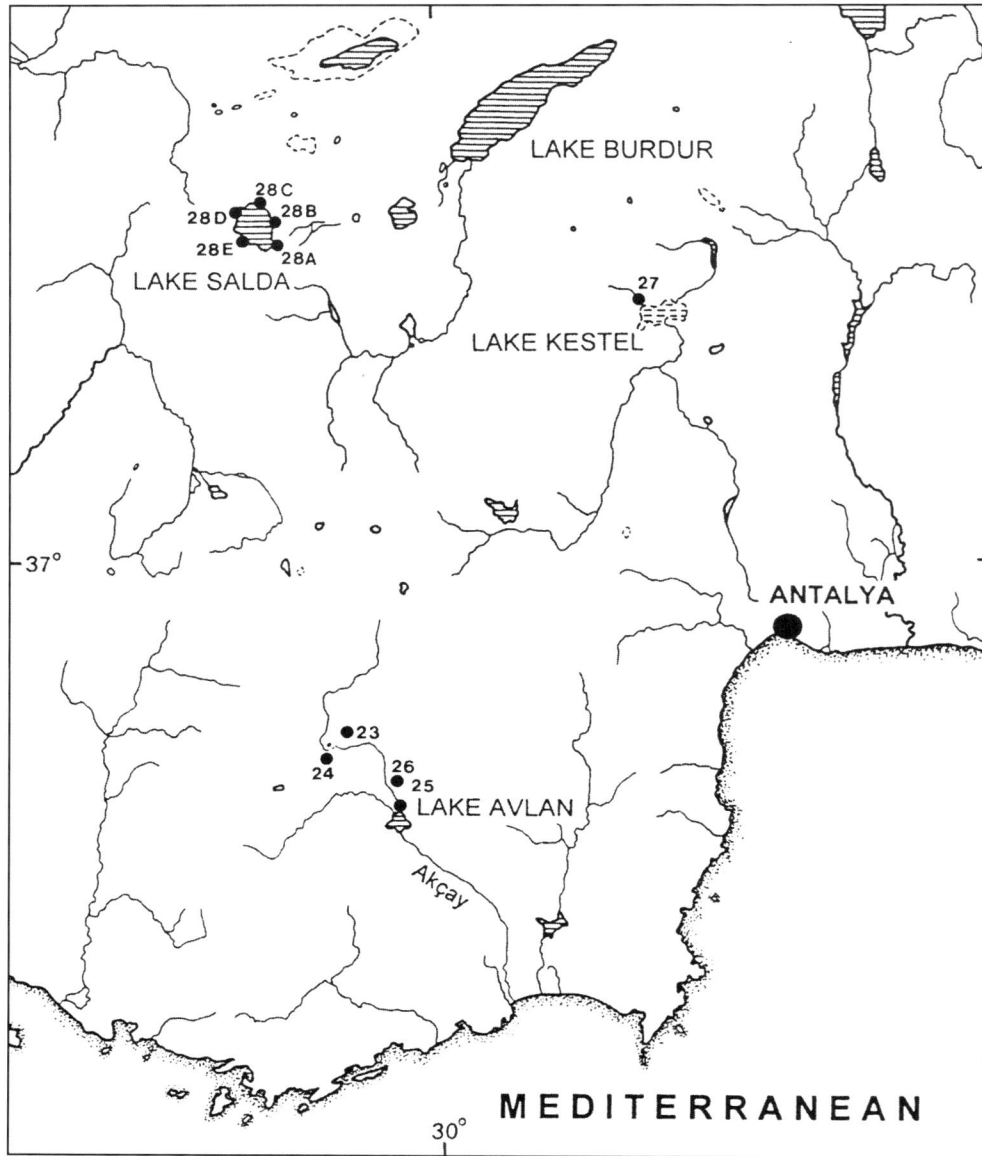

Figure 5: Localities sampled in 1999 (Lake District and Akçay basin).

The nomenclature in this paper is based on the checklists of Eschmeyer (2006) and on the nomenclature used in FishBase (Froese and Pauly, 2007), except for the Cyprinodontidae for which Wildekamp *et al.* (1999) was followed.

3. RESULTS

Tables 4-10 list the fish species that were collected on the various localities during each survey. The data are ordered by basin, and localities that yielded no fish fauna have been omitted. Fish species that were not actually seen by us, but of which the presence was confirmed by experienced fishermen have been indicated in brackets in the tables.

4. DISCUSSION

In the following paragraphs, the various regions that were surveyed are dealt with and attention is focussed on the geographical distribution of species that were already discovered at Sagalassos. In addition to our own field data, information was taken into account of the older literature that was critically reviewed. Of particular importance here are the publications of ichthyologists that were active before the 1960's (i.e., Batalgil, Devedjian, Hanko, Nümann, Kosswig, Steindachner) since at that time anthropic influences on the composition of the fish fauna was still limited. Emphasis is laid here on the species of economic importance. The numerous data that were obtained on smaller species and a detailed discussion of the anthropic effects on the ichthyofauna as a result of irrigation, construction of dam lakes, introduction of species, will be dealt with in ichthyological journals. Partial results of this kind have already been published (Wildekamp *et al.*, 1997, 1999; Van Neer *et al.*, 1999; Hrbek *et al.*, 2002; Hrbek and Wildekamp, 2003).

4.1. The Lake District

Because of their geographical proximity, lakes such as Gölçük, Eğirdir, Beyşehir and possibly also Akşehir and Eber can be considered as potential sources of the fish consumed at Sagalassos. The small volcanic lake of Gölçük is connected with Sagalassos by a small track that already existed in the past (Loots *et al.*, 2000). It could be reached on foot, by donkey or mule, in a few hours time. Although the lake was probably not part of the territory of Sagalassos (Waelkens *et al.*, 1997), the sediment around it was used by the Sagalassians as a temper in their mortars (Viaene *et al.*, 1997; Callebaut *et al.*, 2000) and coarse pottery (Degryse *et al.*, 2000). Domestic carp is found today in Lake Gölçük (Table 5), but during a first survey in the 1940's this species was not reported (Kosswig and Sözer 1945). We therefore

believe that the carp in this lakelet is a recent introduction, an opinion that is shared by Geldiay and Balık (1996: 243). The small cyprinid *Alburnus chalcoides* was introduced into the lake in 1970-1971 (Innal and Erk'akan 2006). We were told that, in addition, Gölçük has been stocked occasionally with eel (*Anguilla anguilla*) and pikeperch (*Sander lucioperca*), but apparently without much succes. Kosswig and Sözer (1945) reported only *Anatolichthys splendens* (synonymized with *Aphanius anatoliae splendens*) and the small cyprinid *Hemigrammocapoeta kemali* from Lake Gölçük, but today both species have disappeared due to habitat degradation and food competition with the introduced species. Thus far no remains of the two aforementioned species, originally living in the lake, have been identified at Sagalassos. They were probably not exploited for food because of their small size.

During the survey carried out previously at the end of July – beginning of August 1996, only few species originally described from Lakes Eğirdir and Beyşehir (Kosswig 1954) could be observed (Van Neer *et al.*, 2000). Many species, including endemic ones that represent ideal indicators of ancient trade relationships, apparently had disappeared as a result of the introduction of the pike perch (*Sander lucioperca*). This piscivorous species was introduced in 1955 in Lake Eğirdir (Nümann 1960: 40; Nümann 1961: 788) and had extremely negative effects on the ichthyofauna (Campbell 1992; Anonymous 1995: 28). Changes in the fish fauna have also been observed in Lake Beyşehir in which the pike perch was introduced in 1978 (Anonymous 1995: 77). It was suspected that relic populations of the missing species would still survive in the small rivers entering the lakes, but they could not be found in 1996. In May 1997, during the spawning season of the fishes, however, we were able to show that all species were still surviving in small numbers, with the exception of *Alburnus akili* from Lake Beyşehir and *Capoeta pestai* and *Pseudophoxinus handlirschi* in Lake Eğirdir (Table 4). Only in the Aksu area of the adjacent Köprüçay, which is linked to Eğirdir Lake through an artificial connection, a *Pseudophoxinus* was found which is morphologically close to *Pseudophoxinus handlirschi*. According to Nümann (1961), *Capoeta pestai* was the commercially most important species in Eğirdir Lake in the early 1950's. Although it apparently disappeared from Lake Eğirdir, this species still survives in rivers emptying in Lake Beyşehir. *Alburnus akili*, a species that was of commercial importance in the past, could not be found despite very intense searches carried out in collaboration with local fishermen that had known the species before. Summarizing, it can be said that these two lakes harbour a number of endemic species that are perfect indicators for former trade connections, namely *Pseudophoxinus handlirschi* found only in Lake Eğirdir, *Alburnus akili* and

	Capoeta pestai	*Chondrostoma beysehirense*	*Cyprinus carpio*	*Gobio battalgilae*	*Hemigrammocapoeta kemali*	*Leuciscus lepidus anatolicus*	*Pseudophoxinus anatolicus*	*Pseudophoxinus battalgili*	*Pseudophoxinus egridiri*	*Pseudophoxinus cf. handlirschi*	*Cobitis bilseli*	*Cobitis turcica*	*Barbatula mediterraneus*	*Seminemacheilus ispartensis*	*Aphanius anatoliae anatoliae*	*Gambusia affinis*	*Sander lucioperca*	*Knipowitschia caucasica*
Eğirdir lake region																		
97-1/ Yalvaç deresi near Madenli	–	–	–	–	–	–	–	–	–	–	–	+	+	–	–	–	–	–
97-2/ Yenice DSİ Canal	–	–	–	–	–	–	–	–	–	–	–	–	–	–	+	+	–	+
97-3/ Karaot, Eğirdir lake	–	–	–	–	–	–	–	–	+	–	–	–	–	+	+	–	–	+
97-4/ Yalvaç deresi rivermouth	–	–	–	–	–	–	–	–	–	–	–	–	–	–	–	–	–	+
97-5/ Aksu area on Köprüçay	–	–	–	–	+	–	–	–	+	–	+	+	–	–	–	–	–	–
Beyşehir region																		
97-21/ Kanlıboğaz, Beyşehir lake	–	–	+	–	–	+	–	–	–	–	–	–	–	+	+	+	–	–
97-22/ Gilet	–	–	–	–	–	–	+	–	–	–	–	–	–	–	+	–	–	–
97-23/ Tol, Gürleviği rivermouth	–	–	–	–	–	–	–	–	–	–	–	–	–	+	+	–	–	–
97-24/ channel towards Beyşehir lake	–	–	–	–	–	–	–	–	–	–	–	–	–	+	+	–	–	–
97-25/ Soğuksu köprüsü	–	–	–	+	–	+	–	+	–	–	–	–	–	–	–	–	–	–
97-26/ Beyşehir–Akseki road	–	–	–	–	–	+	–	+	–	–	–	–	–	+	+	+	–	–
97-27/ Eylikler	+	+	–	+	–	+	–	–	–	–	+	–	–	+	+	–	–	–
97-28/ Sarıöz canal	+	+	–	+	–	+	–	–	–	–	+	–	–	+	+	–	–	–
97-29/ Avşar canal	–	+	–	+	–	+	–	–	–	–	–	–	–	–	–	–	+	–

Table 4: Fish recorded in the Eğirdir and Beyşehir Lake region.

	Oncorhynchus mykiss	Alburnus chalcoides	Alburnus nasreddini	Cyprinus carpio	Leuciscus lepidus anatolicus	Pseudophoxinus ninae	Pseudophoxinus maendri	Cobitis cf. simplicispina	Seminemacheilus cf. ispartensis	Esox lucius	Aphanius anatoliae splendens	A. anatoliae sureyanus	A. anatoliae transgrediens	Gambusia affinis	Knipowitschia caucasica
other lakes in Lake District															
97-10/ Acıgöl, 1st source from east	−	−	−	−	−	−	−	−	−	−	−	−	+	−	−
97-11/ Acıgöl, 4th source from east	−	−	−	−	−	−	−	−	−	−	−	−	+	−	−
97-12/ Acıgöl, 6th source from east	−	−	−	−	−	−	−	−	−	−	−	−	+	−	−
97-13/ Acıgöl at Gemiş	−	−	−	−	−	−	−	−	−	−	−	−	−	+	−
98-50/ Acıgöl, first spring from Gemiş	−	−	−	−	−	−	−	−	−	−	−	−	−	+	−
98-51/ Acıgöl, spring at former teahouse	−	−	−	−	−	−	−	−	−	−	−	−	+	−	−
98-52/ Karapınar near Yeşilova	−	−	−	−	−	−	+	−	−	−	−	−	−	−	−
98-53/ creek emptying in Salda Gölü	−	−	−	−	−	−	+	−	+	−	+	−	−	+	−
99-28/ Salda lake	−	−	−	−	−	−	−	−	−	−	+	−	−	+	−
98-54/ Burdur Gölü	−	−	−	−	−	−	−	−	−	−	−	+	−	−	−
98-55/ Yarışlı Gölü	−	−	−	−	−	+	−	−	−	−	−	−	−	−	−
97-16/ Derekarabağ, Eber lake	−	−	+	(+)	−	−	−	+	+	+	−	−	−	−	+
97-14/ Karamık village, Eber system	−	−	−	+	−	−	−	+	−	(+)	−	−	−	−	−
97-15/ Karamık bridge, Eber system	−	−	+	−	−	−	−	+	−	(+)	−	−	−	+	−
97-17/ Gölçayır, Akşehir lake	−	−	−	−	−	−	−	+	−	−	−	−	−	−	−
97-18/ Karabalut çayı, bridge	−	−	+	+	+	−	−	+	−	−	−	−	−	−	−
97-19/ Karabalut çayı	−	−	+	+	+	−	−	+	−	−	−	−	−	−	−
97-20/ Gölcük lake	−	+	−	+	−	−	−	−	−	−	−	−	−	−	−
99-27/ river near Kestel lake	+	−	−	−	−	+	−	−	−	−	−	−	−	+	−

Table 5: Fish recorded in lakes of the Lake District (others than Eğirdir and Beyşehir).

311

Büyük Menderes basin	97-7/ Dinar Suçıkan	97-8/ Işıklı lake at Beydilli Köyü	97-9/ Karaköprü near Dinar	98-12/ Dinar Suçıkan, pond near restaurant	98-13/ Bülüçalan	98-14/ Gökgöl	98-15/ Gökgöl, at DSI pumpstation	98-16/ Işıklı, large spring area near restaurant at Eumeneia	98-17/ Küfü Çayı	98-18/ Küfü Çayı	98-19/ Hasköy Hamam köprüsü, Banaz Çayı	98-20/ Barsakde ğrmeni, Hanönu, Adıgüzel barajı	98-21/ Yenicekent, DSI regulator on Büyük Menderes	98-22/ Tosunlar köyü, drainage canal	98-23/ Ahmetli köyü, Büyük Menderes	98-24/ Yenice Köyü, Dandalas deresi	98-25/ Akçayı regulator, south of Nazilli
Knipowitschia caucasica	–	–	–	–	–	–	–	–	–	–	–	–	–	–	–	–	–
Lepomis gibbosus	–	–	–	–	–	–	–	–	–	–	–	–	–	–	–	–	–
Atherina boyeri	–	–	–	–	–	–	–	–	–	–	–	–	–	–	–	–	–
Liza ramado	–	–	–	–	–	–	–	–	–	–	–	–	–	–	–	–	–
Syngnathus abaster	–	–	–	–	–	–	–	–	–	–	–	–	–	–	–	–	–
Gambusia affinis	–	+	–	–	–	–	+	–	–	–	–	–	–	–	–	–	+
Aphanius fasciatus	–	–	–	–	–	–	–	–	–	–	–	–	–	–	–	–	–
Aphanius anatoliae anatoliae	–	+	–	–	–	–	+	+	–	–	–	–	–	–	–	–	–
Silurus glanis	–	–	–	–	–	–	–	–	–	–	–	(+)	(+)	(+)	–	–	(+)
Esox lucius	–	+	–	–	–	–	–	–	–	–	–	–	–	–	–	–	–
Barbatula cf. *germencica*	–	–	–	–	–	–	–	–	–	+	–	–	–	–	–	–	–
Barbatula cf. *cinica*	+	–	+	+	+	–	+	–	+	+	+	+	+	–	+	+	+
Cobitis sp.	–	–	–	–	–	+	–	–	–	+	–	–	–	–	–	–	–
Cobitis vardarensis kurui	–	–	–	–	–	–	–	–	–	–	–	–	+	–	–	–	–
Vimba vimba	–	–	–	–	–	–	–	–	–	–	–	–	–	–	–	–	–
Tinca tinca	–	+	–	–	–	+	–	–	–	–	–	–	–	–	–	–	–
Pseudorasbora parva	–	–	–	–	–	–	–	–	–	–	–	–	–	–	–	–	–
Leuciscus cephalus	–	+	+	–	–	–	–	–	–	+	+	–	+	–	+	+	+
Petroleuciscus smyrnaeus	–	–	–	–	–	–	–	–	–	–	–	–	+	+	–	–	+
Hemigrammocapoeta kemali	–	+	+	–	–	+	+	–	–	–	–	–	–	–	–	–	–
Gobio maeandricus	–	–	–	–	+	+	+	–	–	–	–	–	–	–	–	–	–
Cyprinus carpio	–	(+)	–	–	–	–	–	(+)	–	–	–	–	+	–	–	–	–
Chondrostoma meandrense	–	+	+	–	–	+	+	–	–	–	–	–	+	–	–	–	+
Carassius carassius	–	+	+	–	–	–	–	–	–	–	–	–	–	–	–	–	–
Carassius auratus auratus	–	+	–	–	–	–	–	–	–	–	–	–	–	–	–	–	–
Capoeta bergamae	–	–	–	–	–	–	–	–	–	–	–	–	+	–	–	+	–
Barbus cf. *plebejus*	–	–	+	+	–	–	–	–	+	–	+	+	+	–	–	+	+
Alburnus cf. *demiri*	–	–	–	–	–	–	–	–	–	+	+	+	+	–	–	–	+
Alburnoides bipunctatus	–	–	–	–	–	–	–	–	+	–	+	+	+	–	–	–	–
Acanthobrama mirabilis	–	–	–	–	–	–	–	–	–	–	–	+	–	–	–	–	–
Anguilla anguilla	(+)	–	–	–	–	–	–	–	–	–	–	–	–	(+)	–	–	(+)

Table 6: Fish recorded in the Büyük Menderes basin and in adjacent areas.

	98-26/ Irrigation channel between Alamut Köyü and Nazilli	98-27/ Çiftlikburnu, Çine Çayı	98-28/ Topçam Barajı, outlet	98-29/ Bağarası, Sarıçay	98-30/ south of Bağarası, flooded area connected to Sarıçayı	98-32/ Dalyan, Büyük Menderes	areas adjacent to Büyük Menderes	97-6/ Çapalı lake at Eldere	98-9/ Karakuyu gölü	98-10/ Karakuyu gölü	98-11/ Karakuyu, at DSI regulator	98-31/ Bafa Gölü
Knipowitschia caucasica	–	–	–	–	–	+		–	–	–	–	+
Lepomis gibbosus	–	–	+	–	–	–		–	–	–	–	–
Atherina boyeri	–	–	–	–	–	+		–	–	–	–	+
Liza ramado	–	–	–	–	–	–		–	–	–	–	+
Syngnathus abaster	–	–	–	–	–	–		–	–	–	–	+
Gambusia affinis	+	–	+	–	+	–		–	+	+	+	+
Aphanius fasciatus	–	–	–	–	–	+		–	–	–	–	+
Aphanius anatoliae anatoliae	–	–	–	–	–	–		–	–	–	–	–
Silurus glanis	–	(+)	(+)	–	–	–		–	–	–	–	–
Esox lucius	–	–	–	–	–	–		(+)	–	+	+	–
Barbatula cf. *germencica*	–	–	–	–	–	–		–	–	–	–	–
Barbatula cf.*cinica*	–	–	–	+	–	–		–	–	–	–	–
Cobitis sp.	–	–	–	–	–	–		–	–	–	–	–
Cobitis vardarensis kurui	–	–	–	+	–	–		–	–	–	–	–
Vimba vimba	–	+	–	–	–	–		–	–	–	–	–
Tinca tinca	–	–	–	–	–	–		–	–	–	–	–
Pseudorasbora parva	–	–	+	–	+	+		–	–	–	–	–
Leuciscus cephalus	–	–	+	+	–	–		–	–	–	–	–
Petroleuciscus smyrnaeus	+	–	–	+	–	+		–	–	–	–	–
Hemigrammocapoeta kemali	–	–	–	–	–	–		–	–	–	–	–
Gobio maeandricus	–	–	–	–	–	–		–	–	–	–	–
Cyprinus carpio	–	–	+	–	–	–		(+)	–	–	(+)	(+)
Chondrostoma meandrense	–	–	–	–	–	+		–	–	–	–	–
Carassius carassius	–	–	–	–	–	–		–	–	–	–	–
Carassius auratus auratus	–	–	–	–	–	–		–	–	–	–	–
Capoeta bergamae	–	+	–	–	–	–		–	–	–	–	–
Barbus cf. *plebejus*	–	+	–	–	–	–		–	–	–	–	–
Alburnus cf. *demiri*	–	+	+	+	+	+		–	–	–	–	–
Alburnoides bipunctatus	–	–	–	–	–	–		–	–	–	–	–
Acanthobrama mirabilis	–	–	–	–	–	–		–	–	–	–	–
Anguilla anguilla	–	–	(+)	–	–	–		–	–	–	–	(+)

Table 6 (*cont.*)

313

Gediz basin

	Anguilla anguilla	*Oncorhynchus mykiss*	*Alburnus cf. batalgilae*	*Alburnus demiri*	*Alburnus cf. demiri*	*Barbus cf. plebejus*	*Capoeta bergamae*	*Chondrostoma holmwoodii*	*Ctenopharyngodon idella*	*Cyprinus carpio*	*Leuciscus cephalus*	*Petroleuciscus smyrnaeus*	*Rhodeus amarus*	*Vimba vimba*	*Cobitis fahireae*	*Cobitis vardarensis kurui*	*Barbatula cf. germencica*	*Silurus glanis*	*Aphanius fasciatus*	*Gambusia affinis*	*Syngnathus abaster*	*Liza ramado*	*Atherina boyeri*	*Perca fluviatilis*	*Sander lucioperca*	*Knipowitschia caucasica*	*Knipowitschia mermere*
98-39/ Emiralem, DSI regulator, Gediz river	+	–	–	–	–	–	–	+	–	–	+	+	–	+	+	–	–	–	–	+	–	–	–	–	–	–	–
98-40/ Göksu Kaynakları, near DSI station	–	–	–	–	–	–	–	–	–	–	+	–	–	–	–	–	+	+	–	+	–	–	–	–	–	–	–
98-41/ Halitpaşa Köprüsü, Gediz river	–	–	–	–	–	–	–	+	–	–	+	+	–	–	–	–	+	–	–	–	–	–	–	–	–	–	–
98-42/ Hacıveliler, Marmara Göl	–	–	+	–	–	–	–	–	–	+	+	–	–	–	–	–	+	–	–	–	–	–	–	–	+	–	+
98-43/ Akpınar at Gölmarmara	–	–	–	–	–	–	–	–	–	+	+	+	–	–	+	+	–	–	–	–	–	–	–	–	–	–	–
98-44/ Irrigation canal near Salihli draining Marmara Gölü	–	–	–	–	–	–	–	–	–	+	+	–	–	+	–	–	–	+	–	–	–	–	–	–	–	–	+
98-45/ Demirköprü Barajı near Cevizliköy	–	–	–	–	–	–	–	–	–	(+)	–	–	–	–	–	–	–	(+)	–	–	–	–	–	–	+	+	–
98-46/ near Salihli, Gediz river	–	–	+	–	–	+	–	–	–	–	+	–	–	–	+	+	–	–	–	–	–	–	–	–	–	–	–
98-47/ Yurtbaşı, Gediz river	–	–	–	–	–	+	+	+	–	–	+	–	–	–	–	–	+	–	–	–	–	–	–	–	–	–	–
98-48/ Yenişehir Köprüsü, Gediz river	–	–	–	–	–	+	+	–	–	–	+	–	–	–	–	–	+	–	–	–	–	–	–	–	–	–	–
98-49/ Gümüşlü DSI regulator, Gediz river	–	+	–	–	+	–	–	–	–	–	+	–	–	–	–	–	+	–	–	–	–	–	–	–	–	–	–
waters emptying in Kuşadası Bay																											
98-33/ Pamucak, canal	+	–	–	–	–	–	–	–	–	–	+	–	–	+	–	–	–	–	+	+	–	–	+	–	–	+	–
98-34/ Ürkmez dam lake	–	–	–	–	–	–	–	(+)	(+)	+	–	–	–	–	–	–	–	–	–	–	–	–	(+)	–	–	–	–
98-35/ Tahtalı Deresı, near Gümüldür	–	–	–	+	–	–	–	–	–	–	+	–	+	–	–	–	–	–	–	–	–	–	+	–	–	–	–
98-36/ Belevi, Küçük Menderes	–	–	–	–	–	+	–	–	–	+	–	+	–	–	+	–	+	–	–	–	–	–	–	–	–	–	–
waters emptying in İzmir Bay																											
98-37/ Çamaltı Tuzlası	–	–	–	–	–	–	–	–	–	–	–	–	–	–	–	–	–	–	+	–	–	+	–	–	–	–	–
98-38/ Çamaltı Tuzlası, Homadalyanı	–	–	–	–	–	–	–	–	–	–	–	–	–	–	–	–	–	–	–	+	–	–	–	–	–	+	–

Table 7: Fish recorded in the Gediz basin and in waters emptying in Kuşadası and İzmir Bay.

314

Table 8: Fish recorded in the Sakarya basin and in Lake İznik.

Species	99-1	99-2	99-3	99-4	99-5	99-6	99-7	99-8	99-9	99-10	99-11	99-12	99-13	99-14	99-15	99-16	99-17	99-18	99-21	99-22	99-19	99-20
Salarias fluviatilis	-	-	-	-	+	-	-	-	-	-	-	-	-	-	-	-	-	-	-	-	+	-
Sander lucioperca	-	-	-	-	-	-	-	-	-	-	-	-	-	-	-	-	-	-	+	-	-	-
Gambusia affinis	+	-	+	+	-	+	-	+	+	-	-	-	-	-	-	+	-	+	-	-	-	+
Aphanius villwocki	+	-	+	+	-	+	-	-	-	-	-	-	-	-	-	-	-	-	-	-	-	-
Clarias gariepinus	-	-	-	-	-	-	+	-	-	-	-	-	-	-	-	-	-	-	-	-	-	-
Silurus glanis	-	-	-	-	(+)	(+)	-	-	+	-	-	-	-	-	-	-	-	(+)	(+)	+	-	-
Esox lucius	-	-	-	-	(+)	-	-	-	-	-	-	-	-	-	-	-	-	(+)	-	-	-	-
Seminemacheilus sp.	-	-	-	-	-	-	-	+	-	-	-	-	-	-	-	-	-	-	-	+	-	-
Barbatula cf. *angorae*	+	+	+	+	+	+	+	+	+	-	-	+	+	+	-	+	-	-	-	+	+	-
Cobitis cf. *vardarensis*	-	-	-	-	-	-	-	-	-	-	-	-	-	-	-	-	-	-	-	-	+	-
Cobitis simplicispina	-	-	+	-	+	+	-	+	-	-	-	-	-	-	-	-	-	-	-	+	-	-
Vimba vimba	-	-	-	-	+	-	-	-	+	-	-	+	-	-	-	-	-	-	-	-	-	-
Tinca tinca	-	-	-	-	-	-	-	-	+	-	-	-	-	-	-	-	-	+	-	-	+	+
Rutilus rutilus	-	-	-	-	-	-	-	-	-	-	-	-	-	-	-	-	-	+	-	-	-	-
Rutilus frisii	-	-	-	-	-	-	-	-	-	-	-	-	-	-	-	-	-	-	-	-	-	+
Scardinius erythrophtalmus	-	-	-	-	-	-	-	-	-	-	-	-	-	-	-	-	-	+	-	-	-	-
Rhodeus amarus	-	-	-	-	-	-	-	-	-	-	-	-	-	-	-	+	-	+	-	-	-	-
Pseudorasbora parva	-	-	-	-	-	-	+	-	-	-	-	+	-	-	-	-	-	-	-	-	-	-
Leuciscus cephalus	-	-	-	-	-	+	-	+	-	-	-	+	+	-	-	-	-	(+)	-	+	-	+
Petroleuciscus borysthenicus	-	-	+	+	-	+	-	+	-	-	-	-	-	-	-	+	-	-	-	+	-	-
Gobio gobio cf. *obtusirostris*	-	-	-	-	-	-	-	+	-	-	-	-	-	-	-	-	-	-	-	-	-	-
Cyprinus carpio	-	-	-	-	+	-	+	-	+	+	-	-	+	-	-	-	-	(+)	(+)	+	-	-
Chondrostoma angorense	-	-	-	-	(+)	+	-	+	-	-	-	-	-	-	-	-	-	(+)	(+)	-	-	-
Carassius carassius	-	-	-	-	+	-	-	-	-	-	-	-	-	-	-	-	-	-	-	-	-	-
Capoeta baliki	-	-	+	-	-	+	-	-	-	-	+	+	+	+	-	+	-	(+)	+	-	-	-
Capoeta sieboldi	-	-	-	-	-	+	-	-	+	-	+	+	+	-	-	-	-	-	+	-	+	-
Barbus cf. *plebejus*	-	-	+	-	-	+	-	-	+	-	+	+	+	-	+	-	+	-	+	-	-	-
Alburnus escherichii	+	-	+	-	+	+	-	+	-	-	+	+	-	-	+	-	(+)	-	+	-	-	-
Alburnoides bipunctatus	-	-	-	-	+	-	-	-	+	-	+	+	-	-	+	+	+	(+)	-	+	-	-
Abramis brama	-	-	-	-	-	-	-	-	-	-	-	-	-	-	+	-	-	(+)	(+)	-	-	-
Salmo trutta macrostigma	-	-	-	-	-	-	-	-	-	-	-	-	-	+	-	-	-	(+)	(+)	-	-	-
Alosa sp.	-	-	-	-	-	-	-	-	-	-	+	-	-	-	-	-	-	-	-	-	-	-
Anguilla anguilla	-	-	-	-	-	-	-	-	-	-	+	-	-	-	-	-	-	-	-	-	-	-

Sakarya basin

99-1/ Pınarbaşı 1, lake in source area & drainage canal
99-2/ Pınarbaşı 2, small river
99-3/ Küçükhasan river, near bridge
99-4/ Küçükhasan river
99-5/ Ahiler (Sakarya river and floodplain)
99-6/ Seydı çayı, southwest of Yıldızören
99-7/ Sakarya river near Çifteler
99-8/ Seydı çayı at Hamidiye
99-9/ Sarıyar dam lake
99-10/ Çayırhan, Sarıyar dam lake
99-11/ Kirmir Çayı at Taksir, enfenced part
99-12/ Kirmir Çayı at Taksir, small waterfall
99-13/ Aladağ Çayı at Davutoğlan
99-14/ Nallıdere Çayı at Nallıhan
99-15/ Harmankaya river near Köroğlu
99-16/ Göynükçay at Taraklı
99-17/ Sakarya river at Geyve
99-18/ Sapanca lake at inlet of Kurtköy river
99-21/ Porsuk dam lake
99-22/ Ilıca, branch of Porsuk river

İznik lake

99-19/ Kırandere bridge near İznik lake
99-20/ İznik lake near Çakırca

	Anguilla anguilla	*Alburnus baliki*	*Capoeta antalyensis*	*Cyprinus carpio*	*Pseudophoxinus alii*	*Pseudophoxinus* cf. *maeandri*	*Pseudorasbora parva*	*Scardinius elmaliensis*	*Vimba vimba*	*Cobitis* sp.	*Barbatula mediterraneus*	*Seminemacheilus* cf. *ispartensis*	*Clarias gariepinus*	*Aphanius anatoliae anatoliae*	*Aphanius mento*	*Gambusia affinis*	*Mugil cephalus*
basins near Antalya																	
98-1/ Acısu Çayı, Kayaburnu	–	–	–	–	–	–	–	–	+	–	–	–	–	–	–	+	–
98-2/ Acısu Çayı, Kayaburnu	–	+	–	(+)	–	–	–	–	–	–	–	–	(+)	–	–	–	–
98-3/ Acısu Çayı	+	+	–	–	+	–	–	–	–	–	–	–	–	+	–	+	–
98-4/ Yurtpınar, channel connected to Aksu Çayı	–	–	–	–	+	–	+	–	–	–	–	–	–	+	–	+	–
98-5/ Çaybaşı, Tehnelli river	+	–	+	–	+	–	–	–	–	–	–	–	–	–	+	+	–
98-6/ Dereboğaz, Tehnelli river	+	+	+	–	+	–	–	–	+	–	+	–	–	–	+	–	–
98-7/ Güloluk, swamp of Aksu tributary	+	–	–	–	+	–	–	–	–	–	–	–	–	+	–	–	–
98-8/ Güloluk DSI regulator, Aksu river	+	+	+	+	+	–	–	–	+	–	–	–	–	–	+	–	+
97-44/ Kırkgöz	–	–	–	–	+	–	–	–	–	–	–	+	–	–	+	+	–
98-56/ Kırkgöz	–	–	–	–	+	–	–	–	–	–	–	+	–	–	+	+	–
Akçay basin																	
99-23/ Kazanpınarı near Yuva	–	–	–	–	–	+	–	–	–	+	–	–	–	+	–	–	–
99-24/ Karapınar near Elmalı	–	–	–	–	–	+	–	–	–	+	–	–	–	+	–	–	–
99-25/ canal draining from Avlan lake	–	–	–	–	–	+	–	–	–	–	–	–	–	+	–	–	–
99-26/ Yakaçiftlik, canal draining from Avlan lake	–	–	–	–	–	+	–	+	–	–	–	–	–	+	–	–	–

Table 9: Fish recorded in basins near Antalya and in the Akçay basin.

Orontes basin

	Alburnus orontis	*Alburnus sellal adanensis*	*Capoeta barroisi*	*Capoeta angorae*	*Cyprinion macrostomum*	*Cyprinus carpio*	*Garra rufa*	*Hemigrammocapoeta culiciphaga*	*Pseudophoxinus kervillei*	*Pseudophoxinus cf. kervillei*	*Oxynoemacheilus banarescui*	*Schistura namiri*	*Barbatula tigris*	*Clarias gariepinus*	*Aphanius anatoliae anatoliae*	*Aphanius fasciatus*	*Aphanius mento*	*Gambusia affinis*	Mugilidae	*Oreochromis aff. aureus*
Orontes basin																				
97-32/ Çöğürlü köyü, Asi Nehri	+	−	−	+	+	−	+	+	−	−	−	−	−	+	−	−	−	−	−	−
97-33/ canal near Medanköyü	−	−	−	−	−	−	−	−	+	−	−	−	−	−	−	−	−	−	+	−
97-34/ Yeşilada, Gölcük	−	−	−	−	−	−	+	+	−	−	−	−	−	−	−	−	+	+	−	−
97-35/ Yeşilada, Favvar çayı	+	−	−	−	+	−	+	−	−	−	+	+	+	−	−	−	−	−	−	−
97-36/ Demirköprü–Reyhanlı road	+	+	−	−	−	−	+	−	−	−	+	−	−	−	−	−	+	+	−	−
97-37/ Acar köyü canal	−	−	−	−	−	−	+	−	−	−	+	−	−	−	−	−	−	−	−	−
97-38/ Kanal II and ditch	−	−	−	−	−	−	−	−	−	−	−	−	−	−	−	−	+	+	−	+
Others																				
97-30/ small canals east of Sakyatan	−	−	−	−	−	−	−	−	−	+	−	−	−	−	−	−	−	−	−	−
97-31/ Ova Sulaması, Tahliye Kanalı D3	−	−	−	−	−	−	−	−	−	−	−	−	−	−	+	−	−	−	−	−
97-39/ Mersin çayı	−	−	−	−	−	−	+	−	−	−	−	−	−	−	−	−	+	+	+	−
97-40/ Yolçatı bridge	−	−	+	−	−	−	−	+	−	−	+	−	+	−	−	−	+	−	−	−
97-42/ Kurukulak çayı	−	−	−	−	−	−	−	−	+	−	−	−	−	−	−	−	−	−	−	−
97-41/ Tuzla Gölü	−	−	−	−	−	−	−	−	−	−	−	−	−	−	−	+	−	+	+	−
97-43/ Akgöl	−	−	−	−	−	+	−	−	−	−	−	−	−	−	+	−	−	+	+	−
97-45/ Terliksir Köyü	−	−	−	−	−	−	−	−	−	−	−	−	−	−	+	−	−	−	−	−

Table 10: Fish recorded in the Orontes basin and in a number of localities west of that region.

317

Chondrostoma beysehirense typical of Lake Beyşehir, and *Capoeta pestai* found in both lakes. *Vimba vimba*, another cyprinid also identified at Sagalassos, occurs only in Lake Eğirdir, but the species also lives in the Aksu and other rivers north and west of Sagalassos. In addition, Lakes Eğirdir and Beyşehir harbour carp (*Cyprinus carpio*) which was the most commonly imported food fish at Sagalassos. Carp also occurs further north in Lakes Eber and Akşehir, two lakes that used to be connected before (Table 5). The only other economically important species exploited recently in these two lakes is pike (*Esox lucius*). This species was mentioned for the first time from Lakes Eber and Akşehir by Geldiay (1951, not seen). In addition, a small cyprinid (*Alburnus nasreddini*) endemic in Lake Eber (and probably also occurring in Lake Akşehir) is known which could be an indicator for trade with this region. We found this species only in the Lake Eber basin but could not verify if it also inhabits Lake Akşehir. Bogutskaya (1997: 167) believes the species may occur in both lakes since Kosswig (1952) recorded *Alburnus orontis* s.l. from them, meaning that he probably synonymized *A. nasreddini* and *A. orontis*. In order to be useful for archaeological purposes, it remains to be verified to what extent individual bones of *A. nasreddini* differ from those of other *Alburnus* species, since the Eber species was distinguished on external characters such as the number of branched anal fin rays, size of the scales and body depth.

4.2. The major large rivers in western Anatolia

The Büyük Menderes (Table 6), the Gediz, the Küçük Menderes (Table 7) and the Sakarya basin (Table 8) were sampled extensively during the surveys since it became clear that long distance trade of freshwater fishes was practised in antiquity. The European catfish *Silurus glanis*, thus far represented by only one bone fragment at Sagalassos, was observed on a few occasions only during the surveys. For the Büyük Menderes, the species was reported by local fishermen from the Adigüzel dam lake and farther downstream. It is unclear whether the catfish found in Adigüzel lake are an artificial introduction or if they reflect the original distribution. We suppose that the species occurs naturally at least from Yenicekent downstream. Upstream Adigüzel, the tributaries to the Büyük Menderes are likely too shallow to harbor a population of *Silurus*. In the Gediz basin, we found evidence for *Silurus* in the Demirköprü dam lake only. Since it was never reported before from the Gediz and because it apparently only occurs in this artificial body of water, a human introduction is likely here. North of Sagalassos, *Silurus* occurs in the Sakarya basin, downstream from Ahiler; we also found it in Lake İznik. The presence of the European catfish has been reported in the literature from other northwestern Anatolian lakes that

we did not visit during our surveys, i.e. Lakes Apolyont and Manyas (Nümann 1960, 1961). In addition, the species has also been reported from the Kızılırmak river and from Lake Gölhisar (Kosswig 1964). The presence of *Silurus* in the latter lake is said to be also a possible result of human interference, and as source of origin, Kosswig (1964) suggests the Adana-Silifke area. In a later publication, Kosswig (1965) reports the occurrence of European catfish only for the Ceyhan and Seyhan rivers and not for the Tarsus and Silifke area. We have found no evidence at all for *Silurus* during our surveys in that area and suppose that the catfish may have been mistaken for *Clarias gariepinus* which we identified from the basins in that region (see below). In conclusion, it appears that the reconstruction of the original distribution of *Silurus glanis* is hampered by the effects of human introductions, especially in natural and artificial lakes, and by the possible confusion with *Clarias gariepinus*. In addition, we were told that the numbers (and average sizes) have decreased considerably in several parts of the large rivers as a result of overfishing.

Generally speaking, there seems to be a consensus that the wild carp – the most common fish consumed at Sagalassos – was originally confined to the northern part of Anatolia (see map p. 243 in Geldiay and Balık 1996). During the four years that we sampled the Anatolian ichthyofauna, we found the wild form in only one locality (the Karabalut river, emptying in Lake Akşehir). Elsewhere, the domestic form was present, usually the scaled morph, which must have largely replaced (or interbred with) the wild carp, thus hampering the reconstruction of its original distribution. As mentioned above, human introduction of European catfish seems to have occurred in certain areas, but this must have been a relatively rare practice compared to the systematic stocking of carp. In fact, at least since 1976 large numbers of carp fry have been released in natural and artificial lakes. It is hence no surprise that we found this species mainly in lakes and dam lakes during our survey of the region of the Büyük and Küçük Menderes, the Gediz and the Sakarya basins. All these rivers are considered as belonging to the original distribution of the carp (Geldiay and Balık 1996), but details on the parts of the basins populated by the species are lacking. The methods used during our survey were insufficient to estimate population densities in the rivers themselves, but they must be relatively low taking into account the answers obtained during interviews. Of the river systems considered here, localities with carp that are most closely situated to Sagalassos are situated within the Büyük Menderes basin. Carp is common in its upper reaches in the Işıklı area but it is unclear if the wild carp was ever present here. In the other basins, domestic carp was attested in the visited lakes and dam lakes, but again it is not clear where the natural distribution of the wild form would have started exactly. Judging from the properties of the waters (current, depth, temperature, etc.), it appears that the wild carp must have had a wide distribution within each of these large basins. In the Küçük Menderes, the domestic form was attested in the slow running waters at Belevi, but no further details on the distribution in this basin are available. In the Sakarya basin, carp was already found in the Çifteler area which is the section of the river that is in closest proximity to Sagalassos. *Cyprinus carpio* was already mentioned from the Sakarya river by Steindachner (1897) and, more specifically, from the Porsuk branch by Hanko (1924).

Vimba vimba was attested during the 1996 survey in Eğirdir Lake and the Aksu river, and because of the geographical proximity to Sagalassos it was suggested that Lake Eğirdir may have been the most likely source. However, this species has a much larger distribution. During the surveys *Vimba vimba* was found in the Büyük Menderes (the ancient Maeandros river), the Gediz river (the ancient Hermos river), and the Sakarya (the ancient Sangarios river). In addition, the species has been reported in the past from Lake İznik and Lake Sapanca (Nümann 1960), and from the Kızılırmak and Yeşilırmak basins (Geldiay and Balık 1996: 264).

The "*Leuciscus*" finds from Sagalassos have little potential thus far for the reconstruction of former trade connections since these remains could not be identified at species level. Moreover, if the distribution is considered of the various species (*Leuciscus cephalus, L. lepidus, Petroleuciscus borysthenicus*), almost whole Anatolia is covered.

As already mentioned above, pike (*Esox lucius*) occurs in Lakes Eber and Akşehir, but our surveys also confirmed its presence in the upper reaches of the Büyük Menderes in the Işıklı area, and further east, adjacent to the Büyük Menderes, in Lake Karakuyu. It is not clear to what extent these occurrences are natural or not. The presence in the Işıklı area had already been mentioned previously (Kosswig 1969), but the Karakuyu localities are apparently new. Our surveys further confirmed the presence of pike in the Sakarya basin, which had been reported earlier by Steindachner (1897). No evidence was found in the Gediz basin during our surveys and apparently the species was never mentioned in the literature either. The fieldwork of Nümann (1961) showed that pike was present in 1953 and 1954 in Lakes Sapanca, Apolyont and Manyas, and even earlier it had been reported in the early 1940's from Lake Sapanca by Batalgil (*fide* Geldiay and Balık 1996: 229). Kosswig (1969) also mentions pike from the Kızılırmak and, surprisingly, also from small rivers of the upper Seyhan. He believes that transport by man to the latter region is improbable.

4.3. The distribution of *Clarias gariepinus*

The presence of *Clarias* has been attested at Sagalassos from the 1st to the 7th c. AD and was immediately brought in relation with import from Egypt or the Levant (Van Neer *et al.*, 1997). *Clarias gariepinus* is an African species, but its distribution extends into the Syro-Palestinian area (Figure 6). The most northern basin from where it was reported traditionally is the Ceyhan (Kosswig 1969; Skelton and Teugels 1992: 5). More recent data from the literature and from our own surveys has demonstrated, however, that it presently occurs in several waters outside this range. Immediately west of the Ceyhan, in the Seyhan basin, *Clarias gariepinus* is present (Geldiay and Balık 1996), no doubt because it could colonize the latter through the many artificial canals that now connect both river systems. Three specimens found at Terliksir Köyü could not be attributed to either the Ceyhan or Seyhan basin because the Çukurova delta comprises many canals connecting both basins. Local informants told us that the species is also available in the Tarsus river and we obtained a specimen on the fish market of Adana that was said to have been brought in from the Berdan dam lake on that same river. *Clarias gariepinus* was caught during the survey in Akgöl, near Silifke from where it had been previously mentioned by Geldiay and Balık (1996). Much farther to the west, the species had been attested during our 1996 survey in the Aksu basin at Güloluk and again in 1998 (Table 9). It had already been found previously farther south along the Aksu at Kundu Köyü (Küçük and İkiz 1993), and in the Tehnelli river, a branch of the Aksu (Balık 1988). A totally new locality added during our surveys is the Acısu basin. The presence of *Clarias gariepinus* so far west from its 'normal distribution' was considered as a possible result of human introduction (Balık 1988), although no documents seem to exist that such operations were undertaken by the Ministry of Agriculture or the *DSİ* (agency responsible for irrigation and drainage projects which regularly stocks ponds with carp). The new finds between the Ceyhan and the Aksu river might indicate that the catfish species was able to colonize several intermediate coastal streams. If this has been the case, the hypothesis of a putative import from Egypt or the Levant may have to be refuted and import from a much closer distance needs to be considered. It was tried to solve this problem by analysis of mitochondrial DNA (mtDNA) from both modern and archaeological *Clarias* specimens. Fin tissue samples of catfish have been taken during our surveys from the Asi Nehri (Turkish part of the Orontes), the Çukurova area, the Tarsus river, the Akgöl and the Acısu basin. This material has been analyzed in a molecular laboratory, but did not allow to decide whether the presence of the catfish in the basins west of the Ceyhan is a very recent phenomenon due to human interaction,

Figure 6: Original and present distribution of *Clarias gariepinus* in the Eastern Mediterranean area. The basins with recent expansion of the species are indicated separately.

or if it is due to natural colonisation (Arndt *et al.*, 2003). However, the comparison of the successfully extracted ancient mtDNA from catfish from Sagalassos with modern haplotypes from Egypt, Syria, Israel and various Turkish basins, clearly shows that the *Clarias* consumed at Sagalassos was imported from Egypt.

In addition to the finds of *Clarias gariepinus* in rivers emptying in the Mediterranean, a record needs to be mentioned from the Sakarya river. Near Çifteler, the river and the adjacent floodplain form an ideal environment for carp and the introduced Crucian carp *Carassius carassius*. In addition to these species, we observed *Clarias gariepinus* in the river and the adjacent submerged reedbeds. Breeding experiments by Ankara University, using specimens originating from the Silifke area, were started in 1976 at Sakaryabaşi but were finally abandoned. Escaped fishes have found a suitable environment in this part of the river. They were apparently able to survive and reproduce here because of the high temperature of the waters (23°C in the river) which is more or less constant as a result of the nearby presence of springs.

4.4. Implications for the reconstruction of trade

The bones of *Pseudophoxinus handlirschi* that were recently identified at Sagalassos represent a very straightforward indicator of trade relationships, since this species only occurs in Lake Eğirdir. All the other freshwater fish thus far attested at the site have a wider distribution and it is therefore difficult to narrow down the possible provenances. The sources for the traded fish are not necessarily the nearest basins where the species occur since factors other than geographical proximity may have influenced the exchange. Interpretation is also hampered by the recent anthropic influence on the ichthyofauna of Anatolia. For instance, Kosswig (1964) believes that the distribution of carp cannot be used for zoogeographical studies because the species has been too often introduced in various waters. He even questions if carp is part of the original fauna in Lakes Eğirdir, Beyşehir, Eber and Akşehir. It should be noted, however, that the species was already mentioned in the 1920's (Devedjian 1926, not seen) long before systematic stocking started.

In terms of geographical proximity, Lake Eğirdir would be the most likely place of origin for the wild carp. However, it cannot be excluded that the carp was also imported from Lake Beyşehir, Lake Eber, Lake Akşehir, or from the Büyük Menderes or even the Sakarya or Gediz river. These large rivers are a possible source of the carp at Sagalassos, but it seems more likely that the exploitation of the species in

antiquity was mainly carried out in lakes or closed basins, as it is the case today. This is confirmed by geochemical analyses on carp teeth from Sagalassos. Their oxygen and strontium isotope ratios ($d^{18}O_p$ and $^{87}Sr/^{86}Sr$) were compared to those of modern carp teeth and modern water samples from various lakes and rivers (Dufour *et al.*, 2007). The $d^{18}O_p$ values excluded a riverine origin, but the $^{87}Sr/^{86}Sr$ ratios mostly did not match that of any of the local lakes selected as potential origin. Further methodological work will be needed to narrow down the possible provenance of carp and other freshwater species whose origin cannot be established on the basis of zoogeographical information alone.

Lakes Eber and Akşehir, and the Isıklı area on the Büyük Menderes are the localities closest to the site where pike occurs. However, import from other basins such as the Sakarya or lakes in the Marmara region cannot be excluded *a priori*. In addition the species is known from Kızılırmak. For the European catfish *Silurus glanis*, large rivers such as the Büyük Menderes, the Sakarya or Kızılırmak are possible candidates. The localities of *Vimba vimba* closest to Sagalassos are the Aksu river to the southeast, and Lake Eğirdir in the northeast. Elsewhere the species is also found in the Büyük Menderes, the Gediz, the Sakarya, the Kızılırmak and Yeşilırmak.

5. CONCLUSIONS

The conducted surveys of the Anatolian fish fauna and the compilation of ichthyological literature has allowed refining the existing data on the geographical distribution of species, despite the many anthropogenic changes that occurred the last few decennia as a result of introduction of species, damming and irrigation projects, pollution and overfishing. It appears that long distance trade of fishes at Sagalassos was not limited to marine species and Nilotic taxa, but that also Anatolian freshwater fish were commonly traded over long distances. The modern zoogeographical data available thus far allow provenancing of fish in one case, namely *Pseudophoxinus handlirschi* that is limited to Lake Eğirdir. For the other species, that have a wider distribution, multiple provenances are possible and, therefore, the water bodies have been determined that are in closest proximity to Sagalassos. However, since fish trade was also practised at long distances, the closest occurrence of a species does not necessarily indicate its provenance. Further geochemical analyses and possibly also ancient DNA studies may help elucidating where the species were imported from exactly.

6. ACKNOWLEDGEMENTS

The research was supported by the Belgian Programme on Interuniversitary Poles of Attraction (IAP V/9 and VI/22) and the Research Fund of the K.U.Leuven (BOF-GOA02/2 and GOA07/2). We thank Prof. Aksoylar (former dean of the *Fisheries Faculty* at Eğirdir) for his encouragement and the DSİ (*Devlet Su İşleri*, Turkish Water Management Organisation) for logistic support. Dr. T. Nalbant (Bukarest Univ.) is acknowledged for the identifications of the Balitoridae collected.

7. REFERENCES

ANONYMOUS (1995) *Analysis of the Hydrological Balance of the Lakes in the Isparta Region*, Report by BRL Ingénierie for Ministry of Agriculture and Rural Affairs (Turkey) and Ministère de l'Agriculture et de la Pêche.

ARNDT, A., VAN NEER, W., HELLEMANS, B., ROBBEN, J., VOLCKAERT, F. and WAELKENS, M. (2003) Roman trade relationships at Sagalassos (Turkey) elucidated by ancient DNA of fish remains, *Journal of Archaeological Science* 30: 1095-1105.

BALIK, S. (1988) Türkiye'nin Akdeniz Bölgesi içsu balıkları üzerinde sistematik ve zooçoğrafik araştırmalar, *Doğa Tu ZoolojiD* 12: 156-179.

BOGUTSKAYA, N.G. (1997) Contribution to the knowledge of leuciscine fishes of Asia Minor. Part 2. An annotated check-list of leuciscine fishes (Leuciscinae, Cyprinidae) of Turkey with descriptions of a new species and two new subspecies, *Mitteilungen aus den Hamburgischen Zoologischen Museum und Institut* 94: 161-186.

CALLEBAUT, K., VIAENE, W., WAELKENS, M., OTTENBURGS, R. and NAUD, J. (2000) Provenance and characterization of raw materials for lime mortars used at Sagalassos with special reference to the volcanic rocks, in: M. WAELKENS and L. LOOTS (eds) *Sagalassos V. Report on the Survey and Excavation Campaigns of 1996 and 1997 (Acta Archaeologica Lovaniensia Monographiae 11)*, Leuven University Press, Leuven: 651-668.

CAMPBELL, R.N.B. (1992) Food of an introduced population of pikeperch, *Stizostedion lucioperca* L. in Lake Egirdir, Turkey, *Aquaculture and Fisheries Management* 23: 71-85.

DEGRYSE, P., DEGEEST, R., POBLOME, J., VIAENE, W., OTTENBURGS, R., KUCHA H. and WAELKENS, M. (2000) Mineralogy and geochemistry of Roman common wares produced at Sagalassos and their possible clay sources, in: M. WAELKENS and L. LOOTS (eds) *Sagalassos V. Report on the Survey and Excavation Campaigns of 1996 and 1997 (Acta Archaeologica Lovaniensia Monographiae 11)*, Leuven University Press, Leuven: 709-722.

DEVEDJIAN, K. (1926) *Pêche et pêcheries en Turquie*, Imprimerie de l'Administration de la Dette Ottomane de Constantinople, Constantinople.

DUFOUR, E., HOLMDEN, C., VAN NEER, W., ZAZZO, A., PATTERSON, W.P., DEGRYSE, P. and KEPPENS, E. (2007) Oxygen and strontium isotopes as provenance indicators of fish at archaeological sites: the case study of Sagalassos, SW Turkey, *Journal of Archaeological Science* 34: 1226-1239.

ESCHMEYER, W.N. (2006) *Catalog of Fishes on-Line*, http://www.calacademy.org/RESEARCH/ichthyology/catalog.

FROESE, R. and PAULY, D. (2007) *FishBase*, www.fishbase.org.

GELDIAY, R. (1951) Orta Anadolu Göllerinin Balıkçılığına bir bakış, *Biyoloji Cilt* 1, Sayı 5.

GELDIAY, R. and BALIK, S. (1996) *Türkiye tatlısu balıkları*, Ege Üniversitesi Basımevı, Bornova, Izmir.

HANKO, B. (1924) Fische aus Kleinasien, *Annales Musei nationalis Hungarici* 21: 137-158.

HRBEK, T., KÜÇÜK, F., FRICKEY, T., STÖLTING, K.N., WILDEKAMP R. and MEYER, A. (2002) Molecular phylogeny and historical biogeography of the *Aphanius* (Pisces, Cyprinodontiformes) species complex of central Anatolia, Turkey, *Molecular Phylogenetics and Evolution* 25: 125-137.

HRBEK, T. and WILDEKAMP R. (2003) *Aphanius villwocki*, a new species from the Sakarya River basin of the central Anatolian plain, Turkey (Teleostei; Cyprinodontiformes), *Ichthyological Exploration of Freshwater* 14: 137-144.

INNAL, D. and ERK'AKAN, F. (2006) Effects of exotic and translocated fish species in the inland waters of Turkey, *Reviews in Fish Biology and Fisheries* 16: 39-50.

KOSSWIG, C. (1952) Die Zoogeographie der türkischen Süsswasserfische, *Istanbul Üniversitesi Fen Fakültesi Hidrobiologi Araştırma Enstitüsü Yayınlarından B* 1(2): 85-101.

KOSSWIG, C. (1954) Türkiye tatlısu balıkları zoocoğrafyası, *Istanbul Üniversitesi Fen Fakültesi Hidrobiologi Araştırma Enstitüsü Yayınlarından A* 2 (1): 3-20.

KOSSWIG, C. (1964) Bemerkungen zur Geschichte und zur Ökologie der Ichthyofauna Kleinasiens, besonders seines abflusslosen Zentralbeckens, *Zoologischer Anzeiger* 172: 1-15.

KOSSWIG, C. (1965) Zur historischen Zoogeographie der Ichthyofauna im Süsswasser des südlichen Kleinasiens, *Zoologisches Jahrbuch für Systematik* 92: 83-90.

KOSSWIG, C. (1969) New contributions to the zoogeography of fresh water fish of Asia Minor, based on collections made between 1964-1967, *Israel Journal of Zoology* 18: 249-254.

KOSSWIG, C. and SÖZER, F. (1945) Nouveaux Cyprinodontidae de l'Anatolie centrale, *Revue de la Faculté des Sciences de l'Université d'Istanbul* 10(2): 77-83.

KÜÇÜK, F. (1998) The systematic and ecological characters of freshwater fish distribution in inland waters of Isparta

Province, in: Anynomous (eds.) *Isparta'nın Dünü, Bugünü, Yarını* (*Sempozyumu 2, Süleyman Demirel Üniversitesi Publications 15*): 75-88.

Küçük, F. and Ikız, R. (1993) Aksu Çayı ve Kollarında (Antalya) bulunan balık türlerinin saptaması, *Turkish Journal of Zoology* 17: 427-443.

Loots, L., Waelkens, M. and Depuydt, F. (2000) The city fortifications of Sagalassos from the Hellenistic to the late Roman period, in: M. Waelkens and L. Loots (eds) *Sagalassos V. Report on the Survey and Excavation Campaigns of 1996 and 1997* (*Acta Archaeologica Lovaniensia Monographiae 11*), Leuven University Press, Leuven: 595-634.

Nümann, W. (1960) Limnologische Untersuchungen einiger anatolischer Seen, *Internationale Revue der Gesamte Hydrobiologie* 45: 11-54.

Nümann, W. (1961) Die anatolischen Seen und ihre fischereiliche Bewirtschaftung, *Zeitschrift für Fischerei und deren Hilfswissenschaftung* 10(8-10): 773-799.

Skelton, P.H. and Teugels, G.G. (1992) Neotype description for the African catfish *Clarias gariepinus* (Burchell, 1822) (Pisces: Siluroidei: Clariidae), *Ichthyological Bulletin of the J.L.B Smith Institute of Ichthyology* 56: 1-8.

Steindachner, F. (1897) Bericht über die von Dr. Escherich in der Umgebung von Angora gesammelten Fische und Reptilien, *Denkschriften der Kaiserlichen Akademie der Wissenschaften in Wien, Mathematisch-Naturwissenschaftliche Klasse* 64: 685-699.

Van Neer, W., De Cupere, B. and Waelkens, M. (1997) Remains of local and imported fish at the ancient site of Sagalassos (Burdur prov., Turkey), in: M. Waelkens and J. Poblome (eds.) *Sagalassos IV. Report on the Survey and Excavation Campaigns of 1994 and 1995* (*Acta Archaeologica Lovaniensia Monographiae 9*), Leuven University Press, Leuven: 571-586.

Van Neer, W., Wildekamp, R., Küçük, F. and Ünlüsayin, M. (1999) First inland records of the euryhaline goby *Knipowitschia caucasica* from lakes in Anatolia, Turkey, *Journal of Fish Biology* 54: 1334-1337.

Van Neer, W., Wildekamp, R., Küçük, F., Ünlüsayin, M., Waelkens, M. and Paulissen, E. (2000) Results on the 1996 survey of the fish fauna of the Aksu river (Kestros) and some lakes in southwestern Anatolia, and the implications for trade at Sagalassos, in: M. Waelkens and L. Loots (eds) *Sagalassos V. Report on the Survey and Excavation Campaigns of 1996 and 1997* (*Acta Archaeologica Lovaniensia Monographiae 11*), Leuven University Press, Leuven: 828-842.

Viaene, W., Waelkens, M., Ottenburgs, R. and Callebaut, K. (1997) An archaeometric study of mortars used at Sagalassos, in: M. Waelkens and J. Poblome (eds.) *Sagalassos IV. Report on the Survey and Excavation Campaigns of 1994 and 1995* (*Acta Archaeologica Lovaniensia Monographiae 9*), Leuven University Press, Leuven: 405-422.

Waelkens, M., Paulissen, E., Vanhaverbeke, H., Öztürk, I., De Cupere, B., Ekinci, H.A., Vermeersch, P.M., Poblome, J. and Degeest, R. (1997) The 1994 and 1995 surveys on the territory of Sagalassos, in: M. Waelkens and J. Poblome (eds.) *Sagalassos IV. Report on the Survey and Excavation Campaigns of 1994 and 1995* (*Acta Archaeologica Lovaniensia Monographiae 9*), Leuven University Press, Leuven: 11-102.

Wildekamp, R., Van Neer, W., Küçük, F. and Ünlüsayin, M. (1997) First record of the eastern Asiatic gobionid fish *Pseudorasbora parva* from the Asiatic part of Turkey, *Journal of Fish Biology* 51: 858-861.

Wildekamp, R., Küçük, F., Ünlüsayin, M. and Van Neer, W. (1999) The genus *Aphanius* Nardo 1827 (Pisces: Cyprinodontidae) in Turkey, *Turkish Journal of Zoology* 23: 23-44.

LIST OF AUTHORS

ELIZABETH BLOXAM
University College London
Institute of Archaeology
31-34 Gordon Square
WC1H 0PY, London
Great Britain
e.bloxam@ucl.ac.uk

KRISTOF CALLEBAUT
section Geology
K.U.Leuven
Celestijnenlaan 200E, bus 2410
BE-3001 Leuven
Belgium

ANTON CLIJSTERS
section Geology
K.U.Leuven
Celestijnenlaan 200E, bus 2410
BE-3001 Leuven
Belgium

MICKY DEDEREN
section Geology
K.U.Leuven
Celestijnenlaan 200E, bus 2410
BE-3001 Leuven
Belgium

PATRICK DEGRYSE
Centre for Archaeological Sciences
section Geology
K.U.Leuven
Celestijnenlaan 200E, bus 2408
BE-3001 Leuven
Belgium
Patrick.Degryse@geo.kuleuven.be

VERONIQUE DE LAET
Centre for Archaeological Sciences
Physical and Regional Geography
K.U.Leuven
Celestijnenlaan 200E, bus 2409
BE-3001 Leuven
Belgium
Veronique.Delaet@geo.kuleuven.be

MAX FERNANDEZ-ALONSO
Geology Department
Royal Museum of Central Africa
Steenweg op Leuven 13
BE-3080 Tervuren
Belgium
max.fernandez@africamuseum.be

WOUTER HEIJLEN
section Geology
K.U.Leuven
Celestijnenlaan 200E, bus 2408
BE-3001 Leuven
Belgium

JAN HERTOGEN
section Geology
K.U.Leuven
Celestijnenlaan 200E, bus 2408
BE-3001 Leuven
Belgium
Jan.Hertogen@geo.kuleuven.be

TOM HELDAL
Geological Survey of Norway
NGU
NO-7491 Trondheim
Norway
tom.heldal@ngu.no

PIERRE JACOBS
Centrum voor Oppervlaktechemie & Katalyse
Kasteelpark Arenberg 23 – bus 2461
BE-3001 Heverlee
Belgium
Pierre.Jacobs@biw.kuleuven.be

MICHAEL JOACHIMSKI
Institut für Geologie und Mineralogie
Universität Erlangen-Nürnberg
Schlossgarten 5
DE-91054 Erlangen
Germany
joachimski@geol.uni-erlangen.de

EDDY KEPPENS
Geology Department
Vrije Universiteit Brussel
BE-1040 Brussel
Belgium
ekeppens@vub.ac.be

KATRIEN KIMPE
Bodemkundige Dienst van België v.z.w.
Willem de Croylaan 48 – bus 4025
BE-3001 Heverlee
Belgium

HARRY KUCHA
University of Science and Technology AGH
Faculty of Geology
Geophysics & Environmental Protection
30-059 Krakow
Mickiewicza 30
Poland
kucha@geol.agh.edu.pl

FAHRETTIN KÜÇÜK
Eğirdir Fisheries Faculty
Süleyman Demirel University
TR-32500 Eğirdir
Turkey

JOACHIM LAMBRECHTS
Physical and Regional Geography
Celestijnenlaan 200E, bus 2409
BE-3001 Leuven
Belgium

SUZY LENS
section Geology
K.U.Leuven
Celestijnenlaan 200E, bus 2410
BE-3001 Leuven
Belgium

BRANCO MUSIC
Department of archaeology
Faculty of Arts
University of Ljubljana
Zavetiška 5
SLO-1000 Ljubljana
Slovenia

PHILIPPE MUCHEZ
Geodynamics and Geofluids Research Group
section Geology
K.U.Leuven
Celestijnenlaan 200E, bus 2410
BE-3001 Leuven
Belgium
Philippe.Muchez@geo.kuleuven.be

JEAN NAUD
Département de Géologie et Géographie
Bâtiment Mercator
Place Pasteur 3
BE-1348 Louvain-la-Neuve
Belgium
naud@cean.ucl.ac.be

RAOUL OTTENBURGS
section Geology
K.U.Leuven
Celestijnenlaan 200E, bus 2410
BE-3001 Leuven
Belgium.

ETIENNE PAULISSEN
Physical and Regional Geography
Celestijnenlaan 200E, bus 2409
BE-3001 Leuven
Belgium
Etienne.paulissen@geo.kuleuven.be

JEROEN POBLOME
Research Unit Archaeology
Sagalassos Archaeological Research Project
M. Theresiastraat 21, bus 3314
BE-3000 Leuven
Belgium
Jeroen.Poblome@arts.kuleuven.be

YVES QUINIF
Centre d'Etudes et de Recherches Appliquées
au Karst
Faculté Polytechnique de Mons
rue de Houdain 9
BE-7000 Mons
Belgium

PIETER SCHROOTEN
section Geology
K.U.Leuven
Celestijnenlaan 200E, bus 2410
BE-3001 Leuven
Belgium

KRISTOF SCHROYEN
section Geology
K.U.Leuven
Celestijnenlaan 200E, bus 2410
BE-3001 Leuven
Belgium

DOMINIQUE SIMILOX-TOHON
Geodynamics and Geofluids Research Group
section Geology
K.U.Leuven
Celestijnenlaan 200E, bus 2410
BE-3001 Leuven
Belgium
and
Midland Valley
Dominique.similox-tohon@mve.com

MANUEL SINTUBIN
Geodynamics and Geofluids Research Group
section Geology
K.U.Leuven
Celestijnenlaan 200E, bus 2410
BE-3001 Leuven
Belgium
Manuel.Sintubin@geo.kuleuven.be

SIMON SIX
Physical and Regional Geography
Celestijnenlaan 200E, bus 2409
BE-3001 Leuven
Belgium
and
VWM
Simon.Six@vmw.be

PER STOREMYR
Geological Survey of Norway
NGU
NO-7491 Trondheim
Norway
per.storemyr@bluewin.ch

MUSTAFA ÜNLÜSAYIN
Fisheries Faculty
Akdeniz University
TR-07058 Antalya
Turkey

PETER VANDEVELDE
section Geology
K.U.Leuven
Celestijnenlaan 200E, bus 2410
BE-3001 Leuven
Belgium

THIJS VAN THUYNE
Physical and Regional Geography
Celestijnenlaan 200E, bus 2409
BE-3001 Leuven
Belgium

WIM VAN NEER
Royal Belgian Institute of Natural Sciences
Rue Vautier 29
BE-1000 Brussels
Belgium
wim.vanneer@natuurwetenschappen.be
and
Laboratory of Comparative Anatomy and Biodiversity
K.U.Leuven
Ch. Deberiotstraat 32
BE-3000 Leuven
Belgium
willem.vanneer@bio.kuleuven.be

KRIS VANNESTE
Royal Observatory of Belgium
Ringlaan 3
BE-1180 Brussels
Belgium
kris.vanneste@oma.be

MARLEEN VERMOERE
Laboratory for Plant Systematics
K.U.Leuven
Kasteelpark Arenberg 31, bus 2437
BE-3001 Leuven
Belgium

WILLY VIAENE†, deceased 15 March 2000.

MARC WAELKENS
Research Unit Archaeology
K.U.Leuven
Sagalassos Archaeological Research Project
M. Theresiastraat 21, bus 3314
BE-3000 Leuven
Belgium
Marc.Waelkens@arts.kuleuven.be

RUUD WILDEKAMP
Royal Museum of Central Africa
BE-3080 Tervuren
Belgium